Presented by

the

Government of Canada

———

Offert

par le

Gouvernement du Canada

PENDULUM OF POWER

CANADA'S FEDERAL ELECTIONS

J. MURRAY BECK

Department of Political Science
Dalhousie University, Halifax, Nova Scotia

p

PRENTICE-HALL ♦ OF CANADA, LTD.

Scarborough, h *Ontario*

PRENTICE-HALL, INC., ENGLEWOOD CLIFFS, NEW JERSEY
PRENTICE-HALL INTERNATIONAL, INC., LONDON
PRENTICE-HALL OF AUSTRALIA, PTY., LTD., SYDNEY
PRENTICE-HALL OF INDIA, PVT., LTD., NEW DELHI
PRENTICE-HALL OF JAPAN, INC., TOKYO

Library of Congress Catalog Card No. 68-24131
      65566-Pa
      65567-Cl
1 2 3 4 5 72 71 70 69 68

PRINTED IN CANADA

Table of Contents

Preface

This book is intended neither to present a highly sophisticated account of Canadian politics nor to offer original insight into the country's elections. To some readers it may appear to be a repetition of the conventional wisdom about the election campaigns and their chief personalities. It is my hope, however, that within the limitations of space, it presents a panoramic view of the general elections that will give the student and general reader alike a greater understanding of the Canadian electoral process.

I also hope that the book may provide the student with a background for the appreciation and evaluation of the sophisticated books on Canadian politics and elections that have recently begun to make their appearance. It may even suggest avenues for further research into Canadian voting behaviour.

The book demonstrates that, although each of Canada's elections is unique, the factors leading to its outcome may have been set in train the day after the last election. In most elections most of the voters have made up their minds before the formal campaign begins; in fewer than a third of them has the campaign itself determined the outcome or meant the difference between majority and minority government. The crucial factor in deciding most elections has been the capacity of a party to preserve an attractive image in the eyes of the voter in the period between elections. Accordingly the accounts of each election give considerable attention to the events preceding dissolution and the formal campaign itself.

I have made a special effort in my examination of each election to interpret the electoral behaviour of each region or province, particularly Quebec. Admittedly, this has sometimes required me to make judgments that may not stand up under more specialized examination, but I am hopeful that these instances will be few. The tables accompanying each election serve to complement and reinforce the conclusions I have reached relative to the voting patterns of regions and provinces.

The reader should appreciate that the statistics of the first two elections, especially those relating to the popular vote, are little more than informed guesses. In compiling the statistics of succeeding elections, I needed to use less and less discretion, but not until the provisions for taking the armed services vote during the Second World War required each candidate to state his party affiliation could I eliminate it altogether. In exercising discretion, I have tried to be consistent and at the same time produce the most meaningful results. In particular, if a candidate ran as an Independent Conservative, Independent Liberal, or under a similar label of another party, and was unopposed by an official candidate of the party in question, I have treated him in the tables as an official candidate of that party, since he would invariably attract that party's voters; if, on the other hand, he was opposed by an official candidate of the party in question, I have treated him as an "other" candidate. Where two or more candidates ran under the same party label in one constituency and there is no way of determining who was the party's official candidate, I have treated the one who secured the largest number of votes as such, and his opponents as "other" candidates.

I must express my appreciation to Dalhousie University for a grant from its Research Development Fund in the Humanities and Social Sciences to assist in the typing of the manuscript. I must also thank Mr. Ronald Decent, Mrs. Barbara Brougham, Miss Janet Bauer, Miss Linda Norris, and Mrs. Sylvia Haugo of the Production Department of Prentice-Hall of Canada for their capable assistance in bringing the book into print. Any errors of omission or commission are entirely my own.

J.M.B.

First

General Election

VICTORY WITH A QUESTION MARK

The election of 1867 can scarcely be considered a national election. It was, in fact, four separate elections, each conducted in splendid isolation from the others, each taking its tone from the events leading to Confederation in the particular province. It was also a confusing election, particularly because all the provinces were electing Assemblies at the same time and because Quebec and Ontario permitted a person to run for and sit in both the federal and provincial Houses.

It was an election, too, in which highly extraneous influences could be exercised. Nothing else could be expected since each province used its pre-Confederation election law in federal contests and none of them had adopted the secret ballot. Open voting, according to some politicians of the day, was the manly, British way of exercising the franchise. But, as they were too well aware, if facilitated the bribery of voters and the coercion of employees by their superiors and of civil servants by the government.

With the exception of Nova Scotia, no province had a provision which called for simultaneous voting in all constituencies. The government of the day could therefore time most of the contests to improve its own fortunes and it did so unashamedly in 1867. It extended the election over six weeks, "picking the soft spots first and working [its] way cautiously into the hard ones."[1] To make matters worse, Ontario and Quebec held contests lasting forty-eight hours and tabulated the results at the end of the first day. It requires little imagination to conjure up the devices which a governing party, a little behind after one day, would employ in a desperate effort to catch up.

Despite these imperfections, the election played a significant role. In addition to providing the members for the new parliamentary régime, it gave the administration of the day enough support to let it continue the job of consolidating the union. John A. Macdonald, long accustomed to the uncertain politics of the Canadas, found his healthy majority something of a luxury; it was, he told a friend, almost too big.

Of the 181 members in the first House of Commons, 147 came from Quebec and Ontario. These provinces, then, were crucial to the parties' fortunes. George Brown, publisher of the Toronto *Globe* and leader

1

of the Clear Grits of Canada West, could not have fully appreciated it, but he had already ruined his party's chances by a decision he had made on June 22, 1864. That was the day he had entered into a coalition with John A. Macdonald to find a solution for the deadlock which had brought the government of the Province of Canada almost to a halt. The preceding three years had seen four ministries and two elections; it had not seen stable and orderly government. For a long time Brown and his followers had been denouncing "coalitions as dangerous and demoralizing . . . as machinations of weak men with an itch for power."[2] They were especially suspicious that Macdonald – wily knave that he was – might exploit any coalition for his own party purposes. Yet the danger had to be faced. "Party alliances are one thing," said Brown, "and the interests of my country are another."[3]

The deadlock had come about simply because the two contending groups were so nearly in equilibrium that the waverers and independents could upset any ministry. One of them was the alliance between the supporters of John A. Macdonald and A.N. Morin – soon to be succeeded by George E. Cartier – first established in 1854. Destined to become the essential part of the Liberal-Conservative party of the Dominion after 1867, this alliance had the support in Canada East of the Montreal commercial and industrial elements whose spokesmen were Alexander T. Galt and the Montreal *Gazette*. However, its principal component there was the conservative, pro-clerical Bleus of Cartier who, for another two decades at least, continued to constitute a majority of the French-Canadian population.

Meanwhile Macdonald was slowly forging the Canada West component of the party out of the Tories and moderate Reformers, led at one time by Sir Allan MacNab and Robert Baldwin respectively. Unlike the Bleus, they invariably ran second to the Reformers, principally the Clear Grits of George Brown. Egalitarian, pro-democratic and anti-big business, Grittism also took on the anti-Catholic, anti-French posture of its leader. This placed the French liberal element, the Parti Rouge of Canada East, in an exceedingly uncomfortable position. Although its members were pro-democratic and anti-big business, and in varying degrees, anti-clerical, they could maintain little more than an uneasy alliance with a group that was anti-French and anti-Catholic. They also suffered from an even more serious liability: the opposition of a powerful Church. This in itself was enough to keep them in a decided minority. Since, under the best of circumstances, the majority in one section of the province could ally itself only with a minority in another, stable government was quite out of the question.[4]

Brown saw that something had to be done to prevent his own people from being continually sacrificed, as he felt they were in Parliament, by the "moutons" of George Cartier. A desperate situation necessitated a desperate remedy, even the distasteful one of allying oneself with Macdonald, if that was the only way of effecting a union of British North America or, that failing, a federal union of the Canadas. Either would ensure for Canada

West something which Brown and the Grits had long been demanding: representation by population. They would have preferred to give the ministry "outside support" in finding a constitutional solution for the deadlock, but the other side would have none of that. Consequently, Brown entered into his "astonishing agreement"[5] for a coalition with Macdonald.

The result was that the bulk of the Reformers and Conservatives in Canada West became unionists. Opposed were a few Conservatives like Matthew Crooks Cameron, and the moderate Reformers of John Sandfield Macdonald from "central Canada," now eastern Ontario. Their opposition was slight. "Of all the parts of British North America, Canada West was the most powerful and devoted advocate of Confederation."[6]

Brown, not unexpectedly, was never happy within the coalition. On entering it, he had to desert his chief allies, the Rouges and English-speaking Liberals of Canada East, who remained staunchly anti-Unionist. One of the latter, Luther H. Holton, reminded him of his own statement about the long line of gravestones of former colleagues which studded Macdonald's progress. Might there not, he asked, be a "yawning grave waiting for the noblest victim of them all"?[7] As time went on Brown chafed more and more. The inevitable happened in December 1865. Disturbed over the way in which the government was conducting reciprocity negotiations with the United States, he resigned. He had at least waited until his going would not endanger the prospects of union. By that time the Parliament of Canada had approved the Quebec Resolutions and everything depended upon New Brunswick where he exercised no influence at all.

For some time after resigning Brown maintained a parliamentary truce, but he was impatient to end it. "The sooner the better," said his trusted colleague Alexander Mackenzie.[8] When New Brunswick decided for union in June 1866, the Reformers of Canada West were in a position to resume the party warfare in earnest. Already Brown was thinking in terms of a national Reform or Liberal party which would control the first Parliament under Confederation. A little earlier he had broached the subject to William Annand in Halifax, but unfortunately almost all the Nova Scotian Liberals were anti-Confederates.[9]

To have any chance of success he had to extricate the Reformers of Canada West from the coalition intact. By choosing the correct issues in Parliament he made considerable headway. "Half a dozen more such votes," he predicted on one occasion, "and the whole party will be re-united."[10] By early 1867 the *Globe* was calling for the reactivation of the Reform constituency associations, neglected during the years of coalition. A little later the Reform Association of Upper Canada was reconstituted. Finally, the Reformers staged a full-scale convention in Toronto on June 27. William McDougall and William Howland, the Reform ministers who stayed in the coalition, told the convention that "they could not abandon the new-born child, Confederation . . . until they were certain it could stand on its own feet."[11] Was it not better, replied Brown, to abandon Macdonald rather than the Liberals of Canada East? Might the Reformers of Canada West, with a little help from those in the other provinces, not control the first Commons?[12] He carried the convention with him. All but three of the six hundred delegates supported an anticoalition resolution.

For Brown there was one sour note. Only a handful of delegates from east of Toronto had attended the convention. How could he make an appeal to this region, never a centre of Grit strength? How better than by contesting one of its seats, South Ontario, in the first election under Confederation! On the first day of polling he led the Conservative coalitionist T.N. Gibbs by 11 votes. On the second day "money was spent freely; jobs, contracts, favours were promised in profusion," and Brown lost by 96 votes.[13] Anticipating the South Ontario result, Macdonald had staged that contest early. In chopping off "the tallest head" he got exactly what he wanted in propaganda value. Brown might have tried his fortune in another seat but he concentrated on getting his party's candidates elected. Alexander Mackenzie had no trouble in Lambton, nor did the newcomer Edward Blake in West Durham. Yet of Ontario's 82 seats the Liberals could take no more than 30, and in the old Grit area of central and western Ontario they won only 20 of 42.

The timing of the elections and the use of money and patronage undoubtedly played a part in the Liberals' defeat. But their losses, both in South Ontario and elsewhere, resulted mainly from a split in the normal Reform vote. "This in a province like Ontario, when the popular vote for many years has been nearly equally divided," said Richard Cartwright, "was quite enough to turn the scale in favour of the Conservative candidate."[14] What caused the split? The Reformers had to contend with an administration which enjoyed the prestige of having brought Confederation into being. The politically astute Macdonald knew what he was about when he argued against a return to party warfare until Joseph Howe and any others endangering the union had been silenced. In effect he made the "no party" cry an appeal to patriotism and national aspiration. He gave it further substance by inducing the Reformer John Sandfield Macdonald to form a no-party provincial administration. To conduct a successful campaign, the Reformers needed an attractive alternative programme. They had none to offer. That is why many of the Reform voters were prepared to give Macdonald the fair chance he demanded.[15] That is why Brown became "the noblest victim of them all."

In Ontario the merits of Confederation were not an issue in the election. This was true nowhere else. In Canada East, both French- and English-speaking Conservatives had been part of the coalition designed to bring about the union. Still, there had been some differences between them along racial lines in the early stages. Thus, *La Minerve*, usually a spokesman for Cartier, sternly rebuked the Montreal *Gazette* for advocating a highly centralized union which might imperil French-Canadian interests.[16]

Among the Liberals, both French- and English-speaking, there was complete unanimity. Determined at all costs to fight anything inimical to French Canada were the Rouge leaders, and Rouge papers like *Le Pays, L'Ordre*, and especially *L'Union Nationale*, which had been founded in September 1865 by ardent patriots like Louis Amable Jetté and L.O. David to oppose Confederation. The Quebec scheme gave them their chance. As soon as it became public knowledge, they lost no opportunity to inflame the French population against it.[17] Their own past connections with Brown and the Grits, now staunch unionists; the quasi-monopoly of power which the Bleus possessed; and the general lassitude of the ordinary French Canadian all worked against them.[18] Yet they kept arguing that the Quebec scheme was fraught with danger for French Canada and advocated a true confederation with a devolutionary central government and sovereign provincial powers. Also opposed to the Quebec Resolutions was the Montreal *Herald*, which reflected the views of Holton and the English Liberals. Fearing that the Protestants of Canada East would be placed at the mercy of a French-controlled provincial legislature, it strove to preserve the status quo.

By the end of 1864 the Bleu newspapers, and particularly *Le Courrier du Canada* of Quebec, were presenting reasoned arguments, designed to win over the clergy and the better educated public to the Quebec scheme, for, at this stage, many of the Bleus were themselves uneasy. The Fenian scares of December 1864–January 1865 came, therefore, at an exceedingly opportune time for the government; they made it easier to push the Quebec Resolutions through the Parliament of Canada in February and March. The chief opponents were again the Rouges; their main complaint was the centralizing character of the Resolutions. There were also a few dissidents on the government side of the House. The independent Conservative from Brome, Christopher Dunkin, demolished the project article by article, charting almost perfectly the shoals and reefs ahead.[19] Only one Bleu, Henri Elzéar Taschereau of Beauce, separated himself from the government; he called the projected union "un coup mortel à notre nationalité."[20]

The passage of the Resolutions did not end the uneasiness in Canada East. Indeed, it increased in the spring of 1866 when the Nova Scotian Legislature accepted union in principle and left the details to the "arbitrament of the Imperial Government." For a time the issue of "l'arbitrage impérial" threatened to be awkward and possibly become dangerous.[21] It meant that the guarantees to the French Canadians might be jeopardized. It caused the somewhat independent *Le Canadien* to desert the Confederation camp altogether. It led the youthful Honoré Mercier to leave the editorial staff of the Bleu newspaper, *Le Courrier de St. Hyacinthe*. It did more than that: it made him abandon Cartier and the Conservatives forever. As early as 1866, the later nationalist leader recognized "nothing more holy than the national cause" and "no influence . . . strong enough to make [him] sacrifice . . . the future of the French Canadian race."[22] Yet, while "l'arbitrage impérial" was causing alarm in Bleu ranks, the Fenian raids of the spring of 1866 came, and with them disappeared any chance of weakening Cartier's hold on Canada East.

Once the British North America Act had been passed, its more moderate opponents in Canada East accepted union as a *fait accompli*. Holton and the Montreal *Herald* urged that it be given a fair trial and sought to renew their alliance with Brown. At first, A.A. Dorion, the Rouge leader, seemed of like mind; he simply asked that the distribution of powers be modified in the direction of less centralization. This did not suit the party's younger and more advanced members, particularly the group from *L'Union Nationale*.[23] At a Liberal assemblage they expressed their determination to combat Confederation per se and they carried a majority with them. During the election they circulated widely a pamphlet entitled *La Confédération, couronnement de dix années de mauvaise administration*, which sought to prove that the union was simply a device to enable John A. Macdonald to retain power and to realize Lord Durham's plan for the anglicization of French Canada.[24] It made scarcely a dent in the apathy of the ordinary French Canadian.

The Bleus countered with *La Confédération, c'est le salut du Bas-Canada*. It pointed out especially that, since the Americans were casting envious eyes on the Canadians, the latter had no choice but to form a country strong enough to defend itself. The Bleus, however, had a weapon far more potent than pamphlets and that was the episcopacy. A little earlier the French-Canadian bishops had had their own reservations about union. But once it was consummated they left no doubt where they stood. In June, four or five issued pastoral letters which were accorded special prominence in the Bleu press. Typical was that of the Archbishop of Quebec which stated simply that it was God's command to accept what emanated from legitimate authority; the voters ought to refrain, therefore, from supporting anyone who was disposed to combat Confederation or put obstacles in its path.[25] For a time Bishop Bourget of Montreal was silent. His relations with Cartier were cool because the latter's friends and clients, the Sulpicians, were resisting Bourget's efforts to divide their parish of Montreal. However, in July he, too, followed the other bishops.

The reaction of the Rouges was one of indignation. Why should their bishops break with all the traditions of the episcopacy "pour venir faire les petites affaires d'un parti."[26] Thus the Rouges continued the clash with the Church which had always kept them in a minority. It acted strongly to produce this result again in 1867. Add to this the Bleus' entrenched political organization; their control of patronage; and an undercurrent which said, "give the new régime a chance to prove itself," and there were more than sufficient ingredients for victory.[27]

First

And a smashing victory it was too! In Kamouraska an old family feud between the Chapais and the Letelliers led to riots which made polling impossible. Of the 64 seats which declared victors, the Conservatives took 47; 20 of their candidates were returned by acclamation, and 3 of the ministers, Cartier in Montreal East, Langevin in Dorchester, and Galt in Sherbrooke, won without difficulty. The fourth, Chapais, took a seat in the Senate because the troubles in Kamouraska made election to the Commons impossible. Only seventeen Liberals (fourteen Rouges and 3 English-speaking) were elected. Holton won easily in Chateauguay, but Dorion had a bare 23-vote margin in Hochelaga. The results left the Rouges embittered about clerical influence, direct and indirect. According to them, this was why Quebec started out as the banner Conservative province.

What New Brunswick did in the election of 1867 mattered little. Its earlier decision to accept the principle of union was crucial, however, for it made Confederation possible. Government in pre-Confederation New Brunswick, says Professor Waite, "presents the picture of a robust little corporation for the private aggrandizement of its members and the incidental conduct of public business."[28] The issues that divided the province, he continues, were not Liberal and Conservative, but patronage and railways. While the government of Samuel Leonard Tilley from 1861 to 1865 regarded itself as Liberal, the label meant little.

Whether or not he wanted to, Tilley had to go to the electorate in February–March 1865. His hand was forced by Lieutenant-Governor Arthur Hamilton Gordon, who apparently felt it was the best way to get what the British government wanted: a quick decision from New Brunswick in favour of union.[29] How wrong he was! By this time the province had been thoroughly alerted to the supposed ills of the Quebec scheme by Albert J. Smith, the Lion of Westmorland, and Timothy W. Anglin of the Saint John *Morning Freeman*. At first they appealed to a kind of provincial patriotism or, perhaps, parochialism. The proposals, they said, constituted a legislative union in disguise and New Brunswick would soon lose the Assembly it had long possessed. Later they concentrated on the financial bargain of the union; it was so bad, they contended, that the province would soon be forced into odious direct taxation. The substantial Irish Catholic and Acadian populations were distinctly hostile to union, the former because they feared that Protestant Canada West would dominate the federation, the latter because they "trembled at the thought of being submerged in a larger political community."[30] In the election the popular vote was fairly close, but in terms of seats Tilley was utterly routed. "Every delegate to Quebec who was a member of the house of assembly lost his seat."[31]

Even more than its predecessor, the new government of Albert J. Smith defied labelling. The Premier had once been a Liberal; his Attorney General was a Tory; his Provincial Secretary was not much of anything. The ministry cannot be described even as anti-Confederate, only as opposed to the Quebec scheme. Its existence was a troubled one. From the beginning it was on the defensive; it failed to come up with anything that was positive and constructive; rifts soon developed among its members even on the subject of union. By the spring of 1866 the Governor felt it was safe to intervene. He did it so blatantly that his action almost constituted a "coup de main."[32] On April 10 he got what he wanted: Smith's resignation.

Five days later came the first Fenian raid on New Brunswick and any trouble that Tilley might have had with the voters was over. Now he could play down the highly unpopular Quebec scheme and advocate a union best calculated to serve the interests of New Brunswick and protect her from outside aggression. In May and June 1866 he and Peter Mitchell carried the province even more decisively than Smith had the year before. This time the Irish Catholic Bishop of Chatham threw his weight on the side of union. Only three eastern counties, furthest from the border and the dangers of Fenianism, supported Smith. Not long afterwards the new Assembly adopted a resolution calling for union on the best terms that could be got.

These events formed the background of the first federal election in New Brunswick. In terms of results, New Brunswick is the most difficult province to understand. Party lines had never been meaningful and Confederation made them even less so. Two of those elected confounded matters still further; they called themselves Liberals, but supported Macdonald and Confederation. It has been common practice to describe most of the members as "ministerialist" (i.e., prepared to support the government of the day whatever its complexion) or independent, yet seven of the fifteen quite consistently voted with the opposition. The two leading anti-Confederates won easily: Smith in Westmorland and Anglin in Gloucester. However, only four or, at the most, five of the seven antigovernment members could be called anti-Confederates. On the government side four Fathers of Confederation were returned: Fisher and Gray by acclamation in York and Saint John County, Tilley in Saint John City, and Johnson in Northumberland.

In Nova Scotia criticism of the projected union began in the western counties late in the autumn of 1864. But it was the mercantile and commercial elements of Halifax which provided the real backbone of the opposition. By the year's end the Governor found so many leaders of the community opposed to the Quebec scheme that he doubted if it could be carried. Premier Charles Tupper's difficulties increased in January 1865, when William Annand's *Morning Chronicle* joined the anti-Confederate ranks. To this paper Joseph Howe contributed his "Botheration Letters" between January and March. One of several myths surounding Howe and Confederation is that he was the one to rouse his countrymen against the Quebec Resolutions. But the evidence indicates that Nova Scotia had made up its mind by January 1865. In any case, Howe published his letters anonymously and few knew who wrote them at the time of their publication. After March 1865 he made no attempt to influence the Nova Scotian public, even indirectly, for over a year.

Tupper, assessing the situation accurately, ignored the Quebec Resolutions during the session of 1865. Although he had an overwhelming majority in the Assembly, he knew full well that on the issue of union a substantial part of his normally well-disciplined phalanx would desert him. Just as in New Brunswick, the Fenian troubles of March 1866 changed the minds of enough assemblymen to let Tupper have his way. The resolution which he got through the Assembly on April 17, however, did not endorse the Quebec Resolutions; it simply authorized the Nova Scotian delegates to arrange, subject to the arbitrament of the British government, a union which would most effectively protect the province's interests.

By this time Howe had taken over the leadership of the resistance to union. Like other anti-Confederates he sought to demonstrate that the Quebec scheme was a device to solve the political deadlock in Canada at the complete sacrifice of Nova Scotian interests. Furthermore, the union, he feared, would forestall and perhaps prevent forever the organization of the Empire, which he placed first among his political objectives. Neither of these objections brought him back into active politics. What did it was Tupper's determination to take Nova Scotia into union without consulting the people.[33] Howe started out at once on a tour of the western counties, but his function was clearly not to make converts; it was to make more vocal the opinions of people who had already made up their minds. He next proceeded to England where his mighty effort to prevent the Act of Union from being passed proved of no avail.

After these events the first federal election campaign was something of an anticlimax. It had started, after all, in low gear in December 1864 and had been conducted vigorously since April 1866. There was little more to be said in the month prior to September 18, the day of polling for all the Nova Scotian ridings. Howe spoke only once during his tour of inspection of the western counties. He confined his speech-making largely to his own constituency of Hants and to Cumberland, where he supported Annand's all-out effort to beat Tupper. The latter spent a few days in Halifax, but could not afford to absent himself longer from his own county.

The names Conservative and Liberal gave way completely to Confederate and anti-Confederate. The anti-Confederates also dubbed themselves the Nova Scotia Party and the People's Party. The Confederates had a basic Conservative core, but they received two important recruits from Liberal ranks: Adams G. Archibald and Jonathan McCully, both Fathers of Confederation. Those who moved from the Conservative to the anti-Confederate ranks were much more numerous; they included people from all levels of society and particularly from the commercial and mercantile classes. Incongruous among the recruits was the new Attorney General, Martin I. Wilkins, a thoroughgoing Tory if ever there was one.

The hard-pressed Confederates did not miss a trick to strengthen their position. Starting in late August, the *British Colonist* and the *Express* gloated over the government's successes in Quebec and Ontario. Just before the polling in Nova Scotia they recorded the standings in those provinces as 87 government members to 17 opposition.[34] They used with zeal Archbishop Connolly's letter to the Catholics of Halifax which described Confederation as the greatest temporal blessing ever vouchsafed to Nova Scotia.[35] The anti-Confederate press no longer stressed the case against union; it simply implored the voters to punish the traitors who had pushed them into Confederation against their own consent. Otherwise, it said, they would be held in disrespect everywhere.[36]

Punish them they did! Tupper managed to win a narrow victory over Annand, but he was the only Confederate to be returned federally. Provincially the Confederates elected only two members and one of them was later unseated. Archibald, the only member of Macdonald's cabinet to suffer defeat, lost out in Colchester. The *Chronicle* was eminently satisfied: "We, the people of Nova Scotia, have shown that *we own this country* — that Tupper, Archibald, McCully and the rest cannot trample over us."[37] All the *British Colonist* could say was: "Thank God the Union is safe beyond the reach of Howe and all his treasonable pack."[38] It is sometimes said that the electors' disenchantment with Tupper's educational and railway policies was partially responsible for the devastating results in Nova Scotia. Anyone who has read the newspapers of the day knows differently. Union was the only issue which mattered; it alone accounted for the sweeping nature of the results.

Over-all, the election was a victory for the government, but it was a victory with a question mark. The administration had swept Quebec, won decisively in Ontario, and gained something better than an even break in New Brunswick. While the party lines were anything but cohesive, it could count on a majority of approximately 36 in a Commons of 181 Members. The question mark was Nova Scotia. It had not even begun to accept the union. Yet, said Macdonald, it was "powerless for harm." That pestilential fellow, Howe, might, of course, still cause some trouble in England.[39] But perhaps he, too, could be won over.

FOOTNOTES

1. Norman Ward, *House of Commons — Representation* (Toronto: University of Toronto Press, 1950), p. 167.

2. P.B. Waite, *The Life and Times of Confederation 1864-1867* (Toronto: University of Toronto Press, 1962), p. 43.

3. Donald G. Creighton, *The Road to Confederation* (Toronto: The Macmillan Company of Canada, 1964), p. 69.

4. For details see George H. Hougham, "The Background and Development of National Parties," in *Party Politics in*

Canada, ed. H.G. Thorburn (2nd ed., Toronto: Prentice-Hall of Canada, 1967), pp. 2-14.

5. Creighton, *Road to Confederation*, Chapter II.

6. Waite, *Life and Times of Confederation*, p. 132. Chapter IX of this work provides full details of the situation in Canada West.

7. J.M.S. Careless, *Brown of the Globe*, II (Toronto: The Macmillan Company of Canada, 1963), p. 203.

8. Dale C. Thomson, *Alexander Mackenzie: Clear Grit* (Toronto: The Macmillan Company of Canada, 1960), p. 93.

9. Waite, *Life and Times of Confederation*, pp. 220-21.

10. Careless, *Brown of the Globe*, II, p. 232.

11. Thomson, *Mackenzie*, p. 96.

12. Careless, *Brown of the Globe*, II, p. 249.

13. *Ibid.*, p. 255.

14. Sir Richard J. Cartwright, *Reminiscences* (Toronto: William Briggs, 1912), p. 66.

15. For a fuller account see Careless, *Brown of the Globe*, II, pp. 256-59.

16. Waite, *Life and Times of Confederation*, p. 141.

17. *Ibid.*, p. 142.

18. Robert Rumilly, *Histoire de la Province de Québec*, I (Montreal: Editions Bernard Valiquette, 1940), p. 119.

19. Waite, *Life and Times of Confederation*, p. 154.

20. Rumilly, *Histoire*, I, pp. 34-35.

21. Waite, *Life and Times of Confederation*, p. 276.

22. Robert Rumilly, *Mercier* (Montreal: Les Editions du zodiaque, 1936), p. 49. Translated by J.M. Beck.

23. Waite, *Life and Times of Confederation*, p. 277.

24. Rumilly, *Histoire*, I, p. 115.

25. *Ibid.*, p. 118.

26. Waite, *Life and Times of Confederation*, p. 301.

27. Rumilly, *Histoire*, I, pp. 118-19.

28. Waite, *Life and Times of Confederation*, p. 232.

29. See W.S. MacNutt, *New Brunswick – A History: 1784-1867* (Toronto: The Macmillan Company of Canada, 1963), pp. 426-27; Creighton, *Road to Confederation*, pp. 199-203.

30. *Ibid.*, p. 251.

31. MacNutt, *New Brunswick – A History*, p. 430.

32. *Ibid.*, p. 447.

33. For the details see J.M. Beck, *Joseph Howe: Anti-Confederate* (Ottawa: The Canadian Historical Association, 1965), p. 17.

34. *British Colonist*, September 12, 1867.

35. *Ibid.*, September 17, 1867.

36. Halifax *Morning Chronicle,* September 1 to 18, 1867.

37. *Ibid.*, September 19, 1867.

38. *British Colonist*, September 21, 1867.

39. Donald G. Creighton, *John A. Macdonald: The Old Chieftain* (Toronto: The Macmillan Company of Canada, 1955), p. 3.

1867

	Seats	Candidates			Elected						Popular Vote						Total
		Govt.	Opp.	Others	Govt.	%	Opp.	%	Others	%	Govt.	%	Opp.	%	Others	%	
Nova Scotia	19	15	19	1	1	5.3	18	94.7	—	—	14,862	40.9	21,139	58.1	362	1.0	36,363
New Brunswick	15	13	13	3	8	53.3	7	46.7	—	—	9,137	46.7	9,939	50.8	505	2.6	19,581
Quebec	65*	59	44	5	47	73.4	17	26.6	—	—	38,796	53.6	32,654	45.1	962	1.3	72,412
Ontario	82	74	73	12	52	63.4	30	36.6	—	—	71,474	51.1	67,632	48.4	755	0.5	139,861
Total	181	161	149	21	108	60.0	72	40.0	—	—	134,269	50.1	131,364	49.0	2,584	1.0	268,217

* No return in Kamouraska because of riots.

Elected by acclamation (46): Govt. (29): N.B. (2); Que. (20); Ont. (7).
Opp. (17): N.S. (4); N.B. (2); Que. (3); Ont. (8).

First

Second
General Election

UNTIL THE GRISTLE HARDENS INTO BONE

The election of 1872 was crucial to Macdonald. Give him another five years of office, he pleaded, to let him finish the job. By that time Confederation, "now in the gristle, [would] have hardened into bone, and . . . the constitution . . . taken such root as to be able to stand the storm."[1] If nothing else, the first five years had proved that Canada was extraordinarily difficult to govern. The job of completing and consolidating Confederation had produced difficulties and pitfalls galore. Many of them would come back to haunt the government when it faced the electorate.

There was, first, the "better terms" agreement of 1869 – the price of securing Joseph Howe's acceptance of union. While Nova Scotians considered it no more than a simple act of justice, the Toronto *Globe* and the Ontario Grits called it a unilateral breach of the articles of Confederation, a gross injustice perpetrated upon the other provinces.

There were also the problems associated with acquiring the North-West: the insurrection in the Red River colony, the "execution" of the Ontario Orangeman Thomas Scott, the creation of Manitoba, the sending of a military expedition to the West, and so on. Quebec, full of sympathy for the Métis, wanted their rights guaranteed in the new provincial constitution, doubted the necessity of an armed expedition, and expected an amnesty for all the participants in the uprising. Ontario was just as insistent that rebels and murderers get their just deserts and was ever suspicious that the government might yield to a truculent Cartier.

Equally perturbing to the French Catholics of Quebec was the treatment accorded their compatriots in New Brunswick. The government at Ottawa, they noted, had done nothing whatever about the School Law of 1871 which stripped New Brunswick Catholics of the rights they had enjoyed by practice in 1867.

Finally, and worst of all, were the repercussions of the Treaty of Washington of 1871. So concerned were the British plenipotentiaries with settling all the outstanding Anglo-American differences that they were prepared to sacrifice Canadian interests in the process. Macdonald, the only Canadian negotiator, signed the treaty with reluctance and then delayed submitting it to Parliament. His caution was understandable. In Canadian eyes the treaty had little to commend it. It provided no compensation from the Americans for the Fenian raids; it conceded to the Americans the free navigation of the St. Lawrence for practically nothing in return; it opened the Canadian fisheries to the Americans for a purely monetary compensation to be determined by arbitrators. The last was surely the worst blow of all, for the fisheries were to have been Canada's trump card in negotiating a renewal of reciprocity in natural products. No parliamentary opposition could have missed such a grand opportunity for attack. Alexander Mackenzie made the most of it. He dismissed outright Macdonald's contention that a rejection of the treaty might mean Anglo-American conflict. "Had it come to this," he asked, "that the Premier of Canada has to make an appeal to the forbearance of Canadians because of the necessities of that great Empire of which we form a part?"[2]

Scarcely had the session of 1872 concluded when Macdonald betook himself to Toronto to conduct the Ontario phase of the campaign. He knew the direction he wanted it to take. Earlier he had stated that the name Conservative was a little unfortunate. Would something like the Constitutional Union Party not have been better? Certainly it would have been more in line with his basic aim: "the union and expansion of British North America under the protection of the Anglo-Canadian alliance."[3] In his election speeches he intended to pose as the nation-builder. With that end in mind he had already begun to implement two basic programmes: the settling of the West and all-Canadian transportation.

High aims carried with them grave problems, however. The creation of Manitoba had produced nightmarish difficulties; the entrance of British Columbia repeated them in full measure. During the session of 1871 the opposition described the terms of union as outrageous. Canada, they said, could not possibly start the railway to the Pacific within two years and complete it within ten. During the next session they were equally hard on the bill which authorized the government to grant $30 million and 50 million acres of land to the company which built the railroad. In effect, Macdonald said: "If the union is to be complete, permanent and strong, West and East must be bound together by an iron band. . . . Let us not be faint-hearted. Let us borrow freely."[4] In contrast, the cautious, economical Alexander Mackenzie wanted to use the extensive stretches of water along the route. It was, says his biographer, "not an imaginative continent-wide scheme, or one designed to please the British Columbia delegates, but it was realistic."[5]

The calling of the election did not remove Macdonald's railway problems, even temporarily. As the campaign progressed, he sought desperately to effect a fusion between the chief competitors for the contract: Sir Hugh Allan's Canadian Pacific and David Macpherson's Interoceanic Railway Company. After initial resistance, Cartier had succumbed to the Allan influence.[6] He was not alone. Although Sir Hugh received no promise other than the presidency of a merged company, members of the government had compromised themselves badly. To fight a very difficult campaign in Quebec and Ontario, Cartier had accepted $85,000, Langevin $32,000, and Macdonald at least $45,000, from Allan.

Both before and during the election, Sir John suggested a third ingredient in developmental policy: a "National Policy" in tariff matters. Political considerations, he said, prevented him from using the word "protection" for the moment; he simply advocated "a readjustment of the tariff in such a manner as incidentally to aid our manufacturing and industrial interests."[7] Thus far he confined himself to general considerations and ventured nothing specific.

It was a tough fight in Ontario. "Never in the whole of my 27 years of public service," said Macdonald, "have I had such hard and unpleasant work to do."[8] In one respect alone did everything go according to plan. He had observed earlier that George Brown was engaged in strike-breaking activities against the typographical union of the *Globe*. He had noted, too, that in the absence of statutory provisions with respect to unions the common law was operative. It permitted the ready conviction of the striking unionists as parties to an illegal combination in restraint of trade. So, with that "quick instinct for the kind of Tory democracy which Disraeli was to proclaim only a little later,"[9] he had Parliament free the trade unions of their common law disabilities during the session of 1872. Consequently, it was easy to contrast Brown the tyrannical employer with Macdonald the workingman's friend.[10] Not surprisingly, Hamilton gave the Conservatives its two seats, and Toronto two of its three.

Things were different in the rural areas of central and western Ontario, the old centre of Grit strength. There, Macdonald, the Nation-builder, had no special appeal. What concerned the farmers was that the Washington Treaty gave them no outlet for their products and, in fact, conferred no benefits upon them at all. Macdonald's instinct had warned him that the treaty bode him no good and his instinct proved to be right. "I knew Ontario too well to be mistaken," he told the Governor General.[11]

He had to contend also with the determined opposition of the Liberal provincial administration which had assumed office the previous year. Lumber merchants and American railway interests, he said, had filled his opponents' war chest to overflowing,[12] and the provincial government used all its resources, patronage, and influence to beat him. The Premier of Ontario, Edward Blake, was in England recuperating from fatigue, so Alexander Mackenzie directed the Liberal campaign and lambasted the government's record all over western Ontario. Macdonald's confrontation of him on the public platform in Sarnia was anything but a resounding success for the Prime Minister. In the end he had to be satisfied with 40 of Ontario's 88 seats. Western Ontario returned to its old love; in the area where the Grits could get only 20 of 42 seats in 1867, they now won 30 of

45. Macdonald's majority in Kingston dropped to 131; Francis Hincks, his Minister of Finance, lost out in South Brant. Even timing the individual contests to improve his party's fortunes helped him little, if at all.

In Quebec the fray was altogether different. This was because religio-political considerations continually intruded themselves. Continental ultramontanism had gained considerable acceptance among the intellectuals and, early in 1871, some of them produced the "Catholic Programme." The *programmistes* wanted not so much to organize a Catholic party as to purge the anticlerical elements which they felt were creeping into the Conservative party. They insisted, above all, that Catholics vote only for men who would unreservedly support the religious, political, and social doctrines of the Church as interpreted by the bishops. To this, Bishop Bourget of Montreal and Bishop Laflèche of Trois Rivières enthusiastically said "aye, aye," as did *Le Nouveau Monde, Le Journal des Trois-Rivières*, and *Le Courrier du Canada.*

The Liberals – mainly the Rouges of pre-1867 days – had by this time accepted the Confederation which they had once opposed. What they needed most of all was to be accepted by the Church, in whose eyes they were still suspect. In 1871 some of the moderates among them, especially Louis Amable Jetté, took the lead in reorganizing the Liberal party as the *parti national*. According to Skelton, it stood for Canada first and last; advocated a reform of political institutions; favoured the commercial independence of Canada; and expressed kindly feelings for the clergy, while hoping they would not besmirch their robes in the mire of politics.[13] Some old Rouges like Rodolphe Laflamme looked on the *parti national* with scorn; ardent patriots and nationalists like Honoré Mercier welcomed it as a means of placing French-Canadian interests ahead of those of party; the few impatient Conservatives who joined it got out when they realized it was the Liberal party in camouflage.

The *parti national* decided to strike at the kingpin himself. They put Jetté up against George Cartier in Montreal East. In that classic struggle many of the arguments were no different from those elsewhere, but special forces also came into play. The *programmistes* were harder on Cartier than was the *parti national*. Had he not resisted Bishop Bourget's efforts to divide the parish of Montreal which was held by his friends the Sulpicians? Had he not failed to protect the New Brunswick Catholics from the injustice of the school law? The *parti national* took a different tack. Why was Ontario's population increasing at a faster rate than Quebec's? Was the federal government not responsible for the continuing drain of French Canadians to New England?[14]

Cartier was beset with other difficulties, too. Earlier, he had alienated English-speaking Montrealers, long his staunch supporters. Now, as solicitor for the Grand Trunk, he was presumed to be unsympathetic to any railway along the north shore of the St. Lawrence, be it a line from Quebec to

Montreal to Ottawa or the Canadian Pacific itself. This put him in exceedingly bad stead with both French and English, who had visions of Montreal as a great commercial metropolis, the terminus of the C.P.R. and the oceanic shipping routes. It is pathetic to imagine *le grand homme*, his feet swollen from Bright's disease, fleeing before volleys of cabbages and rotten eggs. Eventually Cartier made his peace with both Bourget and Allan, but only at the price of complete surrender. It was too late. Jetté, the little boy in short pants, whom Cartier said he would send back to his history and law books, defeated him convincingly in Montreal East.[15]

Elsewhere in Quebec the government fared somewhat better. They held their own in the district of Trois Rivières, and lost only seven seats in the districts of Quebec and Montreal. None the less, 27 seats out of 65 was not a bad showing for the Liberals. Had they finally managed to cast off some of the anticlerical stigma?

In Nova Scotia the anti-Confederate press at last admitted that there was no immediate prospect of Nova Scotia's release from Confederation. At the same time it bitterly castigated the "red-hot" anti-Confederate M.P.'s from Nova Scotia who had been successfully wheedled into giving an almost unbroken support to John A. Macdonald. Nova Scotians, it said, should not attach themselves to any party to the extent of compromising themselves. Yet, in the very same breath, it told the Nova Scotian M.P.'s they had no choice but to act with one of the two parties at Ottawa, and if they wanted "a purer and more economical government," it would have to be with Mackenzie and Blake.[16] Tupper and the Conservatives ridiculed the idea of Nova Scotians aligning themselves with Grits who had denounced the granting of better terms as "a corrupt act." Above all, they commended the government for "caring with equal fidelity" for every section of the Dominion and for pursuing a strong policy of national development. "We are 'a new nation'! We must not shrink from the duties and responsibilities of our high position."[17]

Some of the members who were returned from Nova Scotia defy labelling, but the anti-Confederate, anti-Macdonald forces undoubtedly lost ground. Howe and Tupper were easily re-elected, even though the ailing Howe had to campaign from Ottawa through the medium of letters to the newspapers. A.W. Savary of Digby and Stewart Campbell of Guysborough, who had been elected as anti-Confederates in 1867, were returned this time as out-and-out Macdonald men. Alfred Jones and Patrick Power, perhaps the leading anti-Confederate members, lost out in Halifax. Even Pictou, supposedly a hotbed of repeal and secession, returned two Macdonald supporters. Nominally it looked as if 11 of the 21 members were Liberals or Reformers. Yet this was grossly misleading. According to the *British Colonist*, 20 of them would usually uphold the administration,[18] and it was not too far off the mark. The Nova Scotia Party was indeed in a state of collapse.

In New Brunswick the situation was no less confusing. Other than the cabinet ministers, the successful candidates appeared to have "professed varying degrees of independence of party ties."[19] While 9 of the 16 had Liberal or Reform leanings, this did not mean very much, since patronage and a low opinion of central Canadian Reformers worked with the same effect as in Nova Scotia. Consequently, the Conservatives claimed 13 or 14 members as their own. Macdonald went one step further; two of his professed opponents, he said, had promised not to vote non-confidence in him.

For the first time Manitoba and British Columbia participated in a general election. Neither province was very much affected, either in this election or the other elections of the seventies, by the party politics of eastern Canada. Their political views, says Escott Reid, were determined by two other forces:

> their desire for the Pacific Railway, and the holding of their elections some weeks after the results in the east had been declared. Until the railway was completed the west could not afford the luxury of party politics. It had to be ministerialist. And as it always knew which party had been sustained by the east, it could be ministerialist without difficulty.[20]

Only when "ministerialism" threatened the railway might it be forsworn. In 1872 all the accounts from the East indicated that the railway party; i.e., the Conservatives, had won. The West knew whom to vote for when its turn came. It is little wonder that Macdonald included among his supporters the six members from British Columbia and the four from Manitoba. He seemed to be certain even of R. Cunningham, who had somehow got himself elected in Marquette while calling himself a Liberal. Richard Cartwright intimated that Macdonald had stolen the election. It was a political swindle of the worst kind, he contended, to have given so many members to Manitoba, which had no more than 25,000 people, and British Columbia, which had 36,000, two-thirds of them Indians.[21] His grievance had some merit. To let 62 voters in Yale elect a member was certainly overrepresentation.

In another way Macdonald found the belated elections in the West useful; they enabled him to find safe havens for the cabinet ministers who had been rejected in the East. A few weeks after their initial defeats, Hincks was returned by acclamation in Vancouver, Cartier in Provencher. Sir George owed his election to Bishop Taché of St. Boniface, who induced Louis Riel and Attorney General Henry Clarke to withdraw as candidates. However, the Bishop expected a great deal in return – nothing less than an amnesty for the ring leaders in the Red River insurrection.

What did it all add up to? The razor-thin majority for Macdonald which the table at the end of the chapter indicates is misleading. The Commons had more than a few "loose fish," "shaky fellows," "inverted Irishmen," or "waiters on Providence." Call them what you will, most of them could be counted upon to sustain a government which seemed secure; they were "ministerialists." The clear-cut nature of the campaigning in Quebec meant an absence of ministerialists in that province; the number in Ontario was also small, except perhaps in eastern Ontario. Few of the 20 members in the eastern provinces who were normally labelled Liberals or Reformers gave regular support to their counterparts in central Canada. Most of them tended towards ministerialism. Western Canada was solidly ministerialist since the government of the day supported the railway. Macdonald exaggerated when he said his margin was about the same as in the first Parliament. None could deny that he had a good working majority, and it was the outlying regions, east and west, which provided it.

To what extent had the parties become cohesive forces? The Conservatives (or more correctly the Liberal-Conservatives) had gone a long way towards becoming a national party. It is true they had run four separate campaigns in the older provinces, but those who conducted these campaigns had worked together for some time in the ministry and had developed a feeling of confidence in each other. They stood for much the same thing and defended the government's record against much the same kind of charges. In Ontario the party had become somewhat more homogeneous since the coalition Liberals had by now either returned to their former party or been swallowed up in the Conservatives. Only in Quebec was there disunity, and there the differences between ultramontane and moderate Conservatives were never to be fully reconciled.

The Liberals had made much less progress towards real unity. Not that they had divisions within the provinces. In Ontario the conflict between the Brownites and the Blakeites had not yet come into the open, while in Quebec the differences between the *parti national* and the old Rouges were not to become significant. The Liberals' real problem lay in the lack of understanding and trust between their provincial segments. It was too much to expect the Rouges to fuse immediately with the one-time anti-French, anti-Catholic Grits; for the moment there was "little more between them than an entente cordiale, at most a dual alliance."[22] In the Maritimes the Liberals still had their suspicions that the Grits were a selfish Ontario party. The Liberal sectional groups were wont to express divergent opinions which their opponents never failed to exploit. Hitherto, the Liberals had not even chosen a parliamentary leader. Perhaps, says Dale Thomson, it was just as well. "The choice of a leader from any one province was certain to be embarrassing to candidates in the others. Without a Dominion leader, the campaign could be adapted to local candidates, and the process of consolidation and unification continued at a natural pace."[23]

1. Macdonald to Lisgar, September 2, 1872, in Sir Joseph Pope (ed.), *Correspondence of Sir John Macdonald* (Toronto: Oxford University Press, 1921), p. 176.

2. Dale C. Thomson, *Alexander Mackenzie: Clear Grit* (Toronto: The Macmillan Company of Canada, 1960), p. 138.

3. Donald G. Creighton, *John A. Macdonald: The Old Chieftain* (Toronto: The Macmillan Company of Canada, 1955), p. 119.

4. William Buckingham and G.W. Ross, *The Hon. Alexander Mackenzie: His Life and Times* [Toronto: C.R. Parish and Company (Rose Publishing Company), 1892], pp. 321-22.

5. Thomson, *Mackenzie*, pp. 135-36.

6. *Infra*, p. 22.

7. Macdonald to Patteson, February 24, 1872, in Creighton, *Old Chieftain*, p. 120.

8. Macdonald to Lisgar, September 2, 1872, in Pope (ed.), *Correspondence*, p. 175.

9. Creighton, *Old Chieftain*, p. 124.

10. Thomson, *Mackenzie*, p. 143.

11. Macdonald to Lisgar, September 2, 1872, in Pope (ed.), *Correspondence*, p. 176.

12. *Ibid.*

13. O.D. Skelton, *Life and Letters of Sir Wilfrid Laurier*, I [Toronto: Oxford University Press (S.B. Gundy), 1921], p. 130.

14. Robert Rumilly, *Histoire de la Province de Québec*, II (Montreal: Editions Bernard Valiquette, 1941), p. 208.

15. For the full story of the contest in Montreal East see *ibid.*, pp. 219-28.

16. Halifax *Morning Chronicle*, July 8, 1872.

17. *British Colonist*, July 25, 1872.

18. *Ibid.*, September 5, 1872.

19. Escott Reid, "The Rise of National Parties in Canada," *Proceedings of the Canadian Political Science Association*, 1932, p. 193.

20. *Ibid.*, p. 198.

21. Sir Richard J. Cartwright, *Reminiscences* (Toronto: William Briggs, 1912), pp. 101-102.

22. Reid, "Rise of National Parties," p. 194.

23. Thomson, *Mackenzie*, p. 140.

	Seats	Candidates			Elected						Popular Vote						Total
		C.	L.	O.	C.	%	L.	%	O.	%	C.	%	L.	%	O.	%	
Nova Scotia	21	17	18	—	10	47.6	11	52.4	—	—	19,939	49.96	19,974	50.04	—	—	39,913
New Brunswick	16	11	15	3	7	43.8	9	56.3	—	—	11,590	46.4	12,705	50.9	684	2.7	24,979
Quebéc	65	58	49	9	38	58.5	27	41.5	—	—	45,092	50.9	41,957	47.3	1,578	1.8	88,627
Ontario	88	78	82	6	40	45.5	48	54.5	—	—	80,896	49.8	81,146	49.9	520	0.3	162,562
Manitoba	4	4	3	3	3	75.0	1	25.0	—	—	646	49.5	583	44.7	76	5.8	1,305
British Columbia	6	6	—	2	6	100.0	—	—	—	—	843	88.2	—	—	113	11.8	956
Total	200	174	167	23	104	52.0	96	48.0	—	—	159,006	49.9	156,365	49.1	2,971	0.9	318,342

Elected by acclamation: C. (27): N.S. (3); N.B. (1); Que. (13); Ont. (6); Man. (1); B.C. (3).
L. (25): N.S. (4); N.B. (5); Que. (6); Ont. (10).

Third

General Election

THE CASE OF THE VIRTUOUS VOTERS

In November 1873 an event took place which is unique in Canadian political history. The government was forced, through the defection of its own supporters, to give way to another party without benefit of an election. The events leading to this denouement had had their beginnings seven months earlier.

On April 2, Lucius Seth Huntington, the Liberal member for Shefford, Quebec, had charged the Macdonald government with gross corruption in the granting of a charter to build the railway to the Pacific Coast. Among other things, he had accused Macdonald and Cartier of demanding and receiving large contributions from Sir Hugh Allan and his associates to assist them during the election of 1872.[1] Macdonald had insisted that there was no connection between these payments and the granting of the charter, but as the investigation continued and the revelations became more incriminating, his majority had gradually evaporated. To avoid certain defeat in the Commons, he presented his resignation early in November.

The Liberals who assumed office in his place, it has been shown, were anything but a cohesive force; in no sense had they been welded into a national party as had the Conservatives. It was not until after the election of 1872 that they had become convinced of the need to have a single leader in the Commons. Even then it was a group of members from Ontario and Quebec alone who made the choice. Antoine Aimé Dorion and Luther Holton of Quebec waived any claim to the leadership on the ground that Ontario provided the chief strength of the party. Edward Blake might have had it, but he felt he had contributed all too little to the Liberal campaign in 1872. So, because the other possible choices had eliminated themselves, it fell to Alexander Mackenzie. Even he doubted his qualifications for the position.[2]

The weaknesses of the Liberals manifested themselves as Mackenzie strove to form a cabinet in November 1873. No other prime minister has had to deal with so many prima donnas. Since the ranking Liberal M.P. from Nova Scotia, A.G. Jones, declined office, two non-entities, Thomas Coffin and William Ross, became Nova Scotia's representatives in the ministry. For personal reasons (or so he said) Luther Holton refused the Department of Finance, and for better or for worse—worse as it turned out—that dogmatic and unbending free trader Richard Cartwright got it. It took the signatures of 104 members of the Liberal caucus to drag Edward Blake into the cabinet and then only as President of the Council without departmental responsibilities.[3] Fortunately for Mackenzie, the political situation was such that this general perversity did him no harm for the moment.

Should a general election be held almost immediately? That was the most pressing decision facing the new Prime Minister.[4] Some of his colleagues wanted a short parliamentary session to permit a new election law to be adopted. Others saw a danger in letting Macdonald manoeuvre in a Parliament in which he had once had a majority. Mackenzie himself favoured a dissolution as a means of presenting a programme to the electorate in precise terms and winning their approval for it. He was also enough of a politician to want to capitalize upon the voters' revulsion against corruption in government. And revolted they were! In 1872 the Conservatives had won West Toronto by almost two to one, but in a by-election in December 1873, the Liberal, Thomas Moss, supported by youthful publicists campaigning for "Canada First" and against partisan corruption, captured the same riding by a decisive margin.[5]

About the same time, word came from Dorion in Quebec and the Liberal leaders in the Maritimes that their forces were ready. By Christmas Mackenzie had made up his mind. On January 7 the writs were issued. In the absence of a general law, complete simultaneous voting proved to be impracticable. Nevertheless, the government saw to it that most Canadians went to the polls within a few days of each other in late January or early February. Certainly there was no timing of the elections to improve the fortunes of the party in power.

As was the custom, Mackenzie unfolded his programme in an address to his own electors of Lambton County.[6] Parliament, he said, had to be "purged of members elected by the corrupt use of Sir Hugh Allan's money." He was resolved, above all, to "elevate the standard of public morality . . . and to conduct public affairs upon principles of which honest men can approve, and by practices which will bear the light of day." None could have been more serious in this intention than Mackenzie. He appointed himself Minister of Public Works so that he could direct the I.C.R. and C.P.R., supervise the extension of the canal system, and resist the pressure of friends and even enemies for favours.[7] Yet in his obsession for honesty and efficiency he had placed upon himself a burden which would impair his ability to give over-all direction to his ministry.

More specifically, Mackenzie promised to introduce clean election laws, simultaneous voting, the secret ballot, the trial of controverted elections by the judiciary, an extension of the franchise, the passage of an insolvency law, the creation of a Supreme Court, and the revision of the militia system. While none of these proposals was highly controversial or especially vote-catching, most of them fitted well into the programme of a government pledged to honesty and efficiency.

In another matter, Mackenzie's address was far more controversial. Negotiations would be undertaken, he said, to relax the "impossible terms of union" with British Columbia. The new agreement would provide that the railway be built "with such speed and under such arrangements as the resources of the country will permit without too largely increasing the burden of taxation on the people." As part of a developmental programme, he promised to facilitate the construction of a railway between the south shore of Lake Nipissing and the mouth of the French River in Georgian Bay, and a branch line from Fort Garry to the United States border. But he would go no further. By utilizing "the enormous stretches of magnificent water communication" between Georgian Bay and the Rockies, he hoped, at least for the moment, to avoid constructing 1,300 miles of railway across the Prairies, thereby saving sixty to eighty million dollars.

No prime minister has ever faced weaker opposition than did Mackenzie in 1874. Macdonald saw that it was the better part of valour to lie low,[8] and that is exactly what he did. Except for the assistance of the party press, the Conservative candidates were on their own. For them there was no hope of an over-all triumph, but merely a desire to save something from the wreckage. Much of their criticism was niggardly or destructive. Why, since the Grits disapproved so much of coalitions, had Mackenzie included seven one-time supporters of Macdonald in his cabinet? How would Canadians like the introduction of complete free trade and the flooding of the Canadian market with cheap American goods?

The opposition attack on the government's railway policy made much more sense. "A gigantic blunder . . . a great crime against the very life of this Dominion," raged the *British Colonist* of Halifax.[9] Why commit the folly of making the Pacific Railway a mere feeder of the Jay Cooke American line? Furthermore, why delude the public that these arrangements would be "only for a time"? It would be only a time before the Dominion was destroyed and became what Huntington, Dorion, and John Young wanted it to be: a feeble fringe of the United States.[10]

As for corruption in government, the Conservatives either condemned the holier-than-thou attitude of the Liberals or conveniently forgot it. However, this was the one issue which the voters would not forget. "A spasm of horror went through an innocent and virtuous public. There appeared to be a general impression that elections were 'made with prayers'. . . . Lord Macaulay declared that he knew of no spectacle so ridiculous as the British public in one of its periodical fits of morality. The Canada of 1874 was in this enviable frame of mind."[11]

An election held in this atmosphere was certain to produce far fewer "loose fish," than the first two elections. Those elected as Liberals understood that they were expected to support Mackenzie and virtue; those elected as Conservatives were generally the hard core, the very backbone of the party, who had somehow managed to escape defeat. Maritime Liberal members, who had hitherto shown little inclination to recognize the Grit and Rouge leaders of central Canada, were more than ready to assist their party in the use of patronage. For these reasons, statistics showing members elected and popular vote by party have far more meaning for 1874 than for 1867 or 1872.

Only British Columbia voted against virtue. There, the railway question dwarfed everything else. Mackenzie's proposal to relax the terms of union prevented the Liberals from securing candidates, much less electing anyone. The province returned six Conservatives to the Commons.

Elsewhere, it was a parade of Liberal victories. Voting for the first time as a province of Canada, Prince Edward Island gave its six seats to the Liberals. In Nova Scotia the Conservatives could elect only the redoubtable Tupper and two of his colleagues – a loss of seven from 1872. Five Conservative stalwarts held on to their seats in New Brunswick – a reduction of two. Manitoba elected two Liberals, one Conservative, and Louis Riel. Through the lieutenant-governor of Manitoba, the federal government had asked Bishop Taché of St. Boniface to prevent Riel's candidature. Obviously, Mackenzie felt it would prove embarrassing, especially in Ontario where the Orangemen were already railing against it. The request annoyed Taché, who had been expecting an amnesty for all the ringleaders in the Red River insurrection and, before he would again intervene, he demanded the promise of a complete amnesty in writing. When that was not forthcoming, Riel ran and was elected in Provencher.[12]

In Ontario the fortunes of the Conservatives touched rock bottom. They let 13 Liberals be elected by acclamation and could win only 22 of 88 seats – down from 40 in 1872. "A little group of veterans," says Donald Creighton, "had alone survived the fleeing disaster of the rout. A solitary square had maintained itself; but it almost lost its weary and unwilling commanding officer."[13] Macdonald had held on to Kingston by a bare 38 votes. In utter disgrace, he could this time give no aid to the other Conservative candidates.

Mackenzie, however, was so busy campaigning throughout western and central Ontario that he did not even attend his own nomination convention at Sarnia. In the end, the only important Liberal from Ontario to suffer defeat was J.D. Edgar in Monck. At a time when the number of voters in each riding was small, the Liberal majorities were unprecedentedly large. Blake's was 321; William Paterson's, 444; David Mills', 463; and so on. The Liberals captured every city riding except for one in Ottawa; they even beat the redoubtable John Carling in London.

The rout of the Conservatives extended to Quebec, although not in the same dimensions. Two years earlier, a serious cleavage had developed between Cartier's moderates and the ultramontane wing of the party.[14] Although he was a nationalist, Cartier stood for the politics of accommodation between French and English, and between Catholic and Protestant. The ultramontanes, whose views were so extreme that the moderates often found the Liberals more congenial, had become "a virtual autonomous faction within the party, seeking its own ends and following its own leaders."[15] Over the next two decades, the differences between the two wings were to produce instability, especially in provincial politics. This schism was never healed and was eventually to have serious consequences for the federal Conservatives.

After the election of 1872 the party had obviously needed reorganization in Quebec. Cartier was not to provide it since he succumbed to Bright's disease within the year. Other leading Conservatives were also ruled out; Masson lacked ambition, Cauchon was shortly to enter the Liberal camp, Chapleau had not yet acquired the necessary experience or prestige. Consequently, Hector Langevin took on the job of putting the party in order. Some accused him of ultramontanism, but although the extremists regarded him with some favour, he stood for almost the same things as Cartier. Langevin managed to reorganize the provincial ministry along moderate lines with Ouimet as Premier and Chapleau as a member.[16] However, these events preceded the Huntington revelations, which stamped Langevin with the same stigma as Macdonald and Cartier. He too had accepted money – $32,000 – from Sir Hugh Allan. Having no offer of a safe seat, he decided not to run in 1874.[17]

For the Conservatives, such a vacuum in leadership was a novel phenomenon. The best known of their members, Théodore Robitaille in Bonaventure, Rodrigue Masson in Terrebonne, and Joseph Alfred Mousseau in Bagot, could not hope to don the mantle of Cartier. Accordingly pressure was put upon P.J.O. Chauveau, the first Premier of Quebec after Confederation and an always willing instrument of Cartier, to resign as Speaker of the Senate and run in Charlevoix. It did no good, for, although the loyal party man consented (albeit reluctantly), he lost out to the demagogic P.A. Tremblay.[18] The Conservatives still had no leader in Quebec.

For the first time, a Liberal, A.A. Dorion, was the most respected federal politician in Quebec. He also had strong lieutenants. In this election the Quebec politicians had to decide whether to sit in the federal or provincial House. By provincial statute Ontario had abandoned the double mandate in 1872. On several occasions the Quebec Legislature had refused to inflict a similar self-denying ordinance upon its members, and it took a federal statute of 1873 to make the provision operative. Most of the leading Quebec Liberals, Laurier among them, opted for federal politics.

In this election the Quebec Liberals did not combat Confederation itself, as they had in 1867, or the annexation of the North-West Territories, as they had in 1872. Instead, they took primarily the same stand that the Liberals took elsewhere: they condemned the Pacific Scandal and asserted the need to re-establish honesty in government. There were some French-Canadian overtones to their campaign, however. They complained of the injustice perpetrated upon their compatriots by the New Brunswick School Law of 1871 and, above all, denounced the harsh treatment of the Métis on the Red River and talked of an amnesty for Riel and his chief supporters.

For the first time, the Liberals won a majority of the seats in Quebec: 35 out of 65, 15 of them by acclamation. Since 14 Conservatives were also unopposed, almost half the seats had no contest on election day. That the Quebec Bleus, even under such adverse circumstances, could win as many as 30 seats, demonstrated convincingly the strength they still possessed.

Nationally, the provincial results added up to a horrendous defeat for the Conservatives by a two-to-one margin, 138 seats to 67. Surveying the carnage, *The Canadian Monthly and National Review* could find only one instance in which the electors had spoken with equal unanimity. That was in 1848 when they had condemned Metcalfe's abuse of powers and vindicated responsible government. The triumph in 1874 was no more a party one than in 1848.

> Now, the country has pronounced its condemnation of the Pacific Scandal. If anyone indulged a belief in the existence of hard-and-fast party lines held more sacred than the interests or the honour of the country, he is now undeceived. The country, when there is any adequate occasion for the exertion of its power, is always found an overmatch for party.[19]

A virtuous public had rendered an unmistakable verdict.

FOOTNOTES

1. *Supra*, pp. 14-15.
2. For details see O.D. Skelton, *Life and Letters of Sir Wilfrid Laurier*, I [Toronto: Oxford University Press (S.B. Gundy), 1921], pp. 162-74.
3. For details see Dale C. Thomson, *Alexander Mackenzie: Clear Grit* (Toronto: The Macmillan Company of Canada, 1960), pp. 170-72.
4. *Ibid.*, pp. 181-82.

5. Donald G. Creighton, *John A. Macdonald: The Old Chieftain* (Toronto: The Macmillan Company of Canada, 1955), pp. 182-83.
6. For the address in some detail see William Buckingham and G.W. Ross, *Life and Times of Alexander Mackenzie* [Toronto: C.R. Parish and Company (Rose Publishing Company), 1892], pp. 356-57.
7. Thomson, *Mackenzie*, p. 171.

8. Creighton, *Old Chieftain*, p. 182.

9. *British Colonist*, January 17, 1874.

10. *Ibid.*, January 6, 1874.

11. Arthur H.U. Colquhoun, "The Story of Eight General Elections," *Canadian Magazine*, XVI (November, 1900), p. 20.

12. Robert Rumilly, *Histoire de la Province de Québec*, II (Montreal: Editions Bernard Valiquette, 1941), pp. 301-302.

13. Creighton, *Old Chieftain*, p. 183.

14. *Supra*, p. 16.

15. H. Blair Neatby and John T. Saywell, "Chapleau and the Conservative Party in Quebec," *Canadian Historical Review*, XXXVII (March, 1956), p. 2.

16. Barbara Fraser, "The Political Career of Sir Hector Louis Langevin," *Canadian Historical Review*, XLII (June, 1961), pp. 101-102.

17. Rumilly, *Histoire*, II, p. 299.

18. *Ibid.*, pp. 299-301.

19. "Current Events," *The Canadian Monthly and National Review*, V (March, 1874), p. 233.

1874

| | Seats | Candidates | | | Elected | | | | | | Popular Vote | | | | | | |
		C.	L.	O.	C.	%	L.	%	O.	%	C.	%	L.	%	O.	%	Total
Nova Scotia	21	15	20	—	3	14.3	18	85.7	—	—	16,466	42.4	22,377	57.6	—	—	38,843
New Brunswick	16	11	15	1	5	31.3	11	68.8	—	—	10,367	42.7	13,872	57.2	30	0.1	24,269
Prince Edward Island	6	3	6	—	—	—	6	100.0	—	—	2,502	25.7	7,226	74.3	—	—	9,728
Quebec	65	50	51	3	30	46.2	35	53.8	—	—	31,449	47.4	34,328	51.7	576	0.9	66,353
Ontario	88	75	86	6	22	25.0	66	75.0	—	—	83,556	46.6	94,736	52.8	1,088	0.6	179,380
Manitoba	4	3	3	2	1	25.0	2	50.0	1	25.0	861	41.7	938	45.5	264	12.8	2,063
British Columbia	6	6	—	7	6	100.0	—	—	—	—	1,264	63.7	—	—	719	36.3	1,983
Total	206	163	181	19	67	32.5	138	67.0	1	0.5	146,465	45.4	173,477	53.8	2,677	0.8	322,619

Others elected: Man. (1): I. (1).

Elected by acclamation: C. (16): N.B. (1); Que. (14); Ont. (1).
L. (39): N.S. (5); N.B. (4); P.E.I. (2); Que. (15); Ont. (13).

Fourth

General Election

THAT "MONSTER" PROTECTION PREVAILS

The election of 1878 was decided long before the campaign started. Four years earlier the Liberals had won, not on their own strength, but on their opponents' weakness. In office they suffered a long series of trials and disappointments. They quickly demonstrated they were not a united party, much less a truly national party. It is unlikely that any prime minister has had greater difficulty in keeping a cabinet intact than did Alexander Mackenzie.

The temperamental Edward Blake resigned on the very day polling was taking place in Ontario in the federal election of 1874. Later the same year, in a celebrated speech at Aurora, he advocated such things as compulsory voting, proportional representation, Senate reform, and a change in Imperial relations. Could it be that he was assuming the leadership of the progressive wing of the Ontario Liberals? Certainly they were chafing under the "old guardism" of George Brown and the *Globe*, represented in the cabinet by none less than the Prime Minister himself. This was not the case, however. In May 1875, Blake was back in office as Minister of Justice, but ill health soon forced him to accept lesser office and then to resign. By election time his commanding presence was missing altogether.

Quebec presented Mackenzie with not one but a multitude of headaches. The chief English-speaking Liberal, Luther H. Holton, declined to enter the cabinet and then quarrelled publicly with Lucius S. Huntington, who did enter it. Worse still were the "kaleidoscopic and unsettling changes" in the French-Canadian ministers.[1] The first three, A.A. Dorion, Télésphore Fournier, and Luc Letellier, moved from the cabinet to high non-political office within a year or two. Two of their successors, Félix Géoffrion and Joseph Cauchon, had equally short tenures; Rodolphe Laflamme remained, despite some peccadilloes, simply because there was not a suitable replacement. The one bright spot was the addition of Wilfrid Laurier in 1877.

Mackenzie's general approach to government, not his difficulties with his cabinet, constituted his basic weakness. None could deny that he placed some valuable measures on the statute book: the secret ballot, simultaneous voting, and the establishment of the Supreme Court. However, as he conceived it, his principal function was to administer honestly and efficiently the departments of government. On this alone he expected to be judged.

Under different circumstances this approach might have been successful, but the times did not favour it. The Liberals' accession to office saw the beginnings of the great depression of the late nineteenth century. As Donald Creighton puts it, "the Conservatives were well out of it."[2] Could Mackenzie cope with it or would Macdonald have another chance? Mackenzie and his Minister of Finance, Richard Cartwright, sought to meet increasing deficits by cutting down expenditures – a course of action which we know today may worsen the very evils they were fighting.

For the moment the Conservatives lay low. Their hopes revived in September 1875, when John Beverley Robinson won an important by-election in West Toronto. Already they were cogitating the proposals which were to become the National Policy. For a time they feared the Liberals might take the wind out of their sails, but they need not have worried. The budget of 1876 avoided any increases in tariff, even for revenue. It was, said Cartwright, "no time for experiments."[3]

Given the chance, the Conservatives delightedly seized the initiative. Macdonald called for "a readjustment of the tariff" to alleviate business stagnation and afford encouragement to struggling industries. Uncertain of public reaction, he was careful, for the moment, not to use the word "protection." Nevertheless, his party had a new policy.

> But it needed a new device, a new method of presentation, which would be as fresh, as striking, as irresistibly attractive as the substance of the new policy itself. And by good luck, and at almost the last moment, the device was discovered.[4]

It turned out to be the political picnic. By invitation of the North York Conservatives, Macdonald attended one at Uxbridge on July 1, 1876. It was an instant success, so successful that Macdonald used a long series of similar picnics to publicize his new policy.

Throughout the session of 1877, the Conservatives expounded the values of incidental protection in such broad terms as to make criticism difficult. Mackenzie did accuse them of trying to "cure a sore on one side of the patient by putting a blister on the other," and in his turn denounced protection as a "monster."[5] Strange it was that the Liberals had "chosen the inappropriate moment of the depression to acquire the fervour and dogmatism of converts to a new religion,"[6] that of laissez faire. The session over, Macdonald betook himself to the picnic grounds of Ontario. Mackenzie delayed; his double duties of Prime Minister and Minister of Public

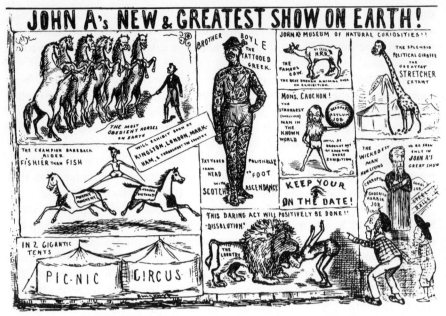

BILLED FOR THE SEASON: OR, BARNUM OUT-BARNUMED.

by J. W. Bengough. Originally appeared in Grip, *June 9, 1877. Reprinted in J. W. Bengough,* Caricature History of Canadian Politics, *Vol. I, pp. 346-347. Courtesy of Toronto Public Library.*

Works had so exhausted him that he looked like a "washed-out rag, and limp enough to hang upon a clothes-line."[7] But by late June he too had joined the picnic parade in Ontario. The election campaign had begun in earnest.

The session of 1878 added little that was new. Cartwright sorely disappointed the Liberal backbenchers by standing adamantly on the existing tariff and curtailed expenditures. "After four years of defending a diet of sparsity they had hoped for a few sweeter morsels to take home to the electorate."[8] Even Laurier admitted that the status quo was deadly dull. In effect, the government was leaving "the field of vision and hope" entirely to the Conservatives. The latter were now actively advocating a National Policy of protection (they dubbed it "N.P.") which would benefit and foster all the industries of the country. Its very vagueness attracted everyone who was dissatisfied with the status quo.

As usual, the political complexities of Quebec dwarfed those of the other provinces during these years. Since the last election political ultramontanism had followed an extremist course. In July of 1875 the ultramontane wing of the clergy intervened actively in the successful campaign of the de Boucherville Conservative government. Two months later the hierarchy united in a joint pastoral condemning Catholic liberalism. Although Archbishop Taschereau and the more liberal bishops had not intended it as such, the document was taken as "a fresh declaration of war on the Liberal party."[9] According to Skelton, clerical intervention in politics amounted to "a reign of terror" during the next few years,[10] so much so that Laurier was hesitant about joining the cabinet in 1877. "I shall be denounced as anti-Christ," he told Mackenzie.[11] He was right; in his by-election in Drummond-Arthabaska he was accused of following the principles of Gambetta and Robespierre and lost by 29 votes.

A few months earlier Laurier had delivered his celebrated address on political liberalism. In it he had pleaded with the clergy not to besmirch their robes in the mire of politics. The Quebec Liberals tried other remedies, too. They appealed to Rome, and Bishop Conroy of Ardagh, Ireland came out to look over the situation. He decided that a halt should be called to clerical intervention; thereupon, the bishops issued a new pastoral in October 1877 declaring that they had never intended to proscribe any specific party. The Liberals also had recourse to the courts which invalidated election after election for undue clerical interference. Yet there were still fears that the Liberals would have to contend with similar interference in 1878.

The timing of the election caused Mackenzie no little concern. Thinking that things would not get better, he himself preferred June, but Blake, whose advice should have been disregarded, counselled delay, as did the Quebec Liberals. Since the recent provincial election had given them only a precarious majority in the Legislature, they did not want to begin a session in the midst of a federal election. There was also the question of whether the nation's leaders should be electioneering at a time when raids by the Fenians were a distinct possibility. So, more than a little reluctantly, Mackenzie postponed the dissolution. In his *Reminiscences*, Cartwright described the delay as "a terrible tactical blunder," to be explained only by the Prime Minister's being "utterly overworked and unfit for any sudden serious responsibility."[12]

Exaggerated as this judgment is, the delay did give Macdonald time to organize Ontario as it had never been organized before. By session's end he was in Toronto where he became "the theorist of the Conservative party's strategy, the improvisor of its tactics, the arbitrator of its disputes, the prophet of its victory."[13] "If we fail in Ontario . . . ," he said, "I for one, shall give up the fight in despair."[14]

After the dissolution on August 17, both leaders confined their campaigning to Ontario. Mackenzie continued to denounce the narrow "Canada for Canadians" policy of the Conservatives, but he was even more appalled by Macdonald's cynicism. Earlier, Sir John had been wary of protection; now he was reputed to have told Goldwin Smith: "Yes, Protection has done so much for us. I must do something for Protection."[15] Mackenzie could not see what made Macdonald so confident, for his own reception in Ontario was invariably good.

The early returns in this, the first election using the secret ballot and simultaneous voting, seemed to bear out Mackenzie's contentions. New Brunswick remained staunchly Liberal and Macdonald lost in Kingston for the first time in 34 years. However, there was no more good news for the Liberals. The results in New Brunswick were not unexpected. Samuel Leonard Tilley, again directing the Conservative forces after a stint as Lieutenant-Governor, had warned Macdonald that flour and coal duties for the benefit of Ontario millers and Nova Scotian miners were not popular in New Brunswick.[16] He prophesied correctly, and ended up with only 5 of 16 seats and a personal majority of only 9 votes in Saint John City. "New Brunswick alone amid the faithless stood faithful," said Mackenzie. " 'Among the faithless, faithful only it.' "[17]

In Nova Scotia Tupper found public opinion running strongly with the Conservatives. While he did not win the 16 seats he promised, he carried two-thirds of the 21 seats. The Conservatives won 5 of the 6 seats in Prince Edward Island and 3 out of 4 in Manitoba; they took all 6 in British Columbia, a not surprising result in view of the government's inaction on the railway to the Pacific.

In Quebec, J. Israel Tarte, who masterminded the Conservative forces, completely altered his party's tactics. Instead of attempting to taint the Rouges with anticlericalism, he stressed economic distress and protection.[18] As usual, he gauged the situation correctly, for Quebeckers were just as perturbed as other Canadians over the economic situation. Tarte did emphasize one distinctly Quebec issue, the *coup d'état* of Lieutenant-Governor Letellier de Saint Just. Letellier, a Liberal, had recently dismissed his Conservative ministry. Everywhere in Quebec, Conservative orators denounced the Governor's action as dictatorial and promised to oust him if their party was returned.[19]

This time the Quebec campaign was as fierce as it had been tepid in 1874. Instead of 29 candidates (15 Liberals and 14 Conservatives) returned by acclamation there were only 4. Giant inter-party *assemblées contradictoires* were common, especially in St. Hyacinthe where Honoré Mercier was the Liberal candidate. Quebec continued to be distinctive also in the number of contests between the same two candidates which occurred election after election.

For all the Liberals' energy in Quebec, they could elect only 18 members to their opponents' 47. The Conservatives captured 18 seats which had previously been Liberal and lost only Argenteuil. The Liberals appeared to have elected Rodolphe Laflamme in Jacques Cartier, until a most ingenious method of ballot-box stuffing was uncovered.[20] Hector Langevin, the only prominent Conservative to suffer defeat, lost in Rimouski. His rival-to-be for the leadership of Quebec, J.A. Chapleau, accused him of not organizing the Quebec district as well as he might have, but in the great triumph this was quickly forgotten.[21] Langevin, it appeared, had succeeded Cartier as the head of the federal Conservatives in Quebec. Tarte, the organizer of victory, had also enhanced his authority in the political world.

In Ontario the campaign was equally vigorous, especially towards the end when the Toronto *Mail* went so far as to call the Prime Minister pigeon-livered.[22] Mackenzie did not mind such editorial comment nearly as much as he did the election returns in Ontario. He had lost his Minister of Finance and seen his party contingent drop from 66 to 26. When he took stock of his losses, he lamented: "All gone. What a splendid lot of men. . . . There are hardly enough left to form a skeletal battalion."[23]

One biographer states of Mackenzie that, "like most active politicians, he was the last to know how he really rated with the public."[24] Surely, few politicians have possessed the same capacity for self-deception. He kept insisting that the adverse verdict was totally undeserved. Had he not sought to disprove that success in politics depended on "intrigue and doing crooked things to countermine the enemy"?[25] All for nothing: even rural Ontario had deserted him.

He considered the results a sad commentary on the intelligence of the people. Could the masses really appreciate an honest administration of public affairs? Had they not defeated a government because it refused to levy more taxes and make commodities dearer?[26] Was it not alarming that they preferred "political chicanery" to "such a course as we pursued"?[27]

These were the thoughts of a man in the throes of bitter disappointment. Years later, a junior colleague of these days, Wilfrid Laurier, took a more objective view. Mackenzie, he said, made an excellent administrator of a department, but it was his misfortune to be called upon to perform other tasks for which he was not as well fitted. "He had not the imagination nor the breadth of view required to lead a party and a country; and he gave to the details of a department the time that should have gone to planning and overseeing the general conduct of the administration."[28]

The Conservatives won a greater over-all victory in 1878 than the Liberals did in 1874. Their majority of 78 gave them more than a two-to-one margin in seats. Though Mackenzie found it incomprehensible, the electors "preferred Conservative optimism to Liberal caution, the 'Kingston Knight's' warm humanity to the ex-stonemason's rigid – though heavily assailed – integrity; they preferred Macdonald drunk to Mackenzie sober."[29] For Macdonald, the victory was especially sweet. His mighty effort had been rewarded. He had revenged a crushing defeat. He had regained office.

FOOTNOTES

1. O.D. Skelton, *Life and Letters of Sir Wilfrid Laurier*, I [Toronto: Oxford University Press (S.B. Gundy), 1921], pp. 182-84.

2. Donald G. Creighton, *John A. Macdonald: The Old Chieftain* (Toronto: The Macmillan Company of Canada, 1955), p. 182.

3. *Ibid.*, p. 211.

4. *Ibid.*, p. 219.

5. Dale C. Thomson, *Alexander Mackenzie: Clear Grit* (Toronto: The Macmillan Company of Canada, 1960), p. 299.

6. Creighton, *Old Chieftain*, p. 230.

7. The words of the Governor General. See Thomson, *Mackenzie*, p. 302.

8. *Ibid.*, p. 323.

9. Skelton, *Laurier*, I, p. 137.

10. *Ibid.*, p. 138.

11. Thomson, *Mackenzie*, p. 295.

12. Sir Richard J. Cartwright, *Reminiscences* (Toronto: William Briggs, 1912), p. 184.

13. Creighton, *Old Chieftain*, p. 240.

14. *Ibid.*

15. Thomson, *Mackenzie*, p. 338.

16. Creighton, *Old Chieftain*, p. 241.

17. Letter to Hon. James Young, September, 26, 1878, in William Buckingham and G.W. Ross, *The Hon. Alexander Mackenzie: His Life and Times* [Toronto: C.R. Parish and Company (Rose Publishing Company), 1892], p. 523.

18. Robert Rumilly, *Histoire de la Province de Québec*, II (Montreal: Editions Bernard Valiquette, 1941), p. 227.

19. *Ibid.*, p. 228.

20. *Ibid.*, pp. 229-30.

21. Barbara Fraser, "The Political Career of Sir Hector Louis Langevin," *Canadian Historical Review*, XLII (June, 1961,), p. 107.

22. Thomson, *Mackenzie*, p. 338.

23. Letter to Hon. James Young, September 26, 1878, in Buckingham and Ross, *Mackenzie*, p. 523.

24. Thomson, *Mackenzie*, p. 329.

25. Letter to a friend, September 21, 1878, in Buckingham and Ross, *Mackenzie*, p. 518.

26. Letter to J.D. Edgar, September 24, 1878, *ibid.*, p. 522.

27. Letter to Senator Hope, September 23, 1878, *ibid.*, p. 520.

28. Skelton, *Laurier*, I, p. 223n.

29. Thomson, *Mackenzie*, p. 339.

	Seats	Candidates			Elected						Popular Vote						Total
		C.	L.	O.	C.	%	L.	%	O.	%	C.	%	L.	%	O.	%	
Nova Scotia	21	20	21	4	14	66.7	7	33.3	—	—	33,226	51.8	28,880	45.0	2,054	3.2	64,160
New Brunswick	16	14	16	4	5	31.3	11	68.8	—	—	17,964	45.0	20,148	50.5	1,768	4.4	39,880
Prince Edward Island	6	6	6	—	5	83.3	1	16.7	—	—	13,978	56.8	10,621	43.2	—	—	24,599
Quebec	65	64	62	4	47	72.3	18	27.7	—	—	78,719	55.8	61,523	43.6	877	0.6	141,119
Ontario	88	88	88	6	62	70.5	26	29.5	—	—	133,633	51.4	125,316	48.2	815	0.3	259,764
Manitoba	4	4	1	—	3	75.0	1	25.0	—	—	546	49.6	555	50.4	—	—	1,101
British Columbia	6	6	—	5	6	100.0	—	—	—	—	2,158	65.0	—	—	1,160	35.0	3,318
Total	206	202	194	23	142	68.9	64	31.1	—	—	280,224	52.5	247,043	46.3	6,674	1.2	533,941

Note: Hughes (L.) was declared elected in Niagara by the returning officer, but the courts awarded the seat to Plumb (C.) before the opening of the first session of the new Parliament. To preserve uniformity in the results, the seat is none the less credited to the Liberals.
Elected by acclamation: C. (8): Que. (3); Man. (3); B.C. (2).
                    L. (3): N.B. (2); Que. (1).

General Election

37

Fifth

General Election

NATION-BUILDERS VERSUS "LITTLE CANADIANS"

The election of 1882, like that of 1878, was uncomplicated. It requires neither searching analysis nor subtle conjuring to understand the voters' behaviour. John A. Macdonald, by now "The Old Chieftain," displayed all the talents of the political master and won a victory with consummate ease.

Once again National Policy was the basic issue, and the Conservatives saw to it that it remained dominant. Well they might, for almost coincidental with its adoption in 1879 prosperity had returned. Though the causal connection between the two was slight, politicians often draw conclusions which cause the economists to shudder. Everywhere the Conservatives rejoiced in "the departure of the dark days of deficits," and attributed it to "the timely adoption of a wise and well-considered National Policy."[1] According to the Halifax *Morning Herald*, "there is not a section of the people which has not been benefitted."[2]

National Policy was not the only weapon in Macdonald's strategic arsenal. A decade earlier he had proposed the two other national economic policies, all-Canadian transportation and western settlement. To give them practical effect he provided the Canadian Pacific with a charter early in 1881. Hence, it was easy for him to pose as the nation-builder during the election of 1882, and it was equally easy to rivet the image of "little Canadianism" on his opponents.

He could do this because the Liberal leadership was still not facing up to the realities of politics. Alexander Mackenzie, after his defeat in 1878, became increasingly lonely and austere, and altogether unyielding on trade matters. Perhaps because his caucus asked him to consider the question of leadership,[3] perhaps because he had become aware of a conspiracy against him,[4] he told the House of Commons on April 27, 1880 that he would henceforth speak and act for none but himself. The caucus had no doubts in choosing Edward Blake to succeed him.

Perhaps it should have had doubts. Blake had already demonstrated that he was temperamentally unsuited for cabinet position; he was shortly to prove that he was equally unsuited for party leadership or, for that matter, politics generally. However, in one respect at least, he was a realist. He saw that the rigid free trade principles of Mackenzie, Cartwright,

Brown, and the *Globe* had to be abandoned. In the session of 1882, he and his followers gave up their general attacks on "N.P." Instead they sought, in separate resolutions, to repeal or lower the duties on coal, coke, breadstuffs, and cotton and woollen goods, with the aim of reducing the burden of taxation on the masses.[5]

Later, when Blake opened his election campaign in a letter to his own constituents of West Durham, he admitted that the issue was not "between the present tariff and absolute free trade"; it was simply that the former was "in some important respects defective and unjust."[6] Macdonald understood at once that the game was in his hands. Blake, he said, was tacitly recognizing that the Canadian people had accepted "N.P." Since the Liberal leader could not admit to a change in views, "he therefore tried to hedge. He tried to wear two faces under one hat – or, as the Yankee sailor said – 'to steer south by north.' "[7]

Conservative orators amused themselves particularly at the expense of Sir Richard Cartwright, who had made dire prophecies about the effects of protection. One of them called him a political Jonah. "And if the whale had swallowed him, the animal would have gone on having annual deficits till nothing was left but its skin."[8] The Conservatives were also gleeful about the split in their opponents' ranks. Even as Blake was assuring West Durham that free trade was impracticable, Alexander Mackenzie was telling East York that any other doctrine was a relic of commercial barbarism. No matter what Blake said, "a counter statement made somewhere else by Mr. Mackenzie, by Mr. Mills, or the Toronto *Globe* [rose] like the ghost of Banquo to confront him; and *vice versa*."[9]

In a second area the Liberal position seemed even less constructive. Blake condemned outright the Canadian Pacific Railway contract; it was, he contended, profligate; it had been made without public tender and in disregard of a more favourable offer; it gave the company a twenty-year monopoly of the trade of the North-West Territories. The correct policy, he declared, was to construct the railway through the prairies immediately; only after these lands had been settled and developed would it become economically feasible to construct the Lake Superior and Pacific coast links.[10] To the end of his days, Sir Richard Cartwright maintained that the bargain with the C.P.R. was the result of ignorance and stupidity.[11] It was simple to denounce such men as Blake and Cartwright as "little Canadians" and this the Conservatives did with alacrity.

Tactically, Macdonald could not be faulted. His timing of the election was superb. A few months before, J.A. Chapleau and his Conservatives had won a resounding victory in Quebec. Good times prevailed and the electors were willing to give National Policy the credit. Satisfied industrialists filled the Conservative campaign chest to overflowing, while Laurier had to rely upon a meagre $2,500 from Blake and the Ontario Liberals to put up any kind of contest at all in the Quebec ridings.

THE GRIT NURSERY.
TROUBLED WITH "HIVES."

by J. W. Bengough. Originally appeared in Grip, *May 20, 1882. Reprinted in J. W. Bengough,* Caricature History of Canadian Politics, *Vol. II, pp. 298-299. Courtesy of Toronto Public Library.*

Nevertheless, Macdonald did not rely completely upon the sunny ways of Providence. He resorted as well to political manipulation of the human variety. Never had gerrymandering been so blatantly practised in Canada as it was in redistributing the seats in Ontario following the census of 1881. Townships were separated from the surrounding territory and "moved out of their own into adjacent counties, partly to adjust differences in population, chiefly to place the supporters of the government where their votes would do the most good."[12] The "Great Gerrymander of 1882" was aimed, not just at the Liberal party in general, but at their tallest heads in particular. Cartwright's seat of Centre Huron was rendered almost unrecognizable; those of Alexander Mackenzie in East York, David Mills in Bothwell, Malcolm Cameron in South Huron, and William Paterson in South Brant became considerably less Liberal, at least on paper. In attacking this "diabolical scheme" in the Commons, the Liberals pictured a Machiavellian Macdonald behind the scenes, gleefully rubbing his hands and ejaculating, "I've hived the Grits! I've hived the Grits!"

Under these circumstances, the over-all result had to be a substantial Conservative victory, and so it was: 139 Conservatives to 71 Liberals and 1 Independent Liberal. Local factors gave the Liberals a majority of the seats in Prince Edward Island and Manitoba, but elsewhere they had little to cheer about. In protest against Blake's stand on the C.P.R., British Columbia continued to send 6 Conservatives to the Commons. New Brunswick followed its usual pattern of supporting the government of the day; 9 of the 16 members it elected were Conservatives. Nova Scotia behaved altogether perversely; it decisively rejected its Conservative provincial government on the very day that it returned 14 of 21 Conservatives to the Commons.

In Quebec the Liberals suffered their worst defeat of all time. A little earlier it had looked as if they might capitalize upon the split in the Quebec Conservatives.[13] Premier Joseph Adolphe Chapleau was, as usual, having his troubles with the ultramontane wing of his party. During these days, he even contemplated a union with the provincial Liberals to give the extremists their quietus. The latter were especially incensed by his attempts to sell the province's railway: the white elephant, Québec, Montréal, Ottawa & Ouest. To them this seemed a betrayal of the French-Canadian race, since the line had a sacred mission: the promotion of colonization. Yet, in the provincial elections of December 1881, moderates and extremists closed ranks to give Chapleau 53 of the 65 seats. Within days, however, Chapleau sold the eastern section of the Q.M.O. & O. to a syndicate in which L.A. Sénécal and other prominent Conservatives had a major interest. In their wrath, the extremists hurled charges of political immorality against members of their own party, but, somehow or other, they managed once more to combine against the common enemy in the federal election of June 1882.[14] Thinking that he had thoroughly subdued the opponents within his own party, Chapleau accepted Macdonald's long-standing offer to join the federal cabinet. Could he, as he hoped, assume the mantle of Cartier and become Quebec's Conservative chieftain at Ottawa?

If Chapleau was sometimes in difficulty in Quebec, Laurier was in despair.[15] Nowhere were the merits of "N.P." expounded more rapturously.

La Minerve gave it the credit for the establishment of thirty-five industrial organizations in Montreal alone and for the return of hundreds of French Canadians from New England.[16] Something else, however, caused Laurier more concern. An eloquent advocate of liberalism of the British type, he had counted upon an alert public which was responsive to rational argument. Sadly, he had to confess that the great mass of the electors "never read, and remain as much in the dark as to what is going on in this country as if they were residing in Europe."[17] It was not much better with the educated class. They received their instruction in *collèges*, which were run by priests who had derived their ideas largely from the continental ultramontanes. Hence, a horror of the very name of liberalism permeated all their teaching. Under these circumstances, asked Laurier, could the *collèges* be anything but hotbeds of conservatism or their pupils anything but fanatical conservatives? He further lamented the lack of newspaper support to counteract this teaching. Of twenty-five French papers in Quebec only five were Liberal, and not one enjoyed more than a precarious existence.[18] Laurier knew well the reasons for the Liberal collapse in Quebec in 1882. His party let 16 Conservatives be elected by acclamation and ended up with no more than 13 M.P.'s of its own. Of the latter, only Laurier in Quebec East, Félix Géoffrion in Verchères, and P.B. Casgrain in L'Islet possessed any stature at all.

Once again, Ontario turned out to be the main arena. Sir John Macdonald gave up his seat in Victoria, B.C., to return to Lennox. After opening his campaign in Napanee, he hied himself to Toronto. From that vantage point, he confronted his chief opponents, Edward Blake and Oliver Mowat, in the chief battleground, central and western Ontario. He found it easier to defend his actions on national than on provincial issues. Why, he was asked, had he permitted the seats in Ontario to be carved up with abandon? Why had he not accepted the findings of arbitrators who had awarded Ontario a large increase in territory along its northwest boundary?

The latter issue was one of many in which Macdonald was to lock horns with Premier Mowat. Recently, they had taken sides on the meaning of Confederation itself. Was it to be the highly centralized edifice which Macdonald had always intended, or were the provinces to enjoy the substantial degree of autonomy which Mowat conceived to be their legal right? They were also battling it out over the Ontario Rivers and Streams Act which Macdonald was to disallow three times before letting it remain operative. Macdonald was even more outraged by the Ontario Liquor Licence Act of 1877; he assured a meeting at Yorkville in June 1882 that "if he carried the country—as he would do . . . he would tell Mr. Mowat, that little tyrant who had attempted to control public opinion by getting hold of every office from that of a Division Court bailiff to a tavern-keeper, that he would get a Bill passed at Ottawa returning to the municipalities the power taken away from them by the Licence Act."[19]

In time the courts were to uphold Mowat in most of his constitutional battles with Macdonald, but in 1882 it was the voters who were making the decision. The Liberals of Ontario missed no opportunity to picture a Macdonald in complete thraldom to Quebec. They "carried through the land a huge *Bleu* Frenchman, who they said was at once the master of the ministry and the ministry itself; and this *Bête Bleue* they affirmed to be jealous of the growth of Ontario, and bent on preventing her further development."[20] They also sang songs which went this way:

> The tricky Tory *Bleus*
> Who Sir John as catspaw use
> Cannot rule the roost in old Ontario.[21]

By these very tactics, the Liberals amply demonstrated that they had not yet become the truly national party that the Conservatives had. Although no Conservative of Cartier's stature had emerged in Quebec, the French Canadians were securing the same accommodation as before within the Conservative party, and nothing had yet occurred which put their faith in that party in doubt. In contrast, the anti-French bias of the Ontario Grits was still suspect in Quebec, and their campaigning in 1882 was hardly calculated to allay the feeling. Not only was the Liberal leadership still Ontario-oriented, but the issues which they stressed often had little attraction outside of Ontario. Thus, the constitutional issue which Mowat considered so vital had little meaning in the Quebec of 1882. Even in Ontario it had dubious vote-getting appeal and the Liberals had little to show for their great effort; they gained only eleven seats while the Conservatives lost seven. Nor could they blame the gerrymander for their relatively poor showing. As is usual when the device is blatantly used, public indignation served to redress the balance. By some mathematical accident, says R. MacGregor Dawson, the end result of the gerrymander was that the Liberals gained seven seats and lost seven seats. Sir John "added votes and obtained exact results, but he failed to count sufficiently on the human element in his equations; he relied on the certainty of mathematics, but his plans were upset by the unpredictability of the human variable."[22]

Why did the Liberals not fare better in Ontario? First, there was Edward Blake himself. He could command the respect but not the support of his hearers:

> The very abundance of his knowledge was his weakness . . . he piled Ossa upon Pelion and threw Parnassus above them both, till everyone became dizzy scaling the heights to which he was being lifted. . . . He could wield the hammer of Thor, but never the lighter weapon of Comus.[23]

Even when ridicule would have been more effective than logic, he could not stoop to levity.

Blake's deficiencies were incidental to his party's failure. The voters of Ontario, like those of Canada generally, were satisfied with the status quo. They preferred a constructive policy to destructive criticism, however valid it might be. As the Liberal George W. Ross put it:

> It was Sir John with the promise of increased prosperity and the development of Canada through the Pacific Railway against Blake with a lofty defence of the sacred character of the Constitution and a denunciation of extravagant expenditure. The people wanted prosperity. They might listen to Mr. Blake some other time.[24]

FOOTNOTES

1. *Dominion Annual Register*, 1880-81 (Toronto: Dawson Brothers, 1882), p. 207.

2. Halifax *Morning Herald*, March 3, 1882.

3. O.D. Skelton, *Life and Letters of Sir Wilfrid Laurier*, I [Toronto: Oxford University Press (S.B. Gundy), 1921], pp. 220-21.

4. Dale C. Thomson, *Alexander Mackenzie: Clear Grit* (Toronto: The Macmillan Company of Canada, 1960), p. 361.

5. See *House of Commons Debates*, 1882, pp. 622, 768, 1162.

6. *Dominion Annual Register*, 1882 (Toronto: Dawson Brothers, 1883), p. 122.

7. Donald G. Creighton, *John A. Macdonald: The Old Chieftain* (Toronto: The Macmillan Company of Canada, 1955), p. 338.

8. J.E. Collins, *Canada Under the Administration of Lord Lorne* (Toronto: Rose Publishing Company, 1884), p. 246.

9. *Ibid.*, pp. 246-47.

10. *Dominion Annual Register*, 1882, pp. 122-23.

11. Sir Richard J. Cartwright, *Reminiscences* (Toronto: William Briggs, 1912), p. 224.

12. R. MacGregor Dawson, "The Gerrymander of 1882," *Canadian Journal of Economics and Political Science*, I (May, 1935), p. 204.

13. For details of the contest in Quebec, see Robert Rumilly, *Histoire de la Province de Québec*, III (Montreal: Editions Bernard Valiquette, 1948), pp. 195-200. Translated by the author.

14. See Barbara Fraser, "The Political Career of Sir Hector Louis Langevin," *Canadian Historical Review*, XLII (June, 1961), pp. 111-12; and H. Blair Neatby and John T. Saywell, "Chapleau and the Conservative Party in Quebec," *Canadian Historical Review*, XXXVII (March, 1956), pp. 5-6.

15. F.H. Underhill, "Laurier and Blake, 1882-1891," *Canadian Historical Review*, XX (December, 1939), p. 393.

16. *La Minerve*, June 5, 1882, as quoted in Rumilly, *Histoire*, III, p. 195.

17. See Underhill, "Laurier and Blake, 1882-1891," p. 394.

18. *Ibid.*, pp. 394-95.

19. C.R.W. Biggar, *Sir Oliver Mowat*, I (Toronto: Warwick Bros. and Rutter Ltd., 1905), p. 359.

20. Collins, *Canada Under Lord Lorne*, p. 247.

21. *Canada and Its Provinces*, VI (Toronto: Glasgow, Brook and Company, 1914), p. 93.

22. Dawson, "The Gerrymander of 1882," p. 215.

23. George W. Ross, *Getting into Parliament and After* (Toronto: William Briggs, 1913), pp. 143-44.

24. *Ibid.*, pp. 122-23.

1882

	Seats	Candidates			Elected						Popular Vote						
		C.	L.	O.	C.	%	L.	%	O.	%	C.	%	L.	%	O.	%	Total
Nova Scotia	21	21	19	2	14	66.7	7	33.3	—	—	28,967	51.4	25,345	45.0	2,058	3.7	56,370
New Brunswick	16	16	13	4	9	56.3	7	43.8	—	—	18,848	48.6	17,625	45.5	2,298	5.9	38,771
Prince Edward Island	6	6	6	—	2	33.3	4	66.7	—	—	15,188	49.9	15,270	50.1	—	—	30,458
Quebec	65	63	45	9	51	78.5	13	20.0	1	1.5	55,476	52.3	44,801	42.2	5,790	5.5	106,067
Ontario	92	92	90	2	55	59.8	37	40.2	—	—	137,947	50.4	134,204	49.0	1,628	0.6	273,779
Manitoba	5	5	4	1	2	40.0	3	60.0	—	—	3,305	45.7	3,855	53.3	73	1.0	7,233
British Columbia	6	6	1	6	6	100.0	—	—	—	—	1,562	55.3	300	10.6	964	34.1	2,826
Total	211	209	178	24	139	65.9	71	33.6	1	0.5	261,293	50.7	241,400	46.8	12,811	2.5	515,504

Elected by acclamation: C. (24): Que. (16); N.S. (1); N.B. (2); Ont. (2); Man. (1); B.C. (2).
L. (1): Que. (1).
Others elected: Que. (1): I.L. (1).
Others (votes polled): N.S. (2): I. (1) 934; other C. (1) 1,124.
N.B. (4): I. (1) 88; other C. (3) 2,210.
Que. (9): I.L. (1) 1,581; I. (3) 1,103; other C. (5) 3,106.
Ont. (2): I.C. (1) 629; other L. (1) 999.
Man. (1): I. (1) 73.
B.C. (6): Other C. (6) 964.

Sixth

General Election

"THE CORPSE OF RIEL" AND NATIONAL UNITY

No Canadian prime minister has faced the voters under more discouraging circumstances than did Macdonald in 1887 and yet emerged from his ordeal successfully. Only a short while before he had been thinking of retiring.[1] It looked then as if the job of nation-building had just about been completed. From late 1885 onwards, however, everything seemed to conspire against him. How much had he accomplished after all?

National Policy had helped him win the previous two elections, but it was a much less effective talking point in 1887 during a period of world-wide depression. Immigration had been reduced to a small trickle and the West was not being settled. Still more serious was the sectional and cultural conflict which was threatening to smash Confederation into its original components.

Macdonald could not know – because only time would demonstrate it – how perilous the position of a party in power at Ottawa is, when it loses a majority of the provincial governments. Nevertheless, he could hardly have been elated with the results of the elections which all the provinces held in 1886. Late in June, it is true, Conservative Premier W.W. Sullivan won his third election in a row in Prince Edward Island, while early in July, William Smithe led a more or less Conservative group to victory in British Columbia.

However, in April, the Liberal-oriented A.G. Blair had triumphed in New Brunswick. He, at least, did not present any threat to Confederation itself, as William Stevens Fielding did in Nova Scotia. There, disillusionment had grown apace as the province continued to stagnate under union. Had the anti-Confederates of the 1860's been right after all? At first, Fielding let his followers talk and move resolutions about the repeal of the Confederation, without committing himself. However, when Ottawa did nothing to help his government out of its financial difficulties, he too became a repealer. In fact, he made it the chief issue in the provincial election of June 15. Macdonald called it blackmail – dangerous blackmail – and sent the federal ministers from Nova Scotia, John S.D. Thompson and A.W. McLelan, to do battle with Fielding. They were unsuccessful and were routed, "horse, foot, and artillery."[2] Fielding's victory, says Donald

Creighton, was "an unqualified repudiation of the very idea of British North American unity."[3]

Disaffection had appeared in Manitoba too. There, a state of financial stringency was not unusual; its government suffered chronically from that condition. Manitobans sought to relieve their frustration in a protest against the monopoly clause in the Canadian Pacific Railway Company's charter. They, too, held a gun to Macdonald's head: let the American railway companies enter the province from the south or give up all hope of political support. The Prime Minister spent July and August in the West, part of it in support of Conservative Premier John Norquay. He would not sacrifice the monopoly clause, but through his extra effort the Norquay government was sustained, after a hard fight, on December 9.

The difficulties in Nova Scotia and Manitoba were purely ephemeral; those in central Canada were, in time, to alter the very balance in Canadian politics – unfavourably, as it turned out, for Macdonald's party. Hindsight makes us wonder if "The Old Man" was finally beginning to lose his grip. Certainly, the eventual collapse of his party in Quebec had its beginning in his handling, or rather mishandling, of his French-Canadian ministers, particularly Chapleau.

The latter came to Ottawa in 1882, confident that he had finally given the ultramontanes their quietus. About this time, they were acquiring a new name. One of their number published the pamphlet "Le Parti, Le Pays et Le Grand Homme," which reaffirmed the group's religious and nationalist views. He signed it "Castor" and the pseudonym stuck. The pamphlet accused Chapleau of overweening ambition and utter sacrifice of political principles. He naturally returned as good as he got. "The uncompromising hostility between Chapleau and the Castors," says Blair Neatby, "was to remain a factor in Quebec politics until the turn of the century."[4] The Castors quickly showed they were anything but dead; within two years they had forced out Chapleau's nominee as Premier of Quebec, the moderate J.A. Mousseau, and installed one of their own, J.J. Ross, in his place.

At Ottawa, too, Chapleau's hopes were dashed. He had expected to become leader of the Cartier school and spokesman for French Canada but he did not make it. Unequalled as an orator on the hustings, save perhaps by Honoré Mercier, he found the House of Commons an uncongenial forum. He lacked the capacity to contribute to the general elaboration of public policy. But he failed primarily because Macdonald never trusted him. The Old Man looked more to his other French-speaking ministers, Sir Hector Langevin and Sir Adolphe Caron, because he knew they would support him through thick and through thin. Mutual loyalty, however, can be expensive in politics. Sir Joseph Pope once remarked that Langevin, more than any man he had ever met, "neatly fulfilled Bismarck's cynical description of Lord Salisbury – 'a lath painted to look like iron,'" while

Macdonald himself admitted that Caron was "too much influenced by his hates – a fatal mistake in a public man." Neither was the equal of Chapleau when it came to wooing Quebec. The relations between the three often resembled a triangular duel in which two of them were pitted against the third; always their dealings were marked by a jealousy and a suspicion that were truly incredible.[5] Even a Macdonald in his prime would have found it hard to keep the peace.

Such were the ministers who were confronted with that *cause célèbre*, the Riel affair, in November 1885. It seems probable that the decision to hang Riel was a political one, at least in the sense that the government decided to risk losing some seats in Quebec rather than to suffer serious political harm everywhere else.[6] Langevin and Caron did not like the decision but, as usual, accepted it without giving resignation a thought. Chapleau summoned his confidants, J. Israel Tarte, Arthur Dansereau, and Senator Alexandre Lacoste and, after an all-night session of agonizing appraisal, he decided to stick it out with Macdonald. "Nous sommes dans la fosse aux ours," he told Tarte.[7] But even this was better than having French Canada excluded from governmental decisions. Yet, he was hardly prepared for the mighty explosion which rocked Quebec for days after November 16, the date on which Riel died on "the gibbet of Regina." His death shocked Quebec as no other event had. The outburst was even greater because French Canada had been led to believe that, at the worst, the sentence would be commuted. Among the explosive ingredients, says Laurier LaPierre, were "a natural psychological *déchirement*, a suggestion of tyranny, and a frustration caused by political impotence."[8] Whose head had the English press been clamouring for, that of Riel or French Canada? Was it Riel or the French-Canadian race which had "stood trial, been condemned, and would ultimately be destroyed"?[9] Did the execution mean that French Canada lacked the bargaining power it always assumed it had?

Initially, all of French Quebec – Bleu, Rouge, and ultramontane – denounced the execution; Macdonald and his French-Canadian ministers were universally execrated as "les pendards" and "les Chevaliers de la Corde." Honoré Mercier assumed the leadership of the *mouvement national* and at an incredible mass demonstration on November 22, at the Champ de Mars in Montreal, he launched a new *parti national*. Leader of the provincial Liberals since 1883, he had always put his nationalism ahead of his Liberalism. Could he get French Canada to unite, for the first time since 1867, in a party with purely nationalist aims?

Chapleau could have had the leadership of the *parti national* simply for the taking, but he continued to warn of the danger of French Canada isolating itself. Time was on his side. No agitation could be kept at such a pitch for long; prudence and moderation soon made themselves felt. Within days, *La Minerve, Le Monde*, and *Le Nouvelliste* (the organs of Chapleau,

Langevin, and Caron respectively) were asking that the ministers be allowed to state their case. Tarte attended only one meeting of the *comité national* in Quebec City and then his own papers, *Le Canadien* and *L'Evènement*, began to backslide. By year's end, the hierarchy was expressing concern about movements which weakened the social fabric and destroyed respect for authority. The Conservative press interpreted the bishops' *mandements* as a condemnation of the *mouvement national*.[10]

The easing of the situation became even more apparent when Parliament convened early in 1886. Initially, all but 11 of the French-Canadian Conservative M.P.'s had denounced the government. Yet, only 3 of them moved to the other side of the House. The Conservatives completely outmanoeuvred their opponents in the Commons by forcing them to debate the government's decision to execute Riel, rather than its policies in the North-West. In the ensuing division, 17 French-Canadian Conservatives deplored the execution, but 23 English-speaking Liberals supported it.[11] The dissident Conservatives had had an opportunity to relieve their pent-up feelings and were content to let it go at that. Who, it might be asked, were more badly split: the Liberals in Ontario or the Conservatives in Quebec?

None of this daunted Mercier. By June 1886, he was already in the field, and from then until the provincial election of October 14, he dragged the corpse of Riel all over Quebec. He made a special effort to win the support of the Castors. Emphasizing language and religion as they did, they found Riel's execution an especially serious affront to their *nationalisme*. At the same time, they were in a serious dilemma, for although Mercier himself had never been a Rouge, they still identified his party with the Liberal Catholicism which they abhorred. None the less, he got the support of a goodly number of them, including François Xavier Trudel and *L'Etendard*, and Jules Paul Tardivel and *La Vérité*. It was enough to transform the small Liberal minority in the last House into a following about as large as the Conservative. Five National Conservatives, largely Castor in sentiment, held the balance of power.[12] To Macdonald this seemed like the last straw. "The triumph of the Rouges over the corpse of Riel," he told Tupper, "changes the aspect of affairs, *quoad* the Dominion government, completely. It will encourage the Grits and opposition generally; will dispirit our friends, and will, I fear, carry the country against us at the next general election."[13]

It was not the last straw! There was to be one final blow in Ontario. That province had reacted strongly to the agitation in Quebec. The extremist views of the *Orange Sentinel* surprised no one, but those of the Toronto *Mail*, for fourteen years a faithful spokesman of Canadian Conservatism, did. Seven days after Riel's execution it said that, rather than submit to the Quebec yoke, "Ontario would smash Confederation into the original fragments." Two days later it wondered if there would have to be a new conquest. This time, however, the victors would not capitulate as in the Treaty of Paris. The French Canadians would lose everything; "the wreck of their fortunes and their happiness would be swift, complete and irremediable."[14] How thin the veneer of national unity appeared to be!

Such comments, made in the heat of the moment, did not worry Macdonald unduly. He was more than a little perturbed, however, in May 1886, when the *Mail* suddenly embarked on a vigorous anti-Catholic, anti-separate school campaign. To him it "sounded altogether too much like George Brown's diatribes of a quarter century ago."[15] His party just could not afford this sort of thing at a time when the Liberals were trying to obliterate the anti-Catholic image they had inherited from the Grits. Had Blake not opposed incorporation of the Orange Lodge and given unequivocal support to Home Rule for Ireland? Had Mowat not done his best to accommodate the Catholics of Ontario and flatly refused to weaken the separate school system? Consequently, Macdonald warned C.W. Bunting, the managing editor of the *Mail,* about alienating the Irish Catholics of Ontario and the Catholics of all the provinces, from the Conservative party; this was all the more likely, he said, because the *Mail* was generally regarded as the organ of the government.[16] It did no good. On September 16, therefore, he publicly disavowed any responsibility whatever for the *Mail*'s editorial policies. Gloomily he confided in Tupper that the paper was having a prejudicial effect upon Catholics everywhere and was introducing "a great element of uncertainty in a good many constituencies."[17]

After the near disaster in Quebec, Macdonald knew that Ontario must be held at all costs. Early in November he began a speaking tour in that province. Mowat responded by calling a provincial election for late December. This kept Macdonald busy on the hustings until December 20. To the Liberals' denunciation, he had one stock answer: National Policy. Scornfully the *Globe* "called the tour 'the Chestnut Combination' because the stories were old, and the arguments sounded like platitudes."[18] Macdonald himself thought the public response was excellent until the returns came in on December 28. Mowat doubled his previous majority.

Under these disheartening circumstances, Macdonald pondered a dissolution of Parliament. Things looked bad, but they might get worse before they got better. If he delayed he might have no opportunity at all to manoeuvre. He decided to gamble and called an election for February 22, 1887. Within days, the five National Conservatives in the Quebec Assembly had voted the Conservative government out of office and brought Mercier to power. Macdonald, therefore, had to face hostile governments in all the original provinces of the Dominion, including the two most powerful.

Seldom has a campaign introduced less in the way of new or constructive ideas. Amidst the growing volume of national discontents, says Professor Creighton, the voters appeared to be in a mood for desperate remedies. Macdonald had given them National Policy in 1878. "But Blake, in similar circumstances and with a similar opportunity, had nothing comparable to offer."[19]

British Columbia and the North-West Territories, not unexpectedly, voted "ministerialist"; the government, which had just completed the C.P.R., got all of their ten seats. Prince Edward Island, on the other hand, returned six Liberals; in a province where provincial matters often predominate over those of national concern, Macdonald's failure to be more generous in the way of financial assistance apparently proved to be the deciding factor. It seems certain that, for the first time, Anglo-Saxon backlash against alleged French-Canadian extremism was an important factor in the other English provinces, but its exact strength is difficult to measure. Manitoba gave the Conservatives four of its five seats for a gain of two, New Brunswick ten of sixteen for a gain of one.

To handle Fielding in Nova Scotia, Macdonald summoned the man he trusted most, Sir Charles Tupper, from his High Commissionership in London. Tupper went to work with his usual vigour in a province in which the *Morning Chronicle* was forecasting the election of 17 Liberals. "Death throes of Toryism" and "Sir John will rule no longer" were its constant themes.[20] As usual, Tupper injected new energy into his own supporters even as he incurred the virulent hostility of his foes. This time the aftermath of the North-West Rebellion helped him immeasurably. Nova Scotia's part in putting it down, says Sir Robert Borden, did more to unite the province to the rest of Canada than any event since 1867.[21] The Conservatives retained 14 of Nova Scotia's 21 seats and Fielding did no more talking about repeal.

Once again, central and western Ontario was the battleground of the two chief gladiators, just as it had been in 1878 and 1882. Blake, as usual, amazed his followers with "the brilliance and sustained power of [his] addresses, filled with exposures of maladministration."[22] He arraigned the government for administrative corruption and political jobbery, for unbridled extravagance, for the ebb in commercial prosperity, and for the rising tide of political discontent.[23] In itself this was all purely negative, and Macdonald quickly perceived that the Liberal leader was "unaccountably failing to take advantage of his enormous opportunities."[24] Blake, however, was superbly confident of victory if he could only convince the manufacturers that their interests were safe under a Liberal government. To this end he said in his Malvern address that he would make no change in the existing system of taxation, "the necessary effect of which [system] is to give a large and ample advantage to the home manufacturer over his competitor abroad." To spike his opponents' guns he added that Sir Richard Cartwright concurred wholeheartedly.[25] However, not all the protectionists believed him.

Macdonald conducted his campaign with none of Blake's logic or oratory, but in a kind of burlesque.[26] The Malvern speech he ridiculed as nothing more than the deathbed acceptance of a religion still abhorred. The *Globe*'s charges that he was in his dotage, he placed on a par with its intimations in previous elections that he was dying of cancer of the stomach or paralysis of the brain. Apart from his campaigning, Macdonald had other factors working for him in Ontario. The Liberal disagreements on Riel carried over from the Commons to the electorate; they ensured that the Conservatives would get more than their usual share of the Protestant vote. The Great Gerrymander of 1882, ineffective last time because of the resentment it aroused, worked decidedly in Sir John's favour this time. The Franchise Act of 1885, by placing the preparation of the voters' lists in the hands of Dominion officials, also helped him, because it meant that any manipulation was in his favour. The result was that the province from which Blake expected so much, returned 55 Conservatives, the same number as in 1882. In all Canada, Quebec excluded, the Conservative majority had gone up from 30 in 1882 to 36.

The big question mark was, of course, Quebec. Could the Bleus hold their usual stronghold despite Riel? Chapleau, said Professor Creighton, chose "this most appropriate moment for a violent assertion of his personality."[27] Yet, Chapleau had a right to be annoyed. Obviously his leader did not appreciate which of his Quebec lieutenants was the real vote-getter. If Chapleau had decided to lead the *parti national*, it would have swept the province, but he chose not to isolate Quebec. Now he expected Macdonald to co-operate with him to prevent that from happening. After the near disaster provincially, he had demanded an immediate reorganization of the party. He had been particularly outraged that two organizations were permitted to exist side by side in Montreal: one centring upon Langevin's organ, *Le Monde*, which received all the official patronage, the other centring upon his own organ, *La Minerve*, which included the true workers of the party.[28] On this occasion Macdonald had ignored him. But not on the eve of dissolution in January, for then Chapleau talked of resigning unless his demands were met. He wanted, especially, the absolute control of the party organization and patronage in the district of Montreal.[29] He got it, as did Langevin in the district of Trois Rivières and Caron in the district of Quebec. He also got his friend Sénécal appointed to the Senate; the latter responded by placing *La Presse* at the disposal of the Conservatives.

For the Liberals, the Riel affair and the treatment of French Canada were almost the sole issues. They could argue them convincingly because they had become indelibly stamped as the provincial rights party.[30] Mercier pressed his way through the winter snows from one end of Quebec to the other carrying the same message as in the previous October. Laurier, who lacked the temperament of a demagogue, could not conduct this kind of campaign at all.[31] The cooling down of heated passions would have made it less effective in any case.

No matter what arguments the Conservatives raised, they were always driven back to the contention that they could best safeguard the interests of French Canada. Their principal assets, says Rumilly, were "le cran de Chapleau, l'habileté de Tarte, et la volonté de Mgr Laflèche."[32] At the outset, Laflèche, Bishop of Trois Rivières and, since the death of Bishop Bourget in 1885, leader of the ultramontanes, had been surprisingly critical of the federal government for executing Riel. Later he had second thoughts. What was one error on the part of trusted friends compared with the permanent danger of a powerful organization in the service of bad, i.e., liberal, doctrines? This time neither his friends, Tardivel and *La Vérité*, nor Trudel and *L'Etendard*, would go along with him. For them it was an agonizing experience to disagree with one whom they regarded as the fountainhead of their views. But, as they saw it, they simply could not submit to such humiliation nor condone the debasement of their race. None the less, Bishop Laflèche returned to his old position that the Liberals were the chief foes. Because of him, the latter found it much harder to maintain the alliance between themselves and the National Conservatives, who were chiefly ultramontane.[33]

Their difficulties on this score were further increased by the tactics of Tarte. He had started out as a member of the school of Cartier, had become an ultramontane when that was the fashion, and had reverted to his earlier position in 1883 when Chapleau seemed to be the rising star. Once again he was the master strategist. On his advice the party did not engage in bitter tirades against the National Conservatives. Three of them were even allowed to win their seats by acclamation. As Tarte predicted, they could be won over later.[34] It was he, too, who weakened the influence of the deserters by quoting the bishops against them. Exultantly his newspapers proclaimed: "L'Episcopat est avec nous."

Then there was Chapleau, upon whom the main defence of the government fell. He spoke to the voters as no one else could; he reconquered hearts. His eloquence paid off in seats. Although the agitation over Riel had been strongest in the district of Montreal, the Conservatives lost only four seats there. In contrast, Langevin and Caron lost thirteen in the eastern districts. Blair Neatby wonders if a railway policy which was distinctly unpopular in eastern Quebec accounts for the regional disparity of the losses.[35] Nothing in the campaign indicates it, however. Why not give full recognition to Chapleau's effectiveness on the hustings?

Over-all it was touch and go for the Conservatives in Quebec. Their defeat in a seat in the Eastern Townships brought their total losses to 18. Although some of the members are difficult to label, it is usual to record the party standings as 33 Conservatives to 32 Liberals. The strong showing of the Conservatives may appear surprising in view of their difficulties.

However, as Sir John Willison points out, "a political party, like an individual, develops character, firmly rooted in its traditions, convictions and sentiments." The Conservatives managed to hold on "because Cartier was a living force in Quebec with the generation which remembered the firm and happy partnership between [him] and Macdonald"; because Quebec was still suspicious of Ontario Liberals as descendants of anti-French, anti-Catholic Grits; "because Macdonald's whole career was fashioned in sincere and courageous racial and religious tolerance"; because Quebec Liberals were still regarded by the hierarchy as exponents of Liberal Catholicism; and "because Chapleau could reach the soul of the French people as even Laurier could not."[36] Yet, some of these factors were losing their strength and some new forces were developing which would not be arrested until a Bleu Quebec was nothing but a distant memory.

In the whole of Canada the Conservative majority was 37. For Blake it was a bitter pill to take. He talked of resigning, but Macdonald hoped he would not. In his mind he "felt he could go on beating Blake, every four or five years, until the end of the chapter."[37] Sir John was most elated, however, that national unity had triumphed over the corpse of Riel. As Tarte put it, "le maintien du parti conservateur au pouvoir signifie la consolidation du grand édifice que nos chefs ont élevé."[38]

FOOTNOTES

1. Donald G. Creighton, *John A. Macdonald: The Old Chieftain* (Toronto: The Macmillan Company of Canada, 1955), p. 444.

2. Macdonald to Tupper, June 21, 1886, in Sir Joseph Pope (ed.), *Correspondence of Sir John Macdonald* (Toronto: Oxford University Press, 1921), p. 382.

3. Creighton, *Old Chieftain*, p. 462.

4. H. Blair Neatby, "Laurier and a Liberal Quebec: A Study in Political Management" (unpublished doctoral thesis, University of Toronto, 1956), p. 29.

5. Sir Joseph Pope, *The Day of Sir John Macdonald* (Toronto: Glasgow, Brook & Co., 1922), pp. 141-43.

6. Laurier LaPierre, "Joseph Israel Tarte: A Dilemma in Canadian Politics, 1874-96" (unpublished M.A. thesis, University of Toronto, 1957), p. 102.

7. J. Israel Tarte, *Le Procès de Mercier* (Montreal: Louis Joseph & Eugène Tarte, 1892), p. 21.

8. LaPierre, "Tarte—A Dilemma," p. 98.

9. *Ibid.*, p. 103.

10. For the details see Robert Rumilly, *Histoire de la Province de Québec*, V (Montreal: Editions Bernard Valiquette, 1942), Chapter II. Translated by the author.

11. Creighton, *Old Chieftain*, p. 450.

12. Neatby, "Laurier and a Liberal Quebec," pp. 49-51.

13. Macdonald to Tupper, October 15, 1886, in Pope (ed.), *Correspondence*, p. 386.

14. O.D. Skelton, *Life and Letters of Sir Wilfrid Laurier*, I [Toronto: Oxford University Press (S.B. Gundy), 1921], p. 316.

15. Creighton, *Old Chieftain*, p. 452.

16. Macdonald to Bunting, May 25, 1886, in Pope (ed.), *Correspondence*, p. 380.

17. Macdonald to Tupper, December 20, 1886, *ibid.*, p. 390.

18. Arthur H.U. Colquhoun, "The Story of Eight General Elections," *Canadian Magazine*, XVI (November, 1900), p. 25.

19. Creighton, *Old Chieftain*, p. 468.

20. E.M. Saunders (ed.), *The Life and Letters of the Rt. Hon. Sir Charles Tupper Bart., K.C.M.G.*, II (New York: Frederick A. Stokes, 1916), p. 85.

21. Henry Borden (ed.), *Robert Laird Borden: His Memoirs*, I (Toronto: The Macmillan Company of Canada, 1938), p. 25.

22. W.T.R. Preston, *My Generation of Politics and Politicians* (Toronto: D.A. Rose Publishing Company, 1927), p. 169.

23. Skelton, *Laurier*, I, p. 333.

24. Creighton, *Old Chieftain*, p. 468.

25. Skelton, *Laurier*, I, pp. 334-35.

26. Creighton, *Old Chieftain*, p. 469.

27. *Ibid.*, pp. 467-68.

28. Chapleau to Macdonald, October 31, 1886, in Rumilly, *Histoire*, V, p. 220.

29. Chapleau to Macdonald, January 15, 1887, *ibid.*

30. Neatby, "Laurier and a Liberal Quebec," p. 44.

31. *Ibid.*, p. 54.

32. Rumilly, *Histoire*, V, p. 229.

33. *Ibid.*, pp. 222-26.

34. *Ibid.*, p. 229.

35. Neatby, "Laurier and a Liberal Quebec," p. 57.

36. Sir John Willison, *Reminiscences Political and Personal* (Toronto: McClelland & Stewart Limited, 1919), pp. 149-50.

37. Creighton, *Old Chieftain*, p. 471.

38. *Le Canadien*, February 23, 1887, as quoted in LaPierre, "Tarte—A Dilemma," p. 125.

	Seats	Candidates			Elected						Popular Vote						Total
		C.	L.	O.	C.	%	L.	%	O.	%	C.	%	L.	%	O.	%	
Nova Scotia	21	21	21	6	14	66.7	7	33.3			41,411	49.7	39,255	47.2	2,584	3.1	83,250
New Brunswick	16	16	15	1	10	62.5	6	37.5			28,884	49.7	28,994	49.9	277	0.5	58,155
Prince Edward Island	6	6	6	—	—	—	6	100.0			17,145	46.5	19,733	53.5	—	—	36,878
Quebec	65	62	62	6	33	50.8	32	49.2			79,155	49.6	78,098	48.9	2,383	1.5	159,636
Ontario	92	92	92	2	55	59.8	37	40.2			181,537	50.7	176,001	49.2	455	0.1	357,993
Manitoba	5	5	4	—	4	80.0	1	20.0			7,712	51.4	7,280	48.6	—	—	14,992
British Columbia	6	6	3	4	6	100.0	—	—			2,571	55.9	603	13.1	1,424	31.0	4,598
North-West Territories	4	4	4	1	4	100.0	—	—			4,217	58.4	2,220	30.7	783	10.8	7,220
Total	215	212	207	20	126	58.6	89	41.4			362,632	50.2	352,184	48.7	7,906	1.1	722,722

Notes: (1) While actual voting took place in Queens, New Brunswick, the returning office later ruled that the Liberal candidate's nomination papers were not in order. In the totals above, the Conservative candidate is treated as having been elected by acclamation.

(2) The three National Conservatives elected by acclamation in Quebec are included in the Liberal totals.

Elected by acclamation: C. (4): N.B. (1); Man. (1); B.C. (2).
                     L. (3): Que. (3).
        Nat. C. (3): Que. (3).

Others (votes polled): N.S. (6): I.L. (1) 206; I.C. (1) 317; I. (4) 2,061.
                        N.B. (1): I. (1) 277.
                        Que. (6): I. (6) 2,383.
                        Ont. (2): I. (2) 455.
                        B.C. (4): I.C. (2) 721; other C. (2) 703.
                N.W.T. (1): .I.C. (1) 783.

Seventh

General Election

DID THE "SHREDS AND PATCHES" REALLY SAVE SIR JOHN?

The election of 1891, more than any other, meant different and even contradictory things to those who observed it. Sir Joseph Pope says it was "not the desperate battle of 1886-7,"[1] but O.D. Skelton calls it "the most bitterly contested since Confederation."[2] For Castell Hopkins, it was "in many respects the most momentous in the history of Canada";[3] for Sir John Willison it was "a campaign of shrieking, of denunciation, and of violence"[4] on a non-existent issue. It is not surprising that Hopkins and Willison would disagree: the admirer of John S.D. Thompson would hardly see it the same way as the admirer of Laurier. For one, it involved "the principles of British unity, British commerce, and British sympathy as against Continental unity, Continental trade, and Continental sympathy";[5] for the other, it was the grossest example of a phony loyalty campaign.[6] No one has summed up the result more neatly than Fred Landon. According to him, the single issue of unrestricted reciprocity enabled "a party already too long in power . . . to snatch another victory at the polls."[7]

Thirteen years of office are likely to build up an accumulation of ills for any administration. So it was with the Macdonald government. Most of its difficulties seemed to centre on Quebec. There, the election of 1887 had not ended Macdonald's troubles with his three-man team of Langevin, Chapleau, and Caron. Between May and October of 1887 their disagreement almost reached the proportions of a crisis. The Old Man's inability to cope as he once did is seen in his attempted solution: he sought to push Langevin and Chapleau in turn into the lieutenant-governorship of Quebec. He should have pushed Langevin a little harder, because, as Tarte indicated, Langevin had had his time.[8] But Langevin refused to budge. So anxious was Sir John to keep the peace that he then made the same offer to Chapleau, even though he was the Conservatives' chief vote-getter in Quebec. Chapleau's friends gave an emphatic "no"; his departure, predicted Tarte, would have meant political disaster.[9] In the end he stayed too, not in the Department of Railways and Canals he wanted, but in the insignificant Department of the Secretary of State.

Inevitably the situation got worse for the Conservatives. In August 1890, Chapleau told Macdonald there was "no political authority in

[Quebec] in federal matters."[10] He was, in effect, suggesting that someone ought to take charge and that he would like the job, but Sir John distrusted him no less than before and did not take the action which the situation required. Yet, as the election of 1891 approached, Macdonald himself admitted that Langevin was "inert and useless" and complained because "he, Caron, and Chapleau [were] allowing Mercier to carry the Province away from them by their want of harmony."[11]

There were other reasons for Mercier's success among the French Canadians. "Nobody since Papineau," says Blair Neatby, "had so roused their latent *nationalisme*."[12] Always more of a Nationalist than a Liberal, he had embarked upon colonization policies which appealed to all species of nationalists. By settling the long-standing Jesuits' Estates question, he proved himself a true friend of the Church. For the first time someone other than a Conservative had "played the role of defender of the French-Canadians' race and religion; indeed, no Conservative had ever done it as aggressively as Mercier."[13] It has been said that the Riel affair destroyed the Conservative hold on Quebec, but it is not quite as simple as that. What Riel's execution did was to bring Mercier to power. Once in office, he destroyed the Conservatives' monopoly position as "defenders of the faith" and thus paved the way for a "solid Liberal" Quebec.[14]

Indirectly, Mercier's acts and speeches were to work in the same direction. With English-speaking Liberals everywhere he was distinctly unpopular. Realizing this fact, and not wishing to alienate themselves from their English counterparts, French Liberals whispered in confidence that they were Rouges, not Nationalists; disciples of Dorion and Laurier, but reluctant followers of Mercier. Yet, in fact, they regarded Mercier's treatment of the Jesuits' Estates question as no more than a simple act of justice. However, when he asserted in the preamble of his bill that the decrees of the Pope were binding, he was being deliberately provocative to English Canada — so provocative as to produce after-effects which would go a long way to alter the very character of the Conservative party.

That party's string of successes had been due to "the historic alliance between a tolerant Ontario Toryism and a conservative Quebec,"[15] fostered and promoted by John A. Macdonald, a man without racial or religious prejudice. For more than a decade, Blake and Mowat had been trying to divorce Ontario Liberalism from its anti-French, anti-Catholic Grit background and hence make it more attractive to Quebec. After 1885 a section of Ontario Conservatism unwittingly helped their cause. First the Riel affair launched the Toronto *Mail* into an anti-French crusade. Then in 1888 the Jesuits' Estates Act was passed.[16] The outcome of these two events was the founding of the Equal Rights League of Ontario, which belied its name by standing for a single language, English, and a single system of public schools. Initially, a few prominent Liberals became members, but most of them got out for fear of embarrassing their party. The same consideration moved not a whit the militantly pro-British, Protestant wing of Ontario Conservatism and particularly D'Alton McCarthy.

Had he chosen, McCarthy might have been Prime Minister of the Dominion; instead he is said to have been more responsible than anyone for the break-up of his party in 1896.[17] President of the Liberal-Conservative Union of Ontario between 1884 and 1888, he resigned when he found himself completely out of tune with his leader and most of his party. Macdonald told him that the Conservatives succeeded federally in Ontario because they carried a substantial portion of the Catholic vote, and that if he persisted in his fatuous course, he would alienate "this saving remnant," assist the Liberals, and ruin the Conservatives.[18] But it did no good. "My view of the duty of the Conservative party," McCarthy replied, "is to hold by and lean on the English Provinces – while, so far as I can understand, yours is rather to depend on Quebec."[19]

To begin with, McCarthy proposed to abolish the dual language clause in the North-West Territories Act, and to let the people of the Territories themselves decide on the official use of French and English. At Stayner on July 12, 1889 he said that, if the ballot did not decide such questions in this generation, bayonets would supply the answer in the next.[20] A little later he went to Portage la Prairie and condemned the "narrow, parochial, French-speaking 'nationalism' " which, through separate schools and special language privileges, worked against the development of a true Canadian nationality.[21] Let the westerners have the power, he said, to "make this a British country in fact as it is in name."[22] It was no surprise, therefore, that his bill to abolish dual language in the N.W.T. contained a preamble declaring it "expedient in the interests of the national unity of the Dominion that there should be community of language among the people of Canada." Thus, the tolerant Ontario Conservatism which used to accommodate itself so readily to the French Catholics of Quebec had been badly eroded by 1890. The Manitoba *Free Press* even prophesied that "a Conservative party founded on an aggressive Protestantism will take the place of the present one, of which Mr. McCarthy will be the leader."[23] For the moment, however, the question was whether or not these developments would affect Macdonald's hold on the province of Quebec. Because the Orangeites had allied themselves with the McCarthyites, the Old Man had even greater reason for worry on this score.

The religious and racial conflict bothered not only the Conservatives. It brought all of the politicians face to face with the very fundamentals of the federation. It made all of them ponder the question: To what extent had the bargain of 1867 intended duality of language and separate schools throughout Canada? Economic matters were raising equally basic considerations. In the elections of 1882 and 1887, Blake had not seen fit to challenge seriously the Conservatives' tariff policies. Discouraged after his second defeat and in uncertain health, he finally gave up the leadership in June

1887. No entirely suitable successor had emerged. Cartwright was unpopular in Ontario because he was a confirmed free trader; in Quebec because he had voted the wrong way on Riel. David Mills lacked personal appeal and was suspected of an anti-French bias. Blake's personal choice was Wilfrid Laurier and the Liberal M.P.'s went along with him, even though they were not highly enthusiastic. While they had much good will for the French Canadian, many of them doubted whether he had the qualities required of a leader. None had more misgivings than Laurier himself.[24] A leader, he said, needed health and money; he had neither. He wondered, too, as he often did later, whether a French Canadian would be fully accepted in English Canada. Yet, within a decade Blake could say that, although he had been a failure in politics, he had done wonders in his choice of successors: Mowat in Toronto and Laurier in Ottawa.[25]

Laurier had just taken over when, during the spring and summer of 1887, a vigorous campaign for commercial union with the United States got under way in Ontario under the special urging of Canadian-born Erastus Wiman of New York. It became the chief topic of the day, says Willison, because this was "a time of gloom and doubt, . . . of hostile examination of the central props and pillars of the national edifice."[26] Cartwright gave the movement his blessing, but early in the session of 1888, Laurier and the Liberal caucus decided they would stand for unrestricted reciprocity and not commercial union. Thus, they turned down the idea of a complete *zollverein*, which would have necessitated a common tariff against the rest of the world, and proposed a system of complete free trade between Canada and the United States, which would let each determine its tariffs with other countries.

Professor Underhill is amazed that a party could have "committed itself to unrestricted reciprocity without first trying to discover what terms could be obtained from the United States."[27] There are several explanations. Economics was not Laurier's strong point and he certainly did not appreciate all the implications of unrestricted reciprocity and what the Conservatives could make of it. In the past his party had failed to provide the positive policy, much less the "heroic remedy," which the times demanded, and it had paid dearly for its caution. It would not make the same mistake this time. Perhaps, says Willison, this is why Laurier and the caucus went further than general feeling within the party dictated.[28] Blair Neatby sees another possibility. Fearful of party disintegration through racial and cultural conflict, Laurier may have felt that by ringing "far and loud the trade question he could keep clear of these irritating questions."[29] Perhaps this is the reason why he kept "u.r." before the public for the next three years.

Such was the cultural and economic situation which confronted Macdonald in 1890. His object was to make his government and party appear in the most favourable light possible, prior to the election which would certainly come in 1891. In one respect the tide of events favoured him – the religious and cultural conflict had begun to ease. At long last the Jesuits' Estates agitation had played itself out. The dual language question in the North-West was settled by a compromise which satisfied all but the extremists on both sides.[30] Although Manitoba had deprived its Catholics of educational rights which they had long enjoyed by practice, if not by law, Macdonald maintained that the question was a legal one and hence to be decided in the courts. For the moment at least the onus was off the government.

Other omens and events, however, were far less favourable for Sir John. He had always watched provincial elections as a barometer of public feeling. This time they were not a hopeful indicator. Early in June Mowat won an easy victory in Ontario. On this occasion, W.R. Meredith, the Conservative leader, went to extremes by climbing on the anti-French, anti-Catholic bandwagon.[31] All he succeeded in doing was to divide the anti-government vote with the Equal Righters, who were themselves in the process of foundering because of internal disputes. Then in mid-June, Mercier, the man responsible for the Inter-provincial Conference of 1887 which had mounted such a dangerous attack on the federal authority, the man whom Macdonald regarded as nothing more than a disturber of the peace, increased his majority in Quebec. Shades of 1886-87! Then, too, the most populous provinces had voted against the Conservatives just before a federal election.

There were also the McGreevy-Langevin scandals to worry Sir John.[32] Thomas McGreevy, a contractor and long-time Conservative member for Quebec West, was accused of having accepted money over the years for furthering the interests of Larkin, Connolly and Company in contracts awarded by the Department of Public Works. The details of the story outdo most works of romantic fiction, for the Minister of Public Works was none other than McGreevy's brother-in-law, Sir Hector Langevin, who, it was alleged, had himself received money from the proceeds of some contracts. That was not all. The whole nasty mess came to light because of a quarrel between Thomas McGreevy and his brother Robert, a member of the firm of Larkin, Connolly and Company, who had been taken into partnership because Thomas had promised to use his influence to secure government contracts for the firm. Out of sheer spite, Robert tried to bring his brother's influence in the awarding of contracts to an end by disclosing the sordid affair to prominent Conservatives at Ottawa, and through them to Macdonald. Thomas McGreevy and Langevin denied everything and nothing happened. Ever persistent, Robert then gave the details to J. Israel Tarte and something did happen.

Beginning on April 30, 1890, Tarte unfolded the facts, bit by bit, in *Le Canadien*. Not until November 19, however, did he mention Langevin by name. Why would the man who had long masterminded the Conservative cause, especially in the district of Quebec, venture on a course so damaging to his own party? Was it from a sense of public duty? Was it because he was a newspaperman first, politician second, and could not afford to pass up a good story? Was it because he saw the handwriting on the wall, realized that Laurier's star was in the ascendant, and decided to hitch himself to it? Was it because he wished to drive Langevin from public life and install Chapleau in his place? If so, was it Chapleau who influenced him or was it Caron, who resented McGreevy's influence in the district of Quebec? According to Laurier LaPierre, it was a combination of all these things which motivated Tarte.[33] In any case, the scandal was an added incentive for Sir John to call an election lest the revelations became even more dangerous.

Economic matters, however, and not scandals, most preoccupied Macdonald. Under conditions of world-wide depression his basic national policies had not promoted the country's development to the extent he had anticipated. Some rural areas actually showed signs of depopulation and there was much emigration to the United States. The McKinley Tariff bill was making its way through Congress during the spring and summer of 1890. For Canada it bode no good. It was bad enough that the American tariff was to be generally increased; it was even worse that heavy specific duties were to be imposed on the cereals and other farm products of which Canada was a chief supplier. Macdonald found the tariff increases to be the major topic of concern during his speaking tour of the Maritimes late in September.[34] Laurier, Cartwright, and Mills also sensed similar consternation in central Canada, since they were now pressing unrestricted reciprocity with a new vigour. It was to be the certain antidote for that worst of all calamities, the McKinley tariff.

Macdonald knew exactly where he stood on Canada's relations with Britain and the United States. He had looked with dubious eyes upon the Imperial Federationists, who had been actively pressing their ideas during the last three or four years. He knew that the movement included the pro-British, anti-French wing of his own party and that it was regarded with deep suspicion in Quebec. None the less, he remained convinced that "the alliance with England and the association with the other developing nations of the Empire-Commonwealth were the surest guarantees both of Canada's political autonomy and its fiscal and commercial independence."[35] He was equally certain that unrestricted reciprocity had political implications which threatened the country's independent status.

He had nothing against limited reciprocity so long as it did not defeat his own basic economic policies for Canadian development. Certainly he had to give the appearance of doing something to counteract the McKinley tariff; but he was not optimistic, for he had it in his mind that the American Secretary of State, James G. Blaine, nurtured a secret desire to make Canada a tributary of the United States. Macdonald had one small success late in 1890. The British government agreed that the negotiations going on between the United States and Newfoundland for a trade and fisheries convention should not be concluded until Canada had a chance to negotiate on its own account. Blaine would not be allowed to play the Empire countries off against one another; he still objected, however, to the appointment of a trade commission, and agreed only to private discussions to determine whether a basis existed for entering into more formal negotiations.

None the less, the Conservatives made the most of Macdonald's small success. On January 16, 1891, the Toronto *Empire*, then the leading Conservative paper in Ontario, told its readers that the Americans had made overtures for developing trade relations with Canada. According to Skelton, the move was "as disreputable as it was audacious";[36] at best it was playing with words. Blaine could, of course, indulge in the same kind of game; to Macdonald's indignation, he told a Congressman that he knew of no negotiations afoot for reciprocity with Canada. Yet, there was no denying that some of the wind had been taken out of the Liberal sails.

By February 2, Macdonald saw he could gain nothing more from this situation. He decided to take the plunge and catch the Liberals by surprise. In his manifesto he boasted, as usual, of the triumphs of "N.P." and condemned "u.r." because it would mean discrimination against Britain and necessitate an annual tax of $15 a family to make up for the loss of revenue it entailed. Thus far he was simply building up to the overriding issue. The voters, he continued, had one question to determine: "Shall we endanger our possession of the great heritage bequeathed to us by our fathers, and submit ourselves to direct taxation for the privilege of having our tariff fixed at Washington, with a prospect of ultimately becoming a portion of the American union?" As far as he was concerned, "A British subject I was born – a British subject I will die." Up to this point Sir John had remained within the bounds of legitimate politics. However, when he accused his opponents of "veiled treason which attempts by sordid means and mercenary proffers to lure our people from their allegiance,"[37] he was undoubtedly hitting below the belt.

Laurier answered these points one by one. What were the real effects of the much-vaunted "N.P"? Nothing less than workers on half time, lowered wages, and a drop in land values. Had "N.P." itself not imposed discriminatory tariffs against Britain? In contrast, unrestricted reciprocity would likely involve little discrimination against the Mother Country, but if it did, he stood for Canada first. As for "veiled treason," this was "a direct and unworthy appeal to passion and prejudice . . . even when presented with the great authority of Sir John Macdonald's name."[38]

The stage was set for the loyalty campaign of 1891. Of one thing there can be no doubt. Macdonald sincerely believed that Canada's very existence as an independent nation was at stake. In what he knew was his last election fight, he stopped at nothing to preserve the edifice he had been building for twenty-five years. Certainly he was not too squeamish about the tactics he used. L.P. Kribbs of the *Empire* came up with just the slogan he wanted for the kind of campaign he intended to wage: "the old man, the old flag, and the old policy."[39] This made it even more certain that the rational and the emotional would be hopelessly entwined.

As usual, Macdonald had summoned Tupper from London to assist in the campaign. As usual, too, he moved to Toronto to direct the proceedings in Ontario. He was not allowed to remain there. In Hamilton, Strathroy, London, Stratford, St. Mary's, Guelph, Acton, Brampton, wherever the going was toughest, all saw and heard him for the last time.

He reserved his bombshell for Toronto on February 17. It had irked him that the same Blaine, who had been unable to see the Canadian government's representatives until after March 4, could grant an interview in January to Edward Farrer, the chief editorial writer of the Toronto *Globe*. Sir John had procured the proof sheets of a pamphlet which Farrer had written at the request of an American friend.[40] In it, the writer for the *Globe* viewed Canadian-American relations as an American might, and even suggested the methods of retaliation which the Americans could use to make the Canadians realize the stupidity of their trade and fisheries policies. This was just the type of document out of which Macdonald could wring the last drop of political advantage. It was people like Farrer, he said, who were responsible for the rejection of Canadian advances at Washington. Farrer was, in effect, telling the Americans that to get Canada "you must concede nothing . . . you must put the screws on Canada, you must coerce the Canadians and bully them in every possible fashion."[41] "I say," Macdonald concluded, "that there is a deliberate conspiracy by force, by fraud, or by both to force Canada into the American Union."

By insinuation Sir John had tainted the whole Liberal party with Farrer's sin; indeed, he acted as if he really believed it was involved in treachery. Farrer assumed full responsibility for the pamphlet; neither the *Globe* nor the party, he said, were bound by anything he had written in a private capacity.[42] Few of the leading Liberals really feared the effects of "u.r." Only Edward Blake had doubts about it, and he was prevailed upon to keep quiet until the day after the election. Oliver Mowat scorned the idea of being "Yankeefied" by "u.r."; he too "was born a British subject and [would] a British subject die."[43] Alexander Mackenzie, now "a broken and pathetic figure passing swiftly towards the end," did not see how reciprocal free trade could possibly be inimical to the interests of Great Britain as the heart of the Empire.[44] Yet, it is difficult to allay charges of disloyalty by mere words. Indeed, says Willison, "the shouts of treason grew louder, the appeal to passion and prejudice more vehement, the charges of plotting and conspiracy more shrill and insistent."[45] At Windsor,

Ontario, Sir Charles Tupper added further fuel to the fire by quoting from the Farrer-Wiman-Hitt correspondence. Among other things, Farrer had told Wiman that many people thought we "had better make for annexation at once instead of making two bites on the cherry"; to which Hitt, the chairman of the House of Representatives' committee on foreign affairs, replied: "we must be very patient with the slow-moving popular mind."[46] Everywhere, the Conservatives forgot about their proposed negotiations with the United States and concentrated on treason.

Willison takes great pains to emphasize that this was "not a contest between British connection and continentalism" and that neither the Liberal candidates nor the Liberal voters were animated by separatist motives.[47] Nevertheless, in denying that "u.r." had any political implications whatever, he tries to prove too much and simply deceives himself. Whether the Conservatives believed in the loyalty cry or not, they were only too aware that it offered them their best, perhaps their only, chance of success. They discovered that Protestant rural Ontario was not kindly disposed towards the Conservative M.P.'s who had failed to take a stand against Mercier and the Jesuits' Estates. The greatest difficulty they faced, however, was the hold that "u.r." had on the farmers. This surprised and grieved Macdonald; "they were carried away," he said, "as the agricultural labourers in England were by the cry of 'three acres and a cow.' "[48] Cartwright had indeed presented his case cogently to rural Ontario.

The Conservatives, however, had several factors other than the loyalty cry going for them. Everywhere, and especially in Ontario, the bankers, traders, and manufacturers were with them. Macdonald's letters expressed indignation that a flood of Yankee money[49] and the "nefarious" influence of the Grand Trunk were being used against him. But this was surely window dressing. He, of all people, knew that the heads of large corporations had filled his party's campaign chest to the brim and that they, of all people, were determined not to accept hands-down free trade with the United States which might "confuse their business connections, swamp their trade, and destroy their industries."[50] The interlocking directorate of the C.P.R. and the Bank of Montreal, which both served and utilized the Macdonald régime, apparently "shelled out" more than ever before.[51] In Montreal West, Sir Donald Smith, the President of the Bank, was again the Conservative candidate. In letters to the Montreal *Witness*, President Van Horne of the C.P.R. put the case against "u.r." as forcefully as anyone. In addition, "all the influence of a great organization [the C.P.R.], the prestige of its directors, the votes of its employees, passes for absentee voters, were exerted without stint,"[52] in an effort to keep the Conservatives in power. Not without good reason. Could the C.P.R. afford not to oppose trade policies which, by encouraging north-south trade, would defeat the very purpose for which it was built? Could it afford to lose Macdonald who, more than anyone, would be likely to provide the financial assistance it needed to expand its empire?

There were more subtle influences at work too. Undoubtedly, Macdonald had the sympathy of the large independent element which "distrusts new men and new proposals, and silently determines the issue of so many contests."[53] The sympathy was even greater because he was an old man putting his last reserve of energy into a cause he believed in. His collapse in Kingston during the last week of February probably added to the store of kindly feeling.

It was this combination of factors, along with a continuing strong federal organization, which prevented the Conservative majority in Ontario from being entirely wiped out. It was very close, however. The popular vote was almost even; the government's majority only 4, down from 18 in 1887. In urban Ontario it lost only London, but unrestricted reciprocity had hurt it badly in the rural areas, where losses or close contests were common. In western Ontario it salvaged only 17 of the 49 seats.

In Quebec, too, unrestricted reciprocity and its political implications were of chief concern. Rumilly sees the contest as partly a battle of the country against the cities; the Liberals, in effect, renounced the urban seats to improve their position in the more numerous rural constituencies.[54] In urban Quebec, where protectionist feelings were strong, the industrialists told their workers they could not carry on without protection. The politicians outdid them; from Langevin and Chapleau down they repeated almost *ad nauseam*: "reciprocity is annexation." Chapleau considered it quite legitimate to use Machiavellian tactics against a party that would hand its birthright over to a foreign power.[55] *La Presse* accused Laurier of being in the line of Papineau who had no faith in the future of Canada and, worse still, of trying to inaugurate the reign of the Yankee on the banks of the St. Lawrence.[56]

Laurier and his followers scoffed at these detractors. Who, asked the Liberal *L'Electeur*, were these Conservatives who claimed a monopoly of loyalty? Had George Cartier himself not been a rebel in 1837? Had John Rose and J.J.C. Abbott not signed the annexationist manifesto of 1849? What could bind French Canada more firmly to Confederation than to have Laurier as Prime Minister?[57]

It was difficult enough to fight the Conservatives; it was doubly difficult to fight the episcopacy. True to their tradition of loyalty towards the British Crown, Archbishop Fabre of Montreal and other members of the hierarchy published pastoral letters warning their flocks against annexationist tendencies. When the Liberals protested, they denied that the letters had political meaning, but their denials came too late. *La Presse* and *La Minerve* had already interpreted the letters as a condemnation of the Liberals.[58]

Mercier postponed a trip to Europe to campaign beside Laurier. Nothing pleased him more than to battle Macdonald who, as a centralizer and a loyalist, stood directly opposed to his own autonomist and nationalist views. He promised Laurier a majority of 15 in Quebec, but had to be satisfied with 9. The Conservatives were, in fact, lucky to get off with a net loss of 5 seats. It was not the loyalty cry, however, that kept their losses down; the aspiration for independence was, after all, a much more respectable idea in Quebec than in Ontario. It was a number of other factors which saved them from collapse. Laurier had not yet made his full impress upon Quebec. Langevin, Chapleau, and Caron managed to put an allegedly decrepit organization in reasonable order in their respective districts. McCarthy and the extremist wing in Ontario kept quiet during the campaign, and French Canada had not lost its confidence in Macdonald.[59]

For all these reasons, the number of voters who switched their allegiance was relatively small. Almost all the veteran members of both parties were re-elected. Among the Liberals was François Bourassa, M.P. for St. Jean since 1867, who continued to trudge over his county on foot, his pockets stuffed with candies for the children.[60] Not unexpectedly, the Conservatives fared very well in urban Quebec; Sir Donald Smith's majority in Montreal West was the largest in Canada. The National Conservatives – Amyot, Godbout, and Vaillancourt – who were Liberal in everything but name, all won re-election. Tarte, although nominally still a Conservative, ran in Montmorency against an official Conservative and was elected by the Liberal organization!

The government had barely held on in the two central provinces. Its majority of 19 in these provinces had become a minority of 5 and its fate depended on the smaller provinces where it previously had a majority of 18. Fortunately, these areas increased that margin to 32. The *Globe* could hardly contain itself; Sir John had been successful only "in the new territories where the voters look to the government for daily bread, in Manitoba where the C.P.R. crushed and strangled public sentiment, and in Nova Scotia and New Brunswick where a hungry people succumbed to the hoarse and blatant prodigality of Tupper."[61] Cartwright, in "one of the phrases he coined with fatal facility," said that "the shreds and patches" had saved Sir John.[62]

Skelton finds it significant that the majority was "secured for the most part from the domains of the C.P.R." He pictures thousands of simple Canadians being duped into believing that the national existence was at stake, and voting to avert the dangers of "u.r." and the diversion of Canadian traffic to American railways. According to him, this is why the Conservatives won every seat but one along the main line of the C.P.R. and, by Van Horne's own admission, lost Marquette solely through oversight.[63] Skelton's analysis suffers from several weaknesses. Seat by seat, the results in western Canada were exactly the same as in 1887. There is no evidence that ministerialism was not still the major determinant of the westerners' voting behaviour, although this time, even more than before, the influence of the C.P.R. undoubtedly added to the government's popular vote.

Skelton fails to consider that the Conservative majority in the West stayed at 13, while in the Maritimes, where the C.P.R. exercised little or no influence, it rose from 5 to 19. The government picked up 3 seats in New Brunswick and 2 each in Nova Scotia and Prince Edward Island. It is perhaps surprising that Nova Scotia and New Brunswick, which had once prospered under reciprocity, should reject the Liberals so decisively. In both provinces the Conservatives argued that "N.P." was inaugurating an era of activity, enterprise, and prosperity, and that "u.r." would necessitate odious direct taxation.

Above everything else, the loyalty cry was heard and heeded. Despite the best efforts of the Halifax *Morning Chronicle* to explain the difference between "u.r." and commercial union,[64] its opponents went on equating the two. No paper in Canada became more British than the Halifax *Morning Herald*. On February 2 it called the election "a contest between the Canadian people, on the one side, and a faction of one of the great parties and their Yankee allies, upon the other"; on February 4 it nailed the red ensign to its masthead for the duration of the campaign; on February 9 it proclaimed that "the people of Canada are brought to the parting of the ways." Would they be bound in vassalage to their foreign foes or prosper as part of the greatest empire the world had ever seen?[65] On the platform the Liberals had no one to cope with Charles Tupper in Nova Scotia and George E. Foster in New Brunswick, and they were both British to the core.

The government had an over-all majority of 27 for a net loss of 10. It had lost two cabinet ministers, Sir John Carling in London and C.C. Colby in Stanstead, but it could carry on comfortably. Superficially, at least, Cartwright was right; the "shreds and patches" had saved Sir John. Fred Landon was also right; "u.r." had enabled the Conservatives to "snatch another victory at the polls." It provided the arguments which minimized their losses in Ontario and gave them a life-saving margin of 21 in Nova Scotia and New Brunswick. Laurier was even more correct in his assessment. He had always said that the Liberals would not gain office while Sir John Macdonald lived.[66] It was Sir John who devised the loyalty cry and became its most effective practitioner; it was Sir John who retained the trust of French Canada despite the aberrations of the McCarthyites; and it was Sir John who attracted the independent vote simply because he was Sir John. Unfortunately for the Conservatives there was no one of his stamp to succeed him.

1. Maurice Pope (ed.), *Public Servant–The Memoirs of Sir Joseph Pope* (Toronto: Oxford University Press, 1960), p. 76.

2. O.D. Skelton, *Life and Letters of Sir Wilfrid Laurier*, I [Toronto: Oxford University Press (S.B. Gundy), 1921], p. 411.

3. J. Castell Hopkins, *Life and Work of the Rt. Hon. Sir John Thompson* (Brantford: United Publishing House, 1895), p. 164.

4. J.S. Willison, *Sir Wilfrid Laurier and the Liberal Party*, II (Toronto: Morang and Company, 1903), p. 160.

5. Hopkins, *Thompson*, p. 165.

6. Willison, *Laurier and the Liberal Party*, II, pp. 160-61.

7. Fred Landon, "D'Alton McCarthy and the Politics of the Later Eighties," *Report of the Canadian Historical Association*, 1932, p. 45.

8. Laurier LaPierre, "Joseph Israel Tarte: A Dilemma in Canadian Politics, 1874-96" (unpublished M.A. thesis, University of Toronto, 1957), p. 128.

9. *Ibid.*

10. Chapleau to Macdonald, August 11, 1890, *ibid.*, p. 125.

11. Macdonald to Thompson, December 9, 1890, quoted in Donald Creighton, *John A. Macdonald: The Old Chieftain* (Toronto: The Macmillan Company of Canada, 1955), p. 545.

12. H. Blair Neatby, "Laurier and a Liberal Quebec: A Study in Political Management" (unpublished doctoral thesis, University of Toronto, 1956), p. 65.

13. *Ibid.*, p. 71.

14. *Ibid.*

15. Lowell C. Clark, "The Conservative Party in the 1890's," *Report of the Canadian Historical Association*, 1961, p. 58.

16. For the details see Skelton, *Laurier*, I, pp. 381-92.

17. Quoted from the Montreal *Star* in Landon, "McCarthy and Politics of the Later Eighties," p. 45.

18. Sir Joseph Pope (ed.), *Correspondence of Sir John Macdonald* (Toronto: Oxford University Press, 1921), pp. 442-43.

19. McCarthy to Macdonald, April 17, 1889, *ibid.*, p. 444.

20. Landon, "McCarthy and Politics of the Later Eighties," p. 47.

21. Creighton, *Old Chieftain*, p. 529.

22. House of Commons, *Sessional Papers*, 1895, No. 20, p. 120.

23. Landon, "McCarthy and Politics of the Later Eighties," p. 48.

24. Margaret A. Banks, "The Change in Liberal Party Leadership," *Canadian Historical Review*, XXXVIII (June, 1957), p. 121.

25. *Ibid.*, p. 119.

26. Willison, *Laurier and the Liberal Party*, II, p. 120.

27. F.H. Underhill, "Edward Blake, the Liberal Party, and Unrestricted Reciprocity," *Report of the Canadian Historical Association*, 1939, p. 136.

28. Willison, *Laurier and the Liberal Party*, II, p. 149.

29. Neatby, Laurier and a Liberal Quebec," pp. 80-81.

30. Creighton, *Old Chieftain*, pp. 538-39.

31. W.S. Wallace, "Political History of Ontario 1867-1912," *Canada and Its Provinces*, XVII, p. 171.

32. For the details see Laurier LaPierre, "Joseph Israel Tarte and the McGreevy-Langevin Scandal," *Report of the Canadian Historical Association*, 1961, pp. 47-57.

33. LaPierre, "Tarte–A Dilemma," p. 146.

34. Creighton, *Old Chieftain*, p. 546.

35. *Ibid.*, p. 526.

36. Skelton, *Laurier*, I, p. 412.

37. Creighton, *Old Chieftain*, p. 553.

38. Willison, *Laurier and the Liberal Party*, II, p. 163.

39. *Ibid.*, p. 160n.

40. For the details see Creighton, *Old Chieftain*, pp. 554-55.

41. *Ibid.*, p. 555.

42. Willison, *Laurier and the Liberal Party*, II, p. 167.

43. Quoted from the *Globe* of February 19, 1891, *ibid.*, p. 170.

44. *Ibid.*, pp. 168-69.

45. *Ibid.*, p. 167.

46. Halifax *Morning Herald*, March 2, 1891.

47. Willison, *Laurier and the Liberal Party*, II, p. 171.

48. Macdonald to Stephen, March 3, 1891, in Pope (ed.), *Correspondence*, p. 485.

49. Macdonald to Stephen, November 10, 1890, *ibid.*, p. 478.

50. Willison, *Laurier and the Liberal Party*, II, p. 172.

51. Skelton, *Laurier*, I, p. 411.

52. *Ibid.*, p. 417.

53. Willison, *Laurier and the Liberal Party*, II, pp. 171-72,

54. Robert Rumilly, *Histoire de la Province de Québec*, VI (Montreal: Editions Bernard Valiquette, 1942), p. 196.

Translated by the author.

55. Chapleau to Macdonald, August 11, 1890, quoted in Neatby, "Laurier and a Liberal Quebec," p. 82.

56. Quoted in Rumilly, *Histoire*, VI, pp. 198-99.

57. *Ibid.*, p. 199.

58. *Ibid.*, pp. 203-205.

59. Neatby, "Laurier and a Liberal Quebec," p. 83.

60. Rumilly, *Histoire*, VI, p. 210.

61. Skelton, *Laurier*, I, p. 417.

62. *Ibid.*

63. *Ibid.*, p. 418.

64. Halifax *Morning Chronicle*, January 13, 1891.

65. Halifax *Morning Herald*, February 9, 1891.

66. Willison, *Laurier and the Liberal Party*, II, p. 171.

1891

	Seats	Candidates			Elected						Popular Vote						Total
		C.	L.	O.	C.	%	L.	%	O.	%	C.	%	L.	%	O.	%	
Nova Scotia	21	21	21	3	16	76.2	5	23.8	—	—	46,934	53.1	40,155	45.5	1,223	1.4	88,312
New Brunswick	16	16	14	2	13	81.3	3	18.8	—	—	34,730	56.0	24,939	40.2	2,377	3.8	62,046
Prince Edward Island	6	6	6	—	2	33.3	4	66.7	—	—	17,892	48.5	18,966	51.5	—	—	36,858
Quebec	65	62	62	6	28	43.1	37	56.9	—	—	94,837	50.8	88,711	47.5	3,097	1.7	186,645
Ontario	92	92	90	9	48	52.2	44	47.8	—	—	183,208	49.4	182,213	49.1	5,658	1.5	371,079
Manitoba	5	5	4	—	4	80.0	1	20.0	—	—	9,369	53.1	8,281	46.9	—	—	17,650
British Columbia	6	6	4	—	6	100.0	—	—	—	—	4,009	71.6	1,592	28.4	—	—	5,601
N.W.T.	4	4	2	2	4	100.0	—	—	—	—	6,752	65.4	1,960	19.0	1,619	15.7	10,331
Total	215	212	203	22	121	56.3	94	43.7	—	—	397,731	51.1	366,817	47.1	13,974	1.8	778,522

Notes: (a) An I.L. in New Brunswick, unopposed by an official Liberal, is treated as a Liberal.

(b) Three National Conservatives elected in Quebec are treated as Liberals.

Elected by acclamation: C. (5): Que. (1); Ont. (1); Man. (1); B.C. (2).

L. (3): Que. (3).

Others (votes polled): N.S. (3): Prohibition (2) 468; other C. (1) 755.

N.B. (2): I. (1) 1,858; other C. (1) 519.

Que. (6): I. (1) 795; other C. (5) 2,302.

Ont. (9): Equal Rights (2) 2,455; Patrons (2) 2,198; I. (5) 1,005.

N.W.T. (2): Other C. (2) 1,619.

Eighth

General Election

"CHOOSE THE BISHOPS OR BARABBAS LAURIER"

"The election of 1896 must remain the classic example of a logical and inevitable end being reached by illogical and almost inexplicable popular processes."[1] So writes J. W. Dafoe. He thinks it logical and inevitable that a government was defeated because it invoked "an obscure constitutional power to impose separate schools upon a province which would not have them." He considers the popular processes to be illogical and almost inexplicable because "the government showed strength where its destruction was looked for," while "the voters for whom it risked its life refused to vote for it." Dafoe notwithstanding, the outcome does not need "a theory of instinctive mass movements beyond the ken or control of politicians"[2] to explain it. Although a mass movement did determine the result, it was neither illogical nor inexplicable, and it was made possible because some politicians were as adroit as others were inept.

Some of the Liberals' new-found wisdom had showed itself when they devised a trade policy. They had not left it to the caucus, which might or might not reflect the general feeling of the party. At a Liberal convention held at Ottawa in July, 1893–the first to be assembled federally by a Canadian political party–the delegates denounced the protective tariff, supported low duties for the purposes of revenue only, and favoured reciprocity with the United States in natural products and a selected list of manufactured goods. They did it in such general terms and in such a low key that they provoked little controversy and caused no alarm. Over the next few years Laurier and, more particularly, Tarte did their utmost to get the adherents of protection to accept a *modus vivendi* with the liberal school of economics.[3] They were successful, at least to the point that the tariff played no meaningful part in the election of 1896.

The Liberal convention of 1893 was symptomatic of something else. Students of politics do not agree on the date which marks the emergence of the Liberals as a truly national party. A plausible time is the early nineties and the chief agent of the process was certainly Laurier. To the "shreds and patches" of the Dominion, Mackenzie and Blake had been remote figures who tended to express an Ontarian rather than a Canadian viewpoint, but it took a French-Canadian Catholic with "sunny ways" and the charismatic qualities of a Macdonald to make these regions feel more at home within the Liberal party. During these years, Laurier's personal visits were creating a favourable impression in all the provinces. The convention of 1893, by assembling nearly every important Liberal in the Dominion, completed the forging of a loose alliance of provincial parties into a coherent, national organization.

One important Liberal did not attend the convention. Honoré Mercier was in disgrace, having suffered a blow from which he would never recover. In December 1891, Lieutenant-Governor Angers had dismissed his government for corruption; soon after the voters routed him at the polls. All too aware of Mercier's weaknesses, Laurier perhaps breathed a sigh of relief. Even so, he was to be the chief beneficiary of Mercier's work, for the fiery Nationalist had destroyed the notion that only the Conservatives could defend the French Canadians' religion and race.[4]

In the short run, however, the Conservatives gained from Mercier's fall. Throughout the "scandal session" of 1891, they had reeled badly from their opponents' accusations.[5] Because of Tarte's revelations, they had had no choice but to expel McGreevy from the Commons and force Langevin out of the cabinet. Now, however, the Mercier affair rescued them from the holier-than-thou attitude of the Liberals. Scornfully, they talked about the pot calling the kettle black. At the same time they were capitalizing upon the seemingly perverse conduct of Edward Blake. The day after the election he had published a letter making known his objection to unrestricted reciprocity. Its very obscurity permitted the interpretation that he thought "u.r." would inevitably lead to annexation. Between them, Blake and Mercier had created a disastrous situation for the Liberals. Starting in February 1892, the Conservatives had a series of successes in federal by-elections that is still without parallel in Canadian political annals. In seventy such contests lasting well into 1895 they built up their majority from 31 to 63. They lost a few seats later but their majority was still 58 on the eve of the general election.[6]

Hence, the common belief that the Conservatives steadily collapsed after 1891 needs qualification, to say the least. It is true that the inter-related problems of leadership, the Manitoba school question, and internal dissent eventually created a situation which put them in complete disarray. But the by-elections clearly indicate that they suffered no loss in popular favour for some considerable time.

None the less, the Conservatives' problem with leadership started shortly after the general election. Within sixty-two days they suffered the worst blow of all; Sir John Macdonald died. His successor ought to have been Tupper or Thompson. Most of the cabinet were opposed to Tupper because "small men did not want a *big* leader."[7] Thompson, himself, felt that in the swelling tide of militant Protestantism, a Catholic – and a convert from Methodism at that – ought not to take the leadership. Such were

the depths to which the once tolerant Toryism of Ontario had sunk. Consequently, Senator J.J.C. Abbott succeeded Macdonald for the somewhat
unique, if hardly commendable, reason that he was "not particularly obnoxious to anybody."[8]

Abbott could be no more than a stopgap. Within a year and a half –
in November 1892 – Thompson got the office he had declined. The politico-
religious climate had not improved, however, and in some respects his
premiership was a nightmare. The appointment meant the complete break
of D'Alton McCarthy from the Conservative party. He got out (so he said)
because he had been completely ignored in the formation of the new
government. By this time the Equal Rights movement had collapsed and a
more sinister Protestant Protective Association (P.P.A.), which drew its
inspiration from an American counterpart, had replaced it. McCarthy would
have nothing to do with it, but he remained no less adamant on separate
schools and the use of the French language.

Because of his Catholicism, Thompson may have been a little too
ready to appease the ultra-Protestant wing. He was even willing to appoint
W.R. Meredith to his cabinet until Archbishop Cleary of Kingston blocked
him because he was "an unpardonable bigot." Instead, N. Clarke Wallace,
the Grand Master of the Loyal Orange Lodge of British North America,
entered the ministry and, according to some observers, was soon creating the
impression that it was composed of P.P.A. men.[9]

Just before Thompson became Prime Minister, the Judicial Committee had laid the Manitoba school question on the cabinet's doorstep. It
called the School Act *intra vires*, holding that Manitoba Catholics had not
been deprived of any rights which they had enjoyed by law when the
province entered the union. Thus, a legacy bequeathed by John A. Macdonald was ready to haunt the government. Naturally, the Catholic minority was quick to petition for the remedial action which the Governor-
General-in-Council and Parliament could provide under section 93 of the
B.N.A. Act and the corresponding section of the Manitoba Act. A cabinet
sub-committee which included Thompson and Chapleau dealt with the
matter. There was doubt whether the Judicial Committee had left the
Catholics any rights which could be restored by remedial action. Hoping
that the government might not have to act at all, Thompson tried to keep
the question on a purely legal basis as long as he could. Although he could
not have foreseen it, it would, in the long run, have been more judicious to
have been less judicial.

Chapleau disagreed strongly with Thompson's handling of the issue.
After Langevin's fall he had expected at last to be master in Quebec. But that
was not to be. When Abbott formed his cabinet, Chapleau had wanted the
portfolio of Railways and Canals as a recognition both of French-Canadian
influence at Ottawa and his own personal prestige. He got Customs instead.
"From this moment," say Neatby and Saywell,"dates his gradual defection

from the Conservative party; and from this moment, until the victory of Laurier, Quebec was without an effective leader in Ottawa."[10]

Manitoba schools completed the rupture. Somewhat unhappily, Chapleau had accepted the earlier decision not to disallow the school legislation, but he had given pledges at the time that, if its legality were upheld, he would see to it that Parliament provided remedial legislation. To regard the matter as one of law, even after the court decision, was repugnant to him. Over Thompson's objection, he had the words "at present" inserted in the subcommittee's report which stated that the matter was not to be considered as political in character. It was not surprising, therefore, that he ended up, not in Thompson's cabinet, but in the lieutenant-governorship of Quebec. For him it was just as well. He had been spurned once too often; he had no desire to stay in a government "where on questions vitally affecting his province he was not recognized as the man who spoke for Quebec."[11] For the Conservatives, it was like committing suicide. Had its English-speaking leaders lost all understanding of the Quebec situation? Did they fail to realize that they were easing out the only man who could speak authoritatively for the majority of Quebec's Conservatives, the school of Cartier? Were they prepared to risk the next election with Quebec dismantled?[12]

The Thompson government proceeded to ask the courts if it still had power to take remedial action, but not before the Manitoba government and its Ontario friends objected to its putting on judicial garb, and not before the Manitoba minority and its Quebec friends opposed the reference to the court as an instrument of delay and an evasion of responsibility. The government's action meant that it could forget about Manitoba schools for another two years and continue to win by-elections. On January 29, 1895, the Judicial Committee decided it still had the power to grant redress. The judgment swept away the last possible excuse for delay. The time for action had arrived.

A month before, Sir John Thompson had died in Windsor Castle, just after being admitted to the Imperial Privy Council. His successor should have been Tupper. Certainly the rank and file of the party favoured him. Yet, like Thompson, he had to wait for a while, this time because he suited neither "the knot of jealous and feuding individuals in the cabinet" nor the Governor General, Lord Aberdeen. The most political of our Governors General, Aberdeen played no small part in the defeat of the Conservatives.[13] Possessed of a violent and unreasoning dislike of Tupper, he was determined that the Nova Scotian would not be Prime Minister. The cabinet, perhaps fearful that he might put Laurier in office, went along with him.[14] As a result, the party was saddled with Mackenzie Bowell, a senator and former Orange leader, whose very modest abilities in no way fitted him to cope with what was perhaps the most difficult of all Canadian political problems. Under him, the government staggered from crisis to crisis and finally began to lose by-elections.

At first the Bowell government acted quickly, if not wisely or decisively. There was good reason for speed because it had become all too painfully obvious that a general election loomed ever closer. Carefully cultivating the idea that it was acting only as an agent of the courts, it ordered the Manitoba government to give redress to the Catholic minority. Showing that it too could play politics, the Manitoba government did nothing for eight months and then, in December 1895, it defied the federal authority outright. During these months the badly-rent Bowell government hesitated on the point of coercing Manitoba, steadily losing support in Quebec as it dilly-dallied. In July 1895, Angers resigned from the cabinet because of its vacillation; in November, Laurier wrote to Willison: "at present in this province we could sweep everything"; in December, the Conservatives lost by-elections in their former strongholds of Jacques Cartier and Ste. Anne.

Manitoba's refusal to provide redress meant that Bowell had no option but to carry out his pledge to call Parliament by January 2, and to try to proceed with remedial legislation. Now, the Protestant wing of the cabinet acted up. Clarke Wallace had left in protest a few weeks earlier. On January 4, seven additional ministers resigned because they had no confidence in Bowell's leadership. The difficulties surrounding this "Nest of Traitors" incident were patched up, but it was questionable patchwork. Bowell was to continue as titular head of the government; Tupper was to lead the Commons during the session and become Prime Minister after prorogation. His assumption of the leadership, already too long delayed, was postponed a little longer. Had the fine hand of Aberdeen or, more accurately, that of his wife, made itself felt once more? Professor Saywell's acount of the situation leaves no doubt. Not only had their influence been felt, but their incredible meddling had made it very difficult for Tupper to "restore the inward harmony or outward presence of the Conseravtive party."[15]

The government let five weeks of the session pass before it introduced its remedial bill. Both parties, says Dafoe, had now to decide, "how best to set the sails to catch the veering winds and blustering gusts to win the race, the prize for which was the government of Canada."[16] The Conservatives had no doubt about the tactics they would use. In the English provinces they would make themselves appear as loyal subjects of the Crown simply carrying out its order delivered through the Judicial Committee; in Quebec they would pose as "the defenders of the oppressed, loyal co-operators with the bishops in rebuking, subduing and chaining the Manitoba tyrants."[17]

Until now Laurier had doggedly kept "behind the lines of Torres Vedras" and not taken a definite position, although he had intimated once that if he had a chance he would "try the sunny way."[18] Already the bishops had presented him with an ultimatum. Through Father Lacombe, the pioneer missionary of western Canada, they had warned him that, if

Eighth

the government were overthrown in granting redress, "the episcopacy, like one man, united with the clergy, will rise to support those who may have fallen in defending us."[19] For some time the faint-hearted among the Liberals had feared that their refusal to adopt any kind of a stand on Manitoba schools might well cause their downfall. Now, it seemed as if the worst had come to pass. Would it not be best to let Clarke Wallace move the six months' hoist which would kill the remedial bill, thus permitting the Liberal members to vote as they pleased? Laurier did not scare so easily, and J. Israel Tarte said "no".

Tarte had not become a Liberal officially until 1893; yet, in short order he was masterminding his new party much as he had the Conservatives in the past. In the early years of controversy on Manitoba schools, he had gone to such extremes that Laurier had to excuse and restrain him.[20] However, "all through the winter and spring of 1895 [he] was sinking test wells in Quebec public opinion with one uniform result. The issue was Laurier."[21] Tarte had also reached the conclusion that coercion was only a second-best remedy for the ills of Manitoba's Catholics and had begun to educate the Quebec Liberals to that point of view. Laurier's sphinxlike silence became a crucial part of the Liberal strategy. Let the government commit itself to a remedial measure and the Liberals could oppose it unitedly without fear of alienating Quebec. When the government's bill combined a minimum of relief with a maximum of coercion, Laurier and Tarte breathed more easily.

Hence, it was Laurier himself, not Clarke Wallace, who proposed the six months' hoist. Seven of his supporters failed to go along with him, while eighteen Conservatives broke with their own party. The bill passed second reading and then bogged down in Committee of the Whole. Tupper cracked the whip and kept the Commons continually in session, but could not prevail over the determined opposition of some Ontario Conservatives. Although Tom Sawyer's school adventures and the Nova Scotia Education Act had scant relevance to the matter at hand, they served the purpose of the filibusterers eminently well. With time running out, even the dogged Tupper had to give up. Parliament prorogued on April 23, just a day before it was due to expire.

Contrary to the usual accounts, Manitoba schools was not the only talking point in the election which followed. In Quebec, it is true, the issue of remedial legislation dominated all else, but in the other provinces the Conservatives avoided it as much as they could and talked about the government's record of development and achievement. Once more their chief stock in trade was "N.P." and the Liberals' chameleon-like conduct on trade matters.[22] These arguments, however, had lost their old appeal. In 1882, 1887, and 1891 the voters had responded positively to "N.P.", but in 1896 they balked. Neither could they be made to believe that the Liberals were revolutionary or disloyal. As Mowat put it to Laurier, "you, like myself, are a Reformer, not a revolutionist, and you recognize the necessity of legislation on the tariff being gradual and cautious."[23] Hardly a terrifying point of view for even the most timid voter! In consequence, the Conservatives could capitalize on neither the positive nor negative arguments from which they had reaped such rich rewards in the past.

In the absence of a fresh, appealing platform the government's chief asset turned out to be Tupper. This was, in fact, his finest campaign. It was this septuagenarian who introduced the leader's cross-country campaign tour. Starting in Winnipeg, he moved eastward to Sydney and then back to Ontario where he delivered 42 speeches in the last 13 days of electioneering. He was indeed an indefatigable campaigner. Once again, says Saunders, "his itinerary exhibited that approach to ubiquity which had characterized his activities in all the political campaigns of his long life."[24] Even the Liberal, Willison, agreed that "no more gallant fight was ever made to save a field than [Tupper's] in 1896."[25]

Both Tupper and Laurier exhibited the sense of responsibility which was especially desirable in a contest involving deeply-felt religious and racial differences. On essentials they spoke with the same voice in Quebec and Ontario. Tupper did try to show that Laurier's remarks at St. Roch contradicted what he said in English Canada. In that Quebec village, Laurier had intimated that, if the situation warranted it, he would take stronger action against Manitoba than the Conservatives had.[26] Nevertheless, in his forays into Ontario, he at no time said he would not intervene if Manitoba refused adequate concessions.[27] Lesser Ontario Liberals were, of course, insistent that federal intervention was unwarranted in any circumstances – a position entirely at variance with that of their counterparts in Quebec. Dafoe, who always maintained that the remedial power was an obscure constitutional provision which ought never to be used for the purposes of coercion, considered the argument of the Quebec Liberals to be pure nonsense.[28] He was equally hard on English-speaking Conservatives who regarded themselves merely as agents of the Judicial Committee. "From their experiences with the electors," he said, "they had good reason to believe that this buncombe would go down."[29] In the past, perhaps it might have, but not this time.

Tupper was beaten before he started. Later he could recount the "fatal mistakes": the decision not to dissolve immediately after the remedial order; the failure to use the parliamentary recess in 1895 to remove the misrepresentation and misapprehension surrounding the school question; the folly of having the remedial bill dealt with by a Parliament "whose life terminated on a specific day, thus offering the greatest possible inducement to obstruction."[30] Nevertheless, he had no little success in parts of English Canada, even though he could induce only one man of prestige – John A. Macdonald's son Hugh John – to enter his cabinet.

The Conservatives lost seats for the first time in British Columbia and the Territories, and a majority of them at that. It was not because the residents of these areas knew the victors in advance, because this time they voted on the same day as eastern Canadians. Good Liberal candidates and the fact that these areas were maturing politically and tending to pursue a more independent line had something to do with it. The results indicate that the West was at last being integrated into the national party structure.

The Conservatives were also disappointed with the results in the Maritimes, where their majority dropped from 19 to 5. Nova Scotia split its 20 seats evenly, leading Bowell to tell Tupper it was a result "not such as you had a right to expect."[31] The regional result was not surprising, however. This time there was no loyalty cry to move the voters and Fielding and Blair, who had recently won decisive victories in Nova Scotia and New Brunswick and who were anticipating being called to Ottawa, worked strenuously for Laurier.

The Conservatives were most elated by the results in Manitoba and Ontario, where they had experienced the strongest opposition. Strange as it may seem, the other English provinces were more perturbed by the threatened coercion of Manitoba than was that province itself. The Manitoba *Free Press*, still Conservative in its sympathies, became almost obsessed with its loyalist attitudes. When Clifford Sifton suggested it was folly for an English court to undertake to direct the House of Commons in the matter of Manitoba schools, it accused him of raising the standard of rebellion.[32] The Liberals suffered because they had neither the leadership nor the organization that had contributed so greatly to their sweeping provincial victory in January.[33] Sifton helped to get D'Alton McCarthy elected in Brandon, but four of the other six seats returned Conservatives, notably Hugh John Macdonald in Winnipeg.

In Ontario, the mere idea of having to defend the forcible imposition of separate schools upon Manitoba was enough to make the Conservative organizers shudder. Clarke Wallace did his utmost to influence the extreme Protestant element against the government, causing Willison to observe how often the Orange Lodge, supposedly the backbone of the Conservative party, had rendered assistance to the Liberals.[34] Even Tupper's booming voice could scarcely be heard above the hecklers. George E. Foster described his meeting in Toronto as "the noisiest . . . of my political career." It had its humorous moments too; when Foster chanced to quote Alexander Pope, he got the instant interjection, "We don't want any Popes here."[35] Oliver Mowat was at his best in demolishing the Conservatives' argument that they were simply acting as agents of the Judicial Committee. The courts, he pointed out, had not indicated how the grievance of the Manitoba Catholics was to be removed. "This is a question between the Protestants and Catholics of Manitoba. It can be healed, but never by the Coercion Bill."[36] The Liberals were given a boost when Mowat agreed in advance to enter a Laurier cabinet. The announcement lost much of its effect because of Mowat's unwillingness to endanger himself; canny Scot that he was, he refused to contest a seat and held on to the premiership of Ontario.[37]

Under the circumstances the results were a triumph for the Conservatives. They polled 4.6 per cent more of the popular vote than the Liberals and won 43 seats: the same number as their opponents. McCarthy's followers contested 9 ridings and won in 2 of them; McCarthy himself was also elected. The Patrons of Industry, a farmers' organization which had come to Ontario from Michigan in 1887, tried in 26 ridings and was successful in 2.

To what factors did the Conservatives owe their good showing in Ontario? First of all, there was Tupper. "How you ever managed in the short time at your disposal to unite and consolidate the party . . . is almost incomprehensible," wrote an admiring Sir Thomas Galt.[38] There was also much temporizing on their part, that helped to prevent the widespread alienation of the Protestant vote. Tupper had no choice but to accept as candidates, men who had opposed the remedial bill in Parliament. At least forty of his candidates in Ontario pledged themselves to vote against similar legislation in the future, while many others gave it only nominal support or declined to discuss it at all. Lowell Clark even doubts whether the Conservatives of Ontario campaigned as a party for remedial legislation.[39] Finally, there was a highly subtle, altogether incalculable factor working for the Conservatives. The strong emphasis on race and religion apparently worked to defeat the purposes of the very people who raised it; it "reinforced the instinctive repugnance of the ultra-Protestants of Ontario and Manitoba to voting for Laurier, Frenchman and Roman Catholic."[40]

In the English provinces the over-all result was 72 Conservatives, 69 Liberals, and 7 others. Everything depended, therefore, upon Quebec. In that province, Tupper's chief lieutenant promised him a majority of 20.[41] This was wishful thinking, for the Conservatives won only 1 seat in the district of Quebec and 15 in the rest of the province. In none of Canada's federal elections have the results in any one province been as far-reaching in their consequences as they were in Quebec in 1896.

The Liberal triumph resulted from a combination of forces, some of which had been operating for a decade or more. Lowell Clark contends that "it was not its ecclesiastical leaders which Quebec repudiated in 1896, but its former Ontario partners."[42] Much of Ontario Conservatism had undoubtedly succumbed to a militant Protestantism and Anglo-Saxon racialism. To the knowing French Canadian it must have appeared thoroughly tainted by the long series of bigots it had produced – the Toronto *Mail*, D'Alton McCarthy, the Equal Rights Association, W.R. Meredith, the Toronto *World*, and, at times, even the Toronto *Empire*. Now that Sir John Macdonald was gone, there was not a single English-speaking Conservative in whom French Canada could confidently put its trust. In addition, there was the temporizing of the Conservative candidates in Ontario. Their conduct did not pass unnoticed in Quebec, especially by *La Presse*. So indignant did it become that it even threatened to desert the party. In the end, its strong protectionist sympathies made it think better of desertion, but its heart was clearly not in the fight.[43] Thus, the evidence is clear that wide cracks had appeared in the cement which bound together the Conservatism of Quebec and Ontario. Nevertheless, an alliance of this kind may survive through inertia alone, long after its original sense of purpose is gone, unless there is a positive force strong enough to lure away its components. Clark's thesis serves only to explain the context in which a Liberal victory became possible; it does not explain the victory itself.

Internally, too, the Quebec Conservatives had a serious disability; despite numerous warnings they went into the campaign with Quebec dismantled. Ironically, the man who gave the warnings was requested twice to take over the Quebec leadership: by Bowell in January and by Tupper in April. The offers came too late. Chapleau informed Bowell that, in view of his earlier pledges, he could not enter the cabinet until a remedial bill had actually been passed.[44] He told Tupper that "the grave reasons which induced me to quit active political life are still sufficient to keep me away from it now."[45] In other words, he would have had to become a colleague of the Castors, whom he detested above all else. As a result, the leadership of the French-Canadian contingent fell upon Angers, ultramontane in sympathy and known to be hostile to the Chapleau group. His colleagues in the cabinet were Desjardins, Ross, and Taillon, all adherents of the Programme Catholique in 1871. For the Conservatives, such French-Canadian representation was unfortunate, if not disastrous. Not one of the four was flamboyant on the platform or possessed natural political ability. Worse still, as Castors, they represented only a minority of their party, and a minority which would have voted Conservative anyway in 1896.[46]

Like the breakdown in rapport between the Ontario and Quebec wings this weakness also served to loosen the Bleu hold on Quebec; it was another of the ingredients in the general situation that made a Liberal victory possible. The strong positive factor that impelled the former Bleus into the Liberal camp was Laurier himself. Willison puts it this way: "Under an English leader the Liberal party would have been defeated and without Quebec Laurier would not have triumphed."[47] The second part of the statement needs no demonstration; even with a policy designed not to alienate English Canada, the Liberals got no better than an even break outside Quebec. The first part is more conjectural, but if a Blake or a Mackenzie had been leading the Liberals, most Bleus might well have gone on voting Conservative, although not with enthusiasm.

It was Laurier who made the difference. Without a deliberate effort on his part he appealed to the French Canadians' *nationalisme*; merely the idea of elevating one of their own to the highest political office in the land filled them with a real sense of pride. But there is more to it than that, because they could have made Laurier Prime Minister in 1891. Since that time, circumstances, some of his own making and some of other people's, had strengthened his position immeasurably. Chapleau's departure from active political life left him without a rival for the hearts and minds of French Canadians. Four years of vacillation on Manitoba schools had created serious doubts about the ability of the Conservatives to act any longer as the defender of French-Canadian interests. Several hundred meetings in every corner of Quebec had stamped Laurier as the one person in whom French Canada could safely put its trust. As Dansereau put it, "le peuple à qui il faut une idole se tourna vers Laurier en 1896."[48]

There has been a tendency to stress Tarte as the strategist, the tactician, and the organizer of the Liberal victory in Quebec. Rumilly, for one, emphasizes the influence of "the most intelligent man of his time."[49] Laurier LaPierre contends that "more than any other politician of his province, Tarte erected around Laurier a national edifice in which French Canadians would find their only refuge."[50] This poses the academic question of what part planning and organization play in an electoral triumph in which they have acted and reacted with other factors strongly working towards the same result. How much, for example, was Laurier's build-up in Quebec due to his own speaking tours, and how much to Tarte's articles in *Le Cultivateur*? The strategy which made reliance on the leader the very foundation of the Liberal campaign was clearly Tarte's doing. None the less, Neatby credits Laurier with the victory. "It was his personal reputation that was being used as the gambling stake, and it must have been he who had made the final decision to take it."[51]

When it came to organization, Tarte was undoubtedly without equal. By July 1894 he had perfected the basic central organization and had turned his attention to the lower levels.[52] His task became much easier in 1895 when deepening disillusionment with the Conservatives was accompanied by a growing confidence in Laurier. Political clubs to which enthusiastic young Liberals flocked, mushroomed all over the province. For once, the Liberals had the manpower to see that the electoral lists were not stacked against them. As the election approached, defections from the Conservatives provided an omen of what was to come. The Bleus had to rely on old-timers, while the Liberals had a healthy infusion of new blood, including candidates of promise like Henri Bourassa and Rodolphe Lemieux. Youthful Raoul Dandurand, the Liberal organizer for the 43 counties in the district of Montreal, had all the assistance he required without payment, except for the students, who timidly requested travelling expenses. In contrast, Frederick Monk of the Conservatives complained because he had to pay fifty dollars to get someone to speak at Lachine.[53]

Tarte did not win the election for the Liberals. Barring major blunders, they would have had a moderate victory without him. But, because he devised the strategy most appropriate for the occasion, brought the organization to a new peak of efficiency, and saw to it that there were no tactical errors, it was a victory of almost astounding proportions.

Tarte also foresaw that Laurier could successfully defy the bishops. Their position was exceedingly difficult because the Conservative leadership was so weak; "if the interests of the Church were to be adequately defended, [they] had to intervene."[54] Archbishop Langevin of St. Boniface prolonged his stay in Quebec to deliver speeches inspired, so the Liberals thought, more by Sir Charles Tupper than by the Holy Spirit.[55] The collective *mandement* of the bishops was relatively mild. Because of the objections of Bishop Emard of Valleyfield, the only member of the hierarchy who was friendly to Laurier, it did not explicitly condemn the Liberals. This did not prevent that sturdy old ultramontane, Bishop Laflèche of Trois Rivières, from mounting an attack on his own. As its basis, he condemned Laurier for saying in the Commons that he took his stand "not from the point of view of Catholicism, not from the point of view of Protestantism, but . . . from motives which may address themselves to the conscience of men loving justice, liberty and tolerance." A man who spoke thus, thundered Laflèche, was a rationalist liberal, the formulator of doctrines opposed to Catholic teaching. Hence, no Catholic could vote for him or his followers under pain of sinning in a grave matter.[56] The other bishops generally went along with Laflèche, but not so the lesser clergy, many of whom were admirers of Laurier.

Although the Liberal papers, *L'Electeur* and *La Patrie*, attacked Laflèche cruelly and relentlessly, Tarte tried another approach. He adopted a respectful attitude towards the old prelate even as he suggested that the Bishop's stand might make it harder for Manitoba's Catholics to get justice.[57] He knew what he was doing, for too harsh treatment of Laflèche might have backfired and created some sympathy for his point of view.

Otherwise Tarte had no doubts. Let the bishops laud the Conservatives as the saviours of French Canada. He knew that the Quebec voters were aware of the government's vacillation for four years on Manitoba schools, and of its stumbling into remedial legislation more through ineptitude than through any desire to ensure justice. Let the curés say that the choice was between the bishops and Barabbas Laurier. Tarte knew that the Quebec voters saw the alternative quite differently, that the velvet glove of Laurier was likely to be more efficacious than the mailed fist of Tupper. He knew, most of all, that they would not consider it a mortal sin to make a French Canadian Prime Minister.[58] He was right.

1. J.W. Dafoe, *Clifford Sifton in Relation to His Times* (Toronto: The Macmillan Company of Canada, 1931), p. 92.

2. *Ibid.*

3. Laurier LaPierre, "Joseph Israel Tarte: A Dilemma in Canadian Politics, 1874-96" (unpublished M.A. thesis, University of Toronto, 1957), pp. 184-87.

4. *Supra*, p. 58.

5. J. Castell Hopkins, *Life and Work of the Rt. Hon. Sir John Thompson* (Brantford: United Publishing House, 1895), Chapter XI.

6. Lowell C. Clark, "The Conservative Party in the 1890's," *Report of the Canadian Historical Association*, 1961, p. 60.

7. Quoted in *ibid.*, p. 61.

8. *Debates of the Senate of Canada*, 1891, p. 12.

9. Clark, "Conservative Party in the 1890's," p. 63n.

10. H. Blair Neatby and John T. Saywell, "Chapleau and the Conservative Party in Quebec," *Canadian Historical Review*, XXXVII (March, 1956), p. 16.

11. *Ibid.*, p. 17.

12. *Ibid.*

13. Clark, "Conservative Party in the 1890's," p. 64.

14. *Ibid.*, p. 67.

15. John T. Saywell, "The Crown and the Politicians: The Canadian Succession Question," *Canadian Historical Review*, XXXVII (December, 1956), p. 331.

16. J.W. Dafoe, *Laurier: A Study in Canadian Politics* (Toronto: Thomas Allen & Son Limited, 1922), p. 41.

17. *Ibid.*, p. 42.

18. O.D. Skelton, *Life and Letters of Sir Wilfrid Laurier*, I [Toronto: Oxford University Press (S.B. Gundy), 1921], pp. 464-65.

19. *Ibid.*, pp. 470-71.

20. H. Blair Neatby, "Laurier and a Liberal Quebec: A Study in Political Management" (unpublished doctoral thesis, University of Toronto, 1956), pp. 101-104.

21. Dafoe, *Laurier*, pp. 43-44.

22. See, for example, the text of one of Tupper's speeches in the Halifax *Morning Herald*, June 6, 1896.

23. C.R.W. Biggar, *Sir Oliver Mowat*, II (Toronto: Warwick Bros. and Rutter Ltd., 1905), p. 649.

24. E.M. Saunders, *The Life and Letters of the Rt. Hon. Sir Charles Tupper Bart., K.C.M.G.*, II (New York: Frederick A. Stokes, 1916), p. 202.

25. J.S. Willison, *Laurier and the Liberal Party*, II (Toronto: Morang and Company, 1903), pp. 255-56.

26. Saunders, *Tupper*, II, p. 202.

27. Sir John Willison, *Reminiscences Political and Personal* (Toronto: McClelland & Stewart Limited, 1919), p. 245.

28. Dafoe, *Sifton*, p. 94.

29. Dafoe, *Laurier*, pp. 41-42.

30. Saunders, *Tupper*, II, p. 208.

31. *Ibid.*, p. 210.

32. Dafoe, *Sifton*, pp. 93-94.

33. *Ibid.*, p. 95.

34. Willison, *Reminiscences*, pp. 251-52.

35. W. Stewart Wallace, *The Memoirs of the Rt. Hon. Sir George E. Foster* (Toronto: The Macmillan Company of Canada, 1933), pp. 98-99.

36. Biggar, *Mowat*, II, pp. 652-53.

37. *Ibid.*, p. 646.

38. Galt to Tupper, June 27, 1896, in Saunders, *Tupper*, II, pp. 209-10.

39. Clark, "Conservative Party in the 1890's," pp. 72-73.

40. Dafoe, *Sifton*, p. 94.

41. Saunders, *Tupper*, II, p. 208.

42. Clark, "Conservative Party in the 1890's," p. 73.

43. See Robert Rumilly, *Histoire de la Province de Québec*, VIII (Montreal: Editions Bernard Valiquette, 1942), pp. 76-77. Translated by the author.

44. Neatby and Saywell, "Chapleau and the Conservative Party," p. 21.

45. Chapleau to Tupper, April 29, 1896, quoted in Neatby, "Laurier and a Liberal Quebec," p. 129.

46. *Ibid.*, pp. 127-29.

47. Willison, *Reminiscences*, p. 246.

48. *La Presse*, November 30, 1901,

quoted in Neatby, "Laurier and a Liberal Quebec," p. 132.

49. Rumilly, *Histoire*, VI, p. 133.

50. LaPierre, "Tarte: A Dilemma," p. 207.

51. Neatby, "Laurier and a Liberal Quebec," p. 135.

52. For the details, see LaPierre, "Tarte: A Dilemma," pp. 212-14.

53. Rumilly, *Histoire*, VIII, p. 77.

54. Neatby, "Laurier and a Liberal Quebec," p. 126.

55. Rumilly, *Histoire*, VIII, p. 60.

56. *Ibid.*, p. 64.

57. See LaPierre, "Tarte: A Dilemma," pp. 201-203.

58. Skelton, *Laurier*, I, pp. 483-84.

1896

	Seats	Candidates			Elected						Popular Vote						Total
		C.	L.	O.	C.	%	L.	%	O.	%	C.	%	L.	%	O.	%	
Nova Scotia	20	20	20	1	10	50.0	10	50.0	—	—	50,772	50.4	49,176	48.8	737	0.7	100,685
New Brunswick	14	14	14	4	9	64.3	5	35.7	—	—	31,399	49.0	28,383	44.3	4,318	6.7	64,100
Prince Edward Island	5	5	5	1	3	60.0	2	40.0	—	—	9,157	49.0	9,194	49.2	321	1.7	18,672
Quebec	65	63	63	1	16	24.6	49	75.4	—	—	102,884	45.8	120,321	53.5	1,485	0.7	224,690
Ontario	92	88	75	54	43	46.7	43	46.7	6	6.5	189,182	44.8	169,480	40.2	63,413	15.0	422,075
Manitoba	7	7	6	4	4	57.1	2	28.6	1	14.3	15,459	47.0	11,519	35.0	5,906	18.0	32,884
British Columbia	6	6	6	2	2	33.3	4	66.7	—	—	8,174	45.0	8,921	49.1	1,057	5.8	18,152
N.W.T.	4	4	3	3	1	25.0	3	75.0	—	—	7,811	43.9	8,191	46.0	1,786	10.0	17,788
Total	213	207	192	70	88	41.3	118	55.4	7	3.3	414,838	46.1	405,185	45.1	79,023	8.8	899,046

Elected by acclamation: C. (1): Que. (1).
                   L. (2): Que. (2).

Others elected: Ont. (6): McCarthyite (3); Patrons (2); I. (1).
               Man. (1): McCarthyite (1).

Others (votes polled): N.S. (1): I. (1) 737.
                    N.B. (4): I. (4) 4,318.
                    P.E.I. (1): Other L. (1) 321.
                    Que. (1): Patrons (1) 1,485.
                    Ont. (54): Other C. (1) 745; P.P.A. (5) 6,233; Patrons (26) 32,337; McCarthyite (10) 14,459; I. (12) 9,639.
                    Man. (4): McCarthyite (1) 3,073; Patrons (3) 2,833.
                    B.C. (2): Other C. (2) 1,057.
                    N.W.T. (3): I. (3) 1,786.

Ninth

General Election

"FULL OF FURY, SIGNIFYING NOTHING IN PARTICULAR"

In 1900, booming prosperity was both the principal campaign weapon of the Liberals and the major determinant of the election results. From coast to coast it was the chief ingredient of Liberal speeches. From the platform and in the press the voters were bombarded with statistics demonstrating the country's development during four years of Liberal rule. Through J.W. Bengough's cartoons, the Toronto *Globe* presented the same theme pictorially.[1] Canadians learned that their foreign trade had increased by $142 million between 1896 and 1900, compared with only $66 million in eighteen years of Tory rule. They were told that Conservative deficits had been replaced by surpluses totalling $13 million in the ordinary accounts; that immigration had increased from 20,000 in 1896 to 32,000 in 1897 to 44,000 in 1898, and so on. They had it drilled into their heads that the great trek of immigrants to the West had already given a strong impetus to business generally, and that manufacturers, merchants, and workingmen in all parts of Canada would benefit still further as western Canada became more productive. Such was the picture of Canada unlimited as it appeared in the Liberal campaign handbook.[2] William Stevens Fielding put it this way: "four years of peace, four years of progress, four years of such prosperity as this country never before knew" – and more to come.[3]

Ironically, this first great period of Canadian development was taking place under the three basic national policies initiated by the Conservatives and once castigated by the Liberals. For the first time, these policies had a chance to be fully effective because the world-wide forces which had so long made for economic stagnation had finally been dissipated. The Liberals, however, did not see it this way. William Paterson, the Minister of Customs, even boasted that the Liberal tariff was a revenue tariff and called it the chief difference between the two parties. Fielding, however, estimated that he had decreased the tariff about 2¼ per cent – hardly a reduction of significance.[4] The Conservatives were right that such changes made scarcely a dent in "N.P."

Yet, the Liberals were caught on the horns of a dilemma. They could hardly cut tariffs with the United States, for in 1897 the U.S. had chosen to superimpose upon the already restrictive McKinley tariff the even higher Dingley tariff. Still, the Liberals did what they could. Fielding's budget of 1897 introduced the principle of a maximum and minimum tariff, the main result of which was to give British goods a preference in the Canadian market. It was a masterly stroke. It cut the ground from beneath the pro-British Conservatives even as it fulfilled the Liberal pledge to cut tariffs. Just before the election the Liberal press published with evident delight editorials, from English newspapers of every shade of opinion, extolling the action of Laurier and his government.[5] This was indeed something new in Canadian politics!

Although the policies of the Liberals were the same old ones, they applied them with new energy and imagination. They had the men to do it. Laurier included four provincial premiers in his first cabinet and, Fielding excepted, they did not compare with some that he had to leave out. Among the talented, none was abler than Clifford Sifton, the Minister of the Interior. "He knew the West; . . . his shrewd insight, his administrative capacity, his power of quick decision, were qualities rare at Ottawa."[6] It was he who reformed the system of land granting, eased and simplified the homestead regulations, and devised the campaigns which were to bring in the settlers in full flood. His innovations had ample time to demonstrate their worth by the time of the election in 1900.

Basically, then, the chief opponent of the Conservatives was prosperity and all it implied. One forecaster correctly observed that their only hope of victory lay in an overshadowing issue which could appeal with crushing force to the electors.

> But of all the issues which Sir Charles Tupper delights to restate, there is not one which the Canadian elector can declare to be of surpassing importance. An Opposition is not nearly as dangerous hacking at the enemy's wall, producing a spark here and a splinter there, as when it concentrates its whole strength at the weakest point. . . . [Because the government had made no serious mistakes] the Opposition must attack an entrenched enemy with small arms, and the conflict promises small success to the attacking party.[7]

Tupper was still leading the Conservatives, but he ought not to have been. His seventy-nine years did not prevent him from waging a vigorous campaign, but, in a different context, he appeared a far less gallant figure than four years earlier. More than anyone, he set the tone of a campaign which, according to Dafoe, was "full of fury, signifying nothing in particular."[8] For Tupper this was just the type of electioneering which used to bring success. "There was a wholesale vigorous denunciation; there were loud and assured trumpetings of victory. But the times were not propitious for such a campaign. In 1900 the people were content; they did not in the mass want any change."[9] Robert Laird Borden, conducting his second successful campaign in Halifax, put it this way: "Our attack possibly was too discursive and lacked force in failing to concentrate on some single issue. But in truth, there was no dominating issue; prosperity prevailed."[10]

Nothing illustrates Tupper's techniques better than his manifesto to the people of Canada on the eve of the election.[11] Only in the last paragraph did he get around to saying what his party stood for positively. In all that went before, he did little more than demonstrate that he stood firmly against sin. The Liberals, he said sweepingly, "have failed in everything they have attempted." "Pledged to free trade, reduced taxation, expenditure and public debt, they adopted protection, increased taxation ten millions per annum, expenditure eleven millions, and debt eight millions." They had perpetrated outrageous election frauds in Brockville and West Huron; they had committed "wanton reckless extravagance" in the contract to build the Crow's Nest Pass Railway; they had administered the Yukon so frightfully as to "disgrace Canada in Great Britain, Australia and America." The list of misdeeds went on almost ad infinitum.

Given this cue by their leader, the lesser Conservatives did what might have been expected of them. They concentrated so much on minor scandals and other shortcomings that, outside of Quebec and Ontario, picayune criticism became their only ware. Such arguments could not cope at all with the government's most effective weapon: the country's prosperity. Even in Prince Edward Island, where the federal cabinet minister, Sir Louis Davies, was suffering an eclipse, the Conservatives took only two of the five seats. In the other Maritime Provinces they fared worse. Nova Scotia had unbounded confidence in Fielding, and its industries were for the moment sharing in the country's development. Hence, it was not surprising that it gave the Liberals 15 of its 20 seats, and inflicted upon Tupper his first personal defeat in 45 years of electioneering. In New Brunswick, A.G. Blair occupied a position analogous to that of Fielding, and he had been indefatigable in seeing that his province got its full share of federal largesse. He ended up with 9 of the 14 seats and personally defeated the Conservative kingpin, George Eulas Foster, in Saint John. It had been part of Tupper's strategy to pit his chief lieutenants against Laurier's ministers, but here as elsewhere it backfired badly.[12]

In the West "the Sifton policies were everywhere vote-getters; 'Sifton' was a name to conjure with."[13] In the Territories the Liberals took all four seats; in British Columbia four of six. Only in Sifton's own bailiwick of Manitoba did they experience trouble. According to Dafoe, some of it lay in disgruntled, time-serving Liberals who had not got jobs; some in Liberals of extreme views who expected more vigorous action from Sifton; but most of it resulted from the Liberals' defeat provincially a year earlier. Sir Charles Tupper and his son Hibbert, who had no love for Sifton, put pressure upon Premier Hugh John Macdonald to oppose the Minister of the

Interior in Brandon. It was the last thing Macdonald wanted to do, but "loyalty to his friends and his party was Hugh John's outstanding characteristic; he felt that Sir John Macdonald's son could refuse no duty laid upon him by his party."[14] To add to the excitement, Sifton and Sir Charles Hibbert Tupper staged a joint debate in Brandon: "the most sensational platform duel ever seen in the West." Hugh John's great personal sacrifice was in vain. He lost out personally and was condemned to political oblivion; his party took only 3 of the province's 7 seats. Disaster had indeed overtaken the Conservatives in the Maritimes and the West. They had won only 17 seats to the Liberals' 39; worse still, they had lost their leader and his two chief lieutenants.

In these provinces, however, the circumstances surrounding the election were simplicity itself compared with those in central Canada. With succeeding elections, the extent to which Quebec was the key to Canadian politics was becoming increasingly evident. Quebec accounted for Sir John Macdonald's great successes in the earlier elections; Quebec trimmed his over-all victories to narrow margins in 1887 and 1891 when it began to doubt his party's ability to serve its interests; Quebec provided all of Laurier's margin of victory in 1896. That election had left a fundamental question unanswered. Was the Liberals' smashing triumph in Quebec simply a passing aberration or was it to become a permanent feature of Canadian politics?

Once in office, Laurier still had to contend with the anticlerical stigma from which the Liberals had never completely freed themselves. Since he himself was less than satisfied with the concessions in education he had secured for Manitoba's Catholics, it was too much to hope that the hierarchy would accept the settlement. Both Archbishop Bégin of Quebec and Archbishop Langevin of St. Boniface were unalterably opposed to it. Laurier's appeal to Rome brought out Archbishop Merry del Val as an apostolic delegate; his visit culminated in the papal encyclical *Affari Vos*, which forced the bishops to accept the compromise. Beyond that, it gained for Laurier the confidence of the authorities at the Vatician; it made the bishops in Quebec change their active hostility to passive dislike, and at times to political neutrality.[15] In the election of 1900 few clerics sought to intervene directly against Laurier. For the Liberals that was a distinct gain.

Given the chance, Laurier had displayed hitherto unsuspected political acumen in other directions. David Mills of Ontario had reason to complain that "no man who had heretofore filled the post of prime minister has cared so little for those who were his colleagues in opposition."[16] Except for Laurier himself, the only representative of the Rouge tradition in his cabinet was C.A. Géoffrion, and he was only a minister without portfolio. But Laurier knew exactly what he was doing, for the "old Liberals," once the very backbone of the party, were now in a minority. To ensure the party's continued success, Laurier saw that it would have to

,appeal to the neutrals and moderates, especially the school of Cartier or the school of Chapleau. That is why he spurned anyone tainted with Mercierism and paid scant attention to the old Rouges when he formed his cabinet. When the latter threatened to erupt with discontent, he simply shuffled them into the lieutenant-governorship, the speakership of the Senate, the judgeships, and the like.[17]

For the leading members of the school of Cartier – Chapleau, Tarte, and Dansereau – he had much more consideration.[18] He would have given Chapleau a second term as Lieutenant-Governor had he not been threatened with dissension from within the party. Chapleau fully understood the difficulty and continued his friendly correspondence with the Prime Minister, in which he reiterated his lifelong views of "une Province unie et forte."[19] Perhaps, before he died in 1898, he had even become reconciled to a Quebec united under Laurier and the Liberal party. Tarte became a senior member of the cabinet as Minister of Public Works and continued his efforts to identify the Liberal party in Quebec with French-Canadian *nationalisme*. Laurier intervened personally for ex-journalist Dansereau, to prevent his dismissal as postmaster of Montreal in 1899. Even at the risk of offending Postmaster General Mulock, he was determined not to have Dansereau resume the editorship of *La Presse* to breathe hot resentment against him. Elsewhere, too, he missed no opportunity to create the atmosphere in which the moderates might be won over. Even before the election of 1900 the development was well on its way; in effect, Laurier was consolidating a new Liberal-Conservative party in Quebec.

Laurier had also managed to avoid the big errors. According to one observer, "when [he] hesitated to send troops to Britain's aid in South Africa he came just as near presenting the Opposition with a fatal issue as is healthy for a Government, but he recovered his judgment in time."[20] The hero of the Colonial Conference in 1897, Laurier had said at an unguarded moment: "Let the watch fires be lit on the hills, and Canada will be the first to respond."[21] He was soon to regret this statement, for as the British difficulties in South Africa worsened and ripened into war, Colonial Secretary Joseph Chamberlain looked to Canada for assistance. Laurier said that nothing could be done without summoning Parliament and hoped that would solve the question.[22] That was wishful thinking. When he returned from an international conference in Chicago on October 12, 1899, he found English Canada thoroughly stirred up in favour of Canadian participation. Hugh Graham of the Montreal *Star* had started it, but the Ontario newspapers, including the Liberal *Globe*, soon followed suit. At the same time the French-Canadian press was saying that the war meant nothing to Canada. *La Presse* put it this way: "We French Canadians belong to one country, Canada; Canada is for us the whole world; but the English Canadians have two countries, one here and one across the sea."[23] This deep-seated difference in outlook was to produce a succession of crises in Canadian national life and markedly affect both national parties.

Laurier now acted quickly and thus avoided the "fatal mistake" which might have cost him dearly. On October 13 his government decided to equip and send one thousand volunteers to the Transvaal. He had little enthusiasm for the war in South Africa, but he foresaw racial cleavage unless some accommodation was made to public sentiment in English Canada. He told Bourassa, "if there is anything to which I have given my political life, it is to try to promote unity, harmony, and amity between the diverse elements of this country."[24] Though his intentions were good, he saw that there were other Canadians who "traded in Imperialism in order to serve paltry political ends, and nursed racial bigotry for party purposes."[25]

This was the first election in which one party overreached itself in presenting two entirely different faces. In Quebec the Conservatives denounced Laurier because he had incurred heavy expenditures for the defence of Imperial interests; they continually quoted out of context Tupper's statement: "Laurier is too English for me"; their newspapers described the Prime Minister as one who had "sacrificed the sweat of our workmen, the backbone of our industries, even the blood of our children" solely to gain British honours.[26] But in Ontario he was the man who was hesitant and faint-hearted about assisting British arms in South Africa. There, however, the Conservative press and politicians generally attacked Laurier through Tarte whom they regarded as the master of the administration and its chief evil genius. They delighted to recall Tarte's earlier remark that Canada should send no troops to South Africa without parliamentary approval, or his later one in Paris that Canada had not sent troops to the Transvaal but merely dressed and transported volunteers.[27]

The Hamilton *Spectator*, the Toronto *World*, and the Toronto *Mail and Empire* sought to outdo each other. The Toronto *News* had no inhibitions whatever; British Canadians, it declared, would have to find a means, through the ballot or otherwise, of "emancipating themselves from the dominance of an inferior people that peculiar circumstances have placed in authority in the Dominion."[28] Even the Governor General, Lord Minto, who was no great admirer of Laurier and the Liberals, called such writings "perfectly monstrous." In England, he said, a man was not considered disloyal if he disapproved of the war. "Here, if he is only lukewarm, and is a French Canadian, he must be a rebel."[29]

The stupidities of the Ontario Conservatives were all grist to Tarte's mill. On the eve of the election he published a 38-page brochure quoting from articles in the Conservative press of Ontario that were hostile to French Canadians. The Conservative candidates in Quebec protested what they called an incendiary appeal to racial hate and prejudice.[30] Tarte's action was not unjustified, and it was certainly good politics. The Quebec Conservatives ought to have found another villain; they ought to have denounced their counterparts in Ontario for giving Tarte an opportunity that no clever politician would miss. It was the first of many similar opportunities that the Ontario extremists would provide their Quebec opponents in the elections to come.

The same Laurier who had done far too little for his opponents in Ontario, had done far too much for some of his supporters in Quebec. Tarte wanted no Canadian participation in British wars unless there was Canadian representation in the councils of the Empire. He went along with the despatch of volunteers to South Africa only because the order-in-council authorizing it contained a no-precedent clause. For Henri Bourassa the government's action was a precedent for all time to come, and he resigned from the Commons in protest. This disagreement between himself and Laurier "contained the seeds of future political crises . . . over the problem of imperialism."[31]

Three months before the election there were rumours that Bourassa would establish a third party which would rally most of Quebec and those English voters who were hostile to the policies of Joseph Chamberlain and who were admirers of the school of Gladstone.[32] Rumour also had it that Dominique Monet, J.A.C. Ethier, and Charles Angers, three Liberal M.P.'s who thought as he did, would join him, but that his chief recruit would be J. Israel Tarte. In the end it all fizzled out. When Tarte returned from the International Exposition in Paris, he went immediately into private conference with Laurier and in short order he was at his old job of masterminding the Liberal campaign in Quebec. As for Bourassa, he was still an admirer of Laurier and, except for the South African issue, he fully supported the government's policies. Consequently, he and his three colleagues were also at Laurier's side when the campaign opened.

No Prime Minister has ever had more factors working for him in Quebec than did Laurier in 1900: prosperity, the absence of clerical opposition, his own appeal to Quebec *nationalisme*, the increasing support of the moderates, a united party, the fanaticism of the Conservative extremists in Ontario, and an incredible act of stupidity on the part of Sir Charles Tupper. When *La Presse*, the most widely-read of the province's newspapers, asked for the journalistic direction of the Conservative campaign, it found that Tupper had already promised it to his friend Hugh Graham, publisher of the Montreal *Star*. Worse still, the chief Conservative organizer in the province was to be the Anglo-Saxon Henry Dalby, an editor of the *Star*.[33] As it turned out, Dalby organized only the English districts: Bergeron the district of Montreal; Caron the district of Trois Rivières; and T.C. Casgrain the district of Quebec. But the damage had been done. While *La Presse* did not support the Liberals, it did not support the Conservatives either. Throughout the campaign it revelled in Laurier's every triumph and gloried in the adulation accorded him across the land.

SIR JOHN'S RIGHTFUL SUCCESSOR.

SPIRIT OF SIR JOHN—My old party may have my effigy with them in this campaign, but the record and influence of my life as a statesman is with you, Sir Wilfrid.

by J. W. Bengough. The Globe, *Toronto, October 26, 1900. Courtesy of* The Globe and Mail, *Toronto.*

The Conservatives had virtually asked to be routed in Quebec; and they were. In the debacle, only eight Conservatives were successful, three of them Anglo-Saxon. What did the Ontario extremists gain by jeopardizing the very foundation of their party in Quebec? They gained only an additional twelve seats in their own province, four of them formerly held by Patrons or McCarthyites. Laurier had expected much more from Ontario. Had he not introduced British preference and assisted British arms in South Africa at the cost of endangering his own position in Quebec? Torontonians, it is true, had cheered him by the thousands in Massey Hall, but had not voted for him. Henceforth, says Willison, "he turned to his own Province and his own people. He never wooed Ontario again. . . . But from 1900 he saw Bourassa as an ever-present menace, against which he believed he could not rely upon Ontario"[34]

Across the Dominion the Liberals had a majority of 53 seats, 49 of which were provided by Quebec alone. It was not only the French of Quebec who voted for them, however. In New Brunswick the Acadians of Kent and Gloucester, once staunchly Conservative, went just as strongly Liberal. So did the French Canadians of eastern Ontario. Sir Charles Tupper had one explanation: the principles of responsible government, he said, had been "momentarily smothered by an appeal of a French leader to his compatriots as Frenchmen rather than as Canadians."[35] An independent Conservative newspaper, the Ottawa *Evening Journal*, knew better:

> When the Conservatives get enough sense to cease attacking Laurier and Tarte ·for alleged disloyalty and Frenchism, which inevitably solidifies Quebec behind the Laurier Administration, they may regain power at Ottawa. . . . The extraordinary spectacle of a politically almost unanimous Province is due chiefly to the tactics of some crazy Conservatives in Ontario who have Francophobia on the brain.[36]

FOOTNOTES

1. See J.W. Bengough, *Cartoons of the 1900 Campaign contributed to the "Daily Globe"* (Toronto: Poole Publishing Co., 1900).

2. J.W. Dafoe, *Clifford Sifton in Relation to His Times* (Toronto: The Macmillan Company of Canada, 1931), pp. 201-202.

3. Halifax *Morning Chronicle*, October 13, 1900.

4. *Ibid.*, September 8, 1900.

5. *Ibid.*, November 3, 1900.

6. O.D. Skelton, *Life and Letters of Sir Wilfred Laurier*, II [Toronto: Oxford University Press (S.B. Gundy), 1921], p. 47.

7. M.E. Nichols, "A Forecast of the General Elections," *The Canadian Magazine*, XV (October, 1900), p. 547.

8. Dafoe, *Sifton*, p. 200.

9. *Ibid.*

10. Henry Borden (ed.), *Robert Laird Borden: His Memoirs*, I (Toronto: Macmillan Company of Canada, 1938), p. 70.

11. See Halifax *Herald*, November 5, 1900.

12. W. Stewart Wallace, *The Memoirs of the Rt. Hon. Sir George E. Foster* (Toronto: The Macmillan Company of Canada, 1933), p. 112.

13. Dafoe, *Sifton*, p. 202.

14. *Ibid.*, p. 203.

15. H. Blair Neatby, "Laurier and a Liberal Quebec: A Study in Political Management" (unpublished doctoral thesis, University of Toronto, 1956), pp. 166-67.

16. *Ibid.*, p. 212.

17. *Ibid.*, pp. 212-13.

18. *Ibid.*, pp. 213-18.

19. *Ibid.*, p. 214.

20. Nichols, "A Forecast of the General Elections," p. 547.

21. Mason Wade, *The French Canadians 1760-1967*, (Toronto: The Macmillan Company of Canada, 1955), p. 474.

22. Neatby, "Laurier and a Liberal Quebec," p. 176.

23. Wade, *French Canadians*, p. 479.

24. *Ibid.*, p. 484.

25. J.S. Willison, *Sir Wilfrid Laurier and the Liberal Party*, II (Toronto: Morang and Company, 1903), p. 329.

26. See quotation from *Le Trifluvien* of Trois Rivières, *ibid.*, pp. 333-34.

27. *Ibid.*, p. 334.

28. Wade, *French Canadians*, p. 486.

29. *Ibid.*

30. Robert Rumilly, *Histoire de la Province de Québec*, IX (Montreal: Editions Bernard Valiquette, 1942), p. 257. Translated by the author.

31. Neatby, "Laurier and a Liberal Quebec," p. 184.

32. Rumilly, *Histoire*, IX, p. 224.

33. *Ibid.*, pp. 228-29.

34. Sir John Willison, *Reminiscences Political and Personal* (Toronto: McClelland & Stewart Limited, 1919), p. 307.

35. E.M. Saunders, *Life and Letters of the Rt. Hon. Sir Charles Tupper*, II (New York: Frederick A. Stokes, 1916), p. 246.

36. Quoted from the Ottawa *Evening Journal* in the Halifax *Morning Chronicle*, November 9, 1900.

	Seats	Candidates			Elected						Popular Vote						Total
		C.	L.	O.	C.	%	L.	%	O.	%	C.	%	L.	%	O.	%	
Nova Scotia	20	20	20	—	5	25.0	15	75.0	—	—	50,810	48.3	54,384	51.7	—	—	105,194
New Brunswick	14	13	14	1	5	35.7	9	64.3	—	—	32,638	47.8	35,401	51.9	228	0.3	68,267
Prince Edward Island	5	5	5	—	2	40.0	3	60.0	—	—	10,139	48.2	10,887	51.8	—	—	21,026
Quebec	65	64	65	7	8	12.3	57	87.7	—	—	103,253	43.5	132,761	55.9	1,306	0.6	237,320
Ontario	92	88	91	8	55	59.8	37	40.2	—	—	212,413	49.7	206,998	48.5	7,762	1.8	427,173
Manitoba	7	7	7	—	3	42.9	4	57.1	—	—	20,117	48.2	21,597	51.8	—	—	41,714
British Columbia	6	6	6	2	2	33.3	4	66.7	—	—	10,814	40.9	12,153	45.9	3,484	13.2	26,451
N.W.T.	4	4	4	—	—	—	4	100.0	—	—	10,606	44.9	13,012	55.1	—	—	23,618
Total	213	207	212	18	80	37.6	133	62.4	—	—	450,790	47.4	487,193	51.2	12,780	1.3	950,763

Elected by acclamation: L. (4): N.B. (1); Que. (1); Ont. (2).

C. (1): Ont. (1).

Others (votes polled): N.B. I. (1) 228.

Que. (7): I. (6) 501; other L. (1) 805.

Ont. (8): Lab. (2) 272; I. (2) 1,893; I.L. (1) 1,180; other L. (3) 4,417.

B.C. (2): Lab. (1) 2,652; other L. (1) 832.

Tenth

General Election

"THE TWENTIETH CENTURY SHALL BE THE CENTURY OF CANADA"

There was no contest in the election of 1904. Canadians, generally, rallied so strongly to Laurier that it was simply a question of how big the government's majority would be. The overriding question was not hard to find. "Perhaps," says Dafoe, "there never was a time when satisfaction with existing conditions and confidence in the future were so general as in the year 1904. There was hardly a cloud in the sky."[1]

By this time the boom had accelerated to unprecedented proportions. All the indices of economic activity – railway earnings, wage rates, employment rates, and so on – pointed upwards. In the preceding year, 130,000 people had come to western Canada and 57,000 homesteaders had taken up land. The West had begun to fill up; yet, despite the influx of immigrants there was practically no unemployment. The Canadian Pacific had, in fact, been unable to carry out its construction plans because of the shortage of labour. Although the government had been anything but niggardly in its expenditures, it had still piled up a surplus of $15 million. Never had a prime minister and his colleagues predicted more correctly. The expanding West had brought prosperity to the whole country, and in the prevailing optimism it appeared as if the good times would go on indefinitely.[2]

Not unnaturally, the election raised the question of whether this happy state of affairs resulted from the acts of government or in spite of them. Laurier attributed the boom to his government working hand in hand with Providence. "We spent our time in action, trying to improve for the Canadian people . . . the benefits which Providence has showered upon us."[3] When Sir George Foster gave the credit to the West, Clifford Sifton retorted: "Well, perhaps . . . but the west was here from 1885 to 1896 without the country being prosperous."[4] The voters, not wanting to disturb the status quo, accepted the government's contentions at face value.

By this time the Liberals had stamped themselves upon the public mind as the party not only of national development but also of national unity. In creating both images Laurier stood out above everyone else. He considered the cementing of the union to be his chief mission in life. His party's newspapers made the most of it. During the campaign they especially played up his speech in St. Paul's Cathedral at the time of Queen Victoria's Diamond Jubilee:

> This cathedral is the image of the nation that I hope to see Canada become. As long as I live, as long as I have the power to labour in the service of my country, I shall repel the idea of changing the nature of the different elements. I want the marble to remain the marble; I want the granite to remain the granite; I want the oak to remain the oak; I want the sturdy Scotchman to remain the Scotchman; I want the brainy Englishman to remain the Englishman; I want the warm-hearted Irishman to remain the Irishman; I want to take all these elements and build a nation that will be foremost amongst the great Powers of the world.[5]

As for national development, even though Laurier was no economist and had no interest in statistics, yet from platforms placarded with "Laurier and the larger Canada" he could talk about Canada, "the star towards which all men who love progress and freedom shall come for the next hundred years," with such fervour and eloquent simplicity that the whole performance was singularly persuasive and highly influential with all who witnessed it. Even the Toronto *News* was led to admit that Laurier had "that strange and mysterious gift, which Sir John Macdonald possessed in almost equal degree, of touching the heart and imagination of the people."[6]

There was another Laurier, less conspicuous and much tougher, whose acts also became election issues. This was the Laurier who in 1903 decided to build the National Transcontinental Railway without consulting his Minister of Railways, A.G. Blair, and then let Blair go when he disagreed. It was also the Laurier who in 1904 defended to the hilt the right of his acting Minister of Militia, Sydney Fisher, to remove an active Tory politician from a list of militia officers, and who decided that the Earl of Dundonald, the officer commanding the Canadian militia, could not be retained after he denounced publicly "this gross instance of political interference." "So long as there is a Liberal government in Canada," said Laurier, "the civil power shall rule the military."[7]

Above all, this was the Laurier who did not hesitate to get rid of Tarte when he grossly violated the conventions of cabinet protocol. Like the school of Cartier generally, Tarte had always been and still remained a protectionist. During Laurier's absence from the country in 1902, he took it upon himself to make a round of speeches advocating an upward revision of the tariff even though the cabinet had decided to maintain the status quo. This was extraordinary conduct even for the extraordinary Tarte. Skelton and Dafoe see it as sheer opportunism.[8] Tarte, they feel, expected a change in leadership, for news had come from Europe that Laurier was exhausted and ill. Would it not have been natural for him to think that he had the advantage in any tussle for the succession? Quebec was already his – or so he believed – and Ontario might well fall to an apostle of protection. But is it really necessary to explain Tarte's actions by sudden excessive ambition? Why not accept, as Blair Neatby does, the views of his contemporaries that this was "merely Tarte being carried away by his convictions again."[9] In any case, two days after Laurier arrived back in Ottawa Tarte was no longer a minister of the Crown.

Laurier's Ontario opponents could no longer doubt that he was Master of the Administration. The Tarte incident is even more far-reaching in its significance; it is one of the reasons why Neatby thinks that 1902 may be singled out as the date when Quebec became solidly Liberal.[10] That is the year in which Laurier spurned Joseph Chamberlain's blandishments at a Colonial Conference and rejected the Colonial Secretary's idea of setting up a permanent advisory council on Imperial defence. To Bourassa and his dissident Liberals, who still held Laurier suspect because he had sent troops to South Africa, the action was reassuring. They may not have been entirely convinced, but they rallied strongly to the Liberal cause. Even though Laurier forced Tarte to resign, he still held on to the school of Cartier. Despite Tarte's confidence that he could lead it back to the Conservative party, he failed. The man who had been so long the kingmaker was kingmaker no longer. He had met his match in Laurier, under whom Quebec had become almost solidly Liberal.

The Blair, Dundonald, and Tarte episodes all played a part in the election of 1904. Apparently Blair was involved in a curious conspiracy which was "turned into *opera bouffe* by Laurier's decisive and timely interference."[11] In the end he spoke not a word during the campaign. The mere mention of Dundonald's name brought cheers at Conservative meetings throughout the Dominion. Yet the affair seems to have harmed neither Frederick Borden, the Minister of Militia and Defence in Nova Scotia, nor Sydney Fisher in the Eastern Townships. In Ottawa, where the *Citizen* played up the incident and urged the voters to "keep both hands on the Union Jack," its tactics may actually have backfired because of the large French-Canadian population. In Toronto, on the other hand, while the issue no doubt helped the Conservative candidates, they would likely have won without it.[12]

From the Tarte incident Laurier suffered even less, if at all. To Tarte's chagrin, he discovered that Frederick Monk, the leader of Quebec's federal Conservatives, would not sit on the same platform with him. Worse still, he found that, after doing as much as anyone to build up Laurier's position in Quebec, he was unable to undo his own handiwork. Try as he might, he could not improve Conservative fortunes in the Quebec provincial elections of 1904. Realizing the futility of struggling against the impossible, he gave up active politicking, and confined himself to writing editorials for *La Patrie*. The one-time mastermind of Quebec politics could devise nothing to cope with the political magic of Wilfrid Laurier.

Another who had to contend with the same formidable antagonist was the new Conservative leader, Robert Borden. The choice of Borden by the Conservative caucus shortly before Parliament opened in 1901, came as a surprise. The veteran George Eulas Foster wanted the leadership, but influential elements in the party had concluded that "his wonderful ability in debate was not always matched by equal good judgment."[13] His personal defeat in 1900, thanks to Tupper's ill-conceived tactics, also told against him. Borden, in contrast, did not want to be leader. He felt that four years' parliamentary experience was not enough. Only reluctantly did he succumb to pressure and accept the position for a year; he still had it almost twenty years later.[14]

Of one thing Borden was certain – the Conservative arguments ought not to be as diffused in 1904 as they had been in the previous election. His own manifesto set the style in this direction.[15] It called for the reform of electoral practices, declared that "the principles upon which Sir John A. Macdonald based his fiscal policy in 1878 guide us today," and promised to seek a preference for Canadian goods in the British market. Apart from these things, the manifesto dealt only with Laurier's proposals for the National Transcontinental. This was the issue to which Borden devoted most of his attention, and the one which altogether dwarfed the other specific issues.

To fit in with Laurier's grandiose concept of Canada unlimited, there had to be a grandiose plan, and the National Transcontinental was part of it. In essence, Laurier proposed a second transcontinental railway from Moncton to the Pacific. The Grand Trunk Pacific, for all practical purposes an adjunct of the Grand Trunk, was to construct, maintain, and operate the western section; it was also to lease, maintain, and operate the eastern section running from Moncton to Winnipeg, which was to be built by a government commission. On the prospects of the line Laurier let himself be completely carried away. It would become, he prophesied, the great highway for trade between Europe and Asia:

> I believe I will live long enough to see that Railway built and to see the merchandise of Europe and Asia passing and re-passing along it as well as the trade of Canada. I hope to see steamers leaving Quebec and Montreal loaded with the products of the Orient and returning again with cargoes for the West to be shipped *via* Port Simpson to the trading centres of the East.[16]

No Canadian, it has been said, is more inconsistent than he who follows one party consistently. The parties appeared to have made full turn between 1882 and 1904; Borden's arguments against the second transcontinental railway bear a striking resemblance to Blake's against the first.[17] History, however, has proved Borden the better prophet. The Liberal folly, he thought, resulted partly from the fact that the Canadian Pacific, which the Liberals still viewed unsympathetically, had proved to be "an enduring monument to the foresight and enterprise of a Conservative administration." Now, in the days of development and prosperity, he alleged, Laurier wanted a second transcontinental line as "an even more conspicuous monument to a Liberal administration."[18]

What perturbed Borden most was that after seven years of delay the government was proceeding without a thorough investigation of Canada's railway needs. It was just not good enough for the Prime Minister to say blithely that "this is not the time for deliberation, this is a time for action," or that "the flood of tide is upon us that leads on to fortune; if we let it pass it may never recur again."[19] It was also not good enough to proceed with a project for which the country supplied nine-tenths of the cash and credit (about $135 million) and then hand over the only portion of the line likely to prove profitable – the section west of Winnipeg – to a corporation that provided only one-tenth of the cost.[20] It was positively dangerous and corrupting to permit what amounted to a partnership between the new line and the Grand Trunk. Even more than before, the Grand Trunk would build up Portland, Maine, at the expense of Canadian ports. Worse still was the prospect of a railway-owned government. "I may go further," warned Borden, "and say that the issue is . . . whether the people shall own the railways or the railways own the people."[21]

What was the Conservative alternative? To say the least, confused. Borden thought the obvious solution was to amalgamate the Grand Trunk, which needed a western outlet, with an entirely western line: the Canadian Northern of Mackenzie and Mann. But Laurier had tried that and failed. So, during the session of 1903, the Conservative leader put forward a proposal that looked like a jigsaw puzzle and had so many pieces that the Liberals called it a crazy quilt. Among other things he would have extended the government-owned Intercolonial Railway to Georgian Bay; brought the section of the C.P.R. between North Bay and Fort William under government ownership and let it be used by the C.P.R., Grand Trunk, I.C.R., and Canadian Northern; granted moderate assistance to the Grand Trunk Pacific to build a line as far west as Edmonton; and proceeded with a line from Quebec to Winnipeg only as a colonization road and only as the circumstances warranted it.[22] Such projects, he argued, were both prudent and adapted to the country's needs.

It is surprising, therefore, that Borden's election manifesto declared his intention of "constructing the new transcontinental railway as a public work,"[23] and that a telegram he sent to Sir Charles Hibbert Tupper promised that he would start it immediately, extend it to the Pacific, and expropriate any private railways which might suitably form part of the project.[24]

Apparently the clamours of his western supporters had borne fruit. Yet, between these assurances and his statements on the hustings there was something of a discrepancy. His speeches still seemed to favour a piecemeal approach, with the added proviso that whatever the public paid for, it ought to own and control.

Such wobbling presented to the Liberals a glorious opportunity they did not miss. Early in the campaign Laurier described Borden's alternative plan as "a perfect Tower of Babel and a confusion of languages."[25] Later, when Borden seemed to change course, he said his scheme "lasted just the life of a rose – bloomed in one morning and the next morning was no more."[26] Laurier also had his innings against Conservative newspapers which denounced the railway monopolists and advocated a "People's Transcontinental."[27]

> Governments [he said] can build railways . . . but Governments cannot operate railways. The reason is very obvious. Railways have been compelled to carry passengers and to carry freight, but it is an act of commerce, and I say to you, my fellow-countrymen, that Governments never were intended to go into business as men engage in commerce. It is not part of the responsibility of government to do anything of the kind.[28]

The Conservative party, he continued, was no longer the party of Macdonald and Tupper; Borden had torn it from its moorings and embarked it on the course of Populism and other demagogical developments imported from across the border.[29]

He had hit upon what was a sore spot for many Conservatives. Although Borden had adopted public ownership in only one instance because of special circumstances, the idea of a government expropriating private enterprise and running railways was quite foreign and altogether repellent to the financial and business interests which were normally associated with the Conservative party. Liberal newspapers had a field day in reciting from the columns of Conservative papers like the Montreal *Gazette*, the Montreal *Star*, and the Toronto *Mail and Empire*, which had condemned public ownership in the past; and in singling out prominent Conservative businessmen like Herbert Holt, J.D. Rolland, and Hugh A. Allan, who had denounced it during the campaign.[30] This raises an interesting theoretical question: how far can a party depart from its traditional policies before it alienates a substantial number of its regular supporters?

The railway issue also indirectly produced an extraordinary conspiracy against the government which "for sheer melodrama and sheer fatuity has never been equalled in Canada."[31] To this day the full extent of its ramifications is unknown. It appears certain, however, that motive lay in Mackenzie and Mann's failure to be recognized as the contractor for the second transcontinental line, and their desire to engineer the triumph of a Conservative government that would be indebted to them. It is also certain that its leading figures were David Russell, well known as a promoter in Saint John and Montreal and as a participant in several Mackenzie and Mann ventures, and J.N. Greenshields, a Montreal lawyer, who was solicitor for Mackenzie and Mann. In part, the plot involved the purchase of several Liberal newspapers and the switching of their support to Borden. There were other ingredients as well. A.G. Blair was to take the stump against the government; charges of corruption were to be made against several cabinet ministers; and Liberal candidates were to resign on nomination day because of these revelations, allowing their Conservative opponents to be elected by acclamation.[32]

Only the first part of the conspiracy got off the ground, and not far at that. Early in the campaign, a former Liberal newspaper in Saint John came under the control of Russell, and presumably Blair. Then, on October 16, came the first real bombshell. *La Presse*, it was rumoured, had been sold to a number of influential Conservatives. Two days later there was a second bombshell. Blair confirmed his resignation as Chairman of the Railway Commission and reiterated his opposition to the Grand Trunk Pacific. Immediately the mystery deepened and excitement heightened. What would happen next? Nothing did; *"La Presse* was practically neutral and Mr. Blair remained a political sphinx."[33] Rumour had it that Laurier called on Blair in Ottawa, and that Blair concluded that silence was golden. The rumour was never denied. As for *La Presse*, Laurier simply told its publishers that if it changed its policy he would give the public the full story about its sale to English-speaking speculators. That would have killed it, for it would have lost much of its circulation, so great was the strength of Laurier in the Quebec of 1904.[34] The conspiracy had fizzled out. None of the other Canadian elections has produced a Hollywood-type melodrama to compare with this misadventure of 1904.

Nothing would have availed against Laurier the man, prosperity, and the National Transcontinental in 1904. In western Canada the Liberals doubted that Borden would build a second transcontinental at all. The *Winnipeg Free Press* asked its readers in bold-face type: "Do you want the [Grand Trunk Pacific] Contract torn up?"[35] Obviously they did not, and they thought it better to be sure of getting the line by voting Liberal than to risk not getting it by voting Conservative. The result was that Laurier got 7 of Manitoba's 10 seats, 7 of the Territories' 10 seats, and all of British Columbia's 7 seats. In effect, the Liberals won all 10 seats which the West gained from the redistribution of 1903.

In the Maritimes, even Conservatives looked on Laurier's railway plans with favour. There, Liberal newspapers followed their western Canadian counterparts in singling out prominent adherents of the opposition party who favoured the government's railway policies. Borden spoke disconsolately of a leading Halifax Conservative who was enthusiastic about temporary prosperity secured through enormous expenditures of money furnished by the people themselves.[36] Prince Edward Island, the only province not directly concerned with any of the railway plans, gave three of its four seats to the Conservatives, largely because of the operation of local factors. In New Brunswick, Blair's defection undoubtedly hurt the Liberals; it lost them Saint John, and they won only a bare majority of the province's thirteen seats. In Nova Scotia, however, the voters totally rejected the Conservatives' contention that the G.T.P. contract would accrue to the advantage of Portland, not Halifax. Borden lost out in Halifax, and his seventeen colleagues all went down to defeat. Nova Scotia returned "a solid Liberal eighteen" – the first time in Canadian electoral history that a province with a substantial number of seats had given them all to one party. Fielding had become a hero in his own right in his native province.

As usual, Laurier was acclaimed in Ontario. This time he chided his Toronto audience: "You cheer me, but you do not vote for me."[37] It did no good. Toronto still gave its 5 seats to the Conservatives, although George Eulas Foster, who had moved from New Brunswick, won the narrowest of victories in North Toronto. Generally the same forces operated in Ontario as elsewhere, enabling the Liberals to reduce the Conservative majority from 18 to 10. They might have done better if it had not been for R.A. Gamey's charges of corruption against the worn-out provincial Liberal administration. Allen B. Aylesworth's defeat in Durham was certainly to be laid at Gamey's doorstep.

This time the Liberals in Quebec could not capitalize upon the utterances of the Ontario extremists because religious and racial peace prevailed. It would not have made any difference, however, for Laurier had made Quebec solidly Liberal. Because of his persuasive powers, the nationalists Henri Bourassa and Armand Lavergne ran under the Liberal banner; Laurier simply told Bourassa he must have him to keep imperialists like Sam Hughes and T. Chase Casgrain in their place.[38] The Conservatives had no leader, for Monk had resigned. They did have two millionaire candidates, but one of them, William Price, went down to defeat in Rimouski. Nevertheless, they managed to increase their Quebec contingent from 8 to 11 members, 5 of them English-speaking.

French Canadians were obviously proud to see all of Canada responding to Laurier's gospel of *la grande patrie canadienne* extending from one ocean to another. He was at the height of his political fortunes. The Quebec Conservatives had been reduced to such a state that they would never again challenge him. Opposition would have to come from another group in another direction. Laurier appeared, above all, to have succeeded in his chief mission: promoting racial harmony. He had done it by taking his cue from John A. Macdonald: he had played down the things that divide Canadians and stressed the material expansion upon which they agree. Many may have had their doubts, but all thrilled to his pronouncement in Massey Hall that "the twentieth century shall be the century of Canada."[39]

FOOTNOTES

1. J.W. Dafoe, *Clifford Sifton in Relation to His Times* (Toronto: The Macmillan Company of Canada, 1931), p. 271.

2. *Ibid.*, pp. 271-72.

3. From his speech in Toronto; see Halifax *Morning Chronicle*, October 15, 1904.

4. Dafoe, *Sifton*, p. 272.

5. Halifax *Morning Chronicle*, September 30, 1904.

6. Quoted from the Toronto *News*, *ibid.*, October 21, 1904.

7. O.D. Skelton, *Life and Letters of Sir Wilfrid Laurier*, II [Toronto: Oxford University Press (S.B. Gundy), 1921], p. 201.

8. *Ibid.*, p. 178; J.W. Dafoe, *Laurier: A Study in Canadian Politics* (Toronto: Thomas Allen & Son Ltd., 1922), p. 117.

9. H. Blair Neatby, "Laurier and a Liberal Quebec: A Study in Political Management" (unpublished doctoral thesis, University of Toronto, 1956), p. 236.

10. *Ibid.*, p. 252.

11. Dafoe, *Laurier*, p. 117; *infra.* pp. 102-103.

12. *Canadian Annual Review*, 1904, (Toronto: The Canadian Review Company, 1905), pp. 204-209.

13. Henry Borden (ed.), *Robert Laird Borden: His Memoirs*, I (Toronto: The Macmillan Company of Canada, 1938), p. 73.

14. *Ibid.*

15. See Halifax *Herald*, October 26, 1904.

16. *Canadian Annual Review*, 1904, p. 175.

17. *Supra*, p. 39.

18. Borden, *Memoirs*, I, pp. 109-10.

19. *Ibid.*, p. 112.

20. *Canadian Annual Review*, 1904, p. 177.

21. *Ibid.*, p. 180.

22. Borden, *Memoirs*, I, p. 116.

23. See Halifax *Herald*, October 26, 1904.

24. *Canadian Annual Review*, 1904, pp. 196-97.

25. *Ibid.*, p. 175.

26. *Ibid.*, pp. 183-84.

27. See, for example, Halifax *Herald*, October 10 and 22, 1904.

28. *Canadian Annual Review*, 1904, p. 196.

29. Halifax *Morning Chronicle*, October 19, 1904.

30. *Ibid.*, October 24, 1904.

31. Skelton, *Laurier*, II, p. 203.

32. Robert Rumilly, *Histoire de la Province de Québec*, XI (Montreal: Editions Bernard Valiquette, 1943), p. 172. Translated by J.M. Beck.

33. *Canadian Annual Review*, 1904, p. 227.

34. Neatby, "Laurier and a Liberal Quebec," pp. 250-51.

35. *Canadian Annual Review*, 1904, p. 198.

36. Borden, *Memoirs*, I, p. 117.

37. Skelton, *Laurier*, II, p. 217.

38. Rumilly, *Histoire*, XI, p. 162.

39. Halifax *Morning Chronicle*, October 19, 1904.

1904

	Seats	Candidates			Elected						Popular Vote						Total
		C.	L.	O.	C.	%	L.	%	O.	%	C.	%	L.	%	O.	%	
Nova Scotia	18	18	18	4	—	—	18	100.0	—	—	46,131	44.5	54,873	52.9	2,647	2.6	103,651
New Brunswick	13	13	13	1	6	46.2	7	53.8	—	—	35,503	48.8	37,158	51.0	138	0.2	72,799
Prince Edward Island	4	4	4	—	3	75.0	1	25.0	—	—	14,986	50.9	14,441	49.1	—	—	29,427
Quebec	65	62	65	4	11	16.9	53	81.5	1	1.5	107,102	41.7	144,992	56.4	4,970	1.9	257,064
Ontario	86	86	86	3	48	55.8	38	44.2	—	—	223,627	50.3	219,871	49.5	759	0.2	444,257
Manitoba	10	8	10	2	3	30.0	7	70.0	—	—	20,119	41.8	23,909	49.7	4,094	8.5	48,122
British Columbia	7	6	7	6	—	—	7	100.0	—	—	9,781	38.8	12,458	49.5	2,945	11.7	25,184
N.W.T.	10	10	10	2	3	30.0	7	70.0	—	—	19,367	41.5	27,173	58.2	136	0.3	46,676
Yukon	1	1	1	—	1	100.0	—	—	—	—	2,113	58.6	1,495	41.4	—	—	3,608
Total	214	208	214	22	75	35.0	138	64.5	1	0.5	478,729	46.4	536,370	52.0	15,689	1.5	1,030,788

Elected by acclamation: L. (4): Que. (2); Man. (1); B.C. (1).

Others elected: Que. (1): I.L. (1).

Others (votes polled): N.S. (4): Lab. (1) 869; other L. (1) 1,653; I. (2) 125.
N.B. (1): I. (1) 138.
Que. (4): I. (3) 522; I.L. (1) 4,448.
Ont. (3): I. (3) 759.
Man. (2): Lab. (1) 1,290; other L. (1) 2,804.
B.C. (6): Soc. (2) 1,077; I. (4) 1,868.
N.W.T. (2): I. (2) 136.

Note: In this table Joseph Girard, the Conservative member for Chicoutimi and Saguenay in the last Parliament and again a candidate in the same riding, is treated as an Independent Liberal. He defeated the official Liberal candidate and was soon recognized as a Liberal M.P.

Eleventh

General Election

THE "MUCK-RAKERS" HAVE A FIELD DAY

The eleventh general election was one of the most unpleasant of Canada's federal elections. Even before the campaign commenced, the *Winnipeg Free Press* expressed its concern about the behaviour of Canadians during elections. It had visions of "a babel of wrangling and abuse, crimination and recrimination," which would "speedily transform the people into a lot of political dancing Dervishes, whirling about in the madness of party hysteria and bereft for the time being of the qualities of kindliness, generosity, sympathy and justice." There would, it feared, be such a "sudden stripping away of the surface conventions and [such a] recrudescence of savage habits of thought" that the astonished onlooker could only conclude that Canadians were still "a primitive people."[1] It prophesied better than it knew.

Laurier did not want it this way. Gutter politics was far from the mind of one who could now assert for himself and his party all three of the roles which successful prime ministers have stressed to justify their continuance in office. He reiterated, for one thing, that his was the party of national development. "We have been 12 years in office," he told the people of Cornwall, "and these years will be remembered in the history of Canada. In them Canada has been lifted from the humble position of a humble colony to that of a nation. . . . In 1908 Canada has become a star to which is directed the gaze of the whole civilized world. That is what we have done."[2]

No less strongly, Laurier extolled his party as a device for promoting national unity. At Strathroy he declared that "the Liberal Party is broad enough, [and] Liberal principles are large enough to give an equal share of Justice and Liberty to all men;"[3] at Sorel he boasted that "if there is one thing of which I am proud it is that I have succeeded in establishing peace and conciliation between all the various elements and races of which our population is composed."[4]

Finally, the Liberals were the party with the leader who best embodied Canada's hopes and aspirations. Laurier had, in fact, re-created his party in his own image. Also, about this time Graham Wallas was showing how important it was for politicians to get the public to feel kindly toward themselves.[5] Laurier had been more successful in exploiting this impulse than perhaps any other Canadian politician. Writing in the Boston *Transcript,* E.W. Thomson said of him: "He makes me feel better, [many people] say. Try to get at what they mean by 'better,' and you discover that they mean just better. Not elated, rather warmed, kinder, more good."[6] In 1908 Laurier was not averse to exploiting this feeling with a bit of pathos:

> Not many years now remain to me. The snows of winter have taken the place of spring; but, however I may show the ravages of time my heart still remains young, . . . I want to carry the coming General Election in order to finish this great work [the second transcontinental railway], and when it is completed I shall be content to say, with the Prophet of old, 'Lord now let Thy servant depart in peace.'[7]

Every Liberal newspaper proclaimed, seemingly without end, "Let Laurier finish his work – Laissons Laurier finir sa tâche," and every Liberal meeting sang with gusto:

Work! Work! Work! Work!
Let Laurier finish his work.
Talk! Talk! Talk! Talk!
Let Borden keep on with his talk.

Although the public exhibited its old kindliness towards Laurier, it was noticeably less enthusiastic for his party and government. The Laurier administration had passed its zenith; it had "come to the end of its programme of big issues."[8] It is true that Laurier did promise the construction of the Hudson Bay Railway and scoffed at those who said it would hurt the trade of the St. Lawrence. "O ye of little faith! the trade of Canada is too great even for these two outlets. What we see coming will be more than sufficient for both the St. Lawrence and Hudson's Bay routes."[9] It is also true that he promised no other project of substance, but contented himself with pleading for time to complete the second transcontinental. This was "old stuff" to the electorate; once again they were subjected to cries of Canada unlimited, but in 1908 the cry lacked its former appeal.

This time, too, Laurier had to face a revitalized opposition. In provincial elections held that year, although the incumbent Liberal governments won everywhere except in New Brunswick, this was their fourth loss, following those of Manitoba in 1899, British Columbia in 1900, and Ontario in 1905. Gradually, the provinces were turning against them. Premiers Roblin of Manitoba and Hazen of New Brunswick accompanied Borden on his campaign tour, while Whitney of Ontario and McBride of British Columbia sent along the Hon. W.J. Hanna and the Hon. W.J. Bowser, in addition to addressing meetings in their own provinces. "Wolves," said Laurier, "hunt in packs; the lions hunt alone. The way of the lion was the way of Sir John Macdonald. To-day the lion is dead, and all the furious howlings of the wolves do not carry one-tenth of the weight of the roar of the lion."[10] The Liberals' derisive references to Borden's "travelling troupe" did not alter the fact that it was a speaking combination of exceptional strength.

Borden was ready for this campaign. In November 1907, he had unveiled "a new national policy" at Halifax. It reiterated his belief in the "N.P." of John A. Macdonald and added to it a system of mutual preferential trade within the Empire. It also called for a system of national telegraphs and telephones, and demanded that the public lands of Alberta and Saskatchewan be turned over to those provinces. However, most of its sixteen articles attacked the Liberals' administration of the public services. A Conservative government would see to it that public moneys were appropriated and expended in the public interest; that the civil service was brought under the regulation of an independent commission; that electoral corruption was reduced by prohibiting corporations and promoters from contributing to party funds; and that the public domain was developed to ensure the greatest possible benefit to the public.

This programme might be regarded as the natural reaction of a minority party to a firmly entrenched party supported by an organization of far-reaching strength. But it also reflected a deep malaise within the society. Skelton puts it this way:

> . . . in some quarters power and prosperity were relaxing moral standards, or at least encouraging men to flaunt their personal misconduct in public. The wave of speculation which was sweeping over the whole country, and particularly the opportunities for getting rich quick in Western real estate, had affected the whole country. . . . It was the seamy side of prosperity, part of the price the country paid for the sudden development of the unexploited wealth of half a continent.[11]

For some time the Conservatives had been attacking the government in the places where it was most vulnerable. The sessions of 1906, 1907, and 1908 had been scandal sessions. Parliament had reverberated with charges and denials in connection with the steamer *Arctic*, the North Atlantic Trading Company, the Saskatchewan Valley Land Company, and so on. Had the supplies for the *Arctic*'s expedition to northern waters been purchased profligately and without tender? Had the government's friends in the North Atlantic Trading Company obtained five dollars per head for immigrants whom they had done nothing to secure? Had 250,000 acres of choice Saskatchewan land been sold to friends of the government at one dollar per acre and later resold to settlers at eight dollars per acre for a profit of $1,750,000?

Broadly speaking, the government was accused of gross abuses in the practice of patronage: of rewarding its friends and sacrificing the public

LET LAURIER FINISH HIS WORK?

In another four years of present financial progress.

by N. McConnell. Toronto News, *October 2, 1908. Courtesy of Toronto Public Library.*

interest in the purchase of supplies, the sale of public lands, and the award of public franchises. There were also charges of election frauds in Brockville and West Huron. Angry scenes took place in Parliament because the government declined an investigation whenever the opposition embarked on a fishing expedition. The latter continually complained about the Dark-

Lantern Brigade in the Commons which sought to prevent disclosures.[12] Laurier refused to act as a detective. Bring him the facts, he said, and he would take action.[13] In the end, extensive peculation on a minor scale was shown to have taken place, especially in the Department of Marine and Fisheries. It also became apparent that the whole administrative machine needed a thorough revamping to cope with the problems of inefficiency, waste, and misuse of public funds. The Conservatives failed, however, in their primary objective; they were unable to come up with a single dramatic, eye-catching act of wrongdoing in high places.

Even before the election, the government acted to remove some of the abuses. Timber leases were to be granted only by public auction; the contributions of corporations to party funds were restricted; a new Civil Service Act went a long way towards eliminating patronage in the "inside" civil service. Most Liberals felt that the best defence was a strong offence; they delighted in assailing Conservative M.P.'s for abuses of private trust and the like. Among their targets were G.W. Fowler and A.A. Lefurgey, but their prime object of attack was George Eulas Foster.

As managing director of the Union Trust Company, Foster had been responsible for investing its funds, which were largely derived from the Independent Order of Foresters. The Royal Commission on Insurance (1907) found that he had been indiscreet in being a member of a syndicate which had dealt with Union Trust, but it did not establish that he had received a commission for his transactions with the syndicate or that he had misused the funds entrusted to his care. None the less, his Liberal opponents acted as if he were a suitable candidate for the penitentiary. Foster called it "one of the most diabolical attempts made . . . to destroy the character of a fellow-Member . . . in the history of Government Commissions,"[14] and took legal action against some of his detractors. The "long tournament of mud-slinging" reached its climax in the session of 1907-8; the session became, in fact, "a vendetta, in which quarter was neither given nor asked."[15]

Such was the background of the general election of 1908. Canadian politicians are never reticent in dealing with scandal and, in the absence of issues of substance, it dominated all else. When Laurier and Fielding called the Conservatives "muck-rakers," they replied: "But who made the muck?"[16]

The Conservative campaign dismayed Laurier. "I do not pretend to be a moral reformer," he said at Jackson's Point, "but I do think I am as good a man as Mr. Borden and as good a man as George Eulas Foster."[17] Later, at Ormstown, he confessed that the petty scandal cry filled him with shame and disgust. "I disdain to discuss these issues. My soul is turned toward greater events and questions, and it is the future of the country I lay before you."[18]

Laurier was not allowed to forget the charges he abhorred. Borden's manifesto, it is true, made attractive promises to both the farmer and the labourer, but it quickly got round to the principal Conservative theme. Laurier, it pointed out, wanted to "turn his soul" towards greater events and questions than that of malfeasance in government.

> Is not honest administration the greatest issue of all? . . . Surely the prime minister of Canada could not occupy himself with considerations of more transcendent importance than those which are concerned with the moral foundations upon which alone the permanency of democratic institutions can securely rest. In all recorded history no nation's greatness has ever proved enduring unless founded upon high public as well as private standards and ideals.[19]

Although Borden himself found this type of campaign revolting, he followed the line of least resistance. Everywhere he insisted that "for every dollar taken from the taxpayer's pocket there should be a dollar received in return."[20] At Kingston he described " 'political pull,' under present conditions, as more valuable than real estate."[21] At Peterborough he stooped in a manner quite uncharacteristic of him: "Sir Wilfrid Laurier says that no man can be half as honest as I talk. . . . Does he speak for himself? . . . Let me tell him that we will no more put up with his shoddy politics than we will put up with his shoddy morality."[22] Borden's colleagues were even more insistent that "the thieves be driven out of the temple at Ottawa."[23] They condemned "the Government of a Hundred Scandals" and said the election cry should not be "Let Laurier finish his work," but "Let Laurier's work finish him."[24]

The Prime Minister and his followers also campaigned on their record, but on a different aspect of it: the constructive policy of Liberalism. They boasted that immigration had increased from 113,000 in the four years preceding 1896 to 852,000 in the four years ending in 1908; that the per capita net debt had fallen from $50.82 in 1896 to $40.50 in 1908; and that the total value of the country's foreign trade had risen from $2.63 billion during the last eleven years of Conservative government to $5.15 billion during eleven years of Liberal rule. To these gains they added a myriad of other accomplishments: the adoption of British preference, the improvement of the St. Lawrence and Great Lakes waterways system, the construction of the Crow's Nest Pass Railway, the passage of the Industrial Disputes Investigation (Lemieux) Act, and the advancement of Canadian autonomy to the point where the country could practically negotiate its own treaties.[25]

At the same time they minimized the charges of wrongdoing. They pointed out that not one minister had been charged with using his position for personal profit and that the discredited systems for the granting of lands and the purchase of goods had been carried over from the last Conservative administration. What right had the Conservatives to adopt a holier-than-thou attitude? Did they not have their own George Eulas Foster? Hon. S.A. Fisher wondered whether "this gentleman, who has been thus manipulating – I might say thimble-rigging – with the Foresters' funds is the same man to whom the Conservative party wants to trust the finances of Canada." So many others said the same thing that the Montreal *Herald* was finally led to observe that the election had "almost simmered down to a question whether George Eulas Foster is to have any further part in the public life of the Dominion."[26]

The muck-raking exhibited many variants. A Liberal administration of thirty-five years had recently been ousted on charges of corruption in Ontario. Now, said the Conservatives, it was the turn of their federal counterparts. Everywhere they hailed Sir James Whitney, the Conservative Premier of the province, as the very paragon of probity and virtue.

Nevertheless, the Liberals also had some things going for them in Ontario. Months before the election, a Board of Strategy, of which Clifford Sifton was the driving force, had planned every aspect of their campaign.[27] Never had they possessed a more efficient organization in that province. They also benefited from the promise of free rural mail delivery, which the Postmaster General, Rodolphe Lemieux, made during the campaign in a speech at Niagara Falls. The Conservatives later contended, with more than a little exaggeration, that seventeen constituencies in rural Ontario had been influenced to vote Liberal as a result.

Perhaps most influential of all was the so-called Hocken pamphlet. On September 10, the *Orange Sentinel* published a full-page editorial calling it the "duty of the hour" to oppose the Laurier candidates and thus prevent further damage to the public school system. Without Borden's knowledge it was republished as a pamphlet entitled *The Duty of the Hour* and circulated in areas where it was thought it might aid the Conservative candidates. The Liberals countered by circulating it in ridings with a large Catholic vote, both inside and outside Ontario. By general admission it did the Conservatives no good and assisted the Liberals in Ontario, Quebec, and Prince Edward Island. Certainly it helped to elect a Liberal in Renfrew South and perhaps in Ottawa.[28]

Borden himself said that without the pamphlet "the Liberal-Conservative party would probably have made such gains as to deprive the Government of a sufficient working majority."[29] This was going much too far, however. More to the point was the fact that the voters grew deathly tired of the endless charges of wrongdoing. As a result, in the province of Ontario where some Conservatives talked enthusiastically of winning 70 seats, they had to settle for 48, the same as in 1904. This was their greatest disappointment.

In Prince Edward Island the voters decided to reject all their sitting members. As a result, the Liberals took three of the four seats. In each case a mere handful of votes brought about the change. The circulation of *The Duty of the Hour* on the Sunday before the election is alleged to have cost the Conservatives two seats on the Island.[30]

The Liberal under attack in New Brunswick was William Pugsley, the federal Minister of Public Works. Allegedly he had drawn more than his entitlement while he served as a provincial minister and had enriched his campaign funds as a federal minister by accepting rake-offs from the beneficiary of a dredging contract. However, Pugsley also had some aces up his sleeve. He had taken steps to acquire the *Telegraph* and the *Times*, leaving Saint John without a Conservative newspaper; he had seen to it that the province was bountifully supplied with public works projects; he had made certain that an unpopular road tax of the Conservative provincial administration received more than its share of publicity. These were sufficient to do the trick. New Brunswick elected 11 Liberals and only 2 Conservatives – a gain of 4 seats for the government.

In Nova Scotia the Liberals found a villain of their own. He was John Stanfield, the winner of a recent by-election in Colchester. Although he pleaded complete ignorance, his opponents decried the acts of his election agent who had distributed supplies of whisky under the label "choice tomatoes." The incident supplied the cartoonist of the Halifax *Chronicle* with his most glorious opportunity for poking fun at the Conservatives.[31] It also took some of the wind out of Borden's sails. Cautious Premier George Murray spoke only once for the Liberals, but Fielding took up the slack. It was too much to expect another "Solid Eighteen," but the Liberals won 12 of the seats.

The Liberals expected to counter possible losses in the East by making gains in the West. They talked about its becoming the Gibraltar of Liberalism. Had they not reduced the tariff; added 6,000 miles to the railway system, mostly in the West; and promoted immigration and settlement? Were they not going to build the Hudson Bay Railway? "If you do not want it," said Frank Oliver, Minister of the Interior, "the Conservatives are good enough for you."[32] Liberal pamphlets proudly extolled the growth of Edmonton, Brandon, Winnipeg, Medicine Hat, and Portage la Prairie between 1896 and 1908. In their turn the Conservatives used the Saskatchewan Valley Land affair and the timber limit deals to the full. Herbert Ames, the Conservative Member for Montreal–St. Antoine, made a big hit by using his stereopticon machine to flash facts and figures about Liberal wrongdoing on the screen. Yet, Oliver and Premier Walter Scott of Saskatchewan, who directed the Liberal forces in Alberta and Saskatchewan, had good reason to be satisfied with the results. Although their party failed to win 3 seats in the former province and 1 in the latter, it did get 13 of the 17 seats.

This was the total of Liberal success in the West. Although no longer a member of the cabinet, Sifton was prevailed upon by Laurier to direct the party's campaign in Manitoba; he found nothing but trouble. Four years without leadership had left a broken and defective organization.[33] Criticism of Laurier's tariff policies was widespread and it did little good to say that a Conservative tariff would be worse. Sifton and more particularly his brother-in-law, T. A. Burrows, the Liberal Member for Dauphin, suffered from the innuendo that they had enriched themselves by plundering the public domain. "What would the great Conservative party have done for an issue in this campaign," asked Sifton, "if I had not had a brother-in-law"?[34] Sifton also had to contend with election lists made under provincial auspices, a strong campaign waged by Premier Rodmond Roblin, and the most potent political organization in Canada, headed by Robert Rogers. Not surprisingly, the Liberals won only 2 seats, down from 7 in 1904. Burrows lost Dauphin and Sifton carried Brandon by only 69 votes.

In British Columbia two issues peculiar to the province dominated the campaign. One was the inability of Premier McBride to get from Laurier the better financial terms he demanded. Even more significant was the failure of the federal government to bar the Japanese from Canada as completely as it had the Chinese. The Liberals argued as best they could that, so long as Japan was tied to Britain by treaty and Canada remained part of the British Empire, complete exclusion of the Japanese was impossible. It did no good. Instead of sweeping the province as they did in 1904, the Liberals won only 2 of the 7 seats. The only cabinet minister in all of Canada to be defeated was William Templeman in Victoria.

The Gibraltar of Liberalism had failed to materialize. The four western provinces gave the Liberals and Conservatives 17 seats each. West of Ontario the Liberals had a majority of 1, and it was provided by the Yukon.

Excluding Quebec, the Liberals had 7 more seats than the Conservatives. Once again they were dependent for an effective working majority on *la belle province*. More correctly, they were dependent on Henri Bourassa, since the Conservatives no longer constituted a genuine competitive force in Quebec. In 1904 Bourassa still had confidence in Laurier; he ran and was elected as a Liberal. But his earlier misgivings soon reappeared. In 1905 he strongly supported the original autonomy bills creating the provinces of Saskatchewan and Alberta, for these bills converted the previous administrative concessions concerning separate schools into constitutional guarantees. Naturally he became highly indignant when the Prime Minister agreed to a compromise which restored some degree of administrative discretion to the new provinces. For the moment his personal affection for Laurier was still such that he refused to criticize the old man and blamed instead the weakness of the Liberal members from Quebec.[35] But the Lord's Day Act of 1906 served to reinforce his doubts. Laurier, it seemed to him, was all too willing to permit the puritanical ideals of Ontario to be foisted on Quebec.

So often had Bourassa and Armand Lavergne been isolated or supported only by a few French-Canadian Conservatives, that they had begun to feel the futility of their actions in Ottawa.[36] Perhaps that is why their political interest turned more and more to Quebec where they were assured of support. By 1907 Bourassa had become embroiled in a heated controversy over the alleged failure of the Liberal government of Quebec to pursue aggressive colonization policies, and in 1908 he was elected to the Quebec Legislature. There, he worked in such close harmony with the Conservative M.L.A.'s that some Liberals feared a union of the Nationalists with Tory-Castor elements.

What would he do in the federal election of 1908? After keeping everyone in suspense for some time, he finally declared that his basic objectives were to replace party spirit by public spirit and to launch a programme of economic, moral, and intellectual development in Quebec in which he would enlist men of all parties. Accordingly he would remain neutral in the federal contest, except perhaps in a few specific constituencies.[37] The Liberals undoubtedly breathed a great sigh of relief at this pronouncement. Yet Bourassa had already weakened their underpinnings in Quebec. As Blair Neatby demonstrates, the Nationalists had made support for the Liberals less enthusiastic. "Pride in the party and the leader, even among Liberals, tended to be replaced by an apologetic attitude."[38]

Nevertheless, Laurier again dominated the election in Quebec, although in a different way. While he complained that the Conservatives were hiding their lack of policies by a resort to scandalmongering, he revealed little of a programme himself. When he was not expanding upon his role in promoting the new grandeur of Canada, he was excusing himself for getting old, asking for time to finish his task, and pleading with his compatriots to "follow my white plume."[39] The Conservatives suffered from Borden's lack of imagination and the weakness of their platform and organization.[40] Although Quebeckers knew that Borden himself was not fanatically anti-French, they were more than suspicious of some of his supporters. On October 17, *La Presse* published a sensational article on *The Duty of the Hour* which described in vivid terms the "Ontario Conspiracy" of the Orangemen and Tories to beat Laurier. Other Liberal newspapers also called upon the Quebec voters to counterbalance Ontario's fanaticism by re-electing Laurier.[41]

The leading Conservatives in Quebec – Frederick Monk, Louis Philippe Pelletier, T.C. Casgrain, E.J. Flynn, and J.G.H. Bergeron – were moderately capable, but they disagreed among themselves and presented nothing of an alternative to Laurier. The conclusion was never in doubt. The Conservatives gained five seats and lost five, and their Quebec contingent remained at eleven. The Liberals had much the better of the exchange of seats, however, for they elected all their ministers and leading members, while their opponents lost Pelletier, Flynn, and Bergeron. The

Conservatives, however, did elect a second millionaire, William Price in Quebec West, to join Rodolphe Forget from Charlevoix. L.J. Papineau, the grandson of one rebel, triumphed in Beauharnois at the same time that William Lyon Mackenzie King, the grandson of another, was being elected in North Waterloo. Again Quebec had provided Laurier with more than the majority he needed. The Toronto *Telegram* called it a stampede to Laurier on the grounds of race and creed, but another Conservative paper, *Le Canadien*, said that Borden was "the victim of the ultra Tories and the men who despise us."[42]

The Liberals had three fewer members in a House which had seven more members. The moral was obvious. It is difficult, perhaps impossible, to defeat a government by parading before the public *ad nauseam* a whole series of misdemeanours which, if taken collectively, indicate deep-seated maladministration but which singly are much less than earth-shattering. Sir Andrew MacPhail put the matter briefly: "The Conservatives failed because their campaign was too picayune. The issues which they presented were too small."[43] The moralistic Montreal *Witness* was perturbed because "the Liberals have not even got the scare they should have had. The election seems to say, like the angel in Revelation: 'He that was unjust, let him be unjust still, and he that was filthy, let him be filthy still.'" It finally concluded that "the people do not elect their best men or their worst, simply those that fairly represent their average morality and aspirations."[44]

FOOTNOTES

1. Quoted from the *Winnipeg Free Press* in the Halifax *Herald*, September 25, 1908.

2. *Canadian Annual Review*, 1908 (Toronto: The Canadian Review Company, 1909), p. 162.

3. Halifax *Morning Chronicle*, September 21, 1908.

4. *Ibid.*, September 7, 1908.

5. Graham Wallas, *Human Nature in Politics* (London: Constable and Company, 1908), pp. 30-34.

6. Quoted in the Halifax *Morning Chronicle*, October 12, 1908.

7. *Canadian Annual Review*, 1908, p. 153.

8. J.W. Dafoe, *Clifford Sifton in Relation to His Times* (Toronto: The Macmillan Company of Canada, 1931), p. 303.

9. *Canadian Annual Review*, 1908, p. 223.

10. *Ibid.*, p. 160.

11. O.D. Skelton, *Life and Letters of Sir Wilfrid Laurier*, II [Toronto: Oxford University Press (S.B. Gundy), 1921], pp. 261-62.

12. Halifax *Herald*, September 18, 1908.

13. Skelton, *Laurier*, II, p. 261.

14. *Canadian Annual Review*, 1907 (Toronto: The Canadian Review Company, 1908), p. 442.

15. Dafoe, *Sifton*, p. 336.

16. Halifax *Herald*, September 28, 1908.

17. *Canadian Annual Review*, 1908, p. 161.

18. *Ibid.*, p. 163.

19. Halifax *Herald*, October 19, 1908.

20. *Canadian Annual Review*, 1908, p. 170.

21. *Ibid.*, p. 172.

22. *Ibid.*, pp. 170-71.

23. Halifax *Herald*, September 25, 1908.

24. *Ibid.*, October 24, 1908.

25. *Canadian Annual Review*, 1908, pp. 174-75.

26. *Ibid.*, pp. 177-78.

27. Dafoe, *Sifton*, pp. 341-42.

28. *Canadian Annual Review*, 1908, pp. 183-84.

29. Henry Borden (ed.), *Robert Laird Borden: His Memoirs*, I, (Toronto: The Macmillan Company of Canada, 1938), p. 227.

30. *Canadian Annual Review*, 1908, p. 234.

31. See, for example, Halifax *Morning Chronicle*, September 2, 5 and 10, 1908.

32. *Canadian Annual Review*, 1908, p. 193.

33. Dafoe, *Sifton*, pp. 342-43.

34. *Canadian Annual Review*, 1908, p. 192.

35. H. Blair Neatby, "Laurier and a Liberal Quebec: A Study in Political Management" (unpublished doctoral thesis, University of Toronto, 1956), p. 278.

36. *Ibid.*, p. 284.

37. Mason Wade, *The French Canadians* (Toronto: The Macmillan Company of Canada, 1955), p. 559.

38. Neatby, "Laurier and a Liberal Quebec," p. 284.

39. Robert Rumilly, *Histoire de la Province de Québec*, XIII, (Montreal: Editions Bernard Valiquette, 1944), pp. 174-75. Translated by the author.

40. *Ibid.*, p. 181.

41. *Canadian Annual Review*, 1908, p. 183.

42. *Ibid.*, pp. 235-36.

43. Andrew MacPhail, "Why the Conservatives Failed," *The University Magazine*, VII (December, 1908), p. 536.

44. Quoted in the Halifax *Herald*, October 28, 1908.

1908

	Seats	Candidates			Elected							Popular Vote						
		C.	L.	O.	C.	%	L.	%	O.	%		C.	%	L.	%	O.	%	Total
Nova Scotia	18	18	18	—	6	33.3	12	66.7	—	—		54,500	49.0	56,638	51.0	—	—	111,138
New Brunswick	13	13	13	—	2	15.4	11	84.6	—	—		34,935	46.2	40,716	53.8	—	—	75,651
Prince Edward Island	4	4	4	—	1	25.0	3	75.0	—	—		14,286	49.6	14,496	50.4	—	—	28,782
Quebec	65	61	65	8	11	16.9	54	83.1	—	—		115,579	40.8	160,485	56.7	7,068	2.5	283,132
Ontario	86	86	83	6	48	55.8	37	43.0	1	1.2		235,765	51.0	217,980	47.2	8,541	1.8	462,286
Manitoba	10	10	10	2	8	80.0	2	20.0	—	—		35,078	51.5	30,892	45.4	2,077	3.1	68,047
Saskatchewan	10	9	10	3	1	10.0	9	90.0	—	—		22,007	36.8	33,885	56.6	3,976	6.6	59,868
Alberta	7	7	7	3	3	42.9	4	57.1	—	—		20,433	44.4	23,100	50.2	2,439	5.3	45,972
British Columbia	7	6	7	5	5	71.4	2	28.6	—	—		17,503	46.8	13,412	35.9	6,453	17.3	37,368
Yukon	1	1	1	2	—	—	1	100.0	—	—		265	10.8	992	40.2	1,208	49.0	2,465
Total	221	215	218	29	85	38.5	135	61.1	1	0.4		550,351	46.9	592,596	50.4	31,762	2.7	1,174,709

Elected by acclamation: L. (2): Que. (1); B.C. (1).
C. (1): Ont. (1).

Others elected: Ont. (1): I.C. (1).

Others (votes polled):
Que. (8): I.L. (1) 2,920; I. (6) 2,457; other L. (1) 1,691.
Ont. (6): I.C. (1) 4,039; I. (2) 708; Soc. (1) 702; Lab. (1) 1,320; other C. (1) 1,772.
Man. (2): I. (1) 100; Soc. (1) 1,977.
Sask. (3): I. (3) 3,976.
Alta. (3): I. (3) 2,439.
B.C. (5): I. (3) 3,947; Soc. (2) 2,506.
Yukon (2): I. (2) 1,208.

Twelfth

General Election

LET'S "BUST THE DAMNED THING"

The election of 1911 brought to an end the second of the lengthy regimes which have characterized Canada's politics. A prime minister who had successfully accommodated the country's major interests for fifteen years appeared to lose his former attraction. Significant groups hitched their wagons to new stars in the political firmament.

Many factors contributed to the defeat of Laurier and the Liberals. There is, according to Sir Andrew MacPhail, "a constant factor or force which makes for the decay of a party, and it grows in intensity, from the moment of triumph until it ends in final defeat."[1] Every time the Laurier government had made an appointment, it had also made one secret ingrate and four open enemies; in its later years it had laboured under countless charges of maladministration; in no small measure it had become infected with the idea that it enjoyed a permanent lease on office; and it had forgotten that the public never likes to have its support taken for granted.

Natural forces of this kind notwithstanding, Laurier would almost certainly have won his fifth victory in a row if two other matters had not intervened. The election of 1911 appeared to be a referendum on a specific issue or its implications: in Quebec the naval question and in the rest of Canada reciprocity. The Liberals could not cope with their more extreme opponents on either question.

Although one issue held the stage in Quebec and another in the English provinces, the two intersected at many points. At the Colonial Conference in 1907, Laurier had turned down the idea of naval contributions by the Dominion. Later, confronted by the growing German threat, he proposed a Canadian naval service and got the Commons to approve the principle unanimously in 1909. The next year, however, when he sought to give it practical effect, he got quite a different reception. He had expected the naval bill to be opposed only by the Nationalists. What could be more reasonable than to create a truly Canadian navy that could be placed on active service only if the Governor General in Council approved, especially as Parliament was to be summoned within fifteen days to sanction such a decision.

He miscalculated badly. Robert Borden now demanded that two dreadnoughts be contributed to the British navy to cope with the existing emergency and, as a sop to the French-Canadian wing of his own party, suggested that the establishment of a Canadian naval service be subject to approval by the electorate. He might have spared himself this meaningless gesture. On this question the French-speaking Conservatives differed so markedly from the rest of the party that they deemed it best for each section to go its own way. Under Monk, who had once again become their leader, they had steadily grown more nationalistic in sentiment and they refused to moderate their nationalism for party unity. Monk remained nominally a Conservative, but as a political ally, not a lieutenant of Borden.[2] He saw the naval bill as a surrender of Canadian autonomy, a victory for Chamberlainism, a pledge of Canadian participation in all British wars. *L'Action Sociale*, supposedly the spokesman of Roman Catholic orthodoxy, took a similar stand, even though Laurier warned the hierarchy behind the scenes of the ills that would follow a renewal of politico-religious strife.

Monk and *L'Action Sociale* were relative lightweights. Soon, far heavier guns were to be levelled against Laurier by Henri Bourassa; the fire power was further increased when the working arrangements between Bourassa and the Conservatives on the provincial level were carried over to the federal sphere. Bourassa was more potent than ever before. In January 1910, his long-held hopes had finally materialized in the establishment of *Le Devoir*. Now he had the means of exercising a more continuing influence than occasional speech-making could ever have permitted. His early writings in *Le Devoir* made one thing perfectly clear: nothing remained of his one-time deep affection for Laurier. It was Laurier himself, not the men around him, whom he now accused of betraying the interests of French Canada.[3] He denounced his former leader for surrendering the rights of Catholics to educate their children in their own faith and for seeking to pitchfork French Canadians into Imperialism. Before long *Le Devoir* was exercising unparalleled influence among the clergy, and Laurier had visions of having to cope with a combination of Conservatives, Nationalists, and ultraclerical elements, not dissimilar to the Castors of old.[4]

Laurier probably tried to prick the Bourassa bubble by calling a by-election in Drummond-Arthabaska.[5] The Nationalists accepted the bait, but not as the Liberals had expected. Instead of importing a prominent Nationalist from the outside, they nominated a local farmer and supported him to the hilt. Showing the importance he attached to the contest, Laurier himself addressed the Liberal nominating convention. He risked his prestige in vain, for the Nationalists won the election of November 3, 1910, apparently on the issue of conscription. Laurier had been right; Bourassa was going to offer him far more formidable opposition than Monk could ever hope to do.

Could he possibly turn attention from the naval question by some kind of diversion? Twenty years earlier he had used reciprocity as a distraction from politico-religious questions.[6] Now, fortuitously, it again entered the realm of practical politics. Months earlier President Taft, apprehensive about the political effects of a tariff war with Canada, had sought arrangements which would relieve him from applying the maximum schedules of the highly restrictive Payne-Aldrich tariff to Canada. At the time that Drummond-Arthabaska was electing a Nationalist, the Americans were returning Democrats in the off-year elections, partly to show their opposition to higher tariffs. The lesson was not lost on Taft.

Laurier himself wanted freer trade for reasons other than as a distraction from the naval issue. Earlier, during a trip to western Canada, wherever he went the farmers had insisted on lower tariffs. Then, in December, the National Council of Agriculture appeared at his door and demanded free trade with the United States in natural products and a selected list of manufactured articles. In contrast with the usual situation, significant interests in each country were anxious for freer trade at the same time. Under these circumstances even politicians can move quickly. By late January 1911, the negotiations between Canada and the United States which had only begun the previous October were concluded; the chief products of the farms, forests, mines, and fisheries were either to be placed on the free list or to have their duties drastically reduced, and a limited number of manufactured articles were to be admitted at a lower rate of duty.

Laurier had good reason to be elated. The bargain seemed to be one that even John A. Macdonald could have accepted and still died a British subject. Just as the Liberals were delighted, so the Conservatives were downcast. When Fielding announced the terms of the bargain on January 26, Borden followed with a short speech which contained the kernel of his party's later objections. However, in caucus the next day he met nothing but the "deepest dejection." George E. Foster admitted that, as Fielding spoke, "his heart had gone down into his boots."[7] The western members were certain that not one of them would be elected if they opposed the agreement.

This was simply the reaction of the moment, however. The hindsight of history makes it clear that in late January there was nothing closely resembling a public opinion on the proposals. It could hardly have been otherwise, for Fielding's statement came almost like a bolt from the blue. It was left to the politicians to convince a largely uncommitted electorate. The Ontario Conservatives who went home that weekend discovered strong misgivings among their constituents, and Borden could soon say that he was "surrounded by a party practically united in firm determination to fight the reciprocity proposals to the bitter end."[8]

It took forces outside the party, however, to convince the Conservatives that it was safe to force an election on reciprocity. Naturally, some weeks elapsed before these forces became fully manifest. But by February 16, Sir Edmund Walker, President of the Canadian Bank of Commerce and a Liberal, told a protest meeting of the Toronto Board of Trade that the proposals put continentalism ahead of the British connection. Four days later eighteen prominent Toronto Liberals issued a manifesto calling the proposals the worst blow ever to threaten Canadian nationality. On February 20, Sir William Van Horne, the former president of the C.P.R., declared that he was "out to bust the damned thing."[9] Within days the country's business, financial, manufacturing, and transportation interests had generally arrayed themselves against reciprocity.

Undoubtedly, the most formidable of these opponents was Clifford Sifton. In the Commons on February 28, he made it clear that he was leaving the Liberal party to conduct an all-out campaign against the proposals. O.D. Skelton, who is distinctly hostile towards Sifton, states that Laurier accused him of being personally motivated in his opposition.[10] Yet Sifton's own biographer, who himself favoured the reciprocity agreement, presents convincing evidence that his doubts about reciprocity dated as far back as 1898.[11] Be that as it may, Sifton inspired the "Revolt of the Eighteen," and hence the Canadian National League which grew out of the revolt; Sifton gave unstintingly of his advice to the Conservative Board of Strategy; and above all, the opposition that Sifton did so much to marshal led the Conservatives to believe they could force an election with some chance of success.

Strangely enough, Borden's decision to accept the aid of the Liberal insurgents led to opposition from within his own party. It came in March from a cabal which had been looking for reasons to repudiate his leadership. Wanting to know where he stood, Borden indicated to Premier McBride of British Columbia his intention to resign. He got what he wanted: a spontaneous, whole-hearted expression of confidence from practically all his followers in the Commons. There was no question that he would continue as leader. Nor did the incident harm the party, for Borden treated the dissidents as if nothing had happened and his party went into the election united. Few leaders have had such an ability to forgive and forget.[12]

For fifteen years Laurier had enjoyed an excellent run of luck. Now fortune turned strongly against him. Had he dissolved Parliament at the first sign of opposition, he would likely have won an easy victory. He was sublimely confident, however, and had no inkling of the disaster which awaited him. Even the method of effecting the proposals turned against him. For a number of reasons, Canada had requested that they be put into effect by concurrent legislation rather than by formal treaty. This would have permitted a quick termination of the agreement if it turned out to be disadvantageous. It also allowed pressure politicians in either branch of Congress to block its passage. Ironically, however, it had made its way through Congress before the end of July, at a time when it was still being obstructed in the Canadian House of Commons. Laurier had no machinery for cutting off debate and, good liberal that he was, would not have used it if he had. He put up with the filibustering for weeks, adjourned the session for two months to attend the Imperial Conference, and then endured another week of endless chit-chat before he requested a dissolution on July 29. The electorate was to pronounce upon reciprocity.

Most writers of the day – largely free-trade liberals (or Liberals) – assumed that there were no rational grounds for opposing the agreement. However, some of the questions of the oppositionists – economic, national, and imperial – did raise serious doubts. Might reciprocity not tend to make Canada a supplier of raw materials for American factories or slow down the movement to set up American branch plants in this country? Might it not delay the establishment of a chilled meat industry and make Canada "the backyard for the city of Chicago"?[13] Might it not require some Canadian agriculturalists, such as the fruit grower and market gardener, to face severe competition? Might it not place Canadian producers in a precarious position by making them dependent on an agreement which could be terminated without notice?

Furthermore, would it not run counter to the country's basic economic policies? Why had millions been spent on a complex east-west transportation system if it was immaterial that the trade went through Canadian channels? Would it not constitute a peripheral attack on National Policy under which Canada had been laboriously developing its own industrial machine?[14] Was it not reasonable for Borden to argue that the agreement would inhibit reciprocity within the Empire, a goal of his party for some time?

Although the Conservatives had other plans – a dozen of them in fact – anti-reciprocity overshadowed all else. In its more rational aspects it probably exercised little influence; it required the ordinary voter to become an amateur economist and that he could not do. Laurier, more than ever addicted to Biblical quotation, pretended to be delighted by his opponents' objections to reciprocity: " 'Surely the Lord is good unto His own, for He has delivered mine enemies into mine hands.' "[15] He would have been right if his opponents had stuck to cold, economic fact. Unfortunately for the Liberals, there were other aspects of the reciprocity argument that permitted the Canadian voter to be subjected to a sentimentality which makes that of 1891 look anaemic. The correspondent of the *Round Table*, who only grudgingly admitted that "possibly there was deliberate exploitation of loyalty for partisan purposes," must have been oblivious to his surroundings. The "exuberant rhetoric, inflated invective and hectic appeals to sentiment and prejudice" of 1911 were not the ordinary manifestations of "that very human performance" which constitutes a general election.[16]

Sir Andrew MacPhail blames the protected interests, who were determined at all costs to "postpone the ultimate downfall of protection in Canada." They realized, so he says, that Laurier's proposals meant free trade for half the community and protection for the other half; the farmer would not continue to pay protection prices for what he consumed when he himself enjoyed no such advantage. And so, concludes MacPhail, they decided that reciprocity had to be defeated and that the loyalty cry was likely to be the best weapon.[17] Surely, however, even the most ordinary Conservative politician must have realized by himself the possibilities of this kind of tactics.

In any case, its practitioners received assistance from distinguished personages across the border. President Taft and Champ Clark, the Speaker of the House of Representatives, became the most-quoted Americans in the entire history of Canadian elections. More than once the President declared that "Canada is at the parting of the ways"; Clark's gem of wisdom was: "I hope to see the day when the American flag will float over every square foot of the British North American possessions, clear to the North Pole. . . . That is the way things are tending now."[18] These remarks may have helped get reciprocity through Congress, but surely only the most obtuse of political practitioners would have failed to realize that they were likely to be veritable dynamite across the border.

The foes of reciprocity also attempted to demonstrate that, if something is dinned often enough into a listener, he will come to believe it. They conjured up the evils of "continentalism," "annexation," and "fusion" *ad nauseam*; they talked so much about Canadians "selling their birthright for a mess of pottage" or becoming "hewers of wood and drawers of water" that the Liberals failed to make the case for reciprocity.[19] In the closing hours of the campaign even Rudyard Kipling joined in the pleas to keep the old flag flying. With bitter irony, Liberal writers pointed out that Sir Edmund Walker or Sir William Van Horne could engage in huge financial transactions in New York without arousing suspicions, but the Canadian farmer who sold his wheat in Minneapolis "inevitably drift[ed] towards a belief in annexation";[20] or that "Kipling could sell his poetry for hundreds of thousands of American dollars without injuring the perfect bloom of his patented patriotism," while a Saskatchewan farmer could not sell a load of grain across the border "without selling his country and his soul with it."[21] Such incongruities were lost on the ordinary voter and they failed to puncture the loyalty cry.

Consequently, says MacPhail, "the naked truth is that the government was defeated by the charge that all who dared to support it were, in *posse* or in *esse*, disloyal."[22] This explanation is too simple. Although the loyalty cry helped the Conservatives everywhere in Anglo-Saxon Canada, it was only one factor – albeit the most important one – in a larger context. This was certainly true in Ontario, where the Conservative victory in 1911 ranks with their successes in 1925 and 1958 as the greatest in the party's history. Only 13 Liberals survived – some, like Hugh Guthrie in South Wellington, solely because of their personal popularity. Even William Lyon Mackenzie King lost in North Waterloo.

In discussing the results in Ontario, Robert Cuff has raised the perennial question of the importance of organization in electoral victory. Undoubtedly, as he says, the Liberal organization in Ontario had crumbled badly, while that of the Conservatives under Sir James Whitney was at its peak. Cuff is impressed – as he should be – by the astonishingly accurate forecast which Frank Cochrane, the provincial Conservative organizer, and his regional organizers made as early as mid-April. They prophesied then, that they would hold the 50 seats they had won in 1908 and, of these, they lost only Norfolk. They conceded 14 seats to the Liberals, who actually won 13. Since Cuff finds no evidence that reciprocity was a controlling factor in these predictions, he calls it "a projection based upon careful consideration of existing Conservative strength, and Liberal constituency weakness." He concludes that "no matter what public issue emerged in 1911, given the existing state of party machinery, the electoral results in Ontario would have remained substantially the same."[23]

Nevertheless, he goes wrong on two points. Cochrane and his organizers were simply gauging party strength in Ontario without attempting to assess the factors which determined it. Also, their forecast undoubtedly reflected the popular attitude towards reciprocity at a time when it had been actively discussed for two months. The reason for this attitude lies deep in the feelings of the people, (that is, outside the cities which, for reasons of self-interest, were protectionist to the hilt just as they were in 1891). Whereas the country voters had reacted less than enthusiastically to Macdonald's "a British subject" plea in 1891, they were strongly for "no truck or trade with the Yankees" in 1911. Undoubtedly, the loyalty cry had its effect in both years, but something else was superimposed upon it in 1911. It has been pointed out that wisdom occasionally comes out of the mouths of babes and sucklings, and that the student newspaper of the University of Toronto hit the mark when it said: "Canada was indignant, and wiped America's eye."[24] The Conservatives managed to rally the slumbering protest against the United States, which tends to prevail widely in Canada. "The relationship of the small boy to the big bully here finds a parallel."[25] In 1891 the Canadian primary producer felt insecure and would have welcomed freer trade with his southern neighbour, but he felt none of the same need two decades later. Why alter a status quo which was distinctly favourable? "Perhaps," says Dafoe, "the determining factor with the man in the street was the conviction that at last he was sufficiently prosperous to be able to sacrifice further gain for himself – or for his neighbours – in order to show his resentment of long years of United States hostility and condescension."[26]

Then, too, there was the longing–to be repeated in 1957–of Protestant rural Ontario for a prime minister neither Catholic nor French.[27] Undoubtedly this was strengthened in the back concessions of Ontario by the no-popery cry, which Skelton unfairly lays at Sifton's door.[28] The

Conservatives made much of the fact that the Speaker of the Commons and a judge of the Supreme Court of Canada had appeared in their robes of office at the Eucharistic Congress of 1910, and that the Roman Catholic Church in Quebec had allegedly assumed the right to annul mixed marriages following the *Ne Temere* decree of 1907. Such tactics, at the very least, neutralized the Liberal attempt to make capital out of a supposed Borden-Bourassa alliance.[29]

Collectively, these were the ingredients which were to produce the massive victory in Ontario: 73 Conservatives to 13 Liberals.

Would the Liberals do better in western Canada, which had provided much of the impetus for reciprocity? Certainly Saskatchewan did all that was expected of it. There the Conservatives were beaten before they started, for their leader, Frederick Haultain, could not live down an earlier speech in favour of reciprocity. Liberal Premier Walter Scott simply said: "Reciprocity means a higher price for our Products and a lower price for our Necessities." At the same time he ridiculed the loyalty cry. "We may remain loyal," he said, "while sending our flax crop over a high tariff wall into the United States but if the wall be removed and we obtain consequent higher prices for our flax we become disloyal."[30] The voters apparently believed him, for the Conservatives polled only 39 per cent of the votes and won but a single seat, Prince Albert.

Alberta was not as favourable to reciprocity as Saskatchewan, a fact explained, perhaps, by its somewhat more diversified interests. None the less, the Liberals took 53.3 per cent of the vote and six of the seven seats. R.B. Bennett rallied the anti-reciprocity forces and won Calgary for the Conservatives.

The Liberals expected little from British Columbia and got nothing. Their opponents strongly denounced the province's federal minister, William Templeman, for relaxing the immigration laws in favour of Orientals – a charge certain to win votes in British Columbia. They also alleged that the American competition resulting from reciprocity would ruin the market gardener and the fruit grower. Most of all, they sought to capitalize upon the strong British sentiment in the province. Premier Richard McBride asked the voters to stand firm by British connection, British liberty, and British free institutions rather than "pander to the many corrupt influences arising and fostered in the United States."[31] One of the placards he used displayed the Union Jack and the Stars and Stripes, and asked "Which?" British Columbia chose the Union Jack and elected seven Conservatives.

Manitoba was the western province which most disappointed Laurier. The *Winnipeg Free Press* – an out-and-out supporter of reciprocity even though Sifton was its owner – said that Canada was coming to the crossroads on September 21. One road led to "the greater happiness and prosperity of the plain people"; the other to "the exaltation of certain special interests; to high protection, restricted markets and trust domination."[32] However good its case, it had to confront perhaps the best political machine in Canada, the Roblin government and its master of organization, Robert Rogers.

Roblin and Rogers pursued several lines of attack. Did Manitobans want to continue the traditional policy of national and imperial development or look southward towards Washington and continentalism? Let them forget about higher prices under reciprocity. Within ten days of its coming into effect, said Roblin, "the prices of wheat at Duluth and Minneapolis will have gone down to the Port Arthur and Winnipeg price."[33] More positively, a Conservative government at Ottawa would accord better treatment to Manitoba, especially in the extension of its boundaries and the transference of its lands and resources to provincial control. Hence "every vote polled for a Liberal candidate [was] a vote polled to shackle Manitoba."[34]

Amidst this bombardment, the Liberal campaign in Manitoba never really got off the ground. The Conservatives had deeper roots here than in the other Prairie provinces, with the result that Borden got 8 of Manitoba's 10 seats. It was not a decisive rejection of reciprocity, however, for the Liberals polled almost 45 per cent of the votes, and lost 3 seats by fewer than 100 votes.

Because of Manitoba, the government made a poor showing in western Canada as a whole: 17 seats to 18 for the Conservatives or one fewer than in 1908. It did little better in the Maritimes, another area where freer trade ought to have proved attractive. High protection, said the Halifax *Chronicle*, had been sucking their very lifeblood and they had been steadily withering for over thirty years. Hence the issue of the election was quite simple: Did the farmer, fisherman, and lumberman "want free access to the markets of the United States for their production, or [did] they not"?[35]

The Halifax *Herald* maintained that "N.P." had operated with a totally different effect; above all, it had facilitated the development of an iron and steel industry having a capital investment of $50 million. This was its only instance of rationality, however, for in its appeal to British sentiment, ·it was as unreasonable as it had been in 1891. The *Herald* accused Laurier of revealing "a personal instinct so hostile to the sentiment of our people" that it would no more trust him to make trade treaties than it would have let him negotiate with Louis Riel or Paul Kruger. After publishing a page of remarks by Americans and Canadian Liberals, it concluded: "If this is not 'Veiled Treason,' perhaps Sir Wilfrid Laurier and Mr. Fielding will tell the Sons of the Blood what it is."[36]

Whatever the reason, the results in Nova Scotia appear quite unintelligible. Two chief beneficiaries of National Policy, Pictou and Cape Breton County, returned Liberals, while the fishing constituencies of

Lunenburg, Shelburne-Queens, and Digby, and the farming constituencies of Hants and Kings elected Conservatives. Apparently, two factors had counterbalanced the arguments in favour of reciprocity. One was the difficulty of making a case for a change in the status quo during prosperous times. The other was the strong residue of British sentiment which even recent elections indicate still exists in Nova Scotia. As a result, it was an election of individual contests in which local factors often dominated. That is why such strong vote-getters as D.D. McKenzie, W.F. Carroll, E.M. MacDonald, and A.K. Maclean could keep Cape Breton North–Victoria, Cape Breton South, Pictou, and Halifax for the Liberals. On the other hand, one of the best-financed campaigns in all of Canada brought down Fielding himself in Shelburne-Queens.

Similar factors operated in the other Maritime provinces. In Prince Edward Island the Conservatives tried to convince the voters that the United States was not the province's natural market. They took 2 of the 4 seats and 51.1 per cent of the votes. In New Brunswick the chief protagonists were William Pugsley, the federal Minister of Public Works, and Premier Douglas Hazen. To counter their opponents' use of the loyalty cry in a Loyalist province, the Liberals denounced the "black compact" between Borden and Bourassa and lauded Pugsley's success in getting public works for New Brunswick.[37] Although the Liberals managed to keep a majority of the province's seats, they fared much worse than in 1908; they lost Charlotte, Kent, and Kings-Albert, and 3 per cent of the vote. In the Maritimes as a whole they likewise retained a majority of the seats (19 to 16) but they dropped 7 seats they could not afford to lose.

Outside of Quebec, the Conservatives won 107 seats. To constitute a majority they needed 4 more, a number which Quebec had never failed to give them even under the worst of circumstances; for them the circumstances in Quebec were not at their worst in 1911.

This time the campaign in *la belle province* was altogether *sui generis*, reciprocity being at best a peripheral issue. While Monk opposed the trade agreement because of the haste with which it had been concluded, Bourassa at first tended to favour it. By blocking the commercial union of the Empire, it was at least an excellent antidote to imperialistic aims. At this stage, "Bourassa favoured reciprocity on anti-imperialistic grounds, while Borden opposed it on imperialistic grounds."[38] A little later, Bourassa said he could not "approve of the motives of Sir Wilfrid Laurier in digging a big ditch [i.e., reciprocity] to hide the nefarious policy of his Naval Bill";[39] finally, during the campaign itself, he became an out-and-out critic of the agreement. Apparently, the alliances he had formed and a temperament which led him to oppose for opposition's sake produced this metamorphosis; yet he never changed his view that reciprocity was a mere herring on the trail.[40]

For the Nationalists, the naval question, involving as they thought

REDUCED TO A JUMPING-JACK,
OR, BORDEN IN THE HANDS OF BOURASSA.

by J. W. Bengough. The Globe, *Toronto, September 18, 1911. Courtesy of* The Globe and Mail, *Toronto.*

it did the preservation of Canadian autonomy, was paramount. At Joliette, on June 12, Bourassa condemned the naval bill because it might drag Canada into wars in which her participation was unwarranted. "It is desired to set up the principle that Canada should be obliged to aid England in all her wars, but I reject that principle."[41] Unless Canada participated in the councils making the decisions which might lead to war, she could not be expected automatically to participate. Give him, he pleaded, twenty-five M.P.'s independent of party and patronage, and within five years he would have the naval law repealed or so amended that it could not possibly endanger the country's autonomy.

The crucial question in Quebec was: Could the antigovernment forces act as a unit to defeat Laurier? A long process of attrition had rendered the Bleus ineffective, but it was quite another matter with the Nationalists. Early in August the Conservative organizer, Charles Beaubien, persuaded the very imperialistic Herbert B. Ames, the less imperialistic C.J. Doherty, the nationalist Fred Monk, and the pronounced nationalist Henri Bourassa to agree to work together against the Liberals.[42] The Conservatives as such would nominate candidates only in the English-speaking ridings of Montreal and the Eastern Townships, and put the rest of the campaign in the hands of Monk, a Monk altogether submissive to the influence of Bourassa.

The tactics used in Canadian elections often raise ethical questions; none more than these arrangements of 1911. Naturally, Laurier denounced the Bourassa-Borden-Monk-Sifton alliance. "Mr. Monk [was] the oil, Mr. Bourassa the vinegar, and Mr. Borden had to eat the dose."[43] It did no good. Borden contented himself with meetings in Montreal and Lake Megantic, while "protectionist and imperialist big business [proceeded] to use the nationalist movement to defeat reciprocity."[44] Big business poured funds into the Nationalist war chest and financed hundreds of additional subscriptions to Le Devoir. This prompted Ernest Lapointe to say that, if he were as bitter as the Nationalists, he might allege that Bourassa had sold himself, all the more so because he had reversed his position on reciprocity.[45]

English-speaking Conservatives who had previously denounced the Nationalists as "rebels" and "traitors" suddenly discovered Bourassa to be the true patriot. C.H. Cahan appeared on the same platform with the Nationalist leader and praised him for judging Canadian politics from a Canadian point of view which was just and wise. Bourassa, he said, was somewhat ahead of Canadian public opinion because he demanded that Canadian military contributions form part of a comprehensive national policy which would ensure Canadian autonomy and intelligently and frankly determine the country's relation with Britain and the Empire.[46] The journalist John Boyd said much the same thing in the Canadian Magazine.[47] But would Cahan and Boyd have agreed with what Bourassa said at Buckingham: "Our duty towards England is accomplished when we have defended our own territories;"[48] or at Ste Rose: ". . . no one – not Laurier or even His Majesty – has the right to ask us to go beyond our shores"?[49] Would they have supported his implication that Canada could and should be neutral when Britain was at war?[50]

Because of Bourassa, conscription became for French Canadians much more than an exaggerated form of Imperialism; indeed, it was raised to the status of "a moral evil, wrong in itself, something equivalent to 'social revolution.' "[51] He could do this because his influence had become immense Within a year of its founding, says Rumilly, Le Devoir was being read by almost all the French-Canadian élite, brandished by the students as a flag, used as a means of liaison between the French Canadians of Quebec and those of the other provinces and New England, hailed by L'Action Sociale, and aided by the financiers of St. James Street.[52] The students found in Bourassa the very personification of their national pride; they even took to singing "O Canada" substituting him for country as the object of devotion.

Bourassa chose to mastermind the campaign in the district of Montreal rather than to offer himself as a candidate. His chief lieutenant, Armand Lavergne, organized the campaign in the district of Quebec in a dictatorial manner. He saw to it that the most imperialistic of the French-Canadian Conservatives, the veteran Thomas Chase Casgrain, did not even get a nomination. Such Conservative papers as *La Patrie* and the Quebec *Chronicle*, which found the alliance with Bourassa distasteful, had no choice but to fall into line. The anti-government French-Canadian candidates – they called themselves *Autonomistes* – cannot be separated into Conservatives and Nationalists, but most of them had a Conservative background. While scandal and the like played some part in their campaign, they generally took their cue from Bourassa and talked almost entirely about *autonomie* in its anti-imperialist, anti-conscription aspects.

In Montreal and its environs, the campaign was especially bitter, more bitter than any since the defeat of Cartier in 1872. The size and exuberance of the Nationalist rallies indicated that the younger French Canadians had found a new idol. Rodolphe Lemieux, Laurier's chief lieutenant in Quebec, found it almost impossible to cope with the Nationalists in his public meetings. Laurier himself discovered that the politics of accommodation had become unattractive simply because it was the politics of the middle way. Almost pathetically he said: "In Quebec I am branded as a Jingo and in Ontario as a separatist. In Quebec I am attacked as an Imperialist and in Ontario as an anti-Imperialist. I am neither. I am a Canadian."[53]

La Presse continually warned its readers: "A vote for Bourassa is a vote for Borden, and a vote for Borden is a vote for imperialism with a vengeance."[54] Its efforts were in vain. Although Laurier appreciated the danger, he told Fielding that the net loss in Quebec would be only three or four seats. "I shall lose the urban counties, but I shall make up for it in the rural counties."[55] However, the situation got worse and he cut short his trip to Ontario to spend the last ten days in Quebec. Yet, try as he might, he could not stem the tide. Two days before the election, from his railway coach in Viger Station, where he had been driven by a horde of Nationalists, he confessed sadly: "We are beaten."[56]

He was right. While he retained 38 of Quebec's 65 seats, that in itself was a defeat, for the victories he had fashioned since 1896, like those of King and St. Laurent after him, were built upon a solid Liberal Quebec supplemented by a substantial number of seats in Ontario. In contrast, the Conservative victories since 1896 (1917 excepted) have had the same common factor in reverse: a solid Conservative Ontario and substantial representation in Quebec. That is the way it was in 1911. The Conservatives or Nationalists or *Autonomistes* (call them what you will) took 27 seats, 16 more than the Conservatives could win by themselves in 1908. Six of their victories were in largely English-speaking ridings, the most notable their defeat of Sydney A. Fisher in Brome.

Laurier was wrong in one respect. The 21 French ridings that he lost were practically all rural. They were not in the area around Montreal where the young Nationalists had caused such a commotion, but largely in northern and eastern Quebec, where the colonization proposals that Bourassa had espoused in the name of nationalism while he was still engaged in provincial politics had apparently borne fruit.[57]

Nevertheless, the results were not really a victory for Bourassa. He had failed to get a bloc of members who held the balance of power in the Commons. The Conservatives had won such an overwhelming victory in Ontario, that Borden would still have had a majority of five if all the *Autonomistes* had deserted him. They gave him such consistent support, however, that they were dubbed "unprincipled office-seekers" by their opponents. All Bourassa could say was that, just as he had beaten Laurier, so he would beat Borden if it proved necessary. However, Blair Neatby points out:

> . . . this was cold comfort to the *nationalistes* who had just helped to establish the more imperialistic of the two national parties, and who would wait many years for an opportunity to undermine it. The third party movement had failed in 1911. It never recovered from the failure.[58]

The Liberal press delighted in taking shots at a discomfited Bourassa. *La Presse* called the results a slap not at Laurier himself but at the whole French-Canadian race; "it is the voice of Toronto which is now going to dominate in the counsels of the nation." A much more bitter *Le Soleil* expressed nothing but contempt for "the pretended patriots of the nationalist school, the Bourassas, the Lavergnes, and all those who, more or less openly preoccupied with the work of hate, have sacrificed to their vengeance the very future of the province of Quebec."[59]

FOOTNOTES

1. Andrew MacPhail, "Why the Liberals Failed," *The University Magazine*, X (December, 1911), p. 567.

2. H. Blair Neatby, "Laurier and a Liberal Quebec: A Study in Political Management" (unpublished doctoral thesis, University of Toronto, 1956), p. 321.

3. *Ibid.*, p. 330.

4. O.D. Skelton, *Life and Letters of Sir Wilfrid Laurier*, II (Toronto: Oxford University Press (S.B. Gundy, 1921), p. 337.

5. Neatby, "Laurier and a Liberal Quebec," pp. 334-35.

6. Robert Rumilly, *Histoire de la Province de Québec*, XVI (Montreal:

Editions Bernard Valiquette, 1945-46), p. 17.

7. Henry Borden (ed.), *Robert Laird Borden: His Memoirs*, I (Toronto: The Macmillan Company of Canada, 1938), p. 303.

8. *Ibid.*, p. 304.

9. J.W. Dafoe, *Clifford Sifton in Relation to His Times* (Toronto: The Macmillan Company of Canada, 1931), p. 364.

10. Skelton, *Laurier*, II, p. 372.

11. Dafoe, *Sifton*, pp. 354-59.

12. Borden, *Memoirs*, I, pp. 309-11.

13. Dafoe, *Sifton*, p. 367.

14. *Ibid.*

15. M.O. Hamond, "The Tragedy of Reciprocity," *The Canadian Magazine*, XXXVIII (November, 1911), p. 88.

16. *The Round Table*, II (December, 1911), pp. 131-32.

17. MacPhail, "Why the Liberals Failed," p. 570.

18. Mason Wade, *The French Canadians 1760-1967* (Toronto: The Macmillan Company of Canada, 1955), p. 596.

19. MacPhail, "Why the Liberals Failed," pp. 571-73.

20. W.L. Grant, "Current Affairs— The Canadian Elections," *Queen's Quarterly*, XIX (October, 1911), p. 171.

21. Skelton, *Laurier*, II, p. 376.

22. MacPhail, "Why the Liberals Failed," p. 570.

23. Robert Cuff, "The Conservative Party Machine and the Election of 1911 in Ontario," *Ontario History*, LVII (September, 1965), p. 156.

24. MacPhail, "Why the Liberals Failed," p. 577.

25. Hamond, "The Tragedy of Reciprocity," p. 89.

26. Dafoe, *Sifton*, p. 374.

27. MacPhail, "Why the Liberals Failed," p. 578.

28. Skelton, *Laurier*, II, p. 372; Dafoe, *Sifton*, p. 374n.

29. Grant, "Canadian Elections," p. 170.

30. *Canadian Annual Review*, 1911 (Toronto: The Canadian Review Company, 1912), pp. 243-44.

31. *Ibid.*, p. 248.

32. *Ibid.*, p. 243.

33. *Ibid.*, p. 241.

34. *Ibid.*, pp. 240-41.

35. Halifax *Morning Chronicle*, August 7, 1911.

36. Halifax *Herald*, August 30, 1911.

37. *Canadian Annual Review*, 1911, pp. 235-37.

38. Wade, *French Canadians*, p. 593.

39. *Canadian Annual Review*, 1911, p. 182.

40. Rumilly, *Histoire*, XVI, p. 75.

41. *Canadian Annual Review*, 1911, p. 183.

42. Rumilly, *Histoire*, XVI, p. 71.

43. Skelton, *Laurier*, II, p. 379.

44. Wade, *French Canadians*, p. 597.

45. Rumilly, *Histoire*, XVI, p. 75.

46. *Ibid.*, p. 85.

47. *Canadian Annual Review*, 1911, pp. 179-80.

48. *Ibid.*, p. 189.

49. *Ibid.*

50. *Ibid.*

51. Neatby, "Laurier and a Liberal Quebec," p. 344.

52. Rumilly, *Histoire*, XVI, p. 86.

53. *Canadian Annual Review*, 1911, p. 165.

54. Rumilly, *Histoire*, XVI, p. 114.

55. *Ibid.*, p. 97.

56. *Ibid.*, p. 111.

57. Neatby, "Laurier and a Liberal Quebec," p. 350.

58. *Ibid.*, p. 351.

59. Rumilly, *Histoire*, XVI, p. 119.

	Seats	Candidates			Elected						Popular Votes						
		C.	L.	O.	C.	%	L.	%	O.	%	C.	%	L.	%	O.	%	Total
Nova Scotia	18	18	18	2	9	50.0	9	50.0	—	—	55,209	48.8	57,462	50.8	351	0.3	113,022
New Brunswick	13	13	13	—	5	38.5	8	61.5	—	—	38,880	49.2	40,192	50.8	—	—	79,072
Prince Edward Island	4	4	4	—	2	50.0	2	50.0	—	—	14,638	51.1	13,998	48.9	—	—	28,636
Quebec	65	63	65	6	27	41.5	38	58.5	—	—	155,779	48.1	162,732	50.2	5,528	1.7	324,039
Ontario	86	85	85	4	73	84.9	13	15.1	—	—	269,930	56.2	207,078	43.1	3,564	0.7	480,572
Manitoba	10	10	10	2	8	80.0	2	20.0	—	—	40,356	51.9	34,781	44.8	2,559	3.3	77,696
Saskatchewan	10	10	10	2	1	10.0	9	90.0	—	—	34,700	39.0	52,924	59.4	1,419	1.6	89,043
Alberta	7	7	7	4	1	14.3	6	85.7	—	—	29,675	42.5	37,208	53.3	2,892	4.1	69,775
British Columbia	7	7	7	3	7	100.0	—	—	—	—	25,622	58.8	16,350	37.5	1,587	3.6	43,559
Yukon	1	1	1	—	1	100.0	—	—	—	—	1,285	60.8	829	39.2	—	—	2,114
Total	221	218	220	23	134	60.6	87	39.4	—	—	666,074	50.9	623,554	47.7	17,900	1.4	1,307,528

Included in the Conservative columns in Quebec are the Nationalist candidates, whom it is impossible to distinguish from the Conservatives.

Elected by acclamation: L. (3): Que. (2); Ont. (1).
                            C. (1): Ont. (1).

Others (votes polled):   N.S. (2): I. (2) 351.
                       Que. (6): Other L. (2) 1,549; other C. (2; both in same riding) 3,520; Lab. (2) 459.
                       Ont. (4): I. (1) 2,281; Lab. (3) 1,283.
                       Man. (2): I. (1) 234; Soc. (1) 2,325.
                       Sask. (2): I. (2) 1,419.
                       Alta. (4): I. (4) 2,892.
                       B.C. (3): Soc. (3) 1,587.

Thirteenth

General Election

". . . TO WIN, AT ANY COST"

A political party normally contends that the national interest depends upon its electoral success. Seldom, however, has a democratic party so equated its own triumph with the well-being of the state as the Conservatives (or Unionists) did in 1917. As they saw it, their defeat would have been disastrous; it would have meant "the virtual withdrawal of Canada from the war, the desertion of her soldiers overseas, the abject surrender of her honour, and the utter loss of her pride."[1] Men acting under the influence of such sentiments may be disdainful, or at least forgetful, of the ideals for which they stand. So it was in 1917.

The election of 1911 had amounted largely to a referendum on two questions; that of 1917 was even more a referendum on one issue: the manpower question. Towards the end of 1915, Borden decided that Canada must step up its war effort, and accordingly he announced that the country's armed forces would be doubled to 500,000 men. No decision has ever had a more far-reaching effect on Canadian politics. Borden had emphasized the idea that Canada was a principal in the war in her own right and that "the country could not set any limits to its exertions that fell short of the totality of its powers." There were undoubtedly others, however, who held that "Canada was in the war on a limited liability basis, and it was for this country to fix the limit of her contribution."[2]

This divergence of opinion did not come into the open until the last half of 1916, when the competitive appeals of agriculture and war industry had caused enlistments to fall behind replacement needs. This was followed by heavy casualties during the early months of 1917. When Borden returned from a meeting of the Imperial War Cabinet on May 15, 1917, he had decided that conscription was the only answer. Within four days he announced his conclusions to Parliament. Almost immediately, conscription became inextricably entwined with the complementary questions of coalition and a further extension of the life of Parliament.

The move towards coalition or national government did not appear Medusa-like before the public in May 1917. Its beginnings, Liberal in origin, dated back to late 1916 when such papers as the *Winnipeg Free Press* came out strongly in favour of it. The movement gathered a full head of steam in 1917 as the belief grew that only an all-party or non-party government would permit Canada to put forth its maximum effort, enable conscription to be enforced, and make it possible to avoid a distracting wartime election.[3] Hence, when Borden proposed union government and conscription to Laurier on May 25, he was reflecting views which were widely held throughout the country.

Laurier waited until June 6 to turn down the offer, though there was never much hope that he would accept it. The man with the abiding belief in individual liberty could not help but find conscription obnoxious. It is true, as Skelton indicates, that he had never let a principle stand in the way of reality, but in this instance "he did not believe that the necessity or expediency of the step had been proved."[4] Naturally Laurier also objected to the idea of having to accept responsibility for a momentous decision which he had had no share in making. "As in the play of children, they asked me: close your eyes and open your mouth and swallow."[5] It might have been pointed out to him that Borden had accepted the primary responsibility for a decision which could not have been avoided. However, Laurier would have replied that he should not be expected to assume any of the onus for a policy which was designed to cover up the government's failures and could only disrupt the national unity it had been his chief mission in life to promote. It was he, after all, who would have had to bear the brunt of the attack in Quebec and, as a supporter of conscription, even he might have been unable to prevent the province from falling completely into Bourassa's hands.

Good as these reasons were for Laurier's decision, there were others, too. Not only might he have forfeited the affection of his own people, but he would also have had to forgo the victory which he anticipated at the polls and with it the prime ministership.[6] As a result, he would not have realized his dream of dying in harness as his country's leader. He reflected this desire in January 1917, when he told the Ontario Liberal leader, N.W. Rowell, that talk of a coalition was nothing more than an attempt to forestall a French Canadian from becoming Prime Minister. A few months later, despite Sir Clifford Sifton's importuning, he opposed the extension of the life of Parliament. He did so even though the extension would have afforded him a means not only of avoiding responsibility for conscription but also of keeping the conscriptionist and anti-conscriptionist Liberals working together and putting them in a good position to win the postwar election.[7] He made his ambition so clear in his rebuffs to Mackenzie King, when the latter attempted to keep the party united, that King gave up trying and went into seclusion.[8] In the end Laurier could prevent neither conscription nor coalition, and he got an election he could not win. King, rather than himself, was to be the beneficiary of his last major political efforts.

By July 6, after less than a month of debate and the use of closure, the Military Service bill had become law. Both Borden and his Secretary of

State, Arthur Meighen, tried to demonstrate that it involved no new principle since the Militia Act of 1904 permitted the conscription of Canadians for the defence of Canada, and the war with Germany involved nothing less than the country's survival as a free, democratic state. This sort of reasoning made no converts. Most French-Canadian M.P.'s would have echoed the words of D.A. Lafortune, the member for Jacques Cartier, who said: "Do not tell me this is Canada's war, Canada did not make war on anybody. . . . The statement that this is Canada's war is just mere imagination."[9]

A vast gulf had, in fact, developed between the country's two major racial groups. "The remoteness from old world quarrels," says Skelton, "was particularly strong in [Quebec] where an old-fashioned economic self-sufficiency . . . was reflected in a parochialism whose barriers could not at once be broken down."[10] Exponents of Anglo-Saxon imperialism and of centralizing imperial federation schemes had helped to drive the ordinary French Canadians back even further into a narrow provincialism. Consequently, when Bourassa told them that the war involved not a single vital Canadian interest, they were more than ready to take him at his word. They were far more concerned that Ontario was restricting the use of the French language in its schools; perhaps they thought it would be better to assist their compatriots in the next province than to fight the Boches in Europe. They were equally resentful of the federal government's ineptitude in dealing with them, especially in its appointment of a Methodist minister as director of recruiting in Quebec.

Understandably, therefore, a "we-have-done-enough" philosophy manifested itself in the speeches of most French-Canadian M.P.'s on the Military Service bill. Laurier, on the other hand, while he condemned the measure, insisted that a Liberal government would prosecute the war to the utmost of the country's resources. Yet, it is doubtful if even he considered Canada a true principal in the war, for Skelton implies that he felt conscription inappropriate for "a country which has gone in, not for its own sake, but Britain's."[11] In any case, he could not divorce himself from his compatriots who held that Canada's role was a purely limited one. Only five French Canadians voted in favour of the bill, and of the 55 members who opposed it 40 were French-speaking.

The real loser was to be Arthur Meighen. In its details, the bill had been his handiwork and he had been its ablest defender in the committee stages. Except for one lapse in which he inferred that its opponents constituted the backward portion of the population and were somehow lacking in red-bloodedness,[12] he said nothing which could possibly have been interpreted as being anti-French Canadian. Indeed, he pointed out that the bill would be less operative in Quebec than elsewhere because its young men tended to be married earlier and because so many of them were engaged in agriculture. None the less, he could never obliterate the image he had built up in that province as chief architect of the Military Service Act.

In July, Borden tested the House of Commons on extending the life of Parliament to avoid a wartime election; when the Liberals objected he abandoned the idea. Now there was nothing to do but call an election, but not "until the ground had been carefully and completely prepared."[13] As Borden put it in his diary: "Our first duty is to win, at any cost the coming election in order that we may continue to do our part in winning the war and that Canada be not disgraced."[14] Two measures were especially designed to ensure his continuance in office.

The Military Voters' Act, which permitted all members of the services to vote and which disfranchised conscientious objectors, could at least be defended without resort to dubious logic or tortuous reasoning. The Liberals did not raise strong objections. Events proved that they should have opposed it more vigorously. By permitting the active service voters to cast their ballots, either for specific candidates, or for the government, the opposition, or another party, and by letting some of them stipulate the constituency in which they wished to vote, this act facilitated manipulation on a gigantic scale.

Much less defensible was the War-time Elections Act; even its architect, Arthur Meighen, was anything but impressive in his attempt to justify it.[15] Clifford Sifton found the measure regrettable but understandable;[16] Skelton describes it as "an attempt without parallel except in the tactics of Lenin and Trotsky to ensure the dominance of one party in the state";[17] Mason Wade calls it "a colossal gerrymander."[18] Essentially, the measure enfranchised the close female relatives of persons on active service overseas, and disfranchised citizens of alien birth or mother tongue who had been naturalized after 1902. To permit female relatives to vote, in order to compensate for the serving men who would be unable to cast ballots, simply made no sense; by spreading service voting over twenty-seven days the Military Voters' Act ensured that few soldiers or sailors would be disfranchised. To deny the vote to naturalized immigrants en bloc seemed to merit the Liberals' criticism that it was a distinct breach of national faith with the immigrant population and "a recrudescence of Krugerism."[19]

Although the idea of the bill probably did not originate with Meighen, it was he who told Borden that "to shift the franchise from the doubtful British or anti-British of the male sex and to extend it at the same time to our patriotic women, would be in my judgment a splendid stroke."[20] It was also he who drafted the measure and rammed it through the Commons by the use of closure. He too had become infected with the "win-at-any-cost" philosophy. The "patriotic women" could easily be made to see the war his way, while persuasion would likely be lost on the large immigrant population which the Laurier government had settled in western Canada and which had strong Liberal sympathies.

The Act had an immediate and probably unexpected result. Both Skelton[21] and Graham[22] are certain that it propelled the conscriptionist

Liberals into a coalition. Despite Laurier's rejection of Borden's advances, negotiations with other Liberals had continued for four months, unfolding slowly "like a great, crowded swirling ballet [as] various Liberals boldly approached and coyly retreated until finally some of them joined their hands to [Borden's]."[23]

That it took so long was due almost entirely to Laurier. Certain of a solid Quebec, he felt that victory was his if he could keep his party united. In the prolonged clash behind the party screen he proved an easy winner during the early stages.[24] His enormous personal influence and the affection of Liberals of all shades of opinion served him in good stead. A meeting of Ontario Liberal members in Toronto on July 20 did not seriously challenge his point of view. More surprisingly, a Liberal convention held the next month in western Canada, where coalitionist sentiment was strong, had the same result. Sifton realized that such gatherings were likely to reflect "the wishes and purposes of the ultra-partisans – the 'hard-boiled' practitioners of the political game."[25] He took upon himself, therefore, the task of educating the public to the serious consequences of a party contest, particularly if it resulted in a victory for Sir Wilfrid. It was only natural, then, that he drew from Laurier and his biographer Skelton all sorts of imputations as to his motives.[26]

Sifton's tactics had come close to succeeding when the War-time Elections Act provided the clinching argument. By making their support less necessary, "it compelled the western Liberals who had sought union on their own terms to accept it on Sir Robert Borden's terms."[27] Laurier had badly miscalculated. "Forces were abroad which he did not understand and which, when he met them, he could not control."[28] He had counted on the strength of party feeling and his extraordinary position in his party, and both had failed him. He attributed the desertion of his followers to political ambition, a desire to further business and personal ends, or conversion to the *Round Table* point of view, and he could not see that it resulted largely from their conviction that united action was essential for a maximum war effort.[29]

The western Liberals came into the government on October 12, and everything was now in order for the election which Borden called for December 17. His manifesto of November 12 maintained that, just as prominent public men had sunk party differences to further a supreme national purpose, so should all other Canadians. As the concomitant of an administration of no party, section, or group it promised the extirpation of patronage and the elimination of expenditures on purely partisan undertakings.[30] Laurier's election address to the Canadian people on November 4, offered to "increase, double and quadruple the output of all that may be necessary for marching and fighting armies." While the Military Service Act would not be used until the people had pronounced upon it in a referendum, Laurier pledged himself to "carry out the wishes of the nation as thus expressed." At the same time he rejected the view that "we must have Conscription or 'quit.' " Give the voluntary system a genuinely fair trial, he said, and it would bring men to the ranks.[31]

As usual, each party's platform had a host of ancillary items. The Liberals, for example, sought to appeal to the West by promising to remove the duties on agricultural implements. In their turn the Conservatives made a bid for the support of labour by coming out for "such conditions of employment as will assure higher standards of living among the labouring classes." When all was said and done, however, the only thing that mattered was the manpower question and particularly conscription.

For both parties this election involved more in the way of tactics than strategy. Outside of Quebec, the Liberals had to conduct a campaign under the most unfavourable conditions: many of their leading lights and, in some cases, the whole of their organization had gone over to the other side; they had lost the support of all the major daily newspapers except the London *Advertiser*, the Calgary *News-Telegram*, and the Edmonton *Bulletin*. In contrast, the Conservatives often had an embarrassment of riches. Their problem was to prevent Liberal-conscriptionists and Conservatives from running against each other and thus dividing the Unionist strength. Since it proved impracticable to allocate seats between the two groups on a provincial basis, they resorted to pressure, persuasion, and patronage. When these devices failed, the appeal was often to Borden himself. The tactics worked so well that competition between the two components of the coalition was almost eliminated.

In the Maritimes the Unionists found the situation murky. The civilian vote gave all 4 seats in Prince Edward Island and 9 of 16 in Nova Scotia to Laurier, and if the military vote had not produced 2 switches in the former province and 5 in the latter, the area would have returned 15 Liberals to 16 Unionists. One reason for the strong Liberal showing was the attitude of the premiers. Although George Murray, the Liberal Premier of Nova Scotia, and A.E. Arsenault, the Conservative Premier of Prince Edward Island, openly favoured the Union government, and W.E. Foster, the Liberal Premier of New Brunswick, was said to favour it, none of the three campaigned actively on its behalf. It was even more significant that in Prince Edward Island and Nova Scotia the conscriptionist sentiment was not substantial enough to break down the strong party affiliations. In both provinces the Liberal organizations remained intact, perhaps because – at least in Nova Scotia – a goodly number of the party candidates could hardly be classified as anti-conscriptionists. This enabled such proven vote-getters as D.D. McKenzie, W.F. Carroll, L.H. Martell, Hance Logan, William Duff, and R.H. MacKay to put up good fights even though not all of them won.

In contrast, there were two New Brunswicks in this election. Apparently, the Anglo-Saxons felt they had to show the flag to the anti-conscriptionist Acadian population. Thus, the province's representative in the cabinet, the Liberal-Unionist, Frank Carvell, won Victoria-Carleton by acclamation and his colleagues more than doubled their opponents' votes in York-Sunbury, Royal, and the dual riding of Saint John–Albert. The Laurier candidates, in their turn, had similar successes in Acadian Kent and Restigouche-Madawaska, won Acadian Gloucester by acclamation, and carried Westmorland with its substantial Acadian population. In no previous election had New Brunswick divided as sharply as this along purely ethnic lines.

In Quebec the Unionists were under no illusions about their difficulties. To protest conscription, E.L. Patenaude had retired from the cabinet and J.H. Rainville from the Deputy Speakership. Even as Parliament debated the Military Service bill, crowds marched through the streets of Montreal shouting "à bas Borden" and "vive la Révolution!"; later someone dynamited the Cartierville home of Lord Atholstan (the former Hugh Graham), whose *Star* vigorously supported conscription.

Never before had the Liberals had an easier time of it in *la belle province*. Because of his uncertain health, Laurier made few speeches and could have absented himself completely. His chief lieutenant, Rodolphe Lemieux, called conscription "a camouflage, under which 'Rule Britannia' could be sung and Quebec insulted as a Province of shirkers and slackers."[32] Premier Gouin said there was "no man strong enough to impose [conscription] upon us if we do not want it."[33] These were the moderates. The extremists went so far as to talk exultantly about the English taking to their heels at Mons and Yprès, but perhaps they were not as bad as the McGill professor who said that "if Laurier were to win he would win leading the cockroaches of the kitchens of Canada to victory."[34]

For once, the Nationalist support went completely to the Liberals. In Bourassa's view, the Unionist programme was "the synthesis of all we detest, of all we despise, both in men, ideas and tendencies in both parties."[35] This time, however, Laurier did not need Bourassa's assistance in Quebec, and indeed found him a liability in other parts of Canada where his utterances were "so freely and widely quoted as to form one of the lesser issues of the campaign."[36]

From the beginning, the position of the government was hopeless. Of the French-Canadian newspapers, it received support only from *L'Evènement*, which thus maintained its long devotion to the Conservative party. The French-Canadian ministers who stayed in the cabinet, Albert Sévigny and P.E. Blondin, and the Unionist organizer, J.H. Rainville, were everywhere denounced as "the triumvirate of traitors," and French-Canadian Unionist candidates were often mobbed or threatened with lynching. Wisely, Borden decided to stay out of Quebec.

Nevertheless, the Conservatives hoped against hope to elect Blondin, Sévigny, Rainville, and a few English-speaking candidates in Montreal and the Eastern Townships. They did return two cabinet ministers, C.C. Ballantyne in St. Lawrence – St. George, and C.J. Doherty in Ste. Anne, as well as Sir Herbert Ames in St. Antoine. Although Blondin put up a good fight in Laurier-Outremont and Sévigny in Westmount–St. Henri, and although Rainville saved his deposit in Chambly-Verchères, that was the full extent of Conservative success. Seventeen Liberals were elected by acclamation, and almost every French-Canadian Unionist lost his deposit. For the first time since Confederation, Quebec had failed to elect a single French-Canadian Conservative; for the first time, too, the party's popular vote fell below 40 per cent. Previously, Laurier had created a "solid Liberal" Quebec, but it had been in seats only. Now the province was veering that way in popular vote as well.

In contrast, Ontario was not as out-and-out conscriptionist as might have been expected, especially at the outset. Indeed, both Meighen and Sifton were surprised by the anti-conscriptionist strength.[37] However, the Liberals laboured under impossible handicaps. The London *Daily Advertiser* was the only daily newspaper that supported them. Except in one or two constituencies, the Conservatives and Liberal Unionists agreed or were induced to present a single candidate. The former provincial Liberal leader, N.W. Rowell, who had entered the Unionist administration, exercised a pronounced influence on the normally Liberal voter. Sir William Hearst and his provincial cabinet ministers actively supported the Unionists on the hustings. Prominent Liberals addressed letters to the newspapers indicating their support for Borden. In the closing days of the campaign, many Protestant pastors (and the Roman Catholic Bishop of London) made the war a holy one which the righteous had no option but to support. Throughout Ontario the opinion leaders were almost all supporters of the government and Laurier had few to press his point of view. Mackenzie King presented himself as a candidate only because Laurier said, "you must run,"[38] but he stayed within his own riding of North York. Sir Allen Aylesworth and the Liberal M.L.A., H.H. Dewart, carried on valiantly for Laurier, but they could hardly be expected to counterbalance the general trend.

The Ontario campaign started out on a reasonable enough level, but in its closing days it almost rivaled that of Quebec in the extremity of its utterances. It was legitimate enough for N.W. Rowell and others to wonder if a Laurier government dependent on Nationalist support could make an all-out contribution to the war effort, but it was surely hitting below the belt for Sir John Willison's Publicity Committee to state that "Laurier, Bourassa and Quebec . . . are in favour of deserting our men, breaking our pledge . . . and trailing Canada's honour in the mud of world opinion."[39] Equally unedifying was the Toronto *News*'s description of Laurier as a "demagogue, a charlatan, and a mountebank"; or the Toronto *Mail and Empire*'s declaration, on election day, that a vote for Laurier was a vote for Bourassa; a vote against the men at the front, the British connexion and

Empire; a vote for Germany, the Kaiser, Hindenburg, von Tirpitz, and the sinking of the Lusitania.[40] At least the Unionist press in the other provinces seldom identified Laurier with Bourassa, let alone with the Kaiser, as the Ontario newspapers did.

Finally, the Unionists had an argument which apparently worked wonders both in rural Ontario and the West. This was the assurance of General Mewburn, the Minister of Militia and Defence, that he would see to it personally that "farmers' sons who are honestly engaged in the production of food will be exempt from military service."[41] This combination of circumstances led to the most one-sided results Ontario has ever known. When the last soldier's vote was counted, Laurier had only 8 of the 82 seats. In the cities the Unionist majorities were enormous, exceeding those of the Liberals in Quebec. Elsewhere, and particularly in western Ontario, the Liberals won few seats, but they did considerably better and, as a result, managed to poll one-third of the province's popular vote. That did not save Mackenzie King in North York. Still he had gone down to defeat supporting Laurier and opposing the Military Service Act. More than he could have believed possible, this fact was to ensure his future success in Canadian politics.

East of Manitoba the government's majority was only 18. Western Canada was therefore crucial, especially as its representation had been increased from 35 to 57 seats since 1911. Suspecting that Quebec and Ontario would counterbalance each other, Laurier, weary and ailing though he was, undertook a western trip in the closing days of the campaign. According to Dafoe, "there is no more gallant episode in Canadian politics."[42] Although Laurier had been told that the War-time Elections Act and the expenditure of $100,000 would enable every government candidate west of the Great Lakes to be elected,[43] he went anyway. Western Canada gave him a reception that frightened the Unionists.[44]

It turned out to be largely a manifestation of personal sympathy, however, for here too the Liberals faced insuperable obstacles. While the four premiers were Liberals, all were Unionists. Even though only one of them, Norris of Manitoba, campaigned actively, coalition had brought into the cabinet three of the most influential of all Westerners: Thomas Crerar of Manitoba, President of the United Grain Growers; J.A. Calder, Saskatchewan's Minister of Railways and Highways; and Arthur Sifton, the Premier of Alberta. For Laurier's Liberals, the result was disastrous. It had been hoped that the farmers, dissatisfied with the government's protectionist policy, would run candidates in opposition, but the entrance into the cabinet of Crerar, one of their leading spokesmen, negated that possibility.

Late in October Laurier's supporters in Manitoba set up a provincial Liberal association, but it lacked anyone with substantial influence. In Saskatchewan Calder took the entire Liberal organization over to the Unionists. In Alberta Frank Oliver and three provincial cabinet ministers campaigned for Laurier, but their organization was split down the middle. The same was true in British Columbia where a strong Liberal nucleus headed by J.H. King could not cope with both the Conservatives and the Liberal Unionists.

Laurier would have had a chance in western Canada only if the two sections of the Unionists could not have presented a united front. Meighen had insisted that he be given the Department of the Interior, which signified western leadership, and that the Conservatives receive the same number of portfolios and run the same number of candidates as the Liberal conscriptionists in the western provinces. He was especially suspicious of Calder who, he feared, was something of a "slippery customer." Yet none proved more accommodating than Calder, who became, perhaps, the government's greatest asset in the West. The Conservatives received twice as many nominations as the Liberal Unionists, and more than the Liberals did even in the Liberal stronghold of Saskatchewan. It took a good deal of persuasion and pressure to prevent them from opposing each other but, except in the Saskatchewan constituency of Mackenzie, the pro-conscription vote was not divided.

Since the Liberal-oriented, foreign-born vote had been taken care of in advance, it is not surprising that the Liberals could win only 2 of the 57 seats in western Canada: Provencher in Manitoba and Victoria in Alberta. The region in which party affiliations had developed less tenacious roots than elsewhere thus proved to be the great bulwark of coalition government. It increased a government majority of 18 in eastern and central Canada to 71.

Of their 153 seats, no one can say precisely how many the Unionists won because of the War-time Elections Act, but certainly they owed 14 to the Military Voters' Act: 5 in Nova Scotia, 4 in Ontario, 2 in Prince Edward Island, and 1 each in Alberta, British Columbia, and the Yukon. These victories resulted from a degree of manipulation which more than exceeded the Liberals' worst fears. W.T.R. Preston, who represented Laurier's interests in the overseas vote, is certainly no unbiased observer, but he adduces enough factual evidence to prove that the Military Voters' Act came close to being "a letters patent for electoral villainy of the first order."[45] He pictures Sir Robert Borden's law partner, Hector McInnes, taking charge of the proceedings and enlisting as his abettors, Lord Beaverbrook, Sir George Perley, the generals in charge of the camps, the commanding officers of the battalions, and some of the floating army of brass hats "whose war-winning activities were confined to wine and women, and drawing their cheques from the Pay Office."[46]

Parliament itself conducted two post-mortems on the manipulation of votes. In May 1918, the Liberals charged the government with devising an organization which transferred a large fraudulent vote to a few selected constituencies in order to overcome a legitimate vote adverse to itself.[47] In

September 1919, they demanded the investigation of a telegram sent by Arthur Meighen, which asked for a thousand service votes to assist four Unionist candidates in Manitoba. Meighen's defence was that the Military Voters' Act permitted servicemen who had not resided in Canada to designate the seats where their votes were to be counted, that these men wanted their votes to be used to the greatest advantage, and that it was the duty of a party organization to assist them to that end.[48] Yet, despite Meighen, it is clear that voters who had been resident in Canada were induced to cast ballots in ridings with which they had no connection. Thus, the entire Ordnance Company at Ashdown, Kent, voted in Cumberland, Nova Scotia, at the insistence of the brother-in-law of E.N. Rhodes, who won the riding by virtue of the service vote.[49] There were other kinds of villainy too.

The Unionist member for Red Deer, Michael Clark, admitted at the time that the methods were "somewhat crude," but entirely in accordance with past practices of both parties to realize highly desirable objectives.[50] More recently, C.G. "Chubby" Power has refused to "attach much condemnation to the acts of fraud" because of the tide of sentiment running in favour of "the patriotic cause."[51] Certainly the public refused to get excited about the manipulation; no less than the government, it apparently felt that the war was all that mattered. It is going too far to say that tactics of this kind won the election. A more correct generalization would be that the opinion moulders in English Canada, especially in Ontario and the West, determined the result. They dinned it into the head of the ordinary citizen, who was not all that enthusiastic about conscription, that to demonstrate his loyalty to Britain, maintain Canada's self-respect, and keep faith with Canada's fighting men, he had no choice but to vote for Borden, the more so because French Canada was not prepared to do its duty.

In this election more Labour candidates – 22 of them – ran than ever before, but the nature of the issues militated against their success. It was much more significant that the election isolated French Canada for the first time since Confederation. Its two cabinet ministers were beaten, and it ended up with only one member, Dr. J.L. Chabot of Ottawa, on the government side of the House. French Canada had practically taken over the Liberal party, however (57 of that party's 82 members were French), and for the next four decades it would use the Liberals to wreak its vengeance upon those whom it accused of callous and unjust treatment in 1917.

FOOTNOTES

1. W.R. Graham, *Arthur Meighen: The Door of Opportunity*, I (Toronto: Clarke, Irwin & Company, 1960), p. 146.
2. See J.W. Dafoe, *Clifford Sifton in Relation to His Times* (Toronto: The Macmillan Company of Canada, 1931), p. 406.

3. O.D. Skelton, *Life and Letters of Sir Wilfrid Laurier*, II [Toronto: Oxford University Press (S.B. Gundy), 1921], p. 496.
4. *Ibid.*, p. 508.
5. Henry Borden (ed)., *Robert Laird Borden: His Memoirs*, II (Toronto: The

Macmillan Company of Canada, 1938), p. 705.

6. J.W. Dafoe, *Laurier: A Study in Canadian Politics* (Toronto: Thomas Allen & Son, 1922), p. 167.

7. Dafoe, *Sifton*, p. 403.

8. R. MacGregor Dawson, *William Lyon Mackenzie King—A Political Biography: 1874-1923* (Toronto: University of Toronto Press, 1958), pp. 260-62.

9. James Cappon, "Current Events," *Queen's Quarterly*, XXV (July, 1917), p. 115.

10. O.D. Skelton, "Current Events," *Queen's Quarterly*, XXV (October, 1917), p. 226.

11. Dafoe, *Sifton*, p. 407; Skelton, *Laurier*, II, pp. 508-509.

12. Graham, *Meighen*, I, pp. 140 and 144.

13. *Ibid.*, p. 146.

14. *Ibid.*, p. 147.

15. *Ibid.*, p. 168.

16. Dafoe, *Sifton*, p. 436.

17. Skelton, *Laurier*, II, p. 529.

18. Mason Wade, *The French Canadians 1760-1967* (Toronto: The Macmillan Company of Canada, 1955), p. 750.

19. "The Union Government," *Round Table*, VIII (December, 1917), p. 175.

20. Graham, *Meighen*, I, p. 165.

21. Skelton, *Laurier*, II, p. 530.

22. Graham, *Meighen*, I, p. 170.

23. *Ibid.*, p. 159. For the negotiations through Borden's eyes see Borden (ed.), *Memoirs*, II, Chapter XXXII.

24. Dafoe, *Sifton*, p. 411.

25. *Ibid.*, p. 418.

26. *Ibid.*, p. 417 and pp. 431-37.

27. Skelton, *Laurier*, II, p. 530.

28. Dafoe, *Laurier*, p. 169.

29. *Ibid.*, pp. 173-74.

30. *Canadian Annual Review*, 1917 (Toronto: The Canadian Review Company, 1918), pp. 589-90.

31. *Ibid.*, pp. 598-99.

32. *Ibid.*, p. 622.

33. *Ibid.*

34. *Ibid.*, p. 623n.

35. *Ibid.*, p. 624.

36. *Ibid.*

37. Graham, *Meighen*, I, pp. 187-88; Dafoe, *Sifton*, p. 437.

38. Dawson, *King*, p. 267.

39. *Canadian Annual Review*, 1917, p. 610.

40. Wade, *French Canadians*, p. 752.

41. *Canadian Annual Review*, 1917, p. 625.

42. Dafoe, *Sifton*, p. 439.

43. Skelton, *Laurier*, II, p. 543.

44. "The General Election," *Round Table*, VIII (March, 1918), p. 358.

45. W.T.R. Preston, *My Generation of Politics and Politicians* (Toronto: D.A. Rose Publishing Company, 1927), p. 365.

46. *Ibid.*, pp. 365-66.

47. *House of Common Debates*, 1918, pp. 2400 ff.

48. *Ibid.*, 1919 (2nd session), p. 547.

49. Preston, *My Generation*, p. 368.

50. *House of Commons Debates*, 1919 (2nd session), p. 566.

51. Norman Ward, (ed.), *The Memoirs of Chubby Power: A Party Politician* (Toronto: The Macmillan Company of Canada, 1966), p. 61.

1917

	Seats	Candidates			Elected				Popular Vote						
		Govt.	Opp.	O.	Govt.	%	Opp.	%	Govt.	%	Opp.	%	O.	%	Total
Nova Scotia	16	16	12	2	12	75.0	4	25.0	57,436	48.4	54,038	45.5	7,282	6.1	118,756
New Brunswick	11	10	10	—	7	63.6	4	36.4	56,593	59.4	38,668	40.6	—	—	95,261
Prince Edward Island	4	4	4	—	2	50.0	2	50.0	17,672	49.8	17,788	50.2	—	—	35,460
Quebec	65	41	65	15	3	4.6	62	95.4	78,808	24.7	231,970	72.7	8,303	2.6	319,081
Ontario	82	82	81	15	74	90.2	8	9.8	509,307	62.7	273,481	33.7	29,012	3.6	811,800
Manitoba	15	15	12	—	14	93.3	1	6.7	106,858	79.7	27,176	20.3	—	—	134,034
Saskatchewan	16	16	11	1	16	100.0	—	—	82,741	72.0	29,812	25.9	2,370	2.1	114,923
Alberta	12	12	12	6	11	91.7	1	8.3	77,912	61.0	45,428	35.5	4,478	3.5	127,818
British Columbia	13	13	12	8	13	100.0	—	—	86,415	68.4	32,324	25.6	7,690	6.1	126,429
Yukon	1	1	1	—	1	100.0	—	—	959	54.3	808	45.7	—	—	1,767
Total	235	210	220	47	153	65.1	82	34.9	1,074,701	57.0	751,493	39.9	59,135	3.1	1,885,329

Elected by acclamation: Govt. (14): N.S. (4); N.B. (1); Ont. (1); Man. (3); Sask. (4); B.C. (1).

Opp. (18): N.B. (1); Que. (17).

Others (votes polled): N.S. (2): Lab. (2) 7,282.

Que. (15): Lab. (2) 917; Nat. (1) 1,343; I.L. (4) 2,702; I.C. (4) 2,857; I. (4) 484.

Ont. (15): Lab. (10) 18,257; I.C. (1) 217; I. (4) 10, 538.

Sask. (1): I. (1) 2,370.

Alta. (6): Non-Partisan League (3) 3,005; Lab. (2) 1,013; I. (1) 460.

B.C. (8): Lab. (6) 7,089; I. (2) 601.

Fourteenth

General Election

"FRENCH CANADA . . . ON TOP . . . WITH A VENGEANCE"?

The election of 1921 was highly significant for three reasons: it removed Quebec from its position of isolation in government, it produced the first House of Commons in which no party had a clear-cut majority, and it gave each party something of a regional character in the Commons.

Such were the results of a contest in which three relatively young men each fought his first election as leader. Laurier died in February 1919, and six months later the first leadership convention of a national party chose William Lyon Mackenzie King to succeed him. His only serious rival, W.S. Fielding, had lost; four-fifths of the Quebec delegation had rejected him because he had deserted Laurier on conscription. The same convention had, among other things, approved the principle of proportional representation, and promised a general reduction in the tariff and the enactment, through co-operation with the provinces, of an adequate scheme of insurance against unemployment, sickness, old age, and other disability. Essential to understanding the new leader was his concept of what a Canadian party ought to do. Its primary function, he felt, was to bring diverse and even conflicting groups sufficiently together to secure a working agreement and a measure of common action, even if it meant that party principles had to be temporarily shelved or substantially modified.[1]

The Conservatives also secured a new leader in July 1920, when Borden retired because of indifferent health. Although the caucus had no doubt that Arthur Meighen should succeed him, some of the cabinet had different thoughts. That most astute of politicians, J.A. Calder, warned that Meighen was lacking in "the necessary qualities to ensure his success as a leader at any time in the future," and that he was "absolutely out of the question in so far as Quebec is concerned."[2] When all the possible alternatives had been eliminated or eliminated themselves, he got the leadership anyway. If he "exaggerated the role of an élite in a democracy" because of his own exceptional ability, as Dawson says he did, and if he "expected the top level of authority to proclaim the policy and the party to accept it and carry it out,"[3] he stood diametrically opposed to King, who tended to regard a leader as an umpire between opposing groups.

Meighen was leader, but of what? The same Unionist caucus which dealt with the leadership also decided to constitute a "National Liberal and Conservative Party," a name as unsuitable for electioneering purposes as it is possible to conceive. To Meighen, who liked the old label "Liberal-Conservative," it was thoroughly distasteful. It was an utterly meaningless gesture, for the Liberal-Unionists now had no choice but to go back to their old party on bended knee and, after a period of penance, be fully accepted, or to submerge themselves completely in the Conservative party. The latter had been left in a bad way by the nonpartisan aura which had surrounded the Union government and which caused it to be "hung in mid-air, sustained by no electoral organization, and isolated from the electorate."[4] Not unnaturally, then, such partisan Conservatives as Robert Rogers of Manitoba were anxious to return to party lines and renew their party's organization. They faced a formidable task, especially in Saskatchewan and Alberta, where the Liberal organization, the stronger of the two, had been used to win the great victory of 1917, and the Conservative one had decayed almost beyond repair.

Other factors made the rebuilding of both the old parties on the Prairies unusually difficult. The events of 1917, it has previously been shown,[5] had disrupted the orderly evolution of the farmers' movement. But this was to be only temporary. In the long run, the nonpartisanship of the Union government had actually assisted those who advocated political action by the farmers on their own. This was because "the electorate of the West came out of the election of 1917 purged of party loyalties. It had undergone a political emancipation, and thereafter the old traditional ties of party were to remain permanently weak across the West." In a very real sense, says Morton, the Union government had created the conditions for the rise of an independent political movement.[6]

Late in 1918 the farmers were returning to their previous discontent. In November the Canadian Council of Agriculture adopted "The New National Policy," which repudiated the National Policy of 1879 and called for substantial reductions in tariffs. In short order its affiliated organizations, the United Farmers of Ontario, the Grain Growers of Manitoba, the United Farmers of Alberta, and the Saskatchewan Grain Growers, accepted the platform, one after the other. What was to be done next? Should an independent agrarian party be constituted to promote the farmers' programme, or should candidates of existing parties be pledged to support it? While it was left to the farmers' locals to provide the answer, neither the Council nor its associations had any intention of setting up an independent, third party at the outset. Indeed, many who drafted the platform hoped to convert the Liberal party to their point of view. However, the movement for an independent party spread so rapidly that nothing could be done to control it. At its head was the official organ of the farmers, the *Grain Growers' Guide*, which kept "whooping it up for independent action."[7]

In June 1919, when the government failed to reduce the tariffs as the farmers wanted, T.A. Crerar resigned from the cabinet and nine western Unionists withdrew their support from the government. In August the Liberal leadership convention also failed to satisfy the farmers, both in its platform and its leader; perhaps nothing more could be expected from a party dependent upon largely protectionist Quebec. In the last four months of 1919 the farmers ventured into politics on their own with unbelievable success. They captured four successive by-elections in three different provinces and became the major partner in a minority Farmer-Labour government in Ontario. It is not surprising that by the beginning of 1920 they were fully committed to independent political action. Their activities were not to be confined to Ontario and the Prairies. Although the United Farmers' organization in British Columbia and the Fermiers-Unis of Quebec were soon stymied by competitive associations, the United Farmers of New Brunswick were admitted to the Canadian Council of Agriculture in 1920, and organizational work was undertaken in Nova Scotia and Prince Edward Island.

The general drift of things became clear on February 26, 1920, when Crerar and ten other farmer M.P.'s formed the "National Progressive Party." This meant that from the spring of 1920 "the farmers' political movement . . . had a national focus and an earnest of what the farmers in politics might achieve."[8] Already there was evidence of the conflict which was to become a critical weakness of the party. On the one side were those, like Crerar, who felt they were creating a reforming, low-tariff party which would make an appeal to Canadians generally and would have an organization and leadership like that of the old parties. Opposed to them were such men as Henry Wise Wood, the "uncrowned King of Alberta," who rejected political parties per se as essentially evil and advocated a Parliament of organized group interests that would bargain openly with each other.[9] Because of Wood, "Crerar and his followers could not obtain anything like a party organization, or a national leader, for the movement."[10]

Meighen had inherited a situation which was troubled enough without having to contend with a second opposing party. The party he led had won the elections of 1911 and 1917 only under the most unusual of circumstances. Now it had to face the disenchantment of a postwar period. As industry slowed down and unemployment mounted, its image became worse. From one thing only did Meighen derive some satisfaction. Convinced of "the utter hypocrisy, absurdity and contemptibility of William Lyon Mackenzie King," he pursued him "so relentlessly, with such savage, ironic scorn, that the pursuit sometimes embarrassed even his own supporters."[11]

However much this may have gratified him personally, it improved his position in the country not a whit. There he had to face the problem of refurbishing a party organization grown rusty through disuse, and of soothing recalcitrant Conservatives like Robert Rogers who were rebelling against that "hybrid monster," the National Liberal and Conservative party. These difficulties paled into insignificance compared with those he faced in Quebec. Because the only French-Canadian minister, P.E. Blondin, could not be elected to the Commons, he had been safely ensconced in the Senate. Clearly something had to be done to strengthen the Quebec contingent. In the late summer of 1920 Meighen sought an understanding with E.L. Patenaude, generally regarded as the leading French-Canadian Conservative. But he could not lure back to the fold the man who had broken with Borden on conscription. He kept trying to attract someone of stature, and early in 1921 he almost made a first-class catch in Georges Boivin. Then, at the last moment, Boivin's friends convinced him that it would be political suicide to join forces with Meighen.[12]

By this time it was clear that no one could resurrect the government. If further proof was needed, the by-elections of 1921 provided it. The first one was in West Peterborough, the next was in Yamaska; but the one in Medicine Hat showed how bad the government's position actually was. There, on June 27, a first-rate government candidate lost by almost 10,000 votes to a Farmer candidate who carried the city of Medicine Hat itself. It did not take Meighen long to make up his mind after his return from the Imperial Conference. Naturally many of his backbenchers wanted to postpone the *dies irae* as long as possible. However, the drop in the government's majority to about 20, its obvious unpopularity in the country, its change of leaders, the revolt of the farmers, and the desire of business to have the political uncertainty cleared up were compelling reasons for consulting the electorate. Meighen was never one to want to sail under false colours. On September 1 he announced that an election would be held.

From the beginning many observers doubted whether any party would gain an over-all majority, although they differed on how the parties should be ranked in order of success. None doubted that the Liberals would take almost all of Quebec's seats, or that the Progressives would sweep the Prairie provinces, or that the Maritimes, Ontario, and British Columbia would provide the best fighting grounds. They also agreed that Ontario with its 82 members was the key to the election. Apparently the leaders did too, for King and Meighen spent more than half their time in that province and Crerar over a third.[13] King, knowing that Quebec was safely his, made only one appearance there; Crerar, realizing his cause was hopeless, none at all; and Meighen, unwilling to create the impression that he had written off Quebec, gave it a week of his time.

As Prime Minister, Meighen had to defend the record of the government, and this he did. But everywhere he made it clear that the preeminent issue was whether Canada would retain its protective tariff against the superior economic power of the United States.[14] According to Dawson, he was "vigorous, bitter, fearless, contumelious, and uncompromising. His was . . . the conviction of unfailing logic."[15] He was so logical, said the *Canadian Forum*, that one could "almost hear the clicking of his brain."[16] In contrast, King concentrated on attacking the government instead of explaining his own programme in specific terms. When asked if he would implement the tariff platform adopted by the Liberal Convention of 1919, he replied: "I do not propose to be thought lacking in frankness and candour.'. . . . I regarded the platform as a chart, upon which was plotted the direction of the course it was expected the Party should take."[17] Even at this early stage King "displayed that verbal voluminousness, that unflagging zeal for drudgery, which was in time to weary and beat down all opponents."[18]

Meighen was emphatically clear on the tariff. Everywhere his unfailing theme was: "If I can but get the people in this country to see that the issue is Protection or no Protection, the battle will be won." The tariff should not be increased, but the existing element of protection should not be eliminated as the Progressives demanded. Let the electorate confirm its decisions of 1878 and 1891, and sustain the country's development. The *Canadian Forum* could say in truth that the old dogma of the National Policy was Meighen's political creed. "The crude protectionist formula remains the one infallible test not only of political orthodoxy but also of political sanity. Mr. Meighen's gaze is fixed upon the past – upon a single aspect of the past."[19]

While Crerar no less equivocally proposed the abolition of protection by degrees, King desperately tried to avoid a specific commitment on the tariff. When he reiterated that he had always favoured "a tariff for revenue only," Meighen commented witheringly that such words were "just the circular pomposity of a man who won't say what he means. He might as well say he favours a perambulating tariff, or an atmospheric tariff, or a dynamic tariff."[20] King came under fire again for a speech at Brantford in which he advocated a revenue tariff which would protect manufacturers, farmers, and people of all classes, but would not create multi-millionaires, monopolies, mergers, and trusts.[21] Meighen indignantly described the Liberal platform as "Protection on apples in British Columbia, Free Trade in the Prairie Provinces and the rural parts of Ontario, Protection in industrial centres in Ontario, [no] Conscription in Quebec, and humbug in the Maritime Provinces."[22] Bourassa, with "that felicity of phrasing and ironic humour for which he is distinguished," had the last word; he suggested that Meighen wanted a tariff for protection that would give revenue, King a tariff for revenue that would give protection.[23]

King sought to make the government's record the dominant issue. "In the mind of the Prime Minister [the tariff] may be the issue; in the mind of the people, however, the issue is the Prime Minister himself and what he and his colleagues represent of autocracy and extravagance in the management of public affairs."[24] It was a government, he said, which had secured office through the nefarious device of the War-time Elections Act, had governed mainly by order-in-council, and had delayed an appeal to the people long after it had lost their confidence. It had permitted appalling waste during war and reconstruction, made enormous increases in taxes and the public debt, and indirectly caused the postwar depression and unemployment. By thus accentuating the negative, King sought to keep below the surface the differences within his own party.

His manner of handling the railway question was typical. Almost of necessity the Union government had taken over, in turn, the bankrupt Canadian Northern and Grand Trunk railways, and run them as public undertakings. In Quebec the Gouin-Lemieux wing of the Liberal party strongly opposed government ownership per se, and Lemieux went so far as to support the Shaughnessy plan, by which the former president of the Canadian Pacific proposed that the C.P.R. run the insolvent lines for the Canadian people, who would, of course, meet the deficit. Publicly King was quick to say that Lemieux spoke for himself; privately he doubted the wisdom of raising the question of government ownership at all. The Liberals, he said, would win everything in Quebec anyway, and by bringing up the matter they might lose something in the West and in rural Ontario, which had more favourable attitudes towards public ownership. For this reason he contented himself with innocuous criticism of the board which was running the nationalized railways.

King's catchall campaign was bound to contain a few silly arguments. He denounced the government repeatedly for permitting the financially hard-pressed Riordon interests to give a note for their federal taxes until he discovered that Gouin had adopted the same course. Then Meighen had his innings. "I am not, as a result, saying the Quebec government is in league with 'Big business.' I wouldn't stand on a platform and talk such rubbish."[25] A second incident verged on the ludicrous. Having personally observed a ship unloading munitions at Lévis, King charged the government with militarism. "Talk about disarmament! The Government . . . are bringing in war materials to an extent we have never known before. . . ."[26] It turned out, however, that the government was simply using a munitions credit it possessed in Britain to replenish the Canadian ordnance depots.[27]

Meighen and Crerar ignored King for the most part and concentrated on battling each other. Outside the Prairies Crerar strove desperately to refute the charge that he advocated class government. Rather, he argued, he stood for a reforming creed, for "the spirit of liberalism . . . that is working its way through every Anglo-Saxon country in the world."[28] Let no one say that the real issue was the tariff. It was whether the government should be free or fettered, whether it should be used to promote the good of special interests, whether railways and manufacturers should make contributions to campaign funds solely in "the sordid hope of getting benefits in the way of legislation and administrative favouritism."[29]

Because King felt that Crerar represented liberal elements who were fighting the same opponents as himself, he sought a working agreement with him both before and during the election. Towards the end of the campaign, when it appeared as if the Progressives might prevent him from getting a majority, his attitude stiffened. Their "wretched movement," he told his brother, might vitiate democratic government in the next Parliament[30] and even keep him out of the office for which he felt destined. It was not just coincidental that Liberal candidates appeared about this time to run for seats which the party had intended to leave to the Progressives.

For two months the three leaders subjected the Canadian people to an unprecedented stream of oratory. They talked on every subject under the sun with the exception of Canada's status within the Empire. Many observers said they used their arts of persuasion in vain. According to Morton, "the electorate, seemingly charmed by none, had made up its mind and waited grimly for the polls to open."[31] W.A. Mackintosh was certain that the voters had decided, not on policies, but on conditions.[32] "The country," said the *Round Table*, "was tired of the Government . . . and the Government was sick unto death."[33]

In most respects the prophets foresaw the outcome correctly. Certainly the Prairies went as strongly Progressive as they said it would. The Liberals undoubtedly missed the *Winnipeg Free Press*, which had deserted them for the second time in a row and had presented a programme closely parallel to that of the Progressives.[34] Manitoba gave all its rural seats, including Meighen's seat of Portage la Prairie, to the Progressives. The Progressives took all of Saskatchewan's seats except Regina and all of Alberta's except the 2 seats in Calgary. R.B. Bennett lost out in Calgary West by 16 votes; this was the closest the Conservatives came to winning a seat in the Prairies. These provinces had spoken with a certain voice; 40 of their 43 seats had fallen to the Progressives or their allies.

Quebec also behaved as the prophets said it would. The Conservatives probably feared the worst, but they could hardly have expected the campaign in Quebec to assume the character it did. There turned out to be only one issue: Conscription and Meighen, "half-man, half-monster." "There was . . . a kind of Meighen phobia . . . ," writes W.R. Graham, "which gripped people and made them anathematize him more bitterly than any public man since Confederation."[35] In the district of Quebec the voters were told that, in the event of a Meighen victory, the Orangemen would "pilfer the consecrated wafers in the churches and feed them to the pigs which they led in the streets on July 12. And the author of this sacrilege is Meighen, the father of conscription, the anti-Christ."[36] Meighen found such conduct incomprehensible, especially as it was practised by a party whose leader preached "unity of class and class, creed and creed, race and race, Province and Province, East and West."[37] Yet this was only a forerunner of future Quebec campaigns.

Because Meighen could attract no one of stature, he had had to settle for second-best in his French-Canadian appointments to the cabinet. Rodolphe Monty, L.P. Normand, Louis de Gonzague Belley, and André Fauteux, respectable though they were, were all nonentities. Early in 1921 there had been hopes that Sir Lomer Gouin would join the federal Conservatives. Recently retired as Premier of Quebec and a friend of the financial interests of St. James Street, he shared Meighen's view of the tariff, as did Rodolphe Lemieux, who had once been Laurier's chief lieutenant in Quebec. Even if Gouin had not differed from Meighen on the public ownership of railways, he was astute enough to realize that anyone who espoused Meighen's cause was condemned to political oblivion. In the end he accepted the Liberal nomination in Laurier-Outremont, determined to "go to Ottawa to make Quebec better known, better respected, better loved."[38] The federal Liberals were not overly enthusiastic about someone allegedly imposed by St. James Street.[39] Both Gouin and Lemieux were actually in the Bleu tradition and would have felt much more comfortable within a genuinely conservative party. King, by no means secure in the leadership, had doubts of Lemieux's loyalty. He kept him out of Ontario, ostensibly because of his views on public ownership, and relied instead on Ernest Lapointe who was more in the Rouge or true liberal tradition.

Henri Bourassa, disgusted with politics and afflicted by ill health. declined to be a candidate and spent much of this time observing the Washington Conference. At the outset he could see no good in any party, be it one headed by the conscriptionist Meighen, one headed by the conscriptionist Crerar, or one which had fallen under the yoke of a venal opportunism in the person of Gouin. Hence he advised his compatriots to vote for an independent wherever possible and to support a Liberal only if the sole alternative was a Conservative. On October 19 he changed his mind and declared that the Progressives offered the best choice to the electorate. For a time some Quebec Liberals feared that a Bourassa-Crerar alliance might foil their efforts to crush Meighen. They might have spared themselves the worry. Because of Meighen's repellent image and his lack of newspaper support – even L'Evènement had deserted him – he had no chance at all in French Canada. Every French-Canadian Conservative, including those who ran as independents to avoid the party stigma, went down to defeat.

Anglo-Saxon Quebec had returned three Unionists in 1917. This time St. James Street, regarding Meighen as unsound in his views on the railway question, had become obsessed with the idea that he had to be replaced. The Montreal Gazette, the mouthpiece of the Canadian Pacific–Bank of Montreal interests, came out strongly against him. It favoured Lomer Gouin, who was "right" on railways and would command a large bloc in the Commons.

At least the Gazette was responsible in its actions. The same could hardly be said for the Montreal Star. Its publisher, Lord Atholstan, once described by Meighen as one who "could turn a corner so fast you could hear his shirt tails snap,"[40] loved to play the part of puppet-master manipulating the politicians. Until November 30 his paper took an equivocal position. Then, because Meighen said openly that Gouin was bent on destroying the national railway system, it became extremely hostile to him. Without a scrap of evidence it charged that the head office of the Grand Trunk would be moved from Montreal to Toronto, as a preliminary to making that city the headquarters of the nationalized railways. The Liberals took full advantage of the *Star*'s revelations, groundless though they were. Montreal, they prophesied gloomily, was to lose one of its greatest assets and 50,000 of its citizens would be jobless.[41] To counteract these charges at such a late date was extraordinarily difficult. Undoubtedly they played their part in English-speaking Montreal's total rejection of Meighen. For the first and only time all of Quebec's seats went to one party.

The prophets also foresaw correctly that the Maritimes, British Columbia, and Ontario would provide the best fighting grounds, although they expected the Conservatives to do better than they did in the Maritimes. There the Progressives ran candidates for 16 of 31 seats, but managed to win only Victoria-Carleton in New Brunswick, where the Liberals helped them by not putting up a candidate. The Conservatives and Liberals split New Brunswick's remaining 10 seats evenly, though the former polled 10 per cent fewer votes than the latter. The Conservatives did this well in seats because they won the Anglo-Saxon ridings by small majorities and lost the Acadian ridings by lopsided majorities. In Nova Scotia and Prince Edward Island, too, their popular vote was well down and they won no seats at all. Their image in the Maritimes was generally poor. In contrast, they made their best showing in British Columbia where they polled 47.9 per cent of the votes and won 7 of the 13 seats. This was not the only time that strong winds on one side of the mountain were not blowing on the other side.

Ontario turned out, as predicted, to be the best fighting ground for all three parties. Not unexpectedly, the protectionist Conservative party kept its hold on the cities of Toronto and Hamilton; it also retained considerable support in rural Ontario. In all likelihood, the fact that the Liberals and Progressives split the anti-government vote helped the Conservatives to win some 15 seats. On the other hand, they won only 2 of the 13 seats where the Liberals chose not to oppose the Progressives, even though some of them were traditionally Tory ridings.

The Liberals and Progressives took comparable portions of the popular vote in Ontario, each about 10 per cent less than the Conservatives. While the Progressives won 24 seats (3 more than the Liberals) this was considerably fewer than they had expected. In their aim at a country-wide total of 75 seats – enough to constitute a genuine balance of power – they were thwarted by Ontario. Part of the trouble lay in the failure of the Drury

Farmer-Labour government in Ontario to accomplish what had been expected of it. There were rumours, too, that the financial interests, convinced of Meighen's fate, had thrown their monetary support to the Liberals and thereby greatly strengthened them against their Progressive opponents.[42]

If an Independent Liberal is included, the Liberals had 117 seats, 1 short of a majority. Even at that, the distortions of the electoral system helped them considerably. On the basis of the popular vote, instead of winning 116 seats, they should have had 96; the Conservatives should have won 71 instead of 50; the Progressives should have had 54 instead of 64. The 260,970 votes that the Conservatives polled in Quebec and the Prairie provinces produced not a single seat for them. This served to magnify their defeat, the most resounding one inflicted upon a Canadian government up to this time. Not only had the Conservative party run third and polled little more than 30 per cent of the popular vote, but the Prime Minister and 8 cabinet ministers had lost their seats. In 6 provinces it had elected nobody and, had Ontario not returned 37 of its candidates, it would have altogether forfeited its position as a national party.

In the battle between the lucidity of Meighen and the obscurity of King, the latter had triumphed. Dawson suggests that Meighen could be lucid only because he had abandoned a primary function of a party leader, "the discovery and maintenance of areas of common agreement which would enable him to build an effective party on a national scale."[43] W.R. Graham replies that Meighen was actually trying to coalesce a broad variety of interests on the tariff question, and in the process do what he felt a party leader was obligated to do: to crystallize rather than to obscure issues in order that the differences between the parties might be debated intelligently.[44] With all apologies to Graham, it is dubious if an extreme stand on the tariff was an appropriate foundation stone upon which to build a national party in the 1920's. In any case Meighen and perhaps King might have reversed their concepts of the function of a party and its leader in the election of 1921 and the result would not have been much different.

Highly significant was the election of a Commons based largely on regional differences. The Liberals were solidly entrenched from the Ottawa River to the Atlantic. The Progressives were not so much a farmers' party as a western farmers' party. Meighen's followers were largely an Ontario group, although not from one section of the province. W.A. Mackintosh concluded that, despite the work of sixty years, "the union of regions is but partially accomplished and the sectionalism apparent in election returns is no mere surface phenomenon but rooted deeply in the fundamental facts of geology, topography, climate, and resulting industrial conditions."[45] As he saw it, a solid West based on economic differences would constitute a more stubborn fact than a solid Quebec based on racial differences.[46] Yet, as it turned out, Quebec long resisted the blandishments of those who had isolated it. In 1921, however, it emerged from its isolation in no uncertain fashion. *La Presse* insisted that its people wanted nothing more than "their fair share, their whole share, of influence."[47] The Toronto *Mail and Empire*, noting the dependence of the Liberals on Quebec, asked: "Are we to be governed on Canadian or just French-Canadian lines?" to which the *Orange Sentinel* replied vehemently: "French Canada is on top now, with a vengeance."[48]

	Seats	Candidates				Elected							
		C.	L.	P.	O.	C.	%	L.	%	P.	%	O.	%
Nova Scotia	16	14	16	8	2			16	100.0				
New Brunswick	11	10	10	5	1	5	45.5	5	45.5	1	9.1		
Prince Edward Island	4	4	4	3	1			4	100.0				
Quebec	65	48	65	18	29			65	100.0				
Ontario	82	79	65	71	16	37	45.1	21	25.6	24	29.3		
Manitoba	15	13	9	12	11			1	6.7	12	80.0	2	13.3
Saskatchewan	16	14	11	16	2			1	6.3	15	93.8		
Alberta	12	12	10	10	6					10	83.3	2	16.7
British Columbia	13	13	11	5	8	7	53.8	3	23.1	2	15.4	1	7.7
Yukon	1	1	1		1	1	100.0						
Total	235	208	202	148	77	50	21.3	116	49.4	64	27.2	5	2.1

Others elected: Man. (2): I.L. (1); Lab. (1).

Alta. (2): Lab. (1); I. (1).

B.C. (1): I. (1).

Others (votes

polled): N.S. (2): Lab. (2) 7,904.

N.B. (1): Lab. (1) 1,224.

P.E.I. (1): Lab. (1) 2,537.

Que. (29): I. (26) 57, 863; Lab. (2) 1,799; I.L. (1) 1,825.

Ont. (16): I.C. (1) 257; I.L. (1) 2,764; I. (6) 6,947; Lab. (7) 23,923; Soldier (1) 3,984.

Man. (11): I.L. (1) 10,570; I. (5) 11,503; Soc. (1) 3,094; Lab. (3) 9,764; I.C. (1) 1,220.

Sask. (2): Lab. (1) 1,896; I. (1) 1,714.

Alta. (6): Lab. (4) 11,790; I. (2) 7,738.

B.C. (8): Soc. (2) 4,565; Lab. (3) 10,484; I. (2) 4,749; Comm. (1) 810.

Yukon (1): I. (1) 18.

Popular Vote								Total
C.	%	L.	%	P.	%	O.	%	
83,928	32.3	136,064	52.4	31,897	12.3	7,904	3.0	259,793
61,172	39.4	76,733	49.4	16,223	10.4	1,224	0.8	155,352
19,504	37.2	23,950	45.7	6,453	12.3	2,537	4.8	52,444
146,236	18.4	558,056	70.2	29,197	3.7	61,487	7.7	794,976
445,175	39.2	338,282	29.8	314,092	27.7	37,875	3.3	1,135,424
42,218	24.4	18,816	10.9	75,578	43.7	36,151	20.9	172,763
37,335	16.7	46,448	20.7	136,472	61.0	3,610	1.6	223,865
35,181	20.3	27,404	15.8	90,791	52.5	19,528	11.3	172,904
74,225	47.9	46,249	29.8	13,917	9.0	20,608	13.3	154,999
707	51.1	658	47.6			18	1.3	1,383
945,681	30.3	1,272,660	40.7	714,620	22.9	190,942	6.1	3,123,903

1. R. MacGregor Dawson, *William Lyon Mackenzie King: A Political Biography 1874-1923* (Toronto: University of Toronto Press, 1958), p. 319.

2. *Ibid.*, p. 340.

3. *Ibid.*, pp. 340-41.

4. W.L. Morton, *The Progressive Party in Canada* (Toronto: University of Toronto Press, 1950), p. 100.

5. *Supra*, p. 144.

6. Morton, *Progressive Party*, p. 60.

7. *Ibid.*, p. 66.

8. *Ibid.*, p. 96.

9. C.B. Macpherson, *Democracy in Alberta: The Theory and Practice of a Quasi-Party System* (Toronto: University of Toronto Press, 1953), pp. 38-54.

10. Morton, *Progressive Party*, p. 95.

11. W.R. Graham, *Arthur Meighen: And Fortune Fled*, II (Toronto: Clarke, Irwin & Company, 1963), p. 10.

12. *Ibid.*, p. 21.

13. Dawson, *King*, p. 351.

14. Graham, *Meighen*, II, p. 120.

15. Dawson, *King*, p. 351.

16. *Canadian Forum*, II (October, 1921), p. 388.

17. *Ibid.*, p. 387.

18. Morton, *Progressive Party*, p. 125.

19. *Canadian Forum*, II (November, 1921), p. 422.

20. Dawson, *King*, p. 351.

21. *Canadian Annual Review*, 1921 (Toronto: The Canadian Review Company, 1922), p. 463.

22. *Ibid.*, p. 454.

23. "The Grand Election," *Round Table*, XII (December, 1921), p. 164.

24. *Canadian Annual Review*, 1921, p. 458.

25. *Ibid.*, p. 501.

26. *Ibid.*, pp. 496-97.

27. Graham, *Meighen*, II, pp. 122-26.

28. *Canadian Annual Review*, 1921, p. 475.

29. *Ibid.*, p. 476.

30. Dawson, *King*, p. 355.

31. Morton, *Progressive Party*, p. 125.

32. W.A. Mackintosh, "The General Election of 1921," *Queen's Quarterly*, XXIX (Spring, 1922), p. 310.

33. "The Federal Election," *Round Table*, XII (March, 1922), p. 388.

34. Ramsay Cook, *The Politics of John W. Dafoe and the Free Press* (Toronto: University of Toronto Press, 1963), p. 115.

35. Graham, *Meighen*, II, p. 142.

36. Robert Rumilly, *Histoire de la Province de Québec*, XXV (Montreal: Les Editions Chantecler Ltée, 1952), p. 225.

37. Graham, *Meighen*, II, p. 143.

38. *Canadian Annual Review*, 1921, p. 486.

39. Rumilly, *Histoire*, XXV, p. 219.

40. Graham, *Meighen*, II, p. 150.

41. *Ibid.*, pp. 162-64.

42. Morton, *Progressive Party*, p. 126.

43. Dawson, *King*, p. 352.

44. Graham, *Meighen*, II, p. 129.

45. Mackintosh, "General Election," p. 314.

46. *Ibid.*

47. *Canadian Annual Review*, 1921, p. 522.

48. *Ibid.*, pp. 518-19.

Fifteenth

General Election

"THE HUNG JURY"

There was no clear-cut issue in the election of 1925. As a result, it turned largely on the image the government had built up during the previous four years. In external affairs Prime Minister King felt he had done especially well. He had said "nay, nay" when requested to assist Britain during the Chanak crisis of 1922 and had got away with it; he had resisted the centralizing influences at the Imperial Conference of 1923; he had done much to set the stage for a new definition of the relations between Britain and the self-governing members of the Empire. Canadians were by no means in general agreement upon these matters and, in any case, few appreciated their significance. Certainly they were not vote-getters in 1925 and they played almost no part in the campaign.

Most Liberals found little to be enthusiastic about in the domestic policy that the government sought to justify. They had won the election of 1921 because of the reaction against the existing ministry, and any Liberal leader would have had much the same success as King. In office he had done nothing to capture the public imagination. It may have been highly creditable that he had been able to form a government from the discordant elements at his disposal and make it work. Certainly such protectionist easterners as Fielding and Gouin had collaborated with such low-tariff westerners as Stewart and Motherwell; Charles Murphy, the fervent Laurier Liberal, had got along with the apostate Fielding. All of them had agreed "not to insist on measures which others could not support."[1] But it was a somewhat negative accomplishment.

By the end of 1923, J.W. Dafoe was still certain that, even if the Prairies returned Liberals, the latter would be subject to the Montreal element "with only the right to make protests in the party caucus, which will be listened to tolerantly and ignored."[2] In 1924, *mirabile dictu*, he discovered the annual Speech from the Throne to be not, as it usually was, "a piece of pretentious humbug, but a document of interest and value to the country."[3] What had caused the Prime Minister to change his position, if only temporarily? King knew the direction in which he wished to lead the party; above all, he wanted to win back the Liberals who had voted for the Progressives in 1921,[4] but only if it brought more gains in the West than losses in the East. In January 1924, he pondered whether the time had come to "cut the Gordian knot to sever this [Montreal] connection completely and bring the Liberals and the Farmers together."[5] The time was propitious. Only a month earlier Fielding had suffered a paralytic stroke and shortly afterwards Gouin had retired, ostensibly because of ill health. Having nothing to fear from the main guardians of the protectionist system, King proceeded to reduce or abolish duties on the equipment used in primary industries and on the material used to manufacture that equipment. With a capacity for self-deception that many considered hypocrisy, he then boasted that he had been "true to Liberal tradition, true to the platform of the 1919 Convention, true to the pledges I gave the electors in 1921 and true to the people – the producers and consumers."[6]

King was prepared to be bold only once on the tariff; the budget of 1925 was completely standpat. It was not in him to risk alienating the eastern elements on the eve of the election. He displayed the same type of attitude towards railway rates. Although he retained the sections of the Crow's Nest Pass Agreement that were applicable to wheat and flour, he terminated the sections that governed westbound goods. The *Winnipeg Free Press* called it "A Complete Defeat for the West."[7]

The Prime Minister's one attempt to provide a dramatic election issue came close to being a disaster. To counteract the monopoly of the North Atlantic Shipping Conference, his government proposed to subsidize ten ships to be built by the independent Scottish shipowner, Sir William Petersen. It turned out to be, as Meighen said, "a hasty, ill-considered, reckless plunge,"[8] and although it taught King not to be bold again, it left him without the issue he wanted.

The government could not point to a single conspicuous achievement. It had lasted for four years under difficult circumstances, but the mere act of survival would hardly win votes. It had tinkered with economic problems, but the country was just beginning to recover from the long postwar recession. Throughout most of Canada "the tide was at the turn, but not yet running."[9] In the Maritimes, where the tide had not even begun to turn, the bad times had provoked a Maritime Rights agitation which the Conservatives had exploited. Beset with problems elsewhere, King had given the Maritimes scant attention. Although he may have strengthened his own position in the party, he had scarcely made himself a popular or heroic figure in the country.

The one factor which was working to his advantage was the split in the Progressives. There had been two motives governing their uprising. "One, represented by the Manitoban Progressives, was the desire to recapture the historic Liberal party of rural democracy and low tariff from the protectionist elements of Quebec and Ontario. . . . The other [represented largely by Albertans] was to destroy the system of party government itself."[10] Partly because of these differences the Progressives had decided not to become the official parliamentary opposition; largely because of them Crerar resigned as leader in November 1922. The usual view has been that this basic cleavage on the proper type of political organization was what splintered the Progressives after 1924. Professor Kenneth McNaught, however, attributes it to "the decisions made with respect to the Liberal legislative programme" by the two wings of the Progressives.[11] That is so, but it is also true that this divergent course on specific matters merely reflected a fundamental difference in principle.

Professor Neatby to the contrary notwithstanding, it seems a distortion of the facts to give Mackenzie King much credit for the split.[12] Not until the budget of 1924 did he make any practical overtures to the crypto-Liberals who formed such a large part of the Progressive movement. Even then it was the Labourite J.S. Woodsworth who engineered the split; by moving an amendment to the budget that incorporated much of the Progressive programme he caused the genuine advocates of change – the so-called Ginger Group – to break with the rest of the party.[13] In the unofficial meetings of Woodsworth with these members Professor McNaught sees the origins of the C.C.F. at Ottawa.[14]

The Ginger Group withdrew from the caucus in 1924. Further withdrawals occurred the next year when seventeen crypto-Liberals voted with the government despite a decision of caucus to the contrary. As the election of 1925 approached, it was apparent that the Progressive movement was spent as a national force. It had not secured the re-alignment of parties it had aimed at, but it had demonstrated the difficulty of independence under the conventions of parliamentary government.[15]

As the Progressives slowly disintegrated, King's major opponents were decidedly on the upswing. By this time the Prime Minister had developed an intense personal hatred of Meighen. This was not surprising. No one would relish being made to "feel fearful and inferior in the House of Commons," and being "subjected there to repeated embarrassments and humiliations,"[16] as Meighen caused him to be. This kind of treatment seemed to intensify as Conservative fortunes improved. In July 1923 a Conservative government was returned in Ontario, and Premier George Howard Ferguson soon left no doubt that he would back Meighen. Revived Conservative organizations in the West also expressed their confidence in the national leader. The fact that the economy was still depressed and that the "ministry ha[d] not impressed itself on the public imagination"[17] gave further impetus to the Conservative comeback. In December victories in by-elections in Halifax and in Kent, New Brunswick, crowned a year of Conservative successes.

The year 1924 brought the Conservatives some setbacks, especially their loss of West Hastings in Ontario and their failure to establish a beachhead in Quebec by again losing in traditionally Tory St. Antoine. Yet the outlook was still favourable for them. That is, except in Quebec. *La belle province* was driving Meighen practically to despair. Although St. Antoine had revealed differences among English-speaking Conservatives, they were nothing compared to those among the French. Rodolphe Monty aspired to be the French-Canadian leader, but he appeared doomed to failure from the start. If anyone were to be successful, it would be Patenaude. He was all too aware of the objections to Meighen in Quebec and there were reports that he was contemplating leading a Quebec Conservative party independent of Meighen and backed by Lord Atholstan. Meighen knew that such a proceeding could not win seats in Quebec and would harm the party elsewhere. Yet all he could do was wait, and Patenaude was an unconscionable time in making up his mind. Meanwhile the Montreal English-language press, especially Atholstan's *Star*, was pursuing its favourite pastime of Meighen-baiting.[18]

Such were the circumstances under which King contemplated an election following the session of 1925. Even as he pondered, matters got worse. On June 25 Nova Scotia's Liberal administration of forty-three years suffered a complete rout. King had no desire to be put in a position where he had no room to manoeuvre; so, "following intuition . . . supported by reason,"[19] he decided on a fall election. The defeat of the Liberal government in New Brunswick on August 10 caused him to have second thoughts. Indeed, the cabinet session of August 15 was so gloomy that Lapointe said it was "like attending our own funeral."[20] However, King concluded that hanging on might lead to the total defeat of his party, and early in September he set October 29 as election day.

Meanwhile he sought to strengthen his cabinet. It needed rejuvenation for it contained too many veterans who were well beyond their prime. Yet he failed to achieve what he had hoped, partly because of the feeling that he was in command of a sinking ship and partly because of his own decision that "there would be no further concessions to the west in the immediate future."[21] The only two additions of note were Vincent Massey and Herbert Marler, but as wealthy protectionists from Toronto and Montreal they would hardly help the Liberals in the West. Charles Dunning, who might have improved the party's chances there, could not be induced to abandon the premiership of Saskatchewan.

The campaign was a dull one. King campaigned on the record of his government, drawing from Meighen the caustic observation that he did not point to one specific achievement because his "page of achievements . . . is a blank."[22] In his initial campaign speech at Richmond Hill, Ontario, the Prime Minister stressed the need for majority government. Group government, he said, might be inevitable in transitional phases of Canadian history, but it was not the kind of government to achieve great reforms or to meet the country's need in 1925.[23] Yet, paradoxically, in the same speech he described the Parliament just dissolved as "the Parliament of large majorities." His statement led the *Canadian Forum* to observe that, if he had chosen to introduce reform legislation, "he could have had the support of every Progressive that ever grew wheat."[24]

More specifically, King asked for a clear mandate to deal with four urgent problems: transportation, immigration, the constitution and powers of the Senate, and fiscal matters, especially the tariff. On transportation, he would see to it that the C.N.R. was divorced from political influence and control, that the C.N.R. and C.P.R. co-operated to reduce operating costs, and that further steps were taken to reduce ocean freight rates. On immigration, his government would initiate vigorous steps to attract settlers. On the powers of the Senate, it would convene a Dominion-Provincial conference and appoint to the upper House only those who were pledged to its reform. It was all delightfully vague and Meighen had his usual blunt comment: "Mr. King says he wants a mandate on these three. What does he want a mandate to do? He has not told us and he is not going to tell us."[25]

On the tariff, King called for a middle path between the extremes of protection and free trade – "a common sense tariff," based on national requirements, and determined by the government and Parliament on the advice of a permanent tariff board. At this point he included a plea for national unity; his course, he said, was designed to reconcile rather than exaggerate sectional differences. It was in essence, says Morton, "a plea for a party majority drawn from all sections of the country, and for a revenue tariff affording incidental protection and for a re-integration of the nation under a Liberal party once more traditional and composite."[26]

In his turn Meighen denounced the King government, calling it the most futile that Canadians had ever had to endure, and demanded a revision of the tariff on a definitely and consistently protective basis. "If this is not right policy for Canada," he said, "the Conservative party should not be in power."[27] Meighen admitted that this was the same programme which had been defeated in 1921. But "I preach it now just as I preached it then and this time the people of Canada are not going to be befuddled by the twisting and shifting practices of Mr. King."[28] As Meighen saw it, the protective tariff would be a fundamental ingredient in consolidating the national fabric; "it was the National Policy as Macdonald had shaped it, and as it had since endured."[29]

Essentially the campaign followed these broad lines, but as usual the leaders adapted their appeals to their regional audiences. While Meighen upheld the protective tariff in both the Maritimes and the West, he emphasized the advantages to those regions of his plan for compensatory freight rate reductions to be financed out of the Dominion Treasury. In the West no politician could ignore the Hudson Bay Railway. King promised to complete it if he received enough support in the West to carry out Liberal policies generally; Meighen lambasted this alleged holding out of a bribe to the electors and promised that, if the line could be completed for $3 million, he would do it.

The *Canadian Forum* was highly critical of Meighen for playing into King's hands. By his obsession with the tariff, he had put King in the position of not having to defend his own poor record and programme. The result, in its opinion, was an election little short of farcical.[30] Fundamentally, however, it considered King to be more at fault than Meighen. Instead of coming to terms with Crerar, he had abandoned the Liberal platform of 1919 and condemned himself to a long series of shaky compromises. The *Forum* measured the stagnation of political life and the lack of enthusiasm for leaders or parties by the fact that three leading newspapers, the Montreal *Star*, the Toronto *Globe*, and the *Winnipeg Free Press* were "each pursuing in their different styles an attitude of cold and critical neutrality."[31]

More than one observer commented upon the general silence on imperial and international problems and on the development of Canadian autonomy. Because the Conservatives were not anxious to cause a further affront to Quebec, they refrained from denouncing King as anti-British; because the Liberals did not want to alienate the other provinces, they purposely avoided any outward show of nationalist fervour.[32] Herbert Heaton was even led to ask: "Do our leaders feel that the best way to solve imperial problems is not to talk about them, but to let them solve themselves?"[33]

The *Canadian Forum* could find little good to say about the Progressives, especially the Easterners, whom it considered to be "camouflaged Liberals who retain the Progressive label to avoid responsibility for the sins of the Government."[34] Although the Progressives went into the election as "groups of independents, scarcely to be termed a party,"[35] Crerar's successor, Robert Forke, put up a bold front. Since his party had been unable to bring about the alignment of political forces it had wanted, he said it was necessary to have strong Progressive representation in the next Parliament; otherwise the reshaping of national policies and the attaining of needed reforms might have to be postponed for a generation.[36] On specific matters, Forke stood for much the same things as Crerar had in 1921. He added one new thing: the Hudson Bay Railway. "The railway to the Bay was in 1925 and 1926 a symbol of the deep frustration of the continental West,"[37] and all the Progressives were for it enthusiastically and unconditionally.

Only 20 Labour candidates contested the election, 4 fewer than in 1921. "With the possible exception of a few backward countries such as Zanzibar and Liberia," said the *Canadian Forum*, "there is probably no state where the political power of Labour is so negligible as it is in this Dominion."[38] Herbert Heaton, after examining recent elections in the Dominions, concluded that in Canada "there was virtually no Labour Party or Labour issue," while in Australia "all, or virtually all, was Labour *versus* anti-Labour."[39]

If the results of the election are considered province by province, the Conservatives generally fared either very well or very poorly. Ontario gave them an astounding victory. They took 57.0 per cent of the popular vote – more than Borden got in 1911 or Diefenbaker in 1958. In the industrial cities they piled up an overwhelming number of votes; in Toronto it was 114,566 to the Liberals' 39,580. They made a strong showing everywhere, losing only 14 seats, 7 of them by small margins and all on the periphery – 3 were along the Quebec border, 2 in northern Ontario, and the remainder in rural western Ontario. Yet this was the province in which King got the most co-operation from the Progressives in the nomination of candidates. As a result, Liberals opposed Progressives in only 8 ridings. In 16 others, only Progressives and Conservatives ran against each other, and in 2 of these, Grey South-East and Huron North, the former won their only victories in Ontario. None the less, the Liberal showing was poor; the 5 cabinet ministers from Ontario, including Mackenzie King himself, all went down to defeat. One observer attributed the result to the province's growing industrialism and the general spread of protectionist sentiment.[40] But the Ontario voter appears to have been influenced less by King's attitude towards the tariff than by the generally lacklustre image he had created.

The Conservatives also fared well in the Maritimes, taking 23 of 29 seats, a result they have bettered only in 1958. The 3 seats they lost in Nova Scotia were all lost by small margins, while in New Brunswick they won even the Acadian seats, Gloucester excepted, and there the result was close. In these provinces the Liberals maintained they stood for every legitimate Maritime right, but the Conservatives had taken over the Maritime Rights movement as their own; in addition, the 3 Conservative provincial premiers campaigned actively for Meighen.[41] It may seem extraordinary that a region which had suffered severely from the effects of "N.P." could support high-tariff Meighen so strongly. But it had recovered even less than the other provinces from the postwar recession and it was simply wreaking its vengeance on the government which it held responsible.

While the Conservative showing in British Columbia was reasonably good–10 of 14 seats–it was no better than could be expected from a province which was traditionally theirs and which gave them strong support in 1921. Possibly the vigorous campaign of Liberal Premier J.H. King helped to limit the number of their victories. The Conservatives were more satisfied with Manitoba where their deep roots enabled them to take 7 seats despite their protectionist stance. But elsewhere their showing was dismal. In Alberta and Saskatchewan they lacked organization and newspaper support; although they increased their popular vote by more than 50 per cent, they started from too low a base to have many successes. In Alberta they managed to win the 2 Calgary and 1 of the Edmonton seats, but although they put up a good fight in Saskatoon and Moose Jaw they remained without seats in Saskatchewan.

King attributed many of his losses in English Canada to the three-way contests involving his party, the Conservatives, and the Progressives. His contention does not bear close scrutiny, except in Manitoba, where the Conservatives took 4 of such contests and the Progressives, 1. Of the 8 three-way fights in Ontario, the Liberals won 5; of the 17 in Saskatchewan, 14 went to the Liberals and 3 to the Progressives; of the 10 in Alberta, 3 were taken by the Liberals and 7 by the Progressives. It was Meighen who should have complained about his lack of success in the multi-candidate contests.

The Progressives also had cause to complain. In Saskatchewan they lost votes, both to the Liberals directed by Premier Charles Dunning and to a reviving Conservative party under J.T.M. Anderson, and their representation fell from 15 to 6. Only in Alberta, where they entered into a co-operative effort with Labour, could they minimize their losses.[42] They ended up with only 24 members, 9 of whom were members of the U.F.A. and ready to go their own way.

The situation in Quebec was still not favourable for the Conservatives. "Meighen needed a coadjutor in that province" and by general consensus Patenaude was the man. Everybody from Borden and Meighen downward had a hand at courting him; yet "week after week, month after month went by and still he did not declare himself, keeping the party in Quebec in a state of suspended animation while he made up his mind."[43] Lord Atholstan also wanted Patenaude to lead the Conservatives in Quebec, but this boded no good for Meighen. Atholstan had made it clear that neither his newspaper nor his pocketbook would be available unless Patenaude remained independent of Meighen and conducted the campaign as he dictated.

When Meighen passed through Lévis on his way to the Maritimes, he announced that he would speak in Quebec City on September 25. However, on September 20, after Patenaude had asserted his intention to further unstintingly "the tradition and the principles which have made the life and the strength of the Liberal-Conservative party," he declared in almost the same breath: "I am in every way free, I am free from Mr. Meighen, even as I am free from Mr. King."[44] The decision meant that the Conservative candidates in Quebec were neither Meighen's nor the party's, but Patenaude's. It meant also that Meighen would not appear in Quebec, for he would not intrude where he was not wanted, especially as Patenaude's tactics were to act as if he did not exist. So on his way back from the Maritimes Meighen made no public appearances until he reached Montreal where a few personal friends greeted him "almost on the sly."[45] Candidates who remained loyal to Meighen and who contested seats in Quebec were snubbed and even threatened for a time with opposition from Patenaude candidates. Those who still persisted, as Rodolphe Monty did in Laurier-Outremont and Grattan O'Leary did in Gaspé, were left entirely to their own resources.[46]

One thing can be said for Patenaude. To the Quebec Liberals he presented a threat such as they had not experienced for a long time. The *Gazette* was friendly towards him, while Atholstan and the *Star* were his avid supporters. On external affairs, he declared that Canada should not be placed in a state of war unless there was first an appeal to the people; on the tariff, he followed the orthodox Meighen line; on railways, he avoided a formal statement of policy, but it was evident that he had the support of the C.P.R. group and Montreal finance. The Toronto *Globe* and the Toronto *Star* alleged that these interests sought to use him much as they had Gouin, their ultimate object being to have the C.P.R. absorb the National Railways and create a gigantic monopoly. Not for patriotism, they said, was St. James Street throwing $2 or $3 million into Patenaude's campaign chest.[47] And he did seem to have plenty of funds. "Tirant sur une caisse inépuisable," says Rumilly, "Patenaude voyageait en train spécial, de comté en comté, de succès en succès, à travers l'or, la rouille, et la pourpre des forêts québécoises."[48] Actually he had made no deal with the proprietor of the *Star* or the Montreal interests. Atholstan, who not only distrusted King but also held him in contempt, was simply hoping that Patenaude's men would hold the balance in the next Parliament and, as a result, that he would be enabled to dump Meighen and possess an instrument to effect his other ends as well.

However, Patenaude had not a chance. King went only to Montreal and Quebec, and needed not to have gone even there. At Quebec Lucien Cannon hailed him as the one who had been "toujours fidèle à Sir Wilfrid Laurier." From Gaspé to the borders of Ontario the name of Laurier cast an incredibly long shadow. Everywhere Liberal speakers talked continuously about the memory of Laurier, the dream of Laurier, the heritage of Laurier. They also refused to accept Patenaude's denial of Meighen at its face value. "On se sert de Patenaude pour passer Meighen en contrabande," was their constant refrain. "Grattez Patenaude," they said, "et vous trouverez Meighen."[49] Premier Taschereau put it this way: "Mr. Patenaude criticizes Mr. King, and does not form a third party; hence he is with Mr. Meighen, no matter what he says."[50] Try as he might, Patenaude could not divorce himself from Meighen or, more particularly, the image of Meighen.

Because the Liberals faced their strongest threat in a long time, they were not squeamish about the tactics they used. Jean Charles Harvey in *Le Cri de Québec* warned of the folly of supporting Meighen and being dragged into adventures which would afford the foolish honour of saving civilization for a second time. *Le Soleil* complained that Mr. Meighen was "always ready to say yes. Let him be installed again as master of our destinies in Ottawa . . . and we will have to march against the Turks, the Egyptians, the Hindus, or other barbarians."[51] Even Premier Taschereau joined in with obvious untruths. It was Meighen, he said, "who, with his conscription law, has filled the cemeteries of Flanders with 60,000 Canadians. Has he grown better since? Has he reformed? Has he had perfect contrition? No."[52]

King was not personally responsible for this type of vilification but, as Blair Neatby admits, he did nothing to moderate it. Neatby, however, excuses him on the grounds that both King and Meighen had accepted the autonomy of their Quebec wings, and that "the Liberal abuse of Meighen was no more misleading or hypocritical than Patenaude's fictional repudiation of his leadership."[53] But surely there was an important difference in that Meighen, although he disapproved of Patenaude's conduct, could do nothing about it. Certainly it was brazen effrontery on King's part to accuse Meighen of raising the race cry; Meighen himself pointed out that the issue in Quebec four years earlier had not been protection but his alleged murder of their children. "For King to accuse [Meighen] of being the author rather than the victim of race prejudice," says Roger Graham, "was a piece of blatant nonsense and a nice illustration of his way of twisting the issue of national unity for his own purposes."[54]

In any case the Liberal Tactics worked. The only Conservatives to win were 4 from principally English-speaking ridings. Bourassa, running for the first time since 1908, was elected in Labelle as an Independent; the remaining 60 seats went Liberal. Despite Patenaude's mighty effort and Atholstan's campaign chest, Quebec failed for the third successive time to elect a French-Canadian Conservative. However, there was a difference this time. The great majority of the Conservative candidates did not lose their deposits, and the party raised its share of the popular vote from 18.4 to 33.7 per cent, but the working of the electoral system kept them from winning seats. Some attributed their failure to the women's vote, some to the lack of a virile French Conservative press, and some to Bourassa and *Le Devoir*. All of these played their part, but what counted most was the bad Conservative image and the ability of the Liberals to capitalize upon it all the more because Meighen remained as leader. He was altogether too much of a burden for Patenaude to carry. Although Meighen was determined never to be kept out of Quebec again, he certainly had begun to have doubts about that province. In 1921 his complete failure in Quebec had made little difference, but in 1925 it was altogether crucial. If he had won even the handful of seats his party had taken in Quebec during the Laurier régime, he would have commanded a bare majority in the Commons. By winning only 4, he had fallen 7 seats short. Was it possible, he wondered, that he would never do much better in Quebec?

The over-all results brought to light an interesting phenomenon, to be repeated in a lesser degree several times later. The Canadian electoral

Le trafiquant de chair humaine

En voulez-vous du Meighen impérialiste ? votez pour les candidats de M. Patenaude

by Arthur Temay. Quebec Le Soleil, *October 23, 1925. Courtesy of* Le Soleil.

system, it seems, is fated to provide membership in the Commons closely approximating the popular vote only when none of the parties possesses a majority. In 1925 the Conservatives got 46.5 per cent of the popular vote and 47.3 per cent of the seats, the Liberals 39.9 and 40.4, the Progressives 8.9 and 9.8. In a sense the Conservatives had hard luck, for a party which gets such a large percentage of the votes can normally count upon a majority

	Seats	Candidates				Elected							
		C.	L.	P.	O.	C.	%	L.	%	P.	%	O.	%
Nova Scotia	14	14	14		1	11	78.6	3	21.4				
New Brunswick	11	11	11		1	10	90.9	1	9.1				
Prince Edward Island	4	4	4			2	50.0	2	50.0				
Quebec	65	58	65		21	4	6.2	59	90.8			2	3.1
Ontario	82	82	65	24	17	68	82.9	11	13.4	2	2.4	1	1.2
Manitoba	17	16	11	12	5	7	41.2	1	5.9	7	41.2	2	11.8
Saskatchewan	21	19	19	21	2			15	71.4	6	28.6		
Alberta	16	15	14	12	4	3	18.8	4	25.0	9	56.3		
British Columbia	14	14	11	3	7	10	71.4	3	21.4			1	7.1
Yukon	1	1	1			1	100.0						
Total	245	234	215	72	58	116	47.3	99	40.4	24	9.8	6	2.4

Note: An Independent Liberal in Quebec, unopposed by an official Liberal candidate, is included in the Liberal columns.

Others elected: Que. (2): I.L. (1); I. (1).
Ont. (1): I.L. (1).
Man. (2): Lab. (2).
B.C. (1): I. (1).

Others (votes
polled): N.S. (1): Lab. (1) 3,617.
N.B. (1): I. (1) 84.
Que. (21): Other L. (1) 768; Farmer (1) 1,130; Lab. (2) 1,681; I.L. (10) 32,175; I. (4) 8,381; Protectionist (3) 12,111.
Ont. (17): Lab. (5) 9,478; I.C. (5) 8,997; I.L. (4) 5,144; I. (2) 9,976; Farm.-Lab. (1) 762.
Man. (5): Lab. (5) 19,325.
Sask. (2): I. Prog. (2) 1,904.
Alta. (4): Lab. (2) 9,750; Lab.-Farmer (2) 4,774.
B.C. (7): Lab. (5) 11,479; Soc. (1) 1,888; I. (1) 4,794.

Popular Vote								Total
C.	%	L.	%	P.	%	O.	%	
125,283	56.4	93,110	41.9			3,617	1.6	222,010
90,489	59.7	61,087	40.3			84	0.1	151,660
23,749	48.0	25,681	52.0					49,430
269,548	33.7	474,192	59.3			56,246	7.0	799,986
694,240	57.0	377,758	31.0	112,022	9.2	34,357	2.8	1,218,377
70,341	41.3	34,554	20.3	46,067	27.1	19,325	11.3	170,287
49,821	25.4	82,283	41.9	62,411	31.8	1,904	1.0	196,419
51,102	31.8	44,277	27.6	50,574	31.5	14,524	9.1	160,477
90,016	49.3	63,374	34.7	11,078	6.1	18,161	9.9	182,629
742	59.4	508	40.6					1,250
1,465,331	46.5	1,256,824	39.9	282,152	8.9	148,218	4.7	3,152,525

of the seats. Regionally there were wide disparities between the number of seats which a party won and the number of votes it polled. In Ontario the Liberals got 31.0 per cent of the votes but only 13.4 per cent of the seats, while the Conservatives won no seats in Saskatchewan even though they polled 25.4 per cent of the votes. Most significantly of all, Quebec gave them 33.7 per cent of its popular vote, but only 6.2 per cent of its seats.

The election appeared to have started Canada on the road back to the two-party system which had been badly shattered in 1921. Yet, paradoxically, the Progressives occupied a much more crucial position in the new Parliament than the preceding one even though they had lost more than half their members. But despite the Progressives' decline in numbers, regionalism still prevailed in the Commons. Neither old-line party had made a successful appeal to all areas of the country. By this time King had made it clear what the principal feature of his politics was to be: if he could possibly avoid it, he would do nothing to alienate Quebec. In hindsight it seems certain that he could have made further concessions to western Canada in 1925 without the slightest fear of endangering his position in Quebec. But to the cautious King that was not so obvious.

Above all, the election had not ended the bitter struggle between Meighen and King. "It had been decided that the post-war era would not be an age of Crerar, but not yet whether it was to be the age of Meighen or King."[55]

FOOTNOTES

1. H. Blair Neatby, *William Lyon Mackenzie King 1924-32: The Lonely Heights* (Toronto: University of Toronto Press, 1963), p. 5.

2. Ramsay Cook, *The Politics of John W. Dafoe and the Free Press* (Toronto: University of Toronto Press, 1963), p. 147.

3. *Ibid.*, p. 149.

4. Neatby, *King: Lonely Heights*, p. 8.

5. Quoted from King's diary in *ibid.*, p. 14.

6. *Ibid.*, p. 19.

7. Cook, *Dafoe and the Free Press,* p. 150.

8. Neatby, *Lonely Heights,* p. 53.

9. W.L. Morton, *The Progressive Party in Canada* (Toronto: University of Toronto Press, 1950), p. 236.

10. *Ibid.*, p. 149. *Supra,* p. 151.

11. W.K. McNaught, *A Prophet in Politics: A Biography of J.S. Woodsworth* (Toronto: University of Toronto Press, 1959), p. 209.

12. Neatby, *King: Lonely Heights,* p. 21.

13. Morton, *Progressive Party,* pp. 190-97.

14. McNaught, *Prophet in Politics,* p. 166.

15. Morton, *Progressive Party,* pp. 208-209.

16. W.R. Graham, *Arthur Meighen: And Fortune Fled,* II (Toronto: Clarke, Irwin & Company, 1963), p. 199.

17. D.A. McArthur, "The Canadian Political Situation," *Queen's Quarterly,* XXXIII (Autumn, 1925), p. 219.

18. Graham, *Meighen,* II, pp. 277-78.

19. Diary entry of July 28, quoted in Neatby, *King: Lonely Heights,* p. 61.

20. *Ibid.*, p. 63.

21. *Ibid.*, p. 68.

22. Graham, *Meighen,* II, p. 329.

23. *Canadian Annual Review,* 1925-26 (Toronto: The Canadian Review Company, 1926), pp. 22-23.

24. "Real Problems and Sham Issues," *Canadian Forum,* VI (October, 1925), p. 6.

25. Graham, *Meighen,* II, p. 330.

26. Morton, *Progressive Party,* p. 238.

27. *Canadian Annual Review,* 1925-26, pp. 24-25.

28. Graham, *Meighen,* II, p. 330.

29. Morton, *Progressive Party,* p. 239.

30. "Real Problems and Sham Issues," p. 7.

31. "Election Notes," *Canadian Forum,* VI (October, 1925), p. 27.

32. Walter R. Sharp, "The Canadian Election of 1925," *American Political Science Review,* XX (February, 1926), p. 112.

33. H. Heaton, "Three Dominion Elections–Some Contrasts," *Dalhousie Review,* V (January, 1926), p. 480.

34. "Election Notes," *Canadian Forum,* VI, p. 26.

35. Morton, *Progressive Party,* p. 240.

36. *Ibid.*, p. 241.

37. *Ibid.*, p. 242.

38. "The Election," *Canadian Forum,* VI, p. 4.

39. Heaton, "Three Dominion Elections," p. 474.

40. McArthur, "The Canadian Political Situation," pp. 219-20.

41. *Canadian Annual Review,* 1925-26, pp. 28-30.

42. Morton, *Progressive Party,* pp. 242-43.

43. Graham, *Meighen,* II, p. 294.

44. *Ibid.*, p. 323.

45. Robert Rumilly, *Histoire de la Province de Québec,* XXVIII (Montreal: Fides, 1955), p. 56.

46. Graham, *Meighen,* II, p. 339.

47. Rumilly, *Histoire,* XXVIII, p. 69.

48. *Ibid.*, p. 67.

49. *Ibid.*, p. 73.

50. *Ibid.*, p. 56.

51. *Ibid.*, p. 71.

52. Graham, *Meighen,* II, p. 343.

53. Neatby, *Lonely Heights,* p. 74.

54. Graham, *Meighen,* II, p. 340.

55. Morton, *Progressive Party,* p. 244.

Sixteenth
General Election

"... IT WAS TO BE KING'S ERA."

The days following the election of October 1925 were anything but happy for William Lyon Mackenzie King. Friend and foe alike questioned his qualifications for the prime ministership. The *Canadian Forum* – certainly no friend – said he had demonstrated beyond a doubt how pitifully inadequate his equipment for the office actually was. Now, it contended, he kept himself in almost monastic seclusion, his days given over to gloomy melancholy. Over in Hull, on any day and in any bar, there could be found groups of mutinous Liberals plotting his deposition; Ottawa itself teemed with "tales of his vanity and pomposity, his love of ceremony and pageantry, his Edward II-like predilection for strange and unworthy favourites, his old-maiden obsession with petty problems of etiquette, and his naive comprehension of politics." It concluded that, although "Mr. King would make an admirable social secretary to some American multi-millionaire who had a humanitarian interest in labour problems, . . . as Premier of Canada he is an absurd and preposterous person."[1]

Yet within a year this allegedly "absurd person" had dealt a mortal blow to his chief rival and, although no one could have known it then, had ensured the King era in Canadian politics. How much of King's success was due to his own clever tactics and sound judgments, and how much was due to luck will always be debatable. Or perhaps, as his diary intimates, it was because "dear Mother and Father & Bell & Max the whole family in Heaven are guiding and directing me."[2]

Despite the misgivings of the Governor General, Lord Byng, King decided to hang on to office, as was his constitutional right, and let Parliament decide who was to govern, himself or Meighen. Until Parliament met he pursued tactics totally unlike those of his rival. Since Meighen considered King's early defeat to be inevitable, he made no overtures to the Progressives and thought only in terms of the next election.[3] In contrast, King did his utmost to get the Progressives, Labourites, and Independents to support him in Parliament. It clearly required a master tactician. "But where is he?" asked Dafoe. "Not I fear in the P.M.'s chair."[4] For three successive elections the *Free Press* had failed to support the Liberals. Now the danger of Conservative ascendancy activated Dafoe. In his opinion Meighen stood for two things that would be positively evil for Canada: extreme economic nationalism and abject political colonialism.[5] Time and again he told the Liberals and Progressives they had "either got to co-operate to sail the ship or they will go on the rocks and the sharks will get them."[6]

With some skill and not a little luck King solved his immediate difficulties. Charles Dunning agreed to play hostage to fortune, relinquished the premiership of Saskatchewan, and entered a ramshackle administration of uncertain life. King himself decided to seek a seat in Prince Albert; "the West having so long refused to come to King, King was at last going to the West."[7] He was extremely cool towards Dafoe's idea that he take several Progressives into his cabinet and thus commit their group to outright participation in the administration. However, when the Progressives asked him and Meighen for their views on a programme of 14 points, he went out of his way to court their favour. Although 12 of 22 Progressives had previously been inclined to support the Conservatives, only 5 of 24 did after the two leaders had commented on the programme.

During the session that opened in January 1926, the executive of the Progressive group met periodically with a cabinet committee and exercised considerable influence on the government's legislative programme, especially on its bill for the establishment of the Farm Loan Board. The two Labourite M.P.'s, J.S. Woodsworth and A.A. Heaps, asked King and Meighen to express their views on old age pensions. This time King gave an assurance that legislation on that subject would be introduced in 1926 even if it had not been mentioned in the Speech from the Throne. "In this kind of popularity contest Meighen was no match for his rival."[8] Try as he might, he could not bring the government down even though it experienced trouble in the early days of the session.

A little later, Providence took a hand. The previous year's bumper wheat crop began to make its influence felt; industrial employment reached its highest level since 1921; an improved economic climate brought markedly higher government revenues. Such was the atmosphere in which James Robb presented his "Prosperity Budget." This time the Quebec wing was not nearly so demanding and its ministers "made it plain that Quebec would go almost any lengths on policy to meeting West."[9] None the less, the cautious King altered the tariff significantly in only one respect and this change – a reduction in the duty on automobiles from 35 to 20 per cent – could have hurt him only in protectionist Ontario, which had rejected him in any case. Even if the more significant changes such as the restoration of 2¢ postage (so-called penny postage) and the reduction in personal income tax were attractive, it was not because they brought substantial benefits to many Canadians. "The budget was popular," says Neatby, "because it responded to a public mood. . . . Prosperity had long been just around the corner and the budget confirmed the feeling that Canada had finally taken the turn."[10]

For Meighen the post-election problem was not so much Parliament as Quebec. Desperate situations require desperate remedies; so in a speech at Hamilton on November 16 he enunciated the principle that in any future war a general election should precede the sending of troops from Canada. For one who had always stood for parliamentary as opposed to plebiscitary democracy, and who believed that Canada should reply "ready, aye, ready!" whenever Britain called, this seemed a startling *volte face*. But Borden and the other Conservatives whom he consulted agreed with him – all but George Howard Ferguson, who thought it "'unwise to disturb a good situation in Ontario."[11] Even the *Canadian Forum* thought it would introduce a greater measure of coherence into the country's politics if the party that espoused economic nationalism moved towards political nationalism.[12]

From the Imperialist wing of the party the reaction was vociferous. Newspapers such as the Winnipeg *Tribune*, the Ottawa *Journal*, and the Toronto *Telegram*, and such politicians as C.H. Cahan, "Tommy" Church, and H.C. Hocken of the Orange Lodge protested the abandonment of the party's traditions. For the moment Meighen stuck to his guns. He reminded some of his followers that "we are jammed in between Quebec on the one hand and the Western low tariff sentiment on the other," and pointed out that there was no remedy if everything done to extricate the party was regarded as "truckling to Quebec."[13] Nothing daunted, he went to Quebec and repeated his new plank during the Bagot by-election of December 1925. All he succeeded in doing was to reduce the previous Liberal majority of 774 to 479 and, mindful of the continuing attacks upon him from within his party, he then let the matter drop. Later he called this abandonment "the only major, or at any rate the most important, mistake I made in public life."[14] Neatby describes the Hamilton speech as "a major blunder,"[15] but this is a dubious judgment. While there was little chance of gain in Quebec if he had campaigned on that plank actively in 1926, the results in the Ontario ridings likely to be most annoyed by the speech indicate he had lost little there.

Although King had easily the better of it so far, the Conservatives had a trump card left: the maladministration of the Customs Department. Early in the session they forced the appointment of a special committee of the Commons to investigate it and after the committee reported in June they were ready to make their final assault on King. The evidence revealed a sorry state of affairs. Furthermore, King had not taken vigorous or courageous action to clean up the mess once he had become aware of it. A majority of the committee, which included Liberals, sought to pin the blame on the former Minister of Customs, Jacques Bureau, whom King had appointed to the Senate the previous year. The Conservatives would have none of this. H.H. Stevens moved an amendment condemning the conduct of the incumbent minister, Georges Boivin, and the cabinet as a whole. On June 25 – one of the most exciting days in the annals of the Canadian Parliament – King lost complete control of the Commons. Eventually he managed to get an adjournment without the House having pronounced on the Stevens amendment. Over the weekend he determined to escape a vote of censure on which he was almost certain to be defeated by asking for a dissolution.

Lord Byng turned down his request and, by refusing, created the constitutional issue that was to occupy the Canadian people for the next two months. King adopted an unprecedented course by resigning forthwith instead of merely offering his resignation, thereby leaving Byng without a prime minister or a ministry. Some writers have pictured Meighen as so anxious to be Prime Minister that he accepted the Governor General's request to form a government without considering the implications. This has no foundation in fact. Indeed, Arthur Beauchesne, the Clerk of the House, advised him through indirect channels to turn down Byng's offer. The result, as Beauchesne saw it, would be to force the Governor General to send for King and grant him a dissolution; in the election which would follow, King would be completely on the defensive and would suffer certain defeat.[16] Meighen felt, however, that King's allegedly improper action had put the Governor General in an exceedingly unfortunate situation and that Byng ought not to be sacrificed. Yet Meighen's so-called "acting ministry"[17] lasted only three days before it fell. He had no trouble getting the dissolution which had been denied King.

On September 14 the Canadian people went to the polls for the second time in less than a year. Just as in 1874 they were asked to pronounce on a government which, in effect, had no record, and just as in 1874 that government hoped to win on a scandal of some magnitude. In one respect the election was unique: the voters were asked to adjudge what was allegedly a major constitutional issue. Whether *demos* is ever competent to decide such questions is dubious; certainly it cannot when most of the constitutional students go wrong and the opinion-leaders generally fail to see straight because of their preconceived notions.

It is tempting to say that there was no constitutional issue in 1926, and, if there was, it was King's action that most seriously departed from proper constitutional practice. After all, no prime minister of any British country had ever requested a dissolution when facing a vote of censure in the elective House. Byng's fault was not that he refused dissolution, but that he refused it for the wrong reason (i.e., if King could not or would not carry on the government, Meighen ought to be given a chance). Most constitutional students reject such a strong use of the prerogative and contend that, had King not been under a vote of censure, he ought to have had his dissolution. But any error on Byng's part was committed in good faith, while King's departure from proper constitutional practice was clearly an attempt to evade responsibility to Parliament for his shortcomings. Nevertheless, King asserted that Byng had taken a course which no Sovereign would have adopted towards a British prime minister and, in effect, had relegated Canada to colonial status once more. This was the constitutional issue as conceived by King. It seems strange that King, who denounced Downing Street domination of Canada, had requested Byng to consult the Colonial Secretary before refusing dissolution. To suggest, as King had done, that the prerogative of dissolution had passed completely to the Prime Minister, displayed an appalling ignorance of constitutional practice. No British prime minister would have offered his Sovereign such bad advice and, if he had, it would likely have been spurned.

It seems astounding that anybody – no matter how pro-Liberal or anti-Meighen he might be – should have fallen in line with the King version of the constitutional question. R. MacGregor Dawson wrote an article generally supporting King's position, but repented in his more mature years. However, he was not in a position to influence the election. That was not true of J.W. Dafoe or Henri Bourassa. Spurred by his dislike of Meighen and everything he stood for, Dafoe returned to the Liberal camp. "In the fury of an election campaign," says Ramsay Cook, "all the important problems of maladministration, economic recovery and even constitutional subtlety were reduced to the simple dialectic of nationalism *versus* imperialism."[18] Using a British incident of 1923 in no way analogous to the Canadian one of 1926, Dafoe contended that equality of status was quite meaningless if the King's representative in Canada could exercise powers that were obsolete in Britain. In Meighen's judgment, said Dafoe, "we . . . must submit ourselves to be 'governed' by an official responsible not to us but to the head of a department of state who sits in Downing Street."[19] Because the West was strongly nationalist, Dafoe saw that "the constitutional issue dressed in nationalist garb provided the opportunity for Meighen's enemies to bury their differences in the face of the Conservative threat."[20]

Bourassa was moved by similar considerations to support the Liberals whom he had spurned in 1921 and 1925. Byng, he said, must be "the election agent of Mr. Meighen"; certainly his actions had imperiled Canadian self-government itself. "It is," he continued, "the slow but gradual conquest of our liberties which is in peril; . . . it is the very spirit of Confederation in its relation with the metropolis of the empire which is being sapped at the present moment."[21] Such were the lengths to which men of great intelligence were carried.

After the election of 1926 it was commonplace to say that the people of Canada returned the Liberals on the constitutional question. Certainly King got a good deal of mileage out of the issue. Some suggested that he had advised a dissolution in the hope that he would be refused, but this indicates foresight beyond even his capabilities. Yet it is true that when Meighen got the dissolution he had been denied King was elated. "I cld not believe [Byng] wd deliver himself so completely into my hands," he wrote in his diary.[22] In his own mind he became a knight in shining armour: "Spent the last hour tonight singing hymns. . . . O God of Bethel. . . . Unto the Hills Around & again Oh God of Bethel – . . . I go into the battle of another election – believing we have a great issue – that the people will respond to – that is the making of our nation."[23] Perhaps King really believed, as Neatby said he did, that responsible government was at stake and that he was fighting for it no less than his grandfather before him.[24] As he toured the country, however, his local supporters told him to go easy on the constitutional issue. Personally he was skeptical: "It is the one thing the people rise to above all else when it is explained."[25] Yet he understood the need to play down specific aspects of the issue, especially in the "loyalist" parts of English Canada. There he took pains to emphasize that he was not casting any aspersions on Byng's honesty or integrity.[26] There he laid stress on Meighen's setting up of an acting ministry, an action, he said, which for gross impropriety made any fault of Byng pale into relative insignificance. "The supremacy of Parliament, the rights, the dignities, the existence of Parliament," he proclaimed indignantly, had been "challenged by the present Prime Minister in a manner that surpasses all belief."[27]

To Meighen it was incomprehensible that the preposterous King could make anything out of such a preposterous issue. In his view his opponent had simply "tried to run away from the just condemnation of himself and his Government by Parliament, but he was not permitted to do so; he thereupon hatched a constitutional issue to act as a smoke screen. This is the case in a nutshell."[28] When it appeared that the public might be taking the matter seriously, Meighen had no choice but to deal with the issue he had hoped to dismiss. The constitutional question permitted the Liberals to assume the initiative and put their opponents on the defensive. In some measure it may have swelled the nationalist tide that had been rising since the war,[29] but it did not directly produce King's victory. What it did do was let King assume a stance which made victory possible.

Above all it served to counterbalance the customs scandal, to which the Conservatives gave most of their attention. Yet, as W.R. Graham points out, "scandals, unless of truly gargantuan proportions, are not particularly good fighting issues in a society not overly preoccupied with political and administrative morality."[30] Besides, after six months of continuing allegations and denials, moral indignation had given way to boredom.[31] Then, too, the exaggeration and excessive zeal of the Conservative candidates worked to destroy the scandal as an effective weapon. A.J. Doucet's attempt to implicate Ernest Lapointe,[32] and G.B. Nicholson's charges of gross immorality in the public service backfired badly.[33] In their turn the Liberals replied with equally unfounded charges against their chief persecutor, H.H. Stevens. Even Meighen and King contrived to create the impression that each was bent on administering a knockout blow to the other.[34]

While the customs scandal and the constitutional issue counterbalanced one another, the Liberals had another issue working in their favour. The *Canadian Forum* had pointed out earlier that the Robb budget had "revived the drooping spirits" of the Liberals and finally offered proof that the King government was "a living functioning administration."[35] Now, during the election, the Liberals could take the credit for the restoration of two-cent postage, the reduction in income tax and the tariff on automobiles, and also the most favourable trade balance in Canada's history. D. McArthur, writing in the *Queen's Quarterly*, considers the Robb budget to have been "the most important single factor contributing to the result of the election";[36] perhaps it did tip the balance.

The best way to evaluate what happened in 1926 is to compare the results with those of 1925. They indicate that the Conservative party did not suffer an overwhelming defeat. It actually polled 9,000 votes more than the year before and its popular vote fell only slightly, from 46.5 to 45.3 per cent. The Liberals (and Liberal-Progressives) secured an additional quarter of a million votes and increased their popular vote from 39.9 to 46.1 per cent; they polled only 0.8 per cent more of the popular vote than their chief opponents, but won 37 more seats. Though the Conservatives lost a mere 1.2 per cent of the popular vote, their representation fell from 116 to 91. Since 22 of these losses were in Ontario and Manitoba, these provinces turned out to be the crucial ones. The Liberals gained substantially from the Progressives in Ontario, Manitoba, and Saskatchewan; other than that, the changes in the popular vote were relatively slight between 1925 and 1926.

The voting in Ontario and the Maritimes showed striking similarities in the two elections. In 1925 the Conservatives won exceptional victories in both regions, largely because of the utter disillusionment with the King administration. It was only natural that the improved economic climate caused some voters to go back to their old party in 1926. Thus, even if other factors had not neutralized the customs scandal, it is doubtful whether the Conservatives could have held their own in 1926. In the Maritimes King's appointment of a royal commission to investigate the area's grievances and his attempted enactment of old age pensions may have won him some votes, but they are not needed to explain the modest improvement in his party's popular vote. Strong candidates enabled the Conservatives to gain Queens-Lunenburg and Antigonish-Guysborough, but every other seat in the Maritimes showed a swing, however slight, to the Liberals. The Liberals restricted their loss in Nova Scotia to 1 seat; they gained 1 in Prince Edward Island and 3 in the Acadian areas of New Brunswick. Despite their net loss of 3 seats, the Conservatives' success in the Maritimes has been exceeded only by the elections of 1930, 1958, 1965, and, of course, 1925.

Much the same sort of thing took place in Ontario, although there the moderate anti-Conservative swing caused the Conservatives to lose 15 seats. The committee of Toronto Liberals who directed King's campaign in Ontario undoubtedly provided him with a better organization than he had enjoyed in 1921 and 1925. Also, the general collapse of the Progressives resulted in arrangements which generally favoured the Liberals. There were three-way races between Conservatives, Liberals and Progressives in only 4 ridings. In 7 ridings the Liberals let the Progressives provide the opposition to the Conservatives; in 6 others a candidate received a joint Liberal and Progressive nomination. But except for Kent and Lambton East, such arrangements accounted for few of the Conservative losses. Most of their losses were in seats where there had been two-party fights in 1925: 6 in ridings with a substantial number of French Canadians, and 8 of the remaining 9 in the old Grit areas of western Ontario. The evidence suggests that in these ridings a considerable number of Liberals returned to the fold from which they had strayed a year earlier. There is little to indicate that the Conservative losses resulted from the defection of "loyalist" Conservatives who objected to Meighen's Hamilton speech. Indeed, in Hastings-Peterborough, Hastings West, and Kingston, where this element was strong, they actually did better than in 1925; in Toronto, even though their total vote was down, they received almost the same proportion of the popular vote.

British Columbia presented quite a different situation. In 1925 the Conservatives had fallen short of their expectations in the west-coast province. King did not like what he saw there in 1926 and called his visit a waste of time. The provincial Liberal government was collapsing and with it the federal organization. The chief federal Liberal, Dr. J.H. King, had lost his hold on the party; the Liberals could not secure the co-operation of the Labourites in the four Vancouver seats, Kootenay East or New Westminster.[37] Perhaps it was not surprising, then, that the Conservatives increased their number of seats from 10 to 12 and their share of the popular vote from 49.3 to 54.2 per cent.

In the Maritimes, Ontario, and British Columbia, the Conservatives took 85 seats to the Liberals' 36 – a creditable showing, but 16 fewer than in 1925. To win they would have to do much better on the Prairies and in Quebec than a year earlier. The Prairies were interested in bread-and-butter issues rather than the customs scandal or the constitutional issue. Meighen attempted to show that his opposition to statutory freight rates such as were contained in the Crow's Nest Pass agreement did not necessarily mean an increase in such rates. He denied that he favoured high and onerous protection. Rather, he wanted "a protective policy that [would] give all classes in this country a fair chance."[38] For the farmer he proposed a "brick-for-brick" policy, which would make it as hard for the Americans to "get into this Dominion as they made it to get into theirs."[39] But this time the unfavourable image of the Conservatives worked against them even more than usual. In 1925 they had been only an opposition party, incapable of doing much harm; now, as the government party, they constituted a positive menace to the West.[40]

No party has ever suffered more from the quirks of the electoral system than did the Conservatives in Manitoba. In 1925, with 41.3 per cent of the votes, they carried 7 seats; in 1926, with 42.2 per cent, they won none. The Liberals (and Liberal-Progressives) took only 37.9 per cent of the votes, but won 11 seats. Largely through J.W. Dafoe's efforts, the Conservatives' opponents co-operated with each other in unprecedented fashion: 7 candidates, including Progressive leader Robert Forke, accepted both a Liberal and Progressive nomination, and no Progressive ran against a Liberal or Liberal-Progressive candidate. In 3 of the 4 Winnipeg seats Liberal and Labour candidates did not oppose each other. The result was that in 13 of 17 seats the opposition to the Conservatives was concentrated on a single candidate. Even Meighen went down to defeat in Portage la Prairie.

In Saskatchewan Premier J.G. Gardiner, who masterminded the Liberal campaign, found it more difficult to co-operate with the Progressives, whom he considered his chief threat provincially. However, by local agreements the number of ridings in which both Liberals and Progressives opposed Conservatives was reduced from 17 to 5. Gardiner concentrated on beating the Progressives in Kindersley, Last Mountain, and Mackenzie – they had consistently supported Meighen in the last Parliament – but failed in all 3 contests. The Liberals (or Liberal-Progressives) took the remaining 18 seats. The Conservatives raised their popular vote from 25.4 to 27.5 per cent, but once again elected no members.

The situation in Alberta did not favour the Liberals, and this was partly their own fault. They had finally reached an agreement for the transfer of the province's natural resources, and then succumbed to Bourassa's demand that the Roman Catholic minority of Alberta be given a definite assurance that it would continue to receive its share of proceeds from school lands. When the agreement collapsed, Dafoe called it "the stupidest performance that any political party was ever guilty of."[41] However, the difficulties the Liberals experienced were due much more to the toughness of the doctrinaire Progressives of Alberta. This time the latter ran as U.F.A. candidates to emphasize their distinctiveness. King talked about bargaining with them, but he actually meant graceful surrender. Outside Edmonton and Calgary the Liberals nominated only 6 candidates. Of these seats they won only Medicine Hat; the U.F.A. won the other 11. But by co-operating with Labour in the two largest cities, the Liberals managed to take Edmonton West, while a Labourite won in Calgary East. R.B. Bennett held on to Calgary West and was the only Conservative to be elected on the Prairies.

Some Conservative candidates in the West blamed their defeat on the Ontario member of their party who contended that immigrants of non-British birth should never be given the right to vote. Although Meighen had not heard the statement, the Liberals created the impression that he had and publicized his failure to repudiate it. According to one Manitoban

Conservative, J.T. Haig, it "played havoc with us in Manitoba; not only the Poles and Ukrainians, but the Swedes, Germans and Icelanders were affected by it and very seriously." Haig notwithstanding, the Conservative setback on the Prairies was so general that this could have been only one of many factors that contributed to it.[42]

In Quebec the campaign differed in one notable respect from that of 1925. This time Patenaude and Meighen worked together in a common cause. The former had come back into the fold on June 10 when he accepted a declaration of principles which Meighen had drawn up on imperial relations and French-Canadian rights. A little later he entered the Meighen cabinet as Minister of Justice.

Other than this there was little change in Quebec. Its electorate showed little interest in economic matters such as the tariff. Nor did it become excited about the customs scandal. Either it accepted the views of Lapointe, Cardin, and Cannon that the scandal was simply a case of peccadilloes or, because the parliamentary committee had had time to investigate the operation of the Customs Department only in Quebec, it concluded that French Canada had been singled out for special inquisition.[43] When Georges Boivin died of complications arising from appendicitis, it was easy to make him a martyr.[44] Bourassa and *Le Devoir* immediately suggested that the ferocity of his adversaries had been partly responsible for his death.[45] King gained more politically by his pilgrimage to the grave of Boivin than he would have by any number of speeches.

Much as the Conservatives would have liked, they could not prevent the constitutional issue from playing a prominent role in the campaign. The alliance of King and Bourassa in opposition to the allegedly arbitrary conduct of an English governor enabled Liberal speakers to recall the uniting of their grandfathers, William Lyon Mackenzie and Louis Joseph Papineau, for a similar purpose in the 1830's. Naturally, this could not but evoke kindly feelings for King. At the same time, the Liberals declaimed against "le coup d'état . . . déclenché à Londres," and Byng's abuse of the Canadian constitution.[46]

Above all, Meighen's opponents once again identified him with war and the conscription of French-Canadian youth. Bourassa said: "[To develop Canada] we need all our money and all our children. That is also the opinion of Mr. King. That is why I have supported him in the course of the last session and why I propose to support him again in the next."[47] One Liberal cabinet minister who noted that Meighen had become fluent in French, said that it was all the better to deceive the simple Quebec habitants. He observed that Meighen had sent his son to Laval, and saw it as part of the boy's training in order that he might head the military school that would be established when the British Imperialists and their Canadian lap dogs brought on the next war.[48]

Although Atholstan still fumed against Meighen, the Conservatives had the support of two French-Canadian newspapers, *La Patrie* and *L'Evènement*. Yet, because these journals launched their main attack against Bourassa rather than the Liberals, they were not overly effective. Even Patenaude did not live up to expectations. His assumption of the top role affronted those who had always been loyal to Meighen, and he failed to attract French Canadians of stature. The Liberals took everything in their stride. They ran 57 of the 60 members whom they had elected in 1925 (two had since died) without even holding conventions. So certain were they of success, that King spoke in Quebec only when he chanced to be passing through the province. Their prognostications were right. Not a single seat changed sides, an unprecedented event. Once again the result was 60 Liberals, 4 Conservatives, and Henri Bourassa. The Conservatives raised their popular vote from 33.7 to 34.3 per cent (they ran 4 more candidates), but they spread their votes so evenly that they again failed to elect a single French Canadian. Quebec had not yet forgotten 1917.

Meighen and King had both contended that only the party they led could provide stable government. Hindsight indicates that Meighen had not a chance. He had reached a peak in Ontario and the Maritimes in 1925, and could only go down. In Quebec and on the Prairies he faced insuperable forces and won a total of only 5 seats. As a result, his following in the House fell from 116 members to 91. The Liberal contingent of 99 was increased to 117 Liberals and 11 Liberal-Progressives who were Liberal in everything but name. In electing only 20 Progressives and 6 others, the Canadian electorate took another step back to the two-party system.

Meighen was accused of running a poor campaign, and perhaps it was uninspired. It was not his election tactics, however, that had led to his defeat, but two decisions he had taken much earlier. The election of 1926 was proof positive that Quebec would never forgive him for the part he played in enacting the Military Service Act of 1917. It also seemed obvious that he would never do well on the Prairies because of the repellent image that his obsession with protection had produced in that area. It may have given him satisfaction that his tariff policy remained unrevised and unrepented, but it also left him unseated. Some of his losses were due, of course, to many voters shifting back from the Progressive to the Liberal ranks. King's support rested in large measure on the rural population and prime producers rather than the manufacturing and financial interests; the former have many more votes.

The election brought criticism of both the electoral system and the length of the campaign. The Ottawa *Journal* commented on the folly of forcing Meighen and King to rush back and forth across the continent "at a body and mind-killing pace" for fifty days. "They talked so often about the same things that their words became a burden upon the newspaper market, with the result that the Press did not print one-tenth of what they said. . . .

	Seats	Candidates				Elected							
		C.	L.	P.	O.	C.	%	L.	%	P.	%	O.	%
Nova Scotia	14	14	13		1	12	85.7	2	14.3				
New Brunswick	11	11	11			7	63.6	4	36.4				
Prince Edward Island	4	4	4			1	25.0	3	75.0				
Quebec	65	62	64		12	4	6.2	60	92.3			1	1.5
Ontario	82	82	72	11	11	53	64.6	26	31.7	2	2.4	1	1.2
Manitoba	17	16	12	4	4			11	64.7	4	23.5	2	11.8
Saskatchewan	21	16	21	10				18	85.7	3	14.3		
Alberta	16	13	9	12	3	1	6.3	3	18.8	11	68.8	1	6.3
British Columbia	14	14	13		9	12	85.7	1	7.1			1	7.1
Yukon	1	1	1			1	100.0						
	245	233	220	37	40	91	37.1	128	52.2	20	8.2	6	2.4

Notes: An I.L. elected in Ontario, unopposed by an official Liberal candidate, is placed in the Liberal columns.

Included in the Liberal totals are 11 Liberal-Progressives: Ont. (6, 2 elected); Man. (7, all elected, 1 by acclamation); Sask. (2, both elected). Also included in the Liberal totals in Ontario are 1 Lib.-Lab. (elected) and 2 Lib.-Lab.-Prog.

The U.F.A. candidates in Alberta are regarded as Progressives.

Elected by
  acclamation: Man. (1): Liberal-Progressive (1).
Others elected: Que. (1): I. (1).
             Ont. (1): I.L. (1).
             Man. (2): Lab. (2).
             Alta. (1): Lab. (1).
             B.C. (1): I. (1).
Others (votes
  polled): N.S. (1): Lab. (1) 6,412.
             Que. (12): I.L. (6) 14,349; I.C. (1) 775; I. (3) 11,331; Protectionist (1) 129; Soc. (1) 672.
             Ont. (11): I.C. (3) 19,028; I.L. (2) 4,481; I. (2) 5,356; Lab. (4) 6,282.
             Man. (4): Lab. (4) 17,194.
             Alta. (3): Lab. (1) 6,707; Lab.-Farmer (1) 1,441; Ind. Lab. (1) 163.
             B.C. (9): Lab. (7) 11,757; I. (2) 4,330.

Half a dozen carefully prepared addresses, delivered at central strategic centres, would have reached twice as many electors."[49] None the less, Canada's leaders are still being required to perform the same antics in the 1960's.

It remained for Professor Frank Underhill to demonstrate the serious consequences flowing from the distortions of the electoral system. "The present system," he says, "exaggerates the sectionalism which is a sufficiently serious problem with us at all times." The Conservatives, who polled one-third of the votes in both Quebec and the Prairie Provinces, should have won 22 and 15 seats respectively; instead they got 4 and 1.

Popular Vote								Total
C.	%	L.	%	P.	%	O.	%	
122,965	53.7	99,581	43.5			6,412	2.8	228,958
87,080	53.9	74,465	46.1					161,545
26,217	47.3	29,222	52.7					55,439
275,280	34.3	500,850	62.3			27,256	3.4	803,386
661,714	54.1	474,885	38.9	50,360	4.1	35,147	2.9	1,222,106
83,100	42.2	74,621	37.9	22,092	11.2	17,194	8.7	197,007
67,524	27.5	139,262	56.8	38,324	15.6			245,110
49,514	31.5	38,451	24.5	60,740	38.7	8,311	5.3	157,016
100,066	54.2	68,317	37.0			16,087	8.7	184,470
823	55.9	648	44.1					1,471
1,474,283	45.3	1,500,302	46.1	171,516	5.3	110,407	3.4	3,256,508

Obviously the Conservative party at Ottawa today would not be so helplessly the tool of manufacturing interests if there were a few more Prairie representatives in it to present the consumer's point of view. Obviously the Liberal party would not be so hopelessly the tool of French Quebec if the solid Quebec were broken up and the Quebec delegation no longer formed the chief component of the Liberal caucus. . . . The dangerous sectional solidity would, to some extent at least, dissolve, had we an electoral system which sent members to Ottawa in proportion to the votes actually cast in the different sections.[50]

Earlier King himself had looked favourably on a reform of the system, but now that he was firmly established in office he forgot that it might some time turn against him. Few of his followers gave him much credit for the victory of 1926 for the very good reason that it had resulted neither from brilliant tactics nor from skill in reconciling group interests. Rather he had adopted a cautious, noncommittal stance and let other factors seal Meighen's doom. For Meighen, unsuccessful in three elections and beset by powerful forces in his own party, the only course was to resign the party leadership. For King victory meant that it was to be his era.

FOOTNOTES

1. "Politics, Parties, and Leaders," Canadian Forum, VI (January, 1926), p. 107.

2. Quoted from King's diary in H. Blair Neatby, William Lyon Mackenzie King 1924-32: The Lonely Heights (Toronto: University of Toronto Press, 1963), p. 88.

3. Ibid., p. 106.

4. Ramsay Cook, The Politics of John W. Dafoe and the Free Press (Toronto: University of Toronto Press, 1963), p. 156.

5. Ibid., p. 160.

6. Ibid., p. 157.

7. W.L. Morton, The Progressive

Party in Canada (Toronto: University of Toronto Press, 1950), p. 247.

8. W.R. Graham, *Arthur Meighen: And Fortune Fled*, II (Toronto: Clarke, Irwin & Company, 1963), p. 378.

9. Neatby, *King: Lonely Heights*, p. 89.

10. *Ibid.*, pp. 123-24.

11. Graham, *Meighen*, II, p. 356.

12. "Politics, Parties, and Leaders," p. 108.

13. Graham, *Meighen*, II, p. 366.

14. *Ibid.*, p. 362.

15. Neatby, *King: Lonely Heights*, p. 105.

16. Graham, *Meighen*, II, p. 421.

17. To avoid having his ministers vacate their seats on accepance of an office of emolument, as the law then required, Meighen made them merely acting ministers without pay.

18. Cook, *Dafoe and the Free Press*, pp. 163-64.

19. *Ibid.*, p. 164.

20. *Ibid.*, p. 168.

21. Quoted from *Le Devoir*, July 19 and September 10, 1926, in *Canadian Annual Review*, 1926-27 (Toronto: The Canadian Review Company, 1927), p. 33.

22. Quoted from King's diary in Neatby, *King: Lonely Heights*, p. 159.

23. *Ibid.*

24. *Ibid.*, p. 160.

25. *Ibid.*, p. 161.

26. *Canadian Annual Review*, 1926-27, p. 34.

27. "The Issues as I see Them," *Maclean's Magazine*, September 1, 1926, in R. MacGregor Dawson, *Constitutional Issues in Canada 1900-31* (London: Oxford University Press, 1933), p. 89.

28. *Ibid.*, p. 91.

29. "Current Politics," *Round Table*, XVII (December, 1926), p. 153.

30. Graham, *Meighen*, II, p. 461.

31. Walter R. Sharp, "The Canadian Election of 1926," *American Political Science Review*, XXI (February, 1927), p. 105.

32. Neatby, *King: Lonely Heights*, p. 162.

33. *Canadian Annual Review*, 1926-27, p. 37.

34. "Current Politics," p. 148.

35. "The Government Takes the Offensive," *Canadian Forum*, VI (May, 1926), p. 235.

36. "The Dominion Election," *Queen's Quarterly*, XXXIV (Autumn, 1926), p. 234.

37. Neatby, *King: Lonely Heights*, p. 165.

38. *Canadian Annual Review*, 1926-27, p. 35.

39. *Ibid.*, p. 34.

40. "Current Politics," p. 154.

41. Cook, *Dafoe and the Free Press*, p. 160.

42. Graham, *Meighen*, II, pp. 467-68.

43. Neatby, *King: Lonely Heights*, p. 166.

44. Graham, *Meighen*, II, p. 461.

45. Robert Rumilly, *Histoire de la Province de Québec*, XXVIII (Montreal: Fides, 1955), p. 239.

46. *Ibid.*, p. 233.

47. *Ibid.*, p. 240.

48. "Current Politics," p. 152.

49. *Ibid.*, pp. 148-49.

50. "O Canada," *Canadian Forum*, X (May, 1930), p. 278.

Seventeenth
General Election

"BLASTING A WAY" TO NATIONAL PROSPERITY

"Man is never less entitled to be called Homo Sapiens than when he is engaged in performing his first duty of citizenship;" i.e., voting.[1] So wrote John W. Dafoe; the election results of 1930 led him to this conclusion. In addition to doubting the ordinary voters' intelligence, Dafoe wondered about King's political capacity. Had he blundered into an election because of the fear of his Quebec ministers that their provincial machine was collapsing?[2] Or, had it come about because R.B. Bennett, the Conservative leader, had "played upon Mr. Mackenzie King's pride, combativeness, and – perhaps – belief in his star in order to get him in the mood to fight a battle on ground chosen by his opponents . . ."?[3]

During the budget debate Bennett had challenged the Prime Minister to get the people's verdict before he represented Canada at the forthcoming Imperial Conference; within fifteen minutes King had accepted the challenge.[4] To regard King's action as impulsive or ill-considered is altogether wrong, for he had been mulling over the timing of an election for some months. Naturally he wanted to represent Canada at the Imperial Conference, particularly because it would take steps to complete the recognition of the country's autonomy along the lines he had been advocating. His influence would be even greater if he had just been accorded a renewed mandate at the polls.[5]

Economic grounds provided an even more compelling reason for the election. Despite the stock-market crash and the economic slowdown King felt that conditions were reasonably good at the beginning of 1930. He did not think they would get worse, but he could not be sure[6] and he did not want to be placed in the position where he had no room to manoeuvre. He had yet another reason for an early election, although its effect is more difficult to gauge. On February 8, he had had a visit from Mrs. Bleaney, a fortune-teller from Kingston, whose oracular prognostications had apparently proved to be right in 1925 and 1926. This time she saw King emerging stronger than ever, whether in 1930 or 1931, but she felt the forces would be more propitious in 1930.[7] Mrs. Bleaney did not determine the timing of the election. What she did was to confirm a conclusion that King had reached on other grounds.

Three days after Mrs. Bleaney's visit, King made known his intentions to Ernest Lapointe, his Minister of Justice, and Charles Dunning, his Minister of Finance, but he did not inform the lesser lights of the cabinet until the third week in March. Dunning had been told in order that he might get "a good budget" ready,[8] and the Dunning budget of May 1 became the very arch upon which the Liberal case rested. It was to be the means of spiking the Conservative guns. Since it failed to estimate revenues and expenditures for the coming year, Bennett naturally called it no budget at all.

Undeniably, however, it did have appealing contents, especially in the announcement of a surplus and the reduction in sales tax from 2 to 1 per cent. But what threatened to steal the enemy's thunder was its catering to more specific sentiments. First, there was a generous increase in the British preferential tariff on 270 items. Ostensibly this was designed to augment trade with Britain, perhaps to the extent of $50 million a year, by encouraging the importation of British tea, china, textiles, and machinery. Its ulterior purpose was to appeal to British feeling in Canada. A party emphasizing autonomy needed something to combat the Conservative charges that it had separatist tendencies.[9]

In addition, the Dunning budget was directed against the United States. Above all, it raised the general tariff on imports of iron and steel goods, nine-tenths of which were American. There were also increases in the duties on fruits and vegetables, apparently to counteract the message of protection which Bennett had been carrying tirelessly to rural Canada since his selection as leader. Also, the voluble protests against the flood of New Zealand butter into the country were not forgotten. By order-in-council such butter had been coming in at a rate of one cent a pound, the same rate chargeable under the trade treaty with Australia; in October it was to be admitted at the normal preferential rate of four cents pending the negotiation of a trade treaty.

It was evident by now that the American Hawley-Smoot tariff would be completed later in the year and that it would provide the upward revision which Herbert Hoover had promised his electorate in 1928. For a Liberal government in Canada to have anticipated such changes by a horizonal increase in the general tariff would have been to negate its past position; for it to have done nothing would have been to play into Conservative hands.[10] For these reasons, the Dunning budget imposed countervailing duties on sixteen items, most of them farm produce. Accordingly, Canada was automatically to apply tariff rates equal to those imposed by another country when the latter's rates on such products were higher than the normal Canadian rates.

King was elated. How could Bennett possibly oppose a policy of freer trade within the Empire and countervailing duties against the United States? "Switch trade from U.S. to Britain, that will be the cry & it will sweep the country I believe. We will take the flag once more out of the Tory hands."[11] The anguished cries of Conservatives who alleged that he had stolen their policies convinced him he was right. More than one commentator felt he had out-generalled his foes. The Liberals have "pleased the low-tariff interest by increasing the British Preference on all articles not made in Canada," wrote Richard DeBrisay, "and they have placated the high-tariff interests by maintaining our protective duties on all articles made in Canada."[12] It was yet to be demonstrated how the ordinary voter would view this "curious shift in the position of the two historic parties."[13]

His grand strategy completed, King was anxious to get into the election. It took only a few weeks to complete the work of the session. This was done by the end of May and an election was called for July 28. For the first time in Canadian history, the leading politicians addressed their countrymen over a nation-wide radio network. Already one observer wondered if a two months' campaign was prolonged "unduly . . . in view of the general use of radio."[14] Professor Frank Underhill was distressed by the use to which the new device was put. Even before its advent he had noted a marked deterioration in the quality of public meetings. Too often the successful orator "approximated to the character of a religious revivalist" and his audiences consisted mainly of "semi-hysterical zealots who turned out only to take part in an orgy of mob emotion."[15] Radio had not improved matters. Why, he asked, if the public demanded "a true matter-of-fact realism from our prose writers," should it not look for "a public man who delivers speeches in the same way that Ernest Hemingway and Morley Callaghan write novels"? It was up to the parties, he felt, to experiment with a new technique of speech-making; otherwise, "until we get television this foaming-at-the-mouth business is going to be terribly tiresome."[16] Another observer pointed out that the unseen audiences became smaller as the campaign advanced, undoubtedly because many radio enthusiasts had "devoted their attention to the lucubrations of 'Amos and Andy,' in preference to Mr. King and Mr. Bennett."[17]

Professor Underhill was especially hard on R.B. Bennett. He felt that "for empty ranting and raving," the Conservative leader's opening speech at Winnipeg in 1930 had "seldom . . . been surpassed in Canadian political history." Did Bennett actually think that a national radio audience was of "the intellectual calibre of a Toronto Tory ward association meeting"?[18] Nevertheless, to the delegates attending the first leadership convention of the Conservative party at Winnipeg in October 1927, Bennett had merits not apparent to Professor Underhill. It did not occur to them, as it did to Dafoe, that his wealth and his identification with big business would constitute too serious a handicap for a Conservative leader.[19] They were also unaware (since experience in office alone would demonstrate it) how little comprehension he had of the psychological aspects of party leadership.[20] They did know that the party had to do well in Quebec and on the

Prairies if it was to win elections. Because Bennett had lived most of his life in the West, he could be expected to have a special appeal to the Prairie voter; because he had played no part in conscription and was free of the curse of Meighen, he would not have two strikes against him in Quebec; because he was a native New Brunswicker, he would undoubtedly evoke kindly feeling in the Maritimes. Certainly he had an abundance of the self-assurance and energy which would stand him in good stead in a campaign like that of 1930.

In deference to the West, the Conservative convention of 1927 had moderated the party's position on protection. Dafoe was quick to warn that this meant nothing because Bennett was an arch-protectionist.[21] Events soon proved him right. Although Bennett's principal lieutenant, Hugh Guthrie, told a meeting at Regina that his party wanted only to "give the people of Canada their own home market,"[22] his own leader appeared to belie him. Indeed, Bennett preached economic nationalism from coast to coast with almost evangelical fervour.[23] A tariff properly framed, administered, and controlled appeared to him to be the one certain remedy that would restore prosperity to the farmer, the workingman, and the industrialist. He would not beg any country to buy Canadian goods, but he would get a market for them. At Winnipeg he said: "I will use tariffs to blast a way into the markets that have been closed to you."[24] At Vancouver he was even more emphatic:

> So will I, when the Government is mine, continue to blast a way through all our difficulties. What else would I be there for; to cringe to others with soft words, and to recoil from each rebuff? That is not Canada's way. That is not my Party's way.[25]

He said he would see to it in the first session of Parliament after July 28 that the Canadian producer had the market of his own country.[26] Indeed, in economic questions it should always be a question of "Canada First". "I give place to no man in my love for our Empire, but there is a greater love in my life, and that is my love for Canada."[27] Such leading Conservatives as Dr. Manion derided King for discovering at long last that there was a British Empire.[28] But Bennett criticized King's extension of British preference per se, especially since it was Canada that had requested that an economic conference be held at the same time as the Imperial Conference:

> If our offer to England and the other Dominions of the Empire . . . means that we are to admit free into our market goods in competition with our own, without securing a real benefit for ourselves, and without obtaining a preferred place in their markets for our products, then I also oppose it as Macdonald did, for it is not good for Canada. What right has the Government, by its premature unreasoned action, to imperil the success of the Imperial Conference?[29]

No one could have been more certain than Bennett that his trade and tariff policies would end unemployment. Until they worked, however, he promised a lavish programme of public works as a stopgap measure. He had the usual bag of miscellaneous promises to offer as well: the full assumption of the cost of old age pensions, the early completion of the St. Lawrence Waterway, and other appeals to regional interests.

Bennett, at least, was able to fight the campaign as he had first planned. King, on the other hand, had hoped to concentrate, as he did in his opening speech, on three arguments: "a record of faithful stewardship," his ministry's vision of the "great mountain peaks of Empire trade and cooperation," and the desirability of having a Liberal government represent Canada at the Imperial Conference.[30] Under normal circumstances he might have succeeded, for although his government had not captured the public imagination, it could point to a series of budget surpluses and tax reductions.

Yet King to the contrary notwithstanding, the circumstances were distinctly abnormal in 1930. Early in the campaign he dismissed unemployment as a world-wide phenomenon. When he reached the West, however, where the number of unemployed stood at about 100,000, and received a rowdy reception at several meetings, his attitude changed. Then for the first time he admitted that unemployment was not solely a provincial or municipal responsibility and promised to assist any provincial government that could not cope with it.[31]

King felt more comfortable when he dealt with Bennett's proposals to blast a way into the markets of the world. "Let me ask you frankly, did you ever hear of anyone blasting a way to trade? . . . Did you ever secure an order [for goods] by force? . . . Is it not an elementary principle of business that trade is not secured by ill-will but by goodwill?"[32] If unemployment were to be satisfactorily solved, it would result from a fiscal policy which would secure for Canada a wider market in Britain and the Commonwealth.[33] At Saskatoon he waxed almost lyrical about British preference, describing it as "nothing less than the royal road of Empire trade, a veritable King's highway of commerce uniting the far-flung communities and possessions of the British Empire. . . .[34] Charles Dunning continued in much the same vein. After pointing out that Canada already sold twice as much to Britain as it bought from her, he concluded that, rather than approach the Commonwealth countries in a spirit of petty bargaining, as Bennett proposed, it should be "in the broad spirit of a willingness to become in ever-increasing measure good customers to those who treat us in like manner."[35]

This was, indeed, a curious change in roles. The autonomist, nationalist Liberals were posing as stout Commonwealth men, while the normally imperialist Conservatives stood, above all, for "Canada First," even though led by the most perfervid of Britons. What could be stranger than to find the Ottawa *Citizen* saying that the Liberals deserved the support of every voter who believed in the British Commonwealth or the Toronto *Globe*, back again in the Liberal camp, denouncing Bennett as a dangerous politician who for the sake of the Commonwealth's future had to be kept out of office?[36]

From the very beginning of the campaign King was put on the defensive. As it advanced, he was "forced to spend more and more time . . . replying to questions on the issues which R.B. Bennett was discussing."[37] At the same time he was meeting determined opposition from the provincial premiers. For some time the elections in the provinces had been going against the Liberals and by July 1930 only the governments of Quebec and Prince Edward Island remained in their hands. But Taschereau of Quebec had disagreed with Lapointe on the St. Lawrence Waterway question and was late getting into the fray. The Progressive premiers of Manitoba and Alberta remained neutral, but not so the five Conservative premiers. King should not have been surprised, for if any prime minister had ever tempted them to intervene strongly, it was he. When told in the House that he should deal with unemployment by giving money to the provinces, he had become indignant. Why should he upset his carefully balanced budget to benefit so partisan a Conservative as George Howard Ferguson of Ontario? In anger he blurted out that he would not give a cent to any Tory government. A moment later he raised the ante a little: "I would not give them a five-cent piece." It was "a surprising slip" and he regretted it almost immediately,[38] but the damage was done. Ferguson denounced this "lowering of public morality" and said it would lead him to campaign actively in the federal campaign. Protesting that he was being misinterpreted, King promised equal treatment to all the provinces "regardless of the complexion of the particular Administration."[39] This did not prevent the hecklers from throwing the "five-cent" statement back at him at almost every meeting.

King had several other difficulties with the Conservative premiers. He became involved in a silly wrangle with Tolmie of British Columbia about whether that province had ever asked for unemployment assistance.[40] He accused Saskatchewan of deliberately delaying public works in order to project unemployment into politics, thereby provoking Premier Anderson to say what a pleasant duty it would be to beat him.[41] Premiers Rhodes of Nova Scotia and Baxter of New Brunswick apparently needed no pretext for their onslaught. The relations between King and Ferguson of Ontario, however, developed into open antagonism. King, who had privately called the Ontario Premier "a skunk," now publicly talked about Ferguson's "great political machine which sought by Tammany Hall methods to secure a monopoly of government in the Province."[42] Ostensibly it was the St. Lawrence Waterway question that caused their angry recriminations and each of them published detailed correspondence which purported to prove that the other had obstructed the scheme.[43]

From the organizational point of view, too, the Liberals were at a disadvantage. Because the Conservative party controlled five provincial administrations, the task of its national organizer, General A.D. McRae, was made easier. His great talents could be put to devising the strongest organization his party had known in years. The same was hardly true of the Liberals. Their convention of 1919 had sought to create a federal organization and had constituted a national committee to that end. Strangely enough, King had shown little interest in the details of organization and the national committee had become largely inoperative. The Liberals were now dependent on their provincial organizations, at a time when there were few Liberal governments in office. In the Maritimes the organization was not so bad, but in Ontario quarrels between the provincial and federal Liberals had left the organization almost impotent. In the West, conditions were so hopeless that King was himself led to say: "It is a crime the absence of organization."[44] In his extremity he left the tasks of party organization and fund collecting to Senator Andrew Haydon, who, though he had resigned as national organizer in 1922, had kept the central office going since that time. The surprising thing is that King regarded inadequate organization and a cabinet with vacancies as no more than minor handicaps. He was confident, says Neatby, because "the political issues, as he saw them, gave his government a real advantage."[45]

In assessing the results of the election J.B.M. Clark was one of the few observers who played down economic factors and emphasized local circumstances. He did so because the victors owed their success to Quebec and the Prairie provinces, and he felt it unlikely that voters of such divergent types would be motivated by basic feelings of an identical kind.[46] Yet economic conditions are the one factor that induces all Canadians to vote· in the same way, and depression and unemployment constituted by all odds the most significant issue in the election of 1930 even though local conditions may have moderated or intensified their impact on the electorate. This does not mean that the voters listened attentively to the specific arguments of the politicians. There was, indeed, something unreal about the campaign. It simply served to confirm a decision that the economic situation had rendered likely. It appears that the voters simply decided that a man who would only grudgingly admit that there were serious economic problems and who gave little evidence of having the capacity or vigour to deal with them was not the leader they wanted. In contrast, his chief opponent crossed Canada exuding energy wherever he went. He promised, promised, promised, in a categorical tone which carried conviction. It may have been windy emotionalism as Professor Underhill suggests but, to the ordinary voter, Bennett looked like the man who might dissipate the crisis and re-establish normality.[47]

In British Columbia, the Maritimes, and Ontario, however, the Conservatives did little better than hold their own. This is not particularly surprising since Meighen had done exceptionally well in these areas in 1926. This time British Columbia gave the Conservatives 5 fewer seats and 5 per cent less of its popular vote. Although they gained Kootenay East, they lost New Westminster, Skeena, and four seats in Vancouver, including those held by H.H. Stevens and General McRae. Dissatisfaction with the Conservative provincial government was a minor factor in these losses; two other circumstances played a far more significant role in the outcome. The preferential features of the Dunning budget naturally found favour in a province where British sentiment was strong, while the shipping, lumbering, and other interests looked askance at the Conservatives for denouncing trade arrangements with Australia and New Zealand which they had found extremely profitable.[48]

The Conservatives also lost a little in Nova Scotia – 2 seats and 1.2 per cent of their popular vote. This, too, was to be expected. In 1926 they had experienced their greatest federal success to date in that province, and since then the provincial Liberals, who had been altogether routed in 1925, had made a strong recovery. In the other Maritime provinces, where the Conservatives had not reached their peak in 1926, economic difficulties helped this time. In Prince Edward Island they gained the dual riding of Queens and won 3 of the 4 seats. In New Brunswick they took a surprising 59.3 per cent of the popular vote and lost only Gloucester, and that by a mere 250 votes. Even French-speaking New Brunswickers seemed to have joined in the desire to have a native of the province as Prime Minister.[49] The Conservatives gained 4 seats in the Maritimes.

In Ontario the Conservatives also won a substantial victory: 59 of 82 seats and 54.8 per cent of the votes – but better than 1926 by only 6 seats and 0.7 per cent of the popular vote. The changes were actually few in number: 9 Conservative gains and 3 losses, generally by small majorities. Undoubtedly the Conservatives' criticism of the increase in British preference and their emphasis on "Canada First" hurt them among the voters with strong British sentiments. Their loss of Toronto West Centre – the first Toronto seat to go Liberal since 1896 – has been attributed partly to this factor.

In British Columbia, the Maritimes, and Ontario the Conservatives were only 4 seats better off than in 1926. Their victory therefore depended on Quebec and the Prairies, which had been Meighen's *bêtes noires*. On the night of July 28 the Quebec Bleus could say that the age of miracles was not over. Not only did they elect 24 members, but they polled 44.7 per cent of the votes. Since the Nationalists had been largely responsible for their electing 27 members in 1911, this was their best showing since 1891. All but 8 of their 24 members were French, the first such members that Quebec had returned in a general election since 1911.

Many factors contributed to this phenomenon; the difficulty is to determine their relative significance. Undoubtedly the Liberals' long tenure of office, especially provincially, had led to an erosion of their strength. The old guard ran the organization as their own, driving able young men into the opposing fold.[50] Then, too, the Quebec Conservatives discovered an unwonted display of sympathy from the Roman Catholic Church. It was not hard to find the reason. On the Prairies strong anti-Catholic sentiment had led to the emergence of an organization not unlike the Ku Klux Klan and, to the defeat, in June 1929, of J.G. Gardiner's Liberal administration, which was charged with kowtowing to the Catholic hierarchy. Some Irish Catholic bishops blamed the anti-Catholic feelings on the racial aggressiveness of the French-Canadian Catholics and, as a result, are said to have tried to marshal the Irish vote against the Liberals in 1930. The French-Canadian church leaders also appeared to have decided that it was desirable to have a French-Canadian component within the Conservative party. So for the first time in twenty years or more the Conservative candidates in Quebec got at least benevolent neutrality and more often practical assistance from many of the Catholic clergy.[51]

The Conservatives would not have had a chance at all had the Liberals been able to do with Bennett what they had done with Meighen. They tried, however, early in the campaign. Such politicians as Lucien Cannon and such newspapers as *Le Canada* reproached Bennett repeatedly for having presided over national registration, the prelude to conscription, as they called it.[52] Quebec Premier Taschereau, after finally entering the campaign, declared: "Mackenzie King is a friend of our race. . . . I have nothing to say against Mr. Bennett, but I must say that I don't like his friends."[53] But this time the Liberals faced the former provincial Conservative leader, Arthur Sauvé, who knew his history: Was it not a Liberal leader who first said: "When England is at war, Canada is at war"? Was it not a Liberal government which in 1899 first made a contribution to a British war? Was conscription not imposed in 1917 as the result of an alliance between Conservative and Liberal politicians? Was it not a Liberal government in Manitoba which had first declared war on French Canadians in the West? Was it not King rather than Bennett who had extended the British preference?[54] There was another factor, too. C.G. Power states that this time "references to conscription bored the audiences"; accordingly, instructions went out to Liberal speakers to play it down.[55]

The attempt to tar Bennett with the same brush as Meighen did not succeed. So in the closing days of the campaign *La Presse* instigated one of the best-known roorbacks in Canadian politics. On July 25 it published a telegram from a correspondent (or pretended correspondent) in London under the heading "Threat of conscription." Its purport was that England, foreseeing a war with Egypt, had reassured itself with the thought that a Conservative government would establish a moderate system of conscription and launch the country into a system of imperial defence.[56] *Le Soleil* immediately took up the cry, but this time the Blues were strong enough to withstand the attack.

All these factors were important, but they simply put the Conservatives in a position where they could win seats. Economic difficulties permitted them to capitalize on their opportunities. On this kind of issue, French Canada reacts much the same as the rest of the country. Despite the serious unemployment in Montreal, however, the Conservatives could add only Jacques Cartier and Ste. Anne to their seats in that area. French Montreal remained what it had been since 1896: the strongest Liberal bastion in Canada.

Hard times had seriously affected the province's pulp and paper industry, but had hit the dairy industry worst of all. The Quebec dairy farmer, relying as he did upon primitive methods on a small holding of land, was already at a disadvantage. To have to face heavy competition from New Zealand butter only added to his woes. This was a most opportune issue for the politician. One defeated Liberal M.P. said that the Conservative speakers had made "a pound of New Zealand butter look as big as a house in the eyes of the Quebec farmers"![57] So they must have, for they took all the seats in the Eastern Townships with the exception of Sherbrooke and did well in all of the St. Lawrence Lowlands area.

Some attributed the Conservative success in Quebec to the quality of the candidates, but this quality was more effect than cause. In politics nothing succeeds like success, and because it was sensed that chances were good in Quebec, the Conservatives found it much easier to attract better candidates and to enrol workers. Ironically, one person miscalculated badly. In 1929 the federal Conservatives had helped to make Camilien Houde the provincial leader of the party in place of Arthur Sauvé, who had divorced himself from the federal wing. Houde, certain that his party was as usual doomed to defeat (and disregarding his wife's advice), declined to take part in the election. Sauvé, on the other hand, was elected in Laval–Two Mountains and entered the cabinet.[58]

To many observers the result in Quebec was "the most happy feature of the whole election."[59] It meant that the solid Liberal bloc had finally been broken. The Quebec *Chronicle-Telegraph* warned its party, however, that it had only five years in which to perpetuate its reconciliation with French Canada.[60]

The Conservatives met with equal success in the Prairie provinces. In 1926 the Conservatives had taken only 1 seat out of 54; this time they won 23, even though they campaigned just as strongly for protection. Perhaps it was not surprising that they could win Winnipeg South and South Centre, Regina, Saskatoon, Moose Jaw, Calgary East and West, and Edmonton East. But, in addition, they took 9 rural seats in Manitoba, 5 in Saskatchewan, and 1 in Alberta. To free traders it was altogether incomprehensible. Richard DeBrisay, in the *Canadian Forum*, understood how

Bennett's "you-be-damned-policy" might appeal to Quebec, "an industrial province, always rather nationalist in outlook and almost [as] protectionist in sentiment as Ontario." He found it quite incredible, however, that it could get support in provinces that were dependent on foreign trade. It was, he felt, "a singular and depressing demonstration of how slight a pressure of adversity is needed to establish the supremacy of prejudice over reason in the electorate of a modern democracy."[61] Dafoe refused to believe that the result heralded an upsurge of Canadian nationalism; he felt that it was the acceptance of a "Sinn Fein policy of 'Ourselves Alone.' " He found it re-grettable that Canadians were "equipped with minds capable of being influenced by the absurdities and crudities of the Bennett campaign." "For the first time in my life," he confessed, "I am a little ashamed of my country."[62] Surely Dafoe and DeBrisay ought to have recognized that during hard times any democratic electorate is likely to insist on change and that it cannot be counted on to examine the alternative as rationally as it might.

The Conservatives won 137 of 245 seats, the most decisive victory they had won by themselves since Macdonald's day. At the same time Canada made another step back to the two-party system. The 3 Liberal-Progressives who were returned were Liberal in everything but name. Out-side the old-line parties, there were only 12 Progressives – 9 of them from Alberta – and 5 other members of varying designations.

Escott Reid felt this election was especially suitable for measuring some of the racial and economic bases of Canadian Liberalism and Conser-vatism.[63] He thought this way because, in his opinion, the alignment of political forces – badly shattered during the First World War – had become very much what it had been in the heyday of the two-party system from 1900 to 1910.

He found, not surprisingly, that in every province, and in every economic region but southern Ontario, French Canadians were disposed to be Liberal rather than Conservative. But not uniformly so. In French-speaking urban seats Liberal strength was overwhelming, in semi-urban seats very pronounced, and in rural areas much diminished. Thus "a Con-servative French Montrealer was even more rare a specimen than a Liberal Torontonian."[64]

In contrast the Conservatives had "safe possession" – more than 52.5 per cent of the vote – of two-thirds of the seats in urban English Canada, but less than a half of the semi-urban and less than a third of the rural. The Conservatives won 13 seats in English Canada because their majorities in the urban and semi-urban parts were enough to overcome Liberal majorities in the surrounding rural areas, while the Liberals won 14 seats there for the converse reason.

Reid's conclusion – although he admitted it was something of an oversimplification – was that "the Conservative party in 1930 was an urban party in English Canada and a rural party in French Canada, while the

	Seats	Candidates				Elected							
		C.	L.	P.	O.	C.	%	L.	%	P.	%	O.	%
Nova Scotia	14	14	14			10	71.4	4	28.6				
New Brunswick	11	11	11			10	90.9	1	9.1				
Prince Edward Island	4	4	4			3	75.0	1	25.0				
Quebec	65	64	64		14	24	36.9	40	61.5			1	1.5
Ontario	82	82	81	2	11	59	72.0	22	26.8	1	1.2		
Manitoba	17	17	13	2	13	11	64.7	4	23.5			2	11.8
Saskatchewan	21	17	21	7	10	8	38.1	11	52.4	2	9.5		
Alberta	16	10	11	11	4	4	25.0	3	18.8	9	56.3		
British Columbia	14	14	12		6	7	50.0	5	35.7			2	14.3
Yukon and N.W.T.	1	1	1			1	100.0						
Total	245	234	232	22	58	137	55.9	91	37.1	12	4.9	5	2.0

Notes: Included in the Liberal totals are 12 Liberal-Progressive candidates: Ont. (2), 12,265; Man. (9, including 3 elected) 49,927, and Sask. (1) 6,905.

One Independent Conservative in Manitoba, unopposed by an official Conservative, is included in the Conservative columns.

Eleven U.F.A. candidates in Alberta are included in the Progressive columns.

Elected by
acclamation: Que. (1): I. (1).
Others elected: Que. (1): I. (1); Man. (2); Lab. (2); B.C. (2); I. (1) and I. Lab. (1).
Others (votes
polled): Que. (14): I. (1 by acclamation); I. (3) 2,935; I.L. (6) 13,608; Comm. (1) 313; I.C. (1) 1,236; Lib. Protectionist (1) 2,723; I. Protectionist (1) 1,294.

Ont. (11): I.C. (3) 6,381; I. (3) 2,404; Comm. (3) 1,495; Lab. (2) 994.
Man. (13): Lab. (5) 19,552; I. Lab. (1) 256; I.C. (1) 715; Comm. (3) 4,365; I.L. (3) 1,139.
Sask. (10): Farmers (5) 11,999; Farmer-Lab. (1) 2,091; I. (3) 11,561; other L. (1) 3,432.
Alta. (4): Lab. (2) 8,769; I. (1) 2,218; Lab.-Farmer (1) 509.
B.C. (6): I. Lab. (1) 15,732; I. (2) 6,338; Farmer-Lab. (1) 429; Prohibition (1) 266; Comm. (1) 861.

Liberal party was an urban party in French Canada and a rural party in English."[65] Yet it is clear, at least in retrospect, that the strong Conservative vote in rural Quebec in 1930 was to be anything but normal. The vital factors were that French Canada was largely Liberal and urban English Canada largely Conservative. To a considerable extent these factors helped to determine the parties' attitudes towards the tariff, Canada's status within the Commonwealth, and like matters.

In contrast with 1926, the electoral system worked to the Conservatives' advantage this time. Though the Liberals polled 260,000 more votes and only 0.9 per cent less of the popular vote, they lost 37 seats. The Con-

Popular Vote								Total
C.	%	L.	%	P.	%	O.	%	
140,503	52.5	127,179	47.5					267,682
109,716	59.3	75,342	40.7					185,058
29,692	50.0	29,698	50.0					59,390
455,452	44.7	542,357	53.2			22,109	2.2	1,019,918
745,406	54.8	590,079	43.4	12,815	0.9	11,274	0.8	1,359,574
111,294	47.7	86,840	37.2	9,228	4.0	26,027	11.2	233,389
124,000	37.6	150,241	45.5	26,854	8.1	29,083	8.8	330,178
67,832	33.9	60,126	30.0	60,848	30.4	11,496	5.7	200,302
119,074	49.3	98,933	40.9			23,626	9.8	241,633
846	60.3	557	39.7					1,403
1,903,815	48.8	1,761,352	45.2	109,745	2.8	123,615	3.2	3,898,527

servatives added 430,000 votes to their total, raised their popular vote from 45.3 to 48.8 per cent, and gained 46 seats. The difference this time was that the substantial vote they polled in Quebec and the Prairie provinces paid off in seats. Although they could not know it, it was a Pyrrhic victory. Indeed, it added to the King myth. For although he had done all he could to win the election, it came to be believed that, anticipating the severity of the depression and the inability of any government to cope with it, he had contrived to lose it. In this way, so the myth goes, he was able to rivet himself permanently upon the Canadian people in the next election.

1. Ramsay Cook, *The Politics of John W. Dafoe and the Fress Press* (Toronto: University of Toronto Press, 1963), p. 192.

2. *Ibid.*, p. 191.

3. J.A. Stevenson, "The Canadian Election," *Queen's Quarterly*, XXXVII (Summer, 1930), p. 575.

4. "Canada: The General Election," *Round Table*, XX (September, 1930), p. 847.

5. H. Blair Neatby, *William Lyon Mackenzie King 1924-32: The Lonely Heights* (Toronto: University of Toronto Press, 1963), p. 321.

6. *Ibid.*

7. *Ibid.*, p. 322.

8. *Ibid.*, p. 323.

9. F.H. Soward, "The Canadian Elections of 1930," *American Political Science Review*, XXIV (November, 1930), p. 997.

10. See Frederick C. Mears, "The Assize of Demos," *Queen's Quarterly*, XXXVII (Spring, 1930), pp. 399-401.

11. Quoted from King's diary in Neatby, *King: Lonely Heights*, p. 325.

12. Richard DeBrisay, "Liberal Claims and Conservative Chances," *Canadian Forum*, X (July, 1930), p. 351.

13. "Canada: The General Election," p. 852.

14. Soward, "Canadian Elections," p. 999.

15. F.H. Underhill, "O Canada," *Canadian Forum*, X (August, 1930), p. 400.

16. *Ibid.*

17. "Canada: The General Election," p. 849.

18. Underhill, "O Canada," p. 400.

19. Cook, *Dafoe and the Free Press*, p. 188.

20. John R. Williams, *The Conservative Party of Canada: 1920-49* (Durham, North Carolina: Duke University Press, 1956), p. 55.

21. Cook, *Dafoe and the Free Press*, p. 188.

22. *Canadian Annual Review*, 1929-30 (Toronto: The Canadian Review Company, 1930), p. 85.

23. Soward, "Canadian Elections," p. 998.

24. *Ibid.*

25. *Canadian Annual Review*, 1929-30, p. 97.

26. *Ibid.*, p. 98.

27. *Ibid.*, p. 95.

28. *Ibid.*, p. 86.

29. "Canada: The General Election," p. 851.

30. Soward, "Canadian Elections," p. 997.

31. "Canada: The General Election," pp. 849-50.

32. *Canadian Annual Review*, 1929-30, p. 89.

33. *Ibid.*, p. 92.

34. *Ibid.*

35. "Canada: The General Election," pp. 850-51.

36. *Ibid.*, pp. 852-54.

37. Neatby, *King: Lonely Heights,* p. 335.

38. *Ibid.*, p. 318.

39. *Canadian Annual Review*, 1929-30, p. 104.

40. *Ibid.*, p. 103.

41. *Ibid.*, p. 87.

42. *Ibid.*, p. 93.

43. Neatby, *King: Lonely Heights*, p. 337.

44. *Ibid.*, p. 330.

45. *Ibid.*, p. 333.

46. J.B.M. Clark, "The Canadian Election," *The Nineteenth Century*, CVIII (September, 1930), p. 342.

47. Robert Rumilly, *Histoire de la Province de Québec*, XXXI (Montreal: Fides, 1959), p. 223.

48. Soward, "Canadian Elections," p. 999; Clark, "Canadian Election," p. 340.

49. Clark, "Canadian Election," p. 336.

50. Stevenson, "Canadian Election," p. 578.

51. "The General Election," *Round Table*, XXI (December, 1930), p. 168.

52. Rumilly, *Histoire*, XXXI, pp. 229-30 and 237.

53. *Canadian Annual Review*, 1929-30, p. 87.

54. Rumilly, *Histoire*, XXXI, p. 230.

55. Norman Ward (ed.), *The Memoirs of Chubby Power: A Party Politician* (Toronto: The Macmillan Company of Canada, 1966), p. 116.

56. Rumilly, *Histoire*, XXXI, pp. 228-29.

57. "The General Election," p. 169.

58. Rumilly, *Histoire*, XXXI, pp. 225-27.

59. Stevenson, "Canadian Election," p. 579.

60. Rumilly, *Histoire*, XXXI, p. 241.

61. Richard DeBrisay, "Nationalism Wins," *Canadian Forum*, X (September, 1930), p. 432.

62. Cook, *Dafoe and the Free Press*, p. 192.

63. Escott Reid, "Canadian Political Parties: A Study of the Economic and Racial Bases of Conservatism and Liberalism in 1930," *Contributions to Canadian Economics*, VI, pp. 7-39.

64. *Ibid.*, p. 26.

65. *Ibid.*, p. 34.

Eighteenth
General Election

THE "POLICY OF HAVING NO POLICY"

If the eighteenth general election was a verdict on the Bennett government, it had to be a verdict on R.B. Bennett himself. Of all the administrations since Confederation his, without doubt, came closest to being a one-man show. Grattan O'Leary, no unfriendly observer, presented this picture of him:

> . . . he never held mastery over his party as Macdonald did, or Laurier, nor appealed to its reason as did Meighen. . . . Respect of his followers he had, and discipline he enforced; but he did not excite, uplift or thrill them. . . . He did not seem to think he needed a party, nor colleagues, nor friendly newspapers, nor propaganda for the public. His work would be enough. *His* work. Thus more and more he became the victim of loneliness imposed by his own nature.[1]

However, it was not Bennett's personal failings that led to his downfall, although they undoubtedly contributed to its magnitude. He had come into office during the first year of a world-wide depression, and no one man could have prevented it from continuing and deepening. J.W. Dafoe prophesied late in 1930 that Bennett would be "the Conservative 'Mackenzie' and his party will be lucky if he does not fix in the public mind for a generation the idea that the Conservative party is a hoodoo and a bringer of hard times."[2] Few prophets have been so accurate.

If energy had had anything to do with it, the Depression would have dissipated before Bennett's frenzied activity. During the campaign of 1930 he had argued that higher protection was a certain guarantee of high wages and employment. Accordingly, "not long after the election, a new, comprehensive and drastically high tariff was bestowed upon Canadian industry."[3] Next, the Prime Minister launched a wider programme. He had got nowhere with his economic proposals at the Imperial Conference of 1930. However, things were different at the Imperial Economic Conference held at Ottawa in July 1932: the British delegates had come committed to the success of the Conference on almost any terms. Canada benefited more from the agreements than any other country. The amount of actual trade diverted from foreign to inter-imperial channels was small; certainly it was insufficient to halt the downslide of the Canadian economy. Not until Roosevelt devalued the American dollar did a hint of recovery appear, first in the United States and then in Canada. By then it was too late to prevent the Conservatives from losing by-election after by-election – 3 in 1933 and 4 out of 5 in 1934 – and too late to halt the apparently irreversible trend to the Liberals.[4]

Bennett had become no less identified with the Depression than had Hoover in the United States. Even the idiom of the day attested all too eloquently to the public scorn and contempt for him. "Bennettburghs" were habitations made of packing cases and kerosene cans which the unemployed used for shelter. "Bennett buggies" were old automobiles that were too decrepit to run on their own power or whose owners lacked the funds to buy gasoline; accordingly, their motors were removed and horses were hitched to them to provide a means of locomotion.[5]

Bennett's dictatorial methods served only to confirm the impression that he was a cold, authoritarian millionaire, who was altogether callous towards the suffering of ordinary folk. No one ever requested more blank-cheque legislation from Parliament than he. He went so far in his Relief Act bill of 1932 that the Liberal C.G. Power said of him: "The place for him is in some South American republic where he can be dictator at his will, or better still in Italy or Russia."[6] A Canadian, James Gray, in an article in the American periodical *The Nation*, accused him of actively flirting with fascism. He said Bennett had every characteristic of a dictator. A millionaire many times over, he had used his own resources and acted like a mountebank in getting his party elected in 1930. He was the first politician anywhere to guarantee a complete cure for the ills of the Depression. Having paid the shot and called the tune, he assumed that the Conservative party belonged to him. He accepted neither criticism nor advice from his own followers or the opposition. He demanded unprecedented delegated power from Parliament. He used Section 98 of the Criminal Code to jail the leaders of the Communist party. He converted the R.C.M.P. from a small police force to a strong private army of storm troopers. Finally, at Regina on July 1, 1935, he used these troopers to break up the relief camp strikers who were on their way to Ottawa to protest the conditions in their camps. "The only explanation that makes sense," said Gray, "is that Bennett, about to be booted into oblivion by an outraged people, was trying to escape from this fate by the dictatorship route."[7] Few Canadians would have gone this far, but many would have agreed with the commentator in the *Canadian Forum* who wrote: "Let us suggest when [Bennett] becomes Baron Bow and Elbow, the College of Heralds quarter upon his armorial bearings a tariff wall and a Bennett buggy, the whole surmounted by an iron heel rampant."[8]

While Bennett floundered in difficulties neither he nor anyone else could have solved, King remained largely standpat and concentrated on criticizing his opponents' efforts. It is true that on February 27, 1933, he had outlined a fourteen-point statement of Liberal policy to the Commons.[9] Except for the promises to reconstitute the Bank of Canada, restore state control over money and credit, establish an investment control board, and adopt a constitutionally valid system of unemployment insurance, there was nothing in this statement that was very new or precise. His principal opponents at least would have concurred with his promise to work for international peace through the League of Nations, and with his promises of a balanced budget, the retrenchment of expenditures, the reduction of principal and interest on the public debt, and the maintenance of the integrity of the C.N.R. Yet the programme had a curious inconsistency that was never satisfactorily explained. By favouring a liberalization of internal trade through the avoidance of such things as artificial price controls, the Liberals seemed to express opposition in principle to state interference in economic matters and to the concomitant increased delegation of power to the executive. But it would have been more than difficult to realize the fourteenth point – a more equitable distribution of wealth in order to further social justice and promote the common good – without substantial governmental interference in economic life. If the exigencies of the time required extensive remedies, they were not to be found in the Liberal programme.

The alleged inadequacy of the old-line parties prompted radicalism to make a fresh start in 1932 by setting up the first party in Canada that was professedly and unashamedly socialist. Socialist ideas had been steadily growing in the farmer organizations and trade unions. The League for Social Reconstruction (L.S.R.) founded early in 1932 by Fabian-oriented professors at McGill and Toronto provided the ideas for the nascent party and lent it intellectual prestige. Late in May of the same year the Labour M.P.'s and the Ginger Group (or "co-operating independents") met with members of the L.S.R. on Parliament Hill to pass the resolutions that led to the founding of the new party. In August a joint meeting of the Western Conference of Labour Parties and the U.F.A. met at Calgary with the representatives of such groups as the L.S.R., the Canadian Brotherhood of Railway Employees, and the United Farmers of Canada (Saskatchewan Section), and formed the Co-operative Commonwealth Federation, soon generally known as the C.C.F. Not until its conference at Regina in 1933, however, did the party draw up a constitution and a manifesto,[10] and make J.S. Woodsworth the first president of its National Council; he also became its parliamentary leader. The Regina Manifesto, which in its original draft was the work of the "most Shavian of Shavians," Professor Frank Underhill, was to become "the party's foundation document and its closest approximation to a sacred text."[11] It left no doubt where the party stood:

> We aim to replace the capitalist system, with its inherent injustice and humanity, by a social order from which the domination

and exploitation of one class by another will be eliminated, in which economic planning will supersede unregulated private enterprise and competition, and in which genuine democratic self-government, based upon economic equality will be possible.

Other criticism of the capitalist system, although less fundamental in nature, was to manifest itself before the election. In January 1934 H.H. Stevens, Bennett's Minister of Trade and Commerce, alleged that large department and chain stores, packing houses, and the like were using their purchasing power unfairly to pare down the prices they paid the manufacturers and producers; as a result, he said, the latter groups paid their employees less than a living wage. Bennett objected and Stevens resigned, but in the end the resignation was withdrawn and kept secret. Stevens became chairman of the Parliamentary Committee on Price Spreads and Mass Buying which was given wide power to investigate his complaints. Its hearings, which received wide attention, soon demonstrated that his allegations had been too modest. After the session, a speech delivered by Stevens to a Conservative study club found its way to the newspapers, which gave it full publicity. It was "brutally frank, and [perhaps] somewhat indiscreet and not wholly accurate."[12] Stevens refused Bennett's demands that he apologize, retract, or correct, and instead resigned. When the committee was transformed to a royal commission to permit it to continue its investigation, Stevens became only an ordinary member and not its chairman. Naturally the man in the street regarded his resignation from the cabinet as a victory for powerful industrial and financial interests.

Then – wonder of wonders – early in January 1935 Bennett himself made a series of radio speeches which recognized the evils of the capitalistic system. "If [capitalism in its present form] does not serve us, we must reform it. . . . I nail the flag of progress to the masthead. I summon the power of the state to its support."[13] Many, such as J.W. Dafoe, regarded Bennett's performance as "one of the most cynical and dishonest . . . recorded in Canadian politics."[14] Why, asked Dafoe, if capitalism was predacious and heartless, did Bennett not find out until he had amassed his millions? None the less, the Speech from the Throne in 1935 promised legislation to "remedy . . . social and economic injustice" and to "ensure to all classes a greater degree of equality in the distribution of the capitalistic system." King was audacious enough to say that the proposed reforms only touched "the fringe of some evils of the system," and they had "long been a part of Liberal policy";[15] others were skeptical, but were prepared to wait and see.

There was reason for doubt. Bennett's radio speeches had been written by his brother-in-law, W.D. Herridge, and his private secretary, R.K. Finlayson, apparently without the knowledge of most members of the cabinet. The legislation about which the Speech from the Throne spoke so optimistically was at best only in a preliminary state of drafting. First,

Bennett's serious illness and then his attendance at the King's Silver Jubilee kept him out of the House from late February to mid-May and deprived the government of its chief directing hand. The unsympathetic attitude of ministers such as C.H. Cahan led to several proposals reaching the statute book "in a somewhat denatured form." Other January promises were entirely forgotten.[16] None the less, the five major acts of the so-called Bennett "New Deal" would have been a major step forward in social legislation had the Judicial Committee in 1937 not declared all of them to be *ultra vires*.

Not so much can be claimed for two other acts of the session. The original version of the Canada Wheat Board Act empowered the Board to control exclusively the interprovincial and export marketing of the grain of western Canada. But the Liberals hearkened to the anguished cries of the grain trade and the Winnipeg Grain Exchange against the compulsory features of the bill, and when it was discovered that the government had put $100 million more into the farmers' hands than the vagaries of the market would have given them, they placed the Conservatives on the defensive and forced them to make the provisions optional.[17]

Far more momentous in its results was the Dominion Trade and Industry Commission Act. The Royal Commission on Price Spreads and Mass Buying had recommended that sweeping steps be taken to protect consumers against various forms of profiteering, and to ensure primary producers and other workers a fair return for their industry. Partly because of constitutional inhibitions, but more likely because of strong pressure from influential interests within the Conservative party, the government's bill was a poor imitation of what the Commission intended. Its utter inadequacy was the clinching factor in the decision of H.H. Stevens to head a new party. "It may sound 'mushy' to say this to a bunch of 'hard-boiled' newspapermen," he remarked on July 7, "but I simply felt I could not desert those 20,000 people [who gave their support in letters]."[18]

Within five days his party had both a name and a manifesto. As the Reconstruction party, its aim was "to help reconstruct Canada's shattered national policy, to wage war with poverty, and to abolish involuntary idleness." It stood in opposition to the old parties which resisted effective change and upheld an obsolete system. But it refused to advocate "panaceas beyond the needs of the situation" or "lend attraction to schemes of rigid state control of life and organization." In other words, it hoped to provide an alternative to socialism for those who rejected the old-line parties. Hence its fifteen-point programme in no way threatened the basis of the capitalistic system. The party would, according to its programme, take action to ensure fair prices for the farmers' products. It would free all primary producers from the oppression of the secondary handlers of their products. It would reduce interest rates and devise a plan of monetary control best suited to Canadian conditions. It would create a federal trade commission which would act as a referee and check unethical business practices and unfair competition generally. In other words, the party was pure Stevens. According to him, it would at last do justice to the five "forgotten" groups of society: the intellectual worker, the farmer, the small merchant, the small manufacturer, and the unorganized clerical classes.

The protest against the established economic order had brought another new entry into the political field on a more limited geographical base. Neither of the old parties had ever been able to weaken the hold which the U.F.A. had had on the province of Alberta since 1921. But on August 22 the candidates of the Social Credit League of Alberta had won a sweeping provincial victory, practically wiping out the U.F.A. in the process. Espousing an unorthodox form of Social Credit tinged with religious revivalism of a fundamentalist flavour, they carried all before them under the leadership of William Aberhart, whom the periodicals of the day described as "a Canadian replica of Father Coughlin."[19] The cultural heritage, the "A plus B" theorem, the unearned increment, the basic dividend, and the just price may have been quite incomprehensible to the economist, but the plausible simplicity with which they were presented made a special appeal to a debt-ridden community subsisting in a sort of quasi-colonial status with respect to central Canada.[20] Certainly Social Credit could be counted on to make a strong fight for Alberta's seats in the next federal election.

Despite the doubts about his health, Bennett told his caucus on June 19: "I'll die in harness rather than quit now. We have a record to be proud of."[21] He was more confident than his ministers, who were fleeing before the storm. On August 17 he filled the vacancies—some of the new members were themselves a little surprised to become Privy Councillors—and submerged himself in the labours of an election campaign.

Shortly Canada was to see a new Bennett, as the old Bennett sought to create a new image.

I am 65 years old. When one reaches my time in life, ambitions dim, the love of power dies, the plaudits of the multitude can scarce be heard, its condemnation is just as meaningless. Therefore I speak without much thought of my place in the national scene after polling day. I want you to think without like or dislike of me. I will speak only as your interests require me to speak.[22]

Later he told a Halifax audience he wanted "nothing more now than eternal salvation."[23] Undoubtedly his listeners would not have denied him that wish, but they had not altered their opinion of him.

To them he was much the same old Bennett. Who else could have boasted how well he had kept his promises of 1930? "We have not only done what we said we would do. We have done far more than we have even told you of."[24] There was also the Bennett who could not be wrong. His promise to "blast a way" into the markets which had been closed had not been amiss in 1930. "It was right then when there were still one or two nations preaching free trade and it is a thousand times more so now when every nation has embraced a doctrine of economic nationalism." Beware, then, of that man King who "would be out smashing down our protective walls so that the commercial invaders of this country might sweep in safety over the ruins of them." Each hard-pressed country must "look after itself first in this world where nations have re-proclaimed the ancient rule–'Each for himself and the devil take the hindmost.' "[25]

But even in his extremity Bennett was not without ideas. Debt, he said, was the basic evil in Canada's economic structure. He proposed, therefore, to ask those of his fellow Canadians who were creditors of the federal, provincial, and municipal governments to "agree to a scheme of conversion upon a substantially lower rate of interest than that now provided for." Although unemployment had fallen from a peak of 738,000 in 1933 to about 500,000, he had "reluctantly but quite inexorably determined on . . . the only prudential solution of the problem . . . to remove from the labour market all those workers who have reached the age of 60 . . . a bold, and, I believe, . . a triumphant attempt to put an end to that cause of unemployment." He made surprisingly few references to that other bold scheme, his New Deal, but he did go on record "now and for all time, as declaring myself against any action which will destroy the Capitalist system." In one of his few references to the Reconstruction party, he condemned, not their objectives, but their attempts to attain them by arousing class prejudice, or by repudiation and destruction.[26]

Stevens and his Reconstructionists campaigned on their fifteen-point programme; Woodsworth and the C.C.F., for the construction of a new social order in conformity with the Regina Manifesto. According to the C.C.F., the Bennett New Deal legislation bore "as little resemblance to the high-flying promises of the radio speeches of January 1935 as do the Government's achievements on unemployment to the promises in the 1930 elections." What were the alternatives?, asked Woodsworth. The Liberals were holding out to "our industrial and financial plutocrats the promise of even less state regulation and control than they have had to fear from the present government." Stevens with his "vote-catching platform of superficial reform . . . refused to face issues and [sought] easy and painless solutions."[27] Surely, he went on, it was now evident that political democracy could not be true democracy unless it was also economic democracy. To effect it, arbitrary, irresponsible plutocracy had to be ousted and economic institutions had to be brought under public control. As a first step, the C.C.F. would socialize the country's banking and financial machinery, and put national credit to use for purposes of national development. Next, it would step in where private enterprise had failed and use the government's financial power to initiate a far-reaching programme for the purpose of increasing employment. And so on.

Eighteenth

When the election was all over, the *Economist* pointed out that King had "not been lavish with promises"[28] and the *Round Table* stated that he had not burdened himself "with an excessive load of commitments."[29] This was true, but it was also a fact that of all the leaders he had shown least concern about the ills of the capitalistic system. This was nowhere better demonstrated than in his keynote address at Kingston in which he saw three perils facing Canada. The first two were national government and third parties. Perhaps King really feared that they would mean the disappearance of a genuine opposition and the obscuring of the issues, but more likely he wanted nothing to stand in the way of government being carried on by Liberals alone. The third peril, dictatorial government, threatened if Bennett continued in office. Unceasingly King denounced the blank-cheque type of legislation which characterized the Bennett régime.

> . . . we have come to the moment where our parliamentary government is at an end. . . . Are we going to let these things go on? . . . As you think of the election to come, ask yourself that little question 'Whither are we tending?' Think of what has happened and ask yourselves if we are making Canada a second Italy, a second Germany, or a second Russia.[30]

King was only slightly less vociferous on trade policies. Bennett, he said, "did not know enough about economics [or] . . . social problems." Worst of all, Bennett regarded trade in the nature of war, rather than exchange. A Liberal government would "work with Mr. Baldwin in freeing the channel of Empire trade" and seek a broad reciprocal trade agreement with the United States. All that Canada needed was "the sympathetic physician's touch. It is from the lack of such consideration that Canada is suffering." And then King remembered that his party had a protectionist wing; so he gave assurances "there would be no precipitate action which might in any way injure a legitimate Canadian industry."[31]

The Liberal advertisements which said, "It's King or Chaos" and "Bennett let us down. Drive him out" simply re-echoed King's campaign speeches. Understandably, there were doubts about whether King had anything positive or definite to offer. The *Nation*, for example, called him a laissez-faire man,[32] while the *Round Table* said he relied on the unpopularity of the Bennett régime rather than the advocacy of bold reformative proposals.[33] Criticism of this kind made him devote his radio address of September 17 to proving that he did have a policy. But all it added up to was his programme of February 27, 1933 which, he boasted, he had "set forth time and again, over a period of years." The simple fact is that King knew that the election was not going to be decided on issues and that "the Liberal party's policy of having no policy" would save him embarrassment both presently and in the future.[34] One aspect of the campaign did disturb

King: the dramatized broadcasts of the Conservatives in which "Mr. Sage" mocked him with libelous overtones. As a result, King had legislation passed making this type of broadcast illegal.

By virtue of accident and history, Quebec, the bastion of conservatism, had become (normally) the mainstay of Canadian Liberalism; everyone expected it to lead the country back to the Liberal party. At least this is what many of the commentators said.[35] To support their view they had only to refer to Premier Taschereau's lament on Bennett, once "a safe man" who had been anxious to "retain the elements which had made the country great," but who had torn "these leaves from the book of his political life and unfaithful to his past, launched into a Socialistic venture bordering on Communism."[36] Could King not behold before his eyes how the mild radicalism of the New Deal had infuriated the Tory Montreal *Gazette* into "steadily turning cold douches on Bennett"?[37]

In the West a principal supporter of King, liberal in terms of some outdated concept, had been denouncing the C.C.F. and state intervention almost fanatically. J.W. Dafoe wanted to remove the stigma, placed on Canadian Liberalism by both the Conservatives and the C.C.F., that it subscribed to some kind of nineteenth-century policy of laissez faire. But as he ranted about the C.C.F. for attempting to "submerge the individual in a collectivism which recognizes and serves nothing but the state,"[38] it appeared that Liberalism, as he conceived it, was little more than laissez faire. Although King went along completely with Taschereau and Dafoe, he need not have done, for they had nowhere to go but the Liberal party. Yet he knew what he was doing. He realized that he had not too much to fear either from the minor parties, which were just establishing themselves and which would in any case split the radical vote, or from the Conservatives, who were clearly on the way out.

Indeed, "no government . . . ever entered an election with the omens so unpropitious."[39] In addition to the Conservatives' poor record in federal by-elections, all their provincial administrations had gone down to defeat since 1930: in 1933 Nova Scotia and British Columbia, in 1934 Ontario and Saskatchewan and finally, in June 1935, New Brunswick. Fighting almost single-handed, Bennett "performed prodigies of oratorical valour, but in times like these a well-groomed prosperous-looking millionaire, who has an autocratic habit of speech, is not a good vote-getter."[40]

Even much of Anglo-Saxon New Brunswick deserted the Conservatives; the only seat they won in the Maritimes—and that by a mere 145 votes—was Royal. In Quebec they lost their entire French-Canadian contingent and elected only 5 Anglo-Saxons. Ontario gave them 25 seats—the worst they had ever done in that province: 11 of these victories came in protectionist Toronto, the Yorks, and Hamilton. However, they also lost 4 seats in these Tory strongholds and, where they won, their majorities were severely reduced. Each of the Prairie provinces gave them only 1 seat and their vote fell by about 50 per cent in Alberta and Saskatchewan, and 44 per cent in Manitoba. In British Columbia their popular vote was cut in half but, because of the total vote being split among 3, and even 4 groups, they managed to hold on to Vancouver South, Victoria, and 3 seats in the fruit belt.

It had been prophesied that the accumulated resentments against Bennett would make "the Meighen of 1921 look like a popular hero."[41] As it turned out, the Conservatives won only 40 seats, 10 fewer than in 1921. One-third of these came from Toronto, Hamilton, and their environs; five-eighths from Ontario; three-quarters from Ontario and British Columbia. Even the most despondent Conservatives had not felt it would be so bad. Many of them blamed the Reconstructionists for the colossal defeat. Probably a majority of the voters who supported Stevens were normally Conservatives. Yet not one Conservative newspaper, M.P., or politician of stature had joined him. If there had been no Reconstruction party, the Conservatives might have held on to Cumberland and Colchester-Hants in Nova Scotia, York-Sunbury in New Brunswick, York West and Victoria in Ontario, and Souris in Manitoba. But in other ridings they would have had to take an overwhelming percentage of the votes that the Reconstruction party polled in order to elect their candidates.

At first, many Canadians indicated sympathy and admiration for Stevens. In a personal contest with Bennett and King he might have won, but Canada does not elect a president.[42] It was soon apparent that Stevens had too much working against him. He did not have time to build up an organization that could cope effectively with those of the old parties, nor did he have "the radical zeal and burning ardour" that animated the C.C.F. Above all, he encountered the strong party attachments existing in Canada. Many. Conservatives who had promised him assistance as a reformer within the party refused him support outside it. Also, a base of small businessmen and shopkeepers was a somewhat limited one on which to build a party. Warren K. Cook and others like him who induced Stevens to embark on this venture said they were "just a lot of business people – amateur politicians if you will – who are trying to help those who have no' politics, and who want to see Canada go ahead."[43] Yet, as Graham Spry said, "a nation of shop-keepers may defeat a Napoleon, but a party of shop-keepers will hardly fool even itself."[44] Stevens did try to broaden his appeal to attract farmers, the unemployed, war veterans, youth, and even individual workers, but with little success. By the end of the campaign the public was becoming tired of his tirades against big business.[45]

The Reconstruction party turned out to be an eastern party. It is true that Stevens, the only member whom it elected, came from British Columbia, but in Alberta and Saskatchewan combined it could find only 6 candidates to run and it polled an insignificant portion of the vote. In contrast, it did best in Nova Scotia where 13.9 per cent of the voters supported it. Ontario gave it 11.5 per cent of its vote, mostly in the cities and larger towns. Its strongest showing in all Canada was in Hamilton and Wentworth County. In Montreal it won almost 17 per cent of the vote and in Toronto 14 per cent, but it made much less of an appeal to the rural areas. Including Stevens, only 11 of the 174 Reconstuction candiates saved their deposits. But perhaps little more could be expected of a party which had few organizations behind it other than the U.F.O. and some associations of retail merchants.

The C.C.F. fared only slightly better. One reason was that the Depression did not act as the C.C.F. expected it would; only four months after the formation of the party, economic conditions showed a slight improvement and "they continued slowly to improve until the date of the election."[46] Another was that it did not have time to organize, especially east of the Ottawa. In the Maritimes it ran no candidates at all. In Quebec it ran only 3, but the time factor probably made little difference there, since the Coadjutor Bishop of Montreal had denounced the C.C.F. as a dangerous movement resting upon "a materialistic conception of the social order which precisely constitutes the anti-Christian character of Socialism."[47]

West of the Ottawa the C.C.F. suffered severely from the competition of the Reconstruction party, and also, in Alberta and Saskatchewan, from the new-fangled Social Credit movement. Although it may have had the most coherent policy, it had "too little command of publicity to make its issues the issue of the election." Its supporters had the feeling that King's "facility for erecting the unimportant into the significant and his capacity for mopping up vague demands for change . . . [had] obscured [it] in a cloud partly of polite commendation and partly of 'red' suspicion."[48]

It was not surprising that it did so poorly in rural Ontario. A veteran member of the U.F.O., Agnes Macphail, had got her organization to affiliate with the provincial council of the C.C.F. in December 1932. However, the radical nature of the Regina Manifesto caused the U.F.O. to have second thoughts. In March 1934 it withdrew its affiliation and later it gave its blessing to the Reconstruction party. In urban Ontario the C.C.F. did considerably better, but it could win no seats in the province and only 5 of its 50 candidates saved their deposits.

In Manitoba and Saskatchewan the C.C.F. polled about one-fifth of the vote and elected 2 members in each province. In Manitoba the labour vote in North Winnipeg continued to elect J.S. Woodsworth and A.A. Heaps; in Saskatchewan the farmers' vote elected M.J. Coldwell in Rosetown-Biggar and T.C. Douglas in Weyburn. British Columbia gave the C.C.F. more support than any other province even though the Liberals "stooped to conquer." Professor H.F. Angus became indignant after 6 Liberal candidates, seeking to take advantage of the province's anti-Oriental sentiment, used advertisements which stated that "a vote for any C.C.F. candidate is a vote to give the Chinamen and the Japanese the same voting rights that you have."[49] Nevertheless, more than one-third of the voters supported the C.C.F., even though it could win only Nanaimo and 2 of the Vancouver seats.

Alberta proved to be the greatest disappointment for the C.C.F. At dissolution 9 of the province's members were C.C.F., all elected under the U.F.A. banner. But the élan engendered by Social Credit's provincial victory carried over into federal politics, and the C.C.F. could overcome it no more than the old-line parties could. Federally, the Social Credit candidates won a total of 17 seats: they defeated the 9 sitting C.C.F. members, and won 6 additional seats in rural Alberta, as well as 2 in Saskatchewan in ridings along the Alberta border.

Except for Alberta, where they lost 2 seats and their vote fell from 30.0 to 21.2 per cent, the Liberals made gains everywhere. In the Maritimes they won 25 of 26 seats, 19 more than in 1930. Of Quebec's 65 seats, 55 went to the Liberals and 5 to Independent Liberals. Ontario gave them 56 of 82 seats for a gain of 34. In Manitoba they increased their number of members elected from 4 to 14; in Saskatchewan, from 11 to 16, even though their popular vote fell from 45.5 to 40.8 per cent; and in British Columbia, from 5 to 6, although their percentage of the vote dropped from 40.9 to 31.8. Altogether, the Liberals won 173 seats – the greatest victory in Canadian history at that time. The election also proved that King was right in thinking he could ride into office without benefit of a coherent programme. "Historic party allegiances, combined with the swing of the pendulum after five years of depression, [had] duly carried the Liberals to their long-expected victory."[50] In speaking of the Liberalism that won in 1936 Professor A.R.M. Lower wrote:

> Here was the great centre group which had received in its ample bosom frightened Conservatives from one side and those who could not go as far as C.C.F. socialism on the other. The victory was not a tribute to Mr. King, it was not a proclamation in defence of Liberty, it was not a pronouncement on the issues of the day. Liberalism, as it emerged in Canada after 1935, was the counterpart of Baldwin Conservatism in Great Britain, of Le Front Populaire in France, and of Rooseveltian democracy: – it represented the huddling together of frightened people, uncertain of their way in a chaotic world.[51]

One wonders, however, if this picture of "frightened people . . . huddling together" is not an exaggeration. Certainly it is just as much the picture of a people determined to inflict retribution on Bennett and the Conservatives, using the Liberals as their agent to accomplish that object. "The magnitude of the poll and the emphatic character of the decision suggest the silent determination of an electorate that had already made up its mind, and that refused to be shaken in its purpose by the blandishments of the platform or the mingled threatenings and entreaties of the Press."[52]

It is also questionable whether the Liberals deserve to be called "the great centre group." Escott Reid, it is true, shows that if the Liberals were to be considered centrists then there were about 30 per cent of the electorate to the right and 23 per cent to the left. But he also makes the valid point that "if the advocacy of state intervention in economic life is a left-wing doctrine, the greater part of the Liberal party lies to the right of the greater part of the Conservative pary."[53] Indeed, if platforms were the determining factor, the Liberals clearly stood to the right of the Conservative, Reconstructionist, and C.C.F. parties. And for that matter, of Social Credit, too, for the commentators of the day, looking at Aberhart's economic rather than his political doctrine, labelled his movement as clearly leftist. In ideological terms the election can be called a centrist victory only if one accepts the views of the Montreal *Gazette*, which described it as "a victory for moderate thought throughout Canada" and "a sweeping repudiation of radicalism and of radical tendencies wherever they had appeared."[54] In any case, as a United Church clergyman pointed out, "so far as the parties of social reform are concerned, if the Canadian people desire amendment of their evil condition, they are like St. Augustine, in his famous prayer for purity, who asked to be set free from his wickedness – 'but not yet.' "[55]

The election proved that a high protectionist policy could no longer provide an adequate basis for a political party since too many groups opposed it. Hence the tariff, which had been a major issue in most elections since 1878, has since ceased to be anything but a minor, sporadic source of contention.[56]

As usual, there were fears that a highly conservative (some said reactionary) French element had once again got control of the Liberal party. It is true that of the 75 seats in which the French were the determining factor, the Liberals took every one but Sir George Perley's Argenteuil. It is also true that the opposition benches did not contain a single French Canadian and that 76 of the 106 seats in which the Liberals had an over-all majority were either French or bilingual. Within months the supposedly dominant influence of Quebec within the Liberal party raised a question of the highest practical significance. On December 1, 1935, when the King government repudiated the proposal of Dr. Riddell, the Canadian advisory officer at Geneva, that the League of Nations' sanctions against Italy be extended to include coal and oil, the question was immediately asked: Is this the voice of an isolationist Quebec?[57]

Once again the electoral system came under severe attack. It was a landslide for Liberalism only if one looked at the number of members elected and not at the popular vote. The Liberals' percentage of the popular vote fell from 45.2 to 44.8 per cent and yet they won the greatest victory to date. The Conservatives polled two-thirds as many votes as the Liberals, but got only 40 seats to their opponents' 173. The C.C.F. polled one-fifth as many votes and won 7 seats, while the Reconstructionists, who polled almost as many as the C.C.F., could elect only Stevens. On the other hand, Social Credit polled fewer than half the votes of either the C.C.F. or the Reconstruction party, but won 17 seats because its strength was concentrated in Alberta and a small section of Saskatchewan. All of the regional discrepancies benefited the Liberals except one: Toronto remained largely Tory even though the Conservatives took only 37.7 per cent of the vote. When the electoral game is going for the Liberals or Conservatives, says Professor Underhill, it is "as if the rule makers in the game of football were to change the rules so that the attacking side was always favoured, so that it could always count on . . . completing every forward pass it made. In a game played under such rules there would be fantastic scores."[58]

In 1930 Professor Underhill castigated the electoral system because it accentuated regionalism in Canada. Now he lamented its tendency to work serious injustice upon the newer and smaller parties such as the one he had helped to found: "A new socialist movement," he said, "can only be built up gradually in Canada, but it has no fair chance at all to get a foothold under the present system." Until it got a sizable number of members elected, its leaders would be prevented from gaining experience in public affairs, and it would be denied the publicity "without which any movement under modern conditions necessarily starves."[59]

The Liberal vote in the English part of eastern Canada remained almost constant, while a pronounced swing away from the Liberals in western Canada was counterbalanced by the swing to them in Quebec. Although the Liberal percentage of the votes in the French part of Montreal actually fell, there was a veritable landslide for the Liberals in the rest of the province. Although, as Escott Reid indicates, the statistics do not indicate the inflow of Conservatives into the Liberal party or the outflow of Liberals into the parties of the left, they do indicate that the Liberal victory was the result "not of a Dominion-wide landslide towards Liberalism but of a Dominion-wide landslide away from Conservatism."[60] The voters had asked not so much to have Mackenzie King back in office as to be rid of R.B. Bennett.

	Seats	Candidates						Elected											
		C.	L.	R.	C.C.F.	S.C.	O.	C.	%	L.	%	R.	%	C.C.F.	%	S.C.	%	O.	%
Nova Scotia	12	11	12	11			1			12	100.0								
New Brunswick	10	10	10	9			1	1	10.0	9	90.0								
Prince Edward Island	4	4	4	3						4	100.0								
Quebec	65	62	64	42	3		42	5	7.7	55	84.6							5	7.7
Ontario	82	80	81	78	50		21	25	30.5	56	68.3							1	1.2
Manitoba	17	16	17	12	14	6	6	1	5.9	14	82.4			2	11.8				
Saskatchewan	21	19	21	3	20	20	1	1	4.8	16	76.2			2	9.5	2	9.5		
Alberta	17	14	17	3	15	17	4	1	5.9	1	5.9					15	88.2		
British Columbia	16	15	15	13	16	2	5	5	31.3	6	37.5	1	6.3	3	18.8			1	6.3
Yukon	1	1	1					1	100.0										
Total	245	232	242	174	118	45	81	40	16.3	173	70.6	1	0.4	7	2.9	17	6.9	7	2.9

Notes: Included in the Liberal columns are two Liberal-Progressives from Manitoba, both elected.

Both candidates in the Yukon prefixed the party label with Independent, but are included in the Conservative and Liberal columns.

Others elected: Que. (5): I.L. (5).
Ont. (1): U.F.O.-Lab. (1).
B.C. (1): I. (1).

Others (votes polled): N.S. (1): Comm. (1) 5,365.
N.B. (1): I.L. (1) 672.
Que. (42): I.L. (20) 65,476; I.C. (4) 2,348; I. Rec. (2) 1,772; I. (5) 7,581; Lab.-Lib. (4) 929; Comm. (1) 3,385; Verdun Party (1) 4,214; Veterans (1) 79; Lab. (4) 6,919.
Ont. (21): I.L. (6) 9,767; other L. (2) 4,614; Comm. (6) 8,945; Anti-Comm. (1) 3,961; Lab. (1) 7,288; U.F.O.-Lab. (1) 7,210; I. (4) 2,708.
Man. (6): I.L. (2) 2,343; I. Lib.-Prog. (1) 2,998; Comm. (2) 9,229; I. (1) 280.
Sask. (1): S.C.-C.C.F. (1) 4,129.
Alta. (4): Comm. (2) 2,672; Tech. (1) 733; other S.C. (1) 378.
B.C. (5): I. (2) 5,196; Soc. (1) 251; Comm. (1) 1,555; Lab. (1) 999.

						Popular Vote						Total
C.	%	L.	%	R.	%	C.C.F.	%	S.C.	%	O.	%	
87,893	32.1	142,334	52.0	38,175	13.9					5,365	2.0	273,767
56,145	31.9	100,537	57.2	18,408	10.5					672	0.4	175,762
23,602	38.4	35,757	58.2	2,089	3.4							61,448
322,794	28.2	623,579	54.4	100,119	8.7	7,326	0.6			92,703	8.1	1,146,521
562,513	35.3	675,803	42.4	183,511	11.5	127,927	8.0			44,493	2.8	1,594,247
75,574	26.9	113,887	40.5	16,439	5.9	54,491	19.4	5,751	2.0	14,850	5.3	280,992
65,078	18.8	141,121	40.8	4,361	1.3	69,376	20.1	61,505	17.8	4,129	1.2	345,570
40,236	16.9	50,539	21.2	1,785	0.7	30,921	13.0	111,249	46.6	3,783	1.6	238,513
71,034	24.6	91,729	31.8	19,208	6.7	97,015	33.6	1,796	0.6	8,001	2.8	288,783
696	55.6	555	44.4									1,251
1,305,565	29.6	1,975,841	44.8	384,095	8.7	387,056	8.8	180,301	4.1	173,996	3.9	4,406,854

FOOTNOTES

1. M. Grattan O'Leary, "Who'll Succeed Bennett," *Maclean's Magazine*, LI (May 1, 1938), p. 10.

2. Ramsay Cook, *The Politics of John W. Dafoe and the Free Press* (Toronto: University of Toronto Press, 1963), p. 193.

3. *Economist*, CXXI (October 19, 1935), p. 742.

4. *Ibid.*, p. 743.

5. J.R. Williams, *The Conservative Party of Canada: 1920-49* (Durham, North Carolina: Duke University Press, 1956), p. 56.

6. Mason Wade, *The French Canadians 1760-1967* (Toronto: The Macmillan Company of Canada, 1955), p. 823.

7. James H. Gray, "Canada Flirts with Fascism," *Nation*, CXLI (October 9, 1935), pp. 406-408.

8. "Notes and Comments," *Canadian Forum*, XV (August, 1935), p. 330.

9. *House of Commons Debates*, 1932-33, pp. 2509-11.

10. For the details, see W.K. McNaught, *A Prophet in Politics: A Biography of J.S. Woodsworth* (Toronto: University of Toronto Press, 1959), pp. 258-65.

11. Leo Zakuta, *A Protest Movement Becalmed: A Study of Change in the C.C.F.* (Toronto: University of Toronto Press, 1964), p. 14.

12. "Capitalism under fire," *Round Table*, XXV (March, 1935), p. 390.

13. Halifax *Chronicle*, January 3, 1935.

14. Cook, *Dafoe and the Free Press*, p. 209.

15. Wade, *French Canadians*, p. 830.

16. "The Record of the Session," *Round Table*, XXV (September, 1935), p. 808.

17. *Ibid.*, pp. 809-10.

18. Halifax *Herald*, July 8, 1935.

19. "The Party Programmes," *Round Table*, XXV (September, 1935), p. 818.

20. For details, see C.B. Macpherson, *Democracy in Alberta: The Theory and Practice of a Quasi-Party System* (Toronto: University of Toronto Press, 1953), and John A. Irving, *The Social Credit Movement in Alberta* (Toronto: University of Toronto Press, 1959).

21. *Canadian Annual Review*, 1935-36 (Toronto: Canadian Review Company, 1939), p. 8.

22. Halifax *Chronicle*, September 7, 1935.

23. *Ibid.*, October 5, 1935.

24. *Ibid.*, September 12, 1935.

25. *Ibid.*, September 7, 1935.

26. *Ibid.*, September 12 and 16, 1935.

27. Halifax *Herald*, July 16, 1935.

28. *Economist*, CXXI (October 19, 1935), p. 743.

29. "Canada: The General Election," *Round Table*, XXVI (December, 1935), p. 171.

30. Halifax *Chronicle*, August 8, 1935.

31. *Ibid.*, September 5, 1935.

32. "Canada's New Deal," *Nation*, CXLI (October 9, 1935), p. 398.

33. "Prospects for the Election," *Round Table*, XXV (September, 1935), p. 814.

34. Escott Reid, "The Canadian Election of 1935—And After," *American Political Science Review*, XXX (February, 1936), p. 116.

35. See "Notes and Comments," *Canadian Forum*, XV (August, 1935), p. 328.

36. "Back to Big Business Normalcy," *Canadian Forum*, XV (November, 1935), p. 351.

37. "Canada: The General Election," *Round Table*, XXVI (December, 1935), p. 169.

38. Cook, *Dafoe and the Free Press*, p. 207.

39. "Prospects for the Election," p. 815.

40. "Canada: The General Election," p. 168.

41. "Notes and Comments," p. 330.

42. Graham Spry, "Politics," *Canadian Forum*, XV (August, 1935), p. 324.

43. John Cripps, "The Canadian Elections," *Political Quarterly*, VI (Winter, 1935), p. 569.

44. Spry, "Politics," p. 325.

45. See "Canada: The General Election," p. 167.

46. Reid, "Canadian Election of 1935," p. 117.

47. Wade, *French Canadians*, p. 827.

48. Spry, "Politics," p. 324.

49. H.F. Angus, "Liberalism Stoops to Conquer," *Canadian Forum*, XV (December, 1935), p. 389.

50. *Economist*, CXXI (October 19, 1935), p. 742.

51. A.R.M. Lower, *Colony to Nation* (Toronto: Longmans, Green, 1946), p. 519.

52. J.S. Thomson, "Topics of the Day," *Dalhousie Review*, XV (January, 1936) p. 494.

53. Reid, "Canadian Election of 1935," p. 113.

54. "Back to Big Business Normalcy," p. 351.

55. Thomson, "Topics of the Day," p. 496.

56. "Canada: The General Election," p. 168.

57. Reid, "Canadian Election of 1935," p. 117.

58. F.H. Underhill, "Our Fantastic Election System," *Canadian Forum*, XV (November, 1935), p. 355.

59. *Ibid.*

60. Reid, "Canadian Election of 1935," p. 115.

Nineteenth

General Election

"MR. KING LOCKED AWAY THE FILES"

The timing of Canada's nineteenth election presented an abnormal complexity. On September 12, 1939, Mackenzie King gave an undertaking to a special war session that Parliament would meet again before a dissolution. It was not long before he called it "one of the most foolish commitments he had ever made."[1]

As late as January 15, 1940, he expected the forthcoming session to go on until May with an election in June. But the next day, after consulting the cabinet, he decided he would call an election in February or March "if we could not carry on the business of Parliament in an orderly fashion." Then fate intervened. On January 18, Premier Hepburn and most Liberal M.L.A.'s joined the Conservatives in the Ontario Legislature to condemn the federal government's war record by a vote of 44 to 10. King was elated because the action "justified an immediate appeal, avoiding thereby all the contention of a [pre-] election session."[2]

Except for J.L. Ralston, the Minister of Finance, who felt that "the Government should present its case, being a good one, to Parliament,"[3] the members of the War Committee of the cabinet all agreed with the Prime Minister. Fearing a leak to the press, King did not even tell the whole cabinet of his intentions. Parliament, he decided, would meet only long enough to provide machinery for taking the armed services vote. On the morning of January 25 – the day on which Parliament reconvened after a long adjournment – he changed his mind again. Why bother passing new legislation? Why not use the War Measures Act to give servicemen the vote? Accordingly, he got the faithful Lapointe to tell the cabinet he had decided on an immediate election. Parliament would meet simply to be told it would not meet again. That is how King met his commitment of the previous September and that is why Canadians went to the polls on March 26, 1940.

Beyond question King's action made a complete mockery of the democratic process. In almost five months of war, Parliament had met for only a few days and then only to agree on the proclamation of a state of war and give the government powers to prosecute it. Professor Frank Scott had already complained that Canada was acting as if an invasion were imminent and was permitting itself to be governed, like the people of France, by decree. While the British government had to defend itself weekly before the Commons, "here we spend more time talking about the need to defend democracy in Europe than we do about what is going on at Ottawa."[4] Even though opposition members wanted answers to almost a hundred questions, King relieved the Eighteenth Parliament of its responsibilities.

Dr. Manion, the Conservative leader, and J.S. Woodsworth, who seldom agreed on anything, spoke as one against "a piece of unscrupulous trickery designed to win a decision for the government by a snap verdict."[5] To King's assertion that the animosities of his opponents in the Ontario Legislature were preventing him from performing his duties effectively, Manion simply replied that a provincial assembly ought not to determine the timing of a federal election. To the Prime Minister's contention that it was necessary to have the election over before serious fighting began on the western front, Woodsworth said he could see no "desperate need for hurrying this thing along."[6] Think of the difference there would have been in the character of the election, said *Maclean*'s "A Politician with a Note-book," if it had been possible first to have questions answered in Parliament, documents and records produced, and officials called to give evidence.

> [Then] the public could have pieced together the picture, would have something to go on – and vote on. . . . Mr. King, for some extra-ordinary reason, locked away the files. The jury must hear the case – or the summing up of the case – without hearing or seeing the evidence. Must take Mr. King's say-so – or Dr. Manion's. No wonder the jury is confused.[7]

Of necessity, then, the election was fought on "vague charges, countered by equally vague replies, of lack of energy and efficiency in the government's conduct of the war."[8] Charge and counter-charge were reinforced by personal abuse and innuendo, all of which produced a good deal more heat than light. King was largely responsible for this nasty type of campaign. Of his two favourite maxims, "Parliament will decide" and "the people will decide," he chose the one that suited his own purposes. But this time, even more than in 1926, the people needed the evidence which Parliament alone could provide to pronounce upon the government's conduct and, as B.K. Sandwell observed: "not a ray of clear and authentic light has been shed" in the only place where that was possible: "by question and answer, by examination and cross-examination . . . on the floor of the House of Commons."[9]

In lesser measure the official opposition – especially its leader – determined the nature of the campaign. Because of the unending attacks upon him, R.B. Bennett had presented his resignation to a national conference of his party in March 1938. That conference indicated which way the wind

Mr. King locked away the files.

by Grassick. Maclean's, *March 1, 1940. Courtesy of* Maclean's.

was blowing. It recommended that the party's name be changed from National Liberal and Conservative to National Conservative – this was later adopted. It discussed a resolution disavowing "the pathway of New Deal economics and policies of the Rooseveltian school," and expressing an intention to "adhere to the traditions that once made [the party] great."[10] Nevertheless, as the leadership convention of July 1938 clearly demonstrated, it had not healed the rifts within the party. The convention's keynote speaker, Arthur Meighen, thoroughly annoyed the French-Canadian delegates with his strong pro-Commonwealth oration rebuking the King government for not letting Britain establish her own flying schools in Canada. At the same time the rightist tenor of the resolutions emanating from the convention led W.D. Herridge to describe them as "a lot of junk" and as proof of the triumph of reactionary forces,[11] and eventually induced him to launch his New Democracy movement.

General Election   225

Most of the delegates, especially those from Quebec, felt that the party must appeal to French Canada, and in Dr. R.J. Manion, a Catholic with a French-Canadian wife, they were sure they had their man. They ignored the elemental fact that French Canadians could not be counted upon automatically to support an Irish Catholic (especially an ex-Liberal who had deserted Laurier on conscription) and the author of the autobiographical *Life Is An Adventure*, which contained passages somewhat uncomplimentary to French Canadians. English Canadians, particularly those who thought Manion had been the nominee of Premier Duplessis of Quebec, also had doubts. The new leader created further doubts by his remark at Fort William on July 26 that "reactionary rich men [were] a great danger to democracy," and by another at Barry Bay a few days later that Canada faced "reform or revolution."[12] The staunchly Conservative Montreal *Gazette* wondered where Manion was going. Why was he talking the language of Bennett and even of Herridge? Why was he being led "away from the great political element in this country upon whose support he must rely"?[13]

Manion's other qualifications for the leadership were his supposed skill in the art of politics and his very considerable personal magnetism. Certainly he mingled the serious with "a bit of whimsy and homespun humour." There was, for example, his picture of King as the man who "never left Kingsmere. . . . We had to bring the King and Queen out to get him to move."[14] But his racy Irish tongue also possessed considerable powers of invective which were to hurt him badly. It was reasonable enough for him to say that Hitler "calls the Reichstag when he wants to make a speech and then dismisses it. That's what Mr. King did."[15] At the outset his criticism of the government's war effort was proper enough. What, he asked, had it to show in defence preparedness for the $188 million it had spent between 1936 and 1939? Why had it not let Britain establish flying schools in Canada? Why had King entered into "that abominable contract with James Emmanuel Hahn for the production of Bren guns"? A royal commission had found no evidence of actual corruption, but it had cast serious doubts on the competence of the Minister of National Defence, Ian Mackenzie, and his deputy. It had also done nothing to allay the suspicion that patronage had spread its tentacles deep into defence contracts. Manion could gleefully point out that the arch-Liberal *Winnipeg Free Press* had been demanding a searching probe of such contracts. He could justifiably castigate King for not ridding himself altogether of Ian Mackenzie and for retaining him in the cabinet even after removing him from the Defence Department.

In quoting chapter and verse of instances of mismanagement in the conduct of the war, however, Manion became unreasonable. He launched into "monstrously exaggerated bickerings" with the new Minister of National Defence, Norman McLeod Rogers, on whether troops of the First

Division had crossed the North Atlantic in mid-December in cotton underwear, and like matters. Understandably Manion became irritated at being continually asked for specific facts by a member of a government which had manoeuvred to conceal those facts. As a results, when his campaign began to turn sour, his Hibernian temper got the better of him. Rogers, whom he had described earlier as "a good teacher become a poor minister,"[16] was later "an irresponsible little falsifier."[17] He wondered how much C.D. Howe, "this American-born genius," had made from cost-plus contracts.[18] Such conduct may have been in keeping with the sobriquet "Fighting Bob," but it did nothing to establish him in the public mind as a suitable war leader.

Manion would have done better to take a consistent stand against the Liberals' abuse of the democratic process. But he let the C.C.F. make this case, while "he indulged . . . in a mass of impossible promises of good things to come."[19] On the east coast he was for a return to local harbour boards; in Calgary for higher subsidies on coal; in Moose Jaw for crop insurance; and in Regina for a wheat price of $1.80, even if it meant hard bargaining with the British government. Manion seemed to have seriously misgauged the temper of the Canadian people. Not only were they not intent on securing material benefits for themselves, but they were quite prepared to accept substantial sacrifices for the war effort.

It was said that Manion developed no programme other than vague proposals for "national government." That is an exaggeration. But in the absence of other eye-catching proposals he did stress his own brain child. Following the Conservative caucus of January 26, 1940, he announced that, if successful, he would form "a truly national government in the sense that the very best brains among our people [would be] drafted to serve in the cabinet."[20] Furthermore, his candidates would be National Government candidates. For the moment his proposal appeared to be a vote-getter. *Maclean's* said it had brought him some support without losing him any,[21] while the *Economist* believed it had widespread approval and that public opinion was "crystallizing in a sense unfavourable to the Dominion government."[22]

Such feelings did not last long. King made it clear that his party would have nothing to do with national government. Where, he asked Manion, were the best brains? "Let him tell the people during the campaign who will be in his government – not after the election."[23] Woodsworth in his turn likened national government to "a ship with three or four pilots at the helm, each of them wanting to go in a different direction."[24] Although Manion could not be faulted for not naming his cabinet in advance, as King was, in effect, demanding, it could be made to appear that the attitude of King and Woodsworth would force him to turn to Hepburn's Liberals, Herridge's New Democracy, and Duplessis's Union Nationale for some members of a national government. This led Liberal newspapers to make invidious comparisons of their Lapointe, Ralston, Rogers, and Howe with

Stevens, Drew, Herridge, Aberhart, and Duplessis, and to ask: "Do the people of the country prefer to trust their future, Canada's future, to these men . . . ?"[25]

As a result, Manion could convince few voters that any good could come from national government. Even Dafoe, although taken a little aback by King's blanket rejection of Manion's proposals, had to admit that there was little merit in them for the moment. The circumstances, he agreed, were totally unlike those of 1917.[26] And so the public-spirited Canadians whom Manion invited to join with the Conservatives in nominating candidates failed to present themselves. The conventions turned out to be Conservative conventions even if their choices bore the National Government label. Only W.E. Landry in Antigonish–Guysborough, George Atkins in Halton, and Dr. John Dewar in Kenora–Rainy River were former Liberals. Naturally the Liberals treated with scorn the latest in the series of name changes by their opponents. The more the Tories tried to look different, they said, the more they remained the same. In many places, it was noted, the pretense of National Government did not last long, as in Nova Scotia, where "the old [Conservative] signs are still up, . . . and the claim that a Manion government will be anything but a Conservative Government, is gradually being dropped."[27]

As the campaign progressed, the *Nation* concluded that "nothing had done so much to bedevil the following of the Conservative Party as this *ignis fatuus* of Dr. Manion."[28] *Maclean's* "A Politician with a Notebook" called national government

> . . . a wraith; a shadow; something which nobody could put his hand upon. In effect, the people were asked to keep a 'blind date' with a government; a government that would become visible only *after* the election. . . . This would be a different sort of government; not a party one. . . . In the net result National Government released Conservatives from their party loyalty. They had no obligation to vote for it.[29]

Undoubtedly the very idea of national government did alienate life-long Conservatives. But in all likelihood Manion would have lost badly anyway. His opposition to railway amalgamation had not endeared him to Bay and St. James Streets, and his campaign chest was empty. By raising the flag of national government he perhaps thought, and not unreasonably, that he might improve his position in two respects. He hoped, for one thing, to overcome the unfriendly attitude of business, which his own radicalism had caused, and to receive its usual contributions for campaign purposes. This hope proved to be a will o' the wisp. "In March, the election was being financed on a day-to-day basis . . . and less than $100,000 was available for the 82 seats in Ontario, the area in which party hopes were highest."[30]

He also had the idea that the national government concept would permit him to forestall the argument-sure to be advanced-that his front bench contained nothing like the wealth of talent and experience that the incumbent government possessed. On January 26 it looked like a reasonable enough gamble.

Observers were certain that King pursued the right tactics in restricting the issues of the campaign. Who else but the Liberals, he asked, could maintain national unity and prosecute the war effort with vigour and efficiency?[31] Above all, he sought to present himself as leader of the nation at a time when great things were demanded of it. Because of the urgency of the situation, he could spend (or so he made it appear) only a limited time away from Ottawa. "We have far too much travel and talk these days," he said, "on the part of many people and from too many sources . . . if I have to gain [the people's] confidence by going back and forth across the country . . . seeking to cater to local casts and prejudices, I do not wish to occupy office for a day."[32]

And so, in the main, King's electioneering took the form of broadcasts from Ottawa. In these broadcasts, as befitted the leader of the nation, he refused to stoop to the methods of the ordinary partisan politician. "I hope," he stated on one occasion, "to be able to say at the close of the campaign that I have not used a word about any person of any political party which may make it impossible for that man or woman to [co-operate with the government]."[33] Only in his last two speeches did he get down from his pedestal and rebuke Manion for his abuse of members of the cabinet. "The deliberate effort to destroy the reputation of public men," he said, "was singularly akin to the language and methods of these very Nazis whose system is endangering freedom the world over."[34]

Otherwise King stuck to his central theme: "There is but one issue – it is Canada's war effort."[35] His government had brought the nation into the war, united and strong, and was in much "the best position to keep Canada united and to achieve the maximum war effort." It had already sent a fully equipped division to Europe and a second would soon follow. It had instituted a huge Commonwealth air training scheme. It had run the country's economic effort smoothly. It had set up a War Supply Board to ensure that there was no patronage or profiteering. It had taken steps to prevent an undue rise in the costs of the necessities of life. National government, it was argued, would draw strength from all sections of the country, but his ministry did that very thing. "Is there any political group or combination, known or unknown, which has the remotest chance of being comparably representative of Canadian opinion as a whole?"[36]

Thus King, despite the obvious lack of enthusiasm for him personally, presented an incomparably better image than Manion. Usually, said one commentator, the electorate votes to throw out a government and disregards the opposition. This time, however, "rather than experiment with

Manion, they voted to grumble with King."[37] It was wrong, however, to blame Manion alone for all the Conservative calamity. Seldom has a leader had so few things going for him as Manion had in 1940.

For one thing he had few lieutenants of stature, although R.L. Maitland, the Conservative leader in British Columbia; M.A. MacPherson, the former Attorney-General of Saskatchewan; and H.H. Stevens did their best. Then, too, George Drew, the Conservative leader in Ontario, was too bitter; at least this is what the observers said, although apparently the test of bitterness "depends upon whether the 'bitter' one is on the winning or the losing side."[38] Premier Hepburn's indirect intervention in the campaign did the Conservatives no good at all. His determination to prove that there had been a disturbance at the R.C.A.F. school at Chatham, allegedly because of inadequate training, led to a declaration by Norman Rogers that each time he "indulge[d] his flair for abuse and for groundless statement . . . , he [was] a party to the betrayal of Canada."[39]

Whereas Manion had no provincial premiers directly backing him, King had six. The Liberals could co-ordinate their organizational work through the National Liberal Federation under the expert direction of Senator Norman Lambert; the Conservatives had no comparable national organization. Indeed, Manion sought desperately to resurrect some sort of party machinery in those provinces where it had virtually disappeared. The Liberals had ample funds, but Manion's campaign chest was "as bare as Mother Hubbard's cupboard; candidates in constituencies with a fighting chance had money sent to them in pitiful instalments."[40] With the disappearance of the protective tariff as a political issue, the Conservatives were no longer able to count on the manufacturing interests, hitherto their financial mainstay. Furthermore, such interests had profited substantially from war contracts and, in anticipation of more to come, took no action to alienate the party most likely to win.[41]

The Liberals had much the better of it in presenting their case to the electorate. In the free-time broadcasts provided for the first time by the C.B.C., M.J. Coldwell of the C.C.F. was the most impressive and persuasive of all the speakers. But King, who had this time received coaching, gave his speeches with something of a lilt and a rhythm which added to their effectiveness. In contrast, Manion's voice, though "musical in conversation, was harsh on the air and he had no real radio technique." The *Canadian Forum* said he was so bad that "if you didn't hear him you wouldn't believe us."[42]

The outstanding feature of the press was its neutrality. Of 100 daily newspapers only some 25 took sides. Yet in two ways this was a gain for the Liberals. Liberal papers such as the *Winnipeg Free Press*, the Toronto *Star*, the Halifax *Chronicle*, and practically all of the French press were militantly partisan. Only the Toronto *Telegram*, the Ottawa *Journal*, and the Winnipeg *Tribune* gave anything that approximated comparable support to Manion. Such normally Conservative papers as the Montreal *Star*, the

Montreal *Gazette*, and the Hamilton *Spectator* "wrapped round them the garb of neutrality." Indeed, it was said of the *Star* that it was "as clear-cut as a black cat on a moonless night in a coalbin."[43]

Coupled with a second development, the lack of newspaper support hurt the Conservatives badly. The war had accelerated the government's practice of issuing official statements on a wide variety of matters. According to Manion, there had been 165 press releases of this kind since the war began. He contended – and correctly – that by their very nature they became a species of propaganda. "You cannot turn on a radio without hearing the words of some minister of the Government who is putting out what is supposedly a description of Canada's war effort, but about two-thirds of those speeches are political propaganda."[44] This consideration led Premier Hepburn to ban the showing in Ontario of the March of Time film "Canada at War." According to him, King already had "control of the press and radio through his censorship. . . . Well, he is not going to control the screen as well. . . . Why should [he and his ministers] be permitted to address theatre audiences when members of other political parties are not?"[45] "A Politician with a Notebook" said that Manion, "in two months of campaigning, could not break down the case thus built up; could not destroy the legends that invariably grow around ministers. Hadn't most people been saying for months: 'The Government is doing a good job'?"[46] Without adequate press support Manion had no hope of weakening that image.

Finally, the Liberals were assisted by the feeling – incalculable but none the less real – that they could be counted on to make an appropriate but not over-extended contribution to the war effort. According to the *Round Table*, two of King's ministers, Lapointe and Gardiner, struck responsive chords when they said that the government had carefully calculated how far it might go without endangering the country's reserves of manpower and wealth. Certainly there were fears that a Manion, subject to the pressures of the British government and imperial zealots, might permit too great a drain on Canada's resources. Conservatives who campaigned on the inadequacy of the war effort were said to have met a lukewarm reception even in Ontario.[47] "Most Canadians," argued the *Canadian Forum*, "are still cool enough to realize that the democracy with which we are primarily concerned is on this side of the Atlantic."[48]

The journalist George Ferguson thought it a calumny on the Canadian people to "imagine that they did not [believe] . . . they were voting for the leadership of men . . . committed to staking the whole resources of the country on the hazard of war." Men like King, Ralston, Rogers, and Howe, he said, would not be guilty of the "disgraceful Machiavellian statecraft of merely pretending an all-out war effort."[49] Yet, if for no reason other than that Quebec is part of Canada, political considerations did play an important part in determining the nature and extent of the war effort. Indeed, this factor accounted for King's cautious approach to the war in September

1939. He made a proclamation of war contingent on its approval by a special session of Parliament, and even then he left the door open for a policy of "aggressive neutrality" if public opinion did not favour more active participation.

Ernest Lapointe, King's lieutenant in Quebec, stated that "for the sake of unity we cannot be neutral in Canada." Yet for some time his own province had been lapsing more and more into isolationism. Its fears of the outside world and the nationalism of Abbé Groulx had helped to revive its old dream of a separate French Catholic state, a "Laurentia."[50] This state of affairs caused a serious miscalculation on the part of Premier Maurice Duplessis, whose Union Nationale had come to power in Quebec in 1936. Two weeks after Canada's entrance into the war he plunged his province into an election in which a vote for him would, in effect, be a vote against meaningful participation in the war. Lapointe called it "an act of national sabotage," and he and his Quebec colleagues issued the warning that if Duplessis were returned they would resign from the federal cabinet en masse.

In October Quebec overwhelmingly rejected the Union Nationale. C.G. Power is convinced that the strong campaign waged by Quebec's federal ministers against Duplessis also had unforeseen dividends. When he and Lapointe visited British Columbia and other provinces during the election of 1940, "we were greeted as if we had been heroes of the war and saviours of the country."[51] By the time of the federal election most of the French press was preaching moderate participation so long as it did not injure the country's agricultural, industrial, and economic life, or pile up massive debts for future generations. On the whole, then, Quebec was reasonably satisfied with the status quo as it existed in March 1940. *Le Progrès du Saguenay* put it neatly that there would be fewer dangers for Quebec under the Liberals.[52] Manion might talk all he liked about his opposition to conscription, but did he not lead a party whose pro-British, proimperialist wing would demand full participation?

The Conservatives were not King's only opponents. The second most formidable was the C.C.F., even though it fought the election with a distinct disadvantage. In 1936 its National Convention declared unequivocally for neutrality in case of war. But at a meeting of its National Council in September 1939 it became obvious that "a deep and wounding split could not be avoided" on the matter. Against J.S. Woodsworth's objections, the Council gave qualified approval to the war effort but rejected the idea of an expeditionary force. "You all know, as I know, what this must mean," said Woodsworth. He was right, for although the Council turned down his resignation, and although he fought the election with much of the old fire, "in effect, September, 1939, ended [his] political career."[53]

It was left to the party's National Chairman, M.J. Coldwell, to present its views on the war. He stated that, although Canada had played no part in making the policies which led to war, none the less it had to do more than defend its own shores since the conflict might well involve the very survival of democratic institutions. It should limit its assistance, however, to economic aid, and not conscript men or send them overseas. Although the C.C.F. was divided on this matter, it was one in opposing the philosophy that the war must be won at all costs and that nothing else mattered. Above all, there had to be economic planning to prepare for the slump that would come with peace. Never again should there be the spectacle of a government which could not find funds for necessary public works or social service benefits suddenly being able to find hundreds of millions of dollars for war.[54]

The C.C.F. insisted also that the method of conducting the war should be determined by Parliament, not by order-in-council. It objected to regulations which practically swept away Magna Charta. "I do not know why Mr. King dismissed Parliament so summarily," said Woodsworth, "but it looks as if the Government had been doing things for a long time which they did not want investigated."[55] He also attacked profiteering. As an outcome of the Bren gun probe, Parliament had decreed that profits in defence contracts should be limited to 5 per cent. But because the government could get no one to tender under these conditions, it had rendered them nugatory. Woodsworth condemned outright "the manufacturers who would not play ball. . . . If men are asked to give their lives in the war, the least that can be done is to see that no one profits out of it."[56]

In spite of a good campaign, the C.C.F. seemed to have little to show for it. Its popular vote remained between 8 and 9 per cent, and its number of members elected increased only from 7 to 8. In taking Cape Breton South it won a seat east of Manitoba for the first time. However, it polled only half as many votes in Ontario as it had in the last election; lost Winnipeg North because of the strong vote polled by a Communist; and dropped 2 of its 3 seats in British Columbia, even though it strengthened itself in that province outside the cities. Only Saskatchewan was highly encouraging; there it got 5 seats and 28.6 per cent of the votes. Perhaps it was surprising that the West, which favoured out-and-out war in 1917, gave as many votes as it did to a limited-war party in 1940.

There were suggestions that both the C.C.F. and Herridge's New Democracy were hurt because they split the radical vote between them. But the returns indicate that this could have cost the C.C.F. seats only in Alberta. More to the point, a party that does not run enough candidates to let it form a government – the C.C.F. nominated only 96 – stands in a weak position before the electorate. However, its equivocal position towards the war hurt it most of all. Its opponents reminded the electorate repeatedly that "a vote for the C.C.F. is a vote to sell goods to Britain, but not to send men to help her."[57] It is true that its candidates presented an opportunity for those voters who were lukewarm about the war to express themselves, but in an election in which most English-speaking Canadians were concerned "with the efficient and whole-hearted administration of the war" and viewed "all other issues with indifference or as likely to prejudice that interest," the C.C.F. was obviously at a disadvantage. R.E.K. Pemberton called it political myopia for so few of the C.C.F. candidates to have said nothing about the war. Why, he wondered, had they devoted "so much time and thunder . . . to damning our profiteers and none at all to damning Hitler?"[58]

The C.C.F. could console itself with only one thing. Of the protest vote (neither Liberal nor Conservative), it took 57 per cent, up from 38 per cent in 1935.

A third Liberal foe was the New Democracy of W.D. Herridge. He had not let the rebuff he had suffered at the Conservative convention of 1938 deter him. On March 1, 1939, he launched his new movement hoping, as he said, to rally the progressive vote and "provide the only answer to the Fascist threat." In the task of re-establishing the principles of democracy, a People's Parliament would co-operate with business as long as it obeyed the laws of progress. But special privilege would come to an end. "The primary producer will no longer be the slave of greedy interests. . . . There will be a minimum price, just as there will be a minimum wage. Alien finances will have no voice in our affairs. Canada will be for the Canadians." Also, New Democracy would undertake whatever economic and monetary reforms were required to "stabilize production upon the maximum level and to raise purchasing power to that level."[59]

Undoubtedly it was this last plank that led to Herridge's appearance on the platform with William Aberhart at Armenia, Alberta in July and to his being presented to the crowd as "our leader." Yet, as Professor Mary Hallett indicates:

> Herridge's and Aberhart's aims for the movement were incompatible. Premier Aberhart thought he saw in New Democracy Social Credit's chance to become a national party. Herridge's speeches convinced him that New Democracy was a monetary reform movement which could be used to attract supporters outside Alberta. Herridge was not and had no intention of becoming a Social Crediter.[60]

At the parliamentary session in September, none other than Mackenzie King sought to explore the relationship between Social Credit and New Democracy, but all he could get from a Social Credit M.P. was: "We are the Social Credit group of the New Democracy."[61]

After the outbreak of war, Herridge conceived a new role for his movement. It was to remain a means of achieving national security, but in war its method was to be national service and that meant conscription of finance, industry, and manpower.[62] Yet, when the Albertan Social Crediters started campaigning, they found national service highly unpopular, and to Herridge's indignation, they proceeded to assert that "conscription of finance without expropriation of individuals' property or money, should precede the conscription of manpower."[63]

The election brought the visionary Herridge down from his cloud in other ways as well. Previously he had shown little interest in organization, expecting his movement to spread spontaneously on its merits. But when the campaign opened, he had to admit that "we are a nation of sleepwalkers" and that New Democracy would have to wait "till events catch up with it." Accordingly it would confine its candidacy to "those constituencies where the electorate is ready for it."[64] Consequently, even if all the Social Credit candidates were included under the label New Democracy, there were only 29 of them, and probably only the 21 in Alberta and Saskatchewan are genuinely entitled to the designation.

One last blow was to tell heavily against them. Five days before the federal election, Aberhart suffered severe losses in a provincial election in Alberta. Not surprisingly, then, New Democracy won only 10 seats in Alberta, where Social Credit had won 15 in 1935, and lost both seats in Saskatchewan, although it did support winning Unity and United Reform candidates in that province. Herridge himself went down to defeat in Kindersley. For all practical purposes, New Democracy was dead.

Thus the main fight, such as it was, took place between the Liberals and Conservatives. The Conservatives, whose fortunes had been at an all-time low in 1935, were able to increase their popular vote only from 29.6 to 30.7 per cent in 1940. In Ontario and the Maritimes, they did add substantially to their share of the popular vote but, except in New Brunswick, this brought them little in the way of seats. In that province the electoral system favoured them and they won 5 of the 10 seats even though they polled only 43.4 per cent of the vote to the Liberals' 54.6. While the latter won most of their seats by large majorities, the former took the 4 Anglo-Saxon seats in the Saint John Valley by small ones and gained Northumberland only because of the intervention of an Independent Liberal. In Prince Edward Island they won no seats at all and in Nova Scotia they were successful only in Cumberland, which the popular Percy Black captured by a mere 12 votes.

Worst of all, in Ontario, where they had talked about gaining 30 seats, their contingent remained at 25, while the Liberals increased their following from 56 to 57 by taking Grey-Bruce from Agnes Macphail, who had sat in the Commons since 1921. Dr. Manion failed to regain Fort William and, for the first time since Confederation, Lanark deserted the Conservatives. While Toronto remained largely Conservative, it was not the Tory Toronto of old, for they lost Eglinton and many of the contests were close. In Ontario, as in the Maritimes, many dyed-in-the-wool Conservatives apparently voted Liberal or stayed at home. They could not bring themselves to support a man who had made their party the National Government party, who was afflicted—so John A. Stevenson said—by what Talleyrand called the "terrible gift of familiarity,"[65] and who campaigned—horror of horrors—on the slogan "Let 'Fighting Bob' take hold." How could their party have descended to such depths?

In Quebec, not unexpectedly, Liberals or Independent Liberals took all the seats but Gaspé, which went to an Independent Conservative because of a division in the Liberal vote. The only surprises were in English Montreal, where C.H. Cahan, R.S. White, and W.A. Walsh lost the traditionally Tory ridings of St. Lawrence–St. George, St. Antoine–Westmount, and Mount Royal by decisive margins. Not only had the Montreal *Star* and the Montreal *Gazette* abandoned them, but also hundreds of true-blue Conservatives who could not abide that "radical" Manion.

The Conservatives fared no better in the West. Their popular vote fell everywhere except in British Columbia, and their number of seats dropped from 8 to 7. They lost R.B. Bennett's old riding of Calgary West, but made up for it when, after many years of defeat, John Diefenbaker took Lake Centre in Saskatchewan. The Liberals won Victoria, another example of a Tory riding which did not like the old party in its new guise.

In all, it was a miserable showing for the Conservatives—an increase of only 1 per cent in the popular vote and 1 additional seat, up from 39 to 40. Were they to be relegated to the status of an Ontario party? Even the sympathetically inclined John A. Stevenson wondered whether they would ever recover or whether they were doomed to extinction as an effective public instrument.[66] The *Canadian Forum*, not so well disposed towards them, said that the deepest emotion of every Canadian Conservative centred on his devotion to Great Britain and it doubted if "a party whose heart is outside of Canada [could] ever become very interested in Canadian reconstruction" after the war.[67]

For the Liberals, it was a victory greater than that of 1935. Although King provided little evidence on which to base a judgment, the voters had no doubt that the Liberals were the best agent to run the war effort. While they lost 4 seats to the Conservatives in New Brunswick and 4, principally to the C.C.F., in Saskatchewan, they more than made up for it by gaining 16 seats in Quebec, Alberta, and British Columbia—thus raising their total from 173 to 181. In addition, they polled 51.5 per cent of the popular vote; this was the first time since 1917 that any party had got the backing of over half the electors.

Yet the very size of the Liberal victory elicited a variety of gloomy forebodings. Previously, the Ottawa *Citizen* had described the Eighteenth Parliament as the most subservient and generally unsatisfactory in Canadian history.[68] Now, said most observers, the situation was likely to be worse. Of the 76 new members, most were Liberals. Practically all the Conservatives' able young candidates were defeated, as were the veterans Manion,

Stevens, Cahan, and Hugh Stewart. According to George V. Ferguson, the opposition would be "paltry in numbers, meagre in ability, and itself divided into three groups."[69] *Maclean*'s "A Politician with a Notebook" said that King would be "a veritable dictator in the House; his nod law, his will supreme."[70] To remedy this sad state of affairs in the Parliament of the future, the *Canadian Forum* again suggested the alternative vote and proportional representation to "that ardent democrat, Mr. Mackenzie King."[71] Even the *Winnipeg Free Press* was despondent because the Liberals had got the support of many who "never were and never wiil be Liberals," especially in Quebec. Since it doubted whether the ministry was any longer entitled to be called Liberal, it called upon the true Liberals to be especially independent and vigilant.[72]

The election results forced observers and commentators finally to wake up to the fact that they had hitherto underestimated Mackenzie King. Only in this, his next-to-last election, did they appreciate his political talents to the full. To T.E. Wood he was the man "whose masterly opportunism has made him Prime Minister of Canada for fourteen of the last twenty years";[73] to John A. Stevenson, "a shrewd political tactician [who] can regard the result as a great personal triumph."[74] But "A Politician with a Notebook" went them one better:

> Meanwhile Mr. King sits in Laurier House, or looks out over the Ottawa River from the window of his West Block office, monarch of all he surveys. He has come a long way from the cub reporter of the old Toronto *Globe*; a long way from the bitter, black years of 1917, when his star was in stygian eclipse. Not since Macdonald and Laurier had any political leader wielded such power; or campaigned with more success; or gauged Canadian sentiment with such uncanny skill. Lapointe, Ralston, Howe—all are potent figures. But King is the Chief; vanquisher of Meighen, Bennett, Manion. Nemesis of the Tory party.
> It hasn't all been chance.[75]

FOOTNOTES

1. J.W. Pickersgill, *The Mackenzie King Record: 1939-44*, I (Toronto: University of Toronto Press, 1960), p. 60.
2. *Ibid.*, p. 62.
3. *Ibid.*, p. 63.
4. F.R. Scott, "Parliament Should Decide," *Canadian Forum*, XIX (January, 1940), p. 311.
5. T.E. Wood, "Canada's Strategic Election," *Nation* (March 23, 1940), p. 391.
6. *House of Commons Debates*, 1940, p. 19.

7. "Backstage at Ottawa," *Maclean's*, LIII (March 1, 1940), p. 10.
8. B.K. Sandwell, "The Federal Election," *Queen's Quarterly*, XLVII (Spring, 1940), p. 93.
9. *Ibid.*, p. 90.
10. Halifax *Herald*, March 5, 1938.
11. *Canadian Annual Review*, 1937-38 (Toronto: Canadian Review Company, 1940), p. 57.
12. *Ibid.*
13. As quoted in J.R. Williams, *The Conservative Party of Canada: 1920-49*

	Seats	Candidates					Elected									
		C. (N.G.)	L.	C.C.F.	S.C. (N.D.)	O.	C. (N.G.)	%	L.	%	C.C.F.	%	S.C. (N.D.)	%	O.	%
Nova Scotia	12	12	12	6		1	1	8.3	10	83.3	1	8.3				
New Brunswick	10	10	10	1		1	5	50.0	5	50.0						
Prince Edward Island	4	4	4						4	100.0						
Quebec	65	53	65	4	2	46	1	1.5	61	93.8					3	4.6
Ontario	82	82	82	24	1	13	25	30.5	57	69.5						
Manitoba	17	17	17	13	4	5	1	5.9	15	88.2	1	5.9				
Saskatchewan	21	9	21	17	4	11	2	9.5	12	57.1	5	23.8			2	9.5
Alberta	17	10	17	15	17	3			7	41.2			10	58.8		
British Columbia	16	15	15	16	1	6	4	25.0	10	62.5	1	6.3			1	6.3
Yukon	1	1	1				1	100.0								
Total	245	213	244	96	29	86	40	16.3	181	73.9	8	3.3	10	4.1	6	2.4

Notes: National Government and Conservative are treated as synonymous, as are Social Credit and New Democracy, even though this may have been strictly true only in Alberta and Saskatchewan.

Four Liberal-Progressives are included in the Liberal columns, 3 (2 elected) from Ontario and 1 (elected) from Manitoba.

An Independent Conservative (elected) from Quebec, who was unopposed by an official Conservative candidate, is included in the Conservative columns.

Others elected: Que. (3): I.L. (3).
      Sask. (2): Unity (1); United Reform (1).
      B.C. (1): I. (1).

Others (votes
   polled): N.S. (1): I.L. (1) 9,217.
      N.B. (1): I.L. (1) 2,679.
      Que. (46): I.L. (29) 128,498; I.C. (4) 2,060; I. Nat. (1) 12,302; I. Anti-Conscription (1) 5,928; I. (7) 22,909; Lab. (1) 3,916; Nat. Lab. (1) 2,354; Comm. (1) 728; Anti-Conscription (1) 642.
      Ont. (13): I.L. (4) 16,012; Lab.-Far. (2) 8,126; U.F.O.-Lab. (1) 4,761; Nat. Lib.-Prog. (1) 2,434; Comm. (2) 3,617; I. (2) 6,144; Can. Lab. (1) 398.
      Man. (5): I. (4) 10,569; Comm. (1) 5,315.
      Sask. (11): Comm. (4) 2,711; Unity (2) 12,337; Nat. Unity (1) 7,534; S.C.-Nat. Unity (1) 241; United Reform (2) 14,137; I. (1) 3,775.
      Alta. (3): Comm. (1) 847; United Prog. (1) 2,727; I. (1) 488.
      B.C. (6): I. Nat. (1) 408; I.L. (1) 145; I. (3) 10,967; Comm. (1) 1,398.

				Popular Vote						Total
C. (N.G.)	%	L.	%	C.C.F	%	S.C. (N.D.)	%	O.	%	
112,206	39.8	142,514	50.6	17,715	6.3			9,217	3.3	281,652
74,970	43.4	94,383	54.6	761	0.4			2,679	1.6	172,793
28,028	44.7	34,664	55.3							62,692
231,824	19.8	741,945	63.3	7,610	0.6	10,781	0.9	179,337	15.3	1,171,497
687,816	42.7	818,154	50.8	61,166	3.8	786	0.1	41,492	2.6	1,609,414
82,240	26.0	151,480	47.8	61,448	19.4	5,831	1.8	15,884	5.0	316,883
52,496	14.1	159,530	43.0	106,267	28.6	12,106	3.3	40,735	11.0	371,134
35,116	13.0	102,060	37.9	35,082	13.0	93,023	34.5	4,062	1.5	269,343
110,619	30.5	135,920	37.4	103,181	28.4	506	0.1	12,918	3.6	363,144
915	53.6	793	46.4							1,708
1,416,230	30.7	2,381,443	51.5	393,230	8.5	123,033	2.7	306,324	6.6	4,620,260

(Durham, North Carolina: Duke University Press, 1956), p. 63.

14. Halifax *Herald*, March 11, 1940.

15. *Ibid.*, February 26, 1940.

16. *Ibid.*, February 9, 1940.

17. *Ibid.*, March 18, 1940.

18. *Ibid.*, March 13, 1940.

19. G.V. Ferguson, "After the Election," *Queen's Quarterly*, XLVII (Summer, 1940), p. 245.

20. Halifax *Herald*, January 27, 1940.

21. "Backstage at Ottawa," March 1, 1940, p. 10.

22. *Economist*, CXXXVIII (February 3, 1940), p. 197.

23. Halifax *Herald*, January 27, 1940.

24. *Ibid.*, March 2, 1940.

25. Halifax *Chronicle*, March 4, 1940.

26. Ramsay Cook, *The Politics of John W. Dafoe and the Free Press* (Toronto: University of Toronto Press, 1963), p. 262.

27. Halifax *Herald*, March 7, 1940.

28. Wood, "Strategic Election," p. 392.

29. "Backstage at Ottawa," May 1, 1940, p. 14.

30. J.L. Granatstein, *The Politics of Survival: The Conservative Party of Canada, 1939-45* (Toronto: University of Toronto Press, 1967), p. 50.

31. John A. Stevenson, "The General Election in Canada," *Fortnightly*, CXLVII (May, 1940), p. 513.

32. Halifax *Herald*, March 1, 1940.

33. *Ibid.*

34. Halifax *Chronicle*, March 22 and 25, 1940.

35. "The Issue as I See It," *Maclean's*, LIII (March 15, 1940), p. 12.

36. *Ibid.*

37. "Backstage at Ottawa," May 1, 1940, p. 14.

38. *Ibid.*

39. Halifax *Chronicle*, March 5, 1940.

40. "Backstage at Ottawa," May 1, 1940, p. 14.

41. Stevenson, "General Election," p. 515.

42. "The Campaign on the Air," *Canadian Forum*, XX (April, 1940), p. 4.

43. "Backstage at Ottawa," March 1, 1940, p. 10; also May 1, 1940, p. 14.

44. *House of Commons Debates*, 1940, p. 11.

45. Halifax *Herald*, March 6, 1940.

46. "Backstage at Ottawa," May 1, 1940, p. 14.

47. "The General Election," *Round Table*, XXX (June, 1940), p. 681.

48. "C.C.F. War Policy," *Canadian Forum*, XX (May, 1940), p. 35.

49. Ferguson, "After the Election," pp. 245 and 247.

50. Mason Wade, *The French Canadians* (Toronto: The Macmillan Company of Canada, 1955), p. 917.

51. Norman Ward (ed.), *The Memoirs of Chubby Power: A Party Politician* (Toronto: The Macmillan Company of Canada, 1966), p. 130.

52. Wade, *French Canadians*, p. 931.

53. W.K. McNaught, *A Prophet in Politics: A Biography of J.S. Woodsworth* (Toronto: University of Toronto Press, 1959), pp. 305-13.

54. Halifax *Herald*, February 28, 1940.

55. *Ibid.*, February 19, 1940.

56. *Ibid.*

57. See speech of J.L. Ilsley, *ibid.*, March 7, 1940.

58. R.E.K. Pemberton, "The C.C.F., the Election, and the Future," *Canadian Forum*, XX (May, 1940), p. 38.

59. Halifax *Herald*, March 2, 1939.

60. Mary Hallett, "The Social Credit Party and the New Democracy Movement: 1939-40," *Canadian Historical Review*, XLVII (December, 1966), p. 325.

61. *House of Commons Debates*, 1939 (2nd session), p. 97.

62. Halifax *Herald*, February 12, 1940.

63. Hallett, "Social Credit Party," p. 321.

64. Halifax *Herald*, February 12, 1940.

65. Stevenson, "General Election," p. 517.

66. *Ibid.*, p. 519.

67. "Grits and Tories," *Canadian Forum*, XX (May, 1940), p. 35.

68. "The Canadian Election," *Round Table*, XXX (June, 1940), p. 686.

69. Ferguson, "After the Election," p. 242.

70. "Backstage at Ottawa," May 1, 1940, p. 51.

71. "The Election," *Canadian Forum*, XX (April, 1940), p. 3.

72. Stevenson, "General Election," p. 518.

73. Wood, "Strategic Election," p. 393.

74. Stevenson, "General Election," p. 513.

75. "Backstage at Ottawa," May 1, 1940, p. 51.

Twentieth

General Election

"QUEBEC SAVES OUR KING"

In the postwar election of 1945, sectionalism displayed itself in an exaggerated form, just as it had in the postwar election of 1921. Just as he had in 1921, Mackenzie King won by a narrow, though workable, margin. And just as in 1921, "Quebec [saved] our King."[1]

Yet there was one significant difference: in 1921 King was supplanting another administration, while in 1945 he was surviving the difficulties of a long period of war to win his third election in a row. Even the *Canadian Forum* paid tribute to some of his achievements. He had avoided a wartime conscription election; he had prevented inflation (or had let his experts do it); and he had not had to do "all the posing" that other democracies had required of their leaders.

> . . . he hasn't travelled à la Winston with his cigar always at the proper angle when the official photographers snap their cameras, and he has deliberately kept his private life to himself in sharp contrast to the goldfish-bowl existence of the Roosevelts. Perhaps a country which manages to go through a world war without needing a Father-Leader at the head deserves some congratulations itself on its sound democratic qualities.[2]

The *Forum* could not, of course, be expected to congratulate King on another of his accomplishments: that he stymied his opponents, especially the C.C.F.

According to the *Round Table*, Canada's old parties were prompt to "reflect new swings of opinion among the people, . . and new wrenches to old political conceptions and procedures."[3] But in King's opinion the contortions the Conservatives were going through would prove ineffectual. Manion had resigned only weeks after the disastrous election of 1940. In November 1941 a meeting of Conservative Privy Councillors, members of the national executive, M.P.'s, and defeated candidates had drafted a reluctant Arthur Meighen as their leader. King was aghast. "I am getting past the time," he moaned, "when I can fight in public with a man of Meighen's type who is sarcastic, vitriolic and the meanest type of politician."[4] Actually, he should have thanked Providence for providing the opponents it did. Within three months Meighen had gone down to defeat at the hands of the C.C.F. in a by-election in York South.

In December 1942, at a full-fledged leadership convention in Winnipeg, the Conservatives decided on an altogether new course of action. They chose John Bracken, since 1920 the Progressive Premier of Manitoba and "a man whose major prior connection with the Conservative party had been the attendance of [his] father at the funeral of Sir John Macdonald."[5] None other than Meighen had undertaken to sell the Conservative party on Bracken and — an even more difficult task — to sell Bracken on the Conservative party. According to Meighen, the Liberals were certain to be beaten in the postwar election and the Conservatives were the only alternative to socialism. Since the C.C.F. would do well in the urban areas, the Conservatives had to make a strong appeal to rural Canada, and who could do it better than Bracken, the man who had kept the farmers of Manitoba solidly behind him for twenty years? In his turn, Bracken had to be satisfied that the party was progressive in his sense of the word. He exacted his price in another change in the party's name, this time to Progressive Conservative.[6]

From these events King concluded that the Conservatives had finally recognized that their party was dead and they were seeking a resurrection through a false leader. Bracken, he felt, was "simply Meighen's puppet" and the choice which would "give [him] the least possible trouble."[7] After 1942 King's diary makes it clear that he feared the C.C.F. more than he did the Conservatives. And with good reason. A dramatic change had occurred in what had seemed a lost cause. According to Professor Leo Zakuta:

> . . . the dark period of the war [turned] men's thoughts to a bright new social order. . . . Although the depression was over, its memory was still fresh, and people everywhere agreed, in language surprisingly like the C.C.F.'s that the world must never return to its prewar state.
>
> The atmosphere was perfectly tailored to the C.C.F.'s appeal for a new society, and, beginning in late 1941, a succession of dramatic C.C.F. triumphs confirmed the public's new mood and made the party's national ascendancy appear imminent and irresistible.[8]

Between 1942 and 1945 it showed substantial strength in federal by-elections; in August 1943 it ran second in an Ontario provincial election by winning 34 seats to the Conservatives' 38; in June 1944 it swept to power in Saskatchewan; and, most surprising of all, in September 1943 it appeared to lead the other parties nationally. The Gallup Poll depicted the rise in its fortunes:

	L.	C.	C.C.F.	Bloc Populaire	O.
1940 March					
(actual election results)	51.5%	30.7%	8.5%	—	9.3%
1942 January	55	30	10	—	5
September	39	23	21	—	17
December	36	24	23	—	17
1943 February	32	27	23	7	11
May	36	28	21	10	5
June	35	31	21	8	5
September	28	28	29	9	6

How was a strengthened C.C.F. to be countered? In King's opinion, by placing increased emphasis on postwar policies and especially social legislation. "I should be happy indeed," he wrote, "if I could round out my career with legislation in the nature of social security." And so the Speech from the Throne in 1943 unfolded, in his words, "a national plan of social insurance to be [a] charter of social security. . . . A magnificent declaration . . . of Liberal policy than which nothing could be better." Characteristically, he said it could all be found in his *Industry and Humanity* of 1918.[9]

Later in the year, when Liberal fortunes had sunk even lower, he consoled himself with the fact that the war would end in time to let him appeal as the leader best equipped to represent Canada at the peace conference and provide suitable postwar policies. To that end in January 1944, he persuaded the cabinet to accept a family allowance bill, which went to "the very root of social security in relation to the new order of things." Because it would cost $200 million annually – half a prewar budget – he expected some opposition. But he knew how to cope with it. In polling the cabinet ministers he started with those whom he "thought would help to give the most support in the first instance" and he easily had his way. Later, when the cabinet discussed his proposed Speech from the Throne, one minister said "there was need of something being inserted which would not cause a large section of the country to say: well, these men are ready to outdo the C.C.F. We might as well join the Tories."[10] But he could not deter King from stealing the thunder of the opponents whom he feared most. In the end the Speech from the Throne promised a national minimum of social security through adequate standards of nutrition and housing, policies to promote full employment, and insurance against privation from unemployment, accident, ill health, and old age.

For some time it looked as if King might not get his customary breaks in the timing of the election. In 1943 and again in 1944, C.G. Power had advised him to call one, but he had found it difficult to justify such a course while actual fighting was still going on. The manpower crisis in late 1944 removed any discretion he might have had. Parliament did not finish its labours until April 16, just hours before it was due to expire and he could only hope for the best when he called an election for June 11. Although he made his announcement on Friday the thirteenth, his traditional luck soon manifested itself. Yet, as Wilfrid Eggleston pointed out, "like a good golfer, [he] plays for the breaks and often deserves them."[11] In any case, German opposition collapsed before the campaign got into high gear, thus minimizing the manpower question which might have hurt him badly in both English and French Canada. If Canadian troops had been suffering casualties during the campaign, his difficulties would have been compounded.

He had already had to weather two serious conscription crises. After Pearl Harbor some members of the cabinet had felt that an emergency might arise in which Canada could best defend itself by sending troops abroad. But one barrier stood in the way: the promise by the government in the autumn of 1939 not to invoke conscription. And so in April 1942 the government asked the people through a plebiscite to relieve it of its pledge. By this time Quebec had isolated itself even more. Wartime controls and centralization had affronted its innate individualism and its devotion to provincial rights. In addition it was aggrieved by the criticism levelled at it in English Canada because of its low rate of enlistments for overseas service.[12] The result was that 72 per cent of Quebeckers voted a resounding "no" in the plebiscite, while four-fifths of non-Quebeckers voted "yes".

Up to now the cabinet had stayed united. But with its decision to repeal a clause of the National Resources Mobilization Act (N.R.M.A.) in order to permit troops to be dispatched overseas by order-in-council, unity disappeared. King's declaration that his policy was "not necessarily conscription, but conscription if necessary," made no difference. P.J.A. Cardin resigned, arguing that parliamentary action should await an emergency. In the parliamentary division most French-Canadian Liberals supported Cardin. Simultaneously, King had difficulty with his conscriptionist wing over the timing of the parliamentary approval that would be sought in case the government decided to impose conscription. It took all his recognized talents for making accommodations to induce J.L. Ralston, the Minister of National Defence, not to press the letter of resignation he had submitted.

But he could do nothing to moderate the repercussions of these events in Quebec. In October 1942 the Bloc Populaire took shape as an outgrowth of *La Ligue pour la Defénse du Canada*, which had been formed to secure a "no" vote in the plebiscite. Broadly speaking, it stood for genuine Canadian independence and for an exaggerated brand of French-Canadian nationalism in both the economic and political spheres. During the provincial election campaign of August 1944, Premier Godbout sought to confine the discussion to provincial issues. But he had not a hope. Everywhere the Bloc Populaire and the Union Nationale depicted him as the bootlicker of an imperialist and centralizing Ottawa.[13] As late as July the Gallup Poll showed the Bloc Populaire far out in front of the Union Nationale. In the end, however, the split between its left and right wings, and the hot-headedness of its youthful urban agitators brought about its defeat. Law-abiding French Canadians in rural Quebec could not stomach such statements as "England has a need of an iniquitous war every twenty-five years, because the English soldier is the worst in the world, and it is necessary for Canadians to fight England's battles and be killed in the place of the English in the hell of Caen."[14] Strange as it may seem, the Union Nationale was a middle way for moderate French Canadians whom the federal Liberals had antagonized, but who feared the Bloc. Duplessis got a small but working majority, the Bloc only 15 per cent of the votes and 4 seats.

Meanwhile, the position of the Conservative party in Quebec had deteriorated still further. It could not be otherwise when its politicians and newspapers in English Canada were advocating immediate conscription and making invidious statements about French Canada. It could expect nothing else when the Montreal *Gazette* was describing as zombies the N.R.M.A. troops who failed to volunteer for overseas service. So, despite the opposition which King had aroused in Quebec, he was clearly preferable to any alternative, provided there were no further serious incidents.

But there were. In October 1944 a shortage of reinforcements for the combat troops in western Europe became obvious. It was a blow to King, who felt his military men had misled him. Was the edifice he had built up so carefully to be destroyed at one fell swoop? Not if he could help it. On October 31 he accepted the two-year-old resignation of Ralston, who was demanding the conscription of N.R.M.A. troops, and left it to his new Minister of National Defence, General A.G.L. McNaughton, to get the needed men by voluntary methods. It could not be done. On November 22 King himself recommended that 15,000 N.R.M.A. troops be sent to Europe. He had no other choice if he were to retain his conscriptionist ministers. But he lost C.G. Power, who held that the need did not justify risking the likely repercussions. Again most French-Canadian M.P.'s voted for a motion of non-confidence in King; again Conservatives and French-Canadian nationalists opposed the Liberals for diametrically opposite reasons.

The government's troubles were not over yet. Early in 1945 absenteeism and desertion were prevalent among the conscripts, not only in Quebec. In late February a draft riot occurred at Drummondville in which an inflamed mob of 1,000 participated. The Montreal *Gazette* said that the chief ill in Canada was "not a failure of military discipline in the army but of moral fiber in the government."[15] This became the chief argument against General McNaughton in his by-election in Grey North on February 5. During the campaign Bracken charged that conscripts on their way to Europe had thrown their rifles overboard. McNaughton lost the election, but Bracken's statement was to hurt him later because of the aspersions it cast on the armed forces.

So stood the manpower question when the election campaign opened. Bracken was the first to get into the fight, since the Liberal and C.C.F. leaders were in San Francisco. Because he was still relatively unknown and his party was to build its campaign around him, the Conservative admen tried to sell him – to Mackenzie King's apparent indignation – like a new breakfast cereal. In successive advertisements McKim Advertising Limited, the first such agency to be used in this way in Canada, introduced the voters to John Bracken the Man, the Worker, the Farmer, and the Administrator. Finally, of Bracken the Progressive they said:

> Born in a log cabin, the life of John Bracken is itself a triumphant vindication of his resolute belief in his fellow men. Never defeated at the polls, he won five straight elections as Premier. How? By consistently practising what he preached – *progress through co-operation*.[16]

Always the emphasis was on Bracken's "deep earnestness, his all-embracing humanity and the almost startling simplicity and sincerity of this Lincolnesque man."[17]

When the C.C.F. accused the new Conservative party of being "the same creature of Big Business," Bracken replied, "If it should ever become so I shall not be its leader." Certainly his "Charter for a better Canada" contained many forward-looking proposals.[18] Indeed it seemed to have something for everybody. But perhaps that was what was wrong with it. The items were so disparate in nature and significance, and so lacking in specificity, that it was difficult to say what the Conservatives stood for. Some of its proposals were simplification of the tax structure, establishment of a national health programme, abolition of radio licence fees, initiation of a large-scale housing programme, and encouragement of the spread of trade unionism. For the primary producer – a special concern to Bracken – there was to be an export board which would pay him the difference between a fair Canadian price and the actual world price. His critics wondered if he ever heard of dumping duties.

Despite the emphasis on progress through governmental intervention, Bracken took care not to alienate the old mainstays of the Conservative party. His appearances with Henry Borden, the party's economic adviser, were probably intended to reassure the country's business interests. Everywhere he asserted that he stood "four square for private enterprise and individual freedom [and] against socialism and state control."[19] In closing his campaign he gave a ringing "guarantee of the rights of private property, the right of individuals . . . to develop their own business enterprises . . . free from unnecessary governmental interference or burdensome restrictions."[20]

When it came to manpower policy, the Conservatives adopted a stance which once again emphasized their Anglo-Saxon character. Bracken's presentation, it is true, had an appealing simplicity. "The policies of the Progressive Conservative Party," he said, "are the same from the Atlantic to the Pacific."[21] Contrast this with King's. Had he not "defied the wishes of the majority of this nation in order to keep the political support of a minority which had kept him in power so long and whose votes he again covets"?[22] Had he not thereby "placed upon the French-speaking people of Canada an undeserved stigma"?[23] Yet the moment that peace came to Europe, had he not abandoned his "vacillating policy of back door conscription . . . [hoping] to recapture, if it was not too late, the last vote of Quebec"?

> Will you [asked Bracken] be faithful to the only sound principle of calling men to war – equality of service and equality of sacrifice – if you fail to judge those, who for no other reason than political gain, fashioned upon your sons double the risk of death and disability that they fastened upon others?[24]

The Conservative leader also became indignant that veterans of the European war were being tempted into the fight against Japan by the promise of an immediate thirty-day furlough in Canada. Was King prepared to "fight the Japs to the last volunteer"? A Conservative government, he declared, would send N.R.M.A. troops to the Pacific theatre and only those veterans of the European who really wanted to go there.

Bracken miscalculated on two counts. To suggest that French Canadians resented not being forced to fight in Europe was preposterous. Also, with the end of a European war – V-E Day coincided with the date scheduled for his first meeting – his conscription argument lost much of its force in English Canada.

This time King's other opponent, the C.C.F., could present itself as a real alternative. Five years earlier it had run only 96 candidates, but in 1945 the number was up to 205, one more than the Conservatives. In western Canada it contested every riding, as was to be expected. What was surprising was that it put up practically a full slate in every province except Quebec.

Undoubtedly the spread of the trade union movement had helped it. During the 1930's its main strength had been in western rural areas, and it had made little headway in industrial urban Ontario. Trade union membership had grown, however, from 385,000 in 1938 to almost 600,000 in 1942, and it had continued to increase as unionism extended itself to medium-sized cities and country towns. Furthermore, the new unionists were enrolled largely in industrial unions rather than trade unions per se, and this made it easier to shift from an exhortation for industrial action to an exhortation for political action.[25]

In the transformation of the C.C.F. from protest movement to major party (as Leo Zakuta says it became), it underwent changes in thinking which are apparently typical of socialist parties undergoing such a metamorphosis. Above all, there was a narrowing of the ideological gap between the party and the public. This was especially marked where the C.C.F. was most distinctive, that is, in its attitude towards pacifism and social ownership. Thus the documents "For Victory and Reconstruction" and "Security with Victory," which the national conventions of 1942 and 1944 had adopted, showed how the party had moved in stages from "pacifism" to "conscription of wealth as well as manpower."[26]

Also, the leadership of the C.C.F. had passed from the altogether idealistic J.S. Woodsworth to M.J. Coldwell, who was more attuned to practicalities. He talked little about the socialization of industry. It is true that he pointed out that fewer than one hundred men controlled the welfare of eleven million Canadians, that big business was threatening to close the giant war plants, that a short feverish boom and then depression might occur, and that only the C.C.F. could prevent such an economic and social disaster. But mostly he talked about the new society his party would build. He called for public planning in time to avoid a postwar recession and, more specifically, for the construction of one million low-cost houses over ten years; the provision of five million new jobs; a vast extension of public health services, especially through the construction of hospitals; and extensive assistance in the building of modern educational facilities.[27]

Like Coldwell, King was late getting into the campaign because he was helping to found the United Nations. He quickly worked that fact into his electioneering. Do you, he asked the voters, want the "change from the known to the unknown to take place before the present world war is at an end" or before "there is brought into being the mighty instrument which now is being forged at San Francisco"? His government had got to know the governments of the Allied countries. "At this of all times . . . are you going to sever relations between these governments and between the past and the future?"[28]

Above all King posed as the leader who could best advance domestic reconstruction. In keeping with the party slogan, "Vote Liberal and keep building a New Social Order in Canada," he said his main task would be to maintain full employment and provide social security.

> [But] the present government did not leave these problems to be solved after the end of the war. . . . The necessary laws are on the statute book; the necessary departments of government have been established; and our policies are in actual operation.[29]

Occasionally there was a personal reference. "I don't intend to even run in another general election," he said at Prince Albert. "But I am heart and soul in this one. . . . I should like to be in office . . . until some of the great reforms I have spoken of to-night are under way."[30] At Saint John he became a veritable crusader: "This world is not going to stand for a few millionaires and poverty side by side. . . . The great natural resources which God has given to all the people are not going to be controlled by a privileged few while great multitudes walk the streets in search of employment."[31] And who, he asked everywhere, could better look after a peace economy than a ministry which had "charge of things from the first, which knew how to unfold the things it had first developed"? Up to his old tricks, he asked Bracken and Coldwell who would be in their cabinets to compare with a ministry two-thirds of whom were trained in war administration and one-third of whom were men with a fresh outlook and with experience as parliamentary secretaries.[32]

King had two methods of dealing with the manpower question. Outside Quebec he accused the Conservatives of being two-faced. Had they not told English Canadians that Quebec determined his policies and were they not now telling Quebeckers that he was their enemy? Were they also not practicing the grossest deception in running candidates in Quebec who were opposed to conscription? In contrast, the Liberal party—embracing as it did great numbers of every section, creed, race, and class—could serve the country's interests better than any other party. As evidence of his genuine Canadianism, he would ask Parliament to approve a distinctive national flag and incorporate a comprehensive definition of what constituted a Canadian citizen in the laws of the land.[33] In Quebec King's plea was to the Liberals who had become disaffected because of his conscription policy. Once again he turned to the name and memory of Laurier. Like Laurier in 1911, was he not being denounced in Quebec as an imperialist and in the rest of Canada for the opposite reasons? "I saw Sir Wilfrid defeated by an unholy alliance between the nationalists of the province and the Tories of the other provinces of Canada. . . . It will be for all time a blot of shame on the pages of the country's history." Would the people of Quebec in 1945 let Mackenzie King suffer the fate of Laurier in 1911? Should they not remember that Laurier owed his defeat to men who spoke of themselves as nationalists or independents and whose campaigns were financed by the Tory party? "I hope history is not going to repeat itself in any success of the alliance between Mr. Bracken and a new generation of independents."[34]

Such were the leaders' appeals to the electorate. In late March Wilfrid Eggleston said no one could hope for a majority even though the Liberals were doing a good deal of squirming and conciliating to make themselves appear as a rallying-ground for moderate opinion in every part of Canada.[35] On the eve of polling, however, he felt that Liberal fortunes had so improved in Quebec that they might get their majority.[36] He was right although there was no consensus amoug Canadians on the broad lines of approach to the basic problems facing the country.

The commentators were convinced that the Maritime provinces would remain strongly Liberal, and so they did. The over-all results were exactly the same as in 1940: 19 Liberals, 6 Conservatives, and 1 C.C.F. The Conservatives lost 2 seats in New Brunswick, but gained 1 in both

Nova Scotia and Prince Edward Island. Partly because it ran 24 candidates instead of 7, the C.C.F. substantially increased its percentage of the popular vote.

Once again the Conservatives pinned their main hopes on Ontario. In the belief that a smashing provincial victory would assist Bracken, Premier George Drew called an Ontario general election for June 11. King, fearing the very same thing, scheduled the federal contest for the same day. Not to be thwarted, Drew changed the provincial election date to June 4, allegedly to avoid confusion. Unable to follow suit because of the time required to stage a federal contest, King could only wait and fear the worst. Not unnaturally, the *Canadian Forum* sputtered about "the clumsy performances of these two high-souled hypocrites" and wondered if "we could adopt the American system of elections at fixed periods."[37] As it turned out, Drew's victory matched all expectations – 66 seats to the Liberals' 14 and the C.C.F.'s 8 – but Bracken fared not nearly so well. He, of course, had to compete with King, while Drew had to compete only with the discredited Mitchell Hepburn and the politically inept E.B. Jolliffe, whose charges that the Premier maintained his own private Gestapo backfired badly. Still, the federal Conservatives held on to all their previous seats in Ontario and gained 23 others: London and 12 rural seats in western Ontario, 8 "loyalist" seats in eastern Ontario, and 2 seats in Toronto. Except for Spadina, Toronto became Tory Toronto once more. The C.C.F. polled over a quarter of a million votes, largely in urban and northern Ontario, and raised its percentage of the popular vote from 3.8 to 14.4. However, it failed to concentrate its strength sufficiently to win any seats.

It was on the Prairies that the man of Lincolnesque virtues was supposed to exhibit his drawing power. Vain hope! While the Conservatives retained their 2 previous seats, their only new rural seat was Bracken's own riding of Neepawa. The 2 Calgary seats that they gained could hardly be classed as rural. Yet King must have found the results on the Prairies equally disappointing, for his own following dropped from 34 to 14. Although the Liberals won 10 seats in Manitoba, they could manage only 2 in each of Saskatchewan and Alberta. The sweeping provincial victory of the C.C.F. in Saskatchewan the previous year had carried over into the federal sphere; the C.C.F. took all of the province's 21 seats, except those of John Diefenbaker, J.G. Gardiner, and one Liberal colleague. Mackenzie King and General McNaughton both suffered personal defeat in Saskatchewan, and King took refuge in Glengarry, Ontario. A rejuvenated provincial party under Ernest Manning enabled Social Credit to take 13 of Alberta's 17 seats, despite Mackenzie King's complaints that it was not internationalist in its outlook.[38] British Columbia spread its political favours more evenly, giving 5 seats to both the Liberals and Conservatives, and 4 to the C.C.F.

Thus Arthur Meighen's plans went completely awry. Perhaps the

Conservatives should not have let him sell them a bill of goods so easily. Bracken, it is true, had been a first-rate administrator, but he had not had a chance to demonstrate his political talents. Drafted as Premier of Manitoba after an election had been won, he had coasted to his subsequent victories against weak opposition. A mediocre speaker and lacking in dynamism, he made no impress, even in the rural areas, when transported to the national sphere. His programme of odds and ends could hardly be described as distinctive except in its criticism of the government's manpower policy and its demand for equality of sacrifice in the Pacific theatre. In the crisis conditions of the previous November, such a stand might have proved a vote-getter in English Canada, but with the end of the war in Europe the atmosphere changed. As the campaign progressed, conscription became an ever-fading issue. In the final analysis, it may have cost the Liberals some seats in Ontario, but these losses may have been more a carry-over from Drew's victory a week earlier.

It has been suggested that Bracken's failure to enter the Commons until the general election worked against him. This meant—so it is argued—that he was unable to construct the entirely new organization he needed, that the Toronto Old Guard retained a large element of control over the party, and that it tailored the party's policies to meet its own wishes rather than Bracken's convictions. Certainly the Conservatives had no difficulty in collecting funds in Toronto and Montreal this time, and they spent at least $1,500,000 in the election.[39] Yet it is still true that Bracken delivered his criticisms of private enterprise as if he really meant them.

For the C.C.F. party the results in English Canada were almost as disappointing as they were for the Conservatives. While it raised its total number of members elected from 8 to 28 and its percentage of the popular vote from 8.5 to 15.6, it fell far short of the expectations held out by the findings of the Gallup Poll in September 1943. The same poll also depicted its subsequent decline:

		L.	P.C.	C.C.F.	B.P.	O.
1943	September	28%	28%	29%	9%	6%
1944	January	30	29	24	9	8
	March	34	30	22	8	6
	June	35	30	24	7	7
	September	36	27	22	5	8
	November	36	28	23	6	8
1945	January	36	28	22	6	8
	April	36	29	20	6	9
	May	38	29	19	5	8
	June 2	40	27	19	5	9
	June 9	39	29	17	3	10
	June 11 (actual results)	40.9	27.4	15.6	3.6	12.5

The C.C.F. had reached its high point under very special circumstances. During a lull in the war the frustrations resulting from governmental restrictions had become less tolerable and aroused greater resentment. The subsequent series of successes in the European conflict helped to make regimentation much more bearable. By this time, too, King had unfolded his own programme to counter the C.C.F.'s plans for a new social order. Not the least of the factors working against the C.C.F. was the Liberal campaign financed by the so-called big interests in support of the status quo. In the earlier stages they used a former general manager of the C.B.C., Gladstone Murray, as their agent; just before the election they turned to B.A. Trestrail's Public Informational Asociation. Trestrail's advertisements warned the voters that a C.C.F. govenment would substitute "a foreign-born scheme of 'State Socialism' for our democratic way of life" and "turn over to the C.C.F. politicians *complete control of our lives*."[40] His last advertisement stated that "under [a C.C.F.] system we would become like animals in a zoo. We would lose our individual freedom just as completely as though we had lost the war!"[41] The pamphlet *Social Suicide* especially irked M.J. Coldwell. He was also critical because the old parties seemed to give aid and comfort to the Labour Progressive Party (the Canadian Communists' new name) in order to split the labour movement and hurt the C.C.F. Whether that is true or not, their 67 candidates polled more than 100,000 votes and they elected Fred Rose in Montreal Cartier. None was more certain than the *Canadian Forum* that the C.C.F. had been beaten before the campaign even began.

> It was beaten by the long campaign of scare-mongering which started just too late to head it off in the Ontario election of 1943, but which got going in full strength immediately thereafter. It was beaten by the bank presidents and the insurance magnates, by the Gladstone Murrays and the Trestrails, by the unanimous newspaper editors who were even more effective in their skilfully slanted news columns than in their righteously indignant editorial articles, by the Citizens Committee urging everyone to vote as he liked but to vote against socialism, by all the combined propagandists who concentrated their efforts month in and month out on the upper and lower bourgeoisie. . . . And [so] . . . the comfortable residential sections of the big and the little towns turned out a monster vote while the polling in the working-class areas was comparatively light.[42]

To convert the public, concluded the *Forum*, there had to be constant education of the kind provided by the Fabian pamphlet, *Facts for Socialists*. In contrast, the *Round Table* wondered if the C.C.F. had been wise in having its National Chairman, F.R. Scott, and its Secretary, David Lewis, write the book, *Make This Your Canada*. Was there still not "political shrewdness in the old wish that 'mine adversary had written a book' "?[43]

Once again the observers marvelled at the anomaly of a socialist party deriving its major support from the rural areas. Of the C.C.F.'s 28 seats, only Cape Breton South, Winnipeg North and North Centre, and Vancouver East could be described as industrial. However, for the first time the C.C.F. drew strong support in industrial Ontario even though it won no seats there.

Of the 180 seats outside Quebec, the Liberals had taken 72, the Conservatives 65, the C.C.F. 28, and Social Credit 13. Since no party other than the Liberal could do well in Quebec, that province would decide whether King was to have an over-all majority. Utter confusion alone described the political state of Quebec. In addition to the candidates of the five major parties (including the Bloc Populaire), 84 others presented themselves; this resulted in an average of 4.4 candidates per riding. King had little fear of the organized opposition groups. Maurice Duplessis had earlier given the Bloc a bad beating, and it had been on the downgrade ever since. While it managed to elect Maxime Raymond and J.I. Hamel, 26 of its 35 candidates lost their deposits. The C.C.F. might have expected a small measure of success, having won Rouyn-Noranda in the previous year's provincial election. Perhaps for this reason Liberal advertisements took the trouble to warn that "the true picture of the C.C.F. is state socialism, the dictatorship of bureaucracy and the death of individual liberty. It is a direct route to the totalitarianism killed in Germany and Italy."[44] Actually the Liberals had little to fear from the C.C.F. Together, the 29 C.C.F. candidates polled fewer than 34,000 votes and they all lost their deposits.

The Liberals' worries about the Conservatives as such were not much greater. In polling only 8.4 per cent of the popular vote, Conservative strength fell to an all-time low. Of the 10 constituencies in which they saved their deposits 8 had substantial English-speaking populations, and they were lucky to win even pluralities in the 2 seats they did. Bracken himself could not have believed his own argument that French Canada resented King's manpower policies because they cost it its self-respect and that conscription for the Japanese war was "in itself an infallible recipe for procuring true national unity."[45] The Conservative policies meant, in effect, the complete abandonment of French Canada in the hope of securing great returns in English Canada.

During the campaign, Paul Lafontaine, the Conservative organizer in Quebec, caused a stir by stating that, in addition to its official candidates, his party would support 33 independents who, he thought, differed from it only on nonessentials. Liberals in English Canada seized upon his pronouncement with glee. According to *Maclean*'s "A Politician with a Notebook," the *Winnipeg Free Press* tried to set the Prairies afire with charges of a deal between total-war Tories and anti-war Nationalists in the style of 1911.[46] In Quebec, this led to pleas on King's part that he should not be permitted to be sacrificed in the same manner as Laurier. Although a number of independent candidates in Quebec were clearly recognizable as ex-Conservatives, King had no fear of them. However, he did fear Liberals disaffected by the government's manpower policy. And this time there was no trusted Ernest Lapointe, nor even a Pierre Cardin, to win them back. Lapointe's successor, Louis St. Laurent, was still a somewhat austere figure who had not yet established a full rapport with French Canada.

On the very day that King had arrived in San Francisco, Cardin had announced the formation of *Le Front National*, and by general consent it was expected to constitute King's most formidable challenge in Quebec. What happened after this is lost in obscurity. There were rumours of a Cardin-Duplessis alliance which would bargain with the strongest English bloc in the next Commons. There was even some prospect of a Bracken-Cardin-Duplessis bloc (or so the Liberals alleged in English Canada).[47] But in the end it all came to naught. Shortly before nomination day Cardin announced his intention to dissolve his Front National and to run as an independent. Certainly, Cardin had lost a good deal of his old fire, but more likely, he had found, just as "Chubby" Power had, that conscription did not remain the same burning issue it had been after 1917. Quebeckers did not approve of King's manpower policies, but among other things they had got used to having their sons away from home serving as N.R.M.A. troops in distant parts of Canada.[48] Then, too, the Liberals had not expelled from the party those M.P.'s who had voted non-confidence in the government on the manpower question in 1942 and 1944; it bore no grudge against them and they did not have to come back on bended knee.[49] Wilfrid Lacroix, who had abandoned them when they declared war in 1939, was elected as a Liberal in Quebec-Montmorency; Jean François Pouliot, who had campaigned successfully for the anti-Liberal nationalist Frederick Dorion in Charlevoix-Saguenay in 1942, was to all intents and purposes elected as a Liberal in Témiscouata. The outcome was that the Liberals got the 53 seats they needed for a bare majority and were assured of support from enough independents to give them a comfortable working margin.

Most commentators were not happy with the outcome. To them the election demonstrated a pronounced lack of national unity. The Conservatives, they said, remained an Ontario party; the C.C.F. drew its support mainly from Saskatchewan, Manitoba, and British Columbia; even the Liberals had got only 40.9 per cent of the popular vote and had fared poorly in the three western provinces. The American professor Lionel H. Laing compared Quebec to the "solid South" in his country's politics, and saw it operating as a brake on the dominant Liberal party, and preventing it from giving the other parts of the country – and particularly western Canada – the bolder policies they wanted.[50] Furthermore, 60.0 per cent of the new M.P.'s, including 51.2 per cent of the Liberals, 59.7 per cent of the Conservatives, 85.7 per cent of the C.C.F., and 92.3 per cent of the Social Credit were elected only by pluralities.

A few observers such as Wilfrid Eggleston felt that Canada had good reason to be satisfied with the results. Both the Conservatives and the C.C.F. had improved their position and could provide more effective opposition in the next Parliament. Better still, "a party of truly national character, drawn from both ethnic groups. . .[would] take responsibility for a program the outlines of which. . .have already been foreshadowed."[51] Although the Liberals got much less than half of the popular vote, they had drawn substantial support from every region, and although the voting was more sectionalized than usual, seldom at any given time has more than one Canadian party been truly national. The miracle of 1945 was that there was one such party. For that King was responsible. This was indeed his finest hour. Not many democratic leaders could have survived the difficulties of conducting a war in a country as complex as Canada. He had won even though saying a kind word about him in the months before the election had been "like a red tie or a campaign button; it got one thrown out of the clubs."[52] The *Canadian Forum* attributed the victory not so much to King as to a preference of the Maritimes and western Canada—often demonstrated in Canadian politics—for being dominated by Quebec rather than Ontario.[53] King himself made much of the argument that a Conservative government at Ottawa would be controlled by George Drew and George McCullagh, the publisher of the *Globe and Mail*. But this is an oversimplification. Actually the business interests of Ontario, whose close tie with the Conservatives had been attenuated in 1940, breathed a sigh of relief when King won, for they knew that under Ilsley, Howe, Gardiner, *et al* they could plan for the future with assurance.[54]

King's great accomplishment was that his skilful handling of the manpower situation, combined with the common sense of the ordinary Quebec voter, avoided the possibility of paralysis. Otherwise French Canada might have turned "off into the darkness behind a motley array of extremists, provincialists, isolationists, demagogs [sic] and crack-pots."[55] When French Canada has a grievance, it tends to support en bloc the party leader who is least objectionable in this connection, and King was that in 1945.[56] He fully recognized that Canada "started out as a partnership and it is too late now to build it on different lines unless we are prepared to consider a divorce."[57] Conscription was undoubtedly the fairest way of raising troops and most of those who advocated it were sincere. But *Saturday Night* was right to doubt their judgment and knowledge of French Canada.[58] In contrast, King both understood and recognized the French-Canadian fact. This is why "Quebec [saved] our King" in 1945.

	Seats	Candidates					Elected									
		P.C.	L.	C.C.F.	S.C.	O.	P.C.	%	L.	%	C.C.F.	%	S.C.	%	O.	%
Nova Scotia	12	12	12	12		5	2	16.7	9	75.0	1	8.3				
New Brunswick	10	9	10	8	1	1	3	30.0	7	70.0						
Prince Edward Island	4	4	4	4			1	25.0	3	75.0						
Quebec	65	29	64	29	43	119	2	3.1	53	81.5					10	15.4
Ontario	82	82	81	80	8	35	48	58.5	34	41.5						
Manitoba	17	17	17	17	8	8	2	11.8	10	58.8	5	29.4				
Saskatchewan	21	19	21	21	9	4	1	4.8	2	9.5	18	85.7				
Alberta	17	16	17	17	17	13	2	11.8	2	11.8			13	76.5		
British Columbia	16	15	15	16	9	21	5	31.3	5	31.3	4	25.0			2	12.5
Yukon	1	1		1		1	1	100.0								
Total	245	204	241	205	95	207	67	27.3	125	51.0	28	11.4	13	5.3	12	4.9

Notes: Three Independent Liberals in Quebec (all elected), unopposed by official Liberal candidates, are included in the Liberal columns.

Four Independent Progressive Conservatives in Quebec (one elected), unopposed by official Progressive Conservatives, are included in the Progressive Conservative columns.

An Independent Liberal in Saskatchewan, unopposed by an official Liberal candidate, is placed in the Liberal columns.

Others elected: Que. (10): I. (6); Bloc Populaire (2); I.L. (1); L.P.P. (1).
             B.C. (2): I. (1); I.C.C.F. (1).

Others (votes polled): N.S. (5): L.P.P. (3) 1,800; Farm.-Lab. (1) 362; I. (1) 488.
             N.B. (1): I. (1) 6,423.
             Que. (119): I. (60) 260,253; Bloc Populaire (35) 181,784; I.L. (12) 21,283; I.P.C. (2) 1,622; L.P.P. (6) 14,641; Lab. (1) 423; I.C.C.F. (1) 279; Farmer (1) 70; Lib.-Lab. (1) 345.
             Ont. (35): L.P.P. (25) 36,333; other L. (1) 6,284; Bloc Populaire (2) 5,038; I.P.C. (1) 295; I. Lab. (1) 241; I. (4) 7,946; Farm.-Lab. (1) 3,258.
             Man. (8): L.P.P. (6) 15,984; I. (2) 2,451.
             Sask. (4): L.P.P. (2) 1,059; Unity (1) 2,124; I.L. (1) 847.
             Alta. (13): L.P.P. (13) 14,136.
             B.C. (21): L.P.P. (11) 25,128; Trade Union (1) 4,679; I.C.C.F. (1) 6,123; Democrat (5) 2,603; Lab. Soc. (2) 459; I. (1) 7,348.
             Yukon (1): L.P.P. (1) 687.

	Popular Vote									Total
P.C.	%	L.	%	C.C.F.	%	S.C.	%	O.	%	
114,214	36.8	141,911	45.7	51,892	16.7			2,650	0.9	310,667
77,225	38.3	100,939	50.0	14,999	7.4	2,300	1.1	6,423	3.2	201,886
30,025	47.4	30,696	48.4	2,685	4.2					63,406
118,933	8.4	717,776	50.8	33,450	2.4	63,310	4.5	480,700	34.0	1,414,169
756,762	41.7	734,402	40.5	260,502	14.4	3,906	0.2	59,395	3.3	1,814,967
80,303	24.9	111,863	34.7	101,892	31.6	10,322	3.2	18,435	5.7	322,815
70,830	18.8	123,344	32.7	167,233	44.4	11,449	3.0	4,030	1.1	376,886
58,077	18.7	67,662	21.8	57,077	18.4	113,821	36.6	14,136	4.5	310,773
128,529	30.0	117,737	27.5	125,945	29.4	9,890	2.3	46,340	10.8	428,441
849	40.0			584	27.5			687	32.4	2,120
1,435,747	27.4	2,146,330	40.9	816,259	15.6	214,998	4.1	632,796	12.1	5,246,130

FOOTNOTES

1. The title of an article by Gordon Rothney in *Canadian Forum*, XXV (July, 1945), pp. 83-84.

2. "The Meaning of the Elections," *Canadian Forum*, XXV (July, 1945), p. 82.

3. "Trends in Canadian Democracy: Political Parties and Policies," *Round Table*, XXXV (June, 1945), p. 264.

4. J. W. Pickersgill, *The Mackenzie King Record: 1939-44*, I (Toronto: University of Toronto Press, 1940), pp. 276-77.

5. John R. Williams, *The Conservative Party of Canada: 1920-49* (Durham, North Carolina: Duke University Press, 1956), p. 72.

6. *Ibid.*, p. 70.

7. Pickersgill, *King Record*, pp. 457 and 459.

8. Leo Zakuta, *A Protest Movement Becalmed: A Study of Change in the C.C.F.* (Toronto: University of Toronto Press, 1964), p. 58.

9. Quoted from King's diary in Pickersgill, *King Record*, pp. 476-77.

10. *Ibid.*, pp. 633-35.

11. Wilfrid Eggleston, "The Ottawa Letter," *Saturday Night*, LX (June 2, 1945), p. 8.

12. Mason Wade, *The French Canadians 1760-1967*, (Toronto: The Macmillan Company of Canada, 1955), pp. 954-55.

13. *Ibid.*, p. 1011.

14. *Ibid.*, the words of Jacques Sauriol, p. 1012.

15. Alzada Comstock, "Election Issues in Canada," *Current History*, VIII (April, 1945), p. 326.

16. See Halifax *Herald*, May 28, 1945.

17. Williams, *Conservative Party*, p. 169.

18. See Halifax *Chronicle*, May 16, 1945.

19. *Ibid.*

20. *Ibid.*, June 9, 1945.

21. *Ibid.*, June 7, 1945.

22. *Ibid.*, May 19, 1945.

23. *Ibid.*, June 6, 1945.

24. *Ibid.*, May 19, 1945.

25. "Trends in Canadian Democracy," p. 266.

26. Zakuta, *Protest Movement*, p. 60.

27. Halifax *Chronicle*, May 22, 1945.

28. *Ibid.*, May 17, 1945.

29. *Ibid.*

30. *Ibid.*, May 21, 1945.

31. *Ibid.*, June 6, 1945.

32. *Ibid.*, May 31, 1945.

33. *Ibid.*, May 25, 1945.

34. *Ibid.*, June 4, 1945.

35. Eggleston, "The Ottawa Letter," *Saturday Night*, LX (March 31, 1945), p. 8.

36. *Ibid.*, (June 2, 1945), p. 8.

37. "The Elections," *Canadian Forum*, XXV (April, 1945), p. 33.

38. Halifax *Chronicle*, May 19, 1945.

39. J.L. Granatstein, *The Politics of Survival: The Conservative Party of Canada, 1939-45* (Toronto: University of Toronto Press, 1967), pp. 190-91, 197.

40. Halifax *Herald*, May 29, 1945.

41. *Ibid.*, June 9, 1945.

42. "Meaning of the Elections," p. 82.

43. "Why Canadians Voted as They Did," *Round Table*, XXXV (September, 1945), p. 361.

44. Rothney, "Quebec Saves Our King," p. 83.

45. *Saturday Night*, LX (June 16, 1945), p. 1.

46. "Backstage at Ottawa," *Maclean's*, LVIII (July 15, 1945), p. 15.

47. *Ibid.*, (April 15, June 15, and July 15, 1945).

48. Norman Ward, ed., *The Memoirs of Chubby Power: A Party Politician* (Toronto: The Macmillan Company of Canada, 1966), pp. 176-77.

49. Rothney, "Quebec Saves Our King," p. 84.

50. Lionel H. Laing, "The Pattern of Canadian Politics: The Elections of 1945," *American Political Science Review*, XL (August, 1946), p. 763.

51. Eggleston, "The Ottawa Letter," *Saturday Night*, LX (June 16, 1945), p. 8.

52. *Saturday Night*, LX (June 16, 1945), p. 1.

53. "Meaning of the Elections," p. 81.

54. Eggleston, "The Ottawa Letter," *Saturday Night*, LX (June 23, 1945), p. 8.

55. *Ibid.*

56. Rothney, "Quebec Saves Our King," p. 84.

57. Eggleston, "The Ottawa Letter," *Saturday Night*, LX (June 16, 1945), p. 8.

58. *Saturday Night*, LX (June 16, 1945), p. 1.

Twenty-first
General Election

FROM "PÈRE DE FAMILLE" TO "PAPPA OF US ALL"

On November 15, 1948, William Lyon Mackenzie King retired as Prime Minister of Canada. At the time, there were many comments about him and his era. Professor A.R.M. Lower said he had based his leadership largely on an "uncanny quality of prescience, a feminine quality of intuition."[1] Professor Frank Underhill described his statesmanship as "a more flexibly adjustable Gallup Poll of Canadian public opinion than statisticians will ever be able to devise." He had been "the representative Canadian, the typical Canadian, the essential Canadian, the ideal Canadian, the Canadian as he exists in the mind of God."[2] But, above all, he had qualified as "the most complete personification of [a] national Canadian characteristic" — a preference for living constantly in an atmosphere of mental haze — and that had permitted him to be the leader who divided Canada least for twenty-five years.[3]

      Professor Frank Scott indignantly objected to King's being permitted, "like Queen Victoria, to give his name to an era," and to his being credited with everything but putting the oil under Alberta. Was a leader "the man who confuses issues, or the one who clarifies them even at the risk of making some enemies?"[4] Earlier Scott had said of King in poetic form:

> He blunted us,
>
> We had no shape
> Because he . . . never took sides,
>
>   . . .
>
> Truly he will be remembered
> Wherever men honour ingenuity,
> Ambiguity, inactivity, and political longevity.[5]

Nevertheless, even though King had contented himself merely with the day-to-day work of seeking balances among sectional interests and had not sought unity through nation-building policies,[6] people would talk of a King era just as they had of Macdonald and Laurier eras.

If King's successor was also to attune himself to the Canadian mood and character, it would be for a different reason. In his mixed Irish-French blood, Louis St. Laurent had, of course, his own equipment for understanding the two main racial groups. Moreover, unlike King's, his speeches had an ordered clarity and reasoned logic that convinced even the House of Commons. But he had liabilities too. The legalistic flavour of his oratory and his habit of saying exactly what he thought might not captivate the ordinary public. Imagine King replying bluntly to Prince Edward Island fish canners who wanted a subsidy: "I have no intention of using public funds to buy up fish."[7]

Until 1941 St. Laurent's vocations had been those of corporation lawyer and *père de famille*. Conscripted into politics after the death of Ernest Lapointe, he had risen in seven years to the party leadership and the prime ministership. He had participated in only one general election, that of 1945, and no one had given him special credit for the Liberal success in Quebec that year. Although perhaps "no man of such intellectual distinction had ever held the office of Prime Minister of Canada," he still had to demonstrate that he possessed "the political finesse and subtle dexterity in the arts of compromise which seem indispensable for long tenure of power in Canada."[8]

There was to be a second unknown quantity in the election of 1949. John Bracken had demonstrated that he was as inadequate in the commons as he had been on the hustings, and his new party soon concluded that its choice of leader had been a serious blunder. And so, early in October 1948 – only two months after St. Laurent's selection by a Liberal convention – George Drew defeated John Diefenbaker and Donald Fleming for the Conservative leadership with about the same ease that St. Laurent had defeated J.G. Gardiner and "Chubby" Power for the Liberal leadership. As Premier of Ontario, Drew had the full support of his own province's delegation and when Ivan Sabourin, the leader of the federal Conservatives in Quebec, nominated him, that province's delegates also flocked to his colours. Many Conservatives saw him as a means of reviving their fortunes in *la belle province*. After all, had he not joined Maurice Duplessis in safeguarding provincial autonomy against a centralizing Ottawa? He had other qualities to commend him. Because of his vigour he was expected to rescue his party from the colourless thing it had been under Bracken. Because he was a true-blue Conservative, he would enable the party to forget its immediate past and would bring it back to its old moorings.

Yet he also had liabilities. His greatest bête-noire, the *Toronto Daily Star*, had already portrayed him as representing the worst kind of conservatism. It was so easy to picture this large, handsome gentleman, immaculately dressed in double-breasted suits and seemingly haughty in manner, as the spokesman of an affluent urbanism. Indeed, the work of the *Star* had already borne fruit in the provincial election of 1948. Initially

Twenty-first

the Conservatives had plastered the billboards with the slogan: "Make Ontario strong with George Drew." But before long they were back-tracking in their personal campaign and complaining that their opponents were making it a Drew election. In the end the Conseravatives won the election, but Drew lost his seat.[9]

The energy Drew displayed as leader drew a mixed reaction. Professor Underhill pictures him rushing up and down the country "like an enraged bull in a pasture field, snorting and bellowing and tossing his head," and suggests that "a bull is both too bellicose and too stupid an animal to be made a model by a man aspiring to the government of a society like ours."[10] On the other hand, the *Round Table* felt that "by his gifts as a debater, his skill as a tactician and his tireless industry he transformed the official opposition into an effective fighting force, which it had not been for years, and made great progress in convincing the country that it could provide a competent alternative administration."[11]

Some Conservatives actually came to believe that only an election was needed to let them take over the government. Perhaps this was understandable. St. Laurent could boast a majority of only 5, and in the session of 1949 he often found himself stymied by opposition tactics that came close to obstruction. In addition to a desire to improve his position in the Commons, he had other reasons for giving the Conservatives the election they wanted. Because he was operating under an electoral mandate given Mackenzie King, he felt that the people should have the earliest practicable opportunity to pronounce on the change. Because Canada was enjoying unparalleled prosperity, he realized it would be wise to capitalize on it before Britain's exchange problems forced her to cut down on Canadian imports.

Douglas Abbott's budget of March 22 made it clear that an election was imminent. Few ministers of finance have been fortunate enough to have a current surplus of $575 million in a pre-election year. Abbott stated his belief that the existing economic situation – and the political one too, he might have added – was "such that it is more appropriate this year to encourage increased expenditure by consumers rather than capital expenditure by business." In consequence,

> . . . almost everybody got something out of [his budget] . . . and in direct ratio to its impact upon the citizen's pocket-book, the reaction was as expected: The 750,000 freed of income-tax payments said, "wow!" The middle-income bracket murmured, "good." Business pondered, "m-m-m-m."[12]

And there are many more voters in the first two groups than there are in the third!

Yet, cautious man that he was, St. Laurent made no decision about an election prior to his speaking tour of western Canada during the Easter recess. He hoped thereby to make himself better known in the part of the country that knew him least and, more important, to determine the response to him in the area where his party was weakest. Sixteen gruelling days in the West transformed St. Laurent. His first speeches were, as usual, "delivered in the tone of a geometry professor lecturing a dull pupil";[13] they evoked applause more polite than spontaneous. Then, mixing with the crowds, he dropped his starchy formality, and chatted easily about crops and the weather just as he had in his father's store in a Quebec village. The second stage in his transformation, says Ian Sclanders, took place when by accident he found out how to reach an audience:

> He talked to the children instead of to their parents–and it was St. Laurent the grandfather talking. Suddenly the adults were cheering and clapping. Here was the beginning of the simple colloquial style of speech he has since used and which is now so familiar to Canadians.[14]

The final stage was his acquiring a nickname. Norman Campbell of the Toronto *Telegram*, watching the new technique being used at Field, British Columbia, remarked: "I'm afraid Uncle Louis will be a hard one to beat." His despatch of the same day contained the phrase "Uncle Louis technique" and "the tag seemed to fit so well that other correspondents picked it up and telegraphed it through Canada."[15]

His doubts obliterated, St. Laurent decided on a dissolution in mid-session. Drew said that to deprive the Commons of its control over expenditures "turned back the clock 100 years to the colonial era,"[16] but he had only got what his parliamentary tactics had invited. A previously balky Parliament quickly approved the North Atlantic Security Pact and the International Wheat Agreement, voted interim supply, and was dissolved in time for an election on June 27.

The election of 1949, to a greater extent than preceding elections, became a contest between two men: St. Laurent and Drew. Although the new election techniques had been tending towards this because of the emphasis they placed on the leader, the personalities of King and the Conservative chieftains of his day had worked to inhibit it. But why a fight between only two leaders? In truth, the altered status of the C.C.F. prevented Coldwell from getting the same attention as St. Laurent or Drew. It had gained 4 seats in by-elections between 1945 and 1948, but it had never fully recovered from its failure to live up to its expectations in 1945. Not only was there a marked drop in membership, but there was also a sharp decrease in involvement among those who remained. At the same time its attitude changed from an offensive and optimistic one to a defensive and pessimistic one. In the midst of continued prosperity it warned repeatedly about an impending depression. Then, too, it must have sensed the growing belief among the electorate that "the C.C.F. had 'no chance' and that a ballot cast for its candidate would be wasted."[17] Consequently it made no pretence of being able to win the election of 1949; it simply said it would supplant the Tories as chief rivals of the Liberals.

Professor Zakuta even suggests that the C.C.F. members were having "trouble finding anything of much interest to say to each other" and that this was "unmistakable evidence that their general viewpoint was not very different from their rivals'."[18] If so, it may have been because the older parties had purloined much of the C.C.F.'s programme. In any case there seemed to be an utter sameness about what the C.C.F. stood for. Had the voters not heard it all before? – a moderate amount of socialization; government subsidies for housing; pensions of $50 a month at age 65; a contributory plan of national health insurance; expansion of international trade through inter-governmental conferences; and so on. "Its campaign," said Professor Underhill, "was not dramatic or colorful, and a party ought to be able to succeed in both without becoming melodramatic or lurid like the Drew shock-troops."[19] It had also failed in educating the public. In Britain, between 1931 and 1945, a flood of books and pamphlets had poured forth not only from the British Labour party itself, but also from the Fabian Society, the Left Book Club, and the Socialist League. Yet, "since the first two or three years of the C.C.F.'s existence, what have we in Canada to show in comparison with that?"[20]

Above all, the C.C.F. found it difficult to convince the voters of the defects of free enterprise during a period of great prosperity. The C.C.F. alone took a stand against the removal of price controls, but this did not help it, even in a time of high prices. A decline in the general strength of socialism and socialist thought definitely hurt it. It found it hard to counter the arguments that Canadians under a non-Socialist government were much better off than Britons under Attlee and that trade unions were coming more and more to dominate the councils of the C.C.F.[21] Also, the public was more than a little suspicious that some members of the C.C.F. were not sharing in the growing distrust of the Soviet Union. When its British Columbian members opposed the Marshall Plan and the North Atlantic Security Pact, they exposed the whole party to the charge that it had become infected with communist sentiment. Professor Underhill wondered why it had not removed such crypto-communists long ago. "It is hard to believe in such innocence in the year 1949, 32 years after the Russian Revolution. And if you do believe in it, how are you to answer critics who say a party with so many innocents in its membership has discredited itself as a party claiming to be considered capable of responsible office?"[22]

Not surprisingly, then, the C.C.F. did badly in 1949. Of its 28 seats it lost 15, 13 of them in Saskatchewan where the quirks of the electoral system – its benefactor last time – worked against it. While it retained Cape Breton South in Nova Scotia and won York South – its first success in

Ontario in a federal general election – it dropped 2 of 5 seats in Manitoba and 1 of 4 in British Columbia.

In popular vote, however, its showing was much more respectable. Its over-all strength dropped only moderately – from 15.6 to 13.4 per cent – and in Ontario and British Columbia it actually improved its position. Nevertheless, it had lost its forward momentum, a matter of no small concern for a party in its stage of growth. Above all, it had failed to make a breakthrough in industrial Ontario. But, at a time when Louis St. Laurent was appealing so strongly to all classes of Canadians, perhaps it could congratulate itself on having done as well as it had.

Basically the Liberals campaigned on their record. Had they not handled postwar reconstruction with skill, raised the gross national product to record heights, ensured virtually full employment, played an active part in bringing into being the North Atlantic Alliance, and conducted the nation's business so carefully as to permit a reduction in debt and taxation? With seeming reasonableness, St. Laurent could therefore say that there were "no outstanding issues in this election"[23] and that his government's attitudes and policies conformed closely to the desires of most Canadians.

> . . . there is a lot more to being really progressive than putting the word 'Progressive' in front of [one's] name. . . . No party has more zeal for social reform than the Liberal party. [Yet] no party believes more strongly . . . that individual initiative and private enterprise are essential to a healthy, prosperous and progressive nation.[24]

Above all, a Liberal government wanted everyone to "share in the good things that Providence had provided in this land." For this reason it was fostering measures to redistribute part of the national income. Already it had paid out a billion dollars in family allowances, "the best piece of social legislation ever put on our statute books."[25] Without becoming very specific, St. Laurent blandly assured his listeners that he would "continue to work for peace and security, for trade and prosperity, for full employment and social security, for complete recognition of Canadian nationhood and the development of all aspects of our national life."[26] While avoiding any fighting comment, "he obviously believed the world would be a better place without Progressive Conservatives. He [had] the attitude that sane people obviously must vote Liberal and it's a waste of time to keep on telling them so."[27]

Naturally St. Laurent made full use of the technique he had discovered on his western tour and it was his election all the way. In the large city auditoriums he seemed lost behind his dark-rimmed glasses and the microphone.

> But in the little places, at the whistle stops, in the fishing hamlets, beside the village war memorials, [the people] came close to him and, the results indicate, he was dynamite. . . .

He spoke 10 and 13 times a day until his throat gave out and then he rested and came back for more. He kissed scores of flower girls, shook tens of thousands of hands, travelled by train and car and air and ship.

But above all he had the people come near him so they could hear him talk and see his face and decide 'if you think you can trust me'. . . .[28]

It was perhaps a little extraordinary for an ex-corporation lawyer to go to the new province of Newfoundland and have Premier Smallwood take him to Spaniard's Bay, Brigus, Bay Roberts, and a dozen other places, and feed him on chocolate bars until three p.m. when they finally lunched on sandwiches beside the road. But the Prime Minister was right at home as he stood up in his car and talked about the responsibilities of the democratic system, the prospects for a young nation "on its way . . . to being the greatest country in the world," and "the rejoicing among the older provinces . . . that you have decided to throw in your lot with us." Perhaps, he went on to say, family allowances "might be the boon which some day will allow Canada to be governed by some man who today is a boy in Newfoundland."[29] This is the type of message which, by election day, the Prime Minister had carried to 190 of the 260 constituencies, an altogether astounding feat of electioneering.[30]

In contrast to St. Laurent, Drew "swept across Canada in a tremendous display of physical vigour and his notable gifts for invective."[31] To demonstrate that he was leading a fight for the survival of the federal constitution, he opened his campaign in Charlottetown where Confederation had started. But it was hard to convince the have-not provinces that tax rental agreements meant the erosion of provincial autonomy. To them St. Laurent's determination to see that "the great sources of tax revenue [were] not monopolized by two or three of the wealthier provinces" made a good deal more sense.[32]

Drew could argue somewhat more acceptably that the Liberals acted as if they ruled by divine right. "Parliament was regarded as a nuisance," he said, "by a government which has had power . . . for fourteen years, and when asked to give account, backed away and denied information to the elected representatives."[33] J.M. Macdonnell, National President of the party, re-echoed Drew's feelings about St. Laurent; "this pleasant, agreeable man has, I think, fallen in with bad companions that have led him astray."[34]

The Prime Minister pretended to be touched by Drew's concern for his alleged deviation from liberal principles. "What I can't understand is why if he wants to be a Liberal he doesn't join the Liberal Party and reform it."[35] St. Laurent was more perturbed because Drew had gone to extremes in criticizing four cabinet ministers: Howe, Abbott, Claxton, and Garson. For this he read him a lecture on the proper behaviour of politicians in a democracy; Drew, he said, "seems incapable of believing that anyone can hold a different view than his and still be honest."[36] His government, rather than being old and tired, was a team of exceptionally able men, constantly invigorated by new blood. In fact, only two of the original cabinet of 1935 remained. He admitted that he, himself, was not as young as he was when he arrived in Quebec in 1905, but he was still able to do a good day's work. "You can ask the newspapermen who have been with me on my campaign tour."[37]

Drew also talked about putting "an end to the minor czars and petty dictators." When challenged on this score, he said he was attacking not the ordinary civil service, but the brains trust, the long-haired boys in ivory towers, "not subject to the supervision of Parliament and in many cases . . . independent even of the government."[38] St. Laurent insisted, however, that the government made the decisions, and charged that Drew "found it more comfortable to make sweeping statements about [civil servants] rather than attack people who . . . talk back."[39]

Most of all, Drew posed as the opponent of statism and socialism. On his western trip St. Laurent had described the C.C.F. as "Liberals in a hurry." In turn, Drew called the Liberals "socialists in low gear" and declared that "a vote for a Liberal candidate is a vote for Coldwell and what his party stood for." Wherever socialism had been tried, it had resulted in "cruel deception and futility," and had opened the way to communism. As for the latter, Drew promised amendments to the Criminal Code so that it would be possible to deal more effectively with it than the Liberals had done.[40] Drew was also in favour of social legislation, if it was properly conceived. Look at his own record in Ontario! Look at the contributory social security programme formulated by the Conservative convention of 1948! Still, the fact remained that such things could "not be fulfilled except from money paid by our people from what they earn" and "only a Progressive Conservative government [could] stem the mounting tide of state control."[41] Even in these matters, however, St. Laurent had the last word. What had been Drew's first comments on family allowances? Had he not sabotaged Ottawa's proposals for a contributory social security system at the Dominion-provincial conferences of 1945 and 1946? And as to handling communism, "we should be careful not to lose our freedom in too vigorous attempts to save it."[42]

Finally, Drew attacked the government's financial and economic policies. Had it not overtaxed the people by $1.5 billion during the past three years and taken $5 for every $4 it needed? Did this not mean that it thought it "knew how to spend your money better than you do"?[43] Worse still, was it not losing the British market and seeking to replace it with the American? If Canadian trade moved north and south, the result would be disastrous for the country's railroads, seaports, and shipping. He would therefore do all in his power to make the dollar and the pound fully convertible. St. Laurent thereupon asked what his specific proposals for accomplishing this end were and, when no reply was forthcoming, he charged that Drew had "no policy but devaluation of the Canadian dollar."[44]

These were Drew's major arguments. According to John R. Williams, he also "swamped the voters with a flood of trivial charges."[45] *Saturday Night* wondered if he thought the main issues were what kind of engine was best suited to T.C.A. requirements and whether Joel Aldred was a good announcer and a loyal employee of the C.B.C.[46] Yet, to be fair, Drew's basic case was much like the one that was to help to bring St. Laurent down in 1957. Unfortunately for Drew, it would not work in the context of 1949. Williams also criticizes him for his resort to invective and his abuse of his opponents; yet, if he had won, they might well have been described as vigour and plain speaking. Finally, Williams says that he campaigned as if the government were going to fall into his hands like an overripe plum.[47] But surely if he felt that way he would not have maintained the pace he did.

Undoubtedly Drew became so obsessed with the Gallup Poll and the outrageously partisan Toronto *Star* that he could not refrain from speaking about them even "in constituencies where most of the voters had probably never heard of the Gallup Poll and seldom saw the *Star*."[48] Everywhere he delighted in telling his audiences that Ontario's Charitable Gifts Act would soon bring about the demise of the *Star*. Just before the election, the Gallup Poll had shown only about one-third of the electors favouring the Liberals, but had indicated that they were making significant gains as the campaign progressed. Drew simply pointed out what had happened to Dewey in 1948 despite the pollsters. Interestingly enough, for that very reason, the Canadian director of the Poll was taking every precaution to ensure accuracy, including polling to the last possible minute.[49] In the end the Gallup Poll's prophecy of the popular vote was, for Drew, all too accurate:

	Gallup Poll	Actual Result
L.	48%	49.5%
P.C.	31	29.7
C.C.F.	15	13.4
S.C.	6	7.4

Nevertheless, the Conservatives felt they had a chance. Because St. Laurent was still an unknown quantity and because Drew was expected to get the support of the Union Nationale, some neutral observers agreed with them. Yet in retrospect it seems ludicrous for anyone to have believed that average Quebeckers would vote for an imperialist Freemason from Ontario rather than one of their own. It implied that they had a concern with provincial antonomy which was altogether unrealistic and that they could be made to believe that St. Laurent had sacrificed their interests. And all this at a time when Liberals were dinning it into their ears that Drew and his party regarded family allowances as "iniquitous" and "a bribe to Quebec."

How much of a Drew-Duplessis axis was there in 1949? The chief organizer of the U.N., J.D. Bégin, made it clear that "the central organization of the Union Nationale Party [had] nothing to do with the federal election," and that "Duplessis was in no way connected with the Progressive Conservative Party organization."[50] He did not want to risk endangering his own prestige in a losing cause. Yet he left his organizers to participate as they pleased on the ground that any other action would have meant taking sides. Bégin readily admitted that in 75 per cent of the ridings the Conservative organizers were U.N. organizers. None the less, the Conservatives could elect only Léon Balcer and Henri Courtemanche, the same number of members as in 1945. The U.N. had made its influence felt, however: the Conservatives ran 69 candidates as against 29 in 1945, and put up genuine fights in 30 ridings compared with 10.

B.K. Sandwell thought it gratifying that Conservatives running under their own label could make such a respectable showing. If they acquired strange bedfellows in the process, he felt that was all to the good; should they not "learn to sleep together without kicking one another out of bed"? Indeed, the more a provincial party became tied to a national one, the more it would become subject to restraints in catering to extravagant local ideas.[51] Yet, despite what Sandwell says, the Conservatives were taking a calculated risk in becoming associated with the U.N. St. Laurent himself commented on their attempt to secure "any, yes, I say any, kind of support in Quebec." Had J.M. Macdonnell not stated that "the U.N. is merely the old Conservative party in Quebec," and had Donald Fleming not told an audience in Rimouski that "Mr. Drew loves your leader Maurice Duplessis"? Let the public study such dubious allies "pretty carefully," he warned.[52]

Naturally the Toronto *Star* was the most bitter critic of the alleged Drew-Duplessis alliance. It also did its best to associate Drew with Mayor Camilien Houde of Montreal. According to J.R. Williams, it reached its low point on the Saturday before the election when it carried on its front page "the picture of a corpulent Camilien Houde with distended stomach and open mouth" beside that of a dignified and paternal St. Laurent. Above them were banner headlines:

> Keep Canada British
> Destroy Drew's Houde
> God Save the King[53]

In this election, too, the Conservative Toronto *Telegram* and the Liberal *Star* engaged in thoroughly unabashed slanting of the news.[54] The

by Arch Dale. Winnipeg Free Press, *June 2, 1949. Courtesy of* Free
Press. *At a brilliant ceremony the Conservative party was recently
united in marriage once more with a beauty of Quebec. Miss Isolation
of 1949, offspring of Mr. Maurice Duplessis. Mayor Houde, a distinguished wartime guest of the Canadian Government, was best man.
The Union Nationale guarded the doors, which were sealed by Mr.
Duplessis's ancestral padlocks. The bride's face was hidden in a veil
worn by her grandmother in 1911 and her mother in 1930. She was
gowned in traditional blackmail and carried a simple bouquet of wild
bigamy. Shotguns were carried by the proud parents, Mr. Duplessis
and Mr. Drew. Mr. Duplessis wore the medal presented to him by
Colonel Peron of Argentina. Mr. Drew wore a boyish smile. Mr. Diefenbaker and Mr. MacDonnell wore sackcloth and ashes. The premises
were tastefully decorated with Fleur de Lis from Mr. Duplessis's
private conservatory. The groom's gift to the bride was a veto over
future Conservative party policy. After the exchange of nuptial vows
the gathering followed the local tradition by burning a copy of the
North Atlantic Pact. In a happy little speech, Mr. Duplessis stressed
the glories of democracy and the need of campaign funds. Mr. Drew
pledged the happy married couple to a long lifetime of convertibility.
The groom modestly remarked that he had not been so pleasantly
married for quite some time. After the cutting of a large cake baked in
St James Street, the bride and groom left for a honeymoon at Niagara
Falls, which the groom will go over, as usual, in a barrel.*

Conservatives also had strong editorial support from the Toronto *Globe and
Mail*, whose publisher George McCullagh took to the radio to aid Drew.

But in over-all newspaper coverage the Liberals had the advantage. The dailies backing them had a circulation of 1,000,000 compared to a circulation of 800,000 for those supporting the Conservatives. The Liberal papers were also more widely distributed and much more vocal.[55]

The end result was that English Canada responded to St. Laurent's pleas in much the same way as French Canada. In consequence, it was one of the greatest Liberal victories on record: 73.7 per cent of the seats compared with 73.9 per cent in 1940. While the Liberals fell short by 0.5 per cent of taking half the popular vote, they gained seats in all provinces except Prince Edward Island, and increased their popular vote in every province, markedly so in Quebec and the four western provinces. Of the seats they had won in 1945, they lost only Beauce, Labelle, and Trois Rivières; they added 71 others, including most of the new ones created through redistribution. Alberta was the only province not to give them a majority of its seats, and even there they gained 3 from Social Credit.

For the Conservatives the results were calamitous. Their popular vote rose from 27.4 to 29.7 per cent, but only because they trebled their portion of the vote in Quebec. Their drop in the other provinces was relatively slight, but it was none the less sufficient to reduce their contingent from 67 to 41, the worst showing they had ever made in percentage of seats. Outside Ontario, they lost 5 of their 19 seats, but they suffered their most serious setback in Drew's own province. There the losses numbered 23, most of them seats Bracken had gained in 1945: 10 in western Ontario, 6 in eastern Ontario, and 7 in Toronto and the Yorks. Perhaps the Toronto *Star* had been as effective as Drew feared it might be.

In his "Morning-After Wisdom" Grattan O'Leary analysed the voters' behaviour as well as anyone, though J.R. Williams said he reflected the fatalism typical of Conservative journalists:

> Mr. Drew lost because there were circumstances which nothing he could do or say or refrain from saying or doing could alter in the time at his disposal – circumstances such as his inheriting the leadership of a party which had become badly run down, plus circumstances such as the prosperity of the country, with no public fear that the prosperity was in danger, plus circumstances such as absence of government scandal, plus the over-all circumstances that many people liked the taste of the "welfare state" which the Government had provided. . . . No strategy by Mr. Drew could have changed them.[56]

O'Leary was not alone in wondering about the political effects of welfare payments. "The more a government gives away to the general body of the voters," wrote B.K. Sandwell, "the more difficult it is going to become to upset it."[57] The Conservatives also had had to meet a whispering campaign that they would eliminate old age pensions and other welfare payments. In

Newfoundland especially, the Liberals had used the role of Santa Claus to good advantage. The irrepressible Joseph Smallwood is reported to have said:

> Ferryland [in St. John's East] has voted against me in two referendums and in the provincial election, but I won in spite of you. Now I don't need you. I've been elected, but . . . you need me. I'm sitting right on top of the public chest and not one red cent will come out of it for Ferryland district unless Greg Power is elected.[58]

Smallwood notwithstanding, Newfoundland's anti-Confederates, primarily the business interests of the capital city, attached themselves to the Conservatives and managed to take both St. John's East and West. But in the five outport ridings, where the voters felt that Canadian welfare payments had ushered in the millenium, they gave all the credit to "Joey" and "Uncle Louis." In places such as Little Heart's Ease, Jo Batts Arm, Seldom Come By, God Almighty Cove, and Horse Chops about 85 per cent of them voted Liberal and continued to do so until 1968.

All observers agreed that it was a great triumph for St. Laurent. They gave him full credit for rejuvenating the Liberal party from within to prevent its suffering the decay which almost inevitably accompanies long tenure of office. Because St. Laurent had qualities of leadership which King never possessed, the *Economist* wondered if he was the man who could unify Canada.[59] But there were some critics of the campaign, the results, and the victorious leader. The *Canadian Forum* thought that the election lacked the sense of a historic moment which had caused all the parties to rise to the occasion in 1945. After pointing out that St. Laurent had described the C.C.F. as "Liberals in a hurry," it pronounced its own judgment: St. Laurent was not in a hurry. Professor Underhill agreed that the old-line parties were charlatans in their professed devotion to social legislation. "Didn't somebody once remark . . . that Talleyrand deceived without lying whereas Metternich lied without deceiving? In this matter . . . the Liberals are our Canadian Talleyrands and the Conservatives our Metternichs."[60] What could be more insulting to the voters' intelligence than to find the federal Liberals and Conservatives belabouring each other as scoundrels at the very time that their British Columbian counterparts were collaborating to keep the C.C.F. out of office and prevent the enactment of social legislation?[61]

There was not much elation either, about the return to the days of weak opposition. Some also noted that, although all kinds of Canadians had voted Liberal and there continued to be little in the nature of class voting, yet voting on the grounds of race and religion was strongly pronounced. Because French Canada was anxious to place its imprimatur on a French-Canadian prime minister, it was not surprising that 73 of the 78 French-speaking members were Liberal. But 13 of the 17 other Catholics in the

	Seats	Candidates					Elected									
		P.C.	L.	C.C.F.	S.C.	O.	P.C.	%	L.	%	C.C.F.	%	S.C.	%	O.	%
Newfoundland	7	7	7	1			2	28.6	5	71.4						
Nova Scotia	13	13	13	9			2	15.4	10	76.9	1	7.7				
New Brunswick	10	10	10	6		3	2	20.0	8	80.0						
Prince Edward Island	4	4	4	2			1	25.0	3	75.0						
Quebec	73	69	73	20		91	2	2.7	68	93.2					3	4.1
Ontario	83	83	83	76	5	19	25	30.1	56	67.5	1	1.2			1	1.2
Manitoba	16	15	16	14		5	1	6.3	12	75.0	3	18.8				
Saskatchewan	20	20	20	20	4	2	1	5.0	14	70.0	5	25.0				
Alberta	17	14	17	13	17	4	2	11.8	5	29.4			10	58.8		
British Columbia	18	15	16	18	2	5	3	16.7	11	61.1	3	16.7			1	5.6
Yukon and N.W.T.	1		1	1		1			1	100.0						
Total	262	250	260	180	28	130	41	15.6	193	73.7	13	5.0	10	3.8	5	1.9

Notes: The Union des Electeurs, which ran 50 candidates in Quebec, 4 in Ontario, and 1 in New Brunswick, is included in the "Others" rather than the Social Credit columns. An Independent Progressive Conservative candidate in Quebec, who was unopposed by an official Progressive Conservative candidate, is included in the Progressive Conservative columns.

Others elected: Que. (3): I. (3).
Ont. (1): I. (1).
B.C. (1): I. (1).

Others (votes
polled): N.B. (3): I.L. (1) 3,084; I. (1) 533; Union des Electeurs (1) 2,172.
Que. (91): Union des Electeurs (50) 80,990; I. (17) 99,219; I.L. (13) 18,959; I.P.C. (3) 4,997; Unité National (1) 5,590; L.P.P. (2) 5,078; Nat. (1) 4,994; Lab. (1) 108; Lib.-Lab. (1) 433; Republican (1) 294; Social Justice (1) 367.
Ont. (19): Union des Electeurs (4) 2,036; L.P.P. (7) 13,613; Lab. (1) 307; Lab.-Soc. (1) 271; I.L. (2) 6,488; I.P.C. (1) 777; I. (2) 1,304; Farm.-Lab. (1) 6,161.
Man. (5): L.P.P. (2) 6,523; I. (3) 6,666.
Sask. (2): L.P.P. (2) 1,531.
Alta. (4): L.P.P. (2) 2,201; I.S.C. (2) 4,598.
B.C. (5): L.P.P. (3) 3,887; I. (2) 11,992.
Yukon and N.W.T. (1): I. (1) 2,283.

	Popular Vote									Total
P.C.	%	L.	%	C.C.F.	%	S.C.	%	O.	%	
29,203	27.9	75,235	71.9	197	0.2					104,635
126,365	37.5	177,680	52.7	33,333	9.9					337,378
88,049	39.4	120,369	53.8	9,450	4.2			5,789	2.6	223,657
32,989	48.4	33,480	49.2	1,626	2.4					68,095
392,530	24.6	961,974	60.4	17,767	1.1			221,029	13.9	1,593,300
757,210	37.4	924,231	45.7	306,551	15.2	3,225	0.2	30,957	1.5	2,022,174
70,689	22.0	153,857	47.9	83,176	25.9			13,189	4.1	320,911
53,624	14.4	161,887	43.4	152,399	40.9	3,474	0.9	1,531	0.4	372,915
56,947	16.8	116,647	34.5	31,329	9.3	126,409	37.4	6,799	2.0	338,131
128,620	27.9	169,018	36.7	145,442	31.5	2,109	0.5	15,879	3.4	461,068
		3,284	49.0	1,140	17.0			2,283	34.0	6,707
1,736,226	29.7	2,897,662	49.5	782,410	13.4	135,217	2.3	297,456	5.1	5,848,971

House were also Liberal, and the constituencies with large Catholic populations almost invariably returned Liberals. The *Round Table* concluded — with some exaggeration — that the Liberals had become predominantly a Catholic party. While it admitted that St. Laurent might be counted on to prevent a Catholic bloc from imposing its will on the party, it wondered if there might not be "important consequences in various spheres."[62]

Why was the Liberal majority so big? B.K. Sandwell was right in saying that, when a party has as many advantages as the Liberals had in 1949,

> . . . the conditions of present-day electioneering, conducted largely by radio and by exploiting the personalities of the national leaders to the exclusion of those of the local candidates, operate with an almost uniform effect in a large number of different constituencies, producing a sort of standard proportion of turn-over which can be resisted only where the normal majority for the losing party is exceptionally strong.[63]

This factor, combined with a context made to order for him, wrought great things for St. Laurent in 1949. A generally satisfied electorate reacted to him much as a crowd did at Hawkesbury, Ontario. There one night he acted the part of a father at the family table and "talked as a wise and kindly father would talk and the people stared at him spellbound. A member of parliament cried . . . and when it was all over, he cried again and said: 'Ah, he is the pappa of us all.' "[64]

General Election

1. A.R.M. Lower, "Mr. King," *The Canadian Banker*, LVII (Autumn, 1950), p. 48.

2. F.H. Underhill, "The End of the King Era—Part I," *Canadian Forum*, XXVIII (August, 1948), p. 98.

3. F.H. Underhill, "The Close of an Era: Twenty-five Years of Mr. Mackenzie King," *Canadian Forum*, XXIV (September, 1944), p. 125.

4. F.R. Scott, "Mr. King and the King Makers," *Canadian Forum*, XXX (December, 1950), p. 197.

5. F.R. Scott, "W.L.M.K.," F.R. Scott and A.J.M. Smith, (eds.), *The Blasted Pine* (Toronto: The Macmillan Company of Canada, 1962), pp. 27-28.

6. F.H. Underhill, "The End of the King Era – Part II," *Canadian Forum*, XXVIII (September, 1948), p. 126.

7. *Time*, September 12, 1949.

8. "The Liberal Convention," *Round Table*, XXXIX (December, 1948), p. 78.

9. G.M.A. Grube, "The Ontario Election," *Canadian Forum*, XXVIII (July, 1948), p. 83.

10. F.H. Underhill, "Vox Populi," *Canadian Forum*, XXIX (July, 1949), p. 77.

11. "The Party Fight in Canada," *Round Table*, XXXIX (June, 1949), p. 222.

12. Halifax *Mail-Star*, March 23, 1949.

13. *Time*, September 12, 1949.

14. Ian Sclanders, "How the Prime Minister became Uncle Louis," *Maclean's*, LXVIII (January 1, 1955), p. 7.

15. *Ibid.*, p. 41.

16. Halifax *Chronicle-Herald*, April 27, 1949.

17. Leo Zakuta, *A Protest Movement Becalmed: A Study of Change in the C.C.F.* (Toronto: University of Toronto Press, 1964), p. 83.

18. *Ibid.*, p. 72.

19. Underhill, "Vox Populi," p. 77.

20. *Ibid.*

21. J.A. Stevenson, "The Canadian Election," *Spectator*, CLXXXII (June 24, 1949), p. 846.

22. Underhill, "Vox Populi," p. 77.

23. Halifax *Chronicle-Herald*, May 12, 1949.

24. *Ibid.*, May 10, 1949.

25. *Ibid.*, May 12, 1949.

26. *Ibid.*, May 10, 1949.

27. The Ottawa *Journal*, June 21, 1940, quoted in J.R. Williams, *The Conservative Party of Canada: 1920-49* (Durham, North Carolina: Duke University Press, 1956), p. 175.

28. Halifax *Chronicle-Herald*, June 29, 1949.

29. *Ibid.*, June 25, 1949.

30. Dale C. Thomson, *Louis St. Laurent: Canadian* (Toronto: The Macmillan Company of Canada, 1967), p. 272.

31. Williams, *Conservative Party*, p. 175.

32. Halifax *Chronicle-Herald*, May 16, 1949.

33. *Ibid.*, May 17, 1949.

34. *Ibid.*, June 4, 1949.

35. *Ibid.*, May 19, 1949.

36. *Ibid.*, June 21, 1949.

37. *Ibid.*, June 7, 1949.

38. *Ibid.*, May 23, 1949.

39. *Ibid.*, May 16, 1949.

40. *Ibid.*, May 11, 1949.

41. *Ibid.*, May 28, 1949.

42. *Ibid.*, May 16, 1949.

43. *Ibid.*, May 17, 1949.

44. *Ibid.*, June 7, 1949.

45. Williams, *Conservative Party*, p. 176.

46. "Reliability in Policies," *Saturday Night*, LXIV (June 7, 1949), p. 1.

47. Williams, *Conservative Party*, p. 173.

48. *Ibid.*, p. 176n.

49. Wilfred Sanders, "A Note on the Public Relations of Election Forecasts," *Public Opinion Quarterly*, XIII (Fall, 1949), pp. 511-13.

50. Halifax *Chronicle-Herald*, May 24, 1949.

51. B.K. Sandwell, "The 1949 Elections," *Queen's Quarterly*, LVI (Autumn, 1949), pp. 427-28.

52. Halifax *Chronicle-Herald*, June 3 and 17, 1949.

53. Toronto *Daily Star*, June 25, 1949,

quoted in Williams, *Conservative Party*, p. 179.

54. See Sidney Katz, "How Toronto Evening Papers Slanted the Election News," *Maclean's*, LXII (August 15, 1949), pp. 10-11, 53-54.

55. Williams, *Conservative Party*, p. 178.

56. Ottawa *Journal*, quoted in Williams, *Conservative Party*, p. 173.

57. Sandwell, "The 1949 Elections," pp. 429-30.

58. Halifax *Chronicle-Herald*, June 14, 1949.

59. *Economist*, CLVII (July 2, 1949), p. 9.

60. "Coming Soon," *Canadian Forum*, XXIX (June, 1949), p. 49.

61. Underhill, "Vox Populi," p. 74.

62. "The General Election," *Round Table*, XXXIX (September, 1949), p. 375.

63. Sandwell, "The 1949 Elections," p. 425.

64. Halifax *Chronicle-Herald*, June 29, 1949.

Twenty-second

General Election

A BENEVOLENT UNCLE BUT NO TIP

Perhaps no two successive elections have had so much in common as those of 1949 and 1953. In many ways the second was merely a rerun of the first. The leaders were the same, as were, largely, the issues and the results. Only the details were different in a political environment that was almost a mirror-image of the one four years earlier.

There were, it is true, more serious complaints about the timing of the election than in 1949. Because so many Canadians were on vacation, M.J. Coldwell felt the results might not be truly representative. The more outspoken George Drew charged the Liberals with "trying to drive the nation in blinkers. . . . Having hidden the truth from Parliament, they now seek to hide the truth from the people."[1] Sardonically Professor Underhill called the comments of Drew and Coldwell a silly performance. "As if any prime minister ever chose an election date without careful calculation of its advantages to his own party! This is the famous feature of our British parliamentary system which provides flexibility. See all our orthodox textbooks." True, much could be said for the American system of regular and fixed elections. "But this is not the British system. And we are all good Britishers in this country, aren't we?"[2]

Nobody seemed so much the same as Louis St. Laurent. A Canadian Press despatch said he had "refined the whistle-stop art to the point where he could give lessons to Harry S. Truman, the old master."[3] Instead of making the conventional speech from the back platform, he preferred to mingle with the people at the station and then deliver a short speech, using a hand microphone hooked up to a loudspeaker on the train platform. Once again his travels were akin to an "oratorical pilgrimage" in which he did his utmost to let "hundreds of people . . . exchange a word with him or touch the hem of his garment."[4] The Liberal campaign managers arranged numerous appearances before schoolchildren, for with them the Prime Minister was an electioneering artist of the first order. As always, he treated the children as serious human beings and talked to them in simple homely language about Queen Elizabeth, the Coronation, and how fine it was to be a Canadian. As always, too, he "conveyed to them the impression that he was their uncle-in-chief, deeply concerned and devoted to their interests and determined to ensure they had happy and prosperous lives."[5]

Parents were no less susceptible than their children to the Uncle Louis technique as it manifested itself in his informal appearances. His former associates were still bewildered to read about the former corporation lawyer making his way among the Newfoundland housewives and shaking their hands – the codfish were running and the boats were out – while a loudspeaker blared forth jazz and hillbilly music. "Your fisherman husbands," he told them, "do not promise a catch when they go out to fish. Well, neither will we. But if there are any fish to be had we will bring them."[6]

> All [he] had to do was to tour the country and talk to people, in the manner of a benevolent uncle, about the greatness of being a Canadian. No one ever thought to ask him for the tip which benevolent uncles are supposed to dispense.[7]

Indeed, he made it clear he would not compete in making "empty promises" or arousing "exaggerated hopes." "We have to submit our accounts to you every few years. I ask you to look [them] over and draw your own conclusions." In 1949 he had promised complete recognition of Canadian nationhood and the development of all aspects of the country's national life. His government had lived up to its undertakings. It had appointed a Canadian to the office of Governor General, made the Supreme Court of Canada the nation's final court of appeal, and begun the "repatriation" of the written constitution. Furthermore, it had provided federal assistance for universities, given price support to agricultural products, expanded the national health programmes, and taken steps to prevent discrimination in industries under federal jurisdiction. It had also been spending $2 billion a year for the preservation of peace. "Most Canadians," he said, would "feel expenditures on this scale are not beyond our capacity nor more than our share." As for trade, it would continue to meet every trade problem as it arose. "And we are certainly fortunate to have a man like Trade Minister C.D. Howe to do that."[8]

So, according to Uncle Louis, it was "roses all the way in the Canadian garden. He [could] detect very few flaws in our civilization and only trivial weaknesses in our national economy."[9] But not everyone was enthusiastic about his attitudes or his type of electioneering. The tough-minded journalist John A. Stevenson said he "conducted a passive campaign," that " 'brown paper parcels of platitudes' were the chief ingredients of too many of his speeches,"[10] that he was "virtually mute" on the subject of reforms. Obviously "fearful of fresh adventures," he elected – like all aging men – to "follow the paths of indolence taken to the grave detriment of his country by Stanley Baldwin."[11] In much the same vein, Professor Underhill said St. Laurent had not Mackenzie King's genius for blurring issues and if he were given time he would make it clear that the major premises of all his political thinking were those of a corporation lawyer.[12]

But in 1953 these were voices crying in the wilderness. In the midst of continuing prosperity the average Canadian was complacent and self-satisfied, not caring to press on with social legislation and reform. If the election of 1953 demonstrated something which that of 1949 had not, it was that St. Laurent was a Liberal of the right. Perhaps because he had so little to offer that was positive, he spent an unusual amount of time in criticizing the policies of his opponents and answering their charges. It might have been supposed that, possessing the veneer of sweet reasonableness that he did, he would not be able to stand up to a good battering from his opponents.

> But the more the Conservatives battered, the better the Liberal veneer looked. There was more than a hint . . . of the 19th century aristocrat turning his condescending gaze on the shouting and vulgar proletarian. Since Mr. Drew himself and many of the more prominent Conservatives are accustomed to be on the aristocratic side of the fence, they must have been particularly galled by the Liberals' calm and successful assumption of superiority.[13]

The Prime Minister dominated the election, and thoroughly outmanoeuvred and outmatched George Drew. This time, apparently by design, Drew was more restrained and less bellicose, though still vigorous. His sixteen-point programme and his campaign itself evoked many memories of 1949. Because the government was four years older, he could argue even more strongly that it was "old and tired in office" and "it's time for a change." He found proof of this in the government's policy for the future, which to him was nothing more than "as you were."[14] Indeed the ministry was not only burned out, but arrogant as well. As Donald Fleming put it, "who is this man [St. Laurent] who sets himself so high that he need not offer the people a program? Do people want to buy a pig in a poke?"[15] Naturally Drew became indignant when the usually accurate St. Laurent went much too far in extolling the accomplishments of Liberal governments. Was it not asking "just a little too much to expect Canadians with any knowledge of their own history to accept [the] statement that our unity, national strength and national stature have been the exclusive achievement of the Liberal party"?[16]

Drew's stand on provincial autonomy was also an old story. In Quebec, especially, he charged the government with deliberately centralizing power in Ottawa.

> That is its purpose. It wants to keep its hand on the money which now represents 78 cents in every tax dollar, leaving only 22 cents for the provincial governments and the municipalities. . . .
>
> Canadian unity demands respect for those principles which

were expressed here in the City of Quebec in the Spring of 1867 [*sic*] and became the terms of the great Confederation Pact. We are pledged to restore the true principles of the Confederation Pact. That is our promise![17]

In reply St. Laurent told his Quebec audiences that "no matter what you hear to the contrary, I am a provincial autonomist but not only for Quebec but especially for Quebec because of special circumstances."[18] It was inconceivable to him that after eight years Drew was still unable to see that the true purpose of tax rental agreements was to strengthen the financial position of the provinces. "Surely provincial rights are stronger and provincial autonomy more secure when the provincial treasuries have assured sources of revenue, when they know what they can count on, when it is safe to plan ahead a few years."[19] He was surprised that Drew persisted in advocating a strengthening of provincial taxing power which, while it would be satisfactory for Ontario, would be disastrous for the other provinces. As for himself, he was not prepared to give up powers that the Dominion Government needed to achieve national goals. Any such change would have to be made by some government other than his. Then, almost as an afterthought, he observed that Drew's successor as Premier of Ontario had gone into the tax rental system in 1952.

The arguments on trade had all been heard before. Gone, said Drew, were Canada's traditional farm markets in Britain and the Commonwealth, and the government had made no effort to regain them. But St. Laurent dismissed as fantasy his opponent's talk about breaking the dollar-pound barrier. That obstacle, he pointed out, was imposed by the United Kingdom, not by Canada," and I don't know how a Conservative government in Canada could lift [it] as long as the Conservative government in the United Kingdom feels it is needed to protect their limited supply of dollars." He dismissed Drew's statement that a Conservative government would not permit barriers to be erected against Canadian goods while its own markets were left open to the dumping of American goods at less than cost prices. Don't let the Conservatives go on another "tariff-raising binge," he warned, and don't give them another chance to blast their way into the markets of the world.[20]

This time, however, charges of maladministration assumed far greater significance than in 1949. The Currie Report, released in December 1952, disclosed a serious administrative breakdown in the engineering detachments of the army works service, especially at Camp Petawawa. For a time all Canada was laughing about its statement that there had been horses on the payroll at this camp. When the Auditor General also complained because eight different systems of accounting were being used in the Department of National Defence, the Conservatives felt they had the government on the run. The entire party demanded a thorough reorganization of the Department, to be followed by an overhaul of other departments as well.

The government replied that it had uncovered the irregularities in the first place and that there was relatively little to indicate that the defence programme had been wasteful or extravagant. St. Laurent charged the Conservatives with picking on defence "because they think it is less popular than other expenditures."[21] However, even after he had shown there were no horses on the payroll, his own audiences snickered whenever he raised the subject and Drew persisted in repeating the charge wherever he went. St. Laurent was equally annoyed because his opponents treated the removal of a few rusty rails at Petawawa as equivalent to the theft of the main line of the Grand Trunk, and because they described the hauling away of a few ramshackle buildings at Farnham, Quebec, as the theft of an army camp. Everywhere he defended his Minister of National Defence, saying there had never been "a more devoted or hardworking or competent minister than Brooke Claxton."[22]

The public was more amused than perturbed by the irregularities. By themselves the ills were not sufficient to convince the voters that it was time for a change. In the end, public attention focused chiefly on Drew's promise to cut taxes by $500 million. At a time when taxation was unusually high, this promise had an undeniable attractiveness. Drew made it sound so simple, too. Since the war, he said, the Liberals had overtaxed the Canadian people by $300 million annually; add that sum to the $200 million that could be saved on defence alone—"this Frankenstein of waste and extravagance"—and his promise would be fulfilled. Independent investigations of other departments would no doubt enable his government to reduce taxation further.

What would be the result? Because the savings would permit, among other things, a substantial reduction in sales taxes, there would be "relief to those on pensions and small fixed incomes in the only way it can be given." There would also be a reduction in municipal taxes through the exemption of the purchases of municipal governments from federal sales taxes and through the payment of municipal taxes on federal property. "We are indeed offering a new deal to the municipal taxpayer," said Drew. For the head of a family of five, a Conservative government would reduce taxes by an average of $170 a year without any reduction in pensions, family allowances, or other social security measures.[23]

St. Laurent described the tax-cutting programme as nothing but "a bare-faced attempt to fool the people." His own government had gone the limit in its recent budget by reducing expenditures by $361 million and personal income taxes by $237 million.[24] If the Conservatives were to cut taxes by reducing the expenditures on defence, it could only mean backing down on Canada's undertakings in Korea and the North Atlantic Alliance, and taking risks with the security of Canada and the Canadian people. If it were done through deficit financing, it would be even worse folly, for the government was already finding it difficult to keep under control the inflationary pressures induced by the Korean War. So "the millions of Canadians who hold Victory Bonds and Canada Savings Bonds [were] not very likely to look on [tax cuts] with much favour."[25]

When Drew went further and promised a host of new undertakings as well as tax cuts, St. Laurent said he was showing contempt for the intelligence of the people. In 1949 Drew had promised to "build a new bridge across every stream he crossed," and since that time his promises had been getting bigger and bigger.[26] For example, he was now proposing a contributory health insurance scheme, a new housing programme, hydro-electric projects, and an independent board which would pay the farmer fair prices related to production costs. When St. Laurent demanded a straight answer explaining how tax cuts and increased expenditures could be provided at the same time, Drew told him he was "the last person to talk about straight answers. . . . We want a straight answer as to when they will get the horses off the payroll."[27]

Drew developed one new technique during the campaign. Realizing the folly of attempting to emulate St. Laurent in whistle-stop campaigning, he used the press conference more than anyone before him. This permitted him to be interviewed on questions of local interest and have the reports appear in the afternoon papers. But, as a vote-getter, it hardly compared to the St. Laurent techniques.[28]

Once again the C.C.F. had difficulty in a period of great prosperity. It had not learned that in such times gloomy prophecies only alienate the public. M.J. Coldwell warned that capitalism works well only during war or the threat of war, and suggested that the end of the Korean conflict might lead to an economic slow down in both the United States and Canada. Although there was "absolutely no necessity for a recession either now or at any time in the future, . . the Liberal government has no plans to keep [the factory machinery] busy."[29] To all of which St. Laurent had a simple stock answer: "They were saying the same things in 1945" but prosperity did not vanish.[30]

Although Coldwell told a meeting in Halifax that his party would nationalize steel – the industry that, according to him, ought above all others to be taken out of private hands – he made no effort to emphasize public ownership. Instead, he launched his party on what was to be its basic strategy of the 1950's: the intensive championship of specific reforms. He came out for "a national health insurance plan, construction of low-cost subsidized housing on a large scale, increased social security benefits, monetary and tariff concessions to Britain to boost trade, long-range price-support programs, and increased aid to underdeveloped countries."[31] He made the first two items his primary concern.

He would not rest content, he said, until there was "a good kitchen sink and a first class bathroom in every house, . . until no Canadian housewife has ever again to bend over an old wooden washboard and break her back every Monday morning doing the family wash."[32] Even more than adequate housing, the C.C.F. promised full health care for every Canadian regardless of his income. "We maintain that it may, in the long run, be just as essential to Canada's defence to have a nation of strong and healthy people as it is to have an air division in Europe."[33] The Prime Minister had stated that he would consider a national health insurance plan whenever all or most of the provinces agreed. To Coldwell that was pure deceit, coming as it did from the leader of a party that had promised it in 1919. Paul Martin had said that the government could not be expected to adopt such a plan overnight. Coldwell retorted: "It's been a long night—34 years."[34]

Such were the arguments of the principal leaders in 1953. Less than a year earlier the Republicans had taken the American presidency for the first time since 1928, using arguments not unlike those of Drew in 1953. But in contrast with the Republicans, the Canadian Conservatives laboured under three disadvantages. For one thing, Drew was no Eisenhower. To the plain folk of Canada who lived on the farms and in the small towns he was still "the perfect pattern of the prosperous urban citizen, who in their view gets too large a share of the national income, and they looked askance at him as a Curzonian type of 'most superior person.' "[35] It was not he but St. Laurent who presented the same kind of father-image as Eisenhower. By arguing in moderate terms free from extreme partisan bias, the Prime Minister attuned himself completely to a public enjoying a high level of prosperity. Canada, said the *Economist*, is so vast that it needs a special kind of leader. "He must be someone with whom every voter can feel he is at least acquainted, and Mr. St. Laurent has become that kind of man."[36]

St. Laurent did make one *gaffe*, a rather surprising one for him. In Calgary he told "a little bedtime story with a moral . . . [about] a political party [which] had been out of office so long it was apparently willing to try any kind of hot air to blow [its] way in," but soon discovered it could not effect the tax cuts it had promised.[37] But *gaffe* though it was, this snide reference to the American Republican party did him no harm in Canada. It made not even a dent in the Liberal slogan, "A Great Leader for a Greater Canada."

Then, too, the image of Herbert Hoover, although unattractive, remained not nearly so repellent in the United States as that of R.B. Bennett did in Canada. Except for five years, the Liberals had guided the evolution of the modern state and in 1953 they were still telling the Canadian public what a disaster those five years had been. Dafoe had been right: Bennett had indeed become the Conservative counterpart of Alexander Mackenzie.

Finally, the Liberals were much more difficult to attack than the Democrats. Although they had blemishes, they had brought about a vast expansion in government without the confusion and corruption that had occurred under the Democrats in the United States. Very early in the campaign it was apparent that the Conservatives were going to get nowhere with their charges of maladministration. "A few cackling geese were alleged to have saved Rome," wrote Professor J.E. Hodgetts, "but surely it will require more than a few disguised horses on a public pay-roll to make an effective election issue!"[38] He was quite right.

The Conservatives had no better luck with their charges that the government had become insolent and arrogant. John A. Stevenson pointed to ministers who had acted like "what Dickens's Sam Weller called 'harbitrary gents.' "[39] The government had promised to use the Emergency Powers Act circumspectly, but used it to pass an order-in-council for the control of shipping only a day or so before introducing amendments to the Canada Shipping Act.[40] When even two Liberals objected, C.D. Howe maintained "we did the right thing and we did it without debate about it." There was also the suspicion that senior "civil servants, unintentionally or otherwise, [had] lost their proper perspective as *public* servants in their zealous services to a party."[41] Prolonged rule by one party does tend to have this effect, but Brooke Claxton might have rendered it a little less obvious by not permitting his deputy minister, C.M. Drury, to make a public reply to a journalist's criticism. Still, in the widely-diffused prosperity of 1953, an apathetic public seemed not a whit interested in such matters.

The Liberals had other things working in their favour in addition to Uncle Louis. Their national organization seemed just as formidable under Duncan MacTavish as it had been under Gordon Fogo in 1949. Campaign funds presented no problem, perhaps because most of the companies that had received defence contracts had "been invited to express their gratitude in tangible form,"[42] and few had failed to respond. In contrast, the Conservative organization creaked badly and, although Richard Bell had returned to the party's central office, its headquarters was badly undermanned. No longer able to count on the financial support of business interests, it was desperately short of money. However, it suffered even more from its opponents' ability to capitalize on their role as creators of the welfare state. Beneficiaries throughout the country simply said: "We won't take chances with another party."[43] Yet the Liberals, by maintaining disinflationary policies during inflationary times to a degree which the *Economist* said would have been regarded as reactionary in England, had also kept the good opinion of business interests.

Indeed, it could be said of the Liberal party under St. Laurent, just as under King, that "no one party has managed to establish itself so broadly across the centre of politics." Governing Canada may be likened to doing a tightrope act: those in office are responsible for reconciling differences, while the opposition has the task of attacking the government's reconciliation without offending any interest more than the government has done. "To get the tightrope walker off his tightrope and calmly take his place in the circumstances of 1953," said the *Economist*, "is a feat which requires either a clumsy tightrope walker or an element of the magical in his substitutes."[44] But if anyone had magic qualities in 1953 it was the Prime Minister himself. Also, for one who lacked experience in the art of politics, he had shown himself surprisingly adept in tightrope walking. Indeed, it was his chief rival whom commentators accused of attempting to score short-term insignificant points instead of keeping his eyes on long-term goals, and of thereby failing to present himself as an acceptable alternative.

By 1953 the C.C.F. was tacitly admitting it was not an alternative to the Liberals and conceding its minor party status. At an inspirational meeting of party workers, all Coldwell would say was, "We're going to have a very good group in the next house."[45] To persuade wavering supporters that the C.C.F. votes would not be wasted, the party speakers could do little more than recount the gains – starting with old age pensions – that had been conceded by the old parties under the kind of pressure that only the C.C.F. could exert.

Under these circumstances the election results were hardly surprising, either regionally or over all. Not even a provincial victory in New Brunswick a year earlier helped the Conservatives much, for although they did regain the traditionally Conservative riding of Saint John, that win was counterbalanced by the loss in Nova Scotia of Colchester-Hants, where the sitting member, a Stanfield, did not choose to re-offer. The benefits of union with Canada served to mute the anti-Confederation sentiment in Newfoundland, and the Liberals took the 2 St. John's seats as well as the 5 outport ridings. Drew's stand on tax rental agreements was not popular in the Atlantic provinces, but it was hardly needed to explain his party's bad showing in the area.

The Conservatives also did poorly in Quebec, where their stand against centralization might have been calculated to win votes and where even Liberal newspapers had been expressing displeasure with the government before the election. Yet little else should have been expected. For although Drew had had some success in his efforts to learn French, he still appeared, or could be made to appear, "like the perfect Canadian pattern of the old fashioned imperialist of the school of Kipling who regarded all people of non-British blood as lesser breeds without the law." In contrast, "racial pride in Mr. St. Laurent's high role [was] strong and deep, often tinged with genuine affection."[46] In English Montreal the Conservatives had never recovered from the defection of the *Star*. In French Quebec Drew suffered because he had no French-Canadian lieutenant of stature and because all attempts to enlist Duplessis's active support had met with failure. Unwilling to risk loss of prestige as an unsuccessful champion of Drew, the

Quebec Premier went on holiday after his substantial by-election victories of July 9. As in 1949, the U.N. organizers were allowed to participate in the federal election just as they pleased. Largely because of them, the Conservatives raised their share of the popular vote from 24.6 to 29.4 per cent, but this permitted them to add only Dorchester and Quebec West to the 2 seats they had won in 1949.

Some commentators loudly proclaimed that the efforts to woo Duplessis backfired strongly in Ontario. However, this is a dubious judgment. Certainly the warnings against a Drew-Duplessis alliance were not pursued as vigorously as four years earlier, and other factors could account for the voters' behaviour. Premier Leslie Frost, who had done Drew no good by entering into a tax rental agreement with Ottawa, remained as neutral as a Conservative Premier of Ontario could be. Convinced that the Ontario electorate had decided it was not time for a change, he had no desire to injure his own prestige. Perhaps, then, the Conservatives were fortunate to raise their popular vote from 37.4 to 40.3 per cent, and to pick up 8 additional seats scattered throughout the province. As for the C.C.F., their vote in Toronto and York County fell from 116,911 to 86,533 and their popular vote in the whole province from 15.2 to 11.1 per cent. Joseph Noseworthy from York South and Claire Gillis from Cape Breton South remained the only C.C.F. members east of the Prairies.

In Manitoba the *Winnipeg Free Press* attacked Drew strongly for favouring tax arrangements which would let Ontario retain all the advantages it derived from being the headquarters of the major corporations, and "the seed of arguments and charges like these [did] not fall on stony ground" in western Canada.[47] Still, the Liberals lost 4 of their 12 seats in Manitoba: 2 to the Conservatives and 2 through redistribution. Saskatchewan, however, gave them an even worse jolt. Their mishandling of an epidemic of foot-and-mouth disease in 1952, their refusal to embark on the South Saskatchewan irrigation project, and the tumbling of wheat prices shortly before the election could not but hurt them. In such circumstances the politically dexterous J.G. Gardiner was powerless to resist the strong campaign waged by the C.C.F. provincial administration. Not surprisingly, the Liberals dropped 9 seats: 6 to the C.C.F. and 3 through redistribution.

In the two western provinces Social Credit put up a strong fight. Earlier it had threatened to provide nation-wide competition, but in the end it nominated only 72 candidates, all but 10 of them in western Canada. In Alberta, where a flourishing oil industry rather than St. Laurent got credit for the boom, Social Credit took 1 seat from the Liberals. In British Columbia, where the old-line parties were provincially in eclipse, the Social Credit party constituting the government and the C.C.F. the official opposition, everything was "fluidity and confusion."[48] The outcome was that Social Credit gained 4 seats and the C.C.F. 4, while the Liberals lost 3.

	Seats	Candidates					Elected									
		P.C.	L.	C.C.F.	S.C.	O.	P.C.	%	L.	%	C.C.F.	%	S.C.	%	O.	%
Newfoundland	7	7	7	1		1			7	100.0						
Nova Scotia	12	12	12	5		1	1	8.3	10	83.3	1	8.3				
New Brunswick	10	10	10	7	1	1	3	30.0	7	70.0						
Prince Edward Island	4	4	4	1			1	25.0	3	75.0						
Quebec	75	71	75	29		53	4	5.3	66	88.0					5	6.7
Ontario	85	85	84	65	9	36	33	38.8	51	60.0	1	1.2				
Manitoba	14	14	14	10	8	10	3	21.4	8	57.1	3	21.4				
Saskatchewan	17	15	17	17	14	9	1	5.9	5	29.4	11	64.7				
Alberta	17	12	17	13	17	13	2	11.8	4	23.5			11	64.7		
British Columbia	22	16	22	22	22	18	3	13.6	8	36.4	7	31.8	4	18.2		
Yukon and N.W.T.	2	2	2		1	1			2	100.0						
Total	265	248	264	170	72	143	51	19.2	171	64.5	23	8.7	15	5.7	5	1.9

Elected by
 acclamation Que. (2): L. (2).
Others elected: Que. (5): I. (3); I.L. (2).
Others (votes
 polled): Nfld. (1): I. (1) 4,459.
  N.S. (1): L.P.P. (1) 794.
  N.B. (1): I.L. (1) 4,317.
  Que. (53): I.L. (17) 58,001; I. (6) 46,532; L.P.P. (25) 10,819; Nat. (1) 7,496; Anti-Comm. (1) 333; I.P.C. (3) 1,636.
  Ont. (36): L.P.P. (29) 18,414; other L. (1) 5,321; I. (3) 6,337; Christian L. (1) 1,505; I.L. (1) 216; Lab.-Soc. (1) 130.
  Man. (10): L.P.P. (7) 6,194; I.L. (2) 1,361; I. (1) 141.
  Sask. (9): L.P.P. (9) 3,906.
  Alta. (13): L.P.P. (12) 9,155; I. (1) 275.
  B.C. (18): L.P.P. (17) 10,340; I.S.C. (1) 422.
 Yukon and N.W.T. (1): I. (1) 421.

	Popular Vote									Total
P.C.	%	L.	%	C.C.F.	%	S.C.	%	O.	%	
31,060	28.1	74,357	67.2	707	0.6			4,459	4.0	110,583
133,498	40.1	176,554	53.0	22,357	6.7			794	0.2	333,203
93,450	41.9	117,619	52.7	6,769	3.0	931	0.4	4,317	1.9	223,086
31,836	48.0	33,874	51.1	552	0.8					66,262
454,052	29.4	944,071	61.0	23,833	1.5			124,817	8.1	1,546,773
772,691	40.3	893,155	46.6	212,224	11.1	5,427	0.3	31,923	1.7	1,915,420
73,644	27.0	109,775	40.2	64,402	23.6	17,260	6.3	7,696	2.8	272,777
41,538	11.7	133,493	37.7	156,406	44.2	18,810	5.3	3,906	1.1	354,153
49,450	14.5	118,941	35.0	23,573	6.9	138,847	40.8	9,430	2.8	340,241
66,426	14.1	145,570	30.9	125,487	26.6	123,278	26.1	10,762	2.3	471,523
1,934	26.7	3,898	53.8			998	13.8	421	5.8	7,251
1,749,579	31.0	2,751,307	48.8	636,310	11.3	305,551	5.4	198,525	3.5	5,641,272

The Liberals had 22 fewer seats in a House enlarged from 262 to 265 members. None the less, it was a decisive victory for them. The Conservatives gained 10 members compared with 1949, but actually only 4 more than at dissolution. The C.C.F.'s 10 gains were all made in Saskatchewan and British Columbia; the Social Credit's 5, in Alberta and British Columbia. The electoral system once again illustrated the Biblical truth: "to him who hath shall be given, and from him who hath not shall be taken away, even that which he hath."[49] Thus the Liberals' 48.8 per cent of the vote gave them 64.5 per cent of the seats, while the Conservatives, with a popular vote of 31.0 per cent, won only 19.2 per cent of the seats. Professor Underhill wondered why the C.C.F., as a reforming party, did not raise its voice in protest. But then he remembered that it had its own "delusions of grandeur"; that the British Labour party – itself a beneficiary of the "first-past-the-post" system – accepted the status quo, and that the C.C.F., "in good, colonial tradition," followed its lead. That Canadians' opposition to p.r. (proportional representation) stemmed largely from their suspicion of coalition government amused him, for the coalition of groups in the Liberal party as engineered by King and St. Laurent was the most formidable in the country's history, although admittedly it had been built up before the election. "What we really mean is that we don't like coalitions among political groups formed by their leaders after the election."[50]

For the first time a party had won five elections in a row. The ills and grievances that had accumulated against the Liberals over a span of eighteen years had little effect in 1953. The results led Professor J.E. Hodgetts to wonder if such longevity tended to "encourage a fatalistic acceptance of the entrenched party as a well-worn but acceptable fixture –

something like the ruler-pigs in Orwell's *Animal Farm*."[51] They also caused Professor Underhill to ask if a new pattern of federalism was developing in Canada. Previously, when the governing party in Ottawa had lost control of the provinces, its days were numbered. By 1949 the governments of Ontario, Quebec, Saskatchewan, and Alberta were not in Liberal hands. Since that time British Columbia had fallen to Social Credit and New Brunswick to the Conservatives. Only provinces with a combined population of 2 million people remained under Liberal control. But St. Laurent sailed blithely on, and "this ancient sword of Damocles seems to have vanished into the air." Apparently Quebec was not alone in wanting a provincial government independent of political ties with Ottawa, one that could negotiate or fight with the federal government as it pleased. Were most Canadians suffering from a form of schizophrenia? Would the end result be that "we shall keep the Liberals permanently in office at Ottawa — to save us from the provincial-rights governments whom we elect in our ten provinces to save us from the Liberals [at Ottawa]"?[52]

Professor Underhill had some practical suggestions as well. Because Canada was condemned to further domination by one party, would it not be well to provide the opposition with a "brains trust" so that it could do its job more effectively? Could Canadians not undertake studies like the Nuffield Studies at Oxford in order to determine how various groups of the community vote and why they vote as they do? Why should not some Canadian motor magnate endow similar psephological studies in this country?[53] Without such assistance, Professor John Meisel of Queen's did make a study of the relationship between religious affiliation and electoral behaviour in Kingston in the federal election of 1953. He found that while "the members of the two largest Protestant denominations supported the Conservatives in greater numbers than did the population as a whole," Roman Catholics voted overwhelmingly Liberal.[54] If his findings are generally applicable, it may well be that Catholics were primarily responsible for keeping the Liberals in office. In the absence of more general studies, however, this can only be conjecture.

When it comes to class voting, the student has little to go on other than the inferences he can draw from occasional surveys of the Canadian Institute of Public Opinion. Even this sketchy information seems to make it clear that the association of social class and voting behaviour is lower in Canada than in any of the other Anglo-American countries. "Class interests," says Professor Robert Alford, "have been cross-cut by so many other politically relevant cleavages — sectional, religious, ethnic — that they have not emerged as the chief basis for political loyalties."[55]

The electorate was apathetic in 1953. Despite an increasing population, 200,000 fewer voters went to the polls than in 1949 — most of the drop occurring in Quebec, Ontario, and Manitoba — and the turnout fell from 74 to 67 per cent. What interest there was centred on the leaders and their

Twenty-second

meetings. The use of modern advertising techniques in electioneering made this inevitable. Admen, not wishing to spread their sales pitch too thin, concentrated on the big names. Interestingly enough, whether they sold St. Laurent or he sold himself, the average voter knew next to nothing about the "father figure." They could say that "he's a fine gentleman, and he was born in Quebec, he used to be a lawyer, and he's got a large family,"[56] but little more. Yet, apparently he could go on winning elections as long as he liked. As Professor Hodgetts put it, the only certain thing about an election in the United States was its date, while in Canada that was the only uncertain thing.[57]

FOOTNOTES

1. Halifax *Chronicle-Herald*, June 13, 1953.

2. F.H. Underhill, "Notes on the August Elections," *Canadian Forum*, XXXIII (September, 1953), p. 121.

3. Halifax *Chronicle-Herald*, July 20, 1953.

4. John A. Stevenson, "The Ottawa Letter," *Saturday Night*, LXVIII (July 11, 1953), p. 10.

5. *Ibid.*, (June 6, 1953), p. 16.

6. Halifax *Chronicle-Herald*, July 3, 1953.

7. "Canadian Tories – I," *Economist*, CLXIX (December 12, 1953), p. 824.

8. Halifax *Chronicle-Herald*, June 23, 1953.

9. Stevenson, "The Ottawa Letter," *Saturday Night*, LXVIII (July 11, 1953), p. 10.

10. *Ibid.*, (August 15, 1953), p. 10.

11. *Ibid.*, (July 11, 1953), p. 10.

12. F.H. Underhill, "How to Vote," *Canadian Forum*, XXXIII (July, 1953), p. 76.

13. "Canadian Tories – I," p. 824.

14. Halifax *Chronicle-Herald*, June 24, 1953.

15. *Ibid.*, July 23, 1953.

16. *Ibid.*, June 24, 1953.

17. *Ibid.*, June 26, 1953.

18. *Ibid.*, July 23, 1953.

19. *Ibid.*, July 1, 1953.

20. *Ibid.*, July 15, 1953.

21. *Ibid.*, August 8, 1953.

22. *Ibid.*, August 1, 1953.

23. *Ibid.*, June 20, 1953.

24. Dale C. Thomson, *Louis St. Laurent: Canadian* (Toronto: The Macmillan Company of Canada, 1967), p. 343.

25. Halifax *Chronicle-Herald*, July 17, 1953.

26. *Ibid.*, July 24, 1953.

27. *Ibid.*, July 13, 1953.

28. *Ibid.*, July 20, 1953.

29. *Ibid.*, July 7, 1953.

30. *Ibid.*, July 17, 1953.

31. *Ibid.*, August 6, 1953.

32. *Ibid.*, July 7, 1953.

33. *Ibid.*, July 30, 1953.

34. *Ibid.*, July 16, 1953.

35. "The General Election," *Round Table*, XLIII (September, 1953), pp. 404-406.

36. "The Liberals Win in Canada," *Economist*, CLXVIII (August 15, 1953), p. 437.

37. Halifax *Chronicle-Herald*, July 13, 1953.

38. J. E. Hodgetts, "The Coming Federal Elections," *Queen's Quarterly*, LX (Summer, 1953), p. 202-203.

39. Stevenson, "The Ottawa Letter," *Saturday Night*, LXVIII (May 23, 1953), p. 14.

40. *Ibid.*, (May 9, 1953), p. 14.

41. Hodgetts, "Coming Federal Elections," p. 204.

42. Stevenson, "The Ottawa Letter," *Saturday Night*, LXVIII (June 6, 1953), p. 16.

43. *Ibid.*, (August 22, 1953), p. 10.

44. "Canadian Tories – II," *Economist*, CLXIX (December 19, 1953), p. 897.

45. Leo Zakuta, *A Protest Movement Becalmed: A Study of Change in the C.C.F.* (Toronto: University of Toronto Press, 1964), p. 85.

46. Stevenson, "The Ottawa Letter," *Saturday Night*, LXVIII (July 25, 1953), p. 10.

47. *Ibid.*, (August 1, 1953), p. 10.

48. *Ibid.*, (August 8, 1953), p. 10.

49. Hodgetts, "Coming Federal Elections," pp. 200-201.

50. Underhill, "Notes," p. 124.

51. Hodgetts, "Coming Federal Elections," p. 199.

52. Underhill, "How to Vote," p. 76.

53. Underhill, "Notes," p. 125.

54. See John Meisel, "Religious Affiliation and Electoral Behaviour: A Case Study," *Canadian Journal of Economics and Political Science*, XXII (November, 1956), pp. 481-96.

55. Robert -R. Alford, *Party and Society* (Chicago: Rand McNally & Company, 1963), p. 101.

56. *Saturady Night*, LXVIII (August 22, 1953), p. 1.

57. Hodgetts, "Coming Federal Elections," p. 199.

Twenty-third
General Election

THE ELECTORS SHOOT SANTA CLAUS

The election of 1957 appeared to justify Peter Regenstreif's description of "luxury election," since it was held in a period of relative calm, economic prosperity, and stabilized international relations.[1] It did not seem an appropriate time for the voters to shoot Santa Claus. The outcome would depend on how well the old master, Louis St. Laurent—now in his seventy-sixth year—could re-create the character of Uncle Louis. To Liberal back-benchers he had attained a status approximating that of a divinity. When Davie Fulton criticized him early in 1955 they treated it almost as *lèse-majesté* and drew the Ottawa *Journal*'s rejoinder that there was "nothing sacrosanct, no human perfectionism hedged by divinity, in a prime minister."[2] The *Journal* had no need to fear, for as the election of 1953 receded, the genuine St. Laurent completely supplanted Uncle Louis. The new mood of the Commons accounted in part for this change.

It began when the government sought, in its amendments to the Defence Production Act, to assume extraordinary powers on a permanent basis. In June and July of 1955 a determined filibuster gave George Drew his first major victory in the Commons. This was the prelude to the pipeline debate (in which the government used closure four times to push its Northern Ontario Pipeline Crown Corporation bill through Parliament) and the events of June 1, 1956, "Black Friday." On that day the Commons almost dissolved in chaos when the Speaker refused to listen to points of order and had the division bells rung instead. As Coldwell, Drew, and their followers advanced angrily upon him, the Liberals sang: "There'll always be a pipeline" and "We've been working on a pipeline." It was, said the Ottawa *Journal*, "the wildest tumult Parliament ever had seen."[3]

At best the government was utterly ham-fisted in getting the bill through Parliament. Long accustomed to dominating the Commons by the sheer weight of numbers, it discovered, when the chips were down, that it had no one to cope with Stanley Knowles and Davie Fulton in arguing points of parliamentary procedure. Through it all the Prime Minister sat sphinx-like, seemingly appalled at what he saw, unable or unwilling to exert moral or any other kind of authority. Because the pipeline bill, like the amendments to the Defence Production Act, was C.D. Howe's, he could be charged with further contempt of the democratic process.

Silent during the pipeline debate, St. Laurent was given to frequent outbursts of temper in the pre-election session of 1957. According to Michael Barkway, he "rose to the most improbable and outrageous questions . . . sometimes sputtering with anger, sometimes saying things that had to be explained away afterward as meaning something quite different."[4] He did himself no good among stout Anglo-Saxons when, in reference to Anglo-French intervention in Suez, he said the day was long past when the supermen of Europe – and that included the leaders of Britain – could conduct international affairs just as they pleased. When he opened his campaign, however, "he and his advisers seemed to feel that all that was necessary was to place on exhibition once more that familiar (to voters only) figure of the kindly patriarch – an uncle perhaps, or a grandfather – radiating kindliness and good fellowship and preaching the soothing syrup doctrine that Canadians had never had it so good."[5]

This time he had his troubles even with children. At Port Hope, as he gave his patented lecture on Canadian history, a couple of them sat at his feet pulling at his trouser cuffs, two stuck old box cameras in his face, and six or seven played tag behind him. Exasperated, he told them that, if they did not want to learn about their country, they would be the losers, "for it's going to be yours to worry about an awful lot longer than it's going to be mine."[6]

Another new experience for him – and one which no father-figure should have to endure – was heckling. His worst moment came in the closing days of the campaign at Maple Leaf Gardens, the scene of some of his greatest triumphs, when sixteen-year-old William Hatton of Malton slowly and deliberately tore up a picture of St. Laurent almost in his face. When a Liberal official grappled with the boy, he tumbled off the platform and landed with a distinct crack on the concrete floor below. The Liberal election campaign ended with a bang, but not the kind of bang its organizers wanted.

Years of office had left its mark on the Liberal party. Its top policy-making committee – the Advisory Council of 236 members – had met only once between the 1953 and 1957 elections: evidence of the "enormous gulf separating fact from fiction concerning the locus of decision-making authority."[7] During the campaign itself, according to the Ottawa *Journal*, the Liberal hucksters thought it old-fashioned for a government with 22 years of office behind it to give an account of its stewardship. Accordingly they tried to present St. Laurent much as they would Gary Cooper or Grace Kelly.[8] The audiences were never as captivated as they were in 1949 and 1953.

Like many fading actors, Uncle Louis started overdoing the part. He kissed too many babies, patted too many little heads, propounded too many platitudes. The press and the crowds began to complain that a prime minister should have something positive to say about current problems.[9]

St. Laurent himself recognized that it was not 1949 or 1953. Beginning at Owen Sound in mid-May he dropped his paternalistic attitude and engaged in genuine debate with Premier Frost of Ontario on federal-provincial relations. Nevertheless, he found it hard to "elbow Uncle Louis's soothing platitudes off the stage,"[10] and soon the newspapers were complaining once again that "never once did he defend with anything like documented argument the actions and record of his government."[11]

The Canadian mood had changed in 1957, at least in English Canada. Could the new Conservative leader capitalize on it? On the advice of his doctor, George Drew had made his "heart-breaking decision" to resign in the fall of 1956. In December John Diefenbaker defeated Donald Fleming and Davie Fulton for the leadership on the first ballot. Paradoxically, a convention which, more than any before it, was designed to be fully bilingual, succeeded in alienating much of the Quebec delegation. *Le Devoir* had earlier uttered its warning that Diefenbaker would be unacceptable because he had never shown any sympathy for French Canada.[12] Hence, to depart from the practice of having a French Canadian either move or second a candidate's nomination, however that course was justified, might have seemed altogether foolhardy. But that is exactly what Diefenbaker did. The result could have been anticipated. Just before the convention was to vote, Henri Courtemanche led a throng of Quebec delegates in the chant: "Jean est mort. John is dead." Later, as the new leader began his acceptance speech, many Quebeckers left the Coliseum. The newspaperman John Bird summed it up this way: "For Quebec . . . the Convention chose the candidate with the weakest appeal. But for the rest of the country it chose the best vote-getter."[13]

One academic, A. Vixen, thought it tragic that the Conservative party, try as it might, could not free itself from its Anglo-Saxon personality; this inhibition was slowly fossilizing the party in a country becoming increasingly less Anglo-Saxon. In Vixen's view, Diefenbaker himself, despite the accident of name, gave "every indication of possessing the annoying Anglo-Saxon faculty of being oblivious to any other group."[14] This was not the Diefenbaker that H.S. Ferns saw. Instead of being a man of the Establishment as Drew was, Ferns said he was perhaps the first genuine outsider since Laurier. In many respects he was a man in a minority: a man with a non-Anglo-Saxon name in a predominantly Anglo-Saxon party; a Conservative in a Liberal or Socialist province; a lawyer in a small town away from the centre of big business; a Baptist in a country where most people are Catholic, United, or Anglican; a man with a law degree from a prairie college in a nation where the leading bureaucrats get their degrees from big-name universities.[15] As it turned out, the varied views of Bird, Vixen, and

Ferns became highly significant at different times and under changing circumstances.

Once the election was announced, the Conservative national campaign became a one-man show. "The posters of party rallies [hailed] John Diefenbaker; only the small print [identified] him as a Progressive Conservative."[16] Unintentionally St. Laurent played into the Conservatives' hands. When he complained because they were not campaigning under their own name, the Conservative national director and campaign manager, Allister Grosart, sent a copy of his remarks in a plain envelope to every Liberal candidate, and was gratified to find them being woven into his opponents' speeches. His political enemies were led to make the very point he was striving to drive home: Diefenbaker was, in effect, leading a new party, not an old one with a repellent image.[17]

The debate between St. Laurent and Diefenbaker evoked much that was reminiscent of 1949 and 1953. This was especially true of their exchanges on federal-provincial financial relations. This time, however, Premier Frost intervened vigorously against the federal government. As usual, the Prime Minister insisted that all Canadians had to be made to feel that they were not penalized for living in a particular province. Because equalization grants helped to create such a feeling in the have-not provinces, they were essential to national unity. Beware, he said, of an understanding between Diefenbaker and Frost which would threaten their very existence.[18] The Conservative leader called this another instance of trying to set province against province, and thereby to divide and rule. "The only deal I will ever make," he said, "is for the betterment of the average Canadian." Whereas the Liberals had adopted a dictatorial attitude towards the provinces, the Conservatives, as the party of Confederation, would cease to make centralizing attacks upon them. They would convene a federal-provincial conference at which the municipalities would be represented and would see to it that the provinces and municipalities were allowed a greater share of the national tax dollar.[19]

Above all else, St. Laurent stressed a basic tenet of the "Liberal interpretation of Canadian history" – only the Liberals were truly representative of the Canadian people and were capable of forming a majority government. "No one wants a one-party state," he said, "but . . . there is only one party which has sufficient strength in every province to assure the country a stable government and that party is the Liberal party." And again: "Do we want a Parliament, like the French parliament, where bargains have to be made between various groups in order to form unstable majorities and where governments change every few months?"[20] In any case, were not the last four years "generally the best ever experienced in Canada"? Had not "our sense of belonging to one Canada . . . grown stronger and stronger"? Were the Liberals not entitled to adopt the slogan "Unity,

by Reidford. The Globe and Mail, *Toronto, May 3, 1957. Courtesy of* The Globe and Mail, *Toronto.*

Security, Freedom"?[21] The Conservatives said it was time for a change; "what kind of a change do they want? Do they want to increase rather than reduce taxes? Do they want to change Canada's growing social welfare program? Do they want to promote federal treasury deficits rather than surpluses?"[22]

In the quiet contentment of 1949 and 1953 an appeal to maintain the status quo had been good enough. It might not be so in the changed mood of 1957. Everything would depend on the kind of appeal the Conservatives made. They had on hand the resolutions adopted by their leadership convention of December 1956. Yet "no attempt was made to give [them] a permanent form and they were not used, as such, in the campaign."[23] Instead, Diefenbaker adopted many of the convention's resolutions one at a time as part of an over-all strategy. As a result, he made news not once, but on several occasions; obtained maximum publicity in the areas in which it did him the most good; and identified himself rather than the party with the resolutions. "The suppression of the convention resolutions was, therefore, another instance of the party attempting to acquire a new physiognomy and of the campaign being linked more to the Conservative leader than to the party."[24]

Diefenbaker concentrated especially on the "average" Canadian discontented with the status quo. For the distressed Nova Scotian coal miner there would be "subventions . . . according to your request and to the demands of the people."[25] For the unhappy western farmer there would be a more realistic crop insurance plan, cash advances on farm-stored grain, and, above all, a system of flexible support prices to ensure a fair price-cost relationship. For the aggrieved old age pensioner there would be something more than the "20 cent a day measure" provided by Finance Minister Walter Harris in his budget. The commentators had said admiringly that, although Harris spread the electoral jam very thin, he had made incredibly good use of it in covering the multitude of voters it did.[26] In Diefenbaker's hands, however, the monthly increase of $6 was made to look like a pittance, not even equivalent to the rise in the cost of living, and it actually redounded to the government's disadvantage.

Tight money was another issue. High interest rates, said Diefenbaker, were having no effect on big business. It was the little man – the farmer, the fisherman, and the small businessman – who was being crushed.[27] Because of discrimination in the distribution of credit, the Maritimes and western Canada were suffering most. Why, he asked at Prince George, were there 3,000 people out of work in the area? Simply because high interest rates had reduced house-building and slowed down lumber operations. "If you've been Liberal in the past, don't you care what's been happening in this constituency? Don't you want your jobs back?"[28]

The abuse of the rights of Parliament, however, most suited Diefenbaker's oratorical talents. St. Laurent might say that the debate on the pipeline bill had been "nearly as long as the pipe-line itself and quite as full of another kind of natural gas."[29] He might accuse the opposition of being the real violators of the rights of Parliament, but Diefenbaker would have

Twenty-third

none of it. "Parliament," he contended, "was made a mockery [of] at the behest of a few American millionaires. . . . A modern Louis says the state is [C.D.] Howe . . ." If the government were to be returned, he warned, "don't ask the opposition to stand up for your rights, because there will be no rights left."[30]

None realized better than Diefenbaker that he had to present a positive side as well. He had been impressed by the suggestion of Dr. Merril W. Menzies that the Conservatives adopt a new national policy. Accordingly, he made Menzies his adviser on speeches dealing with policy, in consultation with Dr. Donald Eldon, the head of the party's research department in Ottawa.[31] To a very considerable degree, therefore, Menzies must be given credit for Diefenbaker's promise to undertake a vast scheme of national development in co-operation with the provinces. While this was clearly an attempt to propound a new dynamic policy that would capture the imagination of the voters, it was altogether lacking in specificity. Equally vague was an assurance that foreign investment would be directed to the maximum benefit of Canada. It led the politician St. Laurent to ask: "What are the Conservatives going to develop that we are not already developing?"[32] It led the academic Denis Smith to say that Diefenbaker's handy stockpile of phrases was "not illuminating [but] often obscure, superficial, contradictory, or meaningless."[33] The Ottawa *Journal*, on the other hand, maintained that an opposition could not be expected to "have a blueprint for this, that or the other thing." Had not Gladstone said: "Call us in, and we will prescribe"? Diefenbaker had provided an approach to problems on the basis of broad principles, which was all there should be.[34]

St. Laurent also criticized the Conservative leader for making promises which St. Laurent said would cost $1.5 billion to implement. An election promise, he warned, was "a mere cream-puff of a thing with more air than substance." As for himself, he would simply get along with the job of providing opportunity in all parts of Canada for Canadians. "The best is yet to be," he prophesied.[35] In his turn Diefenbaker charged the Liberals with making promises that would require an outlay of $750 million.[36] Although this may have been an exaggeration, the Liberals were not nearly so circumspect in the matter of promises as St. Laurent said they were.

In the final analysis, it was not so much what Diefenbaker said that mattered, but who he was and how he said what he had to say. Professor Michel Brunet showed that he had all the qualities required of a principal interpreter for Anglo-Canadians.[37] His non-English origin won favour among all the new Canadians assimilated into English Canada. His deep British convictions appealed to Canadians of Anglo-Saxon origin. He had lived in Ontario and he was a westerner. His great vitality impressed youth. His passionate eloquence and his evangelical style awakened familiar echoes among Protestants, and also permitted him an effective resort to righteous indignation against his opponents' treatment of Parliament.

Such qualities evoked little or no response in Quebec. There, the apathy was such that *Le Devoir* talked about "une campagne électorale au chloroforme."[38] Liberal propagandists dipped deeply into their bag of tricks to make Diefenbaker look bad in French-Canadian eyes. All they could come up with were thirty-year-old excerpts from Saskatchewan newspapers purporting to show he had opposed Catholic teaching in the public schools. He made certain, above all, that the Toronto *Star* could not conjure up the horrible apparition of an alliance with Duplessis. He made no effort to woo the Quebec Premier, and the latter's only comment on the campaign was a none too illuminating "I am sure the party that wins the largest number of seats will win."[39]

In no way whatever did Diefenbaker make special overtures to Quebec. He spent only enough time there to indicate that he was not neglecting it. He spoke just enough French—eight minutes out of fifty-five at Quebec City—to forestall any suggestion that he was not trying. Newspapermen were charitable enough to call his French understandable, but even if he had been more fluent, his evangelical type of presentation was more attuned to English than to French-Canadian ears. Also, the issue which he emphasized with greatest fervour and conviction, the degradation of Parliament, did not reach the same tap roots of deep political tradition that it did in English Canada.

In French Quebec, therefore, the election took on much the same character as the previous two. Once again the Conservatives were dependent on the Union Nationale. Special circumstances, closely bound up with the intricate mysteries of Quebec politics, determined the degree of U.N. intervention. It had to do with "collaboration." Where it was practised, a Liberal M.P. gave only token support to the Liberal provincial candidates within the confines of his federal constituency; in return the U.N. organization made no serious attempt to unseat the federal M.P. Because provincial Liberal leader Georges Lapalme denounced the practice so bitterly during the provincial election of 1956, he got more support than usual from the federal Liberals. Now, in 1957, the Union Nationale had a chance to wreak its vengeance.

The two cabinet ministers who had campaigned against collaboration faced the full onslaught of the Union Nationale. Hugues Lapointe lost out in Lotbinière, but provincial Solicitor General Antoine Rivard could not bring down Jean Lesage in Montmagny-L'Islet. J.D. Bégin, the chief organizer of the U.N., could not save Dorchester for his brother-in-law Robert Perron, nor could Antonio Talbot, the Minister of Roads, get Independents elected in Chicoutimi and Lapointe. On the other hand, the Conservative gains in Bonaventure, Gaspé, Nicolet-Yamaska, and St. Hyacinthe–Bagot were wholly attributed to the U.N. In these contests it used the same tactics it employed in provincial elections: Vote Conservative and get bridges, roads, and schools; vote otherwise and risk the stoppage of work already begun.[40]

In the end at least six provincial ministers had campaigned against the Liberals, and the U.N directed the anti-Liberal forces in twenty to thirty constituencies.

In the few largely Anglo-Saxon ridings the Conservatives were on their own. William Hamilton campaigned in Montreal Notre-Dame-de-Grâce much as he had in 1953, talking to small crowds at bus stops in the morning and canvassing from house to house in the evening.[41] He increased his majority sixfold. In the six seats on Montreal Island which came under his direction (all had large English-speaking populations) the Conservatives improved their position considerably and gained Jacques Cartier–Lasalle. They also showed greater strength in those Eastern Township ridings which still contained a considerable English-speaking residue, notably Brome-Missisquoi and Compton-Frontenac.

The Conservatives increased their Quebec contingent from 4 to 9, including the Independent-Conservative Henri Courtemanche. Yet they improved their popular vote by only 1.7 per cent. If their better showing in English Quebec and the more vigorous support of the U.N. are taken into account, it is obvious that French Quebec was not moved perceptibly by the considerations that operated so strongly in English Canada. Diefenbaker and what he stood for aroused no enthusiasm, and the St. Laurent image shone just as brightly as ever. Although the Liberal popular vote in Quebec fell by 3.4 per cent, the decline occurred largely because of the 24 Independent Liberals who polled 85,674 votes. At a time when a Liberal nomination was almost equivalent to election and a sitting Liberal, like an incumbent American president, was certain of renomination for another term, "it was tempting for those with political ambitions to try their luck as Liberal [candidates], albeit Independent [ones]."[42] If they won they would, after all, soon be recognized as bona-fide Liberals.

To the critical minds of *Le Devoir*, the political process in Quebec was just limping along; "une démocratie boiteuse," they called it. They complained especially about "le nombre substantiel de rates, de cancres . . . qui ont été élus à cause de la popularité du parti [libéral]."[43] Gérard Filion told the voters first, to get rid of "les Beaudry de St. Jacques, les Bonniers de St. Henri, les Denis de St. Denis" and then, to vote for the best candidate, whether Rouge, Bleu, or C.C.F. P. Vigeant wondered if Quebec's federal members would ever give strong support to a French-Canadian cause, so long as they belonged to a national party. Perhaps, he said, only a regional party could serve Quebec's interests.[44]

Markedly different forces were operating outside Quebec. Without being aware of it, English Canada may have wanted a leader belonging entirely to itself. It this is so, Diefenbaker's almost deliberate detachment from French Canada would have rendered him even more acceptable. "This phenomenon, described by Brunet as both a normal expression and a legitimate desire of English Canada, had operated before in the case of Laurier, who was saddened when he became its victim in his later years."[45]

The Conservative mastermind, Gordon Churchill, gave practical recognition to these circumstances in his memorandum of January 1954. He pointed out that in eight of the nine elections in which a government had been beaten, Ontario, the Maritimes, and western Canada had brought about the defeat; only in 1896 was Quebec the deciding factor. The moral was obvious. The party ought not to squander its resources on Quebec where it had been weak since 1891 and almost nonexistent since 1935. In a second memorandum in January 1956, Churchill pointed out more explicitly that of 190 seats outside Quebec the Conservatives held 49. The Conservatives could form a minority government by taking 60 of the remaining 141 seats in Ontario, the Maritimes, and western Canada, where good fights could be waged. "Quebec should not be ignored but it is extremely doubtful that Quebec will be decisive. The military maxim – reinforce success not failure – might well be considered as applicable to political strategy."[46]

This might have been one reason why Peter Regenstreif describes "the Conservative approaches to campaigning in the elections of 1957 and 1958 . . . as classics of ingenuity unequalled in Canadian political history."[47] He gave the credit to Grosart and Diefenbaker. Of course, if the circumstances had not been right, no tactics would have been of any avail. The circumstances were propitious, however, and the Conservative tacticians missed not a trick. Nevertheless, even after the event there was no consensus on the exact circumstances that moved English Canada. The Liberal Ottawa *Citizen* attributed the outcome to "the uneasy talk from the very shores of the Atlantic to the edge of the Pacific that the Liberals had been in too long." Once the collective mind is made up, it said, the electorate has no respect for persons and this time it rejected the ablest men in Canadian public life.[48] Grattan O'Leary of the rival Ottawa *Journal* insisted that time had taken its toll: "I couldn't throw a snowball on Sparks Street . . . without hitting someone as good as half the men they have in the cabinet now."[49]

Liberal Tom Kent thought the government had fallen because it had failed lamentably in explaining its record – the best in the democratic world – to the electorate.[50] This irritated H.S. Ferns, who said it reflected "the materialist, economic interpretation of Canadian politics which has come to influence much Liberal thinking; the assumption that 'Nobody's going to shoot Santa Claus.'" Canadians, he went on, were moved by things other than material interests. Had it not been Diefenbaker's function to show that they wanted to secure greater independence from the United States and to stop the progressive attenuation of the authority of Parliament?[51]

The Liberal Toronto *Star* felt it was best to admit everything. In its opinion the government had ceased to be liberal: witness the pipeline affair. It had also become too sure of its own wisdom and not sensitive enough to people's needs: witness the picayune increase in old age pensions.[52] Neutral observers tended to agree. Eugene Forsey held that a government which had exercised unchallenged power for so long could not resist the conviction that it had arrived at final truth and that it was always and wholly right.[53] St. Laurent, said the *Economist*, "could not be seriously compared to a Hapsburg monarch, nor C.D. Howe to a Metternich, but they and their colleagues exuded an air of established legitimism which made many Canadians itch to put them in their place."[54] Paul Fox felt that four million Canadians wanted to teach their masters a lesson. The Liberals were certain that a docile electorate would not risk its prosperity by voting against them. But this time "you've never had it so good" wore itself out as a winning slogan. The Liberals, like the Democrats in 1952, discovered that " 'no one loves his creditor', especially if he swaggers a bit."[55]

The observers, although certain that the very longevity of the government had much to do with its defeat, did not agree precisely on how the collective mind worked. They had no doubt, however, that Diefenbaker's talents were entirely suited to the circumstances. Much of what Diefenbaker said, when transcribed word for word, made little sense because he often failed to complete his sentences and moved from one idea to the next without indicating where one idea ended and the other began. "The communication, like that of a 'stream of consciousness' novel," wrote Professor Meisel, "was on several levels. Mr. Diefenbaker's speeches were full of words and expressions which undoubtedly released powerful emotions in the listeners. He often employed imagery which was highly evocative to anyone reared in the Christian faith. Indeed much of what Mr. Diefenbaker said had an apocalyptic aura about it."[56] Another observer said of him: "He preaches, he exhorts, he is the modern Jeremiah, the accusing conscience, the prosecutor, the jury lawyer, the man who is for 'human rights' in the corner of the 'little fellow.' "[57] To a third he had "a flair for the telling phrase and the same sort of evangelical fervour as a political crusader that a famous American politician, the late William Jennings Bryan, possessed."[58]

Diefenbaker played two roles that were closely intertwined. The first was his accustomed role of advocate before a jury: he contrived to make the election a jury trial of the St. Laurent government for high crimes in connection with the abuse of Parliament. The other—and perhaps the more important role—was that of the humble, outraged citizen who dared to aspire to the seats of the mighty, largely to chastise his opponents and restore the government to the people.[59] As the spokesman of discontent, "he was able to transfer the sympathy he personally had had in years past, as an underdog member of a party in the shade, to himself as leader of the party. He was the worthy but deprived man."[60]

Diefenbaker's personality was not impressed upon the country solely by the newspapers. This would have taken too much time and, in any case, newspapers depend on events. They did play an important part in the campaign, however. Even Liberal newspapermen had become a little disenchanted with the government over the pipeline affair. Then, "when Uncle Louis' campaign started out as just another baby-kissing job they reported it in merciless damning detail."[61] They also recounted fully Diefenbaker's campaign successes, especially his huge assemblages in British Columbia.

But more significant by far in impressing Diefenbaker the man upon the public was television. In Canada's first T.V. election the Conservatives took advantage of what Alan Thomas has called the "curiously constructed policy of the C.B.C.," which permits only the short, frequent presentation of principals and thereby prevents any thorough discussion of the issues.

> The Conservatives did not confuse the situation by featuring their lesser stars; the major impact of their television shows and public meetings was Mr. Diefenbaker's. There were no distractions from the aspect of the crusader, and the lesser lights merely pointed up his mien and occasionally basked in his reflected glory. . . . Thus the audacity, incredible energy, courage and intensity of Mr. Diefenbaker became the overwhelming centre of attention.[62]

Television demonstrated, above all, that this time there was an alternative to the Liberals. In contrast, the Prime Minister took a dislike to television because of his feeling that its programmes were carefully planned performances similar to stage shows. Hence, although he made three television broadcasts during the campaign, he "read his text with scarcely a glance at the camera, and he looked much older than usual."[63]

The nature of the election was such as to focus attention on the leaders of the old parties. Under these circumstances the smaller parties had difficulty. Social Credit, which aimed to establish itself in eastern Canada, ran 40 candidates in Ontario, up from 9 in 1953. But the much-touted rally in Massey Hall with which it inaugurated its campaign was a dismal failure and the party hardly caught on at all in Ontario.

A year earlier, apparently moved by the affluence of the fifties, the C.C.F. decided that a "re-interpretation" of the principles of the Regina Manifesto was desirable. Its Winnipeg Declaration of 1956 constituted a significant shift to the right, especially in its attitude towards private enterprise. It stated that a C.C.F. government would insist on public ownership only where it was needed to break the stranglehold of private monopolies and facilitate social planning. Elsewhere there would be appropriate opportunities for private business to make a useful contribution to the development of the economy.[64] In the campaign of 1957, however, M.J. Coldwell continued to emphasize specific ameliorative measures rather than theoretical considerations. In particular, he advocated a programme of 100 per cent parity prices for the farmer and measures to counteract the inflation that benefited nobody but a few privileged groups. This time he found it difficult to make the headlines; they went to the leader of the official opposition.

Statistically, says John Meisel, the chances are nearly 99 to 1 that the election results of 1957 indicate a direct causal connection between the increase in the size of the electorate in any constituency and the increase in the Conservative vote. Accordingly, he propounds the hypothesis that Diefenbaker's aggressive style and his promise of a vigorous developmental policy had "a greater appeal to the more expansionist and 'go ahead' communities than to the sleepier and less alive ones."[65] It could also be argued that some of the Conservative success in the areas peopled by New Canadians was attributable to the special attention which George Drew had accorded them.

Nevertheless, there is a simpler and more meaningful way of interpreting the election results. What really mattered was the substantial shift of voters to the Conservatives outside of Quebec, a shift that was generally strong enough to swing those seats which before 1935 had a substantial core of Conservative voters and which normally elected Conservatives when that party was winning elections. In such seats the Liberal party had been getting most of the marginal voters since 1935 because the Conservatives seemed such a distasteful alternative. Although these voters had come to be regarded as part of the Liberal "majority" in the country, they had actually not developed fixed habits of party allegiance and in 1957 they proved it.[66]

In the country as a whole the Conservatives' proportionate increase in the share of the popular vote was 25.5 per cent. By provinces the analogous increases were:

Newfoundland	34.5	Quebec	5.8	Saskatchewan	98.3
Nova Scotia	25.7	Ontario	21.1	Alberta	90.3
Prince Edward		Manitoba	33.0	British Columbia	131.2
Island	9.0				
New Brunswick	16.2				

These increases, though extraordinarily disparate, can be easily explained. In the four western provinces the Conservatives started from such a low base that even a modest improvement in their fortunes appeared to be of large proportions. In Prince Edward Island, where the percentage seems miniscule, it was actually substantial for a static rural population addicted to hereditary voting.

Ontario, as usual, led the way in a Conservative victory. "John Diefenbaker rightfully proclaimed a date with destiny," said the Toronto *Telegram*. "In this Province, Hon. Leslie Frost made it good."[67] The fact is, however, that Frost simply climbed on the anti-government bandwagon. In the closing days Paul Martin, Walter Harris, and C.D. Howe had scurried home to look after their own seats. Lester Pearson had become "the Liberals' hottest campaign commodity; everywhere candidates clamoured for him to 'help out . . . with a personal pitch.' "[68]

In Ontario's 85 constituencies the Conservatives improved their popular vote in all but Cochrane, Lambton West, and Port Arthur. With the exception of Trinity, Toronto became solid Tory Toronto once more. As the Toronto *Star* put it on June 11: "Toronto, this bright June morning, smiles only for Tories. The old girl seems to mean it, too."[69] Except for Trinity, Waterloo North, and Kingston, Liberal successes were confined to the peripheral areas: 5 seats in eastern Ontario where the French-Canadian vote was substantial, 2 in the Niagara Peninsula, 3 in the Windsor area, and 8 in Northern Ontario where Conservative strength had been ebbing since 1930. The voters in the north who wanted a change, as they did in Port Arthur, Timmins, and Timiskaming, turned to the C.C.F. Douglas Fisher of the C.C.F. became the biggest giant-killer of all when he toppled C.D. Howe.

In the Atlantic provinces John Diefenbaker played on the suspicion that the government had not taken enough interest in the region's rehabilitation, and the deprived succumbed to the spell of another who was deprived. Almost heaven-sent for the Conservatives was the *Preliminary Report of the Royal Commission on Canada's Economic Prospects*. Its suggestion that if the resources of the region did not permit a substantial rise in living standards its residents should be assisted to move elsewhere met with a cold reception. "In a region in which voting dispositions were already changing because of general discontent, the report acted as a powerful factor in helping the Conservatives back to power."[70]

Except for three isolated ridings in Newfoundland, the Conservatives improved their position in every seat in the Atlantic area. They won both St. John's East and West; took all of Prince Edward Island's seats for the first time since Confederation; and swept everything in Nova Scotia except Shelburne-Yarmouth-Clare and Inverness-Richmond, the two seats where the Acadian vote is substantial. Even in Acadian Clare they increased their proportion of the popular vote by 43.4 per cent. But because they had made a poor showing among the Acadians in 1953, they started from too low a base to topple the Liberals. Under the circumstances, New Brunswick might have been expected to divide along ethnic lines, but there were two exceptions. Largely French-speaking Restigouche-Madawaska went to Conservative J.C. Van Horne simply because he was Van Horne. Anglo-Saxon Charlotte, however, remained with the government party; it had steadily become more and more Liberal and would now change only in the event of a massive over-all swing.

On the Prairies, too, there was economic discontent. It was only natural that a farmer who was forced to finance the planting of a new crop while he still had unsold wheat on hand would feel dissatisfied. He was also aggrieved because, in terms of constant dollars, he was getting no more for his wheat than at the beginning of the hungry thirties. Not surprisingly, C.D. Howe faced the most hostile reception of his career at Morris, Manitoba. Premier Douglas Campbell of Manitoba, not wanting to be tainted with the sins of the federal Liberals, failed to put in an appearance when St. Laurent opened his campaign at Winnipeg. Meanwhile Conservative leader Duff Roblin was campaigning vigorously for Diefenbaker.

J.W. Dafoe was gone, but his successors on the *Free Press* documented in detail Diefenbaker's meetings with Frost and conjured up dire consequences for western Canada: "Prairie farmers, like wheat, cannot stand too much Frost." But the farmers of Manitoba did not heed the *Free Press*. Of their 8 seats in the last Parliament, the Liberals retained only St. Boniface with its heavy French population. They lost all of their 7 rural seats; the Conservatives took 5 and the C.C.F. took Selkirk and Springfield, where they had built up a strong nucleus of support and ran attractive candidates.

The farmers of Saskatchewan suffered from the same disabilities as those of Manitoba, but the Liberals had only 5 seats to lose in Saskatchewan. Yet although their popular vote fell from 37.7 to 30.3 per cent, they lost only 1 seat. There were only two changes: the Conservatives took Qu'Appelle from the Liberals and Saskatoon from the C.C.F. In both these ridings the Conservatives had residues of strength that they lacked elsewhere. Significantly, the Liberals had no success in Assiniboia, Rosetown-Biggar, Moose Jaw–Lake Centre, and Qu'Appelle, the ridings that contained most of the farm-stored grain. The most spectacular contest was waged in Assiniboia between Hazen Argue of the C.C.F. and Ross Thatcher of the Liberals, but formerly of the C.C.F. In a joint debate at Mossbank between Thatcher and C.C.F. Premier T.C. Douglas, the latter said of Thatcher: "We had him yesterday, you have him to-day, heaven help who has him to-morrow."[71]

A similar reaction against the Liberals in Alberta reduced their representation from 4 to 1. A French-Canadian Liberal took Athabaska which has a substantial French population. Social Credit picked up 2 of the Liberal seats, the Conservatives 1. Again, the Conservatives started from too low a base to win more seats, but the contests were close in Edmonton Strathcona and Bow River.

No province responded more actively to the cry of "it's time for a change" than did British Columbia. It was there that John Diefenbaker outdrew all others; it was there that the "Follow John" slogan made its appearance; it was there that British sentiment arrayed itself against the government. When St. Laurent praised Lester Pearson for the part he had played in devising the United Nations Emergency Force (UNEF), his audience in Victoria interrupted him with cries of "no, no," and asked: "Why did you vote with Russia at the U.N.?" Under these circumstances British Columbians turned to their old love: the Conservatives, a bad fourth in 1953, gained four seats and polled 50,000 votes more than any other party. Three of the gains were in the party's former areas of strength, but the fourth was in Vancouver Centre, where Douglas Jung increased the Conservative vote fivefold to beat Ralph Campney, the Minister of Defence.

Seldom has a tactician of victory diagnosed a political situation as well as Gordon Churchill. His party fell a little short of the 60 additional seats outside Quebec which he said it needed to form a minority government. But it did get 56 (16 in the Atlantic provinces, 28 in Ontario, and 12 in western Canada), and with the 5 seats it gained in Quebec it was able to assume office. Altogether it won 112 seats to the Liberals' 105 though it polled only 38.9 per cent of the vote to the Liberals' 40.9 per cent. Thus the bias in the electoral system which had operated persistently in favour of the Liberals for twenty-two years was suddenly reversed. Quebec behaved as usual: it gave 57.6 per cent of its vote and 82.7 per cent of its seats to the Liberals. But this time "the bias in the electoral system in Quebec could not compensate for an even greater bias against the Liberals in six of the other provinces."[72]

While the minor parties took a back seat during the campaign, they did not suffer on that account. The C.C.F. polled an additional 71,349 votes, most of it in Ontario; the Social Crediters an additional 131,112 votes, spread somewhat evenly among the 5 westernmost provinces. The 5 seats gained by the C.C.F. from the Liberals, 3 in northern Ontario and 2 in Manitoba, more that compensated for their 3 losses to the Conservatives, 1 each in Nova Scotia, southern Ontario, and Saskatchewan. Social Credit held on to its previous 15 seats and gained 2 from the Liberals in both Alberta and British Columbia. The evidence indicates that the electorate willingly availed itself of the most appropriate party to register its protest against the Liberals. According to one post-election survey, "of the persons who abandoned the Grits, 5.1 per cent did so because of the Suez crisis, 38.2 per cent because of the pipeline debate, 26.7 per cent because of the inadequate increase in the old age pension, and 30 per cent because it was 'time for a change.' "[73]

There were some who said that the electorate went further than it intended, that it wanted simply to punish and warn the Liberals, not to drive them out of office. But surely this is to attribute more to the collective mind than can legitimately be done. It is true, of course, that many who voted against the Liberals did not expect them to lose. There were others who pictured the electorate, in its mood of savage resentment against the government, as singling out members of the cabinet for extinction. While this may have occurred in the case of C.D. Howe, Stuart Garson, and Ralph Campney, the other six defeated ministers were simply caught up in the anti-government tide.

In any case it was a transformed House of Commons. Of the 112 Conservatives, 68 had not sat in the last Parliament, a state of affairs which added to the difficulty of forming a cabinet. Yet from one fact the Conservatives could derive great satisfaction. They, who had been dubbed an Anglo-Saxon party, were "now more representative of Canadians generally –except for French Canada–than [were] the Liberals. Their numbers [included] a Jung, a Jorgenson, a Mandziuk, a Kucherepa, and a Martini; a larger number of non-French Catholics than for many years past; and even more French Canadians than in any other election since 1930."[74] In contrast, 95 of the 105 Liberals had sat in the last House. Furthermore, the Parliamentary Guide indicates that 66 of them called French their mother tongue, and at least a dozen others represented seats with a substantial French population. But the Liberal party had not become a French party, as some observers said, since its popular vote was better distributed than the Conservative throughout all ten provinces.[75]

To put it mildly, the election confounded the prophets. *Maclean's*, forced to go to print some time before June 10, found itself in the embarrassing position of having commented on the re-election of "one of the most powerful governments ever created by the free will of a free electorate." The Toronto *Globe and Mail* delighted in labelling the Canadian Institute of Public Opinion a casualty of the election. This poll overestimated the Liberal popular vote by 7 per cent and underestimated the Conservative by 5 per cent. Nevertheless, it was still close, at least in Ontario, until its immediate pre-election forecast reversed the trend which it had indicated in the preceding months. Its director tried to explain its error away by saying this was "a time of yeasty indecision on the part of the voters,"[76] but there is no evidence to indicate that a substantial number of voters had reversed their opinions twice in the closing days of the campaign. Some newspaper reporters had "perceived many of the signs of political upheaval [but] mesmerized, like almost everyone else, by the feeling that the government was invincible, they were altogether too cautious. . . ."[77] When the public makes up its mind, it is not to be thwarted by a strong party organization and a full campaign chest.

The election of 1957 did more than challenge the myth that the Liberals had devised respecting their own unique contribution to the working of the Canadian political process. It also destroyed the notion that Canadians would be content with a Liberal government at Ottawa so long as they possessed a system of countervailing power in the provinces. This idea seemed to have been reinforced in 1956 when Nova Scotia went Conservative, leaving only Manitoba, Prince Edward Island, and Newfoundland with Liberal governments. But then came 1957, and the theory of countervailing power was invalidated. One thing the election of 1957 did not produce was an increase in class voting, for even if the Conservatives were to the left of the Liberals, the strong support they received from the lower income groups was hardly a class vote in the accepted sense. As Alford indicates, voting continued to be largely regional.[78]

The Toronto *Star*, after noting the absence of positive, detailed policies in Diefenbaker's programme, adapted Southey's "The Battle of Blenheim" to the occasion:

> *"And everybody praised the Dief*
> *Who did the great fight win."*
> *"But what good came of it at last?"*
> *Quoth little Peterkin:—*
> *"Why, that I cannot tell," said he*
> *"But 'twas a famous victory."*[79]

Time alone would tell what the victory meant.

	Seats	Candidates					Elected									
		P.C.	L.	C.C.F.	S.C.	O.	P.C.	%	L.	%	C.C.F.	%	S.C.	%	O.	%
Newfoundland	7	6	7	1			2	28.6	5	71.4						
Nova Scotia	12	12	12	6	1		10	83.3	2	16.7						
New Brunswick	10	10	10	2	2	1	5	50.0	5	50.0						
Prince Edward Island	4	4	4	3			4	100.0								
Quebec	75	69	75	22	4	43	9	12.0	62	82.7					4	5.3
Ontario	85	85	85	60	40	6	61	71.8	21	24.7	3	3.5				
Manitoba	14	14	14	14	14	4	8	57.1	1	7.1	5	35.7				
Saskatchewan	17	16	17	17	16	2	3	17.6	4	23.5	10	58.8				
Alberta	17	17	17	15	17	3	3	17.6	1	5.9			13	76.5		
British Columbia	22	22	22	22	21	4	7	31.8	2	9.1	7	31.8	6	27.3		
Yukon and N.W.T.	2	2	2						2	100.0						
Total	265	257	265	162	115	63	112	42.3	105	39.6	25	9.4	19	7.2	4	1.5

Notes: An I.P.C. elected in Quebec, unopposed by an official P.C. candidate, is placed in the P.C. columns.

An I.S.C. candidate in Ontario, unopposed by an official S.C. candidate, is placed in the S.C. columns.

Elected by
acclamation: Nfld. (1): L. (1).
Others elected: Que. (4): I.L. (2); I. (2).
Others (votes
polled): N.B. (1): I. (1) 3, 159.
Que. (43): I.L. (24) 85, 674; I.P.C. (4) 4,777; I. (11) 73,628; L.P.P. (3) 2,377; Capital Familial (1) 237.
Ont. (6): I.L. (1) 5,414; I.P.C. (1) 342; I. (1) 726; L.P.P. (2) 1,432; Lib.-Con. Coalition (1) 252.
Man. (4): I.L. (2) 2,378; I. (1) 205; L.P.P. (1) 1,579.
Sask. (2): L.P.P. (1) 212; I. (1) 122.
Alta. (3): I.S.C. (1) 386; I. (1) 212; L.P.P. (1) 815.
B.C. (4): I. (1) 259; L.P.P. (2) 1,345; Canadian Democrat (1) 628.

FOOTNOTES

1. Peter Regenstreif, "The Canadian General Election of 1958," *Western Political Quarterly*, XIII (June, 1960), p. 352.
2. Ottawa *Journal*, January 31, 1955.
3. *Ibid.*, June 2, 1956.
4. Michael Barkway, "Party 'Break-Up': 1957 Election Danger Signal," *Financial Post*, April 13, 1957.
5. Montreal *Gazette*, June 6, 1957.

6. Ottawa *Journal*, May 21, 1957.
7. John Meisel, *The Canadian General Election of 1957* (Toronto: University of Toronto Press, 1962), p. 38n.
8. Ottawa *Journal*, May 22, 1957.
9. "A Rival for Uncle Louis," *Economist*, CLXXXIII (June 8, 1957), p. 894.
10. *Ibid.*
11. Ottawa *Journal*, May 29, 1957.
12. *Le Devoir*, October 9, 1956.

Twenty-third

				Popular Vote						Total
P.C.	%	L.	%	C.C.F.	%	S.C.	%	O.	%	
34,795	37.8	56,993	61.9	321	0.3					92,109
197,676	50.4	176,891	45.1	17,117	4.4	473	0.1			392,157
114,060	48.7	112,518	48.1	2,001	0.9	2,420	1.0	3,159	1.3	234,158
34,965	52.3	31,162	46.6	680	1.0					66,807
557,356	31.1	1,030,354	57.6	31,780	1.8	3,877	0.2	166,693	9.3	1,790,060
1,104,024	48.8	839,894	37.1	274,069	12.1	38,418	1.7	8,166	0.4	2,264,571
124,867	35.9	90,880	26.1	82,398	23.7	45,803	13.1	4,162	1.2	348,110
90,359	23.2	118,282	30.3	140,293	36.0	40,830	10.5	334	0.1	390,098
118,225	27.6	119,190	27.9	27,127	6.3	161,697	37.8	1,413	0.3	427,652
192,988	32.6	121,301	20.5	131,873	22.3	143,145	24.2	2,232	0.4	591,539
3,611	41.4	5,108	58.6							8,719
2,572,926	38.9	2,702,573	40.9	707,659	10.7	436,663	6.6	186,159	2.8	6,605,980

13. John Bird, "The Conservative Convention," *Commentator*, I (January,1957), p. 2.

14. A. Vixen, "The New Conservative Leader," *Canadian Forum*, XXXVI (January, 1957), p. 218.

15. H.S. Ferns, "The New Course in Canadian Politics," *Political Quarterly*, XXIX (April, 1958), p. 116.

16. Denis Smith, "The Conservatives are Confused," *Commentator*, I (May, 1957), p. 3.

17. *Canadian Politics* (Sackville: Mount Allison University Publications, 1959), p. 30.

18. Halifax *Chronicle-Herald*, May 16, 1957.

19. *Ibid.*, May 27 and June 1, 1957.

20. *Ibid.*, June 6, 1957.

21. *Ibid.*, April 30, 1957.

22. *Ibid.*, June 8, 1957.

23. Meisel, *General Election,* p. 39.

24. *Ibid.*, p. 171.

25. Halifax *Chronicle-Herald*, May 1, 1957.

26. John Bird, "Electoral Jam Spread Thin," *Commentator,* I (April, 1957), p. 2.

27. Halifax *Chronicle-Herald*, May 2, 1957.

28. *Ibid.*, May 25, 1957.

29. *Ibid.*, April 30, 1957.

30. *Ibid.*, June 6, 1957.

31. Meisel, *General Election*, p. 44.

32. Halifax *Chronicle-Herald*, June 8, 1957.

33. Denis Smith, "The Conservatives are Confused," p. 3.

34. Ottawa *Journal*, May 28, 1957.

35. Halifax *Chronicle-Herald*, May 4, 1957.

36. *Ibid.*, May 25, 1957.

37. *Le Devoir*, March 27, 1958.

38. *Ibid.*, May 18, 1957.

39. Ottawa *Journal*, May 25, 1957.

40. Meisel, *General Election*, p. 115.

41. Toronto *Globe and Mail*, May 10, 1957.

42. Meisel, *General Election*, p. 177.

43. *Le Devoir*, June 8, 1957.

44. *Ibid.*, April 30, 1957.

45. J.M. Beck, "Quebec and the Canadian Elections of 1958," *Parliamentary Affairs*," XII (Winter, 1958-9), p. 98.

46. See Meisel, *General Election*, pp. 166-67.

47. Peter Regenstreif, *The Diefenbaker Interlude: Parties and Voting in Canada* (Toronto: Longmans Canada Ltd., 1965), p. 29.

48. Ottawa *Citizen*, June 11, 1957.

49. Ottawa *Journal*, January 17, 1956.

50. Ferns, "The New Course," p. 114.

51. *Ibid.*, p. 115.

52. Toronto *Star*, June 11, 1957.

53. Eugene Forsey, "Never Have So Many Been In So Long," *Commentator*, I (May, 1957), p. 1.

54. "The Ottawa Stampede," *Economist*, CLXXXIII (June 15, 1957), p. 954.

55. Paul Fox, "Why the Liberal Debacle?", *Canadian Forum,* XXXVII (July, 1957), p. 75.

56. Meisel, *General Election*, p. 156.

57. Ottawa *Journal*, May 8, 1957.

58. "Fall of the Liberals," *Round Table*, XLVII (September, 1957), p. 400.

59. Alan Thomas, "TV in Canadian Politics," *Commentator*, I (August, 1957), p. 2.

60. Toronto *Star*, June 11, 1957.

61. John Bird, "When the Liberals Lost the Press," *Commentator*, I (June, 1957), p. 3.

62. Thomas, "TV in Politics," p. 2.

63. Dale C. Thomson, *Louis St. Laurent: Canadian* (Toronto: The Macmillan Company of Canada, 1967), p. 512.

64. Leo Zakuta, *A Protest Movement Becalmed: A Study of Change in the C.C.F.* (Toronto: University of Toronto Press, 1964), p. 93.

65. Meisel, *General Election*, pp. 247-48.

66. Regenstreif, "Canadian General Election," p. 353.

67. Toronto *Telegram*, June 11, 1957.

68. Ottawa *Journal*, May 31, 1957.

69. Toronto *Star*, June 11, 1957.

70. Regenstreif, "Canadian General Election," p. 372.

71. Ottawa *Journal*, May 21, 1957.

72. J.M. Beck, "The Election of 1957 and the Canadian Electoral System," *Dalhousie Review*, XXXVII (Winter, 1957), p. 332.

73. Thomson, *St. Laurent*, p. 519.

74. Beck, "Election of 1957," p. 340.

75. *Ibid.*

76. Wilfrid Sanders, "How Polls Like That Happen," *Commentator*, I (June, 1957), p. 14.

77. Beck, "Election of 1957," p. 332.

78. R.R. Alford, *Party and Society* (Chicago: Rand McNally and Co., 1963), pp. 284-85.

79. Toronto *Star*, June 11, 1957.

Twenty-fourth
General Election

"CATCH THE VISION!"

In one respect the election of 1958 was unusual. The Conservatives, because they had been in office less than a year, found it possible (and, of course, advantageous) to arouse indignation against a Liberal government that no longer existed and to blame it for the ills of the day. Of course, they too came under fire. One critic said that the Prime Minister had not exhibited "anything in excess of an apocalyptic old-style preacher's passionate platitudes."[1] Two others declared that the Conservatives' concern for Parliament had not lasted beyond their accession to office,[2] and the *Canadian Forum* felt they had provided nothing more than "a series of stopgap measures which do not add up to a coherent policy."[3]

Yet even tough-minded newspapermen agreed that an inexperienced cabinet had not done badly and, to all appearances, the general public liked the Diefenbaker flair and his ability to get things done. In short order, he had provided increased pensions for the aged, blind, and disabled; larger allowances for disabled war veterans; cash advances on farm-stored grain; support prices for a number of agricultural products; adjustment grants to the Atlantic provinces; modest reductions in personal and corporate income taxes; and a variety of other goodies. By the end of the year he was anxious for an election. Like other prime ministers he did not wish to have his hold on office dependent on the whims of the opposition parties. Furthermore, a down-turn in the economy had occurred within months of his assumption of office and some Conservatives were already having nightmares that they might be labelled once more as the party of depression.

In the early months, however, they had no excuse for a dissolution. The Liberals made no attempt to challenge them, as Louis St. Laurent, a spent but highly respected figure, "passively [sat] out his term as lame-duck president."[4] But the situation altered substantially in January when Lester Pearson defeated the veteran Paul Martin for the leadership even though he had had little experience as a practical politician and frankly admitted that he was "not an easy or skillful practitioner of the smoke-filled room, machine type of politics." One of his first acts as leader was to promise an all-out attack on the government, and former Liberal ministers echoed the refrain. According to one of them, James Sinclair, "the Tories didn't inherit unemployment from us, they've created it."[5]

At a time when even Liberals were saying that "nobody seems to be sorry we were licked," it might have been discreet for their new leader to lie low. The greater the lapse of time, the more difficult it would have been for the government to blame the current ills on its predecessor. But Pearson, adopting an incomprehensible and, as it turned out, calamitous course, seized the first opportunity to make a scathing attack on the government and concluded with a pusillanimous demand that it resign. It was a heaven-sent opportunity for John Diefenbaker, permitting him to "adopt the congenial role of prosecuting counsel . . . employing all his armory of flouts, jeers and menacing gestures."[6] With evident relish he produced an economic report presented to the previous government by its civil servants, which forecast the economic slowdown. After tolling out a series of quotations in his best courtroom manner, he put it to the Liberal front benchers: "Why didn't you tell the people these things?" While his opponents pretended to be horrified at such use of "secret" or "confidential" information, the public felt they had got exactly what they deserved.

Not surprisingly, Canada found itself in the throes of a general election by February 1. It was not true that the government's position had become intolerable, but the Prime Minister made it sound convincing to the ordinary voter. His opening encounter with Pearson had determined the tone, the character, and even the issues of the campaign to his advantage. Although at the Liberal convention there had been complaints about the brass dominating the grass, none of the ministers defeated in 1957 chose to run again. Except for Pearson and Martin, this left a vacuum in Ontario. The departure of Louis St. Laurent made the situation in Quebec even worse. "Where are the Liberal indispensables?," gibed the *Globe and Mail*. Pearson, it said, was like the shipwrecked sailor in Moby Dick: "I alone am escaped to tell thee."[7] Even 19 of the Liberals elected in 1957 did not choose to re-offer.[8]

Gone, too, were the chiefs of staff who had run the Liberal campaigns behind the scene, and Senators John Connolly and C.G. Power had to step in as co-directors of the national campaign. They concentrated on one big pitch: "Vote the Pearson Plan . . . For Jobs . . . For Peace." Those eight words appeared on every last piece of the party's written propaganda. Pearson himself said repeatedly that the Liberals could provide "the most effective contribution for Canada in the search for peace and security." The new nuclear weapons, he prophesied, would "make the Second World War look like a sham battle" and might even end the world.[9] He would devote all his energy, experience, and talents to preventing such a catastrophe. The Conservatives sought to depreciate Pearson's accomplishments as a diplomat. George Hees went so far as to suggest that the idea of UNEF had been John Diefenbaker's even though Pearson had won the Nobel Prize for it. This was altogether too much for the Conservative Ottawa *Journal*. "The Nobel Peace Prize," it said, "has about as much business in this election as

Halley's comet."[10] Actually the Conservatives had no need to fear the vote-getting appeal of Pearson's diplomatic talents. Canadians did not seem at all worried about the possibility of nuclear warfare; instead they were concentrating on domestic matters.

Pearson had little better luck with the unemployment issue, even though the number of Canadians out of work was somewhere between 565,000 and 855,000 (it depended on which set of government figures suited the politician's purposes.) John Diefenbaker saw to it that the Liberals did not place the responsibility for the situation on him. "They concealed [the economic report]. They covered up. They hid. They knew but they did not act. They were warned that a serious situation was developing."[11] The Liberals were forced to adopt the line that they could handle unemployment better than the Conservatives. On this matter the government's supporters took an optimistic view; the worst effects of the recession, they prophesied, would soon be over as a result of the easing of tight money and the other policies the government had already adopted or would shortly undertake—especially a public works programme amounting to over $1 billion. "As long as I am Prime Minister," said John Diefenbaker, "no man or woman will ever be allowed to suffer, deficit or no deficit."[12]

To the Liberals this was empty rhetoric. Moreover, the Conservatives' public works programme, according to Pearson, consisted largely of routine projects, some of them initiated by the St. Laurent government. In any case, public works would act too slowly; the proper course was to inject money quickly into the economy to get it moving again. As the campaign opened, Pearson promised a tax cut of $400 million, more than half of this to be achieved through a 4 per cent reduction on the first $3,000 of taxable income. To this proposal he later added the idea of a tax holiday. By making the tax cut retroactive to January 1, a Liberal government would be able to forgo income tax deductions for a period of six or seven weeks for most taxpayers, thereby permitting larger expenditures on consumer goods with all the attendant benefits. Pearson's ideas might have been eminently sound on economic grounds, but they simply did not catch on. The Montreal *Star*, Liberal for two decades, said he had committed himself to huge tax cuts which might prove unnecessary; in contrast, the Prime Minister's course was "more moderate and, we believe, more sensible and more appealing to the voter."

This was only the beginning of Pearson's promises. There were also assurances of 2,500 scholarships and 7,500 bursaries; a rail branch to Great Slave Lake; a municipal loan fund to permit municipalities to borrow for long periods at low rates; a farm development bank to provide easier credit for farmers; old age pensions for unmarried women at age 60; and family allowances for students up to age 18. As the Liberal leader travelled throughout Canada, he added a good many items to this list, including two hardy

Liberal perennials: the Saskatchewan Dam and a complete medical insurance plan.

Naturally, Conservative newspapers would not forget that this was the man who, at his leadership convention, had said that government was more than a give-away programme or a national lottery. To add further promises on top of the tax cuts, said the Montreal *Gazette*, was "politics of the old school, the politics of the sawdust trail."[13] Arthur Blakely of the same paper wrote that simply to calculate the cost of Pearson's promises would "keep the adding machines busy for a spell."[14] I. Norman Smith of the Ottawa *Journal* wondered if Pearson would have done better to play it straight as a sober, serious, un-promising intellectual.[15]

The Liberal leader suffered from other disabilities about which he could do little. He had not had time to consolidate his position or give a party in disarray a new look. As first he was anything but dexterous in handling large formal meetings; he was obviously more comfortable in question-and-answer sessions with university students. He spoke more like a United Nations delegate than a candidate for the prime ministership. When he tried to hit the Tories hard he sounded artificial, and when he gave a calm, reasoned discussion of foreign policy, he aroused little enthusiasm. Towards the end of the campaign, however, he did appear at least as "a foreign policy specialist who [was] surprisingly well informed about domestic issues";[16] he was also doing less apologizing and more attacking.

However, it was Pearson's misfortune to be running against a man who, for the moment, had an unparalleled empathy with the Canadian people and whose techniques in this election could not be faulted. Stanley Burke compared Diefenbaker's tactics to those of a strafing fighter pilot "sweeping back and forth across the country, trying with bursts of oratory to keep as many fires going as possible." In contrast, Pearson's tactics were those of an infantryman whose gains might in the long run be more permanent but were not realizable in the immediate future.[17] The opposition was kept on the defensive until the closing days of the campaign. To Liberal criticism Diefenbaker either said: "Why didn't they do something about it while they were in power?" or, "In eight months we have done things that the last government played around with for years and years. . . . They thought of it—we did it."[18] Since Liberals had long taken the credit for Canada's postwar development and the establishment of its international reputation, they thought it sheer ingratitude for the people across Canada to be saying: "The Liberals had 22 years and they didn't do anything. Let's let the other fellows have a try."[19]

The Conservatives had never lost the élan engendered by their recent victory. Voters who had not supported them earlier, because their party did not seem to have a chance, jumped on the bandwagon, especially as Diefenbaker convinced them that he was getting things done. Long before the election the Gallup Poll indicated the trend:

	P.C.	L.	C.C.F.	S.C.	O.
June 1957 (actual)	38.9%	40.9%	10.7%	6.6%	2.8%
August	47	35	10	8	—
November	50	33	9	7	1
January 1958	50	35	9	6	1

A few sophisticated voices did attempt to make themselves heard against the popular trend. James Coyne, Governor of the Bank of Canada, seemed deliberately to inject himself into the election when, in his annual report, he came close to saying that there had not been a tight-money policy under the Liberals, but that, however it was labelled, their policy had prevented an even worse recession. While Pearson was delighted, Diefenbaker and his Minister of Finance Donald Fleming were outraged. They, of course, were seeking to establish a connection between Liberal tight money and the recession.

Academics also joined the fray. Professor B.S. Keirstead was so convinced that the Conservatives were exceeding the proper limits in their campaigning that the Liberals let him use their "free" radio time to say so. Becoming even more emotional than the Prime Minister, he denounced the government for asking the voters "not to weigh the issues but to try to guess the outcome and get on the winning side." Two other University of Toronto professors, Eastman and Stykolt, used the *Canadian Forum* to demonstrate calmly and dispassionately the impracticability of the Conservative trade proposals.[20] Earlier, Michael Barkway suggested that King and St. Laurent, in emphasizing the importance of geography and economics to the exclusion of history, had been negligent of the historic fear of the loss of independence to the United States, and had thus ignored the very reason for Canada's existence. He went too far, however, in suggesting that the vote in 1957 had been, in effect, "a demand for a redress of the balance between historical and economic forces"; after all, the danger of Canada's growing dependence on the United States had played but a minor role in the campaign. Yet he was undoubtedly correct that there existed a "restless, subliminal dissatisfaction" on this score.[21]

John Diefenbaker knew what he was doing (politically, at least) when, after the election of 1957, he proposed to divert a portion of Canada's trade from the United States to Britain. In an off-the-cuff comment at a press conference he said it would be 15 per cent; and he was stuck with that. To the knowledgeable this was utterly impracticable; at the very least it would have required drastic governmental action. To Britons, planning at this very time to get into Europe, it was positively embarrassing. "But the British play rugby, too. They invented it. [Peter] Thorneycroft [the Chancellor of the Exchequer] intercepted Diefenbaker's pass and ran the length of the field for a touchdown."[22] He simply proposed a British-Canadian free trade area and it was then the Canadian Conservatives' turn to be embarrassed. Professors

Eastman and Stykolt might well say it was "time to return to a recognition of reality."[23]

But nothing was to deter John Diefenbaker from using the trade-diversionary argument to the full. Pearson might say: "Let's not do things that may encourage protectionists at Washington to act against us. Let us expand our trade, not restrict or divert it."[24] In the mood of 1958, however, his warning that rough talk might provoke an unfavourable American reaction found little favour. The ordinary voter clearly preferred the Prime Minister's emphasis on Canadian control of the development of Canadian resources to Liberal talk about maintaining a "buddy-buddy" relationship with Washington.[25]

There was nothing specifically anti-American in Diefenbaker's speeches. Rather, there was an appeal to Canadian nationalism at a time when that struck a responsive chord. He could not accomplish his basic objectives – so he said – as long as he depended on the day-to-day support of the Commons. He needed an over-all majority to "provide, through a great national development policy, equal opportunities for all Canadians . . . to create a new sense of national purpose and national destiny . . ." Among the many ingredients were farm rehabilitation from coast to coast; making equity stock in American subsidiaries available to Canadians; the development of power and irrigation projects on the South Saskatchewan and Columbia; the building of branch railways to open untapped resources, especially in the north; an imaginative programme of Arctic research; and so on.[26]

And then there was the "vision." Sometimes it seemed to be associated solely with the development of the Canadian North; sometimes it was "a vision of opportunity" by which Canada could realize the benefits that her great resources made possible. For example, an emotional outpouring at Edmonton began during the playing of "O Canada" when the vast audience became charged with emotion as a blue spotlight played on the Prime Minister. It built up as he lambasted Pearson for describing northern highway development as development from igloo to igloo: was this not like the Liberals of the 1880's who had said the C.P.R. would not pay for its own axle grease? It reached its peak when "leaning partly over the lectern, [he] spoke softly, almost in a whisper at times, as he promised [he] would create . . . a new sense of national purpose."[27]

> Catch the vision! Catch the vision of the kind of Canada this can be! . . . I've seen this vision; I've seen this future of Canada. I ask you to have faith in this land and faith in our people.[28]

Even the Ottawa *Journal* acknowledged there was little of real substance in this kind of oratory. Nevertheless, the *Journal* felt that it did have merits. Did it not possess "the material, the technique, the homage to imagination which makes democracy exciting, vibrant, rescuing it from torpor"?[29] As might be expected, the Toronto *Star* described the main ingredients of Diefenbaker's programme as "humbug and flapdoodle served up with an evangelistic flourish."[30] However, it readily admitted that Pearson seemed unable to communicate himself and his policies to the people, except perhaps in the closing stages of the campaign. Here, then, is the real key to the election. Because the voters could not be induced to show any great interest in issues—not even unemployment—it was, in Peter Regenstreif's terminology, a "luxury" election and hence one in which the personality of the leader was dominant. Since the Conservatives concentrated on their leader, the Liberals had to do the same thing, though it was hardly a fair match.[31] Pearson's polka-dot bow tie could hardly compete with Diefenbaker's personality and techniques in 1958.

Indeed Pearson's own speeches indicate his frustration at the inequality of the contest. "Quivering clichés or evangelistic exhortations;" "oracular fervour and circus parades," were not for him. He relied on the voters' "essential good will and intelligence." Do not, he said, "confuse motion with progress; agitation with action; or platitudes with performance;" reject "the cult of personality, whether expressed in terms of dictatorship or demagoguery."[32] But it was no use. Like other journalists, John A. Stevenson talked about the voters' "flocking to touch the hem of [the Prime Minister's] garment and according him an adoration such as never fell to the lot of either Sir John Macdonald or Sir Wilfrid Laurier." Furthermore, the process was cumulative, for "the plaudits of the crowd . . . inspired him with confidence and fanned the fires of his emotional appeals."[33] Perhaps, as the Toronto *Star* suggested, Canadian politics required the colour that Diefenbaker provided.[34] Certainly the Canadian voters seemed to go on an emotional binge in 1958. But there is another approach to the voters' behaviour. Although there was "plenty of corn" in Diefenbaker's speeches, wrote H.S. Ferns, there was also the assumption that "life is more than a matter of motor cars, deep freezers and gracious living." It may be argued that under Liberal governments material progress had been the only yardstick for measuring Canadian achievement, even though it was achieved at the loss of independence. To many Canadians there was more than mere rhetoric in Diefenbaker's stated intention to "give young Canadians, motivated by a desire to serve, a lift in the heart, and a faith in their fellow Canadians, and in the future destiny of their country."[35]

The effect of Diefenbaker's campaigning, however, ought not to be overemphasized. The pre-campaign Gallup Poll clearly indicated a considerable Conservative victory. The voters' very human reaction to let the "new crowd" have a chance had much effect.[36] None the less, the Prime Minister's personal appeal must be given credit for much of the Conservative increase in popular support—from 50 per cent in January to 56 in mid-March. For once a Conservative leader could campaign on the Poll, and Diefenbaker repeatedly extolled its accuracy. Commenting on the March forecast, he said:

"This is the greatest thing I have ever seen; there has never been anything like it."[37]

Diefenbaker also used the Poll to prove that since Canada was moving back to a two-party system it was folly to vote for the C.C.F. Under such circumstances M.J. Coldwell battled against heavy odds. The spectacle of his having to conduct a national campaign without adequate resources and staff and his becoming ill in the process had a touch of pathos about it. He advocated, as usual, a planned economy to promote stable investment policies and to overcome the ills of "sporadic flood or famine." Above all, he would not enter into "the insincere and hypocritical competition of large-scale tax reductions"; his programme, he admitted, would cost something. Of the government generally, he observed that "never before have so many problems been postponed in so little time by so many cabinet ministers." Its agricultural prices support bill was "only a shell of a program – attractive on the outside but empty inside"; the C.C.F. alone was committed to full parity in agriculture. Especially perturbing was the fact that the Conservatives had allowed the promoters of Westcoast Transmission to make "fantastic fortunes" and commit "a great moral wrong." Had they already forgotten their own denunciation of the Yankee carpetbaggers who had profiteered on the Trans-Canada pipeline? "Only the C.C.F. . . . could fight for the people against . . . vicious exploitation."[38]

Coldwell, however, had not a chance. The personality of the Prime Minister, together with "the combination of advertising, public relations, high-pressure campaigning and a sympathetic press proved irresistible to the voters."[39] Beyond doubt, the Conservatives benefited from the most effective advertising and public relations campaign that a Canadian party had ever enjoyed. They also had the support of Liberal newspapers – especially in Montreal and Vancouver – that thought they deserved a real mandate. Ordinary Canadians must have felt the same way if the excitement that prevailed during the election was any indication. The turn-out was 79.6 per cent – at that time a record in Canadian federal elections.

Such was the national campaign. Regionally, there were differences in approach. The Prime Minister told the Atlantic provinces that "for the first time in history there is a realization by government of your problems. . . . John Sebastian Cabot discovered this part of Canada in 1497 but the Liberal party not until 1957's election."[40] He could point to the lavish treatment that he had accorded the area. He got the response he wanted. His party again took Prince Edward Island's 4 seats and an unprecedented 62.2 per cent of the vote; it won all of Nova Scotia's seats for the first time since Confederation; it gained 2 seats in New Brunswick and reduced the pluralities in the 3 the Liberals retained; it raised its share of the Newfoundland vote from 37.8 to 45.2 per cent and saved its deposits in 3 of the outport ridings.

In Ontario it was much the same. The Conservatives added 6 seats to the 61 they already held there. This time they took all of Toronto and York County. Even in those seats that the Liberals and C.C.F. retained on the periphery, their pluralities were often drastically reduced. The avalanche of Conservative votes was such that the Liberals lost their deposits in 11 of the 18 Toronto and York seats, the 3 Hamilton seats, and such other ridings as Elgin, Halton, Ontario County, Parry Sound–Muskoka, and Peel.

The landslide continued into the Prairies – John Diefenbaker's homeland. This time, in self-defence, Premier Douglas Campbell of Manitoba campaigned for his party. But it was no use. The national Conservative sweep made few exceptions. Even the 2 seats in North Winnipeg, normally Labour or C.C.F. since 1921, went Tory. When Stanley Knowles was defeated there could be little hope for anyone else. All of Manitoba's 14 seats went Conservative and 11 Liberals lost their deposits.

Saskatchewan and Alberta behaved no differently. It was not just a desire to get rid of the Liberals. Never was the complaint so prevalent that splinter groups were a nuisance in Ottawa. Perhaps the voters thought: "What's the use of voting C.C.F.? What did it ever do?" In Saskatchewan, it mattered not whether a Conservative had run first, second, third, fourth, or not at all in 1957; this time he was first in 16 of 17 seats. Only Hazen Argue of the C.C.F. survived, and his closest challenger was a Conservative. The latter might have won, too, if he had appeared to have a chance. But he had polled less than 10 per cent of the vote the year before. Names made no difference. J.G. Gardiner suffered his first personal defeat in 44 years and M.J. Coldwell lost in Rosetown-Biggar. Only 7 Liberals saved their deposits. Alberta's behaviour was even more extraordinary. Since 1921 it had always given a majority of its seats to a third party despite the best efforts of King and St. Laurent. But John Diefenbaker not only won all of its 17 seats, but took 59.9 per cent of its votes, making it the most Conservative part of Canada (Prince Edward Island excepted). Dynamic, fire-eating, and revivalistic, he apparently provided the same sort of style to which Albertans had become accustomed in their Social Credit leaders.[41] The Conservative majorities were something to behold; Douglas Harkness, for example, won by 26,375 in Calgary North. No Liberal saved his deposit, and only 5 Social Crediters saved theirs.

In British Columbia, where the Conservatives had done well the year before, the results also followed the trend. This time the former cabinet minister, James Sinclair, could not stave off defeat in Coast-Capilano. Although 4 C.C.F. members managed to hold their seats, no Liberal was returned and all but 3 lost their deposits; 18 more Conservatives joined the swelling total.

"Embarrass me" with Conservative members of cabinet calibre, was John Diefenbaker's exhortation to Quebec in 1958.[42] The results were overwhelming. The province that had moved almost imperceptibly in his direction in 1957 gave him 50 of its 75 seats and 49.6 per cent of its votes. Not since 1887 had the Conservatives taken even a bare majority of its seats. The Gallup Poll, however, had foreseen such results. In December 1957 it found that Quebeckers, by 44 to 27 per cent, felt that Lester Pearson would not make as good a prime minister as John Diefenbaker.

> The available evidence suggests that in Quebec, as elsewhere, the electorate had made up its mind before dissolution. . . . The differences were that a greater percentage of the Quebec voters remained undecided until just before 31st March – 13 per cent as compared with 10 per cent for all Canada – and that intense ferment was taking place there. . . . As it turned out, the C.I.P.O. forecast the results almost exactly for Quebec, if the undecided voters are allocated in the same proportion as the decided. "We were the first to document the revolution in Quebec," boasted Wilfrid Sanders, the co-director of the C.I.P.O.[43]

There were other indications as well. When Charles-Guy Paré sought to rebuild the Conservative organization in the district of Montreal following the election of 1957, he found an altogether new spirit in evidence. By the time of dissolution he had been able to organize twenty-one associations, mostly in ridings where they had long been defunct. Even more revealing were the circumstances surrounding the nomination of Conservative candidates. In the past the party had relied on "a reserve of perennial candidates who would show up at election time, run in a given riding, and accept defeat with resignation." This time Allister Grosart urged his Quebec wing to "get away from those old-time, hole-in-the-wall kind of conventions" and to spare neither "trouble nor expense to get really wide-open, truly democratic, may-the-best-man-win conventions."[44] Futhermore, he offered to pay the cost of properly conducted conventions. He must have been both surprised and delighted at the results. Instead of the usual corporal's guard, crowds overflowed the meeting places; instead of frenzied efforts to find a sacrificial lamb there were more contested nominations than had occurred within living memory. Yet these "truly democratic" conventions caused much woe to the organizers. In the sprawling Saguenay riding – fifteen times the size of Nova Scotia – their aim was to accord each of the main population centres a share in the nomination. They chartered a plane and travelled 1,300 miles so that the constituency executive and the four candidates might appear in Havre St. Pierre, Sept Iles, Forestville, and Baie Comeau. National Headquarters must have been thunderstruck when it got the bill. But it was a truly democratic convention![45]

The organizers' worst headaches occurred in historic and symbolic Quebec East, the seat of Laurier, Lapointe, and St. Laurent. This time it was also symbolic for the Union Nationale, since the Liberal candidate, "centralizer" Maurice Lamontagne, was one of their principal bêtes noires. More than 5,000 people were in the Quebec Coliseum when the Conservative convention opened at eight p.m.; many were still there when it concluded at six a.m. Despite the long hours spent in regularizing their credentials, the 650 delegates somehow managed to poll 1,100 votes. "One committee functioned efficiently at the rear of the Coliseum, that of costumes. The women went there to change their hats, their coiffure, or even their clothing and returned to vote again. Some ladies voted five and even seven times!"[46] The scandal of the convention was such that its nominee withdrew, allegedly on the intervention of Duplessis himself.

Did the U.N. deserve the primary credit for the results in Quebec? Undoubtedly it fought this election as never before. As Camille Pouliot, the Minister of Game and Fisheries, put it: "And when I say take part, I don't mean a couple of speeches, but I mean work with all my energy." Duplessis did not intervene openly but, as usual, let his supporters participate as it suited them. Perhaps not even he could have restrained them this time. Already some of them had tasted of the lucrative positions which only the federal government has it in its power to bestow. In the past their efforts had availed little against the Liberal steam-roller, but in the altered circumstance they were not hesitant about extending their activities. However, though they helped to magnify the Conservative victory, they did not produce it.

What had caused the change in political climate? For one thing, Louis St. Laurent had retired and his only contribution to the campaign was a message from Florida. According to André Laurendeau, his departure produced an emotional release. "The crown of Wilfrid Laurier has fallen to the ground. . . . The Liberals have tried, as usual, to cry: 'Long live the king,' but everybody felt they had not even a pretender to offer. Our political nationalism, so extraordinarily stable in its primary form ('vote for a French-Canadian Catholic who has chances of succeeding nationally'), did not receive its customary nourishment."[47] With Lester Pearson the Conservatives could take unaccustomed liberties. Sometimes he became "Monsieur Personne" – "Mr. Nobody."

The Liberals again brought out from their arsenal "all the slogans and all the accusations which [had] been hurled against the Conservative party since 1917."[48] One of their advertisements contained twelve outline drawings of the Prime Minister, the first of which had the caption: "Ça, c'est John George Diefenbaker." The second declared that the Conservatives Borden, Meighen, Bennett, Drew, Diefenbaker, and Gordon Churchill were all alike; the others made it clear they were alike in their hostility to French Canada. After attempts to associate Diefenbaker with Saskatchewan's anti-French, anti-Catholic Anderson group of the late twenties failed, his opponents pounced gleefully on a statement of the Orange Lodge of British

Columbia requesting its members to vote for Diefenbaker because he was one of them. They were much chagrined when the Orange authorities apologized for linking the Prime Minister with an organization to which he had never belonged. It was all the more difficult to accuse the Conservatives of being anti-French when four of their English-speaking ministers were campaigning in French in Quebec and Diefenbaker was doing his best in his own brand of French.[49]

The Prime Minister's strategy was well designed and effective. Once again he avoided any hint of association with Duplessis and thereby avoided any suggestion in English Canada of a Diefenbaker-Duplessis alliance. Without according special concessions to Quebec, he had treated it with scrupulous fairness. He had given the province only three cabinet ministers, but that was a relatively high percentage of the Conservatives it had elected in 1957. Early in February 1958 he made one specific undertaking: simultaneous translation into English or French of speeches in the House of Commons. When no others were forthcoming, the French press waxed indignant. *La Presse* accused him of playing the sphinx with Quebec. *Le Devoir* asked repeatedly: "If Mr. Diefenbaker persists in not reassuring us, why should we furnish him the whip with which to beat us?" It was worried that he seemed to favour the "melting-pot" or assimilation of races idea which it violently rejected, and it relented only a little when he spoke in Montreal about "equal respect for our two great cultures" and "equal partners."[50] Clearly Quebec was to come to Diefenbaker, not Diefenbaker to Quebec.

None the less, *la belle province* had been made to feel that its vital interests were not in danger under a Conservative government. And so, because the ghost of Riel and the memory of conscription had lost their old significance, its voters reacted to many of the same forces that moved other Canadians. The image of John Diefenbaker may not have been the same there as elsewhere, but he was undoubtedly the dominant figure in all ten provinces. One Conservative advertisement caught the prevailing mood in Quebec. It showed an outline map of the province, deeply cleft by a hatchet at the Quebec-Ontario border. Above the map were the words: "On prédit un triomphe éclatant à Diefenbaker"; below it: "N'isolons pas Québec." Or, as I. Norman Smith put it, "What about the plain human answer that we all like to be on the band wagon. All signs indicated the Conservatives would win the election. In the face of that near certainty, why would the people of Quebec vote themselves out in the cold?"[51]

Apart from the island of Montreal, the Conservatives won 41 of the 54 seats. Quebec East, Kamouraska, and Témiscouata – Liberal since 1874, 1884, and 1896, respectively – switched to the Conservatives. While the Liberals retained 12 of Montreal's 21 ridings, their losses in the popular vote were proportionately as great there as elsewhere. No Liberal majority on the Island – not even one of the order of 15,000 – was safe in 1958, and the Conservatives won handily even in St. Jacques and Ste. Marie, which had been Liberal since they were created in 1892. In contrast to the 37 Conservatives who lost their deposits in 1953, and the 25 in 1957, only the one in Beauce suffered that fate this time.

Never had there been such a victory. Diefenbaker had secured 208 of 265 seats, clear majorities in every province but Newfoundland, clean sweeps in four provinces, and 117 of 160 seats in Ontario and Quebec. It was phenomenal that Conservatives ran at least second in every seat in Canada but Beauce, that they had lost their deposits only in Beauce and two of Newfoundland's outport ridings, and that Frank McGee had run up a majority of 35,377 in York-Scarborough, the largest ever to be recorded in a Canadian election. While the Conservative popular vote of 53.6 per cent did not seem impressive, this was only the second time since 1921 that a party had taken more than half the votes and, except for the distinctly unusual election of 1917, it was the largest party vote ever to be recorded.

All classes and conditions of people turned to the Conservatives in 1958. Even in Newfoundland's outports and northern Ontario, where they won no seats, they added substantially to their share of the votes. The results in Toronto indicate that the ethnic voter–so strongly wooed by Diefenbaker–also climbed on the bandwagon. Only the service voter remained strongly Liberal. Although in the service polls in Canada the Conservatives came close to parity with the Liberals, the servicemen stationed abroad and therefore isolated from the prevailing mood and attitudes resisted the general trend. Because voting behaviour was virtually uniform across the country, national rather than regional or local factors must be regarded as the primary determinant.[52]

The results were disastrous for all the opposition parties. Social Credit was obliterated, leader Solon Low and all. The C.C.F. did not do much better, even though its popular vote only fell from 10.7 to 9.5 per cent. It was left with only 8 members, and its chief ornaments, Coldwell and Knowles, were gone. The Liberals were reduced to 49 members, the smallest number in their history; 98 of their candidates lost their deposits. Furthermore, they were an utterly unrepresentative group. In 6 provinces they had no seats at all; their only seat west of Ontario was in the North-West Territories; 25 of their 49 members were French-speaking.

It was indeed a political revolution, but was it to be revolutionary in its effects? Certainly, producing a government that could dominate the Commons was not revolutionary. Canada, it appeared, had a penchant for strong government of this sort and if it could not get it through one party it would do so through another. But because of the ills attending one-partyism, perhaps the country was paying too high a price for stability.[53]

Did the results in Quebec simply mean that it had climbed on the bandwagon? Or did they mean the demise of the conscription issue which had given the Liberals a virtual monopoly of power since 1917? As a concomitant, would this victory permit the Conservatives to consolidate a Quebec wing of some substance within their ranks? The apparent reluctance of John Diefenbaker to put French Canadians on a different footing from other ethnic minorities was not a favourable portent. Nor were the dimensions of the Conservative victory. It had been expected that Diefenbaker would have to depend on Quebec for an over-all majority; as it turned out, he needed no assistance from that province at all. Under these circumstances would he make the accommodations needed to keep his party's Quebec wing in a state of health?

Did the results portend radical changes in the nature of the Conservative party? Because the Prime Minister's popularity far exceeded that of his party and because he had attracted thousands who had never considered themselves Conservatives, it was a Diefenbaker victory, not a Conservative one. The Prime Minister was anything but an orthodox Conservative; he had established his prestige as an independent champion of radical causes.[54] Could he pursue a course that would satisfy the business and financial interests of central Canada – the backbone of the party – and still retain his new supporters from western Canada?

Did the results have even wider implications for Canadian politics in general? Dennis Wrong thought they might mean the emergence in Canada of what American analysts called "the nationalization of politics." Like Roosevelt and Eisenhower, Diefenbaker had won a truly national mandate. He had evoked a more positive response than his Liberal predecessors and, unlike them, he had won popular majorities in all regions. Through the technique of "personalization" made possible by radio and television (and by strategists like Allister Grosart) a single election might, as this one did, "crush the opposition party under a plebiscitarian mandate which subordinates party labels as such to the appeal of personalities." But if politics was nationalized and divisions of opinion became the same throughout the country, the next election might produce the opposite outcome. If this were so, the election of 1958 would not mean a restoration of the one-party dominance of the Liberal era. It might, instead, represent a transition to a fundamentally new kind of politics in Canada.[55]

But perhaps this was going too far. Possibly the election might mean no more than a return to the personal element in politics. Who knows, wrote Paul Fox, "the arid rituals engaged in by Messrs. King, Drew, and St. Laurent may be *passé*, and the Aristotelian cycle may yet bring around again those gay old picnics of Sir John A."[56]

"On prédit un triomphe éclatant à Diefenbaker"

les journaux

N'ISOLONS PAS QUÉBEC

Participons largement à la grande victoire du gouvernement conservateur, le seul gouvernement vraiment canadien puisqu'il est le seul à avoir des députés dans toutes les provinces du pays

Des signes infaillibles démontrent sa popularité :

DANS TOUTES LES PROVINCES, dans tous les comtés, il se manifeste un mouvement irrésistible en faveur du gouvernement conservateur actuel dans l'intérêt du Canada tout entier.

DANS LE QUEBEC, un grand nombre d'anciens ministres et députés libéraux ont préféré ne pas se représenter et brillent aujourd'hui par leur absence... sachant bien que leur parti subira la plus humiliante défaite de son histoire.

MALHEUREUSEMENT, pendant 22 ans des libéraux ont réussi à se faire élire dans notre province en nous faisant des promesses et serments qu'ils ont ensuite reniés.

LE QUEBEC ne peut plus se laisser ainsi tromper et donne maintenant son appui à la politique progressive et au parti national de l'hon. John Diefenbaker.

Unissons-nous au reste du pays pour réélire, le 31 mars, un gouvernement véritablement canadien.

LUNDI, VOTONS CONSERVATEUR

Progressive Conservative Campaign advertisement, 1958.

	Seats	Candidates					Elected					
		P.C.	L.	C.C.F.	S.C.	O.	P.C.	%	L.	%	C.C.F.	%
Newfoundland	7	7	7	1		1	2	28.6	5	71.4		
Nova Scotia	12	12	12	4			12	100.0				
New Brunswick	10	10	10	3	3		7	70.0	3	30.0		
Prince Edward Island	4	4	4	1			4	100.0				
Quebec	75	75	75	29	15	25	50	66.7	25	33.3		
Ontario	85	85	85	63	18	10	67	78.8	15	17.6	3	3.5
Manitoba	14	14	14	14	6	1	14	100.0				
Saskatchewan	17	17	17	17	1	3	16	94.1			1	5.9
Alberta	17	17	17	15	17	4	17	100.0				
British Columbia	22	22	22	22	22	5	18	81.8			4	18.2
Yukon and N.W.T.	2	2	2			1	1	50.0	1	50.0		
Total	265	265	265	169	82	50	208	78.5	49	18.5	8	3.0

Others (votes polled): Nfld. (1): I. (1) 263.

Que. (25): I.L. (9) 11,791; I.P.C. (4) 1,844; I. (5) 12,794; L.P.P. (2) 1,162; Soc. (1) 666; Capital Familial (1) 968; Elector's Candidate (1) 8,276; Can. Lab. (1) 243; Radical Christian (1) 687.

Ont. (10): L.P.P. (6) 3,035; I. (3) 1,271; Soc. Educ. League (1) 447.

Man. (1): L.P.P. (1) 1,503.

Sask. (3): L.P.P. (2) 458; I. (1) 146.

Alta. (4): L.P.P. (2) 1,196; I.S.C. (1) 361; I. (1) 253.

B.C. (5): L.P.P. (5) 2,515.

Yukon and N.W.T. (1): I.P.C. (1) 122.

FOOTNOTES

1. Paul Fox, "A New Parliament with Old Ways," *Canadian Forum*, XXXVII (December, 1957), p. 194.

2. H.S. Crowe and S.F. Wise, "What was Heresy in June . . .", *Canadian Forum*, XXXVII (March, 1958), pp. 265-66.

3. "Piecemeal Policies," *Canadian Forum*, XXXVII (January, 1958), p. 217.

4. Fox, "New Parliament," p. 194.

5. Blair Fraser, "The 'Hidden Report' Uproar: What It Really Means," *Maclean's*, LXXI (March 1, 1958), p. 2.

6. John A. Stevenson, "The PM and Parliament," *Saturday Night*, LXXIII (February 15, 1958), p. 4.

7. Toronto *Globe and Mail*, February 26, 1958.

8. The Ottawa *Journal* (February 18, 1958) also notes Pearson's lone battle.

9. Halifax *Chronicle-Herald*, February 14, and March 21, 1958.

10. Ottawa *Journal*, February 25, 1958.

11. Halifax *Chronicle-Herald*, March 10, 1958.

12. *Ibid.*, March 1, 1958.

13. Montreal *Gazette*, February 11, 1958.

14. *Ibid.*, February 12, 1958.

15. Ottawa *Journal*, April 2, 1958.

16. Montreal *Gazette*, March 25, 1958.

17. Halifax *Chronicle-Herald*, March 20, 1958.

18. *Ibid.*, February 28, 1958.

19. *Ibid.*, March 20, 1958.

20. Harry C. Eastman and Stefan

				Popular Vote						Total
P.C.	%	L.	%	C.C.F.	%	S.C.	%	O.	%	
72,282	45.2	86,960	54.4	240	0.2			263	0.2	159,745
237,422	57.0	160,026	38.4	18,911	4.5					416,359
133,935	54.1	107,297	43.4	4,541	1.8	1,711	0.7			247,484
42,911	62.2	25,847	37.5	215	0.3					68,973
1,003,276	49.6	924,090	45.7	45,594	2.3	12,858	0.6	38,431	1.9	2,024,249
1,413,730	56.4	815,524	32.6	262,120	10.5	8,386	0.3	4,753	0.2	2,504,513
216,948	56.7	82,450	21.6	74,906	19.6	6,753	1.8	1,503	0.4	382,560
204,442	51.4	78,121	19.6	112,800	28.4	1,745	0.4	604	0.2	397,712
269,689	59.9	61,583	13.7	19,666	4.4	97,141	21.6	1,810	0.4	449,889
308,971	49.4	100,889	16.1	153,405	24.5	59,762	9.6	2,515	0.4	625,542
5,027	48.9	5,122	49.9					122	1.2	10,271
3,908,633	53.6	2,447,909	33.6	692,398	9.5	188,356	2.6	50,001	0.7	7,287,297

Stykolt, "The Great Disillusion," *Canadian Forum*, XXXVII (November, 1957), pp. 169, 192.

21. Michael Barkway, "Canada Rediscovers Its History," *Foreign Affairs*, XXXVI (April, 1958), pp. 413-15.

22. John Bird, "The Diefenbaker Flair," *Commentator*, I (October, 1957), p. 3.

23. Eastman and Stykolt, "Great Illusion," p. 192.

24. Halifax *Chronicle-Herald*, March 4, 1958.

25. "Flood-Tide for Canada's Tories," *Economist*, CLXXXVII (April 5, 1958), p. 36.

26. Halifax *Chronicle-Herald*, February 13, 1958.

27. Toronto *Globe and Mail*, March 10, 1958.

28. Ottawa *Journal*, March 11, 1958.

29. *Ibid.*

30. Toronto *Star*, April 1, 1958.

31. Peter Regenstreif, "The Canadian General Election of 1958," *Western Political Quarterly*, XIII (June, 1960), pp. 352, 357.

32. Halifax *Chronicle-Herald*, February 15, 1958 and Ottawa *Journal*, March 1, and March 25, 1958.

33. John A. Stevenson, "A Political Revolution," *Saturday Night*, LXXIII (April 12, 1958), p. 6.

34. Toronto *Star*, April 1, 1958.

35. Halifax *Chronicle-Herald*, February 13, 1958.

36. Toronto *Star*, April 1, 1958.

37. Halifax *Chronicle-Herald*, March 18, 1958.

38. *Ibid.*, February 14, 17, 21, 22, and 28, and March 5, 1958.

39. Regenstreif, "General Election of 1958," p. 356.

40. Halifax *Chronicle-Herald*, March 1, 1958.

41. Regenstreif, "General Election of 1958," p. 365.

42. Halifax *Chronicle-Herald*, March 27, 1958.

43. J.M. Beck, "Quebec and the Canadian Elections of 1958," *Parliamentary Affairs*, XII (Winter 1958-59), pp. 91-92. The analysis of what happened in Quebec relies heavily upon this article.

44. Ottawa *Journal*, March 3, 1958.

45. *Ibid.*, February 22, and March 3, 1958.

46. *Le Devoir*, March 21, 1958.

47. *Ibid.*, April 5, 1958.

48. *Ibid.*, March 28, 1958.

General Election

49. Fox, "New Parliament," p. 195.

50. *Le Devoir*, March 1, 6, 24, 26, and 28, 1958.

51. Ottawa *Journal*, April 2, 1958.

52. Regenstreif, "General Election of 1958," p. 356.

53. D.V. Smiley, "One-Partyism and Canadian Democracy," *Canadian Forum*, XXXVIII (July, 1958), p. 79.

54. Stevenson, "Political Revolution," pp. 6-7.

55. Dennis H. Wrong, "Parties and Voting in Canada," *Political Science Quarterly*, LXXIII (September, 1958), pp. 408-12.

56. Paul Fox, "A Promising Campaign," *Canadian Forum*, XXXVIII (April, 1958), pp. 2-3.

Twenty-fifth
General Election

"HE'S NOT THE MAN I THOUGHT HE WAS"

In 1958 Canadians seemed to ascribe to John Diefenbaker some of the qualities of a divinity. By 1960 his clay feet were showing. Statistics in mid-February showed 504,000 unemployed; steadily decreasing farm income had transformed his "halo . . . to no more than a pair of sinister horns," even in the West.[1] The *Globe and Mail* called the parliamentary session of the year "The Idle Parliament" for, despite the government's overwhelming majority, it had let the opposition seize the initiative:

> The cabinet provided little leadership. Its members gave the impression of men baffled by the problems which confronted them, unsure of their course, anxious to put off action in the hope that something would turn up. It is this impression of indecision and fumbling which probably accounts . . . for the disquietude throughout the country.[2]

In September 1960 the Gallup Poll showed the extent of this disquietude: it indicated that national support for the Conservatives had fallen from 57 per cent in January 1959, to 38 per cent, while that for the Liberals had risen from 30 to 43.

The closing months of 1960 brought an economic slowdown and mounting unemployment. Although the government proposed a wide variety of ameliorative measures, it nullified its good intentions somewhat by the disorganized manner in which it sought to implement them in the early months of 1961. According to Professor John Saywell, "the nation seemed to have lost its footing amidst the onrushing tides of domestic and foreign problems. . . . There was, in short, no agreed purpose, no national mood to counteract the divisions, the doubts, the seldom muted cacophany."[3]

Despite all this, the Conservatives had drawn almost even with the Liberals in the Gallup Poll findings of June 1961. This was only temporary, however, for two new circumstances hurt them badly and reversed the trend. It was not their fault, that a Conservative government in Ontario chose this time to impose a sales tax. But only they were responsible for making a martyr out of James Coyne by their ineptitude in seeking to remove him from the governorship of the Bank of Canada. By November

1961 they were less popular than a year before according to the Gallup Poll standings: 37 per cent of national support to 43 for the Liberals.

History is likely to treat the Diefenbaker government more kindly than its contemporary critics did. Certainly the Prime Minister's image would not have taken such a battering if he had been able to operate in the calm unruffled waters of the St. Laurent period. But in having to cope with economic and other difficulties largely not of his own making, he created the impression that he was indecisive. One thing he could not be criticized for was a lack of cabinet meetings. When asked how many of these meetings there had been, a deputy minister replied: "Just one. It started on June 22, 1957, and it's still going on – with occasional brief adjournments."[4]

None the less, because of the Prime Minister's personality, the cabinet could never operate as a genuine team. As Douglas Fisher saw it, John Diefenbaker never "communicated at close quarters in a small gathering of peers. . . . [He] always had a barrier up, partly of mistrust, largely of egocentrism, which his Cabinet colleagues of strength could never pierce with their candor." Conservative backbenchers asked: "How do we get through to him that we've got to be more decisive?"; cabinet ministers and executive assistants said that "getting him to make up his mind is almost impossible"; and speech writers became indignant because "it's always he, himself, and the political limelight: never the content of what's written or the policy context." In short, there could not be that "even-steven, give-and-take exchange of friends and equals" which makes for prompt decision-making.[5]

Professor Frank Underhill added faults he considered even more serious: Diefenbaker's failure to grow with office and his habit of inflating himself. In office, men who are capable of growth usually develop beyond the "corrupting vice of the professional oppositionist, the fondness for making rhetorical and demagogic points against their opponents." In contrast, the Prime Minister and some of his colleagues were marked – so wrote Professor Underhill – by a nasty temper in debate, a self-righteousness, a tendency to whine when things were not going well, and an eternal looking for bogeymen on whom to lay the blame for their own failures.[6]

However unfair or exaggerated these criticisms were, much of the Canadian electorate had reached similar conclusions. Certainly the grand vision of 1958 seemed to have become a hollow mockery. The dreams of a do-it-yourself development of Canada's own resources and a Britain-centred, trade-integrated Commonwealth had dissipated when confronted with cold reality; the promise of a 15 per cent trade diversion had been nothing but a will o' the wisp. Although an economic upswing had begun in the second quarter of 1961, it aroused little enthusiasm, coming as it did after serious unemployment, large deficits, and mounting public debt. During the pre-election session of 1962 the government seemed to be interested mainly in implementing such vote-getting parts of the Speech from the

Throne as those that promised increased pensions, greater aid for municipal winter works programmes, and an extension of the Gaspé Railway. Significantly, the first item of government business to be pushed through was a $42 million acreage payment to western farmers, and the session closed with a promise to build the Prince Edward Island causeway. Journalist John Stevenson thought the latter "established a new peak for electioneering bribery." Did the country have no "statesmen who care for its fortunes when they are dead and in their graves?"[7]

With a good deal of truth Ramsay Cook said the session had done little except for "granting 'better terms' to a few well-chosen sections of the electorate."[8] The Prime Minister had spent a good deal of time in reviving by-gone controversies and denigrating Pearson's inner circle of advisers. After almost a year of guessing, predicting, and teasing about the election, he still kept members in suspense with recurring dark hints about its imminence. Not until April 17 did he "quit playing Pavlov"[9] and announce it for June 18.

Few regretted the demise of the Twenty-fourth Parliament. John Stevenson attributed many of its weaknesses to "a large contingent of second raters who . . . climbed into their seats on the coat-tails of the triumphant Mr. Diefenbaker in 1958." As a generality this was harsh, but the difficulty of keeping a huge horde of backbenchers occupied had led to pronounced absenteeism, silly interruptions, petty backchat, and occasional rowdiness. Stevenson also suggested that John Diefenbaker had failed to live up to Bagehot's dictum that "the greatest elevator of the country as far as Parliament elevates it must be the Prime Minister."[10] The disrespect for the traditional procedures of Parliament, which had begun under the Liberals, got worse under the Conservatives. Few took seriously the Prime Minister's complaint that parliamentary obstruction had brought on the election. If he could not control the House with some 200-odd supporters, it was surely time to give someone else a chance.

In the campaign that followed – the "slickest" to date – the Liberals were easily foremost in resorting to Madison Avenue techniques. All the opposition parties had at least sought to replenish their stock of ideas since the deluge of 1958. To demonstrate that his party was genuinely in search of liberalism, Lester Pearson convened a thinkers' conference at Kingston in September 1960, followed by a non-leadership convention – the second in the party's history – in January. Although Dale Thomson said the Liberals had "ended up relatively where they started from," Pearson felt he had a solid framework on which to build a platform.[11]

Social Crediters, wiped out completely in 1958, met in mid-1960 to draft a new constitution and restate their national policy. A year later they chose Robert Thompson as their national leader. Although Réal Caouette had to be satisfied with the associate leadership, he did get the party's national council to endorse the idea of a $100 basic monthly dividend.

In contrast, the C.C.F. presented itself in a totally different guise. In 1960 the Canadian Labour Congress instructed its executive council to enter into discussions with the C.C.F., farmers' organizations, and like-minded groups or individuals with a view to "creating an alternative force based on the needs of workers, farmers and similar groups." When the founding convention of the new party eventually met in mid-1961, it was quickly apparent that the trade unionists and the liberal-minded Canadians who constituted the New Party clubs had triumphed over the left wing of the C.C.F. The name and leader of the new party were proof enough of that. By calling themselves the New Democratic party the delegates rejected any label that hinted at socialism or social democracy. By choosing T.C. Douglas as leader they showed that they had no intention of taking the cream separator from its owner; "all we want," said Douglas, "is some of the cream." The socialistic Colin Cameron indignantly replied that the owners of private industry "want the cream, not the fun of owning the separator."[12]

Among other things the N.D.P. programme included full employment through economic planning, a national investment board to stimulate economic growth, a new ministry to supervise economic and social planning, progressive taxes to redistribute the national income more fairly, the expansion of public and co-operative ownership in utilities, a comprehensive social security programme, and a national labour code with minimum standards. Seemingly the N.D.P. emerged a little to the right of the C.C.F. in the Winnipeg Declaration of 1956.

In spite of all this emphasis, policies and platforms had little to do with the electoral decisions of 1962. Because John Diefenbaker's study of history convinced him that a lack of major issues favoured the party in power, he deliberately started his campaign in low gear and planned to keep it there.[13] He campaigned, for the most part, on his record. If it had been simply a matter of keeping a large proportion of his election promises – although not some of the major ones – he could have made a good case. In the context of 1962, however, that was not a vote-winning argument.

More positively, the Prime Minister outlined a "16-point prosperity blueprint" as the second stage of a national development policy. "Vast as our program has been in the last five years, it will be even greater in the five years ahead."[14] Yet even his most optimistic supporters did "not see it as the stuff from which victories are wrought."[15] He should have realized he was most effective when he was denouncing sin and sinners. In any case he was soon back on this tack. To voters of East European origin he charged that the Liberals were "soft on communism." Contrast this, he said, with his reply to Khrushchov ("The Speech") at the UN in September 1960. He denounced the "six-buck boys," the socialist experimenters, the ivory-tower people such as Mitchell Sharp, Walter Gordon, and Maurice Lamontagne.

They are your potential masters, a conglomeration of hopeless and hopefuls, a veritable Cave of Addulam, where all the misfits in creation are collected together – a cacophany of jargon.[16]

They've remade Mr. Pearson in their image. . . . This is the same old bunch who showed contempt for Parliament . . . the strong right arm of the government when Canadians were pushed around.[17]

But none of this had the effect he desired.

What he wants [wrote Gerald Waring] is something that clearly portrays him as St. George and Mike Pearson as the dragon. . . . The fact is that none of his oratorical assaults on the 'bureaucrats', the Grit 'socialists', the 'same old bunch' . . . appears to be setting the political heather afire. And this is leaving the P.M. to fight the election on his government's record . . . and on his proposals for a second Tory 'five year plan'. . . .

[These] are not issues of a kind needed to stir a complacent electorate. They lack drama and stark conflict of the kind the pipeline debate produced and put John Diefenbaker on the defensive, where he is least effective – so even at this rather late hour he reaches for the political nostrum that will cure the people's criticism of his record.[18]

For their part, the Liberals started out with no less than 75 proposals, most of them based on the resolutions of their 1961 convention. Among other things they promised measures to promote economic growth and provide a million new jobs, a new approach to federal-provincial relations, a square deal for farmers, and improved welfare services. This was not all. Lester Pearson added to the list almost wherever he went; the Ottawa *Journal* observed that "never in the whole history of electioneering surely, has there been such a plethora of promises. . . . And Mr. Pearson has still six weeks to go! Heaven only knows what his young planners – the boys with 'formulas and gimmicks' – will make him say before we come to the end."[19]

Yet, on the whole, the Liberals followed John F. Kennedy's strategy as outlined in Theodore White's *The Making of a President* in concentrating on a few generalized issues.[20] Their private surveys had indicated that the voters saw little difference in the shape of Canada's prestige abroad under the two parties and little difference in their defence policies. Their surveys did make clear the voters' concern with unemployment, the high cost of living, and budget deficits.[21] Therefore, Pearson laid primary emphasis on Tory bungling and the need to get the economy moving again.

This time the Liberal leader had a much firmer grasp of domestic questions. However, he still had problems. He had developed no great skill as a party manager. He relied excessively on an inner brains trust who, whatever their other abilities, were political novices. According to one displaced veteran, "today in the management of the Liberal party's affairs practical politicians have no place; only 'eggheads' are wanted."[22] To counter his obvious awkwardness before large gatherings and his lack of appeal to the grass roots, Pearson sought to cultivate the homely manner, the human touch. To many he appeared too artificial to be convincing. While Diefenbaker had raised many doubts, Pearson had not convinced the public that he was beyond question the one to supply the leadership that seemed to be lacking.

Meanwhile T.C. Douglas was doing his best to attract the trade unionists within the C.L.C. and retain the support of farmers who were lukewarm about unions. In accordance with the party's philosophy, Douglas put forward a programme of social and developmental legislation, more radical than socialist, emphasizing planning instead of nationalization. As the campaign progressed, he seemed more and more to make medicare the chief issue. In Quebec, following the line of his party's founding convention, he supported a "two-nations" theory, at least in its sociological sense.

In contrast, Robert Thompson asserted repeatedly that he led the only conservative party in the country. While his followers talked as usual about extensive financial reform and increased purchasing power, they emphasized even more a reduction in big government and support of the free enterprise system. Ramsay Cook was led to say they were "on a totally different wave length from the rest of the parties . . . they have just found and been inebriated by Adam Smith (or is it Barry Goldwater?)"[23] While Thompson himself played down the old Social Credit orthodoxy, Réal Caouette was obviously much more of a fundamentalist.

Initially the campaign lacked the crackling tension of 1958, but it steadily increased in tempo. More and more, the Prime Minister made the news, although not in the manner he wanted. He stole the headlines first on May 2 when he announced the devaluation of the Canadian dollar to 92½ cents in terms of the American. Kuch of the *Winnipeg Free Press*, in what Professor John Saywell called the most effective political cartoon in Canadian history,[24] depicted Minister of Finance Donald Fleming nailing to the mast a 92½ cent dollar bearing a picture of the Prime Minister. This was the first of the Diefenbucks or Diefendollars of which thousands were to be distributed.

Politically it would have been wiser to admit frankly the country's financial difficulties, rather than pretend they did not exist. Yet initially the Prime Minister treated devaluation as a gimmick to help the export and tourist industries. "My brother Elmer was in New York the day we did it. He was told *three times* what a marvellous thing this would be for the tourist

by Kuch. Winnipeg Free Press, *May 4, 1962. Courtesy of* Free Press.

trade." But when even the unsophisticated wondered why it was done with such speed in the middle of an election, Diefenbaker adopted another line of argument. His new position was that there were two Canadian dollars, and the dollar "you use to support yourself and your family" retained its old value.[25] When, a little later, Pearson suggested that devaluation was a panic response to a run on the dollar and that other countries were helping to maintain the value of the Canadian dollar, the Prime Minister vehemently denied it. How "unworthy of the leader of a great party" it was "to strike a blow at the financial integrity of Canada!"[26] But he was not out of trouble yet, for his "domestic" dollar did not maintain its value and the prices of essential foods began to go up. Borrowing a leaf from Kennedy's book, he warned that "if, in the next few days, this kind of thing is going on there will be action as effective as it is drastic." Because of a lack of constitutional power, however, he was fighting a battle with an unloaded gun.[27]

Early in the campaign Diefenbaker spurned the Liberal leader's challenge to a television debate. Later, when Pearson adopted another Kennedy tack and posed ten questions for him to answer on devaluation, taxes, deficits, and trade, he totally ignored them in the growing drama of his campaign. At a poorly attended meeting in Edmonton he lashed out against the sinister interests opposing him, and later against Charles King of Southam News, who dared to write: "In the same city where the Conservative campaign caught fire in 1958, the Diefenbaker bubble burst Friday night."[28] Then in Trail, as the Prime Minister put it, some Doukhobor women got down to essentials. Finally, in Vancouver he performed admirably against the ban-the-bombers and unemployed who threatened to turn his huge meeting into a debacle. When, a few days later, a cursing mob assailed him at Chelmsford, Ontario, and Premier Smallwood prevented Donald Fleming from addressing a Rotary convention in St. John's on devaluation, he had all the ammunition he wanted. He could use it both to accuse the Liberals of resorting to their old tactics of closure and to attract sympathy to himself. "It started this time in Vancouver,"[29] was the way he prefixed his exultant prophecies of victory. Naturally he pulled out all the stops when he referred to the variations of his name which his opponents were using: Diefenbucks, Diefenbunkum, Double double Diefentrouble, Diefenboil, and Diefenbubble. To one group of ethnic voters he said: "The playing with my name indicates what they think of those of non-French and non-English origin."[30]

The old parties asked the voters to choose between the Liberals' "Take a stand for tomorrow" and the Conservatives' "Diefenbaker, the man for all Canada." No clear issue emerged and some observers suggested that the voters were lost in the fog. Certainly they got no clarification from the later stages of Diefenbaker's campaign or, as Val Sears described it, the "seven-week run of the greatest political show in Canada." The Prime Minister discussed national issues even less than before; he fell back even more on catch phrases, oversimplification, and "smothering [of] the issues in an eiderdown of words."[31] Again and again he declaimed against the sinister interests that threatened to engulf both him and the average Canadian: the Liberal brains trust, "a collection that had never been seen outside a menagerie"; the American press, which was howling against devaluation because it benefited Canada; the price-raisers—but "I spoke words they understand and there has been no increase in prices";[32] the Russians, against whom he promised a United Nations' resolution calling for the liberation of the satellite countries; and, finally, Khrushchov, who, only days before the campaign ended, had the "colossal effrontery" to protest formally against Canada's alleged preparation to accept nuclear arms. "Do you know why he is annoyed?" asked John Diefenbaker. "He doesn't want this government back because we took a stand on Soviet colonialism that he doesn't like."[33] Donald Fleming went his leader one better and suggested that Khrushchov's intervention was meant to secure the election of Lester Pearson, a man who had said he would "rather be Red than dead."[34] To insinuations that he had gone soft on communism the Liberal leader replied angrily: "I was fighting Communism at the United Nations before John Diefenbaker ever heard of it."[35] Both Pearson and Douglas thought it "cruel and deceiving" to create the impression among the ethnic groups that the satellite countries could regain their freedom easily or quickly.[36] But nothing could stop John Diefenbaker in full flight.

Furthermore, the Gallup Poll seemed to confirm that his campaigning as "a strong, essentially simple person who loves and understands the 'average Canadian' "[37] was not without effect:

	P.C.	L.	N.D.P.	S.C.	O.
May 26	36%	44%	10%	9%	—
June 6	32	42	13	12	1
June 13	36	38	12	13	1
June 18 (actual)	37.3	37.2	13.5	11.7	0.4

The appeal he made was primarily responsible for radical departures from normal Canadian electoral behaviour in 1962. Because of its overwhelming victory four years earlier, the Diefenbaker government might have been expected to suffer losses in all regions. "But the extent, unevenness, locale, and beneficiaries of the swing were sometimes bewildering."[38] Electorally Canada seemed to become four or five countries.

Previously, voting along regional rather than class lines had characterized Canadian politics. But in 1962 only the Atlantic and Prairie provinces conformed to the norm of regional voting. In a turn-about of the usual order of things the Conservatives were strongest in the rural areas, growing progressively weaker as the size of the community increased; with the Liberal and N.D.P. parties the converse was true.[39] Even more startling, the upper-middle and upper income voters in urban Canada—once so Conservative that they had stamped their party as the party of the rich—were in full revolt. They simply could not condone high deficits and what they considered to be indecisiveness and poor management; they looked askance on the Prime Minister's denunciation of expertise, of which they saw too little evidence. As an insurance office manager in Hamilton put it, "I pay taxes for that man down there and he throws the money around." Disillusionment with Diefenbaker himself was rife among these groups. "He's not the man I thought he was," one Halifax lady stated bluntly. Especially reflecting these attitudes was the St. Antoine–Westmount riding of Montreal, where the Liberal candidate did poorly in the low-income district of St. Henri, but more than made up for it in wealthy Westmount.

The pronounced drift away from the government manifested itself in all levels of urban society, at least in central Canada. As Peter Regenstreif points out, when change is in the air, city dwellers are more susceptible to it because of the greater likelihood of political discussion outside the family environment and the greater contact with the mass media.[40] Not surprisingly, then, the Conservatives did poorly in Montreal, Toronto, Winnipeg, and Vancouver, and lost any possibility of securing an over-all majority. In these four major centres the Conservative contingent dropped from 41 to 8, while the Liberals elected 37 members instead of 12 and the N.D.P. 10 instead of 2.

In the Atlantic and Prairie provinces regional and economic considerations were intertwined. Normally the Maritimes exhibit a type of rationality (or prescience if you will) in ending up on the winning side. This time, despite the Gallup Poll, they had the feeling that the Conservatives would win with a reduced majority.[41] The Conservatives also benefited from the slogan, "Diefenbaker – the best friend the region ever had." The swing towards the Liberals, however, was so strong that they won back most of the normally strong Liberal seats. Thus in New Brunswick, Restigouche-Madawaska, Westmorland, and Charlotte returned to the Liberal fold, as did Inverness-Richmond and Antigonish-Guysborough in Nova Scotia. Cape Breton South went to the N.D.P. but, somewhat surprisingly, the Conservative Felton Légère held on to usually Grit Shelburne-Yarmouth-Clare – perhaps because of the public works he had jollied out of the ministers and their deputies. "Why, the whole French Acadian coast is a wharf,"[42] was one comment. With the assurance of a causeway, Prince Edward Island did what it was expected to do and re-elected 4 Conservatives. In Newfoundland, Term 29 became the chief issue. Premier Smallwood alleged that Diefenbaker had sabotaged his province by putting a time limit on the payments to be made by Ottawa under this term. The Conservative avalanche of 1958, he continued, was "like the great plague, the black death. . . . Now the voters are healthy again . . . and we're going to keep the black death away from our voters." Yet, for all his efforts, the Conservatives held on to St. John's East, and it took the service vote to beat them in St. John's West.[43] All told, the Conservatives lost 7 seats in the Atlantic provinces, not a bad showing as things went in 1962.

In the Prairie provinces they did even better. "Johnny's going back," exulted one Saskatchewan farmer. "I was for him last time. I'm for him again."[44] He and his fellows noted with satisfaction that several years' accumulations of unsold grain were rapidly dwindling; they gave full credit to John Diefenbaker and his Minister of Agriculture Alvin Hamilton for the sales of wheat to China and other Communist countries that made this possible. To the urban dweller of central Canada the government may have looked indecisive, but not to the Saskatchewan farmer.[45] In the three months preceding the election other factors, some of which could hardly be credited to the government, contributed further to a "counter-revolution" in Saskatchewan. In March there came an increase of 12.5 cents in the basic price of wheat and a record-breaking final payment on the 1960 crop; in May, devaluation and with it a further increase of 6 cents a bushel; an announcement that acreage payments would be on an annual rather than an *ad hoc* basis, and a general rain, which made crop prospects bright.[46] No wonder the Conservative candidates did not overwork themselves in the campaign; no wonder they retained all their rural seats. They failed, however, by a mere 353 votes to take Assiniboia from Hazen Argue, now running as a Liberal. The sense of well-being that pervaded rural Saskatchewan extended to the urban areas. There the Conservatives were also helped by their refusal to become involved in the bitter medicare dispute in which the Liberals and the N.D.P. were embroiled. They had no trouble holding on to the city seats, beating T.C. Douglas decisively in Regina.

For the same reasons operating in rural Saskatchewan, all of Manitoba's rural seats remained Conservative. However, Winnipeg North, Winnipeg North Centre, and St. Boniface returned to their old moorings, the first two to the N.D.P., the last to the Liberals. The Conservatives barely held on to the 2 seats in South Winnipeg, Gordon Chown's plurality in Winnipeg South being reduced from 19,784 to 392. In Alberta the 5 mainly urban Edmonton and Calgary ridings remained with the Conservatives, but they lost heavily in the high income areas, especially in Edmonton West. They also lost 2 of their rural seats to Social Crediters Robert Thompson and H.A. "Bud" Olson, but these were personal victories more than anything else.

John Diefenbaker won 42 seats in the Prairie provinces, a loss of 5 but a phenomenal showing in terms of any election other than 1958. The other 3 parties had to be satisfied with 2 seats each.

The Conservatives also fared well in the largely rural areas of old Ontario. Of the solid Conservative contingent which metropolitan Toronto returned in 1958 only Donald Fleming, George Hees, and Frank McGee survived; the others were replaced by 12 Liberal and 3 N.D.P. members. Northern Ontario again returned Liberals except for the N.D.P. members in Port Arthur, Timmins, and Timiskaming. However, away from the big centres in southern Ontario it was another story. Granted there was a swing towards the Liberals, but it met stout resistance, even though these areas had not benefited from the bounty of John Diefenbaker to anywhere near the extent the Atlantic and Prairie provinces had. Much of the Prime Minister's glamour had worn off in these parts, but he was still preferable to Lester Pearson, no matter what Madison Avenue techniques were used to improve the latter's image. Almost without exception, the Conservatives retained the primarily rural seats they had won in 1958. In the mixed urban-rural ridings the Liberals did much better and picked up such seats as Peel, Lincoln, Brant-Haldimand, Kent, and Lambton-Kent. None the less, the Conservatives held on to 12 of their 17 seats in eastern Ontario and 20 of their 31 seats in western Ontario. This gave them 35 seats in the whole province, down 32 from 1958. But rural Ontario had saved them from utter rout.

The remaining provinces, British Columbia and Quebec, were disaster areas for the Conservatives. British Columbia, which had led the way in "following John," turned more strongly against him than any other province. Its upper income groups went the same way as those in central Canada, while its trade unionists resumed their leftist posture. Only Howard Green's vote-drawing abilities enabled him to retain the higher status riding of Vancouver Quadra, and the party's other victories resulted from either the personal strength of the candidates – such as Davie Fulton in Kamloops – or from a fairly even split of the vote among four parties, as in the Okanagans.

The N.D.P. was the real victor in British Columbia: it took 30.9 per cent of the vote and almost half the seats. The obvious reason for its strength, wrote Professor Walter Young, lies in the urban nature of the province and the urban orientation of the N.D.P.[47] The province's urban-industrial economy, he continued, is based on primary production and is highly dependent on export trade. Hence, management is peculiarly sensitive to costs, and this leads to rancorous labour-management relations in the most unionized of the provinces. At the same time the anti-union bias of the Social Credit provincial government has solidified the labour movement and strengthened its desire for more vigorous political action.[48] Prior to the founding of the N.D.P., the British Columbia Federation of Labour and the C.C.F. had worked in close collaboration. In the absence of N.D.P. clubs such as those which sprang up in Ontario, the Federation assumed the primary responsibility for setting up the new party. So "the B.C. Federation of Labour is, in a real sense, a wing of the provincial N.D.P. – or, as some have argued, vice versa."[49] The result was to give the N.D.P. the strongest base it has in Canada, but not without cost. The antipathy between labour and management led to a strong anti-labour bias in the middle class, which may act as a limiting factor on future growth of the N.D.P. Not surprisingly, 9 of the 10 N.D.P. seats were won in areas of C.C.F. strength, and the only new ground to be broken was Vancouver-Burrard, which the N.D.P. won by a mere 94 votes.

Of the remaining seats in British Columbia, the Conservatives took 6, the Liberals 4, and Social Credit 2.

In an election of surprises, Quebec provided the biggest one of all. In 1958 French Canada decided to go on a venture; it returned to the party of Macdonald without really attaching itself. However, it did not like the fruits of its escapade. It got a few minor concessions, but it also got serious unemployment. Moreover, at a time when it was bursting forth from Duplessisism, first under Paul Sauvé and then under Jean Lesage, the government at Ottawa seemed utterly remote. French Canada talked about realizing itself, but the Prime Minister "thought only Canadian."[50] Quebec could not identify with him or any of his lieutenants. A Conservative party that appealed to Quebeckers on its past record and promised more of the same could hardly expect success in 1962.

However, the Liberals did not look much better. Although their provincial wing had thoroughly rejuvenated itself, their federal wing had not. They proposed nothing to inspire the imagination, and for new blood they presented only Lionel Chevrier. Yet, although he was French, he came from Stormont, Ontario and was hardly acceptable to Quebeckers as the leader's chief lieutenant. Clearly the Liberals expected Quebec to return automatically to their fold.

Most Quebeckers were not impressed by Pearson despite his improved French. His tacticians must have realized this, for his picture never appeared in the party's advertisements; instead they referred to the team of Liberal candidates, "les 75."[51] The Liberal leader might have helped if he had avoided making platitudes in his speeches; but he echoed the old refrain that under the Conservatives, French Canada had not been allowed to play the role which was its right and that the Liberals would redress this wrong. He said little that appealed specifically to emerging Quebec.

For all these reasons "political interest, in Quebec, except for the few New Democrats, was uniformly low." Robert Alford wondered how much of this lack of interest might be due to "the apolitical character of Quebec" and how much to its "alienation from the nation to the point where elections to a national parliament have less importance for them" than for the rest of Canada.[52] The latter feeling explained much of it; except when the leaders were in the province, the metropolitan press was almost silent on the Liberal, Conservative, and N.D.P. campaigns and except for Réal Caouette, "no Quebec candidate aroused more than local interest."[53]

Almost no one took Caouette seriously until towards the end. This is understandable; although a radical tradition exists in Quebec, in the past it had little success in electing third-party members to Parliament.[54] There was a feeling in 1962 that when the voters "get behind that curtain . . . they'll think that if they don't vote *rouge* or *bleu* they'll be excommunicated."[55] But non-academic Caouettism had a different fate than the academic radicalism that preceded it.

Caouette had established Le Ralliement des Créditistes de Québec in June 1958 and had begun at once to present his views on Rouyn-Noranda's TV station. As membership dues permitted, he bought time on the stations in Trois Rivières, Sherbrooke, New Carlisle, and Quebec City. During the winter of 1961-62 there were 12,000 members and he was using 9 stations. "By the time the election was called, [he] was as popular in rural and small-town Quebec as Boom-Boom Géoffrion."[56] Without a doubt the Social Credit phenomenon was one man. "More than any one man influenced any other area, Caouette's personality shaped and colored the campaign through a vast piece of Quebec."[57]

Caouette did not write out his speeches, but quickly sensed how to approach a crowd. He told them they came into the world on a finance plan and died on a budgetary plan. The first bought the layette; the second paid the undertaker. If they lost their jobs at 45, they were too old for family allowances and too young for old age pensions. What they needed was liberty and security through money. At that point he ventured into his version of Social Credit monetary theory or, as someone put it, "he pronounced a few words in Latin."[58] Although he insisted that his hearers could be for Social Credit without understanding it, they always went away feeling they had understood. Like the other leaders, Caouette borrowed from John F. Kennedy: "Don't ask what Social Credit can do for me. Ask what I can do for Social Credit."[59] But his clinching argument was: "You have nothing to lose by voting Social Credit."

Peter Regenstreif was the first to draw attention to Social Credit. In the Montreal *Star* of May 19 he stated that Caouette had the support of 15 per cent of the urban voters and 30 per cent of the rural voters in the 28 seats east of Trois Rivières. A little later some journalists – including Gérard Pelletier of *La Presse* and Fernand Bourret of *Le Devoir* – expressed similar opinions. The Gallup Poll had recorded a marked increase in the popularity of Social Credit a year and a half earlier as the table below shows. The Poll's finding of June 9, based on interviews compiled by May 26, indicated a further gain of 7 percentage points in Social Credit strength, apparently at the expense of the Conservatives. However, the immediate pre-election poll simply talked about "an abnormally turbulent electorate" and rapid gains for Social Credit, this time, as it turned out, at the expense of the Liberals.

	P.C.	L.	S.C.
1958 (actual)	49.6%	45.7%	0.6%
January 1961	25	65	8
September 1961	32	47	16
November 1961	33	50	13
May 1962	32	53	12
June 9, 1962	25	52	19
June 18 (actual)	29.6	39.2	26.0

Despite the warnings of growing Social Credit strength, the counterattacks were slow in coming. Not until June 11 did Jean Marchand denounce it to his trade unionists; not until June 13 did André Laurendeau call it "une monumentale duperie" in *Le Devoir*; and not till June 14 did René Lévesque take to television to condemn it.[60] Only at this late date did the Liberals spend what was left of their advertising budget proclaiming: "Créditistes, your leaders are deceiving you."

By then it was much, much too late. On June 18 Quebec, for the first time in its history, gave a substantial number of seats—26—to a third party. Their victories were not marginal: in 14 seats they polled more than 50 per cent of the vote. Their successes—all within Caouette's TV coverage—were contiguous seats in the form of half an ellipse starting north of Trois Rivières and moving east to take in all the seats of Northern Quebec, dipping south to include all the Quebec City seats except Quebec South, extending south of the St. Lawrence to the United States, dipping deep into the Eastern Townships, but not including the 5 isolated ridings of Gaspésie. Their percentage of the popular vote varied from 6.2 in Metropolitan Montreal, through 26.9 in the Trois Rivières Region and 48.0 in Quebec City, to 54.6 in Abitibi-Témiscamingue.

When the election was over Caouette got the attention he had not had before. He was variously described as a French-Canadian combination of William Aberhart, Pierre Poujade, Dale Carnegie, and Juan Péron; as a Hitler; as a Don Quixote; and as an ignorant and unscrupulous demagogue. André Laurendeau, though no admirer of Caouette, wondered if he was any more demagogic than the Liberals had been in their long-time resort to the conscription issue.[61] The fight in Quebec had been between the Liberals and Social Credit. Although the Conservatives polled a slightly higher percentage of the popular vote than the Social Crediters, they spread it over 75 ridings, while Caouette's followers concentrated theirs in about half as many. This time John Diefenbaker pulled no one to victory; the 14 Conservatives who got in did so by their own efforts.

On the Island of Montreal the vote was overwhelmingly Liberal, although Conservative Georges Valade held on to Ste. Marie. Even if Caouette had used TV in Montreal, the result would have been no different. The Liberals had too many things working in their favour: the support of the opinion leaders, the good record of the Lesage provincial government, and the tendency to blame the economic difficulties on the Conservatives. Also, as Gérard Pelletier indicated, Caouette appealed to the folklore culture that is so characteristic of Quebec's small communities,[62] but almost nonexistent in Montreal.[63] On the Island the more English-speaking a seat was, the less its shift to Social Credit. Jewish voters were especially anti-Social Credit presumably because of its anti-Semitic tendencies. There was a slight shift to Social Credit in Montreal, but it occurred in less affluent French constituencies.[64]

In areas that depended on stagnant industry or that were too remote from Montreal for market gardening, the situation was quite different. Small farmers, who in more prosperous times had gone into debt to buy agricultural machinery, found themselves squeezed between increasing costs and stable returns for their products and could see no way out.[65] Workers in areas dependent on one dominant industry, which was itself dependent on world markets, felt equally helpless, as pulp and paper, aluminum, and textile plants cut down production in the face of declining sales abroad. Such people could not see that anything would be lost by voting Social Credit.

Professor Vincent Lemieux, in his study of the election in the riding of Lévis, found three components present everywhere in the Social Credit wave: economic protest and aversion to the old parties, Caouette's speeches, and the transmission of his ideas to workers whose enthusiasm for them contrasted with the weariness of the old parties' organizations:

> [Caouette's] speeches took place on Sunday night at supper time when families were all together. A very popular broadcast (L'Heure des Quilles) preceded Caouette. . . . [He] was also followed by a very popular program (Robin des Bois): there was, therefore, a strong tendency to leave the set turned on during the Social Credit program. . . .
>
> Many people who were very hostile at first and who regarded Caouette as some sort of deranged person, came in this way to agree with one or two of his ideas. During the week they would have the chance to discuss them with friends, neighbours, or fellow workers. It was in these primary groups that opinion leaders, who had previously been converted . . . convinced the others to pay closer attention to Caouette. Many would do this the following Sunday, thus making themselves even more receptive to the Social Credit opinion leaders.[66]

If Lévis was typical, conversions took place inversely proportional to the size of the community, and largely among those who had turned to Diefenbaker in 1958, perhaps for analogous reasons. However, Professor Lemieux indicates there was an urban as well as a rural créditisme, and that it was marked not only by economic protest and political disaffection, but also by dissatisfaction with the social order. Since it resulted not from low earnings but from a feeling of being dominated, it was more a social than an economic phenomenon; and where English-speaking owners or managers were doing the dominating, it assumed the form of nationalistic discontent.[67] W.P. Irvine's analysis plays down the importance of economic protest alone and suggests that Caouette's success primarily depended on a combination of nationalistic and economic frustrations. While he seems to go too far, he does show that the seats that went Social Credit invariably had a large centre or two containing industry owned and managed by Anglo-Saxons, and that the nationalism of these centres could be easily communicated to the rural areas around them. It is also true that Social Credit did poorly in Gaspésie where, although the people's economic lot was poor, the lack of communications prevented them from comparing it with the lot of people elsewhere.[68] Thus urban créditisme added another dimension to Social Credit support. In addition to unskilled workers, farmers, village shop-keepers and the like – generally those with incomes under $3,000 – it brought in blue- and white-collar workers who were more culturally than economi-cally deprived. However, few professional people and intellectuals took Caouette seriously.

Connected to the economic and nationalistic aspects, there was also a religious one. Social Credit was clearly strongest in areas where the clergy clung to traditionalism and were fearful of the reforming Pope John XXIII. Here, because of clerical influence, the people had become suspicious of socialism. Their poverty also made them dislike big capital; yet, if they tried to be small capitalists, they encountered the Anglo-Saxon trusts. Social Credit, as the party of both free enterprise and the French Canadians, resolved their dilemma.[69] Its leader was a French-Canadian tribune who spoke the people's language, in contrast to the distant aristocrats and nota-bles who had previously dominated Quebec politics. Likewise Social Credit candidates were "firmly rooted in the local community, prominent in civic affairs, members of local clubs, known for their good works, and respected for their large families."[70]

Caouettism may have been a strange mixture of *poujadism*, conserv-atism, protest, leftism, and fascism;[71] it may have produced an anarchist vote, a vote of ignoramuses and political minors, a vote of feeble people who felt persecuted.[72] But whatever it was or did, it took 26 seats that the Liberals had counted on, limiting their total in Quebec to 35 and thereby preventing them from having the most seats in the Commons. They won 100 seats to the Conservatives' 116. John Diefenbaker would carry on, at least for the moment.

For some time Canadian periodicals had abounded with appeals for systematic analyses of Canadian electoral behaviour comparable to studies in the United States. For the election of 1962, two professors in American universities, Robert Alford and Peter Regenstreif, provided separate studies of this kind.[73] Because they had to rely largely on a Canadian Institute of Public Opinion (C.I.P.O.) survey not specially designed for their purpose, they were unable to use a political science approach based on the voter's indi-vidual perception; they used a sociological approach and assumed that "the behaviour of social collectivities or aggregates . . . is the most important way to examine the social basis of support for political parties."[74] Never-theless Regenstreif was struck by "the seeming instability of voter commit-ment over time" and the "very few constants which can be relied upon in terms of individual party support,"[75] while Alford found "literally no stable bases for the Canadian parties . . . except on a very *local* basis."[76]

Commenting on the studies, Professor Meisel concluded that "almost any statement made about Canadian voting behaviour as a whole can be shown to be strongly contradicted in some region or among some sections of the population."[77] For example, 49 per cent of Catholics across Canada voted Liberal and 24 per cent Conservative. However, in Ontario 70 per cent of them voted Liberal to 10 per cent for the Conservatives; in Alberta only 36 per cent of them voted Liberal, and 42 per cent voted Conservative.

Alford's study of occupation, education, and socio-economic status demonstrated once again the lack of any significant class basis in Canadian politics. In all the social class groups the Liberals drew almost identical support—36 to 40 per cent. Differences in support were in the Conservative and N.D.P. totals, the latter polling more votes in the lower income groups than the former. Despite the defections in 1962, Protestant Conservatives still constituted "the highest status group of any in Canada, comprising a high proportion of businessmen, professionals and of people largely English in background." However, even in broad generalities of this kind there are inconsistencies and lack of uniformity. Certainly "voting patterns could not be easily predicted from a knowledge of the class status of the voter."[78] Religious, regional, and ethnic variations distinguished party support most consistently.

None of the four leaders could have exulted over the outcome. Robert Thompson's party had, in effect, become an expression of French-Canadian disillusionment; 26 of its 30 members owed their election and their first loyalty to someone other than their national leader. For T.C. Douglas the election was disappointing, partly because of his personal defeat, partly because of his party's somewhat poor showing in polling only 13.5 per cent of the vote. Since all of its 19 seats were won with strong trade union support, some observers were already calling it a labour party. However, its task of converting the unionists had only begun; it had secured only 22 per cent of their votes across the country, 4 percentage points fewer than the Conservatives and 16 percentage points fewer than the Liberals.

Lester Pearson had done much better than in 1958, but not nearly so well as the early Gallup Poll findings had led him to anticipate. The election confirmed his inability to communicate to voters in rural areas and smaller communities; he had done well in urban Canada, but this seemed to be due less to any appeal that he possessed, than to the voters' rejection of the Prime Minister.

As for John Diefenbaker, he had dropped no fewer than 92 seats and his party looked as if it might become a rural-based movement. Certainly it had lost its élan or, as Blair Fraser put it, it "looks beaten, it feels beaten, and nobody is afraid of it any more."[79] The result must have been especially disappointing to one who had boasted of a deep understanding of the Canadian people as John Diefenbaker had. According to Peter Newman, he seemed to think that the melodramatics of 1957 and 1958 would work in the sober circumstances of 1962–and they did not. Likewise, he totally misjudged the sophistication of urban voters by failing to talk to them frankly about Canada's financial difficulties. In other words, "he thought he understood the voters better than he did."[80]

As in 1925 and 1957, the results did not permit one party to form a majority government. Because of the ever-growing complexity of political forces in the country, Professor Meisel wondered if in the future minority government would become the rule rather than the exception.[81] However, the results in 1962 appeared to be due more to the personalities of the two leaders, especially John Diefenbaker, than to anything else. What Diefenbaker had done was to divide Canada along rural-urban lines more than had ever been done before. Almost everything about him had contributed to this type of cleavage. In office, he had been especially solicitous of Atlantic and Prairie Canada; he had gratified them by his decision to sell grain to the Communist countries and his promise to build the Prince Edward Island causeway. But in matters of concern to urban Canada he appeared quite indecisive, lacking the capacity to conduct a business-like government. Devaluation, which in urban eyes seriously damaged Canada's prestige, was hailed by western farmers as a means of increasing their income. Also, the Diefenbaker brand of oratory had worn much less well in the urban parts than in the less sophisticated rural areas.

Lester Pearson's role, it turned out, was to reinforce rather than reduce the cleavage that the Prime Minister had done so much to create. The Liberal leader could not communicate to the rural dweller in either English or French Canada. Urban Canada, which wanted nothing so much as business-like management in government, could see nothing wrong in Pearson's surrounding himself with a brains trust. But rural Canada was highly suspicious that he might rely excessively on experts and bureaucrats, especially since John Diefenbaker lambasted them so derisively. Seldom have two leaders been so antithetical in the images they have presented to different sections of the electorate; the outcome was a deeper rural-urban cleavage than the country had heretofore experienced.

FOOTNOTES

1. Toronto *Globe and Mail*, March 8, 1960, in *Canadian Annual Review* (Toronto: University of Toronto Press, 1960), p. 19.

2. *Ibid.*, August 12, 1960, in *Canadian Annual Review*, 1960, p. 20.

3. *Canadian Annual Review*, 1961, p. 3.

4. Blair Fraser, "Is Diefenbaker Running a One-Man Government?," *Maclean's*, LXXII (March 14, 1959), p. 14.

5. Douglas Fisher, "What Makes Diefenbaker Run?," Toronto *Telegram*, February 9, 1963.

6. F.H. Underhill, "P.M. Didn't Grow—He Inflated Himself," Toronto *Star*, March 16, 1963.

7. John A. Stevenson, "Ottawa

	Seats	Candidates					Elected							
		C.	L.	N.D.P.	S.C.	O.	C.	%	L.	%	N.D.P.	%	S.C.	%
Newfoundland	7	7	7	4	1		1	14.3	6	85.7				
Nova Scotia	12	12	12	12	7		9	75.0	2	16.7	1	8.3		
New Brunswick	10	10	10	7	8	1	4	40.0	6	60.0				
Prince Edward Island	4	4	4	4	1		4	100.0						
Quebec	75	75	75	40	75	18	14	18.7	35	46.7			26	34.7
Ontario	85	85	85	81	70	9	35	41.2	44	51.8	6	7.1		
Manitoba	14	14	14	14	13	3	11	78.6	1	7.1	2	14.3		
Saskatchewan	17	17	17	17	15	1	16	94.1	1	5.9				
Alberta	17	17	17	17	17	3	15	88.2					2	11.8
British Columbia	22	22	21	22	22	4	6	27.3	4	18.2	10	45.5	2	9.1
Yukon and N.W.T.	2	2	2		1		1	50.0	1	50.0				
Total	265	265	264	218	230	39	116	43.8	100	37.7	19	7.2	30	11.3

Others (votes polled): N.B. (1): I.L. (1) 441.

Que. (18): I.L. (5) 9,654; I.P.C. (4) 2,713; I. (4) 3,442; Parti de la Confédération (1) 636; Candidat Libéral des Electeurs (1) 1,836; Capital Familial (1) 393; Comm. (1) 347; Ouvrier Indépendant (1) 152.

Ont. (9): Comm. (5) 1,836; I. (3) 1,038; Co-op. Builders of Canada (1) 261.

Man. (3): Comm. (2) 2,153; I. (1) 1,144.

Sask. (1): Comm. (1) 317.

Alta. (3): I.L. (1) 311; I. (1) 497; All Can. Party (1) 189.

B.C. (4): Comm. (3) 1,707; I. (1) 224.

Letter," *Canadian Forum*, XLII (May, 1962), p. 38.

8. Ramsay Cook, "An Election Without Issues," *Canadian Forum*, XLII (May, 1962), p. 27.

9. *Canadian Annual Review*, 1962, p. 8.

10. Stevenson, "Ottawa Letter," p. 38.

11. *Canadian Anual Review*, 1961, p. 77.

12. Colin Cameron, "The New Party Will Die If It's a Mere Liberal Splinter," *Maclean's*, LXXIV (July 29, 1961), p. 5.

13. Peter Newman, "How to Win Voters and Avoid the Election Issues," *Maclean's*, LXXV (June 16, 1962), p. 65.

14. Toronto *Globe and Mail*, May 3, 1962.

15. *Canadian Annual Review*, 1962, p. 14.

16. Ottawa *Journal*, May 14, 1962.

17. *Ibid.*, May 10, 1962.

18. Kingston *Whig-Standard*, May 17, 1962.

19. Ottawa *Journal*, May 7, 1962.

20. *Canadian Annual Review*, 1962, p. 11.

21. Newman, "How to Win Voters," p. 65.

22. "Nearing Dissolution," *Round Table*, LII (March, 1962), p. 203.

23. Ramsay Cook, "Old Wine and Apathy," *Canadian Forum*, XLII (June, 1962), p. 49.

24. *Canadian Annual Review*, p. 13.

25. Peter C. Newman, "Why Diefen-

		Popular Vote								Total
C.	%	L.	%	N.D.P.	%	S.C.	%	O.	%	
55,396	36.0	90,896	59.0	7,590	4.9	158	0.1			154,040
198,902	47.3	178,520	42.4	39,689	9.4	3,764	0.9			420,875
115,973	46.5	110,850	44.4	13,220	5.3	9,016	3.6	441	0.2	249,500
37,388	51.3	31,603	43.3	3,802	5.2	153	0.2			72,946
617,762	29.6	818,760	39.2	91,795	4.4	542,433	26.0	19,173	0.9	2,089,923
1,056,095	39.3	1,122,222	41.8	456,459	17.0	49,734	1.9	3,135	0.1	2,687,645
161,824	41.6	121,041	31.1	76,514	19.7	26,662	6.8	3,297	0.8	389,338
213,385	50.4	96,676	22.8	93,444	22.1	19,648	4.6	317	0.1	423,470
214,699	42.8	97,322	19.4	42,305	8.4	146,662	29.2	997	0.2	501,985
187,389	27.3	187,438	27.3	212,035	30.9	97,396	14.2	1,931	0.3	686,189
6,769	47.6	6,506	45.7			948	6.7			14,223
2,865,582	37.3	2,861,834	37.2	1,036,853	13.5	896,574	11.7	29,291	0.4	7,690,134

baker Lost Canada," *Maclean's*, LXXV (July 28, 1962), p. 45.

26. Ottawa *Journal*, June 6, 1962.

27. Toronto *Globe and Mail*, June 9, 1962.

28. Toronto *Telegram*, May 28, 1962.

29. *Canadian Annual Review*, 1962, p. 17.

30. *Ibid.*, p. 20.

31. Toronto *Star*, June 16, 1962.

32. *Canadian Annual Review*, 1962, p. 21.

33. Toronto *Globe and Mail*, June 15, 1962.

34. *Canadian Annual Review*, 1962, p. 21.

35. *Ibid.*, p. 104.

36. Toronto *Star*, June 13, 1962.

37. *Ibid.*, June 16, 1962.

38. J.M. Beck, "The Democratic Process at Work in Canadian General Elections," in J.C. Courtney, (ed.), *Voting in Canada* (Toronto: Prentice-Hall of Canada, Limited, 1967), p. 30.

39. S. Peter Regenstreif, "Group Perceptions and the Vote," in John Meisel, (ed.), *Papers on the 1962 Election* (Toronto: University of Toronto Press, 1964), p. 237.

40. *Ibid.*, p. 239.

41. *Ibid.*, pp. 242-43.

42. Toronto *Globe and Mail*, May 1, 1962.

43. The courts later invalidated this result.

44. Regenstreif, "Group Perceptions," p. 242.

45. Norman Ward, "The Counter-Revolution in Saskatchewan," in Meisel, *Papers*, p. 179.

46. *Ibid.*, p. 175.

47. Walter D. Young, "The NDP: British Columbia's Labour Party," in Meisel, *Papers*, p. 182.

48. *Ibid.*, p. 184.

49. *Ibid.*, p. 200.

50. See André Laurendeau, "Le Québec se paie une escapade avec Dief," *Le Magazine Maclean*, III (April, 1963), p. 1.

51. Léon Dion, "The Election in the Province of Quebec," in Meisel, *Papers*, p. 117.

52. Robert Alford, "The Social Bases of Political Cleavage," in Meisel, *Papers*, p. 231.

53. Dion, "Election in Quebec," p. 111.

54. Laurendeau, "Le Québec paie," p. 2.

55. Peter Gzowski, "Hung Jury: A

Strongman's Road to Power," *Maclean's*, LXXV (July 28, 1962), p. 35.

56. *Ibid.*, p. 33.

57. *Ibid.*, p. 11.

58. *Le Devoir*, June 6, 1962.

59. *Canadian Annual Review*, 1962, p. 19.

60. Dion, "Election in Quebec," p. 120.

61. Laurendeau, "Le Québec paie," p. 2.

62. As quoted in *Canadian Annual Review*, 1962, p. 27.

63. Regenstreif, "Group Perceptions," p. 241.

64. W.P. Irvine, "An Analysis of Voting Shifts in Quebec," in Meisel, *Papers*, pp. 131-32.

65. Vincent Lemieux, "The Election in the Constituency of Lévis," in Meisel, *Papers*, p. 36.

66. *Ibid.*, p. 37.

67. *Ibid.*, p. 51.

68. Irvine, "Analysis," pp. 129-30, 132.

69. Adèle Lauzon, "Le Canada pris au piège de sa prospérité," *Le Magazine Maclean*, II (September, 1954), p. 54.

70. *Canadian Annual Review*, 1962, p. 27.

71. Lauzon, "Le Canada pris," p. 55.

72. Jean Paré, "Le vote créditiste a ses racines dans notre vieille insécurité," *Le Magazine Maclean*, II (September, 1962), p. 51.

73. Robert R. Alford, "The Social Bases of Political Cleavage in 1962," and Regenstreif, "Group Perceptions," in Meisel, *Papers*, pp. 203-34, 235-52.

74. Alford, "Social Bases," p. 233.

75. Regenstreif, "Group Perceptions," p. 249.

76. Alford, "Social Bases," p. 232.

77. John Meisel, "Conclusion: An Analysis of the National (?) Results," in Meisel, *Papers*, p. 286.

78. Alford, "Social Bases," pp. 216-17.

79. Blair Fraser, "What Pearson Won by Losing," *Maclean's*, LXXV (July 28, 1962), p. 39.

80. Peter C. Newman, "Why Diefenbaker Lost Canada," *Maclean's*, LXXV (July 28, 1962), p. 10.

81. John Meisel, "The June 1962 Election: Break-up of our Party System?," *Queen's Quarterly*, LXIX (Autumn, 1962), pp. 329-46.

Twenty-sixth

General Election

"SNATCHING DEFEAT FROM THE JAWS OF VICTORY"

"A strange, rowdy, expensive, emotional, bruising campaign" and an electorate that was "restless, secretive, demanding, undecided, prone to heckle savagely" – such was Mark Gayn's description of the election of 1963.[1] Arthur R. Ford of the London *Free Press*, an experienced political historian and journalist, said he had "never seen an election where the voters were so confused, so puzzled and so deeply anxious over what course to take . . . to bring about stable government."[2] When the Diefenbaker government fell on February 5, it seemed as certain as anything can be in politics that it would go down to calamitous defeat.

The *Canadian Annual Review* – with some exaggeration – described the events following the election of 1962 as "mid-summer madness":

> . . . a nation apparently hovering on the brink of financial collapse, a government rejected by two-thirds of the electorate refusing to meet Parliament, a defeated ministry borrowing millions of dollars and levying new taxes by unusual means, a Prime Minister presuming to speak for the nation in London before his dubious mandate had been confirmed, and the life of the administration hanging by a thread held by the whimsical Réal Caouette.[3]

Only six days after the election, the Prime Minister announced the details of his so-called "austerity programme." To relieve the pressure on the Canadian dollar and to strengthen Canada's badly depleted exchange reserves, there were to be temporary tariff surcharges on about half the country's imports, substantial cuts in governmental expenditures, and the imposition of a tight-money policy; in addition, there were arrangements for credits totalling about $1 billion from the International Monetary Fund and American and British governmental agencies. Although the government had talked about the country's prosperity and stability during the election, the situation was anything but good. Little wonder that *Le Devoir* criticised "une lamentable supercherie qui fait peu honneur à la démocratie."

Not until September 27 – more than three months after the election – did Parliament have a chance to discuss these matters. John Diefenbaker did his best to show that the major loss of exchange reserves had occurred after his last television address of the campaign, that the gloomy picture of the economy painted by the Liberals had led to the loss of confidence in Canada's stability, and that a clear-cut victory for his government would have quickly restored it. But his donning a martyr's garb convinced no one. Parliament's failure to do much more than pass interim supply bills prior to Christmas hardly improved the government's stature. Although this was partly due to the Liberals' efforts to embarrass and bring down the government, it was equally true that the government had "given no evidence of having any real plans."[4] Not surprisingly, the Gallup Poll reported in October that Conservative support had fallen from 37 to 33 per cent, while Liberal strength had risen to 47 per cent.

The government did not last long after Parliament reconvened on January 21; nuclear arms provided the *coup de mort*. Shortly after the Diefenbaker government came to power, it agreed to switch the role of Canada's air division in NATO from air defence to light bombing. Accordingly the division was to be equipped with CF-104 Starfighters, designed to use tactical nuclear weapons only. Although the Honest John short-range rockets to be used by Canada's Infantry Brigade in Germany were to have both a nuclear and non-nuclear capacity, no non-nuclear warheads were ordered for them.

In the summer of 1957 the Canadian and American governments agreed to establish an integrated North American Air Defence Command (NORAD). Two years later Canada cancelled the construction of the Avro-Arrow interceptor, which was to have been its chief contribution to NORAD; it agreed, however, to substitute two squadrons of anti-aircraft missiles, the Bomarc-B, and five squadrons of CF-101B Voodoo interceptors. No conventional warhead was developed for the Bomarc-B's, and the Voodoos would have been fully effective only with nuclear weapons. By the time the R.C.A.F. was taking over the first Bomarc base at North Bay and establishing its first Starfighter squadrons at Zweibrücken in December 1962, the cabinet still had not made up its mind about acquiring nuclear warheads for any of its weapons systems. It had, in fact, been joked about for some time that the Prime Minister was vacillating between the anti-nuclear views of External Affairs Secretary Howard Green on Mondays and Wednesdays, and the pro-nuclear views of Defence Minister Harkness on Tuesdays and Thursdays.

Things moved quickly to a climax in the new year. At Ottawa, on January 4, General Lauris Norstad, the retiring Supreme Commander of NATO, said bluntly that Canada had committed itself to a nuclear role. Eight days later Lester Pearson reversed his previous position and proposed that Canada accept nuclear warheads for "those defensive tactical weapons, which cannot effectively be used without them but which we have agreed to use."[5] Cynics said he had an eye on the Gallup Poll, which showed that 54 per cent of Canadians favoured the acquisition of nuclear weapons. Although the Prime Minister presented his views in the Commons on January 25, no one was much the wiser after he had finished. He appeared to say, however, that as a result of the Nassau understanding between President Kennedy and Prime Minister Macmillan, Canada could somehow postpone arming its CF-104's until the NATO Council considered the whole question of nuclear deterrence.

Some of the Prime Minister's points did not pass unchallenged for long. On January 30 the American State Department made a statement that was almost unprecedented in its contradiction of a friendly government. The Voodoos, it said, could not perform effectively without nuclear weapons; the Nassau understanding cast no doubts on Canada's nuclear role; negotiations for Canada's acquisition of nuclear weapons were not going ahead "forcefully."[6]

Repercussions came thick and fast. On Sunday February 3, Douglas Harkness resigned from the cabinet because his views were irreconcilable with the Prime Minister's. The next day Lester Pearson moved non-confidence in the government because of its confusion and indecision in dealing with national and international problems. On Tuesday Réal Caouette did what he had long threatened to do: he helped to bring down the government. Why did the leaders of the minor parties decide on such a course with "the awful example of 1958 before them"? In part it was consideration of the national interest. Perhaps, too, Robert Thompson had visions of the sixty seats in Quebec that Caouette was assuring him he would win in the next election. Perhaps he was annoyed at not being consulted about the basis on which he might support the government. In any case, he was being offered "Diefenbaker's head on a platter," and "this was heady stuff to a relative greenhorn [who] didn't seem to understand that his role of a kingmaker would end," once Pearson's motion was adopted. As for T.C. Douglas, he knew the non-confidence motion was like a bee-sting; "it would be effective alright [sic], but it would kill the bee." Yet, optimist that he was, he did not think there could be a repetition of 1958.[7]

Peter Stursberg described the events of a fateful week in this manner: Great Power blasts deception of Little Border Country's nuclear policy. Government of L.B.C. begins to crack with defence minister first to go. A palace revolt occurs with a group of ministers (variously estimated at six, nine, and eleven) plotting at midnight to overthrow their flamboyant leader and save the government. Faithful Alvin Hamilton rallies the western back-benchers to foil the rebel coup. On Tuesday the leader becomes the Dief of old as he flails both the Liberals and the Americans in an amazing come-back. The government falls in a setting reminiscent of an Eisenstein movie, "with the crowds in the Gothic setting of the Parliament Buildings, and the dark mutterings of conspiracy and treachery." On Wednesday the *Globe and Mail* confirms the western members' suspicion of a Bay Street take-over with its front page editorial that Diefenbaker must go. The same day Senator Grattan O'Leary, almost single-handed, rallies the Conservative caucus to the side of the Chief. George Hees emerges from the meeting saying "we've never been such a united party" and "we are going to knock hell out of the Grits." On Saturday Hees and Pierre Sévigny resign from the cabinet on the nuclear arms question.[8] And so,

> . . . with the three resignations, with Messrs. Fulton, Fleming, and Halpenny deciding not to test the election, and with such Tory stalwarts as the *Globe and Mail*, the Toronto *Telegram* and the Montreal *Gazette* imploring him to resign, Prime Minister Diefenbaker moved into battle in the vanguard of his tattered army.[9]

No one gave him much of a chance as he travelled west to start his campaign. Most people felt that, like Sir John Macdonald in 1874, he could do no more than conduct a salvage operation and attempt to maintain his party's base in the rural West. But the straitened financial condition of his party turned out to be a blessing in disguise, for it made him resort less to the chartered aircraft and more to a type of campaign congenial to his talents. The crowds he drew as he whistle-stopped towards Prince Albert exhilarated him. "In 1962 I flew over the people at about 30,000 feet. . . . This time I'm with the people where I was in 1957 and 1958."[10] So far he was in the friendly territory of the rural Prairies. But when he drew crowds of 6,000 in Winnipeg, 5,000 in Vineland, 1,500 in Chatham, and 1,800 in Guelph, he became almost intoxicated. At Vineland he said exultantly: "You heard the stories . . . of how sick I was. But I want to tell you that the way the crowds are turning up in this campaign, somebody else is going to be sick, and it isn't going to be me."[11] At Londonderry, N.S., he exclaimed: "It's rolling—it's rolling everywhere."[12]

In 1962 "a sour and dispirited flavour" had permeated his whole campaign and "the smell of impending disaster hung over everything, affecting his staff, [and] poisoning his relations with the press." Not so in 1963.

> The way John Diefenbaker is behaving, it's as though he had found the politician's Eldorado, the fount from which he could draw inexhaustible reserves of energy, optimism and self-confidence. . . . When he says he detects something of the spirit of '57 and '58 he really means it . . .
> . . . There he is, night after night, cavorting on the platform as though he were in the springtime of his career, slaying dragons left and right, chuckling about his difficulties with his cabinet, sentimentally reminding his audience that he is one of them, a humble farm boy moved by some predestination to come forth and protect the "average man."[13]

While no prime minister has ever made such an amazing comeback, no prime minister has ever discussed the issues less meaningfully than Diefenbaker did in 1963. He did talk about a programme of national purpose designed to create a million new jobs, but only in the most general terms. Instead he concentrated on knocking down three strawmen which he treated as evil incarnate: the Liberals, the Americans, and the "sinister interests."

The Liberals, he contended, had brought about the exchange crisis by their cries of doom and gloom, and none was more to blame for it than J.W. Pickersgill. That man, he said, was supposed to have a sixth sense; "if only he had the other five."[14] But for the most part he attacked the Liberals because they "stalled, stultified, torpedoed Parliament. They didn't want a budget. All they wanted was to budge the government out."[15] Actually, John Diefenbaker had some explaining of his own to do. Why had he waited until September 27 to meet Parliament when he might have called it for July 31? Why had he prolonged the Christmas recess to January 21, two weeks longer than usual? No one but he was responsible for this loss of fifty-six sitting days. The *Globe and Mail* thought the voters might conclude that many of his tales were myths, "that there never was a Budget, there never was a progamme of legislation, and that Mr. Diefenbaker is barren of constructive ideas and incapable of action."[16]

The Americans were his second target. For a time it appeared as if the Prime Minister had the stage set for the same kind of campaign as Macdonald had waged in 1891.[17] However, some of his own ministers warned him they would resign if he came down too hard on Uncle Sam. Therefore, he contented himself mainly with isolated insinuations rather than full-blown anti-Americanism. The Ottawa *Journal* concluded that "aside from a few too extreme phrases, . . the Prime Minister has kept the operation within fairly reasonable bounds."[18]

Occasionally, in the tones of a Biblical prophet, he would proclaim that "our nation must not be made a puppet," and Alvin Hamilton would echo that the Americans "think we're a Guatemala or something. . . . Don't push us around chum."[19] Diefenbaker would also remind the Americans that "Canada was in both wars a long time before some other nations were. . . . "[20] Surprisingly, his words had some effect, for Liberal meetings more than once echoed with hecklers' shouts of "Yankee Lover."

Such anti-Americanism as there was was closely bound up with the defence issue. Here, said Charles Lynch, The Old Conjurer was at his trickiest best. "Audiences cheer, hecklers jeer, and students of the military art gasp with incredulity at the Prime Minister's handling of [the] central issue of the election."[21] At no time did he provide the coherent statement on defence he had promised; he relied instead on peripheral debating points and derision of his opponents. Thus, in referring to Pearson's altered position on nuclear weapons, he said that "never since Saul, at his conversion on the road to Damascus, has there been such a change in the thinking of one person."[22] Yet he somehow managed to create an impression of decisiveness by suggesting that he was against nuclear weapons for Canada's home defence forces and leaving the question wide open for its NATO forces. To the knowledgeable, however, there were all sorts of inconsistencies. For example, he said: "Canada had no . . . commitment [to accept nuclear weapons] and [Pearson] knows that . . . Canada keeps her word and always will."[23] But surely Canada's allies had the right to infer that if Canada accepted the delivery vehicles for nuclear arms, she would not reject the warheads that alone could make them useful.

This instance could not compare with his treatment of the Bomarc. Early in the campaign he quoted American reports to the effect that there were conventional warheads for the Bomarc. But this was not true of the Bomarc-B which Canada had acquired. Later he said that the bomber threat was finished and with it the Bomarc; on the other hand, he insisted that the U.S. Strategic Air Force was "our only hope of survival." He exulted in the testimony of American Defense Secretary Robert McNamara, which was made public at the end of March; in his opinion it meant that the Bomarc would be useful only to draw ballistic fire from other North American targets. In other words, Liberal policy would make Canada a decoy for intercontinental missiles, a burnt sacrifice as it were. "I told you the Bomarc was no longer an effective instrument, and Mr. Pearson said the Prime Minister lied. . . . I wish I could look into Mr. Pearson's heart today."[24]

Obviously John Diefenbaker thought he had a winning argument. McNamara's statement, he said, made Pearson's case look "like a sieve—you can see right through it." Five weeks ago "the Liberals were picking out their cabinets. Now they're picking out a hole to hide in."[25] Yet, as Pearson kept insisting, it was not he who had had the rug pulled out from under him. "The Bomarc," he said, "is Mr. Diefenbaker's rug—not ours."[26]

More than anything else the Prime Minister campaigned against a variety of sinister interests plotting to harm himself and Canada. At Vineland, Ontario, he took a cue from Harry Truman's "give 'em hell" campaign of 1948 and borrowed the line "Everybody's against me but the people."[27] From then on he became "a politician of the . . . Truman image of 1948, whistle-stopping across the country, appealing for the support of the electorate against the powerful, sinister but unnamed interests at home and abroad that are fighting against him and, by implication, against 'the little man.' "[28]

Although Diefenbaker was never explicit about the "great interests," "some powerful interests," and "an invisible incognito," by the time he was finished they seemed to include the State Department, the Pentagon, *Newsweek*, Bay Street, the Toronto newspapers, and even Pearson's Liberals. When he told an audience at Chatham, Ontario, that pleasing the big interests was not one of his first concerns,[29] it was Bay Street that he had in mind. The villains in this instance were those who did not like his requirement that half the equity stock in enterprises developing Canada's northern resources must be Canadian-owned. When he railed against those who had falsely accused him of deceiving the public about Canada's financial situation in the 1962 elections, those who had started a whispering campaign about his alleged ill health, and those who had sponsored a photographic campaign designed to depict him as a Machiavellian monster,[30] it was the Liberals he meant.

To counteract the suggestion that he was ill, he started his campaign by presenting a medical report indicating that his physical health was excellent. Then Lionel Chevrier played right into his hands by suggesting there were forms of health other than physical. Diefenbaker sought to capitalize on the "photographic campaign" in *Newsweek* which, he said, tried to "destroy me with [its] savage caricature."[31] The reference was to the issue of February 18 in which an article accompanying a photograph suggested that in full oratorical flight he was "a sight not soon to be forgotten [as] the India-rubber features twist and contort in grotesque and gargoyle-like grimaces." All of it was in poor taste and the Prime Minister made the most of it. In good humour he said Satan had looked at the picture and exclaimed: "I've got competition on earth."[32] But he was thoroughly serious when he talked about the origin of the article: "Who were the progenitors? . . . I say, – and they haven't denied it – that it was the members of the Liberals' Who's Who."[33]

Never (save in 1917) has the press been so one-sided as it was during this election. Except for the Ottawa *Journal*, the Winnipeg *Tribune*, the Vancouver *Province*, and the Fredericton *Gleaner*, the Conservative dailies had switched to the Liberals because of the Prime Minister's lack of leadership and the need for majority government. This infuriated John Diefenbaker. "No," he said, "I haven't got the big Toronto papers with me, but a crowd like this makes it pretty clear that the people are reading other papers."[34] And again: "It would have been so easy to do what these two or three newspapers wanted [on nuclear weapons] – easy but wrong. And if the time ever comes when such newspapers dictate or control the thinking of Canadians on national issues, then freedom ends."[35]

The forces working against Diefenbaker were grist to his mill. Once he had wooed Prairie juries with consummate skill. Now the Canadian people were his jury, "and he [was] working on their sympathy, their instinct tending to side with an underdog – especially an underdog hard done by."[36] To them John Diefenbaker was saying: "I've been derided. I've been condemned. Some of my colleagues left. If they thought I would leave the helm because of their action, now they know that they were wrong."[37] There he was, a poor man with an empty campaign chest: "We have no funds from which to draw." Do not, he pleaded, ask for money to work on election day. "In all my years of public life I have never had to pay my workers." Why were he and Michael Starr in public life when the financial return was so small? Simply because "there is tremendous satisfaction in trying to help others."[38]

J.W. Pickersgill accused the Prime Minister of trying to weep his way back into office.[39] Lubor Zink of the Toronto *Telegram* thought that his attempt to ride to power on a wave of sympathy was "an undignified role for a Prime Minister."[40] The Toronto *Star* told him to forget about the shapeless genie persecuting him and spell out his programme for the next five years.[41] However, it was useless to say that the Liberals had had nothing to do with the *Newsweek* article, that Bay Street had a representative in his own cabinet in the person of Senator Wallace McCutcheon, or that two Toronto dailies had given him full support until he had made a mess of things. Nothing could deter him from attempting to establish a rapport with those who like himself had been pushed around; according to Walter Gray of the *Globe and Mail*, "the country must be filled with the downtrodden, judging by the response the Prime Minister is getting."[42]

The Prime Minister's single-handed fight seemed to be proving altogether too successful for his newspaper foes. The man they had counted out was reviving the melodramatics of 1958, garbing his villains in dress of the darkest hue, providing light touches with an impish sort of humour, and getting unexpectedly enthusiastic responses.[43] Two weeks before it was over, a worried Toronto *Telegram* conceded that Diefenbaker's position had improved and that Pearson was "not putting his message across."[44] There was even talk about the frailties of ordinary folk. What did they want in a prime minister – asked the Toronto *Star* – "a television performer, a melodramatic actor . . . [who takes] even to reviving the gibes of 40 years ago, about U.S. slowness in entering World War I" or a responsible, sensible leader?[45] Lubor Zink complained that Diefenbaker's "fury of emotionalism . . . had struck a responsive chord in a politically illiterate public." Zink could appreciate that the farther one went from Ottawa the hazier became the picture of events since the last election and the more easily were people prey to electioneering demagoguery. However, he could not understand the city crowds' acceptance of "the blatant distortions of truth and the hollow slogans of the 'Power si, Puppet no' type."[46]

Undoubtedly the Liberals were worried too. On February 2 the Gallup Poll indicated they had nation-wide support of 44 per cent compared with the Conservatives' 33 and they talked airily of winning 175 seats. But remembering how they had squandered a lead of 8 percentage points in 1962, they were determined not to reach their peak too soon. They also knew they needed a programme that would appeal to voters in a serious frame of mind. Their strategy, as it emerged from a meeting of the Council of the National Liberal Federation on February 11 and 12, was twofold. In Quebec they would advocate a reorientation of Confederation designed, so Lionel Chevrier said, to recognize French-Canadian demands "after all

HOBSON'S CHOICE

by Macpherson. Toronto Star, *March 2, 1963. Reprinted with permission*—Toronto Daily Star.

these years [for] admittance to full partnership";[47] Pearson's promise to set up a royal commission on biculturalism emphasized this aspect of their campaign. In Canada as a whole the Liberals would contend that they alone could provide stability and restore purpose and direction in the management of the country's affairs. Strategist Tom Kent told them to talk about "decisive" rather than "strong" government, and to picture Lester Pearson as the one best equipped to provide it "without appearing to sell him as a cellophane-wrapped package."[48]

As his opening assignment, the Liberal leader chose to address a luncheon meeting of the Quebec Liberal Federation. Although Quebec was by no means enamoured of his new stand on nuclear weapons, his reception was highly encouraging. Moreover, Premier Lesage, who had ignored the campaign in 1962, sat at the head table and smiled broadly at Pearson's contention that Canada needed "a stable government, a decisive government, a Liberal government," the same kind that Quebec had in Quebec City.[49]

Thereafter Pearson set about developing a hard-line approach. To a Moncton audience he said that, in order to clear up the mess he was going to inherit, "we'll have to take decisions and some of them won't be very pleasant ones."[50] The *Globe and Mail* was all smiles. Pearson, it was sure, had recognized that the major problem in Canada was economic and would not spend a nickel after the election "unless it [contributed] to the expansion of the economy."[51] Most of Pearson's new promises – such as submitting a design for a national flag to Parliament within two years – involved no large outlay of funds. However, he did not abandon his programme of 1962; he merely delayed it for the time being. At Port Arthur, for example, he stated that a Liberal government would not introduce a national medicare plan until its fourth year of office unless "the necessary economic improvement is achieved."[52] Naturally he did not escape gibes for his retreat. Ramsay Cook suggested that, after such spokesmen of Canadian conservatism as the *Financial Post*, the *Globe and Mail*, and the Montreal *Gazette* had climbed on the Liberal campaign train, Pearson's "high hard line became increasingly one of economic conservatism."[53]

In spite of all their strategy, the Liberals' chances of getting an overall majority seemed to slip from their grasp. The Gallup Poll of March 9 indicated a drop of 3 percentage points in their popularity, down from 44 to 41 per cent. When things did not improve in the days that followed, there was anxious soul-searching. It was generally agreed that their gimmick campaign had not helped them. Apparently the brain child of national campaign director Keith Davey, bemused by American electioneering methods, the chief gimmick was a truth squad which was to attend the Prime Minister's meetings and report on his inaccuracies.

"Pity the poor P.M. with this crew onto him," wrote Douglas Fisher. Apparently he was thinking of Judy La Marsh and her habit of "seeing politics in terms of invective and hatchet."[54] But John Diefenbaker and the Conservatives could look after themselves. At the squad's first test in Moncton on March 13, a spotlight played on it incessantly, and the crowd yelled in derision as the opening speaker quoted poetry at it:

> Some other men had ghost squads too
> > Herr Hitler used them well. . . .
> So note the truth, you ghostly three,
> > Then change it into lies.
> And rest assured that you will be
> > The light in Lester's eyes.

The crowd continued to hoot as John Diefenbaker rattled off reams of statistics indicating what he had done for Canada and added: "They're after the truth and now they are getting it."[55]

From all sides there came immediate denunciation of the squad. The Montreal *Star*, for example, said it would repel more people psychologically than it would convince factually. But the critics had no need to worry. At Halifax the crowd kept yelling, "throw out Judy La Marsh"; the police had to be called in, and that was the end of the truth squad. "It's a great thing when people find the truth in two days," said the Prime Minister, "and then return to the place whence they came."[56]

Keith Davey had other gimmicks too. One involved homing pigeons, but the pigeons had sense enough not to co-operate. There were colouring books, supposedly 65,000 of them, designed to ridicule Diefenbaker. The first cartoon pictured him as a faceless man with curly, flowing hair:

> This is a Prime Minister.
> He is at breakfast.
> Should he have orange juice or grapefruit?
> It is a hard decision. He dreads decisions.
> Perhaps he will never have breakfast.
> Colour him hungry.

To the Toronto *Star* it was incomprehensible that a Canadian party would use silly gimmicks that had failed in the United States.[57] For a party claiming to be a party of responsibility facing up to the hard truths ahead, it was sheer folly.

The Liberals sought also to present Pearson as the "Man of Decision." Imitating the "King or Chaos" slogan of 1935, they talked about "Pearson or Paralysis." But, because the intellectual Pearson could not see political matters in black and white, he appeared something less than decisive. The Toronto *Telegram* wondered if he was another Adlai Stevenson. "Face-to-face, Mr. Pearson is warm, friendly and easy to talk to. It is not until he starts making campaign speeches that the frosty remoteness of an ordained egghead descends upon him."[58] Pearson's newspaper supporters felt obliged to remind their readers that, although he could not play the demagogue, he was an intelligent, honest man, who could bring the same talents to Canada's crises as he had brought to world crises. They also pointed out that, while Canada occasionally flirted with men of words, its political leaders for long periods of time were "solid men who talked little and sometimes badly, but who had the power of decision—and therefore the will to act. Mr. Pearson qualifies."[59]

One of Pearson's difficulties was how to cope with a man of words who resorted to "every ploy, every strategem, every trick in the political book—and some that haven't been written yet" and who, in the process, not infrequently distorted and misrepresented facts and defied logic.[60] Yet the same man of words provided no opportunity for interrogation—he refused to face either a C.B.C. panel or Pierre Berton. Pearson disliked being distracted from a discussion of the issues but, if for no other reason than psychological ones, he felt he could not let some of the Prime Minister's statements go unchallenged. Starting at Barrie on March 15, he criticized

John Diefenbaker for avoiding discussion on the basic issues of the day and for tactics "beneath the dignity of a head of a party." Come out from behind "the smokescreen of excitement and emotion," he continued. "Canadian voters are not going to be impressed by a campaign of personalities and prejudices, excitements, and emotionalism and drama. They are thinking and wondering and worrying."[61] Later, at Kingston, Pearson released a sheet of facts setting the record straight on matters of defence.

None the less, at this stage in the campaign it was not so much a question of the Liberals' peaking too soon as it was one of their being able to get their campaign off the ground at all. There were even suggestions that Pearson had "snatched defeat from the jaws of victory."[62] However, in the closing days, as the Liberal leader outlined the specifics of the "60 days of decision" which would follow his accession to office, the situation improved. Among other things he put forward a four-point programme for full employment which included the establishment of a department of industry, a municipal loan fund, a national development corporation, and the expansion of foreign trade. It seemed to catch on. In Vancouver on April 1 he made the best platform appearance of his career. Across Canada he had been heckled by anti-nuclear exponents. In Vancouver he met organized opposition both from these people and from the Communists, and he fought them to a standstill. He who had "never been magnificent before on a public platform," wrote Christopher Young of the Liberal-oriented Ottawa *Citizen*, was, "in a word, magnificent." In this respect Young was correct, but it was much more difficult to agree with him that this was the turning-point of the campaign or to agree with Richard O'Hagan, Pearson's special assistant, who said that "we won the election tonight!"[63] After March 9, the findings of the Canadian Institute of Public Opinion hardly changed at all and still conformed closely to the actual results.

In a campaign such as this one, the smaller parties were at a disadvantage. Voters who are anxious about existing conditions and want more decisive government are likely to turn to the strongest of the opposition parties. For this reason the N.D.P. seemed to direct its fire as much against the Liberals as against the Conservatives. In urban Canada, where the N.D.P. drew most of its strength, the Liberals were its chief rival. Therefore, while T.C. Douglas criticized Diefenbaker for "procrastination and indecision," he also lambasted Pearson for his failure to present constructive proposals. Most of all he denounced the Liberals' plea for majority government. Some of the best governments Canada ever had, he said, were those of Mackenzie King when he was "hanging on by the skin of his teeth."[64] In contrast, governments with big majorities had tended to "lapse into a state of suspended animation."[65] Under the Liberals Canada had stable government for twenty-two years, "so stable it never moved. . . . When you remember how a stable smells, I don't think you'll want stable government."[66]

More positively Douglas proposed to attack the problem of unemployment through a national investment plan that would create funds for building highways, housing developments, and other essential national projects. He was insistent, too, that welfare measures be placed ahead of business profits. "We do not accept the proposition that what is good for General Motors is necessarily good for the nation."[67] Pearson's proposal to postpone welfare measures because of economic difficulties especially aroused his ire. "Why, in a country so richly endowed as Canada and so far behind already in the field of public welfare, [should we] get even further behind?"[68]

At times Douglas seemed to put the nuclear question ahead of unemployment. Pearson, he said, should "explain why, after opposing nuclear weapons from 1959, he suddenly [found] on Jan. 12, 1963, that we had a so-called commitment which we must honor."[69] As for him, he would forthwith negotiate out of any such commitment since it served neither to defend nor deter, but only increased the likelihood of nuclear war.

The stand of the N.D.P. on nuclear weapons was viewed with particular favour in Quebec, as was its support of a more generally bicultural Canada and the position of T.C. Douglas on relations with the United States. "I like the Americans," he said. "I like my relatives, too, but I don't want them to move into my house."[70] Hence, when trade union leader Gérard Picard agreed to assume the leadership of the N.D.P. in Quebec, there were hopes that the party might make at least a small breakthrough. Picard, it was said, would be to T.C. Douglas what Cartier was to Macdonald and Lapointe to King.

Like Douglas, Robert Thompson of Social Credit lambasted the leaders of both the old parties. The last Parliament had not worked, he charged, because they "didn't try to make it work."[71] To solve the country's unemployment and development problems he proposed to create a social capital bank as an arm of the Bank of Canada. However, Thompson found himself in serious difficulties on the nuclear issue. He advocated removing defence policy from partisan politics and entrusting it to a parliamentary committee; on the other hand, Réal Caouette had adopted the slogan: "Bread and Butter but no Bombs." When Thompson went to Montreal, he promised to do everything in his power to prevent Canada from becoming a nuclear power. Stanley McDowell of the Ottawa *Journal* said that he "looked the part [of a national leader] as much as a man looks the master of a house when he is in his wife's kitchen."[72]

In contrast with 1962, everyone ganged up to defeat Caouette this time. The Liberals felt they had "the antidote" for him in Member of Parliament Yvon Dupuis, who used the same flamboyant, off-the-cuff style that Caouette did. Dupuis pretended the task was an easy one. "I bucked Duplessis for years and came out on top, and as far as I'm concerned that Créditiste Caouette is a bushleaguer."[73] His mission was to shadow Caouette across

Quebec and reply to him in public meetings and on television. For the most part, his message was: "Caouette has lied to the people of Quebec; now I'm here to tell you the truth." Once, to illustrate the inflation that could occur under Social Credit, he threw a bundle of worthless German marks into the air, thereby creating a short-lived blizzard before the TV cameras.

Lester Pearson also directed his fire against the Caouettists. On his first trip to Quebec he called them "the most insincere group ever elected to Parliament," and emphasized that Quebec had everything to gain by not voting Social Credit. On his return trip he criticized Caouette's promise to distribute dividends and at the same time cut taxes without causing inflation. "If this were possible every government in the world would have gone Social Credit. Even Khrushchov would have traded Karl Marx for Major Douglas."[74]

But interest focused most of all on Jean Lesage. Both *Le Devoir* and *La Presse* told him not to intervene in the election for fear he might identify himself with Pearson's changed stance on nuclear weapons. They were also opposed to reviving the old "automatisme partisan"–Liberal at Ottawa and Liberal at Quebec City.[75] When Caouette denounced the provincial government's take-over of the power companies, however, Lesage could no longer hold back. To the Legislature he stated that Quebeckers who wished to improve their economic lot had only one course, to "vote for the only party that can give a stable government in Ottawa, the Liberal party." Later on television he warned Caouette not to meddle in Quebec politics or "we'll prove he doesn't know any more about provincial affairs than he does . . . about other matters."[76]

By this time the leaders of the Quebec Federation of Labour (C.L.C.) and the National Trade Unions (C.N.T.U.) had come out strongly against Caouette, and Eric Kierans, President of the Montreal and Canadian stock exchanges, had ventured into Social Credit territory to denounce the party's monetary theory. "I wonder how many oats or potatoes he has grown to achieve his present situation," was Caouette's reaction. "Suck the blood of the poor–that's the only way finance has become so prominent in Canada."[77] Caouette also accused the Liberals of opening their campaign chest to the N.D.P. in order to split Social Credit, but Keith Davey called it "a preposterous suggestion."

The Liberal newspaper advertisements in Quebec were directed mainly against Social Credit. "Le Crédit Social, c'est la Misère" and "Le Paradis du Crédit Social, ce serait l'Enfer"–such were the warnings blazoned in large type. But as James M. Minifie saw it, the Liberals talked in global terms rather than in terms of Chicoutimi. Caouette, on the other hand, spoke the language of the habitant. "And when he tells the habitant, 'we have nothing to lose,' he is stating a demonstrable fact. When he enunciates his inalterable opposition to nuclear weapons, he arouses atavistic memories of traditional opposition, to 'fighting the foreigners' war,' whether that foreigner be British, American or English-Canadian."[78] That is why one often heard: "Caouette—he knows how to speak to us." And the more one doubted his theories the more his partisans gathered around him.

Professor Léon Dion felt that Créditistes had "added a new and most effective weapon. They have appointed themselves champion of extreme nationalism."[79] Although their support of the French-Canadian cause had resulted in only minor triumphs—the printing in French of the menus used in the Parliamentary restaurant and a commitment to have parliamentary procedures translated into French—Caouette boasted that "la preuve est faite," or roughly, "we have proved our worth." However, Dion went too far. Undoubtedly Social Credit rested on "a mixture of economic dissatisfaction and ethnic identification canalized by powerful oratory";[80] certainly Caouette did emphasize that French Canadians were second-class citizens in nine provinces and French Canada must assert itself. But even he admitted that ethnic insecurity was only a secondary theme of his campaign.[81] Claude Ryan of *Le Devoir* had no doubts that Social Credit support came primarily from an economic rather than a nationalist reflex.[82] Perhaps the Liberals would have devised a better election strategy if they had recognized that Social Credit had not created economic instability, but rather was a result of it throughout much of Quebec. In any case, there was no doubt that Caouette continued to make a strong appeal to the unemployed, to the unskilled, to marginal farmers, and to the self-employed classes hard hit by high interest rates. Under these circumstances it was debatable whether he should have travelled all over Quebec in an $8,000, 1963-model car, even though it was a demonstrator owned by the finance company.[83]

The big questions in Quebec in 1963 were whether Caouette could hold his 26 seats, and at the same time extend his victories into the Eastern Townships, Gaspésie, and the lower income ridings on Montreal Island. Certainly he tried to make a real fight of it in all 75 seats. Yet to some observers it became apparent that he was losing much of his higher income support. Social Credit defectors of this type, wrote Peter Regenstreif, "now seem to be yearning for respectability after a wild night on the town."[84] The result, as he saw it, was "the development of genuine and passionate class consciousness on the part of both Socred supporters and opponents alike. Political preferences are almost always expressed in terms of 'we' and 'they'. . . . In French Canada, there is the party of the rich, the business community, the professionals and the skilled—and a party of the poor. It goes without saying that Caouette is a master of intensifying this cleavage."[85]

Regenstreif also felt that Social Credit would cost the Liberals more in terms of votes than seats, and he. was proved correct: their popular vote went up from 26.0 to 27.3 per cent, but they gained only Labelle and

Rimouski while losing 8 others; their representation fell from 26 to 20. Although they increased their vote on Montreal Island, the best they could do there was to save their deposits in the low income ridings of Hochelaga, Laurier, Mercier, St. Henri, and St. Jacques. A furious Réal Caouette attributed his party's setback to American finance allied to Premier Lesage and to "the lying and infamous propaganda of the Liberal party." To the insinuations made against him personally, he replied: "I haven't any arms, I haven't any army, I am not a Hitler or Mussolini, I am not a dictator, I am a French Canadian who wishes to aid his country."[86]

Not surprisingly, the Conservatives' popular vote fell from 29.6 to 19.5 per cent, and their 8 victories were all personal ones. The Liberals gained 12 seats, but their 47 seats left them 3 short of what Lionel Chevrier had expected. According to Peter Desbarats, the Liberal success, such as it was, might have been a vote for stable government, a vote against Social Credit, or a protest against Diefenbaker, but it was definitely not a vote for Pearson.[87]

Some writers interpreted the election to mean that national unity was Canada's most pressing problem. Only a few weeks before, Dr. Marcel Chaput had launched his separatist party, le Rassemblement pour l'indépendance nationale (R.I.N.). At the same time terrorists of the Fédération pour la libération du Québec (F.L.Q.) were planting bombs in federal government buildings and mailboxes, and were threatening to blow up the Prime Minister's train on its way to Cap-de-la-Madeleine. It was altogether paradoxical that the returns of 1963 in no way reflected the split between English and French Canada, which might threaten Confederation itself, but revealed, in an even more accentuated form than previously, the split between rural and urban Canada, which did not seem to have serious long-range implications.[88] Professor Saywell suggested that John Diefenbaker skilfully used "the revulsion of professional elements, the business community, and the lords of the press [against the government] . . . to build up urban-rural antagonisms in a desperate Machiavellian attempt to retain power."[89] But this is an oversimplification. What rift there was had been developing over the preceding four or five years and stemmed "naturally from the unique phenomenon of having a prairie radical as leader of the Progressive Conservative party and from other personal characteristics of Mr. Diefenbaker."[90]

As Professor Underhill pointed out, the Prime Minister's strong point was his attachment to the little man. But this emotional commitment worked in a peculiar way. His "populist democratic emotions make him too suspicious of expert civil servants and central bankers. He too easily assumes that the nobility of these emotions, which identify him with the ordinary citizen, is a satisfactory substitute for expert knowledge and for action based on that knowledge."[91] Just as Laurier had come to feel that he should not be expected to do anything that might imperil his standing with his compatriots, John Diefenbaker made certain that the "little man" – especially the Prairie wheat grower – would not suffer at his hands. To an audience at Duck Lake he said: "I'm not asking for the support of the powerful, the strong and the mighty, but of the average Canadian – the group to which I belong."[92]

In all the rural seats on the Prairies, the reaction was much the same. A small farmer in Selkirk put it this way: "I think Diefenbaker has done more for this country in the last few years [than the Liberals did in 22 years] but they didn't give him a chance."[93] The Liberals who said "we're floating on Cloud Nine" when they induced Rudy Usick, the former president of the Manitoba Farmers' Union, to be their candidate in Selkirk were doomed to disappointment. The Conservatives took that seat and all the other rural seats in Manitoba. In Saskatchewan a typical reaction was that of half a dozen farmers talking in a garage at Antler: "It is not Pearson, this 'blanc-bec' of the East, who changes ideas as he changes shirts, who will get our vote."[94] Saskatchewan gave all its seats, including Assiniboia, to John Diefenbaker and Alvin Hamilton.

Except for the support of the upper income voters, Lester Pearson also did very poorly in Alberta. One observer suggested that the Conservative M.P.'s from the province were "not the grey little farmers at home they have sometimes appeared to be in the Commons," but represented the "new kind of Conservative in the west, tough, astute, caring not for Bay Street and, above all, with the confidence of knowing it is *possible* to be elected."[95] The outcome was that the Conservatives reduced the Social Credit majorities in Red Deer and Medicine Hat, and easily captured the other rural seats in Alberta. In all the Prairie provinces in general, and in practically every rural seat within these provinces, they increased their share of the popular vote.

Diefenbaker's sympathy for the underdog continued to be reflected in Atlantic province attitudes, although strong cross-pressures were operating in the region. While the nuclear commitment was not much of an issue, even Conservatives were saying: "I'm not a turn-coat. But things are in a hell of a mess. It all seems to be pulling apart."[96] The indications that Pearson would have the largest contingent in the House also helped the Liberals, for these provinces have always found it wise to be on the winning side. However, there were factors working in the Conservatives' favour, also: their government's considerate treatment of the area, the absence of a positive reaction to Pearson and, in Nova Scotia, the popularity of Robert Stanfield. Hence, the Liberals had to be satisfied with gaining St. John's East in Newfoundland, Kings and Prince in Prince Edward Island, and Shelburne-Yarmouth-Clare and the dual riding of Halifax in Nova Scotia. The Conservatives regained Cape Breton South from the N.D.P., but improved their standing in only one other seat. Regionally the result was 20 Liberals to 13 Conservatives.

In contrast, the almost complete collapse of the Conservatives in large parts of urban Canada stemmed from the side of John Diefenbaker's character portrayed by Professor Underhill. The Conservatives' loss of their customary support could not be as great as in the last election, because this time there was not so much of it left. However, traditional Conservatives of the upper-middle and upper income brackets had been further alienated by Diefenbaker's apparent concealment of the crisis in international payments until after the election of 1962, by his failure to formulate coherent economic and defence policies, and by the prospects of continued instability. One member of this group told Samuel Lubell that the Prime Minister was "so irresponsible he makes me ashamed I am a Canadian."[97]

The upper-middle and upper income voters flocked to the Liberals as the surest means of getting stable government and responsible fiscal management. The Liberals received strong competition from the N.D.P. for lower income and working class votes, but even here – particularly with the "ethnic vote" – the Liberals did well owing to their image as the "party of the common man." Diefenbaker's hold on the Southern European ethnic vote had collapsed in 1962 because these voters are more interested in the opportunity to get work than in tirades against communism; in 1963 even Eastern European voters deserted him in large numbers despite his none-too-subtle appeal for their support. The over-all result was that in metropolitan Toronto the Conservatives were buried under a landslide of Liberal and N.D.P. votes. So many upper income voters shifted to the Liberals in Forest Hill that Marvin Gelber managed to beat N.D.P. David Lewis in York South. The N.D.P., however, compensated for this loss by winning Hamilton South. For the first time since 1874 the Conservatives failed to win a seat in Toronto and York County. They also lost all their seats in Hamilton and Wentworth County and dropped Carleton for the first time since Confederation. As the city of Ottawa expanded into Carleton County, it brought with it a class of voters who were in revolt against the Conservatives.

The rural areas of Ontario exhibited surprisingly little anti-Diefenbaker sentiment. Eastern Ontario, almost as traditional in its voting habits as the Maritimes, did give 4 additional seats to the Liberals. However, in 3 of these ridings – Carleton, Northumberland, and Hastings South – the urban voters overpowered the rural ones. In the 35 ridings west of Toronto the Conservatives did even better; they retained all their seats except Wentworth and 2 in Hamilton, and actually regained the mixed urban-rural seats of Kent and Lambton-Kent. Except for northern Ontario, where the N.D.P. again took 3 seats and the Liberals the rest, the Liberal seats were to be found along a thin highly-populated strip running from Ottawa along the Lakes to Windsor. The net result in Ontario gave the Liberals 8 more and the Conservatives 8 fewer seats. Once again, rural Ontario prevented the Conservatives from being utterly routed.

The results in Ontario were indicative of the national trend. In English Montreal the rout of the Conservatives was such that they lost their deposits in traditionally Tory Mount Royal (where they were even out-polled by the N.D.P.!), Notre-Dame-de-Grâce, St. Antoine–Westmount, and St. Lawrence–St. George. Gordon Churchill managed to retain the lower income seat of Winnipeg South, but Liberals Margaret Konantz and Harry Hays captured the higher income ridings of Winnipeg South Centre and Calgary South. Howard Green lost in a similar riding, Vancouver Quadra, to the Liberals. However, there were exceptions to the normal pattern in urban Canada. The Conservatives won by wide margins in Regina and Saskatoon, indicating that, in Saskatchewan, "the attitude that the world revolves around the farmer is not confined to the tillers of the soil."[98] The Conservatives also increased their majorities in the three Edmonton seats, including high-income Edmonton West. "These last results point out the danger of treating in the aggregate special segments of the population, such as the urban voter, without reference to special regional conditions."[99]

The situation in British Columbia was unusual in several respects. It was "in a state of political flux equalled by no other area . . . other than Quebec."[100] Moreover, many of the voters switched their loyalty – from Conservative to Liberal and from Liberal and floater to N.D.P. – solely on the nuclear issue.[101] The net result was that the Liberals gained 3 seats in the province, 2 from the Conservatives and 1 from the N.D.P.

As the *Spectator* put it, "Canada's electors have almost made up their minds this time. It's a pity they did not do so completely."[102] Although the Liberals gained 29 seats for a total of 129, they were still 4 short of an over-all majority. All the opposition parties lost seats: the Conservatives 21, Social Credit 6, and the N.D.P. 2. American newspapers breathed an audible sigh of relief at the outcome; British reaction was reflected in the *Economist*: "The best that can be said for the Canadian election result is that the good guy won."[103] However, in most Canadian newspapers there was reluctant admiration for the fighting qualities of John Diefenbaker. "What an unbelievable recovery from the doleful days of the Hees-Sévigny resignations," said Douglas Fisher of the Toronto *Telegram*.[104] Even though the Conservatives had alienated most of the national élites, John Diefenbaker had kept his party in the fight. Despite his ups and downs, the Gallup Poll indicated that the Canadian people, by 34 to 32 per cent, preferred him to Pearson as Prime Minister. "This election," wrote Peter Regenstreif, "has been simply a case of man against party. It was an unequal struggle."[105] Only the rabidly Liberal Ottawa *Citizen* could not say anything good about the Prime Minister. His defeat, it said, would "serve as a warning to future politicians against the use of such divisive tactics."[106]

Between 1962 and 1963 the Liberals increased their share of the popular vote by 4.5 per cent, while that of the Conservatives decreased by a similar amount. Samuel Lubell suggested that two acts of the Diefenbaker

	Seats	Candidates					Elected							
		P.C.	L.	N.D.P.	S.C.	O.	P.C.	%	L.	%	N.D.P.	%	S.C.	%
Newfoundland	7	7	7	3		1			7	100.0				
Nova Scotia	12	12	12	9	2		7	58.3	5	41.7				
New Brunswick	10	10	10	7	10		4	40.0	6	60.0				
Prince Edward Island	4	4	4	4			2	50.0	2	50.0				
Quebec	75	75	75	60	75	10	8	10.7	47	62.7			20	26.7
Ontario	85	85	85	80	68	13	27	31.8	52	61.2	6	7.1		
Manitoba	14	14	14	13	13	1	10	71.4	2	14.3	2	14.3		
Saskatchewan	17	17	17	17	16	3	17	100.0						
Alberta	17	17	17	17	17	4	14	82.4	1	5.9			2	11.8
British Columbia	22	22	22	22	22	5	4	18.2	7	31.8	9	40.9	2	9.1
Yukon and N.W.T.	2	2	2		1		2	100.0						
Total	265	265	265	232	224	37	95	35.8	129	48.7	17	6.4	24	9.1

Others (votes
 polled): Nfld. (1): I.L. (1) 1,943.

Que. (10): I.L. (1) 1,320; Libéral des Electeurs (1) 496; I.P.C. (1) 1,616; I.S.C. (2) 717; Ouvrier Ind. (1) 1,064; I. (2) 2,823; Nat. (1) 540; Comm. (1) 327.

Ont. (13): I.L. (2) 7,808; I.P.C. (3) 1,508; I. (2) 760; Soc.-Lab. (1) 43; Comm. (5) 1,777.

Man. (1): I. (1) 826.

Sask. (3): I. (1) 135; Comm. (2) 308.

Alta. (4): I. (2) 460; Comm. (2) 795.

B.C. (5): I.L. (2) 3,587; Comm. (2) 1,027; I. (1) 232.

government—its increase in old age pensions in 1957 and 1962, and its sale of wheat to Communist China—stood like two solid walls blocking a strong Liberal surge.[107] The age categories employed by the Canadian Institute of Public Opinion do not permit a verification of Lubell's thesis. Perhaps the old age pensioners did remain strongly Conservative, but in the 50-and-over group the Liberals share of the vote increased from 34 to 44 per cent, and that of the Conservatives fell from 44 to 38 per cent. In most other categories there was a similar swing away from the Conservatives. They took 6 percentage points less of the Catholic vote and 4 less of the Protestant; the Liberals increased their proportion of votes in these groups by 3 and 5 percentage points, respectively. Among executive and professional people the Conservatives suffered a disastrous decline from 43 to 30 per cent, while the Liberal percentage went from 40 to 49. But among the farmers the Conservatives actually raised their vote from 43 to 49 per cent, while the Liberal share dropped from 35 to 33.

Twenty-sixth

Popular Vote										Total
P.C.	%	L.	%	N.D.P.	%	S.C.	%	O.	%	
45,491	30.1	97,576	64.5	6,364	4.2			1,943	1.3	151,374
195,711	46.9	195,007	46.7	26,617	6.4	401	0.1			417,736
98,462	40.4	115,036	47.3	8,899	3.7	21,050	8.6			243,447
35,965	52.0	32,073	46.4	1,140	1.6					69,178
413,562	19.5	966,172	45.6	151,061	7.1	578,347	27.3	8,903	0.4	2,118,045
979,359	35.3	1,286,791	46.3	442,340	15.9	56,276	2.0	11,896	0.4	2,776,662
169,013	42.3	134,905	33.8	66,652	16.7	28,157	7.0	826	0.2	399,553
224,700	53.7	100,747	24.1	76,126	18.2	16,110	3.9	443	0.1	418,126
249,067	45.3	121,473	22.1	35,775	6.5	141,956	25.8	1,255	0.2	549,526
172,501	23.4	237,896	32.3	222,883	30.3	97,846	13.3	4,846	0.7	735,972
7,783	53.8	6,114	42.3			560	3.9			14,457
2,591,614	32.8	3,293,790	41.7	1,037,857	13.1	940,703	11.9	30,112	0.4	7,894,076

Thus the Ottawa *Citizen* was justified in suggesting that the Liberal party, more than any other, was "a coalition in the Canadian tradition that embraces people of all classes and regions [and is] built around a programme and the solution of issues rather than a person," while the Conservative party was "built around the personality of Mr. Diefenbaker, whose greatest strength resides in the country's rural areas, especially on the Prairies."[108] This rural-urban split prevented Pearson from having an overall majority. Just as in 1962, the matter of personality more than anything else had frustrated the Liberals. Everywhere Samuel Lubell went he found people who were saying: "Diefenbaker has shown he isn't fit to be a prime minister but Pearson is no leader either."[109] Peter Regenstreif likewise discovered that the Liberal leader's inability to draw potential Tory defectors had become "a national chant."[110]

Two countries, an urban and a rural one, had voted in 1963, and there were many warnings of the dangers of disunity. For the moment the basic French-English conflict was producing nothing more than strong rumblings. In the long run, however, it represented a far greater threat to Confederation than the urban-rural cleavage.

FOOTNOTES

1. Mark Gayn, "The Canadian Elections," *Nation*, CXCVI (April 20, 1963), p. 319.

2. See column of Gerald Waring in Kingston *Whig-Standard*, February 28, 1963.

3. *Canadian Annual Review* (Toronto: University of Toronto Press, 1962), pp. 27-28).

4. Toronto *Globe and Mail*, December 8, 1962.

5. *Canadian Annual Review*, 1963, p. 287.

6. *Ibid.*, p. 294.

7. Peter Stursberg, "Postmark Ottawa," *Saturday Night*, LXXVIII (May, 1963), pp. 7-8.

8. *Ibid.*, (March, 1963), p. 7.

9. *Canadian Annual Review*, 1963, p. 16.

10. Ottawa *Journal*, March 16, 1963.

11. *Ibid.*

12. *Ibid.*

13. Ottawa *Citizen*, March 23, 1963.

14. Toronto *Telegram*, March 16, 1963.

15. *Ibid.*

16. Toronto *Globe and Mail*, April 6, 1963.

17. John Saywell in the *Financial Times*, March 11, 1963.

18. Ottawa *Journal*, April 4, 1963.

19. *Ibid.*, March 7, 1963.

20. Montreal *Gazette*, March 25, 1963.

21. Ottawa *Citizen*, April 2, 1963.

22. Kingston *Whig-Standard*, March 6, 1963.

23. Ottawa *Journal*, March 26, 1963.

24. Ottawa *Citizen*, April 1, 1963.

25. Toronto *Star*, April 1, 1963.

26. Ottawa *Citizen*, March 30, 1963.

27. Ottawa *Journal*, March 6, 1963.

28. Toronto *Globe and Mail*, March 11, 1963.

29. Montreal *Gazette*, March 8, 1963.

30. Toronto *Star*, March 9, 1963.

31. Ottawa *Journal*, March 6, 1963.

32. Toronto *Star*, March 9, 1963.

33. *Ibid.*

34. Ottawa *Journal*, March 6, 1963.

35. *Ibid.*, March 29, 1963.

36. Gerald Waring in Kingston *Whig-Standard*, March 12, 1963.

37. Montreal *Gazette*, March 8, 1963.

38. Toronto *Telegram*, March 9, 1963.

39. Toronto *Globe and Mail*, March 9, 1963.

40. Toronto *Telegram*, March 20, 1963.

41. Toronto *Star*, March 16, 1963.

42. Toronto *Globe and Mail*, March 18, 1963.

43. Arthur Blakely in the Montreal *Gazette*, March 30, 1963.

44. Toronto *Telegram*, March 23, 1963.

45. Toronto *Star*, April 2, 1963.

46. Toronto *Telegram*, April 1, 1963.

47. Toronto *Globe and Mail*, February 12, 1963.

48. *Ibid.*, February 14, 1963.

49. Ottawa *Journal*, February 25, 1963.

50. Montreal *Gazette*, March 1, 1963.

51. Toronto *Globe and Mail*, March 4, 1963.

52. Kingston *Whig-Standard*, March 9, 1963.

53. Ramsay Cook, "A New liberal Government?", *Canadian Forum*, XLIII (May, 1963), p. 25.

54. Toronto *Telegram*, March 16, 1963.

55. Toronto *Globe and Mail*, March 14, 1963.

56. Kingston *Whig-Standard*, March 18, 1963.

57. Toronto *Star*, March 16, 1963.

58. Toronto *Telegram*, March 11, 1963.

59. Toronto *Globe and Mail*, March 30, 1963.

60. Bruce Macdonald in Toronto *Globe and Mail*, March 11, 1963.

61. Toronto *Star*, March 16, 1963.

62. "The Four-Way Stretch," *Economist*, CCVII (April 6, 1963), p. 27.

63. Ottawa *Citizen*, April 3, 1963.

64. Ottawa *Journal*, March 6, 1963.

65. Toronto *Globe and Mail*, March 28, 1963.

66. Ottawa *Journal*, March 4, 1963.

67. Toronto *Star*, March 16, 1963.

68. Ottawa *Citizen*, March 9, 1963.

69. *Ibid.*

70. *Ibid.*, March 30, 1963.

71. Kingston *Whig-Standard*, March 4, 1963.

72. Ottawa *Journal*, February 26, 1963.

73. *Ibid.*, February 22, 1963.

74. Toronto *Globe and Mail*, March 18, 1963.

75. André Laurendeau in *Le Devoir*, March 22, 1963.

76. Toronto *Globe and Mail*, March 22, 1963, and Montreal *Gazette*, March 23, 1963.

77. Ottawa *Journal*, March 5, 1963.

78. James M. Minifie, "Quebec's in Turmoil," *Commentator*, VII (April, 1963), p. 4.

79. Toronto *Telegram*, March 16, 1963.

80. Peter Regenstreif in Kingston *Whig-Standard*, April 5, 1963.

81. Montreal *Gazette*, March 28, 1963.

82. *Le Devoir*, April 8, 1963.

83. Kingston *Whig-Standard*, March 28, 1963.

84. Ottawa *Journal*, April 5, 1963.

85. *Ibid.*, March 11, 1963.

86. *Le Devoir*, April 9, 1963.

87. Toronto *Telegram*, April 3, 1963.

88. J.M. Beck, "The Election of 1963 and National Unity," *Dalhousie Review*, XLIII (Summer, 1963), p. 152.

89. John Saywell, "Canada's Disunity Now Our Most Pressing Problem," *Financial Times of Canada*, April 29, 1963.

90. Beck, "Election of 1963," p. 146.

91. Toronto *Star*, March 16, 1963.

92. Peter C. Newman, "Whistle-stop Magic at Work in the Prairies," *Maclean's*, LXVI (April 6, 1963), p. 1.

93. Peter Regenstreif in Ottawa *Journal*, March 26, 1963.

94. Roger Nantel in *La Presse*, April 2, 1963.

95. Doug Sagi, "In Alberta Social Credit is Gaining," *Commentator*, VII (April, 1963), p. 9.

96. Peter Regenstreif in Ottawa *Journal*, March 2, 1963.

97. Ottawa *Citizen*, April 2, 1963.

98. Peter Regenstreif in Ottawa *Journal*, March 15, 1963.

99. Beck, "Election of 1963," p. 151.

100. Peter Regenstreif in Ottawa *Journal*, March 22, 1963.

101. Walter Young, "B.C.–Liberals and N.D.P. Up," *Commentator*, VII (April, 1963), p. 11.

102. "A Change for the Better," *Spectator*, CCX (April 12, 1963), p. 452.

103. "Mr. Pearson's Problem," *Economist*, CCVII (April 20, 1963), p. 221.

104. Toronto *Telegram*, April 9, 1963.

105. Kingston *Whig-Standard*, April 6, 1963.

106. Ottawa *Citizen*, April 9, 1963.

107. *Ibid.*, April 1, 1963.

108. *Ibid.*, April 4, 1963.

109. *Ibid.*, April 3, 1963.

110. Kingston *Whig-Standard*, March 30, 1963.

Twenty-seventh
General Election

"IT ISN'T MUCH TO COME OUT OF AN ELECTION"

On September 7, 1965, Prime Minister Lester Pearson announced Canada's third election in four years. Those who heard him wondered if he was trying to convince himself of a decision he had declared to be his and his alone. At any rate, Canadians would pronounce upon two and a half years of Pearson rule. Undoubtedly his government had shown both imagination and courage in tackling some of the country's problems, but in the process it had also demonstrated an astonishing lack of political finesse. Its early troubles hinged around the Prime Minister's promise of "sixty days of decision." He might have wanted to forget that promise, but the newspapers did not; "a daily tabulation of the administration's accomplishments became a favourite sport"[1] with them. On the fifty-third of those days Minister of Finance Walter Gordon presented a budget incorporating some of his own novel ideas. His ill-starred proposals and their administrative unworkability forced him into a series of embarrassing retreats and "by the time the budget resolutions were passed they contained little or nothing out of the ordinary."[2] Furthermore, Gordon, though a political novice, had adopted such an arrogant attitude towards the record of the preceding administration that he had aroused the ire of even the moderate Conservatives. Parliament had got off to a bad start and the drift was steadily downward. By June 1964 the *Round Table* was calling it "an addled Parliament." Acrimony marked its debates and the time it wasted on partisan squabbles about petty matters became a national disgrace.[3]

On the other hand the Liberals accused the Conservatives of deliberate obstruction to make the government look bad; they accused John Diefenbaker of desperately trying to bring down the government so that he might lead the country during its centennial year. On the other hand, the government was quite capable of obstructing itself. Pearson and many of his cabinet had been civil servants and their experience in the art of politics had been minimal. Douglas Fisher thought that the Prime Minister behaved "too often like a nineteenth-century colonial administrator negotiating with Hottentots through *billets doux*."[4] The Toronto *Star* said that "the government stumbles on its own legislation and then crowds the opposition against deadlines. Abuse replaces reason, and our governors no longer govern."[5]

Fate also conspired to confront the Pearson government with difficult problems. In its earliest days Premier Lesage presented the demands of Quebec's Quiet Revolution in a so-called ultimatum. Desperately the government sought to "find the unmarked channel of co-operative federalism between the Scylla of national needs and the Charybdis of provincial rights."[6] History may later credit Pearson's diplomacy with doing much to save the Canadian federation in these troubled days. However, to such papers as the Toronto *Globe and Mail* it appeared that secretive, behind-the-scenes negotiations between the emissaries of the federal and Quebec governments had supplanted the open and aboveboard federal-provincial conference, and to many Anglo-Saxon Canadians it appeared that Quebec was always the chief beneficiary of any new arrangements with Ottawa.

The bitter controversy over the flag further exacerbated the relations between the Liberals and the Conservatives. Parliament heard 270 speeches in 33 sitting days spread over 6 months, before the Prime Minister decided that public opinion permitted him to invoke closure in December 1964. The debate served to increase the antipathy between Pearson and Diefenbaker. By this time Peter Newman was questioning the capacity of either man to lead, and however exaggerated his generalizations, they had a germ of truth. Diefenbaker, he felt, regarded "time spent in Parliament as a necessary respite between elections[,] and legislation as a posture instead of a process"; the Conservative leader also "considered French Canada as just another ethnic group, who happened to get here first." Pearson, on the other hand, treated Quebec like "some giant lobby, which must be appeased into line," and "behaved as though his main job was to conserve the powers of his office rather than expend them in the interests of survival." Newman concluded that whichever party had the courage to choose a new leader— "a mid-Twentieth-Century man who truly speaks for this era"—would inherit the nation.[7]

The Conservatives did not get a new leader, but it was not because many of them did not want one. The dissatisfied had come to believe that, because of the Liberal record, they could win the next election under new leadership. But when they challenged John Diefenbaker at the annual meeting of the national association in February 1964, he confronted them with piercing eye, stabbing finger, and wagging head, saying: "I want to know where I stand with you. I want to know where you stand too." In the end only about thirty delegates dared show they stood against him. During 1964 the party's internal difficulties became worse as its leader consulted only a few intimates about policies and strategy. At the meeting of the national executive in February 1965, the anti-Diefenbaker faction tried its luck again, and this time narrowly failed to secure a leadership convention. A Quebec M.P., Rémi Paul, left the party in disgust, but Léon Balcer was induced to stay because of the closeness of the vote.

Meanwhile, Lester Pearson was having his own troubles in the way of scandal. In November 1964 there was the sordid case of an active worker for the Liberal party in Quebec, Lucien Rivard, whom the United States was seeking to extradite for narcotics smuggling. Had an executive assistant to a cabinet minister offered a bribe to secure his release on bail? Had a parliamentary assistant applied pressure to the same end? Had Guy Favreau, the Minister of Justice, dealt properly with the evidence in his possession? Eventually, Chief Justice Dorion, acting as a one-man royal commission, found that the executive assistant had offered the bribe, that the parliamentary assistant had applied improper pressure, and that Guy Favreau had shown bad judgment in not seeking an opinion from his legal advisers on the evidence. The executive assistant was charged, the parliamentary assistant resigned from the Commons, and Favreau left the Justice Department but remained in the cabinet. In December there was the case of two other ministers, Lamontagne and Tremblay, who had been involved in curious transactions involving the purchase of substantial quantities of furniture to be paid for as and when the purchasers chose. Although the ministers' explanations were not entirely convincing, Pearson let them remain in the cabinet. He was tougher in January 1965, however, when Yvon Dupuis was accused of accepting money to accelerate the granting of a racecourse franchise by the Quebec government; he demanded and got Dupuis's resignation from the cabinet.

Despite all its troubles, the government's position remained surprisingly stable. In March 1965 the Gallup Poll indicated its support had fallen only from 47 to 45 per cent, while that of the Conservatives had fallen from 32 to 29. Bad as the Liberals appeared, the feeling existed that the Conservatives would not be a suitable alternative until they changed leaders. By mid-year, reported the *Round Table*, the Liberals had got "their second wind" and were becoming more and more "cocky."[8] They could boast of positive accomplishments: the Canada Pension Plan, a distinctive national flag, a new system of redistribution, and so on. There was, in addition, a high level of prosperity, an improvement in the government's financial position, an abundant harvest, and a marked reduction in unemployment. Not unnaturally, Liberals in high places wondered if it would be well to have an election while the Tory party was still split. As early as March 10, Pearson pondered the situation with some of his ministers: "To go while Diefenbaker [was] still there? To risk facing a new Conservative leader? To wait out the aftermath of the Dorion inquiry? . . . To take time to build a new image in Quebec? . . . To wait for the advantages—and fairness—of redistribution? To continue to face a hopeless Parliament? Indeed, to go or not to go?"[9]

In succeeding months the omens continued to be good for the government. On July 30 the Gallup Poll reported its strength to be undiminished and on August 11 big wheat sales were announced. Fearing that Pearson was about to take the plunge, the Toronto *Globe and Mail* warned that there were no issues for an election, that the government was obligated to wait until the new redistribution scheme came into effect, that it was in no danger of defeat in the Commons, that there was no evidence of any strong swing to the Liberals, and that the outcome might be "a fracturing of Canada." Pointedly it asked: "Is it worth gambling so much in the hope of a Liberal win?"[10] Nevertheless, strategists Walter Gordon, Tom Kent, and Keith Davey wanted a dissolution, and at a cabinet meeting on September 1 only one minister strongly opposed it.

This election, wrote Peter Desbarats, was the first to bear the authentic Pearson imprint. In his three previous campaigns as leader, Liberal strategists had tried to give him "at least a glimmer of glamour and . . . put [him] through all the hoopla of American-style electioneering," but the surveys had shown that his popularity actually decreased during the campaigns.[11] This time the Liberal high command decided he would conduct what virtually amounted to a non-campaign. Above all, they did not want it to "deteriorate into a titanic duel between two aging political gladiators" in which their man would be no match for John Diefenbaker. Instead they proposed to present Pearson as a man above politics, "as a personification of the national consensus on all of the broad basic issues. His main function . . . will be to spread a large umbrella over the centre of Canadian politics and invite the majority of voters under it with him." Pearson was to persuade the voters that he, like Charles de Gaulle, was so identified with the good of his country that he personified the national will. But "to put it as mildly as possible," wrote Peter Newman, "Lester Pearson is no Charles de Gaulle. . . . His negotiable approach to leadership contrasts sharply with the image his image-makers now hope to project . . . he has failed to become a central figure in the national conscience. He remains smaller than life – as if he were the agent of forces greater than himself."[12]

Pearson none the less spent an unprecedented amount of the election period in Ottawa "prime ministering," and the result was to cut drastically the number of his public appearances. Eddie Goodman, who was running the election for the Conservatives, charged him with running a big-city campaign and ignoring the small towns. "Three weeks ago Mr. Pearson was ready to go to India or Pakistan. Today he is unwilling to go to Lévis or Kelowna." "Who's Mr. Goodman?", retorted Pearson. "I happen to be Prime Minister. . . . I'll be visiting every province. I'll be in small places as much as I can but . . . my first obligation is as Prime Minister."[13] Scornfully, John Diefenbaker talked about the Buddha at Ottawa and prophesied that public pressures would force him out.

When the Prime Minister did participate in the campaign, he emphasized, above all, the theme of majority government. "We need in this country," he said, "a five-year plan for action, rather than a five-month plan." And again, "I am asking for a clear mandate so that our country can have the leadership and strength in Ottawa to get on with the basic tasks" –

economic expansion, improved social security, equal opportunity for all Canadians.[14]

> Our record in 2½ years has been good. With a majority we could have done more and, I think, done it better. It took six months to pass the flag resolution. If it had been done in two months, we should have had four months for some of these other matters.[15]

The minorities were saying, he continued, that the great challenges facing the country were less important than giving third, fourth, and fifth parties a veto over everything the government tried to do. Should this become the permanent situation, negotiations among political parties might replace Parliament as the basis of government decisions. "I believe this is bad for the democratic process in this country."[16]

Naturally he thought it was the Liberals who deserved the majority. "We have made mistakes, have suffered disappointments, have had our setbacks and delays. . . . But . . . we have done things. We have tackled the tough problems, have faced up to those things on which action was needed."[17] Of the six major undertakings he had put before the electorate in 1963, his government had realized five and hoped to bring the sixth, medicare, into effect by July 1, 1967. The Prime Minister exulted particularly in the improved economic conditions. "The signs of growth are all around us – vital constructive achievement. . . . Let's keep things going ahead with a strong central government at Ottawa able to go ahead and operate over a period of years."[18] The Conservatives talked about cleaning up the "mess at Ottawa," but did the people want to go back to the Diefenbaker era? "That was a record period. Record disputes . . . record confusion . . . record stagnation."[19]

Pearson rejoiced also in the general accomplishments of Canadians.

> Nearly every pull in Canada is north and south, not east and west. We Canadians have refused to accept the dictates of nature, of economics and of geography. We have built out of this northern part of the continent one country – from ocean to ocean – from the southern border to the Arctic sea. There are not many people in this world that could have done that. And we are going to keep it Canadian . . . a strong, a separate state that shares a continent and counts in the world.[20]

A Liberal government, he continued, could best ensure that Canada would stay strong and united. "If we can't build up unity between French-speaking and English-speaking and any-other-kind-of speaking, how can we expect to have unity and brotherhood in the world?" And French Canadians agreed with him. "I told them straight, not about what they [should] expect Canada to do for them as French Canadians, but what Canada expected them as

French Canadians to do for her. . . . And you know, they cheered me for telling them."[21]

But Canada could never be a united country while some of its people were poor and others rich. If a family of four required $3,000 a year for reasonable living, between three and a half and four million Canadians lived poorly. That was why he had begun a war on poverty. That was why his government was trying to ensure greater equality of opportunity through its manpower training programme, its policy of providing greater mobility for the unemployed, its area development policy which offered industries tax incentives to settle in underdeveloped areas, and its extension of the Agricultural Rehabilitation and Development Administration in rural parts. That was why his government had provided $100 million to the Atlantic Development Board.

A Liberal government that was itself united, the Prime Minister continued, could best keep the country united. "It is not necessary for us to restore unity in our party. We have it. We do not have to put even a candle in the window, let alone a high-powered searchlight, to show the way home for the exiles."[22] As leader, he did not have to sing: "Won't you Love Me in November as You Didn't in May?"[23] His government was a team and his idea of leadership was to "keep the party united for going ahead, to give my colleagues the responsibility for doing their part, to be the quarterback and call the signals on the team but not trying to carry the ball on every play and also be ticket taker, cheer leader and the St. John Ambulance Brigade as well."[24]

In accordance with the general concept of his campaign, Pearson promised at the outset not to "indulge in smears, sneers, slander and scuttlebutt." But if he hoped thereby to avoid a discussion of honesty in government, he deceived himself. At Edmonton on October 19, after emphasizing his own adherence to moral values, he went on to say that politics was the noblest of professions and the meanest of trades, and that "there [were] some pretty mean practitioners."[25] Three days later in a national television address, he made it clear, without mentioning names, that John Diefenbaker was the meanest of practitioners; when he denounced "smear tactics," "whispering campaigns," "witch hunts," and "malicious invective," it was clearly the Conservative leader whom he had in mind. "No charge," he continued, "has been made that has not been investigated. Nothing was revealed, that should have been dealt with, that was not dealt with, and the rest is insinuation and misrepresentation."[26] Pearson could not be made to see that no one had ever attacked his personal honesty and integrity, but there were serious doubts whether he had genuinely sought to uncover all the factors or taken decisive action against those whose conduct was not above reproach.

Pearson's boast of a united cabinet also came under attack from the Conservatives. Did he and the rest of his ministers favour the Maurice

Sauvé–Walter Gordon–Tom Kent concept of "a planned economy" and did Mitchell Sharp accept Walter Gordon's prescription for national survival, which was allegedly to increase Canada's independent status by reducing its trade with the United States?

Even Pearson's ascription to the Liberal party of a pre-eminent role in forging national unity was scoffed at by Claude Ryan of *Le Devoir*. Ryan insisted that the government did not deserve the mandate it expected to get in Quebec and that any such mandate could only aggravate "the imbalance which already exists between the support enjoyed by the Liberals in the rest of the country and [that] which they obtain only too easily, alas, in Quebec."[27] Accordingly Quebeckers should forget about party and vote for first-rate candidates like Sauvé, Pépin, Marchand, and Pelletier of the Liberals; Martineau, Asselin and Grafftey of the Conservatives; and Cliche, Taylor, and Gifford of the N.D.P.

Pearson's real failure, however, was not in his arguments but in his manner of presenting them. Why his strategists believed he could enact the exacting role they had assigned to him in 1965, after his disappointing performances of 1962 and 1963, is somewhat mystifying. Indeed, their own action indicated they did not believe he could do it. Realizing his inadequacy before the television camera, they resorted to a gimmick that John F. Kennedy had used successfully; they filmed informal living-room encounters between Pearson and "typical" citizens who wanted to have specific issues explained to them. But it seemed too artificial. Scoffingly Charles Lynch wrote that "given a few more elections, the party brass may fathom some of these hitherto impenetrable mysteries."[28]

The strategists had likewise failed to find a solution to Pearson's ineffectual performance before large audiences. This time his speeches were short, and virtually the same night after night. To one observer he seemed "even more adept than usual . . . in ringing all the flat notes in the oratorical scale."[29] To Peter Newman he conveyed the impression of having made a political and intellectual commitment to his policies without revealing the extent of his emotional commitment.[30] At a meeting in Humboldt, Saskatchewan, Premier Ross Thatcher spoke first and filled the room with excitement. Then, when the Prime Minister began, "the old wall slammed down before the platform and the audience began to shift in their seats and murmur among themselves." Journalists covering him found little to write about; they felt that the atmosphere of genteel touring surrounding his entourage was quite unprofessional, and that his refusal to "work himself into an exhausted froth at this late stage of the campaign" was un-American.[31]

Pearson's chief rival was anything but unprofessional. His defects were of another kind, and one of the first tasks of the Conservative national campaign committee was to repair a party riddled by the defections he had caused. It succeeded far beyond its wildest expectations. As the defectors came back in a flood Charles Lynch likened them to "The Ghost Riders in the Sky."[32] One ex-rebel Eddie Goodman, agreed to run the party's national campaign.

Powerful assistance was forthcoming from those who had not defected. Davie Fulton, no enthusiastic admirer of "The Chief," returned from British Columbia politics saying: "I am anxious to serve again in Ottawa under John Diefenbaker."[33] Premier Robarts of Ontario announced that he and his organization would give "full throttle" to the Conservative campaign; Premier Stanfield of Nova Scotia threw himself into the election as he had never done before; and Premier Roblin of Manitoba – although he declined to enter federal politics at a time "when important new provincial policies are in the process of formation" – promised all-out support to John Diefenbaker.

In 1963 only five newspapers had supported the Conservatives; this time twenty-one did, compared to eighteen for the Liberals. On October 30 the influential Toronto *Globe and Mail* returned to the fold in a belaboured, tortured editorial entitled "The Instruments of Power." It arraigned Lester Pearson for letting federal powers slip away in behind-the-scenes negotiations, for not ridding himself of ministers who had been found wanting, and – worst of all – for giving no assurances that he was "not intending to move – indeed gallop – into a controlled economy," guided by the Walter Gordons, the Tom Kents, and the Maurice Sauvés. Surely it could not support John Diefenbaker whom it had denounced for so long? But yes. "Can we expect [the return of the magician of 1957 and 1958 who] was able, for a time, to give this country sound leadership? . . . The party has admitted it needs a leader. The leader has admitted he needs a party. There is, at least, ground for hope."[34]

Although John Diefenbaker held out the olive branch to the rebels, he promised them nothing. To him it was simply a case of the disloyal returning to a fold they ought never to have left. According to the Toronto *Star*, George Hees "achieved what appeared to be a painfully one-sided reconciliation only after [he] grabbed the party leader's hand and shook it."[35] "The Chief" did not put out the welcome mat for everybody. When two hundred Conservative candidates and organizers in Quebec invited Marcel Faribault, President of the General Trust of Canada, to be a candidate, Diefenbaker told newspapermen he was the kind of man his party wanted to attract. However, at no time did he extend a personal invitation to Faribault, whose views on the constitution were anathema to him. Noticeably, too, the rebels did not come back in Quebec, where the party needed them most. Rémi Paul said he would lose his deposit if he ran under Diefenbaker, and Léon Balcer also gave up, saying: "There is no place for a French Canadian in the party of Mr. Diefenbaker."[36]

The defectors were returning not to Diefenbaker, but to the Conservative party. Except in the Prairie provinces, "Conservative spokesmen tended to follow one of three courses: to ignore their leader altogether; to argue that he was a changed man; or to point out that he would soon be stepping down."[37] The Conservative party, which had been masquerading for some time as the Diefenbaker party, emerged in its old true-blue colours in newspaper advertisements. "The Chief" none the less got into the campaign early and stole the show almost from the start. Indeed, it is a sad commentary on democratic elections – or on his opponents' lack of political talents – that one offering so little could be so successful. From being almost down and out, wrote George Bain, he came back "bouncing like an Ed Sullivan trampoline. . . . His resilience is part of his extraordinariness."[38] His intense pride drove him to redeem his lost reputation, to justify himself. Even Charles Lynch, a hard-boiled journalist, responded with the rest "when [Diefenbaker] spoke about lifting up the eyes of all Canadians to the greatness of this nation, or pleaded that his mission was to show the people the way and the truth."[39]

Once again whistle-stopping figured extensively in the Conservative leader's campaign. Once again he moved slowly across the country from grain elevator to oil tank, grasping every hand in sight for twelve hours a day, "tireless, enthusiastic, obviously recharging his emotional batteries from contact with people eager to shake his hand." It may have been, as he called it, a meet-the-people campaign, but it was not, as he also claimed, a campaign to put the issues before the people. No one could have done this meaningfully in one, two, or three minutes.[40] It was equally difficult to accept his appraisal of these relatively small crowds: "It's the spirit of '57 and '58 again" or "This is a reception the like of which I have never before received." In 1965 John Diefenbaker believed what he wanted to believe. On November 2, as he was still whistle-stopping in western Ontario, Anthony Westell wrote: "The last of the whistle-stoppers rolled through Ontario yesterday and into the history books . . . almost certainly the end of a tradition that stretches back to Sir John A. Macdonald and the building of the first railroads."[41]

The romantic side of John Diefenbaker's campaign was its most attractive side. Peter Newman summed up its other side thus: "John Diefenbaker's campaign remains more style than substance," and he "acted throughout as though he believed that Canadian governments are defeated and not elected."[42] More than ever before, he attacked the Liberals on every conceivable matter. In the old British city of St. John's he denounced them for whittling away the monarchy and associated institutions: "The [November] 8 election represents the last chance to stop it. There isn't going to be any second chance."[43] In the Maritimes he belaboured Walter Gordon for offering their people a one-way ticket out of the area.

Why did Pearson want an election anyway? "He had a majority. We didn't know until Dr. Marcoux's revelations that it had been purchased . . . either by blandishments or otherwise."[44] Here Diefenbaker was referring to

Social Credit M.P. Marcoux's charge that Premier Smallwood and J.W. Pickersgill had participated in negotiations by which six Social Credit M.P.'s were induced to sign a document pledging support to the Liberals shortly after the election of 1963, a charge which both of them vehemently denied. The Conservative leader criticized Pearson again for stating that, if he did not get a majority, there would be another election within eighteen months. How very like Louis XIV's statement: "L'état, c'est moi"! Pearson denied making it, but a tape recorder proved that he had. Diefenbaker intimated that he had tried to get out of the situation by saying in effect: "I said what I said when I said it but I did not mean what I said when I said it."[45]

The Conservative leader conducted much of his campaign as a witch hunt for criminals in the government. Always he conjured up the picture of an administration riddled through with criminal influence, and then added: "When I was Prime Minister no one ever said there was lack of honesty in government." Anthony Westell took him to task because, even though he had solid material with which to work, "he conjures up from a mass of non-facts" the evidence for his charges. Thus, in referring to such unsavoury persons as Minaudo, Bonanno, and Stonehill, Diefenbaker wondered "if the welcome mat has been laid out by government for these people coming from outside." But if coddling had occurred in some of these cases, it had actually been done by his own government.[46] Similarly he had little evidence to substantiate his charges of a connection between bankruptcies and murder and arson cases in Quebec. Yet that did not stop him from saying: "Today there have been murders, most callous murders. In the face of violence and crime, what did the Government do? . . . They covered up, they concealed, they didn't want to talk about it."[47] When Pearson accused him of waging a campaign of "sneers, smears, scuttlebutt and slander," he wondered if the Prime Minister considered C.J. Dorion's findings as "guilty of that collection of s's."[48] Reporters, said Westell, bent over backwards to be fair to the Conservative leader, "but what is fairness in reporting a politician who puts aside his truly remarkable memory for detail when he climbs on the platform and pours forth a private version of the facts?"[49]

Diefenbaker did have a positive program to present as well. Indeed, the *Globe and Mail* said the Conservative programme was "so full of planks that the voters not equipped with a computer may lose track of them": old age pensions of $100 a month for everyone at age 65, the additional $25 to come from the Canada Pension Fund; income tax exemptions for home-owners to the extent of their municipal tax bills; increased university grants and more money for medical and dental educational research facilities; larger basic wheat quotas; acreage payments on crop losses to eastern farmers; removal of the 11 per cent sales tax on production machinery; a conference to draft a made-in-Canada constitution; and so on *ad infinitum*. Apparently most of the programme was inspired by Alvin Hamilton and his policy committee, who sold it to the national campaign committee, but John Diefenbaker adopted as much or as little of it as he chose.

Indeed, the party platform was largely peripheral to Diefenbaker's campaign. Because of public pressure – so he said – he concentrated on integrity in government and the Liberals' failure to bring about national unity. When he did get round to the party programme, some reporters found it "hard to escape the conclusions that [he had] been armed with brief summaries of the policy planks and [knew] little of the background thinking."[50] In any case, he was not inhibited in devising his own programme to suit the needs of each particular region except Quebec. Thus, after "taking a surveyor's look at the Atlantic landscape, [he] promised to trap tides, dig canals, and provide unlimited funds to spur the Maritimes' economic development."[51]

More than anywhere else, however, John Diefenbaker displayed his inadequacy in the wooing of Quebec. His decision to remain in politics, he said, resulted from his belief that he had "something to offer for the preservation of the union." Yet he had little to offer. Strangely enough, he attracted larger crowds than Pearson did in Quebec City, leading Conservative Raymond O'Hurley to say: "I am still trying to figure that one out myself." Naturally Diefenbaker was ecstatic: "They said I wouldn't come into Quebec. . . . Tell me of a province where the welcome to my wife and me has been greater than in the last two days."[52] Generally his strategy was to campaign in specially selected rural areas where his party might retain a seat or two. According to the reporters, the little knots of people who gathered at the stations as he whistle-stopped through *la belle province* consisted of long-time Bleus who had never been disloyal to any leader. He ought not to have felt he was genuinely communicating with French Canadians when he said "grand plaisir" to a few of them in his fractured French. The Quebec of the Quiet Revolution was not at all interested in his reminder that he had given Canada a French-Canadian Governor General and provided simultaneous translations in the Commons.

Most of all, Quebec was suspicious of his "One Canada" theme. The Montreal *Star* told him that utterances along this line in Quebec would "kill him dead. . . . 'One Canada' is interpreted here as being an attempt to extinguish French-Canadian rights . . . this theme of Mr. Diefenbaker goes straight back to Lord Durham."[53] Actually, the Conservative leader was completely irrelevant to most of Quebec. As Gérard Pelletier put it, "French Canadians do not even take the trouble to detest him. They find him so profoundly foreign, so completely out of touch with French-Canadian opinion, so totally incapable of understanding its uneasiness and its new mood that they treat him like a Martian."[54]

Meanwhile T.C. Douglas of the N.D.P. was saying that to give the Liberals a big majority would be "just like giving them a tranquillizer" and encouraging them to "push things under the rug." For him the real issues were leadership and the development of a sense of national purpose. "We've never had any over-all national goals in the last 40 or 50 years. . . . Can you imagine any recent Prime Minister pressuring Parliament and the country to undertake a project as enormous as the Canadian Pacific Railway? Macdonald did. . . . Can you imagine a leader today flying in the face of the religious and cultural prejudices of his own supporters? Laurier did in 1896."[55]

Douglas asked what was wrong with the present system. Drawing from the findings of John Porter in *The Vertical Mosaic*, he found that the chief evil was that fewer than one thousand persons made the basic decisions in our society. "The real Government of Canada doesn't sit in Parliament [but] in Bay Street in Toronto and in Jesse James Street in Montreal." Douglas had the ammunition he wanted when the CTV network, influenced by John Bassett, declined to show an N.D.P. film attacking misleading advertisements. "If these vast agencies of the mass media can refuse to let us present this issue, what prevents them from denying us or any other party the right to present any other issue . . . ?"[56]

More positively, the N.D.P. maintained that "the only limitations on how far a student should be allowed to go in pursuit of his education should be the brains in his head and not the money in his father's pocketbook."[57] It favoured a comprehensive manpower programme as an essential ingredient for its plans to banish poverty and want, and to improve the quality of life. It advocated a redistribution of income and increased purchasing power for lower income groups through higher income tax exemptions and social services such as medicare. It also wanted to achieve greater Canadian independence through an independent foreign policy evolved by the federal government itself. Most of all, it stood for planning over a wide area as a means of enriching "human life and improved living standards while at the same time preserving the cultural identities of the two founding races." To this end it proposed a permanent federal-provincial planning and development council; a planning council in the office of the Prime Minister to set guidelines for industry, agriculture, and labour; and an immediate inventory of the country's natural resources to provide the basis for a national plan for management of resources.

As for Quebec, the N.D.P. continued to boast that it was "the first party to call for a two-nations concept in confederation and for the principle of co-operative federalism which recognizes the equal partnership of English and French Canadians within the bosom of a single state."[58] It was taken aback for a moment when Jean Marchand, Pierre-Elliott Trudeau, and Gérard Pelletier, who were considered to be sympathetic with the N.D.P. point of view, threw in their lot with the Liberals. However, it soon concluded that its prospects in Quebec were rosier than ever before. This was not, it admitted, because many Quebeckers had embraced socialism, but rather because Caouette had been discredited, the electorate was confused and uncertain, and the N.D.P. had come up with an effective leader and excellent speaker in Robert Cliche.

So optimistic was T.C. Douglas that for the first time he saw the possibility of his party's forming a government. Early in the campaign he said that this would come about if N.D.P. could capture three-quarters of the 40 per cent of the electorate that was uncommitted at the time. Later he was more realistic and indicated that, if he held the balance of power, he would be willing to "sit down with whichever party is most amenable to implement our program . . . in exchange for voting support." But there would be no formal coalition because that would make the N.D.P. "like the canary inside the cat."[59]

In this election Social Credit made no pretence to being a national party. The long-threatened split between Thompson and Caouette had finally taken place in September 1963. At that time Caouette and 12 of his Quebec supporters left the national party and assumed the former designation of Le Ralliement des Créditistes, Robert Thompson led a Social Credit rump consisting of himself and 10 others, and the House of Commons had 5 parties instead of 4. Although Thompson's partly ran only 86 candidates in 1965 – all but 5 of them west of Quebec – he promised that if they were elected the result would be nothing less than the regeneration of Canada. In the existing state of affairs, he said, an election could no longer be called a national election. "It is really 265 by-elections where the citizens in their frustration are beginning to look at the candidates on the basis of local issues."[60] The old-line parties, in trying to coexist on the principles of private enterprise and the policies of the welfare state, were dying out. In the guise of bringing in social legislation, they had introduced socialism by the back door. Already Canadians were spending more than one-third of the gross national product in welfare; projected plans (in this election there were "six billions worth of promises to buy your vote") would add to that proportion. Yet it had been shown, warned Thompson, that a state that spends over 25 per cent of the G.N.P. in this area will surely fail.[61] Clearly Thompson was presenting his group as the party of private enterprise against socialistic Liberal, Conservative, and N.D.P. parties.

More than once Thompson emphasized that Caouette "has no connection with us" because the Ralliement had adopted a provincial rather than a national viewpoint. In reply, Caouette denounced Thompson for saying to Social Crediters from Quebec who sought to speak in the Commons: "Sit down, sit down; you'll hurt us out West."

> For too long Quebec M.P.'s have been straw men and yes men who have crawled behind their parties, rallying to caucus decisions because they were told they had to do so for the sake of national unity. . . . I ask you can you eat national unity? . . . Can you plow your fields with national unity?[62]

And so "Quebec First" became a fundamental ingredient of Caouette's campaign.

At the outset the Créditiste leader charged that the government had made an agreement to conscript 100,000 Canadians for Viet Nam. Pearson would deny it, he said, "but look at what the Mackenzie King group did in 1942. They were elected opposing conscription and then imposed it. I remember it like it was yesterday."[63] Otherwise Caouette limited himself to extolling the virtues of private enterprise and advocating old age pensions of $100 a month to everyone at age 65, higher income tax exemptions, and interest-free loans for public bodies from the Bank of Canada. Yet none of this evoked much enthusiasm, and newspapermen pondered the question: "Is the old magic gone?" At Caouette's grand opening in Quebec City only 1,000 attended, contrasted with 5,000 in 1963; there was "a feeling of ritual, a lack of spontaneity" about the meeting.[64] Where once he had only to speak to bring roars of adulation, this time he had to work for applause. In desperation he tried a new device. He asked his partisans to flood the mail with letters publicizing the Ralliement's cause throughout Quebec. "The newspapers don't like us and we can't afford to advertise like the other parties, but we will do things ourselves–by letter."[65]

However, nothing came of this, and Caouette fought more and more with his back to the wall. At Mégantic he drew only 400 (it had been 4,000 in 1962), at St. Anselm 240, at Rimouski 300 and no applause. Peter Cowan of the Montreal *Star* found it unreal that a man "guiding his ship downwards towards the inevitable crack" should talk about winning 50 seats in Quebec and holding the balance of power in the next Parliament. To Cowan, Caouette's words sounded "somewhat hollow as they echo through halls where all the seats are not filled and the crowds are less than enthusiastic."[66] His listeners had once accepted his theories without attempting to understand them; they now appeared to think there was little to them. Even the Créditistes' threat to enter provincial politics worked against them, for in some counties U.N. organizers who had previously helped them against the Liberals told their followers to support the N.D.P.

"A bore for the voters, but for the politicians . . . a nightmare," was Peter Newman's description of the campaign.[67] George Bain of the *Globe and Mail* found that the voters were not greatly concerned with programmes but were mainly interested in the personalities of the leaders and the candidates.[68] Even the normally Liberal Leslie Roberts felt that Pearson had accepted the advice of his strategists to stage a general election over nothing. "Hence the national yawn. Hence the state of boredom which has laid its heavy hand on the Canadian people."[69] What, wondered the *Globe and Mail*, were the issues? The politicians "do not debate. They are little men posturing a hundred sideshows up and down the country, while the country yawns. It had better weep." Yes, said the same paper, it was "a long, shabby, sham of an election campaign," and "there has been little in the tide of words that eddied around [the voters] that offered their country any clarity, any purpose, any dignity."[70] The evidence bears out this dismal picture to some extent; issues such as defence and foreign policy were not discussed at all, and voter turn-out, which had been 79 per cent in the three previous elections, fell to 75 per cent.

Both Pearson and Diefenbaker campaigned with serious liabilities. Pearson's apparent reluctance to deal firmly with lapses in conduct had created doubts that he could be sufficiently hard-hearted. Consequently he had to "maintain the fiction that all is well in his government."[71] John Diefenbaker had the even more difficult task of persuading the voters that he was credible as a prime minister in view of his previous record in that office. It had been said during the British election of 1964 that all a Labour candidate had to do was say, "Think of another five years of Sir Alec Home," and he would be greeted by stunned silence to be succeeded shortly by rage and, finally, by despair. "Substitute John Diefenbaker for Sir Alec Douglas Home in this harsh context," wrote Peter Newman, "and you have one expression of the nation's mood on the eve of its 27th general election."[72] Indeed, this factor led some observers to feel that Pearson would get at least a small majority. For the first time John Diefenbaker was not running ahead of his party. The Gallup Poll indicated that only 29 per cent of the electorate approved of his conduct as leader of the opposition, the same percentage that supported the Conservatives in the immediate pre-election poll.

The feeling that Pearson would win heavily in Quebec governed the thinking of most observers. They thought this result was inevitable because of the collapse of the Créditistes, the rejection of John Diefenbaker, and the Liberal recruitment of "The Three Wise Men" – Marchand, Pelletier, and Trudeau. Peter Regenstreif's surveys confirmed that "the Liberals [dominated] across the entire social spectrum, showing no group-specific weaknesses."[73] In contrast, Caouette, who had lost his upper income support to the Liberals in 1963, suffered a further desertion of the lower income groups in 1965. Naturally the improved economic climate took a good deal of steam out of his campaign. His too obvious attempt to capitalize on the "Quebec First" argument also hurt him. Many former supporters no longer felt that his ideas were capable of practical application or that he led a credible movement. Not surprisingly, then, Caouette lost two seats in his northern kingdom of the Saguenay, three in Quebec City, and six others. In holding nine of his twenty seats he did better than was expected. Only one of "the six" managed to get elected, but their accuser, Dr. Marcoux, also failed miserably in Quebec – Montmorency.

Because John Diefenbaker was unacceptable to Quebec, it was felt that only the most popular and hard-working of the incumbent members would have any chance at all to win seats for the Conservatives. On this basis Clément Vincent, Heward Grafftey, and Théogene Ricard retained their

by Macpherson. Toronto Star, *September 9, 1965. Reprinted with permission*—Toronto Daily Star.

seats. However, the Conservatives were also able to re-elect Georges Valade in Montreal – Ste. Marie and, although they dropped Paul Martineau's seat and those that Léon Balcer, Rémi Paul, and L.J. Pigeon failed to contest, strong candidates won in Argenteuil – Two Mountains, Charlevoix, and Gaspé, as well as in St. Jean – Iberville – Napierville, which deserted the Liberals for the first time since Confederation.

Partly because the Conservatives and Créditistes ran stronger than was expected, the N.D.P. was unable to make a breakthrough. However, in rural Quebec Robert Cliche and Raymond D'Auteuil saved their deposits; on Montreal Island the N.D.P. outpolled the Conservatives in 8 ridings, and Charles Taylor and Charles Gifford made strong showings. The party could also boast of an increase from 7.1 to 12.0 per cent in its popular vote. Its improved showing was due, in part, at least, to the quality of its candidates.

Since Independents won Sherbrooke and Trois Rivières, there were only 56 Quebec seats left for the Liberals, 9 more than the last time but fewer than they had expected. Once again Pearson had been unable to make

General Election   389

a strong positive appeal to Quebeckers; yet, if his party held its own elsewhere, then Quebec would at least provide him with the margin he needed for majority government.

As it had been doing in recent years, Ontario responded as three or four separate regions. In Metropolitan Toronto there was a great deal of indecision, and the voters appeared to view the candidates with "disdain, disinterest, mild amusement."[74] Though in the end the booming economy led many of them to vote Liberal, Peter Regenstreif found that the Liberals were less solid with the upper income groups than they had been in 1962 and 1963.[75] Scandals in government and fears of Walter Gordon's policies had much to do with this. On the other hand, the N.D.P. made some inroads in the middle and especially the lower income groups; this enabled the party to take Broadview from the Liberals. In York South David Lewis regained much of the upper income Jewish vote he had lost in 1963 and, aided by a highly efficient organization, won that seat back from the Liberals. These two N.D.P. gains were the only shifts in seats in Toronto and York County.

The once Tory Toronto remained Tory-less Toronto. Despite the Liberal losses in the upper income levels and despite his personal popularity, Frank McGee could not win back York Scarborough. Dalton Camp ran strongly against Mitchell Sharp in Eglinton, saying: "You do not make weak men stronger by giving them more backbenchers to prop them up,"[76] but he failed to get elected. The Conservatives ran third in seven ridings instead of three as in 1963, and had no reason for jubilation. The Liberals did well among middle class voters, the chief beneficiary of prosperity, and Peter Regenstreif felt this might "turn out to be the most welcome development of the campaign" for them.[77]

Northern Ontario was as static as Metropolitan Toronto. The N.D.P. dropped Port Arthur, where Douglas Fisher had retired, but picked up Nickel Belt. Although these were the only changes, the N.D.P. did well in the unionized areas of the region, especially in Cochrane and Sudbury.

Altogether different forces were operating in tradition-oriented eastern Ontario. The French ridings in the very east of the region remained Liberal, but in the seats with a Loyalist background – anti-French and anti-Catholic as they were – the evidence of corruption by French Canadians and the suspicion that Pearson had catered to Quebec had an effect on the voters. However, there was no wholesale shift to the Conservatives. Pauline Jewett, who had won Northumberland by 505 votes in 1963, lost to George Hees by 563, and a Conservative loss by 646 in Hastings South became a win by 255. Additional factors were operating in Carleton – especially the discontent of civil servants at the steps being taken to ensure a bilingual public service – and it returned to the Conservative ranks. However, the three Conservative gains in eastern Ontario were partly counterbalanced by their loss of Peterborough to the Liberals.

It was in western Ontario that the Liberals expected their chief gains. Since the Diefenbaker albatross still hung around the neck of the Conservatives in the urban parts, it was not surprising that they lost Waterloo North and Middlesex East to the Liberals and Waterloo South to the N.D.P. They also dropped Elgin, which as a major beneficiary of the automobile pact with the United States was to acquire a giant Ford assembly plant. But they could not be budged from their hold on the rural and mixed seats. The N.D.P. helped the Conservatives by drawing votes away from the Liberals; corruption in government and some Anglo-Saxon backlash did the rest.

The net over-all result in Ontario was a gain of three seats for the N.D.P., two from the Conservatives and one from the Liberals. Clearly Ontario had not hearkened to Pearson's plea for majority government.

On the Prairies the Liberals did even worse. Peter Regenstreif said they had "gotten themselves into a terrible bind here and it is going to take a lot more than an election campaign or two to get out of it." He found the rejection of Pearson and his government altogether astonishing in its intensity; sometimes they were described as "caring only for themselves," or even as "a bunch of crooks."[78] According to John Diefenbaker, Mitchell Sharp could announce ten wheat sales without helping the government, and he was right. The Conservative leader had himself suffered a loss of popularity in the West. Nevertheless, although he was running behind his party, he was "still by far the best liked leader for the post of prime minister." Interestingly enough, the Prairie voters were answering "Conservative" when asked how they would vote. This time it was not Diefenbakerism alone that was determining their electoral behaviour.[79]

Not surprisingly, then, party changes in the West were minimal. In Manitoba the Conservatives lost the rural riding of Springfield to the N.D.P., allegedly because of the incumbent member's erratic attendance at Ottawa. However, television personality "Bud" Sherman made up for the loss by toppling Liberal Margaret Konantz in a circus type of campaign in Winnipeg South. In Alberta the Conservatives increased their popular vote by 1.3 percentage points, and they actually improved their position in the high-income ridings in Edmonton and Calgary where they were thought to be in danger. They even managed to topple Minister of Agriculture Harry Hays in Calgary South by 115 votes. Otherwise there were no changes in Alberta. In Saskatchewan the Conservatives slipped a little in the popular vote, but once again they won all the province's 17 seats.

British Columbia's economy was booming during the time of the campaign and the Liberals should have pulled far ahead of the other parties. However, Pearson's failure to exert any strong positive attraction stood in the way.[80] John Diefenbaker was no longer an issue and the Conservatives were beaten before the campaign started. Not unexpectedly, the real fight was between the Liberals and the N.D.P. but, as it turned out, the only seat to change hands was Okanagan–Revelstoke, which the Conservatives lost to Social Credit. Howard Green came close to winning back Vancouver Quadra from the Liberals, but the Diefenbaker albatross was just too heavy a burden to bear.

Western Canada, like Ontario, failed to respond to Pearson's plea for a majority. Although the Liberals gained the Mackenzie River seat from the Tories, the over-all result in the West was a loss of one seat.

Perhaps the Maritimes would help them out of their difficulties. As a have-not region, these provinces usually climb on the bandwagon, but this time they were in some doubt about the winner. Charles Lynch's visit to Nova Scotia convinced him that the Liberals would pick up most of the Conservative seats. Peter Regenstreif, on the other hand, who travelled about the area shortly after dissolution, felt there would be relatively few changes. He thought he detected a slight Liberal wind blowing and that it might lead to Conservative losses in York-Sunbury in New Brunswick, and Digby-Annapolis-Kings, Colchester-Hants, and Cape Breton South in Nova Scotia, but nothing more than that.

Instead, the wind turned out to be slightly Conservative, and that party gained about 2 per cent of the vote in each of the Atlantic provinces. This gain was insufficient, however, to wipe out any of the big Liberal majorities in New Brunswick and Newfoundland, and the party standings in these provinces remained the same. Premier Robichaud, like Premier Smallwood, campaigned actively on the theme: "I could not stand for one moment another Diefenbaker government," but he was unable to change any of the Conservative seats.

The situation was altogether different in Prince Edward Island and Nova Scotia, where the Liberal majorities were smaller and hence easier to overcome. In the latter province the Conservatives gained Shelburne-Yarmouth-Clare and the dual riding of Halifax, and failed to take Antigonish-Guysborough only because of the service vote. Their success was not attributable to any one factor. Pearson's impact on the province had been slight, while the revulsion against John Diefenbaker had not gone nearly as far as it had in central Canada; indeed, his trip from Truro to Yarmouth late in the campaign was nothing less than a triumphal tour. Then, too, the charges of corruption in high places tended to be "treated much more seriously in a less urbanized society . . . than in a highly urbanized one, which is more tolerant of the foibles and laches of big business and big government." Probably even more significant was the Anglo-Saxon backlash, "a wide-spread suspicion that the government had been kow-towing to French Canada."[81] Also, partly through political ineptitude, the Liberals had created the impression that they were not nearly so solicitous as their predecessors in dealing with Nova Scotia's problems. Premier Stanfield, by this time the province's trusted leader, spoke in almost every riding in the province, criticizing the Pearson government's failure to take thought for the Nova Scotian interest in such matters as offshore mineral rights and full recognition of the province's fiscal incapacity. At the same time, the federal minister Allan MacEachen was creating the impression that he was on the defensive and confined himself to his Cape Breton bailiwick. The Liberals had not recovered completely from their defeats in 1956 and 1957, provincially and federally, while Stanfield had developed the most formidable organization the Nova Scotian Conservatives had ever known. Certainly there was some truth in Keith Davey's lament that "the Stanfield machine creamed us."

Many of these factors also operated in Prince Edward Island, but there was another that made not a few Islanders' blood boil – the failure to invite Premier Shaw to attend the ceremonies initiating the construction of the causeway to the mainland. The Conservatives regained Kings and Prince, and the whole Island was theirs.

Nova Scotia and Prince Edward Island had foiled Pearson's purpose in calling an election. The Liberals' gain of 9 seats in Quebec had been almost counterbalanced by losses of 1 in Ontario, 1 in the West, 2 in Prince Edward Island, and 3 in Nova Scotia. Their net gain of 2 seats had left them with 131, 2 short of an over-all majority.

"It isn't much to come out of an election."[82] When Arnold Edinborough wrote these words, he was expecting something more than a net Liberal gain of 2 seats; otherwise he might have written that nothing had come out of the election. The Ottawa *Journal* described the election in terms that had been used to describe the 1900 election: "Full of Sound and Fury, Accomplishing Nothing."[83] Professor Kenneth McNaught said it was more like another scandal election, that of 1908, yet with a significant difference: "its total exclusion of issues in a time when significant issues abound."[84]

"Pearson wins but loses" was the Montreal *Gazette*'s description of the outcome.[85] Eddie Goodman put it still another way: "I think anyone would say that if the Liberals don't get their majority, they've been defeated."[86] The *Globe and Mail* was certain that "the Liberals will be psychologically weaker"[87] in the Commons, and even the Ottawa *Citizen* admitted that "the Prime Minister's position is infinitely more difficult than it was before he called the election."[88] There was general agreement, too, that although Pearson's advisers had pressed the election upon him, he had to accept full responsibility for it, because "the judgments he makes or the judgments he accepts are one and the same."[89] For the third election in a row Pearson suffered a loss of substantial support during the campaign itself, from 48 to 44 per cent, according to the Gallup Poll, and to 40.2 per cent, according to the actual returns.

The results caused Charles Lynch to resolve that he would never again overestimate the political appeal of Lester Pearson or underestimate that of John Diefenbaker.[90] Even Diefenbaker's enemies grudgingly conceded that the lawyer from Prince Albert—one of the best political campaigners Canada has ever produced—had again confounded the pollsters. As the results came in, Eddie Goodman said exultingly, "So far we have beaten MacNaught, Regenstreif, and Gallup";[91] when they were in, John Diefenbaker donned a chef's hat and cut a celebration cake. Charles Lynch showed how much of a victory it was:

> The election was not of [Diefenbaker's] choosing, nor were the issues of his making. He went forth into what many thought would be a hostile atmosphere and put up one of his classic campaigns. He may have been less on his own than in 1963, but the kind of campaign he waged was very much his own idea and his own inspiration. . . . The enemy sounded the battle cry, named the weapons and chose the field of battle—Mr. Diefenbaker emerged from the fray stronger than when he went into it.[92]

But without denigrating the Conservative leader's performance, his party gained only 2 seats, while losing 0.4 per cent of the vote. Social Credit was the big loser; together its two sections polled 3.5 per cent less of the vote and won 10 fewer seats. On paper at least, the chief winner was the N.D.P., for it gained 4 seats and raised its popular vote from 13.1 to 17.9 per cent. T.C. Douglas thought the party's gains were good, but not good enough for a big grin and certainly not enough for wild cheers. Perhaps he appreciated that a party that lost its deposits in 186 of the 255 seats it contested had a long way to go. Yet he did say, "We will have a labor Government in Canada within two or three elections."[93] Whether his allusion to "labor" was intended or not, it was significant because, except for Springfield, the N.D.P. successes continued to be confined to ridings where unionism was strong.

Most newspapers echoed the sentiments of the Montreal *Gazette* that there is "little reason for satisfaction" in the results.[94] Some prophesied another Parliament of bickering and wrangling; others feared a chronic state of administrative instability and a weakening of the federal government at a time when it needed to give positive direction. A surprising number of papers of varying shades of opinion called for the retirement of both Pearson and Diefenbaker. "Canada needs new men at the top," ran the leading editorial in the Toronto *Star* on November 9. Substantially it said that men of 68 and 70 were not the men to catch the new feelings abroad in the land and give them heart and substance. Because of the electoral disaster, the Montreal *Gazette* questioned the value—either to his party or his country—of further leadership by Pearson. It got at Diefenbaker more obliquely: "It is not enough for any party—and it is not enough for the country it serves—to be suitable as an Opposition, but not as a Government. There have to be two parties, the one always capable of replacing the other."[95]

All the newspapers assumed that the problem of Canadian government was minority government. But to Professor Bruce Hodgins minority government was only a symptom of the real problem: "consensus politics." According to him, the basing of an election on a plea for majority government was "perhaps a logical if depressing consequence of having elections merely as a contest between one set of brokers and another." While some of Canada's most eminent political scientists had lauded the system of competition between two opportunistic political parties, Hodgins was inclined to accept the propositions of Professor John Porter in the *Vertical Mosaic*: that the most significant feature of Canada's two major parties is their espousal of the same conservative values; that reform and progressive legislation are achieved through "the spirit of opportunism" rather than "from a basic orientation to social progress and change"; and that, by eliminating social differences, the Canadian party system obliterates the creative source of Canadian politics.[96]

Whatever the ills of consensus politics, time alone would tell whether Professor Hodgins was on good ground in suggesting that, barring the appearance of a charismatic leader, minority government was likely to continue. For just as in 1962 and 1963, it was arguable in 1965 that minority government was the result of a peculiar juxtaposition of qualities in the persons of Lester Pearson and John Diefenbaker.

> Seldom has there been so strange a contrast as exists between Mr. Pearson and Mr. Diefenbaker. The Liberal is richly endowed with good sensible ideas about the direction of Canada's future. He is also, perhaps, the worst strategist and tactician who has ever held high place in this country. Mr. Diefenbaker is utterly absorbed with these latter matters but has few glimmers about policy. . . . If our two leaders could be placed in a blender – and thoroughly shaken up, we might get an ideal prime minister – unless of course, what emerged was the worst in both of them.[97]

FOOTNOTES

1. *Canadian Annual Review* (Toronto: University of Toronto Press, 1963), p. 50.

2. J.M. Beck, "The Pearson Government after Six Months," *Queen's Quarterly*, LXX (Winter, 1964), p. 470.

3. "An Addled Parliament," *Round Table*, LIV (June, 1964), p. 293.

4. *Ibid.*

5. Quoted in *Canadian Annual Review*, 1964, p. 21.

6. *Canadian Annual Review*, 1963, p. 65.

7. Quoted in "Leadership in the Doldrums," *Round Table*, LV (December, 1964), p. 76.

8. "Government's Second Wind," *Round Table*, LV (September, 1965), p. 379.

9. Quoted from the Montreal *Star* in *Canadian Annual Review*, 1965, p. 66.

10. Toronto *Globe and Mail*, August 21, 1965.

11. Montreal *Star*, October 26, 1965.

12. Quoted from the Toronto *Star* in

	Seats	Candidates						Elected											
		P.C.	L.	N.D.P.	S.C.	R.C.	O.	P.C.	%	L.	%	N.D.P.	%	S.C.	%	R.C.	%	O.	%
Newfoundland	7	7	7	3		4	1			7	100.0								
Nova Scotia	12	12	12	12			2	10	83.3	2	16.7								
New Brunswick	10	10	10	10	1	1		4	40.0	6	60.0								
Prince Edward Island	4	4	4	4				4	100.0										
Quebec	75	75	75	71		75	31	8	10.7	56	74.7					9	12.0	2	2.7
Ontario	85	85	85	84	19	1	16	25	29.4	51	60.0	9	10.6						
Manitoba	14	14	14	14	11		1	10	71.4	1	7.1	3	21.4						
Saskatchewan	17	17	17	17	12		1	17	100.0										
Alberta	17	17	17	17	17		3	15	88.2					2	11.8				
British Columbia	22	22	22	22	22		8	3	13.6	7	31.8	9	40.9	3	13.6				
Yukon and N.W.T.	2	2	2	1				1	50.0	1	50.0								
Total	265	265	265	255	86	77	63	97	36.6	131	49.4	21	7.9	5	1.9	9	3.4	2	0.8

Others elected: Que. (2): I. (1); I.P.C. (1).

Others (votes
polled): Nfld. (1): I.L. (1) 1,022.

N.S. (2): I. (2) 1,249.

Que. (31): I. (10) 42,966; I.L. (9) 15,716; I.P.C. (3) 12,541; I.S.C. (1) 194; Ind. Worker (1) 298; Indépendantiste Ind. (1) 669; Comm. (2) 570; Rhinoceros Party (2) 618; Lib. Worker (1) 352; Droit Vital Personne (1) 465.

Ont. (16): I. (7) 5,391; I. Con. (1) 373; I.P.C. (1) 657; Comm. (3) 1,038; New Capitalist Party (3) 1,009; Soc. Lab. (1) 147.

Man. (1): I. (1) 237.

Sask. (1): Comm. (1) 179.

Alta. (3): Comm. (2) 782; I. (1) 493.

B.C. (8): Comm. (4) 1,716; I. (2) 1,150; I.S.C. (1) 228; Progressive Workers' Movement (1) 274.

Halifax *Chronicle-Herald*, September 22, 1965.

13. Toronto *Globe and Mail*, October 5, 1965.

14. Halifax *Chronicle-Herald*, September 20, 1965 and *Globe and Mail*, September 22, 1965.

15. Toronto *Globe and Mail*, October 6, 1965.

16. *Ibid.*, November 3, 1965.

17. Halifax *Chronicle-Herald*, September 20, 1965.

18. Toronto *Daily Star*, October 28, 1965.

19. Ottawa *Citizen*, November 6, 1965.

20. Toronto *Globe and Mail*, September 22, 1965.

21. *Ibid.*, October 27, 1965.

22. Halifax *Chronicle-Herald*, September 20, 1965.

23. Toronto *Globe and Mail*, September 22, 1965.

24. Halifax *Chronicle-Herald*, September 20, 1965.

25. Toronto *Globe and Mail*, October 20, 1965.

26. Toronto *Daily Star*, October 22, 1965.

27. Quoted in the Toronto *Globe and Mail*, November 5, 1965.

Twenty-seventh

Popular Vote												Total
P.C.	%	L.	%	N.D.P.	%	S.C.	%	R.C.	%	O.	%	
47,638	32.4	94,291	64.1	1,742	1.2	2,352	1.6			1,022	0.7	147,045
203,123	48.6	175,415	42.0	38,043	9.1					1,249	0.3	417,830
102,714	42.5	114,781	47.5	22,759	9.4	352	0.1	1,081	0.4			241,687
38,566	53.9	31,532	44.1	1,463	2.0							71,561
432,901	21.3	928,530	45.6	244,339	12.0			357,153	17.5	74,389	3.7	2,037,312
933,753	34.0	1,196,308	43.6	594,112	21.7	9,791	0.4	1,204	0.0	8,615	0.3	2,743,783
154,253	40.7	117,442	30.9	91,193	24.0	16,315	4.3			237	0.1	379,440
193,254	48.0	96,740	24.0	104,626	26.0	7,526	1.9			179	0.0	402,325
247,734	46.6	119,014	22.4	43,818	8.3	119,586	22.5			1,275	0.2	531,427
139,226	19.2	217,726	30.0	239,132	32.9	126,532	17.4			3,368	0.5	725,984
6,751	45.2	7,740	52.0	431	2.9							14,922
2,499,913	32.4	3,099,519	40.2	1,381,658	17.9	282,454	3.7	359,438	4.7	90,334	1.2	7,713,316

28. Ottawa *Citizen*, November 2, 1965.

29. Montreal *Star*, October 26, 1965.

30. *Ibid.*, October 16, 1965.

31. *Ibid.*, October 26, 1965.

32. Ottawa *Citizen*, September 16, 1965.

33. Toronto *Globe and Mail*, October 18, 1965.

34. *Ibid.*, October 30, 1965.

35. Toronto *Daily Star*, October 23, 1965.

36. *Canadian Annual Review*, 1965, p. 97.

37. *Ibid.*, p. 98.

38. Toronto *Globe and Mail*, September 18, 1965.

39. Ottawa *Citizen*, November 6, 1965.

40. Toronto *Globe and Mail*, October 19, 1965.

41. *Ibid.*, November 3, 1965.

42. Ottawa *Citizen*, October 12, and December 24, 1965.

43. Halifax *Chronicle-Herald*, September 25, 1965.

44. Toronto *Globe and Mail*, October 23, 1965.

45. *Ibid.*, November 2, 1965.

46. *Ibid.*, September 21, and October 19, 1965.

47. *Ibid.*, October 21, 1965.

48. *Ibid.*, September 22, 1965.

49. *Ibid.*, October 19, 1965.

50. *Ibid.*, October 18, 1965.

51. Toronto *Star*, October 28, 1965.

52. Toronto *Globe and Mail*, September 29, 1965.

53. Montreal *Star*, October 9, 1965.

54. As reported in *Canadian Annual Review*, 1965, p. 99.

55. Toronto *Star*, October 29, 1965.

56. Toronto *Globe and Mail*, November 2, 1965 and Toronto *Star*, October 28, 1965.

57. Toronto *Globe and Mail*, October 1, 1965.

58. *Ibid.*, September 27, 1965.

59. *Ibid.*, November 1, 1965.

60. *Ibid.*

61. *Ibid.*, October 9, 1965.

62. *Ibid.*, October 14, 1965.

63. *Ibid.*, October 2, 1965.

64. *Ibid.*, October 9, 1965.

65. *Ibid.*, October 4, 1965.

66. Montreal *Star*, October 18, 1965.

67. Toronto *Star*, October 23, 1965.

68. Toronto *Globe and Mail*, November 5, 1965.

69. Montreal *Star*, October 16, 1965.

70. Toronto *Globe and Mail*, October 13, and November 8, 1965.

71. Toronto *Star*, October 23, 1965.

72. *Ibid.*, November 2, 1965.
73. *Ibid.*, October 16, 1965.
74. Toronto *Globe and Mail*, November 6, 1965.
75. Toronto *Star*, October 30, 1965.
76. Toronto *Globe and Mail*, September 28, 1965.
77. Toronto *Star*, October 30, 1965.
78. *Ibid.*, October 24, 1965.
79. *Ibid.*
80. *Ibid.*, October 28, 1965.
81. J.M. Beck, "The Electoral Behaviour of Nova Scotia in 1965," *Dalhousie Review*, XLVI (Spring, 1966), p. 35.
82. Arnold Edinborough, "The Unpopular Election," *Saturday Night*, LXXX (November, 1965), p. 11.
83. Ottawa *Journal*, November 9, 1965.
84. W.K. McNaught, "National Affairs," *Saturday Night*, LXXX (December 1965), p. 13.
85. Montreal *Gazette*, November 10, 1965.
86. Ottawa *Journal*, November 9, 1965.
87. Toronto *Globe and Mail*, November 10, 1965.
88. Ottawa *Citizen*, November 9, 1965.
89. Ottawa *Journal*, November 9, 1965.
90. Ottawa *Citizen*, November 9, 1965.
91. Ottawa *Journal*, November 9, 1965. MacNaught, the Minister of Mines, was beaten in Prince, Prince Edward Island.
92. Ottawa *Citizen*, November 9, 1965.
93. Toronto *Globe and Mail*, November 10, 1965.
94. Montreal *Gazette*, November 10, 1965.
95. *Ibid.*
96. Bruce Hodgins, "The Bankruptcy of Consensus Politics in Canada," *South Atlantic Quarterly*, LXV (Summer, 1966), pp. 326-27.
97. Quoted from the Montreal *Star* in *Canadian Annual Review*, 1965, p. 119.

Twenty-eighth
General Election

"HIS IMAGE HAS EVERYTHING"

In 1964 Peter Newman said that whichever party dared to choose a new leader—"a mid-Twentieth-Century man who truly speaks for this era"—would inherit the nation.[1] Prior to the election of 1968 both major parties changed their leaders. Which had better attuned itself to the modern era?

The Conservative leadership convention of September 1967 demonstrated disillusionment with the incumbent federal politicians. John Diefenbaker had fought the determined efforts of the party's National President, Dalton Camp, to have "a reconfirmation or otherwise of leadership." On the third ballot, after his vote which had started at 271 fell to 114, Diefenbaker withdrew and the real contest developed between Premier Robert Stanfield of Nova Scotia and Premier Duff Roblin of Manitoba. Stanfield won on the fifth ballot, 1,150 to 969.

Things started auspiciously for the new leader. In October, the Gallup Poll reported that 43 per cent of Canadians preferred the Conservatives to 34 per cent for the Liberals. Dalton Camp concluded that the party had "triumphed over its trauma and seems headed for electoral victory." Under a leader with a "creative sense of policy-making," it would practise "the new politics," a politics "indifferent to dogma, cool to partisanship but alive to social and economic problems."[2]

However, by March 1968 the Gallup Poll found the Liberals leading the Conservatives 42 to 34 per cent, and the nagging doubts of those who had thought it unwise for Stanfield to leave Nova Scotia returned. It had taken him fourteen years to conquer his native province and then it had not been through charisma or eloquence. While his audiences had foreborne to cheer, they listened in rapt attention, for in him they recognized "the man of sincerity, the voice of reason and good sense."[3] But did he have time to make such virtues known throughout Canada?

Newspapermen talk about the jinx that besets provincial premiers who become national leaders. Actually they generalize on the cases of John Bracken and George Drew, who encountered Mackenzie King and Louis St. Laurent at the height of their power. None the less, a premier makes the transition to national politics with difficulty. Stanfield found it hard to acclimate himself to the halls of Parliament. "You walk out and they shove a bunch of microphones in your face and in 30 seconds you're expected to produce a profound and intelligent answer to . . . an extremely complicated national issue."[4] Glib commentators were appalled by his inarticulateness; one of them suggested he needed an immersion course in English, rather than one in French. His "obsession with the fear of expressing erroneous, uninformed opinion" made him appear to evade even simple questions, and prompted newspapers, headed by the usually Conservative Toronto *Globe and Mail*, to criticize him for having nothing of moment to say on national problems. Outside the Maritimes, his public image seemed to be "rapidly hardening into a picture of colorless, indecisive conservatism."[5]

The Liberals' turn to select their Mid-Century man came when Lester Pearson announced his retirement in December 1967. On April 6 they chose Pierre Elliott Trudeau, whose very existence had only dawned on English Canadians a few months before. "Never in our history [has] a man risen from the herd to grasp supreme political power with such dazzling notoriety."[6] Late in 1965, when he decided to give Quebec federalists a stronger voice at Ottawa, he was not even a member of the Liberal party. Not until April 1967 did he enter the cabinet as Minister of Justice. Circumstances and accident had provided him the best possible stage to display "his qualities at a time when the public [was] unimpressed with the familiar faces of the declared candidates" for the leadership.[7] Towards the end of 1967 he caught the eye of English Canada with his proposal to broaden the divorce law and his omnibus bill to liberalize the Criminal Code with respect to homosexuality and abortion. Then, at the constitutional conference of February 1968,

> . . . before a spellbound nation . . . he sparred with steel wits against the member from Bagot, Premier Daniel Johnson . . .[and] burst upon the consciousness of tired, discouraged federalists of every background as a leader to defend the citadel of eroding federal power.[8]

The confrontation between Trudeau and Johnson catered to the Anglo-Saxon backlash everywhere: here was a Frenchman who could put the trouble-making Frenchmen in their place. However, this merit simply reinforced his more intangible qualities of charisma and style. It has been suggested that the mass media produced the Trudeau boom for the leadership. Anthony Westell denies it: "the press and TV began to hear about Mr. Trudeau from the grassroots before they took him seriously as a possible candidate."[9] But once they did he was irresistible. "Through sheer force of personality, the demagogue malgré lui appropriated the nation's attention for six weeks. . . . One can't deny he got [power] with the eager complicity of nearly all the country's media outside his native province."[10] An avid public got its fill of

> . . . the Mercedes sports car, ascot ties and sandals. The racy reputation as wealthy bachelor surrounded by beautiful women. The academic achievements at some of the world's best universities. The judo brown belt, and acquaintance with yoga. . . . The crusading intellectual who campaigned against Duplessis, helped launch Quebec's Quiet Revolution, went to work as a trade union adviser in the struggle for social justice, [and] opposed nuclear arms in 1963.[11]

Only "the chicken syndrome" – as Charles Lynch put it – stood between him and the leadership. Was he too big a gamble for the Liberal establishment? Knowledgeable Conservatives watched their television screens hopefully as the opposition coalesced against Trudeau, the only candidate they really feared. But all efforts to stop him were ineffective. Once established as Prime Minister, Pierre Elliott Trudeau was free to pursue his "love-in" with the media and the public. When he presented a makeshift cabinet consisting largely of hold-overs and decided on an immediate dissolution without presenting a programme to Parliament, he largely escaped the shellacking that such action would have normally produced.

The excitement he had injected into politics extended to the nominating conventions. Furthermore, the new system of representation which required constituencies to be more nearly equal in population, had produced a genuinely new electoral map. Some former members found themselves with a radically different riding, and some with no riding at all. Although many former members chose not to run, there was the largest number of contested nominations in history. In Vegreville, Alberta, it took 3,000 Conservatives until 5:15 a.m. to nominate Don Mazankowski; in Red Deer a convention of 2,500 persons chose former Social Credit leader Robert Thompson as the Conservative candidate.

But the Liberal conventions produced even more pandemonium. In Calgary South an experienced M.L.A. lost to political novice Pat Mahoney, who was "wildly cheered by hundreds of teen-agers carefully choreographed by one of the city's better theatrical directors."[12] In Peel South the sheer volume, the confusion, and the miniskirted teeny-boppers recalled the Liberal and Conservative leadership conventions.[13] In Toronto Davenport, where the membership of the riding association rose from 150 to 5,445 in a few weeks, the convention was held in the C.N.E. Coliseum. Here, as elsewhere, the outcome may have been determined by nonresidents and ten-year-olds who, under the rules, could not be debarred from voting. As one official put it, "You must remember that laws are always passed after the crime."[14] In St. Boniface Roger Teillet suffered the unenviable distinction of being the first cabinet minister in Canadian history to be denied renomination. Another minister, Maurice Sauvé, whose riding had disappeared through redistribution, lost the nomination in the Montreal riding of Gamelin. The Prime Minister called it an unavoidable concomitant of the open party and the participatory politics that he favoured, but cynics felt that the ministers had paid the price for not supporting him initially for the leadership.

Just as the Prime Minister dominated the election, so he must dominate any account of it. During his campaign for the leadership he had shown he could "turn the people on"; prior to his formal electioneering he caused "frenzied scenes of clutching, pushing and shouting"[15] wherever he went. As George Bain told an American audience, "Canada has a case of Trudeaumania."[16] All sorts of people succumbed: teeny-boppers, students, young businessmen, working men, elegant women, academics – even older people. But Pied Piper Trudeau aroused most excitement among the young. Kids, it was said, had found a new kick: politics. "It beats LSD, glue-sniffing, Beatles and transcendental meditation, they find."[17] Trudeau told "the young people that politics is more fulfilling than pot, and they seem to agree."[18]

The Liberal organizers, wrote Gary Oakes, would have had to have "rocks in their heads not to capitalize on Mr. Trudeau's greatest asset – the exciting response his presence evokes everywhere."[19] In his first formal campaigning – a swing through metro Toronto – he discovered the ideal forum for what Dalton Camp called "a non-campaign":[20] the shopping plaza. But although his opponents derided him as Pierre de la Plaza, there was nothing wrong in itself in his going where the people were, to plazas, parks, and city hall steps, "finding the people who [were] not committed and [wouldn't] go to a rally in the evening because it [was] miles away from the suburb in which they [lived]." Largely abandoning the concept of the formal meeting, he sped across the country in a DC-9 jet – thus reinforcing his modern, glamorous image – sometimes visiting three provinces in one day. By using helicopters to reach small centres, he created "the anticipatory excitement of a god descending from the sun into the midst of his people. . . . This is the jet age, man. And there is the jet age candidate."[21]

A superb organization masterminded by William Lee ensured that everything went according to plan. Action Trudeau girls in orange and white miniskirted costumes acted as guards of honour. Introductory speeches were short and snappy. There was the ovation as the Prime Minister moved to the podium; he gave a quiet smile, a slow wave, and a few minutes of a soft-toned and usually slight message. He made another surge through the crowds, signed a few autograph books and Trudeau pictures, and went on by jet to the next shopping centre.[22] Reporters said this "mad mod election campaign [with its] exploding color and excitement" was "like looking at a psychedelic film."[23]

In other respects, too, the Trudeau campaign was unconventional. He declined to lay out a catalogue of specific policies but concentrated on describing and indicating his attitudes towards the problems and challenges he delineated.[24] As George Bain put it, "he has said, in effect, these are the attitudes I bring to public questions, this is the turn of my mind: never mind the specifics, take a chance, we'll deal with the problems as they come up."[25] At places such as Oakville he appealed to Canadians' spirit of adventure. A young, dynamic, progressive people possessing a wealthy country should not be afraid of change. "We don't want to buy back the past like the old parties with old ideas. . . . If [Canadians] want to take a bit of a risk, if they want to take a chance on the future, then we're asking them to vote for us."[26]

The absence of promises also made the Trudeau campaign unusual. From the outset he warned that "there will be no give-aways. . . . It is more important to have a sound dollar than to satisfy this or that particular interest."[27] More than once he said he had no wish to govern if he had to make promises he could not fulfil. When, at Regina, Premier Thatcher urged a higher price for wheat and asked, "What other segment of our society hasn't had a wage increase since 1945?" the Prime Minister replied: "We have to make sure that the budget is balanced and to do that we can't make costly promises. . . ."[28] He did admit that additional expenditures would be needed to deal with regional disparity, but the aim would be to make the weak regions competitive, not provide them with artificial crutches concocted in government buildings at Ottawa.[29] Governments, he warned, had no money of their own, only that which came through taxation. His audiences seemed to find it refreshing, and they cheered him even at Regina.

This was the man and the stance against which the opposing leaders had to contend. Basically, Robert Stanfield and T.C. Douglas conducted conventional campaigns, although holding the normal type of meeting itself constituted a risk. When projected through the media it might appear to be a failure – "no great crowds, no wild cheering, no color or drama or excitement."[30] Anthony Westell even wondered if Stanfield's reliance on a propeller-driven DC-7C hurt his image. Had Canadian politics "vaulted straight from the train to the jet?"[31]

Newspaper readers must have tired of hearing about the quiet, unassuming person that Stanfield was – a man who conducted a low-key campaign that underwhelmed his listeners, whose "gothic mask of unconcern [hid him] from public scrutiny," and who continued to deliver halting, strained, monotonous speeches "with here a tired joke, there a platitude."[32] Stanfield suffered, of course, from comparison with Trudeau. It might have been better, however, if he had avoided projecting an artificial image on television and had altogether spurned the "sock-it-to-'em" type of oratory. Some thought he needed a communicator to help him project his virtues, and suggested that Dalton Camp would have been ideal if it had not meant reviving the allegations that Stanfield was his puppet.[33] But T.C. Douglas needed no communicator, and he was not being heard either. In this election public and newspapermen alike had eyes for the performance of only one man.

Both Stanfield and Douglas hoped to make the government's record on economic questions a major issue, but failed: As Dalton Camp put it, "One could not have imagined how artfully, and completely, it would be buried."[34] The voters themselves assisted in the process. They showed only passing interest in inflation, high interest rates, unemployment, and the lack of housing; furthermore – astonishingly enough – they divorced a Trudeau government consisting almost entirely of hold-overs from anything that preceded it. Some Liberals even asked to be elected to help Trudeau get the country moving again, forgetting that a Liberal government had held office for five years.

When it came to making promises that cost money, both Douglas and Stanfield were judged in terms of the Trudeau standard. The former quickly lost the favour of the financially orthodox for promising old-age pensions of $125 per month,[35] but Stanfield remained circumspect until the last week of the campaign, even though the *Globe and Mail* lambasted him for promising a feasibility study of a link between Newfoundland and Labrador.[36] On June 17 the *Financial Times of Canada* said there were two credible national leaders, only to have Stanfield later disqualify himself with "his preposterous pledge" to give tax deductions to everyone paying more than 7 per cent for a residential mortgage. "Then there was one."[37]

In their policies neither opposition leader escaped unfavourable comparison with the Prime Minister. Douglas was labeled "an echo of yesterday"[38] even though his party's "Minimum Program for a New Canadian Society" sought to come to grips with new conditions. Perhaps it was because among the national leaders he alone revived the memories of 1911, accepted the conclusion of the Watkins Report that "our independence is being eroded," and condemned Trudeau as a "continentalist" who talked about a continental economic entity – "and that eventually means one political entity, dominated by the United States."[39] Or perhaps it was because his call for "a new society, where excessive privilege and wealth for the few" would be eliminated, revived the slogans of the class war which, his critics said, was an anachronism.

Similarly, Stanfield was "a figure out of the pre-Edisonian age,"[40] even though he had raised policy to top priority instead of treating it as "a sub-branch of rhetoric" as his predecessor had.[41] Although his party's new policy advisory committee headed by President T.H.B. Symons of Trent University had scarcely begun its work, Stanfield presented proposals on housing, agriculture, regional development, and an eventual guaranteed annual income, all seemingly reasonable if not eye-catching. Anthony Westell of the *Globe and Mail* wondered if the "good, dependable, intelligent man of integrity with no instant policies" was harming his image by suddenly producing "policies by the bucketful."[42] It seems ironic, however, that Westell's newspaper, which had been Stanfield's severest critic for his failure to be specific on policy, was supporting Trudeau who spurned the idea of a platform of specifics.

Both the Conservatives and the N.D.P. took pot shots at the concept of the "just society," which Trudeau had used to win the leadership. A nebulous concept, it obviously included the amelioration of regional disparity. In addition, if a Liberal policy paper was any indication, it meant protection for the individual in his dealings with the state.[43] President Symons felt that Trudeau was "more concerned with legal justice than social justice. What we need is a 'society of concern,' a society in which people genuinely care about one another."[44] Likewise, T.C. Douglas suggested that "justice sees only categories and laws. Justice lacks compassion";[45] in any case "you can't have a just society unless you get a just tax structure,"[46] and Trudeau had not accepted the Carter Report and its proposals for a capital gains tax. Douglas also lashed out at the Prime Minister's fiscal conservatism: his penchant for a balanced budget was "an echo from the days of . . . R.B. Bennett and the orthodoxy of the 1930's";[47] his statement that Canadians wanted no more of "that free stuff" indicated that "behind the facade [of swinger] he has turned out to be a Barry Goldwater."[48]

By far the strongest criticism was leveled at Trudeau's campaign. According to Douglas, the greatest problem of the election had been to get the Prime Minister to discuss the issues.[49] "Nothing but a theatrical performance . . . contemptuous of the democratic process," said Stanfield.[50] "For the first time in Canadian history a prime minister has asked the people for a blank cheque."[51] Anthony Westell thought that if criticism was justified it should be put in other terms. The Prime Minister had issued long statements on policy, but perhaps they were so nonspecific as to suggest that he had only attitudes and not new ideas. Accordingly, the problem for the voter was whether "Mr. Trudeau's philosophical attitude – there are no magic solutions to be produced by governments, and while problems can be defined, they can be solved only by people participating in the democratic process – is more or less acceptable than specific proposals made by the other leaders."[52] However, Trudeau did not even spend enough time elaborating his attitudes.

Professor Ramsay Cook had said that if the Prime Minister "just plays the image game he won't do so well. I think I know him well enough to say he won't do that."[53] Apparently the original plan was to divide his campaign into two stages: an early one in which he was to travel at top speed across Canada "satisfying the enormous public curiosity about himself," and a later one in which he was to be more prime ministerial and deliver his major addresses.[54] But he never reached the second stage.

His advisers may have decided to obtain maximum exposure out of a "hot property" at the least risk. Knowing his incapacity to indulge fools, they may have had second thoughts about letting him come to grips with specifics.[55] Perhaps they recognized that he performed indifferently in delivering long, set speeches to formal meetings, but was "an instant pop hero" when mingling with crowds. Or they may have concluded that they had the commitment of sophisticated people, that they needed to sustain the enthusiasm of the less sophisticated, and that they could best do it by letting their prime exhibit be seen and touched by the greatest numbers. Whatever the reason, some newspapermen became uneasy over the Prime Minister's electioneering. Content, said Charles Lynch, was being sacrificed on the altar of the shopping centre; Trudeau's capsule speeches (with rare exceptions) were designed to "prove that the dreamboat can really float."[56] Christopher Young wondered why a philosopher king was behaving like a pop musical hero and thought it was "faintly insulting" to Canadians to assume that they could be satisfied with so little.[57] Peter Newman complained of his pedestrian speech before 50,000 at Toronto. "The kid . . . holding up a lonely sign that read 'Fifty to One He Says Nothing' turned out to be dead right."[58]

The Prime Minister felt that the enthusiasm he generated was part of a new politics of involvement. Everywhere things were changing. In other lands there were purges and strikes; Canadians did not want them and were therefore plugging themselves into the decision-making process. Even the kisses bestowed on him so liberally would lead to a higher stage of political involvement.[59] George Bain was skeptical; the so-called new politics was "rather too personal, suggesting the leader himself in communion with the stimulated (and perhaps manipulated) throng, taking these decisions." He also dismissed the "high-sounding McLuhanesque blather about involvement," saying that Trudeau wanted some explanation of his appeal other than charisma.[60] President Symons was certain that the Trudeau campaign did nothing to "halt the alienation between the voters and the parliamentary system."[61]

What was the source of the enthusiasm for Trudeau? It had much to do with both the mood of the country and the image of the leader. Supposedly, "the Canadian style changed in 1967. The Quiet Canadian became the Confident Canadian during the Centennial."[62] Instead of cynicism, the Diefenbaker-Pearson period had left a legacy of accumulated psychic energies.[63] Erick Ericson has suggested that when old beliefs weaken and dim the people become "charisma-hungry" and want a reassuring leader-symbol.[64] In the mood of 1968 they were not likely to turn to Robert Stanfield whose image, according to Marshall McLuhan, may be "Abe

Lincoln," but is also that of "an archeological exhibit." In contrast, the Trudeau image had everything.[65] Perhaps Professor Paul Fox put it even better than McLuhan: The Prime Minister, although a man full of contradictions, was "the consensual man, because there is something in him for everybody."

> . . . [he] embodies a mixture of contradictory truths like the Canadian political system and reality itself. There is the key. Trudeau is not a comfortable middle-of-the-roader. He is not a bland average which is an artificial concoction with highs and lows eliminated. He is an aggregate of conflicting interests which is very different.[66]

Trudeau managed to utilize to his political advantage the contradictory qualities of swinger and fiscal and economic conservative. His unconventionality—he wore an ascot and sandals in Parliament—and his ability to communicate "like crazy" brought out the frenzied crowds to see the exciting male who, like the Kennedys, plunged fearlessly into the idolatrous mobs.[67] It was not Trudeaumania that struck Place Ville Marie but Trudeauphilia, "a vast outpouring of friendliness towards the Prime Minister."[68] At a higher level, the brilliance and vigour of his intellect, the apparent modernity of his style and thought, and his lucidity in French and English attracted those who felt he would "whisk away the stale aroma of cigar smoke that has surrounded politics for too many decades,"[69] and produce a Kennedy-type rebirth in Ottawa.

According to the *Globe and Mail*, Canadians had seen "a new side of themselves, a readiness to gamble on the unknown," and had intuitively felt that the Prime Minister could best lead them into areas not yet explored.[70] Because Trudeau was "tuned in" and his opponents were not, the Montreal *Star* contended that a gamble with him was "in fact less of a gamble than a sure thing with . . . Stanfield."[71] But would either paper have supported such a gamble or would the business interests have filled the Liberal campaign chest with such alacrity if Trudeau the modern man had not also been Trudeau the fiscal conservative?

The Montreal *Star's* test of Trudeau's modernity was highly revealing: it was that he spoke of Mozart and the brave and generous St. Exupéry, while Stanfield dealt with material things like interest rates.[72] Unconsciously it was admitting Trudeau's attractiveness to the affluent who knew no financial worries. The Prime Minister did offer a Marshall Plan to residents of low-income areas, but they treated him as one more politician making more promises. The same areas were flooded with pamphlets associating the Prime Minister with socialism, communism, and hostility to Christian morality, but this so-called hate literature had little effect on their voting behaviour.

Another contradictory image was that of a French Canadian and a Quebecker putting other French Canadians and other Quebeckers in their place, even though he was devoted to his race and his province. In February Canada had taken a strong stand against Gabon because it had sent an invitation to attend an international conference on education to Quebec City rather than to Ottawa. As the campaign opened, France extended a similar invitation, and the Prime Minister appreciated that he must show English Canada he meant business. The device he used was a white paper entitled "Federalism and International Conferences on Education." Stanfield, making no attempt to defend the stance of Premier Daniel Johnson in the matter, accepted the basic points of the white paper: that Ottawa alone is responsible for Canada's foreign policy and that no province can conduct relations with another country as a sovereign state or use precedents to acquire that status. But he was opposed to reversing the practice followed by the provinces since Confederation. He was amenable to allowing the provinces to continue to consult and make arrangements and agreements with other countries if they remained within their jurisdiction, did not conclude formal treaties, avoided conflicts with Canada's foreign policy, and stayed within guidelines set by the continuing constitutional committee.[73] Stanfield's position did not, in fact, differ much from Trudeau's. However, at the level of political debate the impressions the two leaders left came to be markedly different. Partly because he lacked lucidity in explaining a complex position, and partly because he wanted discussion of the issue rather than confrontation, the Conservative leader was the target of numerous editorials like the Toronto *Star*'s "Mr. Stanfield is too mushy on Quebec,"[74] and came more and more to be linked with Daniel Johnson. Meanwhile, Trudeau simply reinforced his image as unifier of Canada. "When Canada's participation is sought for an international conference there is only one address for the invitation – Ottawa."[75] What is more potent than the simplistic statement of an articulate charismatic politician?

Trudeau's confrontation with the Quebec government led the prestigious Marcel Faribault to become a Conservative candidate and led the Union Nationale to give strong support to the Conservatives. Meanwhile Stanfield had sought to alter his party's stance towards Quebec. Personally he disliked the terms "two nations" and "special status," but he had accepted the statement of his party's Montmorency Conference that Canada consisted of two founding people who had been joined by peoples of other cultures. To his misfortune "two peoples" translated into French becomes "deux nations" which, when translated back into English, is "two nations." This circumstance led to difficulties from John Diefenbaker at the leadership convention and to further difficulties during the election. While rejecting special status, Stanfield suggested that the practice recognized in the B.N.A. Act of permitting a province particular arrangements to meet its unique circumstances might be followed in the case of the Quebec of today, but only if the other provinces were offered the same arrangements and the essential federal powers were retained. This position seemed defensible; of more concern was the calculated risk of becoming allied with Marcel Faribault. While Faribault opposed special status, he favoured such enhanced powers for all the provinces that he seemed to negate Stanfield's concept of a strong central government. However, Stanfield had an even heavier cross to bear.

Trudeau stressed the lack of logic in two nations and special status; even in a sociological sense the former would lead to two nation-states, while the latter would reduce Quebec's influence in Ottawa and limit the French fact, juridically and politically, to Quebec. His theme of "one Canada" and "one nation" evoked such a favourable response that it became his chief stock-in-trade. Conservatives said he was catering to the Anglo-Saxon backlash, and so he was. But he was saying the same thing in French Canada, and even telling English Canadians that if they expected him to be hard on Quebec they should not vote for him. He always left the impression that his position stood in stark contrast to the Conservatives'. His followers were less reticent about pinning a two-nations policy on their opponents, and put Conservatives across the country on the defensive, refuting the charges that Diefenbaker had made at the leadership convention, labouring to show that "deux nations" did not mean "two nations." Eventually Liberal advertisements, especially in Calgary, accused Stanfield himself of espousing a two-nations policy. Trudeau did not repudiate them until Stanfield called him "an accomplice to a smear campaign."[76] However, the Liberal tactics probably did less to enlist new supporters than to retain those whom Trudeau the unifier had already won.

Trudeau pressed his case with such assurance that listeners did not question its reasonableness.[77] However, in telling his compatriots that his linguistic proposals would do much to eliminate their ghetto existence, he was leading them astray. Also, despite what he inferred, constitutional arrangements seldom rest on strict logic. The English Canadians who applauded his stand on special status may, in the future, want greater federal involvement in provincial fields such as education, only to be stymied by Quebec. Adventurous Canadians might have been expected to welcome the idea of a distinctive form of federalism uniquely suited to the country's needs. It is paradoxical that, in the mood of 1968, they showed such enthusiasm for a rigid, simplistic stance.

Early in the campaign Peter Regenstreif stated that Stanfield looked like a "shoo-in" throughout the Maritimes.[78] A little later a national poll reported that the Conservatives led 56 to 32 per cent in the Atlantic region. However, this was before the Prime Minister evoked some manifestations of Trudeaumania in the area. Moreover, Maritime voters – usually an excellent bellwether – believed, 44 to 40 per cent, that the Liberals would win,[79] and Charles Lynch reported that "Mr. Stanfield's power base [was] being eaten into by reports of how well Mr. Trudeau [had] been doing in other parts of the country."[80]

Liberal candidates shelved the designation "Liberal" and became Trudeau candidates. The Liberal establishment of Halifax – although it did not identify itself as such – sponsored an advertisement that made it appear almost a duty to support Trudeau.[81] But they were stymied because Trudeaumania was largely an urban phenomenon and the Maritimes are not highly urbanized; and because the Maritime press – conservative with both a big and a small "c" – would not provide the large headlines, the oversized pictures, and the long front-page stories that carried the Trudeau phenomenon elsewhere.

Most of all, they ran up against "Bob" Stanfield. Many a Maritimer felt he would not be much of a Maritimer if he did not support him, and that Stanfield could do for Canada what he had done for Nova Scotia. Suggestions that he stood for two Canadas or two nations carried no weight in an area where he was trusted. In contrast, the conservative Maritimer did not feel that Trudeau possessed the image a prime minister ought to have – "You know, this business of kissing all the girls all the time."[82] Hence, the Conservative candidates had a stronger running mate in Stanfield than the Liberals had in Trudeau.

In Nova Scotia the Conservatives added more than 6 per cent to their popular vote and lost only Cape Breton Highlands–Canso to Allan Mac-Eachen. In Prince Edward Island, they retained the 4 seats, although their popular vote fell by about 2 per cent. In New Brunswick even Acadians said: "I like Stanfield. He didn't do badly in Nova Scotia."[83] However, the swing to the Conservatives in all ridings was only sufficient to give them 1 more seat: they gained Moncton, where they benefited from redistribution.

Newfoundland was a major surprise of the election. At dissolution the Conservatives held none of its seats and they had never won any of its five outport ridings. This time they took all the seats except Burin-Burgeo. Stanfield's reputation helped. "He's one of us and he understands our problems." Ottawa's failure to take decisive action in relief of a hard-pressed fishing industry also played a part. But most telling was the unfavourable image of the provincial government, resulting from its unpopular new taxes and a hit-and-run approach to economic development. It was strange to hear of "Pierre for People committees" designed to "whisk the traditional Newfoundland Liberal ammunition – the Smallwood record – out of current campaign literature."[84] The tide had gone out for the Liberals in Newfoundland.

The Conservative victory in the Atlantic region – 25 out of 32 seats – was the party's only cause for elation. Elsewhere – especially in Quebec – the Stanfield pull was negligible. Ostensibly, Quebeckers were to choose between the points of view of Claude Ryan and the Prime Minister.

Ryan contended that, if French Canadians had made themselves count for anything and if they constituted a distinctive force in Canadian politics, it was not because they had minority representation at Ottawa, but because they controlled the government at Quebec City which, through every vicissitude, had never lost sight of their aspirations. It still best understood their historic position and unique vocation in the Canadian federation. Recently, to realize broad new objectives, the Lesage and Johnson governments had requested a reasonable extension of Quebec's power within the federal structure, and almost all French Canadians had concurred. Now the Prime Minister was seeking to reverse the process with his symmetrical concept of federalism.[85]

Trudeau replied that it was insulting to Quebeckers to be told they required greater privileges than other Canadians to make their way. "The people of Quebec . . . don't need a wheel chair or a crutch to get along."[86] Neither did their members at Ottawa need to be straw men; they could be full interpreters of French Canada in federal matters.[87] While it was good to be master of one's province and proud of its achievements, French Canadians should be sharing in great developments across Canada.[88] The Prime Minister inferred that Ryan, as a member of the traditional élites, claimed, as usual, to represent the people's views on the constitutional question. "Do we really know what the people of Quebec think?" he asked.[89]

Because Marcel Faribault attracted so many high-calibre candidates, especially in Montreal, there was anticipation that the two positions would be fully joined. However, the intrusion of other factors prevented it. Everywhere, though in varying degrees, French Canadians said, "Trudeau's a French Canadian and that means a lot."[90] Anglo-Saxon and Jewish voters, fearful of their future in Quebec, turned en masse to Trudeau as a saviour. The Prime Minister carried one-time Conservative Mount Royal by a margin of 20 to 1; C.M. Drury took Westmount by 5 to 1. The Conservatives lost their ablest Quebec members, Roger Regimbal and Heward Grafftey, because the English vote deserted them in Argenteuil and Missisquoi (Grafftey also lost some low-income French-Canadian support to the Créditistes). In this election the N.D.P. hoped to make a breakthrough in Quebec on the Island of Montreal, and Stephen Lewis went to Dollard riding to conduct a "saturation campaign" for Charles Taylor.[91] But it was futile to contend with the Liberals in middle-class ridings with large English populations, and Taylor, Laurier LaPierre, and Charles Gifford all lost by 3 to 1 margins.

More than any other city, Montreal was infected with Trudeau-mania. Some stemmed from the constitutional issue, but ultimately it resulted from Trudeau's personal appeal, especially among women.[92] Faribault, lacking popular appeal, could not catch the public eye with his constitutional views and lost his deposit in Gamelin. The only genuine contests were in Duvernay, where the N.D.P. Quebec leader Robert Cliche lost to Eric Kierans, and Ste. Marie, where Conservative Georges Valade's personal popularity let him retain his seat. Montreal remained the most Liberal part of Canada by voting more than 65 per cent for that party.

In contrast, Trudeau had his coolest reception in rural Quebec. Partly responsible was his omnibus bill. Les Pélérins de St. Michel said in their organ *Vers Demain* that "it is the beast of Sodom that inspires his legislative projects."[93] But mostly responsible was the cynicism of residents of a chronically depressed area. "When Mr. Trudeau spoke to them of his 'Just Society,' they reacted with an arms-folded, show-me attitude."[94] Initially the Conservatives expected to do well, but they faded steadily. This was partly because the Union Nationale, which conducted much of their campaign, seemed interested only in beating Trudeau. In addition, the constitutional issue proved to be a boomerang: when Julien Chouinard, their candidate in Matane and former Deputy Minister of Justice in Quebec, spoke of it, all he got was a blank stare. But for the most part the Conservatives did poorly in Quebec because, in talking about economic issues, they could not compete with Réal Caouette.

Caouette's fortunes had risen even before the nationally televised debate of the four leaders on June 9. The favourable response he evoked on that occasion accelerated the move towards him. Consequently he took many votes and seats that the Conservatives expected. The latter won only 3 ridings outside Montreal to the Créditistes' 14. Because of the divided opposition vote, the Liberals elected about 12 members – including cabinet ministers Jean Luc Pépin, Jean Marchand, and perhaps Jean Chrétien – who might otherwise have lost.

Although the Liberal vote in Quebec increased by about 8 per cent, they did not add to their previous 56 seats; the Conservatives retained roughly 21 per cent of the vote but lost 4 of their 8 seats. The results meant that a Quebec federal politician could take a strong stand against special status and not be harmed. They also indicated that French Canadians were generally apathetic towards the constitution. Did these results also mean that the constitutional question had been laid to rest?

In urban Ontario the Conservatives were rid of the Diefenbaker albatross, but they had an even worse handicap: Trudeaumania. In metropolitan Toronto it produced incredible Liberal strength "in the upper-middle and middle areas, in suburbia and in the inner city"; among upper- and middle-income females it was "wild and completely uninhibited." They had other reasons, but in affluent urban Ontario many supported Trudeau because they had been "turned off by the traditional politics of the country."[95] There was only a minor erosion of the N.D.P.'s working-class vote, but it lost so much middle-class support that it retained Waterloo and its 3 Toronto bastions only with difficulty. It also gained Oshawa-Whitby, but lost Hamilton-Mountain and, in the North, Timmins, Sudbury, and Nickel Belt.

Metro Toronto gave half its votes to the Liberals – up from 42.9 per cent in 1965 – while the Conservatives polled slightly more, and the N.D.P. slightly less than one-quarter of the vote. None of a strong Conservative slate headed by Dalton Camp came close to being elected. Each might have said, "I'm not conceding to my Liberal opponent; I'm conceding to Mr. Trudeau." Camp lost because the mobile young couples in the 15,455 high-rise apartments of Don Valley voted overwhelmingly for Trudeau, as they did throughout Toronto. Camp thought his party was hurt because the C.B.C., instead of enforcing the 24-hour ban on political broadcasting before the election, "rolled over and fawned." He referred to the telecast of separatist violence in Montreal on election eve: "The Liberal organizer who said the affair was worth 40,000 votes in Toronto alone may have been guilty of understatement."[96] Actually, the Conservatives were beaten before this episode. The only one to survive the trend was Lincoln Alexander in Hamilton West, the first Negro to be elected to the Commons and the only Conservative to win a wholly urban seat in Ontario.

In rural Ontario the Conservatives missed John Diefenbaker even though the dose of Trudeaumania was mild. The Tory losses appeared substantial. Even in Frontenac-Lennox and Addington, where it was said that a coat on a rack could be elected if it had a Tory blue ribbon in the button-hole, they had trouble. However, their losses resulted mainly from the elimination of rural seats or the dilution of rural strength in mixed ridings. Most rural voters resisted the trend: "Farmers don't go for that [swinger image]. They're smarter than city people."[97] None the less, the results in Ontario were disastrous for the Conservatives. Their total of 17 seats was 5 fewer than their previous low of 22 in 1874; their popular vote was about 2 per cent below its previous low of 34.0 per cent in 1965.

For four elections John Diefenbaker had sublimated other issues and kept the Prairies speaking almost as one, but he had been tossed aside, it was alleged, by an eastern establishment. Hence the outcome this time would be the net results of a variety of forces operating with differing effect. The biggest asset of the Liberals was Pierre Elliott Trudeau. He had "an iconoclastic political style that has always gone over well in the West";[98] he had taken a hard line towards Quebec and had not given hostages to a Faribault, not inconsiderable virtues in an area suspicious of French Canada. However, rural dwellers frowned upon "all this mod stuff." Mindful of 900 million unsold bushels of wheat, they said: "The only thing that matters is who can sell the most wheat."

In Manitoba, unpopular provincial tax measures hurt the Conservatives. When Liberal James Richardson circularized the voters of Winnipeg South, he found this issue uppermost.[99] Taxes combined with the Trudeaumania that enveloped Winnipeg caused the Conservatives in the South and South Centre ridings – Duff Roblin was one – to be soundly defeated. Taxes also helped the Liberals to gain Provencher and Portage from the Conservatives. The Liberals polled about 10 per cent more of the total vote than the Conservatives, instead of 10 per cent less as in 1965.

In Saskatchewan unsold wheat and Premier Thatcher's introduction of deterrents into medicare limited the Liberals' gain in popular vote to about 3 per cent, but they did win 2 seats. The N.D.P. surprised everyone by winning 6 seats and polling almost as many votes as the Conservatives. It was largely due to the westerners' penchant for supporting third parties when the old parties are in disfavour. The Conservatives fared quite well in the rural areas, where their slogan was: "Alvin Hamilton will sell your wheat," but they lost all 5 seats containing the large urban centres. They suffered from their attitude towards medicare and Dalton Camp's statement that the federal scheme was a "dead duck." Alvin Hamilton said that each Conservative candidate had lost 1,000 votes as a result,[100] and he may have been beaten himself in consequence. In all, the Conservatives lost 12 seats – almost half their net national loss – 8 to their opponents and 4 through redistribution.

In Alberta the Conservatives capitalized on the objections to federal medicare. However, they benefited most from the collapse of Social Credit, which ran only 3 candidates and polled only about 2 per cent of the vote, down from 22.5 per cent in 1965. While the Liberals won 2 rural seats, generally they fared badly in this area: of the 8 Liberal candidates throughout Canada who lost their deposits, 6 had run in rural Alberta. In Calgary and Edmonton the Liberals took full advantage of Trudeau's coattails and used "two nations" with abandon, but they won only 1 seat in each city. The Conservatives polled half the province's vote and won 15 of the 19 seats. None the less, Conservative strength on the Prairies fell from 42 seats to 25.

Both urban and rural British Columbia succumbed to Trudeau-mania. While the N.D.P. retained about 33 per cent of the popular vote and the Conservatives – better organized than in 1965 – about 19 per cent, the Liberals added about 12 per cent to their previous 30, largely at the expense of the Social Credit. The shift enabled the Liberals to win the 3 Social Credit seats, the 3 Conservative seats (including Davie Fulton's), 1 new seat, and, in effect, 2 N.D.P. seats for a gain of 9. Although the N.D.P. lost some working-class support, it held on to all its working-class ridings except New Westminster and Comox–Alberni. Challenged personally by former provincial Liberal leader Ray Perrault, T.C. Douglas said: "I'm running for a seat in the Commons and he's running for a seat in the Senate."[101] However, redistribution had altered the balance in Burnaby–Seymour from working to middle class, and Perrault won a narrow victory.

The election of 1968 had meaning for every Canadian politician. For the provincial premiers, it augured anything but good. Only G.I. Smith of Nova Scotia could have been pleased with his province's voting; the others must have found the results disquieting or even alarming. For Social

Credit, which elected no members, the election may have meant its end as a national force. For the Créditistes – their number increased from 9 to 14 as a result of the same forces that caused their rise in 1962 – the future would be inversely proportional to the success of the Prime Minister's war on poverty in low-income rural Quebec. For the N.D.P. it was a holding election: its representation rose from 21 to 22, but its popular vote fell slightly below the 17.9 per cent of 1965; its working-class support stood the test, but not its middle-class vote.

For the Conservatives, the election produced nothing but problems. Some said that Stanfield had been mismanaged, but actually he was beaten the night that Trudeau became leader. Trudeau's campaign was designed to keep the support he had amassed at that time, and the political novice made no mistakes. Also, as Dalton Camp put it, "when all goes well, you are . . . courted by good luck. The sun beamed down on Trudeau. The rain poured down on Stanfield."[102]

One problem that the election forced on Stanfield and the Conservatives was whether a man of integrity and good sense, not adept in the art of communication, would be able to win an election in this electronic age, even if the Canadian mood were to change. Another problem was to present a credible opposition in the Commons. Numerically, the Conservatives with 72 members (down from 97 in 1965) were not badly off, but they had lost men of ideas such as Alvin Hamilton and Davie Fulton, and had failed to elect their first-rate candidates in Toronto, Montreal, and elsewhere. Currently a non-urban party, they suffered because their best nominees often ran in the cities where they could not be elected. More than ever before, the election had been presidential rather than parliamentary – a contest between Trudeau and Stanfield – and candidates of quality had counted for naught. [103] In the days following the election there were suggestions that Canadians should "look closely at the congressional system, or some derivative of it, as an alternative to a parliamentary system which gradually is being twisted out of shape."[104]

However, the Conservatives' most serious problem was Quebec. No leader had risked more to create "a credible presence for conservatism in Quebec" than had Stanfield, but the election negated his effort.[105] The constitutional problem had not been resolved simply because Trudeau had willed it, but clearly the 4 Conservative and 14 Créditiste M.P.'s would be incapable of presenting an alternative point of view. There was danger that René Lévesque would "take advantage of the opposition vacuum to polarize the Quebecois voters into Trudeau federalists and anti-Ottawa Souverainistes."[106] That is why Claude Ryan and others talked about proportional representation or other electoral reform after June 25. Even the French type of run-off elections might have elected Conservatives or Créditistes instead of Liberals in much of rural Quebec.

by Macpherson. Toronto Star, *May 29, 1968. Reprinted with permission*—Toronto Daily Star.

For the Liberals the problems were of a different order. Their 155 members not only ensured majority government but greater representativeness than they had enjoyed in any election since 1953; they were particularly elated that they had won 11 seats on the Prairies. A pre-election survey indicated that they fell behind the Conservatives in only two groups – the 65-and-over age category and the small town and rural electorate – and that they were particularly strong among the young, the residents of metropolitan areas, Roman Catholics, Jews, French Canadians, and better-off and better-educated persons.[107] This was nothing new, but Trudeau's image and style of campaigning had accentuated the division. The Liberals had clearly become the party of the haves: they received twice as much support as the Conservatives from voters with incomes over $10,000. Not surprisingly, then, Peter Regenstreif said of the results that "the election pitted haves against have-nots."[108]

Some expected Trudeau to establish clear-cut differences between the Liberals and Conservatives, but in this election he was, if anything,

Twenty-eighth

further to the right than Stanfield. However. it would be naive to believe that Trudeau – pragmatic on everything but the constitution – would normally differ on fundamentals from the equally pragmatic Stanfield. Crucial to Trudeau's success will be his ability to satisfy the demands of the rational exponents of Trudeauism for a new kind of politics. In the election of 1968 he employed his own contradictory qualities to attract conflicting interests and groups; will he appear equally attractive to them when the chips are down?

FOOTNOTES

1. *Supra*, p. 375.
2. Toronto *Telegram*, November 27, 1967.
3. J.M. Beck, "The Electoral Behaviour of Nova Scotia in 1965," Dalhousie *Review*, XLVI (Spring, 1966), p. 38.
4. Toronto *Globe and Mail*, April 22, 1968.
5. *Ibid.*
6. *Ibid.*, April 23, 1968.
7. Anthony Westell in *ibid.*, February 12, 1968.
8. Keith Spicer in *ibid.*, April 23, 1968.
9. Anthony Westell in *ibid.*, February 12, 1968.
10. Keith Spicer in *ibid.*, April 23, 1968.
11. Anthony Westell in *ibid.*, February 12, 1968.
12. Toronto *Globe and Mail*, May 9, 1968.
13. *Ibid.*, May 10, 1968.
14. Toronto *Star*, May 11, 1968.
15. Ottawa *Citizen*, May 13, 1968.
16. The title of an article in *The New York Times Magazine*, June 16, 1968.
17. Toronto *Star*, May 11, 1968.
18. Ottawa *Citizen*, May 14, 1968.
19. Gary Oakes in Toronto *Telegram*, May 18, 1968.
20. Dalton Camp, "Why We Lost," Toronto *Star*, June 29, 1968.
21. Anthony Westell in Toronto *Globe and Mail*, June 22, 1968.
22. Halifax *Chronicle-Herald*, June 5, 1968.
23. Ottawa *Citizen*, May 31, 1968.
24. Toronto *Globe and Mail*, May 17, 1968.
25. George Bain in *ibid.*, June 22, 1968.
26. Toronto *Globe and Mail*, June 15, 1968.
27. Ottawa *Citizen*, May 13, 1968.
28. Ottawa *Journal* and Toronto *Globe and Mail*, June 11, 1968.
29. Halifax *Chronicle-Herald*, June 19, 1968.
30. Toronto *Globe and Mail*, May 29, 1968.
31. Anthony Westell in *ibid.*
32. See Toronto *Star*, May 14, 1968; Ottawa *Journal*, May 22, 1968; and Toronto *Star*, May 31, 1968.
33. Toronto *Globe and Mail*, June 22, 1968.
34. Toronto *Star*, June 29, 1968.
35. For his defence, see Toronto *Globe and Mail*, June 20, 1968.
36. *Ibid.*, May 27, 1968.
37. *Financial Times of Canada*, June 24, 1968.
38. Toronto *Star*, June 20, 1968.
39. Toronto *Globe and Mail*, May 14, 1968.
40. Montreal *Star*, June 18, 1968.
41. Peter Newman, in Toronto *Star*, June 14, 1968.
42. Anthony Westell in Toronto *Globe and Mail*, June 22, 1968.
43. Toronto *Globe and Mail*, June 14, 1968.
44. Toronto *Star*, June 14, 1968.
45. Ottawa *Citizen*, June 11, 1968.
46. Toronto *Star*, May 10, 1968.
47. Toronto *Globe and Mail*, May 23, 1968.
48. Ottawa *Journal*, June 22, 1968.
49. Montreal *Star*, May 28, 1968.
50. Toronto *Star*, May 31, 1968.
51. Halifax *Mail-Star*, June 25, 1968.
52. Toronto *Globe and Mail*, June 22, 1968.

	Seats	Candidates						Elected											
		P.C.	L.	N.D.P.	S.C.	R.C.	O.	P.C.	%	L.	%	N.D.P.	%	S.C.	%	R.C.	%	O.	%
Newfoundland	7	7	7	7		1		6	85.7	1	14.3								
Nova Scotia	11	11	11	11			1	10	90.9	1	9.1								
New Brunswick	10	10	10	10	1		2	5	50.0	5	50.0								
Prince Edward Island	4	4	4	4				4	100.0										
Quebec	74	74	74	73		70	32	4	5.4	56	75.7					14	18.9		
Ontario	88	87	87	88	3		20	17	19.3	64	72.7	6	6.8					1	1.1
Manitoba	13	13	13	13	5		4	5	38.5	5	38.5	3	23.1						
Saskatchewan	13	13	13	13			2	5	38.5	2	15.4	6	46.2						
Alberta	19	19	19	19	3		7	15	78.9	4	21.1								
British Columbia	23	23	23	23	19		8			16	69.6	7	30.4						
Yukon and N.W.T.	2	2	2	2				1	50.0	1	50.0								
Total	264	263	263	263	31	71	76	72	27.3	155	58.7	22	8.3			14	5.3	1	0.4

Notes: A Lib. Lab. elected in Ontario, unopposed by an official L. candidate, is placed in the L. columns. Lucien Lamoureux was elected as an Independent in Stormont-Dundas, preparatory to becoming the first Speaker of the Commons divorced entirely from party ties.

Others elected: Ont. (1): I. (1).

Others (votes polled):

    N.S. (1): I.P.C. (1) 294.

    N.B. (2): I.P.C. (1) 268; I. (1) 553.

    Que. (32): I. (15) 13, 545; I.L. (5) 4,452; I.R.C. (1) 290; Rhinoceros (1) 355; I.P.C. (1) 279; Dem. Econ. (5) 2,671; Cons. (1) 339; Comm. (1) 191; Franc. Lib. (1) 2,141; Esprit Social (1) 311.

    Ont. (20): I.P.C. (1) 571; I.L. (3) 3,714; I. (7) 18,419; Comm. (6) 1,573; Nat. Soc. (1) 89; Soc. Lab. (1) 202; New Canada Party (1) 147.

    Man. (4): I. (2) 1,207; Comm. (1) 869; I. Cons. (1) 632.

    Sask. (2): Comm. (1) 230; I. (1) 689.

    Alta. (7): I.L. (3) 8,599; I.P.C. (1) 1,349; I. (1) 1,206; Comm. (1) 410; Cons. (1) 3,575.

    B.C. (8): Comm. (4) 1,196; I. Canadian (1) 403; Republican (1) 175; Republican Party of Canada (1) 425; I. (1) 526.

53. Toronto *Star*, April 27, 1968.

54. Toronto *Globe and Mail*, June 12, 1968.

55. Ottawa *Citizen*, May 31, 1968.

56. Charles Lynch in Hamilton *Spectator*, June 1, 1968.

57. Christopher Young in Ottawa *Citizen*, June 22, 1968.

58. Peter Newman in Toronto *Star*, June 20, 1968.

59. Toronto *Globe and Mail*, June 13, 1968.

60. George Bain in *ibid.*, June 22, 1968.

61. Toronto *Star*, June 14, 1968.

62. Anthony Westell in Toronto *Globe and Mail*, June 22, 1968.

63. Peter Newman in Ottawa *Journal*, June 1, 1968.

64. Quoted by Max Lerner in Halifax *Chronicle-Herald*, July 3, 1968.

65. Montreal *Gazette*, June 12, 1968.

66. Paul Fox, "The Liberals Choose Trudeau – Pragmatism at Work," *Canadian Forum* (May, 1968), p. 27.

67. Ottawa *Citizen*, June 15, 1968.

68. Montreal *Gazette*, June 22, 1968.

69. Ottawa *Citizen*, June 15, 1968.

	Popular Vote [Preliminary]											Total
P.C.	%	L.	%	N.D.P.	%	S.C.	%	R.C.	%	O.	%	
84,521	52.8	68,492	42.8	7,035	4.4	126	0.1					160,174
186,071	55.2	127,920	38.0	22,683	6.7					294	0.1	336,968
125,263	49.7	111,847	44.4	12,262	4.9			1,769	0.7	821	0.3	251,962
26,283	51.8	22,786	44.9	1,639	3.2							50,708
466,259	21.3	1,170,610	53.6	164,363	7.5			358,116	16.4	24,574	1.1	2,183,922
942,755	32.0	1,372,612	46.6	607,019	20.6	889	0.0			24,715	0.8	2,947,990
125,713	31.4	166,022	41.5	99,974	25.0	5,969	1.5			2,708	0.7	400,386
153,228	37.0	112,333	27.1	147,950	35.7					919	0.2	414,430
283,997	50.4	201,015	35.7	52,688	9.3	10,940	1.9			15,139	2.7	563,779
155,350	19.4	334,171	41.8	261,253	32.7	46,105	5.8			2,725	0.3	799,604
5,325	33.5	9,067	57.0	1,523	9.6							15,915
2,554,765	31.4	3,696,875	45.5	1,378,389	17.0	64,029	0.8	359,885	4.4	71,895	0.9	8,125,838

70. Toronto *Globe and Mail*, June 20, 1968.

71. Montreal *Star*, June 15, 1968.

72. *Ibid.*, June 18, 1968.

73. Ottawa *Journal*, May 17, 1968.

74. Toronto *Star*, May 10, 1968.

75. Toronto *Globe and Mail*, May 15, 1968.

76. Halifax *Chronicle-Herald*, June 20, 1968.

77. George Bain in Toronto *Globe and Mail*, May 25, 1968.

78. Peter Regenstreif in Ottawa *Citizen*, May 22, 1968.

79. Toronto *Star*, June 20, 1968.

80. Charles Lynch in Ottawa *Citizen*, June 22, 1968.

81. Halifax *Chronicle-Herald*, June 24, 1968.

82. Peter Regenstreif in Ottawa *Citizen*, May 22, 1968.

83. *Ibid.*

84. Halifax *Chronicle-Herald*, June 14, 1968.

85. *Le Devoir*, June 22, 1968.

86. Toronto *Globe and Mail*, June 21, 1968.

87. Ottawa *Citizen*, May 18, 1968.

88. Halifax *Chronicle-Herald*, June 17, 1968.

89. Toronto *Star*, June 17, 1968.

90. Ottawa *Journal*, May 31, 1968.

91. Toronto *Globe and Mail*, May 23, 1968.

92. Peter Regenstreif in Montreal *Star*, May 24, 1968.

93. Toronto *Globe and Mail*, June 8, 1968.

94. Montreal *Star*, May 29, 1968.

95. *Ibid.*, June 14, 1968.

96. Toronto *Star*, June 29, 1968.

97. Toronto *Globe and Mail*, June 8, 1968.

98. Toronto *Star*, April 27, 1968.

99. Toronto *Globe and Mail*, May 31, 1968.

100. *Ibid.*, July 6, 1968.

101. Toronto *Star*, May 30, 1968.

102. *Ibid.*, June 29, 1968.

103. See Larry Zolf in Toronto *Star*, June 26, 1968, and Anthony Westell in Toronto *Globe and Mail*, July 13, 1968.

104. *Ibid.*

105. Dalton Camp in Toronto *Star*, June 29, 1968.

106. Toronto *Globe and Mail*, July 13, 1968.

107. Toronto *Star*, June 20, 1968.

108. Peter Regenstreif in *ibid.*, June 26, 1968.

Conclusion

"... TO DEPEND ON QUEBEC"

What light do Canada's general elections shed on the nature of Canadian politics? They indicate that, although Canadian society is in no sense polarized along class lines, class cleavages do exist and classes have expressed themselves, at least to a small degree, in political demands and through political parties. Yet the elections demonstrate no less clearly that support for the major political parties has not diverged sharply along class lines.[1] Much as V.O. Key, Jr. wrote about politics in the United States,[2] so Underhill, Dawson, and Corry have written about politics in Canada: that it can most suitably be viewed as a process of sectional reconciliation and that Canadian political leaders have acted as brokerage politicians to that end even more than their counterparts in the United States.

The resulting brand of politics, says John Porter, has been thoroughly unsatisfactory. As he puts it, "to obscure social divisions through brokerage politics is to remove from the political system that element of dialectic which is the source of creative politics,"[3] and to have the effect of bringing about change through sheer opportunism rather than through response to genuine needs.

Yet parties adapt themselves to the environment in which they have to function, and in a society such as the Canadian one, which is not sharply polarized along class lines and in which demands tend to be made on a regional basis, it would have been surprising if the parties had developed differently. Even if the parties had started out sharply divergent in ideology, they would have moderated their position with each succeeding election and moved towards each other. In any case, it is a dubious assumption that creative politics can emanate only from the dialectic of a party system based on class divisions or on a polarization along leftist and rightist lines. For there is a dialectic of another kind – the debate at any given time about the kind and scope of federal participation in regional undertakings and development, which in Canada may be creative in another way. This kind of politics may be opportunistic, but not necessarily more so than class politics, for parties of the left and right often prove to be highly opportunistic as they appeal for the middle-class support without which they are unable to govern.

The succession of minority governments in the 1960's reinforced the position of those who felt that brokerage or consensus politics had failed in Canada. They argued further that it was deficient in producing a genuine consensus even when it produced parliamentary majorities. As factual evidence, they pointed out that only twice since 1921 – in 1940 and 1958 – had a winning party been able to get 50 per cent of the popular vote. This fact led Professor S.M. Lipset to suggest in 1954 that "the peculiarities of Canadian politics . . . must be seen as the failure of the British Parliamentary system to work in a society with complex internal divisions."[4] Accordingly he proposed that Canada, like many European countries that started with the same system, should at least adopt some form of proportional representation in lieu of more radical changes, and therefore allow every significant group to be represented by its own party.

Recently Professor Alan Cairns has levelled more serious charges against the first-past-the-post electoral system. He suggests that the stimulation of the politics of sectionalism and the manner in which the party system has evolved have been closely connected with the electoral system. His basic theme "in its simplest form, and somewhat crudely stated, is that all statements about sectionalism in the national party system are, at a deeper level, statements about the politics of the single member constituency system."[5] He has no difficulty in showing that the Liberal and Conservative parties have often received rich dividends in seats, altogether out of proportion to their percentage of votes, from particular sections and provinces. Thus, the Conservatives dominated Canadian politics prior to 1896 because they consistently won a large number of Quebec seats; since 1896 the government has usually been Liberal for the same reason. Except in rare instances, the major parties cannot each win a substantial number of seats in Quebec at the same time, and the electoral system is almost entirely responsible for this phenomenon.

Furthermore, Cairns says that, when a politician feels he will gain significant political benefits by addressing himself to the special needs of an area, he will not fail to make at least a partial response. Sometimes, in fact, "the sectional nature of party support imposes on politicians the necessity of making a cruel choice between sections, a choice recognized as involving the sacrifice of future representation from one section in order to retain it from another section."[6] Thus, the electoral system has the tendency to foster "a politics of opportunism based on sectional appeals and conditioned by one party bastions where the opposition is tempted to give up the battle and pursue success in more promising areas."[7] The dominant party in a region may also make mendacious appeals to the voters even though the effect is to exacerbate divisive sectional and ethnic cleavages. All this leads Cairns to wonder if the usual interpretation of the Canadian party system as an agent for performing a nationalizing function is valid. "Does the party system, in performing its conciliatory brokerage function [he asks], stimulate the very cleavages it is alleged to bridge?"[8]

Conclusion

It seems obvious that Cairns draws these conclusions because of the strategy and tactics of the major parties in Quebec. Undoubtedly Laurier in his later years felt he should not be expected to take any action that might weaken his hold on his native province. Nevertheless, this thesis was seldom used as an operating principle, and his government usually performed the brokerage function without undue concessions to Quebec in formulating its legislative and electoral programmes.

Perhaps even more than Laurier, King had an eye on Quebec, and that province was primarily responsible for his victories in 1921, 1926, and 1945. Sometimes he went further than necessary in ensuring Quebec support. In the twenties he could have done more to placate the free trade West without fear of endangering his hold on protectionist Quebec. However, in most aspects of public policy King was a master in the art of accommodating many shades of opinion — so much so that his party came to cut a wide swath across the centre of Canadian politics. The crudity and mendacity of the Liberal appeals in Quebec relating to Meighen the Monster did not prevent King from making his party representative of all the significant interests in the country. Because these appeals were crudest in the rural areas of Quebec, they largely escaped public attention and were not the divisive factor Cairns suggests they were. Also, the stand of both parties on conscription was initially not opportunistic. Laurier's position was thoroughly in accord with the liberal creed he had espoused throughout his life, and the attitude of the Conservatives was equally understandable in terms of their past.

It is none the less true that the successes of King and St. Laurent in Quebec tended to make the Conservatives an Anglo-Saxon and sometimes even an Ontario party in Parliament. The lack of Conservative French-Canadian M.P.'s during the Second World War affected the party's attitude in Parliament, where, despite the best efforts of Manion, Hanson, and Bracken, it exuded an Anglo-Saxon and often anti-French-Canadian outlook which further tarnished its image in Quebec. Yet, 1917 excepted, it was not true that the Conservatives wrote Quebec off. Their leaders have always known that they cannot govern without Quebec, and until 1957 the Conservatives lavished about half their financial resources in that province on what they must have feared was a hopeless cause.

Furthermore, the political behaviour of the different regions of the country belies the picture that Cairns describes. For, excepting 1963, whenever power has been transferred from one party to another, each region has swung away from the party in power.

> Sometimes, as in the Maritimes in 1896 and 1911, or in Quebec in 1911 and 1930, the swing might have been insufficient to give the victorious party a majority of the regions' seats, but it was none the less clear-cut. Sometimes, as in western Canada in 1921, the victori-

ous party might not have been the chief beneficiary of the governing party's losses, but it nevertheless improved its position. . . . With a few minor exceptions, Prince Edward Island in 1896, Alberta in 1911, and Nova Scotia in 1911 and 1930, every province moved in the direction of change when change did occur.[9]

This phenomenon would not have been likely if there had not been a conscious and successful effort on the part of the winning party to create a favourable image in all regions.

The crucial questions seem, therefore, to be: Is Canadian politics characterized by the operation of a brokerage function which, in its task of reconciling interests, is only slightly impeded by counterforces of a divisive nature growing out of the electoral system? Or, does Canadian politics suffer seriously from the divisive effects of an electoral system which are only slightly counterbalanced by the major parties' performance of the brokerage function? Or, does some intermediate position more closely approximate the true picture of Canadian politics? More studies are needed to provide definitive answers to these questions.

Cairns also suggests that a politics of sectionalism is a politics of instability. He argues that the self-interest that causes a party to write off a section of the country may be highly unfortunate for national unity; furthermore, that sectional politics is more disruptive than class politics because it tends to call into question the very nature of the political system and its legitimacy. "Classes, unlike sections, cannot secede from the political system, and are consequently more prone to accept its legitimacy."[10]

In reply, it should be noted that the major parties seldom write off entire regions. Also, it is dubious that a region having so strong a sense of discrimination that it is thinking of secession will continue to be divided along class lines. At any rate, there would be another kind of instability under the system of proportional representation that Cairns appears to favour. Minority government would almost certainly become a common phenomenon and it would be minority government as it exists in Europe, rather than the kind resulting from the Canadian elections of 1962, 1963, and 1965. However, Cairns may well be right that the instability resulting from proportional representation would be less likely to attack the legitimacy of the political system than the instability growing out of the politics of sectionalism.

The election of 1968 illustrated the problems and doubts arising from the electoral system and consensus politics. Quebec might have had a second voice in the Commons on constitutional matters if the Conservatives had elected the 15 members to which their popular vote in the province entitled them. Also, dissatisfaction with a kind of politics that concerned itself with making deals and blurring issues led many Canadians to vote for Pierre Elliott Trudeau and, hopefully, for a new brand of politics.

Conclusion   *423*

TABLE I

Elections in which the campaign is not likely to have determined the outcome or meant the difference between minority and majority government.	Elections in which the campaign is likely to have determined the outcome or meant the difference between minority and majority government.
1872	1867?
1874	1891
1878	1911
1882	1917
1887	1957
1896	1962
1900	1963
1904	1965
1908	
1921	
1925	
1926?	
1930	
1935	
1940	
1945	
1949	
1953	
1958	
1968	

To what extent has the campaign itself played a significant part in determining the outcome of Canada's elections? How would the results have differed had the polling taken place on the day of dissolution? At the risk of deflating the country's leading campaigners and the key party organizers, past and present, only eight elections appear to have had their outcome substantially affected by the campaign (see Table I). Moreover, four of these eight elections have occurred since 1957 and in each of them the crucial factor has been a charismatic leader, adept in the use of the mass media, especially television. In any event, the strength of party organization seems to have been not so much an independent variable as a function of the type of image, favourable or unfavourable, that a party was reflecting at a particular time.

The classification of elections along these lines is often a matter of judgment, and none more so than the election of 1867. In Nova Scotia, the voters had made up their minds long before the campaign started and the election was largely an anticlimax. However, in Ontario the outcome was determined by a substantial number of Grits temporarily throwing in their lot with the Conservatives, and with them, Macdonald's arguments on the hustings against a return to normal partisan warfare until the pressing problems of the new federation had been resolved seem to have proved effective. In Quebec, too, Cartier's Bleus campaigned successfully on the bishops' injunction not to support those who opposed Confederation. Certainly the Rouges were loud in their denunciation of clerical interference which, they felt, had cost them the election. While no exact measurement of these forces operating in Quebec and Ontario can be made, they may well have given Macdonald his majority.

In 1872 there were no issues of substance and, under the circumstances, the governing party which alone had a claim to be called a national party and which knew how to use the possession of power to its own advantage, held on to office. Two years later, a "virtuous" electorate had decided in favour of Liberal Alexander Mackenzie long before the campaign started, and Macdonald devoted all his efforts to saving what he could from the wreckage. By 1878 the electorate was so disillusioned with Mackenzie and stagnation that the Conservatives would have won even without National Policy. Long before the campaign of 1882 began the voters had rejected Edward Blake's negativism and decided to give the Conservatives and "N.P." full credit for the improvement in the economic climate. In 1887 the Conservatives barely managed to hold on to Quebec despite the nationalistic outpourings of Honoré Mercier; in Ontario the Anglo-Saxon backlash against the Riel agitation in Quebec, the delayed effects of the gerrymander of 1882, and the advantages accruing from the Franchise Act of 1885 were responsible for the Conservative success. The campaign itself was not the determining factor.

In 1891, however, the circumstances were very different. It was not in Quebec that the campaign was important, for there the continuing trust in Macdonald and Chapleau's ability to counteract Laurier prevented more than a slight drift away from the Conservatives. However, in Ontario the rural areas found the Liberals' platform of freer trade highly attractive, and Macdonald's "a British subject" plea prevented the opposition's inroads from being greater. In Nova Scotia and New Brunswick similar loyalty cries by Tupper, Foster, and the Conservative newspapers helped to give the Conservatives their over-all majority.

Five years later Tupper's success in uniting and consolidating his party in English Canada in a few short weeks might have been, as Sir Thomas Galt said it was, "almost incomprehensible,"[11] but all it did was to give him an even break in these provinces. The key to the election was Quebec and, as Dafoe pointed out: "The issue was Laurier."[12] The province that determined the election knew what it was going to do long before the campaign started. The election of 1900 was held amid booming prosperity and the electorate readily gave the Liberals credit for "four years of peace, four years of progress, four years of such prosperity as this country never before knew."[13] The situation was much the same four years later; in Dafoe's words, perhaps there was never a time when satisfaction with existing conditions and confidence in the future were so general as in the year 1904. There was hardly a cloud in the sky."[14] By 1908 a series of scandals had darkened the sky, but in the public mind the Liberals were still the party of national development, the party of national unity, and the party with the leader who best embodied Canada's hopes and aspirations.

If reciprocity had not been an issue in 1911, Laurier would likely have won his fifth election in a row. In much of English Canada and certainly in Ontario the campaign had the effect of rallying the slumbering protest against the United States that always exists in this country. This development had started before the election, but the campaign served to complete the process. In Quebec, even before dissolution, Bourassa had been saying that the naval bill might drag Canada into wars that she would do better to stay out of. But the campaign itself, in which funds from imperialist and protectionist sources aided and abetted the Nationalists, was what led to the extensive Liberal losses in *la belle province*.

Again, in 1917, the campaign had a decisive effect upon the outcome. This was not true in Quebec, where conscription had made Borden's position hopeless from the start and where, because of poor health, Laurier had made few speeches and could have absented himself completely from the hustings. In contrast, English Canada and especially Ontario were not nearly as solidly conscriptionist as might have been expected. Changing this state of affairs took a campaign that was in some areas as extreme as that in Quebec, and a promise not to conscript farmers' sons honestly engaged in agriculture. Opinion-moulders in English Canada determined the result by emphasizing that to demonstrate loyalty to Britain, maintain Canada's self-respect, and keep faith with Canada's fighting men, the ordinary citizen had no choice but to vote for Borden.[15]

The postwar election of 1921 reflected a disenchantment with the Unionist administration. There is little to indicate that King's campaign was materially responsible for the Conservatives' losses or for the Progressives' inroads not being greater. Four years later the voters in English Canada indicated they had become disillusioned with Mackenzie King. While it could be argued that the Liberal campaign of vilification in Quebec determined the outcome in that province, it is more likely that memories of the Conservatives' handling of conscription did.

The effect of the campaign on the outcome in 1926 is more difficult to assess. Although Bourassa's argument that the Governor General was returning Canada to colonial status may have had some effect in Quebec, it seems likely that Meighen was still the determining factor. In English Canada it appears that the Conservatives had already reached the highest peak they could under the circumstances, and that the slight reaction away from them was a natural phenomenon that had little to do with the campaign itself.

In 1930, mounting depression rather than Bennett's campaign appears to have determined the result in all parts of Canada. In Quebec a number of factors apart from the campaign conditioned the province for change, but it was primarily the economic difficulties that impelled a large number of Quebeckers to alter their voting habits. Five years later the positions of the parties were reversed and King's "policy of having no policy" indicated that he knew he could win on the general dissatisfaction with Bennett and the repellent image his ministry had created. In 1940 Quebec would have nothing to do with the Conservatives, the party of conscription, while English Canada reflected its general satisfaction with the Liberals' conduct of the war. Manion, it has been pointed out, "in two months of campaigning, could not break down the case thus built up; could not destroy the legends that invariably grow around ministers. Hadn't most people been saying for months: 'The government is doing a good job'?"[16] The radical and intemperate nature of the closing part of Manion's campaign actually harmed the Conservatives, but only by making the Liberal majority bigger than it otherwise might have been.

In 1945, as the campaign advanced – but not as a result of it – the government's handling of conscription became an ever fading issue both in French and English Canada. Because this was the question that had threatened to hurt them most, the Liberals managed to win a narrow victory on their record, rather than on their campaign. Four years later it was a foregone conclusion that the Liberals would win again because of their success in postwar reconstruction, and because of an ever rising gross national product, virtually full employment, and substantial reductions in debt and taxation. Louis St. Laurent's appearances on the campaign trail as "pappa of us all" did enhance the victory, but it would have been a splendid one anyway. In 1953 "only the details were different in a political environment that was almost a mirror-image of the one four years earlier."[17]

In 1957, for perhaps the first time since 1917, the campaign played a key role in the election. The way had been prepared by such things as an alleged tight-money policy and the abuse of Parliament during the pipeline debate. But it took one of the country's greatest campaigners, John Diefenbaker, aided by television in Canada's first television election, to make the appeal required to bring down the Liberals. By the time the election of 1958 was called, all the factors had already been set in motion to ensure a substantial Conservative victory. However, it was Diefenbaker's prowess on the platform that made it the greatest of all Canadian election victories.

In each of the elections that produced minority government in 1962, 1963, and 1965 the campaigns played a significant part. In 1962 the Gallup Poll seemed to indicate that Diefenbaker's campaigning as "a strong, essentially simple person who loves and understands the 'average Canadian' "[18] was not without its effect, for it showed Liberal strength ebbing from 44 to 38 per cent during the campaign. Hence it is altogether likely that, if polling had taken place at dissolution, the Liberals could have formed at least a minority government. For most of the 1963 campaign Pearson performed badly, while Diefenbaker, "the man they had counted out, [by] reviving the melodramatics of 1958, garbing his villains in dress of the darkest hue, [and] providing light touches with an impish sort of humour," got unexpectedly enthusiastic responses. Once again the Liberals dropped a few percentage points of support during the campaign and, as a result, fell a few seats short of an over-all majority.[19] Something of the same sort happened in 1965 because of Pearson's inability to exert a strong positive pull. Consequently, Liberal support – up to 48 per cent in September – dropped to 40 per cent in November, and Canada had another minority government.

In contrast, Pierre Elliott Trudeau had won the election of 1968 the night he became Liberal leader. Indeed, his campaign was conducted so as not to lose the support he had amassed at that time (about 50 per cent according to the Gallup Poll) and, except for a few percentage points, he retained it.

The moral of all this seems to be that Canada would lose nothing in having shorter and, hence, less expensive campaigns.

As in any other country, each of Canada's elections is unique in nature, meaning, and consequences. Perhaps it is not surprising, then, that students of elections define them in varying ways. Professor V.O. Key, Jr., for example, saw an election as "a formal act of collective decision that occurs in a stream of connected antecedent and subsequent behaviour."[20] In behaviour prior to voting, he continued, elections differ in such things as the proportion of the electorate that is psychologically involved, the intensity of the attitudes associated with the cleavages within the electorate, the nature of the expectations about the consequences of the voting, and the impact that objective facts have on the voters' choice. However, to develop a typology of elections based on such antecedent behaviour is out of the question because of the difficulty in measuring quantitatively the various elements that go to make up that behaviour.

It is more fruitful to use the technique adopted by Professor Angus Campbell in classifying American presidential elections.[21] Underlying his technique is the idea that the vote cast by the electorate or specific groups within the electorate may be split into two parts: the normal vote division to be expected from the electorate or a specific group, other things being equal, and the current deviation from that norm, which is a function of the immediate circumstances of a particular election. The election outcome may be construed, then, as "the result of short-term forces acting upon a certain distribution of party loyalties which have characterized the population."[22] At any one time there is a majority party, which can count among its adherents a majority of the "normal vote" throughout the country, and a minority party, which is in a minority in the "normal vote." In any specific election there are short-term forces producing fluctuations of varying size from this normal vote. "Depending on whether the movement of the vote results in the election of the [presidential] candidate of the majority or the minority party, and on whether this movement is associated with a basic shift in long-term partisan attachments," Campbell classifies each election as maintaining, deviating, or realigning.

> In a maintaining election the pattern of partisan attachments prevailing in the preceding period persists, and the majority party wins the Presidency. . . . In a deviating election the basic division of party loyalties is not seriously disturbed, but the influence of short-term forces on the vote is such that it brings about the defeat of the majority party. . . . In . . . a realigning election, popular feeling associated with politics is sufficiently intense that the basic partisan commitments of a portion of the electorate change, and a new party balance is created.[23]

To illustrate his classification scheme, Campbell used quantitative surveys of the 1948, 1952, 1956, and 1960 elections, and, less confidently, impressionistic inferences drawn from earlier elections. In Canada the data is even more scarce and less reliable; yet on the surface the federal elections fit neatly into his scheme of things. In applying it to the Canadian scene (see Table II), the basic assumption is made that 1896 is the great watershed in Canadian politics, and that up to that time the Conservatives were the majority party in the country and since then the Liberals have been.

Shortly after Confederation, Macdonald coalesced significant elements of all the major groups in the country into a national party. The circumstances of history assured him of the support of a majority of French Canadians from the start. Early in the 1870's he won the good opinion of the urban proletariat by freeing the trade unions of their common-law disabilities against strike-breaking activities.[24] The "National Policy" of 1879 cemented the support he received from the manufacturers and allied financial and commercial elements, and also from the urban workers, who felt that their livelihood depended on the protective tariff. However, none of these groupings was a solid bloc in support of the Conservatives, and when the latter offended the electorate, the number of shifting voters was sufficient to bring the Liberals to power. That was what happened in 1874, the only instance of a deviating election prior to 1896.

In contrast, the Liberals did not become a genuinely national party until the 1890's. Laurier managed it, but he had help from Blake and Mowat, who divorced Ontario Liberalism from its anti-French, anti-Catholic

TABLE II

Maintaining Elections	Deviating Elections	Realigning Elections
1872	1874	1896
1878	1911	1917?
1882	1917	
1887	1925	
1891	1930	
1900	1957	
1904	1958	
1908	1962	
1921		
1926		
1935		
1940		
1945		
1949		
1953		
1963		
1965		
1968		

Grit background. Ontario Conservatism played into their hands by producing a series of bigots who, despite Macdonald's efforts, adopted a point of view that alienated both the French-Canadian and Catholic vote. D'Alton McCarthy said that the Conservative party should "hold by and lean on the English Provinces," while Macdonald's view, so it appeared to McCarthy, was "rather to depend on Quebec."[25]

In 1896 Quebec did not hesitate to repudiate its former Ontario partners, and the election of that year was a realigning one. In effect, the school of Cartier (or of Chapleau) moved from the Conservative to the Liberal camp in sufficient numbers to make the Liberals the majority party. For the time being, however, over 40 per cent of Quebeckers still continued to vote Conservative. That party's failure to reach an accommodation with French Canada on conscription in 1917 led to an even more massive swing to the Liberals than in 1896. Thus, the election of 1917 may also be regarded as a realigning one in the sense that it produced a further substantial shift in voters to the majority party, though not to such an extent that special circumstances could not lead to deviating elections.

Some sort of unconscious or, perhaps, instinctive force appears to have operated in English Canada such as to injure the party that is the chief beneficiary of French-Canadian voters. Thus western Ontario has been considerably less Liberal since 1900 than it was in the last century. But the Liberals have more than made up for this loss elsewhere. The good terms accorded to Saskatchewan, Alberta, and Newfoundland on their entrance into Confederation enabled the Liberals to develop deeper roots in these provinces than the Conservatives; Bennett's "New Deal," Manion's radicalism, and C.D. Howe's rapport with the business community broke the close connection between the Conservatives and the manufacturing, financial, and commercial elements; the removal of the protective tariff as a vital issue of domestic politics led to Conservative losses among the urban proletariat in English Canada – to the C.C.F. as well as the Liberals. Even more important was the shift in the non-French, Catholic vote to the Liberals, perhaps because the Conservatives were increasingly reflecting an Anglo-Saxon Protestant image after 1900. More than is generally appreciated, non-French Catholics became a significant part of the Liberal coalition and, if the surveys are correct, may account for much of the Liberal success nationally.

In recent years the intensity of party identification has declined even in the traditionalist provinces. Largely because of John Diefenbaker, the Conservative party is presently in the peculiar position of holding its own with the Liberals only among the older and the less well-to-do people. However, this need not be permanent because of the volatility of the contemporary Canadian electorate; Peter Regenstreif thinks it "doubtful that more than half the electorate voted the same way [in 1968] as it did in 1965."[26] None the less, the key to Canadian politics is still Quebec. The canniest of politicians, William Lyon Mackenzie King, read the situation right when he felt it his "duty . . . to depend on Quebec."

FOOTNOTES

1. See Robert Alford, *Party and Society* (Chicago: Rand McNally & Company, 1963), Chapter IX.

2. V.O. Key, Jr., *Politics, Parties and Pressure Groups*, (3rd ed.) (New York: Thomas Y. Crowell Company, 1952), Chapter IX.

3 John Porter, *The Vertical Mosaic* (Toronto: University of Toronto Press, 1965), p. 374.

4. S.M. Lipset, "Democracy in Alberta," *Canadian Forum*, XXXIV (December, 1954), p. 198.

5. Alan C. Cairns, "The Electoral System and the Party System in Canada: 1921-1965," a paper presented at the annual meeting of the Canadian Political Science Association, June 7, 1967, p. 18.

6. *Ibid.*, p. 11.

7. *Ibid.*, p. 14.

8. *Ibid.*, p. 6.

9. J.M. Beck, "The Democratic Process at Work in Canadian General Elections," in John C. Courtney, (ed.), *Voting in Canada* (Scarborough: Prentice-Hall of Canada, Limited, 1967), p. 25.

10. Cairns, "Electoral Systems," p. 15.

11. *Supra*, p. 80.

12. *Supra*, p. 77.

13. *Supra*, p. 87.

14. *Supra*, p. 97.

15. See *supra*, p. 146.

16. *Supra*, p. 231.

17. *Supra*, p. 276.

18. *Supra*, p. 337.

19. *Supra*, p. 360.

20. V.O. Key, Jr., "A Theory of Critical Elections," *Journal of Politics*, XVII (February, 1955), p. 3.

21. See Campbell, Converse, Miller and Stokes, *Elections and the Political Order* (New York: John Wiley and Sons, Inc., 1966), Chapter IV, "A Classification of the Presidential Elections."

22. See *ibid.*, Philip Converse, "The Concept of a Normal Vote," p. 15.

23. *Ibid.*, pp. 64, 69, and 74.

24. *Supra*, p. 15.

25. *Supra*, p. 59.

26. Toronto *Star*, June 26, 1968.

Cook, Warren K., *215*
Co-operative Commonwealth Federation (C.C.F.), *165*; origins, *208-209*; election of 1935, *212, 215-19*; 1940, *232-34, 236*; 1945, *242-43, 246-48, 250-55*; 1949, *262-64, 266-67, 271*; 1953, *281-82, 284-87*; 1957, *302, 304-306*; 1958, *318-19, 323*; gives way to N.D.P., *332*
Corry, J.A., *420*
Courrier de St. Hyacinthe, Le, 5
Courrier du Canada, Le, 5, *16*
Courtemanche, Henri, *268, 293, 299*
Cowan, Peter, *387*
Coyne, James, *315, 329*
Creighton, Donald, *25, 46-47, 50, 52*
Crerar, T.A., *144, 168, 175*; formation of Progressive party, *151*; election of 1921, *152-56*; resigns, *165*
Crow's Nest Pass Agreement, *164, 184*
Cuff, Robert, *126*
Cunningham, R., *18*
Currie Report, *279*
Customs scandal of 1926, *179, 182, 184, 186*

D

Dafoe, J.W., *72, 76, 78, 88, 89, 97, 98, 126, 144, 163, 177, 181, 185, 191, 193, 201, 206, 209, 214, 228, 282, 305, 425-26*
Dalby, Henry, *93*
Dandurand, Raoul, *82*
Dansereau, C.A., *48, 82, 91*
D'Auteuil, Raymond, *389*
Davey, Keith, *361, 364, 377, 393*
David, L.O., *5*
Davies, Sir Louis, *89*
Dawson, R. MacGregor, *43, 152, 158, 181, 420*
De Brisay, Richard, *193, 200*
Defence Production Act, *291*
Desbarats, Peter, *366, 377*
Devoir, Le, 121, *131, 172, 293, 298, 322, 351, 364*
Dewar, John, *228*
Dewart, H.H., *143*
Diefenbaker, Elmer, *334*
Diefenbaker, John, first elected, *236*; Conservative leader, *293-94*; rejected as leader, *399*; election of 1957, *294-305, 308, 427*; 1958, *311-24, 427*; 1962, *329-41, 343-47, 427-28*; 1963, *351-58, 360-62, 366-71, 428*; 1965, *374-84, 388, 391-95*; 1968, *409, 412, 413*
Dingley tariff, *88*
Dion, Léon, *365*
Disraeli, Benjamin, *15*
Doherty, C.J., *130, 143*
Dorion, A.A., *6, 7, 22, 24, 26, 30, 58*
Dorion, Frederick, *254, 376, 383*
Doucet, A.J., *182*
Douglas, T.C., *216, 305*; N.D.P. leader, *332*; election of 1962, *334, 346*; 1963, *353, 362-63*; 1965, *384-86, 394*; 1968, *403-405, 414*

Drew, George, *228, 230, 250, 255, 303, 321, 324, 399*; Conservative leader, *260*; election of 1949, *260-62, 265-70*; 1953, *276, 278-82, 284-85*; resignation, *293*
Drury, C.M., *283, 411*
Dual language in N.W.T., *59, 61*
Duff, William, *141*
Dundonald, Douglas Mackinnon Baillie Hamilton Cochrane, Earl of, *98-99*
Dunkin, Christopher, *5*
Dunning, Charles, *166, 170, 178, 195*; budget, *192*
Duplessis, Maurice, *226, 228, 245, 254, 260, 268, 298, 321, 341, 363, 401*
Dupuis, Yvon, *363, 376*
Duty of the Hour, 113-14, *116*

E

Eastman, Harry, *315, 316*
Economist, 213, *227, 271, 282, 301, 369*
Edgar, J.D., *25*
Edinborough, Arnold, *393*
Eggleston, Wilfrid, *244, 249, 255*
Eisenhower, Dwight, *282, 324*
Eldon, Donald, *297*
Electeur, L', 66, *83*
Elections, maintaining, realigning and deviating, *428-30*; luxury, *291, 317*
Electoral system, bias of, in 1925, *172-75*; 1926, *185, 188-89*; 1930, *202*; 1935, *218-20*; 1940, *235*; 1953, *287*; 1957, *306*; 1958, *323*; 1968, *415*; general, *421-23*
Emard, Joseph Médard, Bishop, *83*
Empire, Toronto, *63, 64, 80*
Equal Rights Movement, *58, 74, 80*
Ericson, Erick, *406*
Etendard, L', 49, *53*
Ethier, J.A.C., *93*
Evènement, L', 49, *142, 156, 187*
Express, Halifax, *10*

F

Fabre, Edward Charles, Archbishop, *66*
Family allowances, *243, 264, 265, 266, 342*
Fariball, Marcel, *381, 408, 409, 411*
Farrer, Edward, *64, 65*
Fauteux, André, *156*
Favreau, Guy, *376*
Fenians, *5, 6, 8, 9, 14, 33*
Ferguson, George V., *231, 237*
Ferguson, George Howard, *165, 179, 196*
Fermiers-Unis de Québec, *151*
Ferns, H.S., *293, 300, 317*
Fielding, W.S., *46, 51, 79, 87, 88, 89, 104, 111, 114, 122, 128, 129, 132, 149, 163, 164*
Filion, Gérard, *299*
Financial Post, 360
Financial Times of Canada, 404
Finlayson, R.K., *209*
Fisher, Douglas, *304, 330, 360, 369, 374, 390*